THE BOATMAN'S MANUAL

The NEW
BOATMAN'S
MANUAL

A Complete Manual of Boat Handling,
Operation, Maintenance, and
Seamanship

By CARL D. LANE

Illustrated by the Author

THIRD EDITION, REVISED AND ENLARGED

W · W · NORTON & COMPANY · Inc · New York

ISBN   0   393   03163   2

PRINTED IN THE UNITED STATES OF AMERICA

5 6 7 8 9 0

NOTICE

The reader of this Manual *is cautioned that no words and none of his time are wasted in it. Facts are stated once and not repeated.*

In addition to a complete index, each chapter is divided into subheads and numbered paragraphs. Illustrations bear the same figure number as the number of the paragraph to which they refer. The first component of the number signifies the chapter number; the second, the paragraph or illustration number.

⚓

PREFACE TO THE THIRD
REVISED EDITION

The need which prompted the original publication of this manual is even greater today, some twenty years later. The small craft fleet of our country—from outboards to spit-and-polish yachts—has multiplied in fantastic numbers, and boating has moved from an obscure sport to one as common as bowling or skiing. Thousands of men and women have discovered the pleasures of boating and demand an accurate, concise and well-arranged handbook to help meet the myriad problems of sailing and navigating.

In this edition, its second major revision, *The Boatman's Manual* becomes the most complete guide available for the small-craft skipper, owner, and crew member. It is still the book which thousands of seamen have come to rely upon and keep, above all others, on the chart table, but has been thoroughly modernized, with much new material added and new drawings and diagrams included.

It was pointed out by the many organizations and individuals who reviewed this manual in outline that two things above all were essential to its usefulness: (a) that it be concise yet give all information however basic, elemental, or obvious it may appear to the boatman of long experience, and, (b) that its arrangement and illustration be truly in manual or handbook form, the contents quickly available, clear and bare of all narrative writing.

What is here presented for the first time is neither startlingly new nor in any way novel. It is merely the gleaning, the assiduous gathering, of all information vital and necessary to the small-boat operator, owner, or crew member. Over a hundred books, pamphlets, articles, and other publications were consulted in its preparation. This manual, together with the proper *Coast Pilot,* charts, and tables, should enable the small-boat mariner to take his boat, in safety, anywhere in American and British waters, and should enable him to be prepared to meet any one of the scores of situations even the shortest of passages raises.

For help in preparing and reviewing this manual, the author is gratefully indebted to many, and especially to the following:

Mr. Felix Cornell, The Cornell Maritime Press, Cambridge, Md.
Lieut. Roger N. Ryley, USN
Mr. Robert S. Graves, United States Coast Guard Auxiliary
The Gray Marine Motor Company, Detroit, Michigan

The author freely acknowledges the great help received from the publications of the United States Navy, the United States Coast Guard, the Department of Commerce, the United States Hydrographic Office, the United States Army Engineer Office, the service pamphlets and the specially prepared material on the marine engine by the Gray Marine Motor Company; from many articles appearing in *The Rudder, Yachting, Motorboating,* and *Boats;* from H. I. Chapelle's *Yacht Designing and Planning,* and his *Boatbuilding;* and, of course, those great source books, Knight's *Modern Seamanship,* Riesenberg's *Standard Seamanship for the Merchant Service,* and Dutton's *Navigation and Nautical Astronomy.*

For the reviews and critical readings which assisted so much in the preparation of this revised edition, I thank many but especially:

Mr. John H. Montgomery, my respected collaborator on other works
Mr. H. W. de Fontaine, of *Yachting*
Mr. Roland Birnn, of Washington, D.C.
Mr. T. P. Sanders, of Chestertown, New York
Mr. Robert Lane, my son, of the Penobscot Boat Works, Rockport, Maine

—and to many readers who have over the years been kind enough to write me many a helpful thought or suggestion.

Carl D. Lane

Rockport, Maine

CONTENTS

PART I
BOAT HANDLING

⚓

⚓

CHAPTER I

HANDLING SMALL BOATS

A boat is defined by Webster as "a small open vessel, or watercraft, usually moved by oars or rowing."

A deepwater man considers a boat any small craft, usually auxiliary to his own larger ship, which can be bodily lifted from the water and stowed on a large vessel.

With the coming of power and modern sail rigs, replacing oars, the "boat" has reached far beyond its meaning of only a few decades ago. For the purposes of this manual, a boat shall be considered any hull however moved which is not a ship. This, of course, raises the question: how small is a ship; as well as other questions even more embarrassing. So, rather than place a limit of size or tonnage to the vessels to which this manual applies, let us merely state that the canoeist, the small-sailboat man, the powerboat man should find this work advanced and complete while the deepwater merchant or naval sailor should find it elemental and complete, lacking only full treatment of specialized subjects.

In most cases the boat is operated singlehanded; the lone operator must be his own deck man, navigator, reefer, engineer, and cook; serve his vessel as owner, master, and crew. He must thoroughly understand the elements of a great many subjects—be his vessel a dinghy, a 40-ton schooner, or a dragger—and he must have a basic working knowledge of them all.

Before he ever steps foot on his boat, certainly before he will require a knowledge of detailed seamanship, navigation, or maintenance, he will need to understand the handling of the boat of his choice.

Logically, a manual purporting to be complete and useful should commence at the beginning—at boat handling.

Logically, the subject of boat handling should commence at the beginning also—with the handling of the basic elemental type of boat, that which is propelled by man power.

HANDLING BOATS UNDER OARS

The ancient, straddling his logboat, without doubt first propelled his rude craft by a setting pole, a satisfactory device until he sailed into deep water. Once "off soundings" he was up against trouble, and his answer was to kick his feet violently and discover that the broad bulk of his calves actually moved his boat independently of any contact with the solid land beneath him. It was a short step from this discovery to the conversion of his spare setting pole to a paddle by attaching a wide, flat section of bark to it. The need for an efficient means of propelling larger craft led to a further evolution of the paddle to an oar.

The types of rowing boats are myriad. Each region has developed its own peculiar type best suited to wind, weather, and beaching conditions as well as to basic purposes. In general the dory is considered the safest deepwater boat. It is high-sided and has marked *flare,* making it a good weight carrier and a fairly dry boat. Its construction is strong enough not to depend upon thwarts for strength, and so it can be nested or banked, four or more dories to a bank. It is generally rowed by pushing the oars rather than pulling them, the boatman facing forward in a standing position. Dories will sail only moderately well, and they require a small sail with low centers.

In very small sizes the flat-bottomed rowboat is satisfactory and is easily pulled except in very rough water. It is a good carrier and is strong, but it can seldom be towed satisfactorily. However, it has the advantages of cheapness, ease in building and repair, and of being able to take a lot of punishment on a beach or at a wharf; and is a common type. Properly designed and taken out of the "box" class, the flat-bottomed, or sharpie, rowboat makes the best all-round boat for most small-boat uses.

Round and V-bottomed small boats are treacherous, cranky craft until they reach a length of about 12 feet. In the smaller sizes they have most of the bad characteristics of the canoe and none of its good characteristics. They tow fairly well, they can be sailed, and they look well in conjunction with a smart yacht when davited or decked. Repairs are difficult. Unless very lightly built, they are heavier than the flat-bottomed boat and therefore offer more difficulty in beaching and stowing. In larger sizes, such as cutters and whaleboats, the advantages of round-bottomed construction and design become apparent, and they become able boats.

In selecting the small boat the prime consideration should be that it fit the uses to which it will be put.

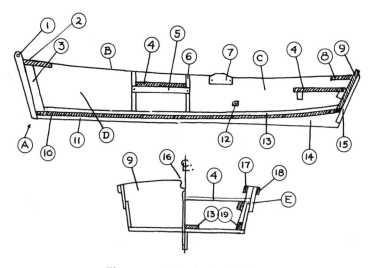

Figure 101. Parts of a Small Boat

 1. False stem
 2. Breasthook
 3. Stempost
 4. Thwart (seat)
 5. Riser
 6. Rib (or frame)
 7. Socket block
 8. Quarter knee
 9. Transom

10. Bottom plank
11. Keel
12. Stretcher
13. Keelson
14. Skag
15. Sternpost
16. Sculling notch
17. Gunwale (or clamp)
18. Rub mold (or gunwale)

19. Clintle (nailing strip)

A. Forefoot
B. Sheer (curvature)

C. Stern sheets
D. Foresheets

E. Sheer strake

101. The Flat-bottomed rowboat up to 12 feet. For lake and river recreation and fishing, protected salt-water fishing, dinghy use, work boats; outboard motors up to about four hp. Sail well except to windward in a rough water.

102. The Dory up to 21 feet. For exposed waters and offshore. Tenders for deepwater boats. Unless sections are modified (*see* Figure 102) will not sail well except off the wind.

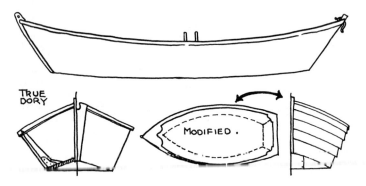

Figure 102. The Dory. Right, Modified for Sailing or Outboard Motor

103. The Round-bottomed boat (and V-bottomed). Good, "fancy" dinghies in small sizes. Drive well under power and tow well. When so designed will sail very well. (Example: the "Frost-bite" dinghies.) Boats carried by ships are always round-bottomed and reach the length of 40 feet.

The Oar

104. Ash makes the best oar material. It may be kept white and clean by rubbing with sand and canvas. Always stow oars flat. For long life, the leather (which may be of leather, canvas, or fiber) is necessary. (Figure 104.)

Rules for length:

In a single-banked boat (whaler)—twice the width of the thwart from which it is rowed plus the freeboard at the rowlock.

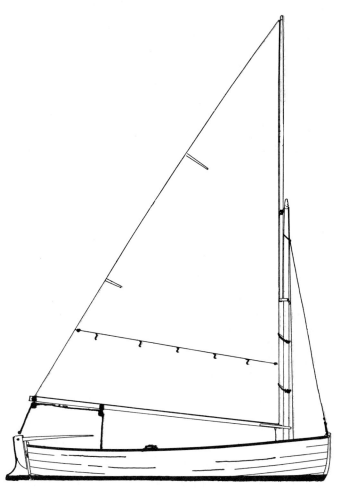

Figure 103. 13-Foot Utility Round Bottom Dinghy for Sail, Power, or Rowing

In a double-banked boat (cutter)—twice the length of the thwart from which it is rowed.

In a single-hander (dinghy)— 7′ OA   6′ oar
                                                9′ OA   6½′ oar
                                                11′ OA   7′ oar
                                                13′ OA   7½′ oar

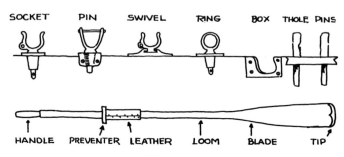

Figure 104.

Rowing the Small Boat

105. Most good oarsmen prefer to have the ends of the oar handles touch each other or even overlap slightly. Either way, the result will be considerably more power than when the handles are widely separated.

The complete stroke is made up of four distinct parts:
Catch—Place the blade in the water, ready to pull.
Pull—Sweep the blade aft to give headway.
Feather—Raise the blade out of the water and turn flat.
Recover—Swing oars to position of *Catch*.
To give the stroke power it is essential to:
1. Keep the upper edge of the blade at the surface of the water.
2. Keep hands about level. They move fore and aft as if in a fixed groove.
3. As the stroke is completed, the wrist is given a smart flip so that the blade comes out of the water at about a 45° angle. The elbows are in close to the body.
4. Keep the back straight, chin up and in, and the feet against the stretcher.
   Your weight should be centered slightly abaft the center of buoyancy; never so that the boat trims down by the head.

The pin-type lock (Figure 104) will not permit proper rowing form. It is popular on lakes for trolling where the oars must be trailed at times. Better is a ring rowlock and a preventer inboard of the oar leather.

Learn to set a course and head the boat exactly for it (making due allowances for tide or wind if necessary). From then on steer by the

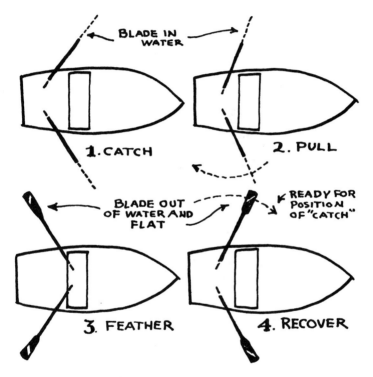

Figure 105. The rowing stroke

wake or by taking ranges over some point of the quarter. It is lubberly and tiresome to peer forward after every few strokes.

Long pulls can be made less tedious by changing the position of the oars slightly or by facing forward and push-rowing for a while. More progress will be made against a head sea by quartering into it rather than meeting the seas head on. This is especially true with a flat-bottomed boat of generous beam.

Sculling

106. A single oar, properly handled, can move a boat almost as fast as a pair of oars used in the usual manner. This maneuver is called sculling, and it is especially useful in congested waters, such as near a busy dock or in a narrow creek or channel.

The oar is shipped over the stern, or the quarter, in a rowlock or through a grommet that has been spliced into the transom, the

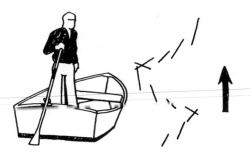

Figure 106. Sculling. Right, the Successive Blade Positions

sculler standing and facing aft. The oar is placed with the blade athwart the boat. Grasp the handle in the right hand, turn the knuckles down, and move the handle to the right. At the end of the stroke, turn the knuckles up and move the handle to the left—knuckles up, push left; knuckles down, push right. Continue, and keep the oar blade pressing outboard—that's all there is to sculling. Steering is accomplished by easing the motion right or left, and so directing the boat.

Boat Orders

107. Boat orders are given by the coxswain. Their practical use is in training for rowing in unison with a pulling boat's crew, such as that of a life boat or a surf boat. "Oars" is a hold position midway between the stroke parts of "feather" and "recover." "Stand by" is the commencement of "pull" but the oars are not yet dipped awaiting the command "Give way." It is smart to flip the oars from "pull" to "recover" with a slight upward turn of the blade.

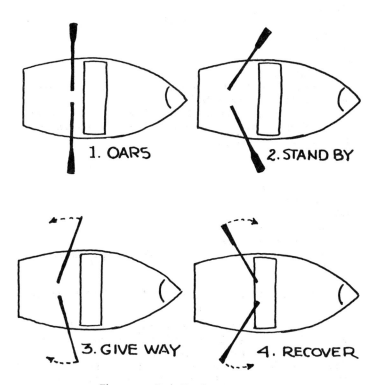

Figure 107. Basic Rowing Commands

Handling Ship's Boats Under Oars

108. Boats manning four or more oars use a set form of commands in handling. These are given by the coxswain (steersman) and are used according to the following tables:

TABLE I

Used by cutters with sunken or box rowlocks.

(1) *Stand by the oars.*
(2) *Up oars.*
    (1 and 2 *given before the boat is reported ready.*)
(3) *Shove off.*
(4) *Let fall.*
(5) *Give way together.*
(6) *In bows.*
(7) *Stand by to toss, Toss,* or *Oars* (followed by *Boat the oars* or *Way enough,* without the command *Oars*).

In all other cases the commands in Table II shall be used to shove off and go alongside. Boats with swivel rowlocks will not toss oars, and boats with awnings spread cannot toss oars.

TABLE II

(1) *Stand by the oars.*
(2) *Shove off.*
(3) *Out oars.*
(4) *Give way together.*
(5) *In bows,* or *Trail bow.*
(6) *Oars* (followed by *Boat the oars* or *Way enough,* without the command *Oars*).

THE SPECIAL COMMANDS FOLLOWING ARE FOR USE IN THE SITUATIONS INDICATED.

Out oars.—To rig out the oars in the rowlocks ready for pulling.

Oars.—(1) To salute. (2) To stop pulling for any purpose, keeping the oars out, horizontal and blades feathered.

Give way together (starboard, port).—To commence pulling.

Trail.—(1) To salute. (2) To pass obstructions. For the latter, oars of either side may be trailed independently.

Hold water.—To check headway or sternway. The oars of either side may hold water independently. If boat has much headway, care is required.

Stern all.—To acquire sternway. Should not be given when boat has much headway. When boat has headway, should be preceded by *Hold water.*

Explanation of the Commands:

Figure 108A

Stand by the oars.—Every man except the bowman seizes his oar by its handle and sees the blade clear of other oars. The oars should be shoved forward over the gunwale far enough to bring the handle in the proper position, but should be kept fore and aft. The blades will be kept clear of the bowmen's boat hooks.

Figure 108B

Out oars.—Given when the boat is clear of the ship's side. Thwart-men throw blades of oars horizontally outward, allowing the leathers to fall in rowlocks, place both hands on handle, and quickly trim blades flat and directly abeam. This is the position of *Oars.* Bowmen throw their oars at the same time as rest of crew, if they are ready; otherwise, they swing their oars out together, touching their blades forward to insure making the movements in unison, and bring them to the position of *Oars* to take up the stroke with the remainder of the crew, as the case may be.

Figure 108C

Trail.—Given when blades are in the water. Finish that stroke, release the handle of the oar, allowing it to draw fore and aft and trail alongside. If no trailing lines are fitted, retain the handle of the oar in the hand. With a cutter having sunken rowlocks, lift the handle of the oar quickly when blade is in the water at middle of stroke, throw oar out of rowlock, and retain handle in hand.

Figure 108D

Point the oars.—To shove off a boat that has grounded, stand facing aft, point the blades of the oars forward and downward to the beach at an angle of about 30°, ready to shove off at the command. If waves lift the stern of the boat, the united effort to shove off should be made just as her stern lifts.

Figure 108E

Give way together.—All the oarsmen take the full stroke, keeping accurate stroke with the starboard stroke oar. Feather blades habitually. Bowmen get out their oars together and take up the stroke. (They may have got them out before the command *Give way together,* in which case they give way with the other members of the crew.)

14

Figure 108F

Way enough.—If the crew has the skill, the command *Way enough* makes a fancy and snappy landing at a dock or gangway. Ordinarily, the command *Oars* is given, whereupon the stroke is completed and the oars brought to the position of *Out oars.* (Figure 108B.) *In bows* is given as the boat drifts to its objective, the bowmen boating their oars and, manning the boat hooks, springing to position in the foresheets, ready to fend or hold on. The command *Boat the oars* (the reverse of *Stand by oars*) will permit the landing to be made.

Back starboard (port).—To turn. Should *Hold water* before backing, if boat has much headway.

Back starboard, Give way port (or vice versa).—To turn quickly when boat has little or no headway.

Stand by to toss, Toss.—Used only in cutter, with sunken rowlocks. (1) To salute. (2) In going alongside, when it is not desirable to boat the oars. The habitual command to be used when coming alongside. Given from position of *Oars.*

Boat the oars.—To get the oars into the boat. Given when lying on oars, or when oars have been tossed or trailed.

Point the oars.—To shove off a grounded or beached boat.

Way enough.—To cease pulling and boat the oars. Given only while pulling, and for proper execution must be given just as the blades enter the water.

Let fall.—To go from *Up oars* to *Oars.*

(*Note.*—Thwarts and oars are numbered from forward. Doublebanked thwarts are designated by No. 1, starboard, No. 1, port; No. 2, starboard, No. 2, port, etc. The thwarts next to the bow and stroke are also properly designated as second bow and second stroke.)

UNITED STATES COAST GUARD ROWING INSTRUCTIONS

Pulling by Numbers

109. The crew is first taught to pull by numbers as follows: From the position of *Oars* the order is given to *Stand by*. At this order the body is bent forward at the hips and between the thighs, back straight, shoulders braced back, the arms extended to the full extent, the knees well apart, chest and belly full and prominent. The blade of the oar should be at right angles to the water and about one foot above it. Both hands should grasp the oar handle with the thumbs underneath. The head must be kept erect, the eyes on the back of the man in front.

1.—Drop the blades of the oars into the water without chop or splash. As the oar enters the water (keeping the surface of the blade perpendicular), put the weight of the body on the oar, arms and back remaining straight; drive with the legs against the stretcher until they are straightened out and the body is about $22\frac{1}{2}°$ past the perpendicular. The body must then remain stationary, while the arms bring the oar home by bending the elbows and keeping them close to the body until the root of the thumb touches the breast about one inch below the nipple.

NOTE:—The knees during this movement should close slightly. This movement is an excellent exercise for strengthening the muscles of the back, thighs, stomach, and loins, which play such an important part in rowing. The stroke should be begun by trying to feel the water, and it should then develop into a hard, steady pull.

2.—Drop the arms until the blade is clear of the water.

3.—Turn the wrists by dropping them, bringing the knuckles up, and feathering the oar.

4.—Shoot the arms out sharply, but without a jerk, and swing the body slowly and steadily forward to the position of *Stand by*. Care should be taken that the body comes steadily aft, otherwise the oarsmen will drop their shoulders and heads, and the blades, instead of being as close to the water as possible on the return, are uneven and cannot enter the water together.

After the motions have been distinctly taught, combine the first, second, and third at the order *Stroke,* completing the fourth motion at the word *Recover*.

When the crews have been thoroughly practiced in the combination, pulling in quick time should be carried out, the order being to *Give way*.

Cadets should always remember that the main object is to pull correctly, and that pulling hard and for a long distance is merely a matter of practice; but that a bad style once contracted is like a bad habit, hard to get out of. It must be impressed upon the boat's crew that their oars are to be pulled more by their legs than by their arms, and that both hands, both arms, both shoulders, each loin, and both legs and feet should bear an equal strain throughout the stroke.

The stroke should be finished with the shoulders and the muscles that work them, and the biceps should be passive throughout the stroke.

The whole secret of pulling lies in the body swing and good leg work against the stretcher.

LAYING ON OARS:—At the order *Oars* the crew will come to the position *Oars,* as previously described, taking time from the stroke oars.

1. SWING:—The aim in this should be to swing the body as far as possible from the hips without bending the back, being careful to let the head swing with the body. The swing must be slow and balanced, for the time occupied in coming forward should be the body's rest, when the easy, measured swing, erect head, braced shoulders, and open chest enable heart and lungs to work freely and easily, in preparation for a definite beginning of the next stroke. As the body swings, the hands should be at the same time stretching and reaching out, as if striving to touch something which is constantly evading them.

2. STRAIGHT BACKS:—As far as possible, a straight back should be acquired. The values of a straight back are as follows:

(a) The swing must be from the hips, and not from any point in the middle of the back as a secondary pivot.

(b) The straightness of the back eases the respiratory organs.

3. USE OF ARMS:—The arms must be straight when swinging back. They must be considered as merely connecting rods between the body and the oars. The use of the biceps in rowing should be discouraged, as the man who finishes his stroke by the aid of the biceps invariably

sticks his elbows out at right angles to his ribs, thus giving a weak as well as a cramped and ugly finish.

4. DO NOT MEET YOUR OARS:—i. e., keep your body back until your hands have come in. *If you pull yourself forward to meet your oars, you will certainly shorten your stroke prematurely.*

5. TURNING OF HANDS TOWARD END OF STROKE:—Hands must be dropped before the wrists are turned to get the blade clear of the water first, and to insure a neat, clean feather. If the oar is feathered properly it comes out like a knife.

6. USE OF LEGS:—When the beginner has been taught the use of his body and has begun to get used to the swing of it for the main motive power of the stroke, he can be taught to apply extra power with his feet at the right time, to increase the power and the swing of the body. As soon as the body feels the strain of the oar, legs instinctively stiffen themselves against the stretcher. They should be kept in this rigid posture, supporting the body throughout the stroke. The rigidity should commence at the instant the oar touches the water and the strain begins to fall upon the shoulder.

7. RECOVERY:—This is largely dependent upon the abdominal muscles, and to get quick recovery these muscles must be exercised and developed. The muscles of the legs, thighs, and loins should all join with those of the abdomen in the recovery. The first part of the recovery should be the most rapid.

8. CATCH:—The beginning of the stroke should be the most forcible part. This *catch* should be driven from the body as if the whole body were to be lifted off the seat by the joint support of the oar and stretcher. Avoid striking the water in the *catch*.

9. FORM:—May be defined and made up of square shoulders, straight swing from the loins, elastic recovery, and absence of doubling up at the finish.

10. DISTANCE OF SWING BACK:—In deciding this, two things must be considered. Viz.:

(a) Whether the man is physically capable of maintaining his length of *swing back* without sacrificing some of his *reach forward*.

(b) Whether his powers of recovery are adequate to the distance through which his body has to be recovered for the next stroke.

If both of these can be done, then the man who fulfills these conditions is doing his work to best advantage, if his body, when straight at the end of the stroke, makes an angle of about $22\frac{1}{2}°$ with the perpendicular, the reach forward being full.

It is more economical to recovery to swing fairly well back and to row a fewer number of long strokes than a large number of short strokes.

In teaching a man to swing back, he should be told to hold his head well up. The weight, if thrown back, assists his swing, while if hanging forward, it acts in a contrary direction.

> *Insist on Silence Being Kept in the Boat.*
> *Insist on Eyes Being Kept in the Boat.*
> *Allow No Inattention.*

Special Notes on Handling Boats under Oars

110. In going into a crowded or difficult landing, pull easily and keep the boat under control with the oars as long as possible, laying on oars if necessary, and boating oars only at the last moment.

In going through a narrow entrance, get good way on the boat, then trail or toss the oars.

A loaded boat holds her way much longer than a light one.

In pulling across a current, try to make good a straight line by steering up stream from the line you want to make good.

Having a long pull against the tide, run near shore where the tide is slacker than in midstream, and where there is sometimes an eddy.

There should always be a lantern, filled and trimmed, in the boat, and boats should never leave for a trip of any great length without a compass. Weather is liable to thicken at any time, and a boat without a compass would have difficulty in reaching a landing or returning to the ship. For this reason, coxswains should at all times know the compass course between the ship and landing; and if they are away from the ship and it begins to thicken, they should at once observe the compass course before the ship is shut in.

Never go alongside a vessel which has sternway or which is backing her engines.

In coming alongside in a seaway or when a strong tide is running, warn the bowman to look out for the boat line which will be heaved from the ship.

If caught in a gale in an open boat, rig a sea anchor by lashing the spars and sails together, sails loosed. Fit a span to this and ride by the painter. If there is oil in the boat, secure a bag of waste saturated with oil to the sea anchor.

Towing, Decking, Daviting Small Boats

111. Towing the small boat has ever been a problem of the cruiser, especially in a sea or offshore. Dangers include swamping and filling and consequent strain and perhaps parting of the towing hawser and,

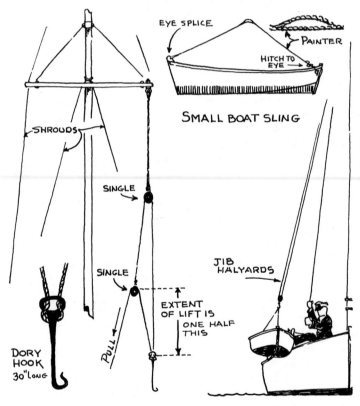

Figure 112. Two Methods of Decking a Small Boat

under certain conditions, the towed boat actually coming aboard the towing craft or ramming her stern.

Experienced deepwater men insist upon a deck design which allows the small boat to be carried there or in davits.

If the boat must be towed it is best secured to a quarter bitt. Towed off center thus it exerts somewhat less pull and is less apt to "wander" in its course astern. Sometimes this inclination to veer can be cured quite easily by:

1. Dragging a length of line from the *center* of the towed boat.

2. Affixing a deeper or longer skeg.

3. Ballasting the towed boat a trifle out of trim, port, starboard, or by the stern.

4. Lashing the tiller (if so equipped) to keep the towed boat edging slightly off the true course.

5. Towing the boat at "just the right" point aft, the point to be found by experimenting, and depending upon speed, sea conditions, tide, and current. In a towing boat having a distinct wave drag this spot is likely to be the forward side of the second following wave.

Most small boats tow best if provided with a towing ring on the stem near the waterline or even below it. This gives a lift to the fore-foot which prevents the boat from "nosing" (burying the forefoot) and veering wildly.

112. Some method of actually taking the dinghy aboard the larger boat is necessary for any extended coastwise work. Davits are an abomination on the small cruiser unless there is beam enough to davit the small boat thwartships across the stern in chocks on deck, in preference to its merely hanging over the water from the davits.

Side davits on the small boat are not practical in general, as the first sea aboard will sweep the dinghy away. The dinghy, if it can be accommodated on deck, is best stowed about amidships and on the center line, overturned, if possible. Methods of decking the small boat are shown in Figure 112.

The most practical davits for the small cruiser are the ones of the round bar or radial type. A modification of the quadrant type, in which the davits hinge inboard and deliver the davited boat directly over its skids, is in use but cannot always be handled by one man.

113. With the small boat actually on board, it should always be provided with its own permanently secured skids and hold-down arrangement.

If the boat is carried upright, the skids take the outside shape of the sections at which they grip the boat and are padded to minimize chafing. These skids fold to the deck to facilitate handling the boat. They should always be high enough to permit swabbing the deck under the secured boat; say, at least 10 inches.

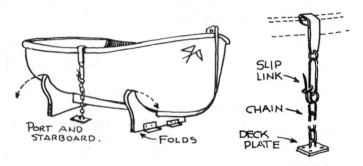

PORT AND STARBOARD.

FOLDS

SLIP LINK →

CHAIN →

DECK PLATE →

Figure 113. Chocking a Small Boat on Deck

A boat carried this way is held down by gripes which are easily cast off by releasing the locking link (*see* Figure 113). A boat cover must be provided, rigged over a ridgepole. It is usually fitted with canvas straps passing under the boat for lashing down.

A boat carried upside down needs chocks as well as some method of lashing to the deck. Unless the boat is of canvas-covered or plywood construction, a cover is desirable to prevent undue drying of the planking. On the sailboat a cover is necessary to prevent soiling sails and running rigging.

Modern yacht designers have recognized the dinghy and its problems as a serious handicap to successful cruising and are gradually coming to include the dinghy and making provisions for its stowage in the original design. This is accomplished by adjusting sail or deck plans to accommodate a small boat. Pram-type dinghies which fit over a part of the trunk, or become part of the cockpit or the deck, have been tried with some success.

Launching from a Ship

114. The launching of a heavy life boat presents special problems. Launching mechanism may be quadrantal davits, gravity davits or the common radial davits. The first two types operate by means of gears or levers which place the boat in position for lowering. The radial davits require careful maneuvering and drill in order to have them function to their designed purpose. Figure 114A gives the steps in diagrammatic form.

When the boat is swung out ready for lowering it should be in such condition as to become waterborne without further effort. The cover should be removed and it, with the spreaders, stowed within the boat, the boat plug in, the painter lead forward and outboard of all encumbrances, rudder hung and Jacob's ladder ready to drop into the boat when afloat.

If the boat is to be carried swung out for some time before launching, the strongback should be relashed to the davits and the boat lashed to the strongback by gripes. It is usual to leave the boat plug out if the boat is to be carried swung out. If an immediate launching is contemplated lash the strongback out of the way to some part of the ship if there is time; if not, cast it overboard as far clear of the side as possible.

Frapping lines leading from the lower (or movable) block of each fall will prevent the boat from swinging in a seaway or in the case of a severe outboard list. Such lines should lead from the swivel of the block or from a bight taken around the fall and should be handled from the boat deck.

Lowering is accomplished by paying out the boat falls from a sitting position and with the heels braced if possible. Gloves should be worn to avoid rope burns and the falls should be properly turned on a cleat to avoid a quick drop. The Jacob's ladder should be payed out as the boat is lowered from between the davits to the midships of the boat. If the ship has headway the after end of the boat should be a trifle lower than the forward end and should reach the water first.

Releasing gear should be operated *before* the boat is completely waterborne and when the ship has reached the limit of a downward roll. If the ship has way on, the proper rigging of the sea painter from the boat to the ship will see the boat lying parallel to the ship, riding

1. Clear Away. Falls are manned and the boat raised several inches above the chocks. Falls belayed. Chocks folded or knocked out. The after guy is cast off. (Boat plug checked.)

2. Launch Aft. The boat is swung forward, helped by a haul on the forward guy, and as it clears the after davit the forward guy is let go. Without loss of motion, the next step—

3. Bear out Aft. Haul away after guy—is completed. The stern is swung out.

4. Launch Forward. The boat is pushed aft, helped by a haul on the after guy.

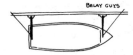

5. Bear out Forward. The boat is pushed outboard and both fore-and-aft guys securely belayed. The boat then can be lowered away.

(If the boat has been lashed to a strong back, the spar must first be removed from the davits before attempting to launch overboard.)

Figure 114A. Launching a Davited Boat

easy. Crashing may be avoided by use of the boat's rudder, putting the helm toward the ship slightly but not enough to cause a wild outward sheer and consequent danger of swamping or capsizing. The crew may board by the ladder or by sliding down the falls.

Way is made by placing two oars ready for use and hauling ahead on the painter. When the painter is "up and down" it is cut smartly, the rudder put smartly away from the ship and the oars put into use. Get away from the ship at once on a right angle course to avoid propeller suction and to make room for other boats.

Whenever possible launch from the lee side or from the lowest side.

Always release the stern falls first when the ship has headway on.

If launching from the low side of a listed ship no special instructions are required save to rig frapping lines to the falls.

If launching from the high side of a listed ship keep a strain on the falls while the boat gripes are cast off lest the boat slide to the low side. A "skate" of some design is necessary to launch from the high side so that the boat will clear extending members of the ship, port hole rims, bolts and plate edges and will not capsize as it is lowered. If the boat is not equipped with the usual iron midship skate the strongback or another spar may be lashed along the inboard gunwale as a jury skate. It is almost hopeless to attempt to launch from the high side without a skate.

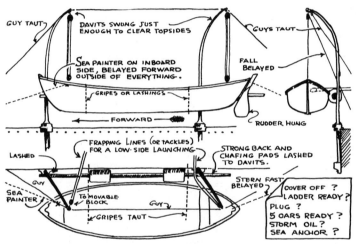

Figure 114B. Life Boat Swung Out Ready for Emergency Lowering

Handling Rowing Boats at Sea, Beaching Them, etc.

115. In heavy sea conditions, the chief concern of the rowing craft is to meet the wave crests end on and so avoid a fatal "broaching to." The secret is to have way on when meeting crests, either by moderate forward motion or actual "holding" so that the crest passes ahead of the boat. Rudder or oar action can often "dodge" a crest of white

tumbling water and this is recommended practice provided that in so doing the boat is not turned sufficiently to be endangered by receiving a sea on the beam and broaching to.

Running before a sea is always dangerous, the problem being to maintain course as the seas attack from astern. Rudder work and constant way are the best safeguards. If the bow seems to wish to "bury" get weight aft. Be sure the boat is dry, since water weight flowing fore-and-aft as the boat pitches adds to the bow weight when buoyancy there is most needed.

To make a landing in heavy surf, make a careful study of the situation and estimate of the power of the sea. One of these methods, all designed to prevent the fateful broaching to which spells disaster in beach landings, should be used:

1. Turn the heading of the boat end for end in smooth waters; then back in, pulling a few strokes ahead to meet the heavier seas.

2. Come in bow first but back upon the charge of each sea; then allow the "back" of the sea itself to carry the boat shoreward. This would be similar to the surf-boarding of the Pacific islanders.

3. Come in bow first dragging a drogue (basket, life-preserver, boat sea anchor, etc.), thus holding the stern into the wave crests.

116. Beaching the small boat, up to 100 pounds or so, presents no difficulties, except in surf or heavy seas. Within limitations the remarks in paragraph 115 relating to the beaching of large pulling boats relate to small boats also. However, it is foolhardy to attempt beaching the small, light dinghy of ten or twelve feet in length in heavy surf conditions unless it is of undisputed seaworthy design and build. The various dory types might possibly fall into this class; any boat with a broad transom stern decidedly does not.

Sometimes a landing can be successfully made stern first, keeping the bows to the incoming seas and the weights slightly toward the bow. Headway and steerageway must be maintained under any conditions. Such a landing would probably only be made under emergency conditions, and the rower or passengers should be equipped with life preservers and resigned to a ducking and possible loss of the boat and/or its equipment.

117. The actual handling of the small boat on the beach is not particularly difficult, especially with man power available. Alone, the boat's safe removal to a point beyond danger may present some problems. Some hints for handling follow:

1. Use rollers (logs, branches, tubular fenders, large tin cans, etc.) if at all possible. Oars, with the blade end boosted slightly by riding on a driftwood stringer or another oar, can sometimes be made to work.

2. A boat will slide easily on wet kelp, or other seaweed, or on dry marsh grass.

3. Pull the boat, never push.

4. A fairly heavy boat can be "jogged"; i. e., lift one end and carry ahead, pivoting on the remaining end; then lift the pivot end and repeat.

5. Always secure the boat to a stake or a rock, no matter how high on the beach. If on a rocky shore, with danger of the tide rising, boost the boat up on its oars, using them as beams spanning a low spot between high-flanking rocks.

6. Hide the oars or lock them in the boat. Leave a note or some other indication showing the Coast Guard patrol or police that the boat is not abandoned nor shipwrecked.

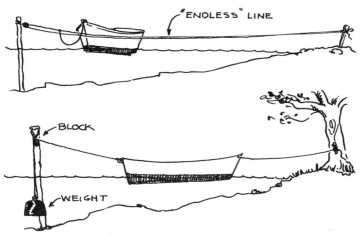

Figure 117. Mooring to Stakes

118. The boat which is regularly beached or taken ashore upon landing should be handled by gear designed especially for that purpose. A dock or a float should be provided with a wide flush roller to facilitate the hauling to a safe position. Where there is a great rise and fall in the tide a "dinghy launch" serves well. The boat is usually handled by a tackle and possibly a small winch or capstan. (Figure 118A.)

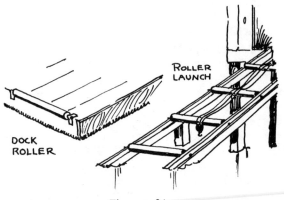

Figure 118A

119. Carrying boats on public highways. It is generally dangerous to carry even very small boats on the roof of a passenger car, especially at high speeds. In some states it is forbidden—and wisely.

The common carrying devices make use of gear which (a) grips a certain part of the car, usually the drip gutters, or (b) attaches by means of rubber suction caps. Both are weak in that they do not provide for the great strains of windage. The pocketing effect of an overturned boat being driven into the wind or against wind of the car's own making is tremendous and frequently has resulted in serious accidents.

The safest method of transporting boats over highways is by the use of a boat trailer. Such a trailer must be heavy enough to amply carry the boat and its gear (spars, oars, ground tackle, or outboard motor) and be provided with a self-gripping cradle and adequate lash-down devices.

In all states the following regulations apply to trailers:

1. They must be rubber-tired.
2. They must be attached to the towing car by a "hitch" of approved design and manufacture. (Some states require chain attachment in addition, in case of failure of the hitch.)
3. They must be licensed and their license plates displayed.
4. They must carry an electrically lighted taillight, stoplight, and license-plate light. (Some states further require a tail-reflector light.)
5. They must not exceed eight feet maximum width. (Boats wider than this require special permits for each haul, secured generally from police bureaus or state highway departments.)

(In some states, trailers over certain weights, or having four wheels, require their own braking systems operated by the car driver.)

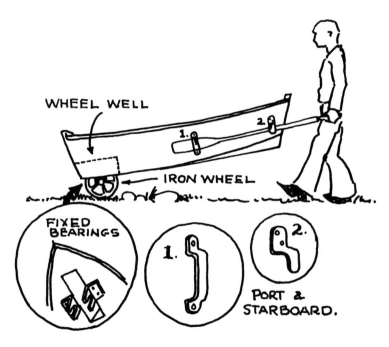

Figure 118B. Trundle Skiff

120. Boats shipped by rail, if heavy, must be provided with a suitable cradle mounted on skids. Handling, placing on the car, and chocking are usually done by the railroad company and always under the direction of an experienced foreman. Before rolling, they must be examined and approved by a representative of the freight department.

Tanks must be empty and no gasoline is permitted to be carried aboard. Unless especially insured, the contents of a boat (gear, navigating equipment, stores, etc.) are not covered by ordinary transportation insurance. Ordinarily, the contents of boats carried on a flat car must be removed from the boat. Watchmen or boat tenders, in the employ of the shipper, may not sleep or live on the boat while it is being transported. Sometimes, such a tender may travel in the caboose, paying regular passenger fare.

Small boats shipped by rail need not be crated but must be covered, usually by a burlap wrapper, sewn on. Husky, sharpie-type boats and dories are sometimes shipped without any wrapping.

Spars, shipped separately, must be wrapped and protected. Rigging should be removed, especially blocks, spreaders, and winches.

In shipping via express, the rules of the express company apply and may vary from the requirements of railroad freight departments.

Under special conditions, such as in the case of a large shipment of dinghies to a port on the racing circuit, or outboard racers, or a flotilla of canoes shipping against the current or around rapids, exceptions are made and usual rules do not apply.

In preparing a boat for railroad shipment, seal every space against cinders and usual railway dust. Large glass areas should be reinforced or braced. Reduce the boat to its barest form, removing cowl ventilators, bowsprits, military masts, etc. Awnings and dodger cloths should be removed. If the hull travels wet, that is, soaked and the planks fully swollen, vibration and jarring will do less damage to caulking and fastenings than when dry. A light cover over the boat, securely fastened, will not only keep the boat reasonably free of cinders but will help to prevent the too rapid drying out of the planking.

Canoes

The handling of the American canoe, the design of which is based upon those of the North American Indians, is an art. Its handling calls for the nicest sense of balance. The man who can handle a canoe well, especially under sail, has learned a great deal of basic seamanship, which he will unconsciously apply to the handling of other and much larger boats.

Paddling Positions

121. The safest and fastest paddling position is the one in which the paddler kneels, usually on soft pads attached to the knees or on a cushion about 24" x 15". Kneeling positions keep the center of gravity lower than when sitting on the seats, sometimes provided, and permit the upper leg muscles to add their power to those of the arms and back. Cruising positions call for one or both knees on the pads, but the buttocks rest against a thwart. Racing positions call for the knee on the paddling side to be on the pad and the body generally more erect than in cruising.

Double paddles are used from a full kneeling position only, or from a seat. Such a seat is generally portable, is raised but three to five inches from the bottom, and sometimes has extensions to which a cross foot brace is attached.

When both paddlers of a team sit upon the caned seats found in many canoes, the boat becomes a very unstable and cranky craft. In general, unless there is cruising duffel low down to bring the center of gravity lower, it is best to have at least one paddler in a kneeling

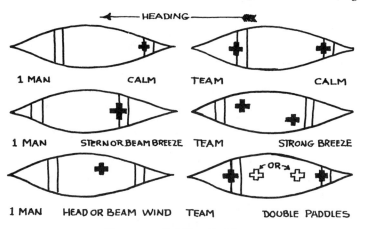

Figure 121. Paddling Positions

position. Expert canoeists, men with thousands of miles of water behind them without a spill, invariably use the kneeling positions as a matter of basic safety. The comfort of the sitting position, however, should not be denied, and many canoeists rehang the cane seats so that they are several inches below the gunwales. This is a simple operation, involving only longer carriage bolts from gunwale to seat frame and sometimes the removal or lowering of the thwart forward of the stern seat.

In white water and in rapids, the expert finds that a standing position will permit him to quickly counteract capsizing efforts by throwing his body weight from one leg to the other. A long, light pole rather than a paddle is then often used, the current being permitted to move the boat, the pole being used more or less as a fender or a setting pole.

Canoe Strokes

122. *The J Stroke*. Used for single paddling. Its curve is adjusted according to trim, windage, or current so that the boat is propelled forward on a straight course. After completion, a slight drag—using the paddle as a rudder, directing the bow in the opposite direction from that given it by the stroke—is given.

The Bow Stroke. Used by the bowman of a team. It is perfectly parallel to the keel. The bow stroke sets the pace for the stern paddler. Regardless of the maneuver in the offing, the bow stroke is kept up in this manner and not changed until so ordered by the stern paddler, who is considered the helmsman.

The Sweep. Used for wide slow turns without loss of speed. Sometimes is terminated in the draw stroke for quicker turning.

The Backwater. Simply the reverse of the bow stroke. The paddle is not removed for the back stroke but kept submerged and feathered.

The Draw. Used to move the canoe sideways or to a dock or float.

The Push-over. Used to move the canoe away from a dock or float. The gunwale is used as a fulcrum, the paddle as a lever. The stroke is feathered upon the return.

The Bow Rudder. Used by the bow paddler to swing the stern or to make quick turns. Also, for the same purpose, the paddle is extended forward of the stem and the blade projected into the water on the opposite side of the keel.

Sculling. To move the canoe sideways but at a 45° angle forward or backward.

Figure 122. Canoe Strokes

Lie on surface, bear down on gunwale and kick forward

Press right hand hard, keeping elbow above gunwale—then—

Spring and draw body on gunwale, with as much weight as possible on right hand—and—

Flop in!

Figure 123. Getting into a Canoe in Deep Water

Canoe Accidents

123. The canoe is its own life preserver in a sense. Even when it is filled, it will float and afford flotation to a man in the water. Overturnings are common, especially with the inexperienced. But they need not be dangerous—unless, of course, the canoeist is not a swimmer, in which case he has no business being in a canoe anyway.

Most canoe tragedies occur because the canoeist does not know how to right and reboard his boat. When understood, this is a simple trick. If the canoe has filled in upsetting (as is most likely) it must first be freed of water. The first step is to swim to either the bow or stern and take a vertical position facing the opposite end. Now, place one hand on the stemhead and the other beneath the curve of the stem under water. Slowly submerge the canoe, keeping it in even thwartship trim; as soon as possible bring your full weight on the end and with the free hand and legs start swimming forward. Most of the water will rush toward you and spill over the submerged end. Do not let go of the canoe or it will sheer wildly from you and make its recovery necessary. The gunwales will now be several inches above the water and the canoe out of an "awash" position.

Now swim to a point about amidships, on the leeward side, and using your full weight, rock the canoe from side to side, splashing the water out in small dallops. The trick is to time the application of your weight with the natural thwartship rush of the water, giving it a flip as the water bulk reaches its extreme surge at the near gunwale. Patience will soon reduce the water in the canoe to the amount where it can be dipped or sponged out.

Once the canoe has been emptied, it is reboarded, as shown in Figure 123. Immediately upon a canoe's upsetting and swamping, at least one paddle should be retrieved and wedged into the bow or stern. Other gear can be picked up after the boat is again under way. If the canoe has not filled upon upsetting, under no circumstances let go of it. Even a gentle breeze will carry it away much quicker than you can swim after it. With one hand always on the canoe and dragging it with you, go after the paddle.

Canoe Sailing

124. Canoe sailing has developed many forms of rigs, some of them of amazing and dangerous sail areas. For ordinary day sailing or cruising, a safe but efficient rig, such as the one shown in Figure 124, should suffice. Decked-in canoes, or canoes equipped with "hike boards" upon which the skipper may crawl to create windward ballast, of course, might have sail areas several times as large as that shown.

The leeboards are detachable, and each is pivoted so that the leeward board alone is down when sailing. When running free, both boards are up or slightly trailing.

The sail center and leeboard center (center of lateral resistance) must have a certain definite relationship to each other and to the hull itself. (*See* Chapter II.) In a canoe these are easily adjusted by shifting the leeboards fore and aft until the perfect balance has been achieved. With your own weight approximately amidships and the leeboards vertical, the canoe, without rudder effort (the paddle is used for a rudder), should tend to round to into the wind or have a "weather helm."

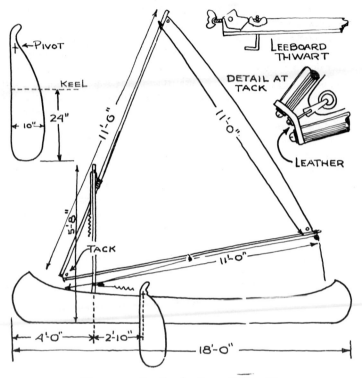

Figure 124. Details of a Canoe Sailing Rig

Centers can be further shifted by pivoting the leeboard in use forward or aft of the pivot center until little or no rudder effort is required. A canoe sails best upright, not heeled. Do not hesitate to add to her stability by shifting your weight to windward, or by hooking a leg over the gunwale. Do not sit on the gunwale. The wind resistance will deaden the boat and a sudden slackening of the wind, or a pocket, might easily capsize you to windward. Windward courses are helped by shifting your weight slightly forward. Off the wind, a weight shift aft will help.

The expert sailor does not use his paddle for coming about. He stows his paddle, slides forward and, as the canoe heads into the wind, he sheets the sail in, keeping it full. With the boom amidships and the sail luffing, the leeboard is raised and secured, then, pushing the boom slightly to windward, he again slides aft. With the bow well around on the new tack, the boom is released, the paddle shipped, and, with the foot, the leeward leeboard is pushed down.

Spars should be of Sitka spruce or of stock of equal weight, and running rigging should be very light, preferably of cotton line. Sails are of 1-oz. canvas or so-called "balloon cloth," without bolt ropes, and grommets should be of brass machine set. Leeboards are generally of one-inch stock, mahogany being the favorite, though spruce, white pine, or Spanish cedar are sometimes used.

Outboard-Motor Boats

125. The outboard motor is today a thoroughly reliable mechanism and has brought forth a host of hulls designed to be used with the "portable engine." These range from small yacht tenders to step hydroplanes capable of speeds of 60 MPH and more using souped-up engines of the hot rod variety. In general hulls suitable for outboard-motor use are of the planing or semi-planing type and almost all are characterized by a broad flat stern section capable of floating the engine and operator in the after end. V-bottomed construction is common for wooden boats since this type hull readily accommodates itself to the flat surfaces of plywood sheets or aluminum. Lapstrake wooden boats are both V- and round-bottomed. Fiberglas and plastics have opened new horizons for small boats and hull forms are unlimited, the round-bottomed hull being the commonest form in "glass" boats. All outboard hulls are lightly built and lightly decked as the accent is on speed, and in these sizes relatively small weight economies can result in marked speed increases. Lightness also is desirable for handling, launching and towing purposes.

Some designers have turned out successful outboard cruisers in the 17- to 22-foot class, weighing up to 2000 pounds and performing well with single 75-HP engines or twin-50s. Most designs suffer from a forced poor weight distribution, i.e., light cabins and low density masses forward and most real weight (engine, fuel and passengers) concentrated in the stern. Enormous power is required to reach plan-

ing trim; once reached the boats perform well enough. However, reduced to sane sea speeds by heavy weather, some of these craft become floating coffins, breaking every rule of safe naval design.

Stern transoms on stock outboard boats have been more or less
standardized at 20 inches from waterline to motor clamp, readily
accepting the trade standard "long shaft" motor. The older 15-in.
transoms are now provided only for low-power small fishing and
the smaller speed boats. Clamps fit transoms of from ⅞-in. to 2⅛-in.
and the higher powered engines bolt to the transom.

As outboard power grew higher and higher with the demand for
speed, fuel economy became a concern. The cost of the two-cycle engine in low horsepowers was not prohibitive; but in the 75-HP class
fuel consumption rose to as high as 12 gallons an hour when water
skiing or "hot-rodding." As a result the far more economical four-
cycle engine was re-investigated and the industry came up with various
four-cycle power heads hooked to angle transfers similar to the familiar

Figure 125A. Modern Outboard Cruiser

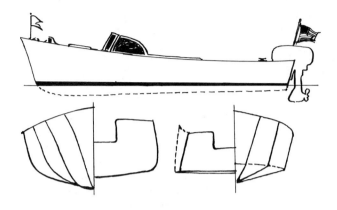

Figure 125B. An Outboard Runabout and Typical Lines

outboard motor drive. Thus there are numerous "inboard-outboard installations available which appear to perform well in a hull originally designed to carry weight in the stern. Some manufacturers experimented with Diesel outboard power heads.

A trend is now under way to consolidate both power and hull in a single package from a single manufacturer. Such a move will probably result in a better boat and motor combination than when each component is bought separately. Unfortunately, the marine dealer is not always a technical expert and may put together a boat and motor combination gauged to move merchandise rather than produce a safe, well-balanced and durable investment. The buyer is cautioned to investigate most carefully the advertising claims of the mass producers as to speed, quality and performance, to seek advice, and to consult with a naval architect before making a final decision.

A question becoming more acute each year is the one of the relative merits of construction and materials. Here are some guides:

Aluminum sheet construction. Very satisfactory for slow speeds and in fresh water; or for trailer use in fresh or salt water. It "drums" and makes noises not present in conventional construction. It is hot in summertime and cold in winter. The weakest factor is the skin fastening. Rivets of a certain alloy *must* be used or fatigue and corrosion will soon ruin the outfit. However, for a fishing boat, for lake use or as part of a camping outfit, the aluminum-hulled boat is probably the best.

Sheet plywood construction. Inexpensive and reasonably satisfactory. Plywood will eventually break down—much sooner than solid wood planking. Drums and is noisy. Repairs not difficult. Bottoms tend to "work" and hence fastenings *must* be large-headed screws, or so-called annular construction nails. Plywood edges must be protected at all times. Teredo worms adore the glue between the laminates of some plywoods. The plywood grade should be "marine," i.e., with solid core and selected faces and backs. Mere "exterior" grade is not good enough. Douglas fir is cheapest but will not take a smooth paint job; for that use mahogany-faced marine plywood, at least 5-ply.

Good for trailer boats. Begins to fail at ultra-high speeds; say 40 MPH and up. The quality in a sheet plywood boat is found in the framing and ribbing more than the skin itself.

An inherent criticism of all sheet materials is that the sheet, unbendable into compound curves, dictates the hull form. Therefore such a hull must be a compromise between what a designer considers safe, fast and weatherly and what form the sheet of material will permit. This is why some plywood and metal boats can truly be characterized as "boxes." Some of them are unsafe; indeed man-killing. Lapstrake construction somewhat solves this very basic problem.

Lapstrake construction. A very strong hull form, yet not unduly heavy. Look for good glue bonds at laps and a sensible manner of clinching, namely, rivets and burrs or clinch nails. Adjustable bolts and nuts seem to be a sales gimmick only. Some glues today stand without metal fastenings of any kind; lessons learned from the airframe industry. Plywood or solid will provide an equally good hull form. Solid plank will soak water and become much heavier than plywood in time; further, it will not take as much soaking and drying as plywood and is better for a boat which is to be left at a mooring rather than trailed home or beached.

There is no merit whatever in the claim that the laps of the boat actually are a planing surface or "lift" the boat and increase speed. These are claims for the unthinking.

A weak area is the fastening of the planks (a double plank, really) to the relatively light bent frames of a round-bottomed lapstrake boat. A rivet and burr is best here; the usual screw works out under stress of a speed-wracked hull. Keep sand and litter out of the bilges; once it is allowed to creep or sift between the laps (as when the boat is dry), the boat can be made tight again only by external gunks and compounds made to correct such leaks.

A lapstrake topside with a smooth bottom, on a chine-form hull (V-bottom), makes the fastest, lightest and most satisfactory boat for normal uses. Round bottom is usually good at sea but slower than the above form in smooth or lake waters.

"Glass" construction. The early glass and plastic boats were sorry affairs indeed. The public seems to have shied away from them to some extent, undoubtedly disappointed in the lavish claims of some suppliers that there are no maintenance costs, that the hulls are indestructible, that nothing can affect the beautiful polished hulls. But glass boats *do* disintegrate—sometimes under heat, or fire, or cold, or oil spillage. Glass boats *do* crack—all by themselves on some cold winter night. Glass boats become "crazy checked" in time, from vibration, from temperature changes, from road shock and from improper laying up. There isn't a boat plastic available that will not eventually become as hard and brittle as a porcelain plate. The curing process can be slowed up—as much as five or ten years—but, eventually, flexibility will vanish and the boat is finished. This is built-in obsolescence, along with annual style changes, color schemes and accessorial notes.

There are good glass boats. They always cost 20% or more than the same boat in wood or plywood. If not, they may be suspect of poor quality, thin sides, unfinished edges and a waxed rather than polished surface.

The material lends itself to endless hull forms. It is astonishing that, with fine, safe, sea-kindly hull designs available for a few dollars from capable naval designers, so many manufacturers choose to market untried, unsafe and impractical hull forms. The glass boat industry may one day inherit the boat business of the world—but until they concentrate on better design that day is a long way off.

Glass boats can be quite readily repaired; home kits are available for a few dollars. They are not a good investment value, however, possibly because too many owners have believed the fable of "no maintenance" and their turn-ins show extreme lack of even ordinary care.

Composite construction. This is very new and as yet untried form. The hull is often of conventional wood, with decks and cabin tops glass covered, or exterior trim and joiner work glass covered. Some designers have placed conventional accommodation plans of wood into glass hulls. These have always cost far, far more than wooden boats and nobody knows if they will outlast a wooden boat or not. Sailing craft have also been made of glass, with some success, but many of the applications do not seem to make sense. Why fabricate a spar out of glass, for example? Wood is standard, reasonably priced and quite satisfactory, and aluminum extrusions are just as good but lighter than either wood or glass.

In general, be wary of experiments with new construction methods and materials. There is one final answer and that is cost—when newer methods really compete with conventional wooden construction, dollar for dollar, feature for feature, we may see a firm trend and a departure from what is now considered satisfactory, safe and sound. Until then it seems to be all gadgets and gimmicks, bubbling and stewing in claims, with an occasional truth or virtue rising to the surface.

Yacht Tenders

126. In combination with the small rowing-type dinghy, the smaller-size outboard engines serve the cruising yachtsmen well. Engines up to 3 HP are sufficiently powerful for a ten- to twelve-foot displacement dinghy and do not offer a great problem in finding stowage space aboard the mother vessel. It is essential to keep such a motor in the true lightweight class (23 to 35 pounds, tank filled). A bracket in a vertical locker or a cradle in the lazarette should be provided. Be certain that such a space is ventilated and always wipe off oil and gas film before stowing. Store outboard-motor gas on deck and in metal cans only.

A yacht tender requiring a number under the latest state or Federal Motorboat Act is governed by the same rules which apply to the parent vessel, except that if the tender is under 16 feet, it may in some cases not need a number. Under no circumstances does it arbitrarily take the number of the parent vessel; nor should it be assumed that since the parent vessel is numbered, the tender is exempt. Conflict exists in the case of a documented vessel. Obviously the tender cannot also be documented (since it is under 5 tons), therefore it must be numbered under state or Federal law. In such a case, it would be best to number and/or license the tender just as if it had no parent vessel.

For complete details of registering and numbering, see Chapter IV.

Outboard Motors as Auxiliary Power

128. The detachable motor has come into wide use as auxiliary power for sailboats up to 30 feet. While hardly capable of driving a heavy hull into a head wind or tide, the outboard serves faithfully when the wind dies and calm waters prevail. The open sailboat has no problem in attaching the motor. However, the decked craft requires some type of extension bracket or false transom on the stern. Ship chandlers stock various devices applicable to flat transom craft. Avoid the large "contraption" of the Rube Goldberg variety too often seen; they require more space for stowage than the motor itself. As neat and clean a device as there is consists of a small removable panel of deck in the way of the transom, just large enough to receive the motor clamp. It may be off-center to clear rudder and traveller. Steering is done by the ship's rudder, the engine being set in its "straight ahead" notch.

Some larger sailing cruisers use a dinghy–outboard-motor combination as a push boat. Pad the bow of the dinghy at the transom and rig lines from the dinghy quarters to the ship's quarters, lashing the dinghy bow amidships. These bridles may be used as steering lines, the dinghy itself becoming the rudder.

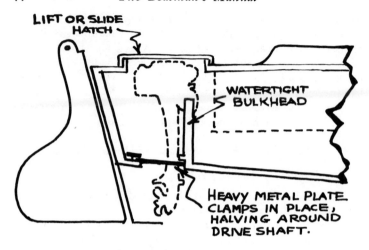

Figure 128A. Typical Motor Well on a Small Sailing Craft

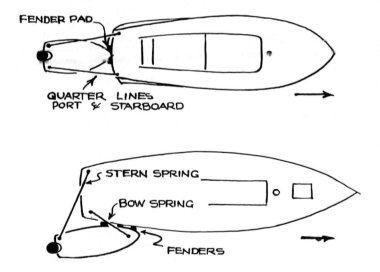

Figure 128B. How to Use an Outboard-Motor Dinghy as Auxiliary Power

If the dinghy and motor are lashed 'longside, lay against fenders and rig a spring line from the dinghy bow to the ship's quarter on the same side; then a stern line from the dinghy stern to the opposite quarter. Let the propeller extend somewhat aft of the ship's waterline (stern) and tighten the spring line so that the dinghy "toes" in to compensate for the extreme off-center power application.

Sailboats under 16 feet need not be numbered even though regularly using a detachable engine as auxiliary power nor, if the dinghy is a rowing dinghy, need it be numbered. It must carry the required equipment of its class. However, if the sailboat is over 16 feet and its engine, though a detachable motor, operates in or through a built-in motor well it may be fairly considered a powerboat and come under powerboat regulations. The matter of engine space ventilation in such a case is determined by common sense; if the engine is confined, as under a hatch, or its fumes can reach and settle within the boat, ventilation must be provided. Flame arrester and fire extinguisher, though not required, should be provided as a part of prudent seamanship.

Figure 129. A Good Type of All-Metal Boat Trailer

Boat Trailers

129. While it would appear that the factor of portability has been lost sight of in many outboard-motor boat combinations (motors 110 pounds and boats 1,200!), most owners find easy transportation and launching one of the chief advantages of the outboard outfit. Boat trailers should be light weight, preferably factory fabricated of tubing or angle stock, have a positive car hitch and be rubber-tired. Mud guards on the wheels and a tight boat cover are essentials. Be sure that the tires do not tend to float the trailer when launching. The cradle should be well padded and a secure hold-down provided.

Such a trailer must be licensed and, at night, show a red tail light and reflector in accordance with state laws.

Look with caution on car-top carrying devices. Since most depend upon an anything but firm grip on the narrow rain gutters plus a few rubber suction grips, they fall short of sound engineering. The added weight aloft sometimes dangerously affects steering, and windage, pocketed under an overturned boat, has been responsible for many accidents. Car-top devices, even though they may be safe, still do not solve the problems of launching and hauling.

Motors are rather neatly handled by a wheel and handle device related to the longshoreman's case truck. The most convenient are collapsible.

GLOSSARY

The recognized nomenclature of the principal parts of boats and their fittings is as follows:

Apron.—A timber fitted abaft the stem to reinforce the stem and to give a sufficient surface on which to land the hood ends of the planks.

Beams.—Transverse supports running from side to side to support the deck.

Bilge.—The part of the bottom, on each side of the keel, on which the boat would rest if aground.

Binding strake.—A strake of planking, usually thicker than other planks, fitted next to and under the sheer strake.

Blade, oar.—The broad flattened part of an oar as distinguished from the loom.

Boat falls.—Blocks and tackle with which the boats are hoisted aboard at davits.

Boat hook.—A pole with a blunt hook on the end to aid in landing operations or hauling alongside.

Boat plug.—A screwed metal plug fitted in the bottom planking of the boat at the lowest point to drain the bilges when boat is out of the water.

Bottom boards.—The fore-and-aft planks secured to the frames, or to floor beams, forming the floor of the boat, frequently removable.

Braces, rudder, upper, and lower.—Strips of metal secured to the rudder, the forward ends of which fit over the rudder hanger on the sternpost, thus securing the rudder and forming a pivot upon which the rudder swings.

Breaker.—A small cask for carrying potable water.

Breasthook.—A wood or metal knee fitted behind the stem structure.

Capping.—The fore-and-aft finishing piece on top of the clamp and sheer strake, at the frame heads, in an open boat.

Carling.—A fore-and-aft beam at hatches.

Chock.—A metal casting used as a fair-lead for a mooring line or anchor chain.

Clamp.—A main longitudinal strengthening member under the deck in decked-over boats and at the gunwale in open boats.

Cleat.—A horned casting for belaying lines.

Cockpit.—A compartment, usually for passengers, in an open boat.

Deadwood.—Timber built on top of the keel or shaft log at either end of the boat to afford a firm fastening for the frames and to connect the keel to the end timbers.

Fenders.—Portable wooden or rope sennit bumpers hung over the side during landings to protect the hull.

Floors.—The transverse timbers which reinforce the frames and carry the strength athwartships across the keel.

Foresheets.—The portion of the boat forward of the foremost thwart.

Frames.—The ribs of the boat; curved timbers, frequently steam-bent, secured to the keel and extending upward to the gunwale or deck.

Garboard.—The lowest strake of outside planking next to the keel.

Grapnel.—A small multiple-fluked anchor used in dragging or grappling operations; a common small boat anchor.

Gripes.—The fitting used to secure a boat in its stowage position on board ship. For boats secured at the davit heads, gripes are made of tarred hemp woven with a wood mat, backed with canvas, to hold the boat against the strongback. For lifeboats, the lower ends of the gripes are usually fitted with a slip hook. For boats secured in cradles, the gripes are usually of metal, tightened with turnbuckles, and arranged to prevent the boats from lifting from the cradles when the deck becomes awash.

Gudgeons.—Small metal fittings, similar to eyebolts, secured to the sternpost of very small boats on which the rudder hangs. Used in place of the rudder hanger of larger boats.

Gunwale.—The upper edge of the side of an open boat.

Hanger, rudder.—A vertical strip of metal, secured to the sternpost, forming the traveler upon which the rudder braces are secured.

Hoisting pads.—Metal fittings inside the boat often attached to the keel to take the hoisting slings or hoisting rods.

Horn timber.—The after deadwood (often called counter timber) fastening the shaft log and transom knee together.

Keel.—The principal timber of a boat, extending from stem to stern at the bottom of the hull and supporting the whole frame.

Keel stop.—A small metal fitting on the keel, at the after end, to act as a stop in locating the boat in a fore-and-aft position on the keel rest when stowing the boat in the cradle.

Keelsons.—Fore-and-aft structural timbers either above or outboard of the keel.

Knee.—A shaped timber for connecting construction members installed at an angle to each other. Some knees are sawn from straight-grained wood, while in other cases the grain follows the natural bend of the tree at a limb or root.

Leather.—The portion of an oar which rests in the rowlock. This is sometimes covered with canvas, but is usually covered with leather.

Loom.—Rounded portion of an oar between the blade and handle.

Norman pin.—A metal pin fitted in a towing post or bitt for belaying the line.

Painter.—A rope used in the bow for towing or for securing the boat.

Pintles.—Small straight pieces of metal secured to the rudder and fitting in the gudgeons on the sternpost of very small boats, thus supporting the rudder. Pintles and gudgeons are used in place of the rudder braces of larger boats.

Plank-sheer.—The outermost deck plank at the side.

Risings.—The fore-and-aft stringers inside a boat, secured to the frames, on which the thwarts rest.

Rowlocks.—Forked pieces of metal in which the leathers of oars rest while pulling. *Sunken rowlocks* are those which are set down in the gunwale of the boat. *Swivel rowlocks* rotate, the shank of the rowlock fitting in a socket in the gunwale.

Sheer.—The line of form at the side which the gunwale or deck edge follows in profile.

Sheer strake.—The uppermost strake of planking at the side following the line of sheer.

Side fender.—A longitudinal timber projecting beyond the outside line of the hull planking, often metal faced, to protect the hull.

Slings.—Gear made of wire rope and close-linked chain for handling boats at booms or cranes.

Spars.—Masts, booms, and gaffs upon which, when stepped in the boat, the sails are spread.

Steering rowlock.—A form of swivel rowlock, fitted near the stern of a whaleboat or motor whaleboat, in which the steering oar is shipped; sometimes called a crutch.

Stem.—The upright timber in the forward part of a boat, joined to the keel by a knee.

Stem band.—A metal facing or cutwater fitted on the stempost.

Stem heel (The forward deadwood).—A timber, often called the sole piece, used to connect the stem knee to the keel.

Stern fast.—A stern painter for use in securing the stern of a boat.

Stern hook.—Same as breasthook, for stern on a double-ended boat.

Sternpost.—The principal vertical piece of timber at the after end of a boat, its lower end fastened to the keel or shaft log by a stern knee.

Stern sheets.—The space in the boat abaft the thwarts.

Strakes.—Continuous lines of fore-and-aft planking. Each line of planking is known as a strake.

Stretchers.—Athwartship, movable pieces against which the oarsmen brace their feet in pulling.

Stringers, bilge.—Longitudinal strengthening timbers inside the hull.

Strongback.—The spar between the davits to which a boat is griped.

Tarpaulin.—A waterproof fabric cover to keep stores dry while being transported.

Tholepin.—A pin fitted in the gunwale plank for use in place of a rowlock. Used with Manila ring about five inches in diameter, called a *tholepin grommet*.

Thrum mats.—Mats made of a small piece of canvas, with short strands of rope yarn sewed on them, called *thrumming*. These are placed between the rowlocks and the oars to prevent noise in pulling.

Tiller.—A bar or lever, fitted fore and aft in the rudder head, by which the rudder is moved.

Towing bitts (Often called towing posts).—A vertical timber securely fastened for use in towing or mooring.

Trailing lines.—Small lines secured to the boat and around the oars to prevent the latter from getting adrift when trailed from swivel rowlocks.

Transom.—The planking across the stern in a transomed boat.

Yoke.—Athwartship piece fitting over the rudder head, by which the rudder is moved by yoke ropes when the tiller is not shipped.

CHAPTER II

HANDLING BOATS UNDER SAIL

Boat sailing is done today almost entirely under fore-and-aft rigs. The square rig has always been the sail dress of ships capable of carrying the large crew necessary to handle the rig. It was essentially the rig of deep water where the ship had sea room enough to "go find a breeze"; and with one of the trades or other steady and predictable winds abeam or astern, long, fast passages were made with regularity and safety.

Wind conditions near the land are never predictable except in so far as they generally provide breezes either from the land or toward the land in normal stormless periods. Any sailing vessel sails best with the wind abeam or *reaching*. Small vessels, fishermen and coasters which did not sail foreign seas nor engage in an overseas trade, soon learned that in their normal trade between coastal ports this beam wind, permitting fast reaching courses on either board, called for the fore-and-aft rig. Not only did this rig give them maximum day-in and day-out speed and safety, but it was also very handy for quick maneuvering in tight harbors and rivers, and required an absolute minimum of hands to sail.

Deepwater ships in island or short-run service, making many ports per voyage, learned the advantage of the fore-and-aft rig for inshore work and well knew the advantages of the square rig in the ocean trades. Hence, we find such combinations as the topsail schooner, the brigantine, the barkentine, and the jackass bark; rigs which were efficient for deepwater or coasting.

The sail rig for the boat has always been the fore-and-aft rig for obvious reasons. Occasionally, as in the case of a deepwater cruiser or an offshore banksman, a combination rig is carried which makes use of one or more square sails, known, on yachts, as trade-wind sails and raffees. A sail often carried by fore-and-aft boats is the spinnaker in one of its several forms; a sail directly related to the square sail, though not modernly rigged to a yard nor sheeted as an out-and-out square sail.

The working rig of all sailboats is the fore-and-aft rig. The principle and the basic handling of all fore-and-aft rigs are the same. If

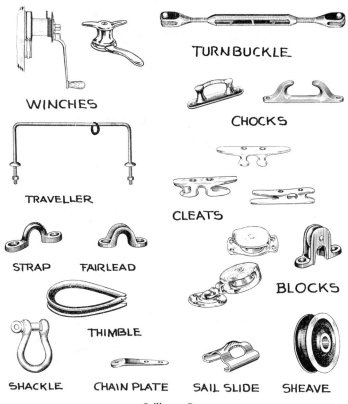

Sailboat Gear

a sailor understands the handling of a catboat, the simplest form of the fore-and-aft rig, he can, with but little additional practice, also handle more complex forms, such as the sloop, the cutter, the yawl, the ketch, and the schooner.

201. Men have been sailing for centuries without understanding the force which drove them. Only recently, with the subject much aired by the scientific approach of airplane and yacht designers, have we begun to understand the action of moving air or wind on our sails.

There is nothing strange in the phenomenon of a sailboat moving before the wind. The pressure of the wind on the spread sail is suffi-

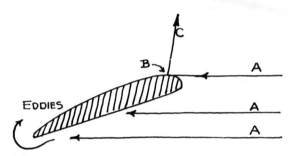

Figure 201. The Force of Wind on an Airplane Wing. Note Change of Direction of Force AB

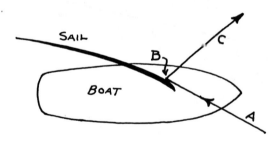

The Same Force on a Sail

cient to overcome the retarding effect of the water on the hull, and the entire assembly, sail, spars, and hull, moves in the direction of the wind.

However, when the wind is on the beam or ahead and the assembly actually moves *against* the force which is moving it, entirely different, and until recently unknown, principles come into play.

What happens when a boat moves against the wind is simply that the direction of the force of the wind has been changed. A certain proportion of this force or power is dispersed and wasted. A remaining proportion is conserved (through efficient design, setting, and handling of the sails) and becomes useful power.

In the language of the layman, this useful force is in the form of a vacuum, on the leeward side of the sail, which exerts a suction or pull. In Figure 201 is represented an airplane wing. The wind A exerts some force on the undersurface, "holding it up," but a far

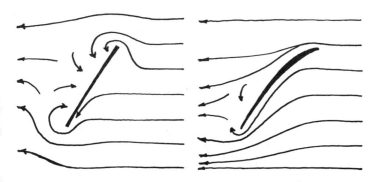

Figure 202A. Excessive Eddy Making of a Flat Surface   Reduced Eddy Making of an Airfoiled Surface

greater force is exerted at point B where a negative or lifting force comes into play because of the change in the direction of the force. This direction is approximately shown by the arrow C.

If we now stand the wing on end, so to speak, as if its leading edge were lashed to a boat's mast, this same force would exist but its changed direction would exert a suction not upward but forward—resulting in progress against the driving force.

Because our sail is of one thickness, without a "bottom" and different in contour from the top surface (as in the airplane wing), it has certain advantages over the wing. Its inside or after shape is taken, as allowed by the suction on the opposite or forward side, as a result of the pressure of the wind against it. Being flexible, the sail becomes air-foiled, that is, perfectly balanced between the two components of the wind. This air-foiling is all-important, as it reduces to a minimum the eddies which tend to destroy the suction power on the forward side.

202. Some eddies cannot be entirely eliminated. These are chiefly those caused by the leach or after edge of the sail. These form the "dead areas" present to some degree in all sails, no matter how well designed or bent. (Figure 202A.)

The leading edge of the sail does most of the work, for here, on its leeward side, occurs the pull or suction. The leading edge of a sail

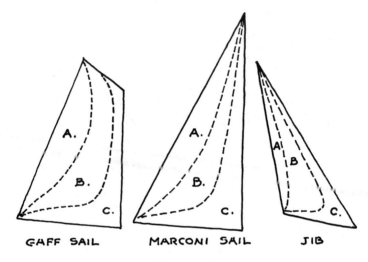

GAFF SAIL   MARCONI SAIL   JIB

Figure 202B

A. Little or no drive
B. Moderate drive
C. Much drive

is called the *luff*. The efficiency of the luff is somewhat impaired by the eddies set up by the mast (in the "much-drive" area of the sails shown in Figure 202B).

In order to eliminate these hindering eddies, a foresail or a jib is used. The air spilling from the leach of the foresail or jib destroys the eddies and restores the drive of the sail aft of it. To some extent, the foresail, or the jib, helps the drive of the sail aft of it in another way. The wind velocity is increased in the narrow "funnel" between the two sails, and results in an increased pressure at the luff of the mainsail, exactly where it is needed most. If this funnel is made too narrow by excessive sheeting-in of the foresail or jib, or by the use of a jib which overlaps the mainsail too much, it back-winds the mainsail and invades the luff vacuum, destroying its suction power. Excessive narrowing of the funnel will so pocket the wind as to form a vacuum on the *after* side of the mainsail, drawing the boat *backwards*.

203. By applying the parallelogram of forces to the wind force (Figure 203) of a vessel sailing *into* the wind, the force is broken into

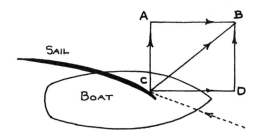

Figure 203. The Parallelogram of Forces

its component parts. Its forward drive in a direction parallel to the keel is represented by lines AB and CD. Its side drive (called leeway) is represented by lines AC and BD.

The boat is somewhat like a watermelon seed squeezed between the fingers, the force in each finger pushing an opposite side and the watermelon seed shooting forward along a line which is roughly a neutral force line; one along which the seed meets the least resistance. The force CB drives the boat ahead but also sideways.

The object is to have the boat sail ahead as much as possible and sideways as little as possible. This is accomplished by designing the hull to offer the *greatest* resistance to the wind's force, as represented by the lines AC and BD; to resist side motion; and also to design the hull so that it offers the *least* resistance to the wind's force, as represented by the lines AB and CD; the direction in which we wish the boat to go, or to windward.

Resistance to side motion (lines AC and BD) is accomplished by
fitting the boat with a keel or a centerboard so that a large surface
or plane is presented to resist forces AC and BD. Inasmuch as this
large surface is presented in water, a fluid of much greater density
than air, it is obvious that the forces AC and BD cannot move the boat
as quickly nor as much through the water as through the air.

In order to have the boat present the least resistance to being driven
along the lines AB and CD (or ahead) its hull and upper parts are so

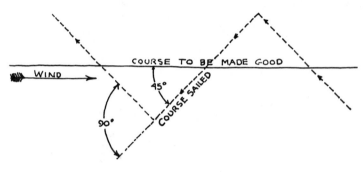

Figure 204. Tacking

designed as to offer the least resistance to the water and air through
which it is to be driven.

Good hull design, sharp bows, easy runs and sterns, minimum *flat*
planes and minimum areas of wetted surface are some of the elements
combined to permit easy motion forward through the water.

Minimum above-the-water parts (such as deckhouses, spars, and
rigging), and these of streamlined design, permit the easy motion
forward through the air.

A happy combination of proper design will find the boat sailing
approximately along lines AB and CD, the direction in which the
boat is required to go. The forces AC and BD cannot be entirely
overcome, and the boat will make a certain amount of leeway or side
motion.

204. It is evident that the boat will not sail directly into the wind;
or *against* its driving force. Consequently, tacking must be resorted
to; that is, the boat is steered as closely into the wind as possible

(about 45° from a true windward course), with the wind's force on one side and then the boat "put about" or veered about 90° into the wind, until the wind's force is exerted on the opposite side of the boat. Thus, in a series of steps or jogs, motion is made directly into the wind. Such a course represents a greater distance sailed than a straight line to windward, of course. (Figure 204.)

205. The study of aerodynamics (which includes sailing) is a complicated and involved one, of course; but it is an exact science. This manual can hardly do more than mention the subject in presenting the foregoing elemental ideas.

However, it is entirely possible to sail, and sail well, without understanding any part of the theory of sailing. Anybody can sail—it becomes an art only when a person can sail well, that is, when sailing is done in the most efficient and safe manner, when there is nothing lubberly in the handling, and when the "boat and skipper become one." When that occurs the theory of sailing is utilized, though it may not be understood; the skipper has acquired a "feel" or a sixth sense, and the practical results are exactly the same as if the complicated phenomenon of sailing were thoroughly understood.

206. No book and no set of diagrams can teach anybody to sail. There is but one school—the school of experience. Armed with the messages of the printed page, the student *must* sail to become a sailor. Text and diagrams, at best, can merely ease some of the knocks and bumps of the school of experience.

In giving the rudiments of sailing, the sloop will be used as an example in the following pages. Subsequent parts of this chapter will deal with only the special characteristics of other fore-and-aft types, as the basic handling is exactly the same as for the sloop.

THE SLOOP

207. Sails are sheeted (adjusted in relation to the center line of the boat) to meet four general conditions: (Figure 207B.)

1. On the wind (or close-hauled).
2. Off the wind (or reaching).
3. Running before it (sailing free, scudding).
4. To give maximum drive to the mainsail.

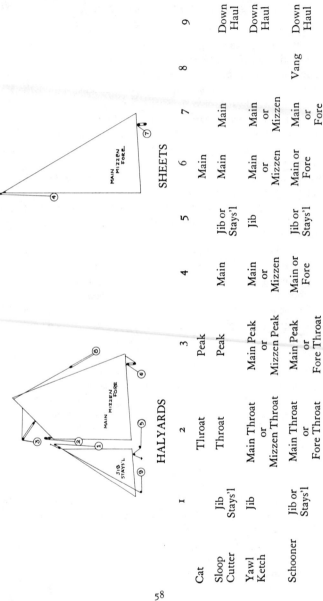

| | HALYARDS | | | SHEETS | | | | | |
	1	2	3	4	5	6	7	8	9
Cat		Throat	Peak			Main			
Sloop Cutter	Jib Stays'l	Throat	Peak	Main	Jib or Stays'l	Main	Main		Down Haul
Yawl Ketch	Jib	Main Throat or Mizzen Throat	Main Peak or Mizzen Peak	Main or Mizzen	Jib	Main or Mizzen	Main or Mizzen		Down Haul
Schooner	Jib or Stays'l	Main Throat or Fore Throat	Main Peak or Fore Throat	Main or Fore	Jib or Stays'l	Main or Fore	Main or Fore	Vang	Down Haul

Figure 206. Principal Running Rigging of Sailboats

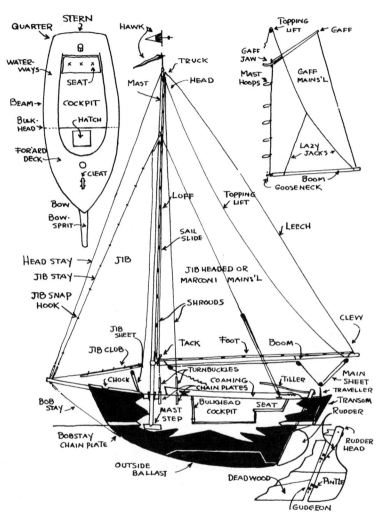

Figure 207A. The Parts of a Sailboat

59

208. A boat is sailing on the wind when the wind comes from a point forward of six points on the bow (Figure 208A). The sails are sheeted flat, that is, almost parallel to the keel of the boat. The general rule for sailing on the wind is to keep the sails full, sheets not too flat, but every sail drawing, and the boat definitely alive and moving. This trim is reached by having the boom somewhere between the rudder-

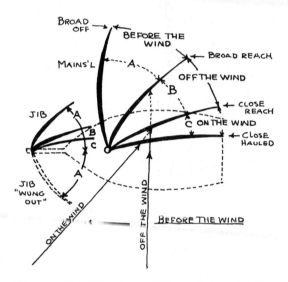

Figure 207B. Sail Position on Different Points of Sailing

head and the quarter, and the boat pointed, by steering, in a direction in which the luff of the mainsail is just about to flutter.

To actually permit it to flutter or collapse indicates that its power has been destroyed (by eddying). To permit the wind to strike the sail too broadly when close-hauled will cause excessive leeway, and thus loss of forward speed and forward distance.

A good helmsman steers by the luff. He keeps the boat headed so that there is neither flutter nor undue fullness on the after side of the sail. Helping to keep this course, in addition to constant watchfulness of the luff (using eyes and that sixth sense which all good sailors develop), is a wind pennant. This is a small flag of bunting or light metal mounted on the masthead and extending well beyond the eddies of the sail peak. It indicates the true direction of the wind, and the helmsman endeavors to maintain the angle which he found by experimentation between it and the boat's course. The wake also indicates the true course in relation to the wind. Ranges of any fixed object ashore or afloat also serve as a bearing, but when so used allowance

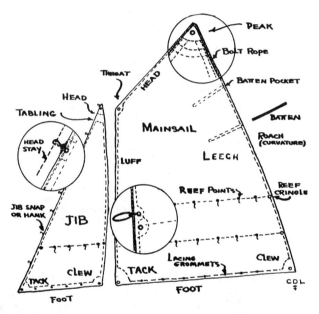

Figure 207C. The Parts of Fore-and-Aft Sails

must be made for tide, current, and leeway. Generally, a range is useful only for a short hitch. As current, tide, or leeway remove the boat from its first observed course to the range, allowance must be made and another bearing taken, even though to the same object.

209. While sailing close-hauled, the sail should be as flat as possible; topping lift slacked off, and luff stretched fully along the mast, and foot stretched fully along the boom. This point of sailing is the most dangerous of any, and the sheet is never belayed while close-hauled

or "pointing." The boat heels most on this point, and any sudden puff of wind, or any combination of normal wind and steep sea may see the boat heeled to dangerous angles.

This is parried by: (1) Immediately heading the boat directly into the wind, so that the sails flutter over their entire surfaces. The boat will "stand up straight" at once; and will also lose its headway if the

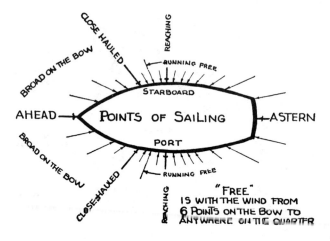

Figure 208A

course is held into the wind; (2) letting the sheet run out but keeping the basic course. The boat will at once stand up but not as straight as in maneuver (1), because the jib and part of the mainsail are still under wind pressure. However, not as much headway is lost; if the sail is promptly sheeted-in, there will be practically no time or speed lost. The sheet is never "let fly," merely slacked off a few feet. To "let fly" might permit the boom to strike the water and kill steerageway entirely, and create a dangerous situation.

A boat is designed to sail in a heeled position. To have the seas lapping the rail is not a sign of danger nor an indication to shorten sail or luff up. Keelboats are in no danger until the seas actually begin spilling into the cockpit. However, nothing is actually gained by sailing with the rail buried for a long period, as the contours of the deck and deck fixtures decidedly slow the boat's speed. Centerboard boats generally become dangerous when the seas begin reaching inboard of the rail. They are then approaching a critical angle beyond which it is unsafe to go. The factor of stability is relatively small in a centerboard or unballasted boat; it very quickly turns from a safe to a dangerous boat. Live ballast, of course, well to windward very much increases the safe heeling angle of the centerboarder.

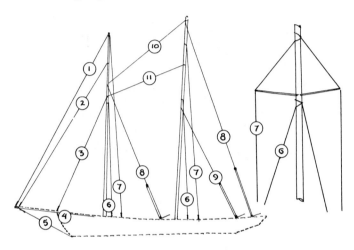

Figure 208B. Principal Standing Rigging

    1. Headstay
    2. Jibstay
    3. Forestay
    4. Bowsprit shroud
    5. Bobstay (sometimes ends in chain)
    6. Lower shroud
    7. Upper shroud
    8. Backstay (partly running rigging)
    9. Lowermast backstay
   10. Springstay
   11. Triatic stay

Note: Each stay takes its name from the mast it supports, thus:

    No. 7 on a schooner—main upper shroud
    No. 6 on a yawl—mizzen lower shroud

210. In strong winds it may become apparent that the boat is over-canvased, in which case reefing will have to be resorted to. Figure 210 shows how to reef all common sails. If for some reason reefing is not possible, it is still possible to continue sailing safely and with reasonable speed by the following maneuver: Trim in the jib flat amidships. Start the mainsheet until the sail is about 50 per cent luffing, or until

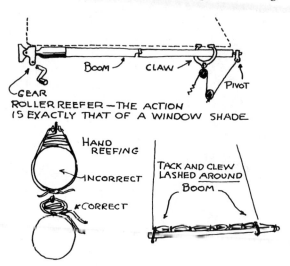

Figure 210.

the "much-drive" area has been destroyed. The boat will sail on providing it is not pinched too closely into the wind. This is called lazy reefing. What it lacks in windward qualities it makes up for in speed, and it will see the same point reached in about the same time as in usual reefing.

211. A well-designed boat almost steers herself when close-hauled. Very little rudder effort is required to keep a straight course. However, this quality can be utterly destroyed by the improper sheeting of sails, as related to each other. Each boat has a different point at which the sails are set exactly right—which point is to be found by experimentation. Any unbalance in this set is reflected in undue rudder effort. If the rudder "pulls" hard (always providing that the boat is correctly hung, and that the cause does not lie elsewhere, a matter to be discussed later), it usually can be eased by adjusting the set of the jib. This position is somewhat of a compromise between a position of the utmost drive and one of least rudder effort. Sharp rudder angles slow a boat enormously, and it is wise to sacrifice some jib drive to gain fair underwater lines.

212. If the wind is blowing on the starboard (right) side of the boat and the boom extends to the port (left), the boat is said to be sailing on the starboard tack.

If the wind is blowing on the port (left) side of the boat and the boom extends to the starboard (right), the boat is said to be sailing on the port tack.

213. Tacking consists of the steps required to put a boat on the opposite tack from which she has been sailing. It is called *coming about* and is carried out as follows:

1. Warning is given by the hail *Ready about!* and the boat headed slightly away from the wind to give it maximum speed.

2. Just before commencing the evolution a further warning of *Hard alee* is given and the helm pushed hard down to leeward.

3. When the boat points directly into the wind (sails will be luffing), it is permitted to run ahead under its own momentum with the helm amidships.

4. As way is lost, the helm is moved gently and the boat's head brought around so that the wind reaches the opposite side of the sail, and she at once moves off on the new tack.

As most small boats have self-trimming sheets, no adjustment of sheet positions will be required. Overlapping jibs (called Genoas) will need to be cast off on the leeward side as the boat enters the maneuver, and the new leeward sheet will need to be trimmed as it enters upon the new tack.

214. Failure of the boat to complete the maneuver will find her without headway, possibly sternway, and inclined to remain in a permanently luffing position. To again get her sailing it is necessary to:

1. (*a*) Trim the jib in as flat as possible.

(*b*) Push the boom slightly away from the direction in which you wish the bow to swing. The boat will slowly swing on the tack desired. Appropriate rudder action must follow as soon as headway has been regained and the sails are drawing.

2. Go forward and hold the jib away from the direction in which you wish the bow to swing, permitting the mainsail to luff the while.

A boat in the position just described is said to be in irons or in stays. Properly handled no boat should ever go into irons. Persistence in so doing may be cured by centerboard adjustments or by slacking off the jib sheets before going about. In strange waters boats go in irons because of unfamiliarity with local tides and currents which upset the maneuver calculations of sometimes even the most careful helmsman. Small boats, willing to be branded as a lubber's ship, sometimes work out of irons by using the rudder as a sculling oar, or by actually paddling the stern or bow around with an oar.

Wearing

215. Wearing is another method of tacking or coming about onto the opposite tack. In a light or moderate breeze, the boat is slowly rounded to a position with the wind aft. As the head is brought around and the wind begins to cross the stern, the sails are sheeted in smartly, being held amidships as the wind actually reaches and passes the center line of the boat. Now, as the head swings round to the new course, the sheets are slowly paid out and belayed when at the proper point of trim. The boat is kept sailing during the entire maneuver.

Reaching or Off the Wind

216. Reaching is the fastest and sportiest point of sailing for most sailboats. The boat not only moves ahead faster but makes considerably less leeway than when sailing close-hauled. In consequence, a course can be sailed by bearings or by compass with more accuracy than when close-hauled.

No special sailing instructions are required to sail on a reach. Under certain conditions of sea, a boat on a reach will roll quite easily, and it is always good therefore to look to the topping lift and see that the boom is kept well out of the sea. Ordinarily, only about 60 per cent of the centerboard area is required on a reach (the sheathing of the board alone contributing much to speed), but exposing its full area will often lessen the roll.

.In entering other points of sailing from a reach, it is of the utmost importance that the skipper know his boat well before attempting to skip a step. While a boat can be brought from a port reach to a starboard reach without loss of motion or without going into stays, the tyro would do best to first close-haul the boat, then come about in the usual manner, and then slowly come from the new tack to the new reach.

A boat can also be got around by wearing, or, as it would be called under these circumstances, gybing. In this manuever, the very nicest timing and seamanship are required in order that the sails are not dashed violently from one board to the other, causing parted sheets, broken spars, bashed heads, or any other combination of these disasters. Such a violent gybing, with or without disastrous results, is called an accidental gybe. If the manuever is carefully planned (*see* paragraph 215) and is successful, it is called an intentional gybe.

Ordinarily, boats cruising or day sailing do not use the intentional gybe unless forced to. In racing, however, it is often used, and it provides an extremely fast manner of changing tacks or courses.

Before the Wind

217. When running before the wind, or sailing downhill, as it is called, the mainsail should be at approximately right angles to the keel of the boat. While the boat will still continue to sail downhill if the sail is sheeted in, it will then begin to make leeway and not sail a straight down-wind course. Very little leeway is made, however, by sheeting the sail aft just enough to clear the shrouds. Such leeway can be compensated for by setting the jib out on the opposite side from the mainsail by rigging a temporary boom (a boat hook or whisker pole). Speed will be increased as well.

If the jib is not boomed out it will hang idle from its stay and have no driving value whatsoever.

When sailing before the wind, the topping lift should be set up to prevent the boom from dragging in the water and to give the sail more pocket or belly, a desirable feature on this point of sailing.

A danger always present when sailing before the wind is that of an accidental gybe. A sudden wind shift or a yaw of the boat may very easily bring the wind to bear on the forward side of the sail and whip it against its sheet on the opposite board. A gybe under these conditions may well result in capsizing, and almost certainly the carrying away of spars or rigging or both.

If the jib is not "wung out" (boomed out or sailing wing and wing) it becomes an ideal gybe warning. As long as it remains quietly asleep forward of the mainsail there is no danger of gybing. If, however, it suddenly fills on the opposite side from the mainsail, or lashes forward against the head or jibstay (called a scandalized jib), it is giving timely warning that the point of a gybe is being approached. In general, in sailing before the wind it is safest to keep the wind over the quarter opposite to the side over which the mainsail is boomed. This may necessitate a slightly longer course, seldom more than a few yards per mile, however, and is called tacking down wind.

In light airs, the boom can be kept on the side where it belongs by heeling the boat (by live ballast) toward the boom. In heavy weather, a down-wind course can be made under jib alone with more safety than under a reefed mainsail.

Give Maximum Drive to the Mainsail

218. To get the greatest drive out of a mainsail it is essential that the area of "much drive" be in no way violated. The sail must be bent

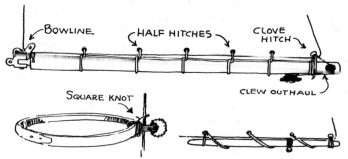

Figure 218. Sail Bending
Top—lashing to a gaff or boom
Left—lashing to a hoop
Right—lacing to a jib club

and hoisted so that this area is free from wrinkles. The luff should be fitted with ample track slides or mast hoops so that it does not present a scalloped effect. (Figure 218.)

When sheeting the mainsail, the important angle is that of this "much-drive" area to the keel rather than the angle of the boom. This angle must be correctly reached and maintained, even at the cost of a slight flopping of the leach.

On the wind and off the wind, the mainsail drives best if it is reasonably flat, its foot and gaff lacings secure and tight, and the foot and head boltropes hauled tight. Before the wind a belly or pocket effect is more efficient. Generally, these conditions can be achieved by the use of the topping lift; slack for the two first-mentioned points of sailing, and taut, carrying the boom, for the last-mentioned.

The drive of small boats is very easily killed by the injudicious placing of passengers or crew. In general, sitting high on the rails, or hanging in the shrouds, or sprawling on the forward deck or cabin top, creates eddies which reduce the efficiency of the sail. Objects placed on the deck (like dinghies or bundled spare sails) have a similar effect. In racing boats, such as the Stars, this idea is carried out even to streamlining or eliminating most of the common small-deck fittings, guardrails, combings, etc.

The jib often kills the drive of the mainsail. As a rule the jib (or any foresail) is set at an angle of about 15° greater to the wind than to the mainsail.

When a boat is on the wind, it is a decided advantage to so dispose the live ballast as to bring it as near to an even keel as possible. Eddies from the lifted windward topsides sometimes completely kill the drive along the foot of the sail.

Centerboard and Keels

219. The keelboat has its underwater parts permanently fixed. Its skin friction cannot be changed. However, the boat which is equipped with a centerboard can greatly increase its sailing speed by the proper use of the centerboard. The correct positions for various points of sailing are shown in Figure 219.

Trim

220. By trim is meant the position in which the boat will sail best after the distribution of the ballast, both live and otherwise, and after the correct setting of the sails.

Thwartship trim should find the fixed ballast low down and the boat standing with its mast plumb when viewed from bow or stern. Thwartship trim on small boats can be adjusted to suit sailing conditions by the disposal of the live weights to windward in breezes and winds, amidships in gentle breezes, and to leeward in calms or near calms.

Fixed ballast (inside ballast in the form of iron or lead pigs, bags of sand or stone) is never adjusted to meet sailing conditions requiring thwartship trim. Certain racing boats, called sandbaggers, now almost obsolete, are an exception to this statement. Thwartship trim is seldom

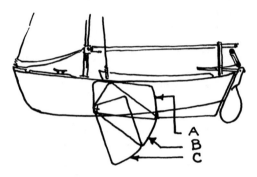

Figure 219. Correct Centerboard Positions for Various Points of Sailing

A. Before the wind
B. Reaching
C. Close-hauled

If, while reaching, the boat rolls excessively, lower board to position C.

If, while before the wind, the boat rolls excessively, lower the board to position B.

required in the well-designed and properly sailed boat except after a certain point of heeling has been reached, when the shifting to windward of passengers will extend the margin of the safe heeling angle.

221. Boats are considered in trim when the waterline is parallel to the water, always assuming that the hull then presents its best form for driving. However, in boats up to about 25 feet waterline, the shifting of fore-and-aft ballast will have a marked effect upon sailing. Centerboard or shallow boats are more sensitive to this ballast adjustment than keelboats.

The ballast adjustment is usually made by shifting passengers or crew (and occasionally sandbags) fore or aft under the following conditions:

1. Shifting the ballast forward will give the boat a tendency to head into the wind. It will relieve a lee helm.

2. Shifting the ballast aft will give the boat a tendency to fall away from the wind. It will relieve a weather helm. When running before

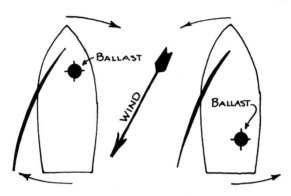

Figure 221. Effect of Ballast Shift on Helm

the wind, the ballast moved aft will give the boat a beneficial drag by the stern and hold the rudder deeper in the water.

Lee and Weather Helm

222. A boat which, without rudder effort, tends to head into the wind is said to carry a *weather helm*. All boats are designed to carry a slight weather helm, so that if for any reason the tiller must be abandoned the boat will immediately cease sailing (by heading into the wind and luffing). A weather helm is desirable.

A boat which, without rudder effort, tends to swing her bow away from the wind is said to carry a *lee helm*. Boats are designed so as not to carry a lee helm. If, for any reason, the helm must be abandoned, the boat will fall off *on the wind,* wear, and possibly gybe. Lee helm is undesirable and dangerous.

Lee or excessive weather helm can be cured by:

1. Adjusting fore-and-aft ballast (trimming).

2. Adjusting the set of the jib or other headsails.

3. Checking the balance of the sails to see that one end does not overpower the other. This balance is usually perfect under plain or working sails. It is often upset when carrying light airs, or storm canvas, or when reefed. (For example, when tucking in a reef in the mainsail, its area is so reduced that the jib will upset the sail balance. The jib must be reefed as well, or a storm jib of reduced area set.)

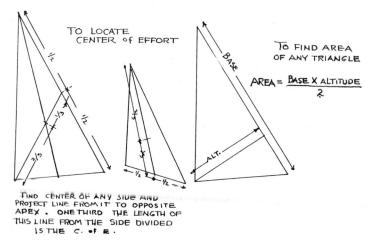

TO LOCATE CENTER of EFFORT

TO FIND AREA OF ANY TRIANGLE

$$AREA = \frac{BASE \times ALTITUDE}{2}$$

FIND CENTER OF ANY SIDE AND PROJECT LINE FROM IT TO OPPOSITE APEX. ONE THIRD THE LENGTH OF THIS LINE FROM THE SIDE DIVIDED IS THE C. of E.

Figure 223A. Jib-headed Sail

4. Checking the relationship of the center of effort of the sails to the center of lateral resistance of the hull.

223. This relationship is established according to well-known engineering rules. If an engineer or naval architect has designed the boat and the boat has been built according to design, these relationships are probably correct. However, changes in rig, in hull, in trim, in mast positions may have upset this relationship with resultant objectionable lee or weather helm, poor sailing, dangerous sailing, or failure to sail at all.

In calculating the factors entering into this relationship, both the sails and the hull profile are considered as flat planes; the sail plane subject to pressure by the wind, and the hull plane subject to resistance in making leeway through the water. Each is given a reference point, this point being the center of the pressure of the wind and the center of the resistance of the water pressure.

These centers are found by the methods shown in Figures 223 A, B, C, D, and E.

If transferred to drawing paper, the relationship can readily be checked. The center of sail pressure is called the center of effort and

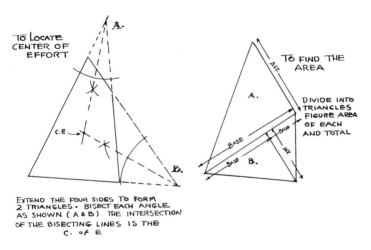

TO LOCATE CENTER OF EFFORT

C.E

A.

B.

EXTEND THE FOUR SIDES TO FORM 2 TRIANGLES · BISECT EACH ANGLE AS SHOWN (A & B) THE INTERSECTION OF THE BISECTING LINES IS THE C. of E

TO FIND THE AREA

DIVIDE INTO TRIANGLES FIGURE AREA OF EACH AND TOTAL

A.

ALT

BASE

BASE

ALT

BASE

B.

Figure 223B. Gaff Sails

is a common center of the effort of all working sails. The areas of roaches and the overlap of overlapping sails (such as a Genoa) are not considered in calculating the area of sails. The center of hull resistance is called the center of lateral resistance. The rudder is not considered in the calculations but the centerboard, fully dropped, is. Large rudders, such as those found on catboats, are sometimes partly considered, and the forward one-third of the area is calculated as part of the lateral plane.

Upon being diagramed on paper the center of effort should lead the center of lateral resistance. No fixed amount can be determined beforehand as it varies with every design. The separation, or lead, will, however, be somewhere around 6% of the waterline length separation

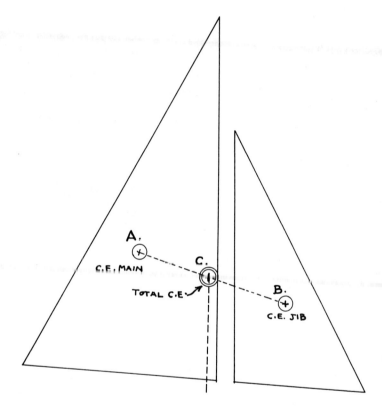

Figure 223C. Finding the Total Center of Effort

Draw the sails in their exact relationship and connect the two centers by the line A-B. Divide the product of multiplying the area of the jib by the scaled length of A-B by the sum of the areas of the jib and the main- sail. The result is the scaled distance from C. to A.

$$\text{Rule: } AC = \frac{\text{Area of jib} \times \text{A-B}}{\text{Area of jib} + \text{area of mainsail}}$$

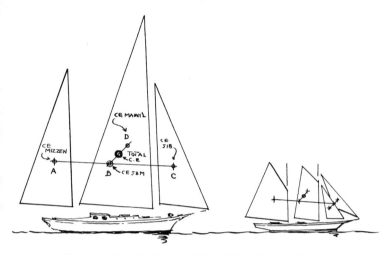

Figure 223D. Finding C. of E. of Two-Masted Vessels

In sail plans of more than two sails the following practice is used: The sail areas are treated in rotation for CE. The common center of any two is found; then this is taken as a single area and combined with the next, and so on.

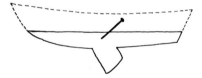

Figure 223E. Finding the Center of Lateral Resistance

Cut out of cardboard, metal, or plywood the exact *underwater* shape of the hull drawn to scale. Balance at the outer edge with a pin or needle. The point from which the waterline hangs level is the C.L.R. The point is transferred to the master drawing. The C.L.R. is anyplace along a vertical line drawn through the point.

between the two points. The important point of such a check is to find out whether the center of effort actually does lead the center of lateral resistance. If a safe boat, having a weather helm, is required, the CE *must* lead the CLR.

224. A radical upset of the relationship must be corrected by redesigning the sail plan.

A slight upset of the relationship can be corrected by adjusting the

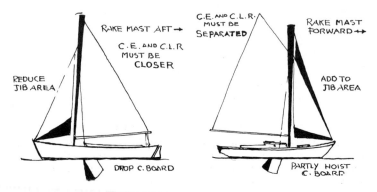

Figure 224. To Cure Mild Lee Helm   To Cure Mild Weather Helm

present sail plan or by adjusting the rake of the masts, the position of the centerboard, etc.

Heavy Weather Sailing

225. Heavy weather sailing on the wind is always made easier and more comfortable by quartering into the seas rather than by meeting them head on. To attempt to "buck" steep seas will only result in the boat's being stopped by each attacking sea and perhaps even being thrown backward, if headway has not been regained between attacks.

If the boat becomes too hard-pressed, assuming a dangerous angle of heel, sail shortening must be resorted to. This is called reefing. Careful and smart sailors reef before it is absolutely necessary. Not only does such a course give them a fairly large margin of safety, but it results in a better course and faster time. The boat carrying full sail in reefing weather must frequently luff or spill her wind. She then heads directly into the seas, stops dead, and must be gotten under way again. This may or may not be possible to accomplish before the next sea attacks. The reefed boat will not need to luff, and she can maintain course and speed without loss of time.

It is time to reef an open boat when the seas begin to approach the lee rail; not after the water has actually come aboard.

It is time to reef a decked boat when the seas begin to regularly flood the deck; not after the cockpit has been flooded.

It is time to reef a cabin boat when any part of the deck or deck fixtures (trunks, cabins, etc.) regularly are submerged.

226. Reefing is accomplished by reducing the areas of existing sails by mechanical means (Figure 210). Balance must always be maintained; the reefed-sail plan must have its common center of effort at approximately the same place as the full-sail plan.

(Multisailed craft reduce areas by reefing and also by various sail combinations. Figure 226.)

Small boats are best reefed by dropping all sails and tying in the reefs without way on. When tied, the mainsail is hoisted first, acting somewhat like a weather vane and tending to swing the bow into the wind. The jib is then hoisted, the main sheeted in, the jib sheeted in, and the boat put on its course.

A reef on a small boat is best shaken out (or untied) by reversing the above procedure.

When reefing under way, the boat must be sailing close-hauled in order to have the boom inboard. The helm should be manned constantly while reefing under way.

A hand reef is tied in by first lashing the tack and the clew, passing several turns of light line through the cringles and *around* the boom. The reef points are then tied in, starting foreward and proceeding aft, the points passing between the boom and the foot boltrope and being tied, all on the same side, with a square or reef knot. A loop (or half bow) will permit easy shaking out again.

A hand reef is shaken out by casting off the points first, then the clew lashing, then the tack lashing.

227. Running before a sea is always dangerous.

There is danger of rolling the boom into the sea, in which event it will act like a rudder, take charge of the boat, and result in a gybe.

To prevent this danger:

1. Top the boom sharply by means of the topping lift.

2. Steer with a long oar instead of the rudder (which frequently "rolls" out of the water).

3. Lower the centerboard to prevent rolling.

4. Ballast the opposite side to the one on which the boom is.

There is danger of being "pooped."

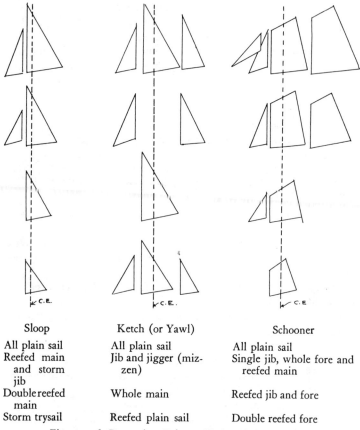

Sloop	Ketch (or Yawl)	Schooner
All plain sail	All plain sail	All plain sail
Reefed main and storm jib	Jib and jigger (mizzen)	Single jib, whole fore and reefed main
Double reefed main	Whole main	Reefed jib and fore
Storm trysail	Reefed plain sail	Double reefed fore

Figure 226. Preserving Balance Under Shortened Sail

A boat sailing down the back of a wave submerges her stern and quarters, and the next sea (especially if it is breaking) is liable to come aboard and flood the cockpit by the stern. Tacking down wind so as to take the seas on the quarter, parting them, will help prevent pooping; so will ballast forward (but not too far forward lest the rudder be raised out of the water), or running under jib alone.

There is danger of broaching to.

A hard sea striking the quarter opposite to the one on which the sail is set will drive the bow around and tend to push the boat beam to the seas. Broaching to often results in capsizing. If the jib is sheeted in flat it will help somewhat by making the bow hard to swing; as the boat flies against the rudder, the wind pressure on the jib helps to pay her off again and take the boat out of its yaw. A drag of some kind, trailed from astern, will help to prevent excessive yawing, the primary cause of broaching to.

228. If the sea makes up so that progress becomes impossible or too dangerous, boats may resort to *laying to*.

Laying to is a maneuver calculated to stop the boat from sailing and to keep her approximate position without the use of an anchor. While laying to the boat makes leeway and is also carried by tide or current. Sea room is needed to leeward, and laying to is not recommended in confined sounds, bays, or estuaries.

To lay to, the boat is headed into the wind to the point where she begins making sternway. The tiller is then lashed down or to leeward, and the sheets are trimmed so that she does not sail.

The boat is then said to "go to sleep." What she is doing, in endless cycles, is this: She starts moving backwards. As the helm is lashed down, the bow will slowly fall off, whereupon the boat will slowly sail ahead and again round into the wind, and then repeat the process over and over.

The trick is to so adjust the helm and the sheets that both a minimum of sternway and a minimum of sailing ahead take place. This point can be found only by experimenting, but once the point is found, the boat will lie quietly and not sail. In practice, the sail will be fluttering, the sheets slightly started and the boom about over the quarter (about in the same position as in a close reach).

On small boats, even though hove to and "in the groove," the shifting of live ballast will upset the balance entirely. The helm and sheet adjustments are made from the hatch, the skipper remaining in the approximate position from which he made the adjustment while laying to.

229. If the boat will stand no canvas at all, a safe and fairly comfortable lay can be made by laying to a sea anchor.

The effect of a sea anchor is to keep the bow of the boat heading into the seas rather than beam to. As in laying to, leeway is made, and the tide and the current affect the boat's position as well. (Figure 229.)

A long warp is required so that the surge of the boat, as she pitches, does not snap too smartly and part the line or tear the canvas cone of

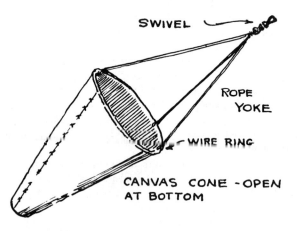

SWIVEL

ROPE
YOKE

WIRE RING

CANVAS CONE - OPEN
AT BOTTOM

Figure 229. A Sea Anchor or Drogue

the anchor. When rigged the anchor should be invisible, from five to twelve feet beneath the surface. Chain should not be used for the warp of a sea anchor.

A jury sea anchor, having a similar effect, can be made by lashing together spare spars, timbers, hatch covers, etc., and launching over the bow. These should be rigged so that they present the greatest resistance to the tugging of the boat. A swamped small boat, towed by a bridle from its stem to sternpost, can readily be used for a jury sea anchor.

230. The use of oil reduces seas and prevents their breaking, and oil bags are often called into service when either laying to or laying to a drogue (sea anchor). Its use for small boats is described in paragraph 117, Chapter I.

Large boats pump the oil overboard, using the bilge pump, or discharge it from watercloset or sink drains.

231. Thunderstorms seldom make permanent heavy weather. They rise and disappear quickly, and it is not necessary to lay to during one. Upon the approach of a thunderstorm, and during the calm that always precedes it, all sail should be taken in, stopped down, and extra lashings placed on the boom.

If at all possible lay to an anchor with plenty of warp. Thunderstorms seldom build up great seas, and the strain is from the wind alone. If no bottom is found, the approach of a storm should send the boat sailing away from the shore which will be a lee one when the storm breaks. Prepare to scud before it if there is sea room, using a small jib to maintain steerageway.

If in really tight quarters, without sea room or the possibility of anchoring to bottom, a sea anchor may be used. Removing the mast will greatly reduce the windage and slow up the boat's motion. Unless forced to do so, do not anchor on a lee shore. Lightning is an ever-present danger during thunderstorms, and it is wise to keep away from masts, halyards, and shrouds. Lightning will not harm you if your body is generally at or below the waterline.

A thunderstorm expends most of its wind before the rain. If the rain comes first, then the wind, look out for dirty weather; the storm is more than merely a local thunderstorm. Beware of the split storm, one with two centers, or one at the turn of the tide, as there is liable to be a repetition almost at once. Sail had best not be made until the storm has definitely passed away—and then quickly—for thunderstorms often are followed by long periods of dead calm or confused light winds.

Fishermen use the verse below to diagnose the severity of and length of thunderstorms:

> *If the wind before the rain*
>   *Soon you may make sail again.*
> *If the rain before the wind*
>   *Shorten sail and halyards mind.*

Light-Weather Sailing

232. The jib and mainsail of a sloop are referred to as the *plain sails* or *working sails*. In light airs they are of insufficient area to efficiently drive the boat. Working sails are designed to meet average weather conditions with safety and ease of handling. When the wind drops to below average, additional sails are called into use, generally called *light sails*.

They are made of lighter-weight canvas than the working sails and are designed for temporary use. Except on very large boats, the gear

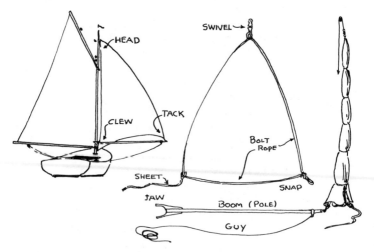

Figure 232. The Spinnaker

to handle them is simple, and tackles are not used for hauling or sheeting.

The largest of the light sails is the spinnaker. (Figure 232.) This is a triangular sail, secured at or near the masthead, at some point inboard forward of the mast, and to a boom or spinnaker pole rigged athwartships (or nearly so) to the keel.

It is generally used before the wind or with the wind slightly on the quarter. It is set on the opposite side from the main boom, and sheeted fore or aft by means of the spinnaker guy or by the sheet, so that it keeps filled and drawing. The jib is either dropped or "wung-out" on the same side as the main boom, so that the spinnaker spills its wind into it.

Small spinnakers are set as follows: The bundled sail is carried forward, with the two clews exposed. The head is made fast to the spinnaker halyard; the clew snap (or the sheet, if provided) is secured and the tack made fast to the outboard end of the spinnaker pole, which has been laid on the deck, parallel to the keel, and pointing forward. The after spinnaker guy is now passed aft, outboard of the shrouds and backstays, and is manned by the helmsman or another hand aft.

Now, the spinnaker is sent aloft and it hangs as an idle sail, possibly billowing forward somewhat. Without loss of time, the boom is run forward, the spinnaker jaws placed against the forward side of the mast and helped by the man forward, the man aft hauls away on the guy. As the boom swings to its thwartship position, it will suddenly fill and draw, and when drawing correctly, the after guy is belayed. It is taken in in exactly the reverse way and smothered as it comes down to deck. Forward guys and lift guys are used on heavy spinnaker gear or in a seaway or in a calm to reduce the wild thrashing of the boom.

The spinnaker may also be set in stops. This procedure is common on large yachts and on all yachts when racing. It can be hoisted and made ready some time before it is needed and very quickly set to draw. To put a spinnaker in stops, it is laid out (along the waterways or ashore), the leech and luff matched, the sail rolled in from the center to the edges, very small and tight. The clew and tack will be aft; the head forward. It is now tied at intervals with single turns of light-cotton thread.

The boom is then rigged outboard and guyed aft, held by the luff rope of the bundled spinnaker. To set the sail (as when rounding a racing mark), haul away on the sheet, breaking the thread stops; then adjust both sheet and guys for maximum draft.

The spinnaker can be used without the mainsail. It cannot be used when the wind is forward of the beam. As the wind veers from dead aft, both the tack and the clew will have to be adjusted to give maximum draft. It is time to douse it when it refuses to stay filled.

233. The balloon jib (ballooner or reaching jib—Figure 233) is a light sail used when off the wind. It is sheeted outside of the shrouds as the spinnaker is, but, since it sets on the same side as the main boom, it requires no boom. Its forward edge is hanked to the jib or head stay, and it is handled exactly like a working jib except that it cannot be self-trimming. It must be resheeted after every tack. Small boats

Figure 233. Balloon Jib   Genoa Jib   Parachute Spinnaker

often carry a combination spinnaker-ballooner, a sail designed to be used as either.

234. The Genoa jib (Figure 233) is a jib which overlaps the mainsail and is not quite as large as a ballooner. It is used for sailing on the wind and is handled exactly like a ballooner. The sheet must generally be a tackle, even on a small boat, to correctly trim or flatten the sail.

235. Parachute or twin-spinnakers are carried by modern yachts quite frequently, especially racers. These are simply huge, baggy sails, boomed out to port and starboard, sometimes in two parts and sometimes in one. Working sails are not carried while these sails are set.

Handling a Sailboat in a Tideway

236. Waters affected by tide or current are moving *en masse*. Sailing in such waters is no different from sailing in any other waters. Nothing is changed except the relative position of the boat to the land.

However, if a land objective is sought, certain problems arise which the sailor must solve in order to make the best course to such an objective.

In sailing across the tide, that is, with the tide on the beam, the course must be laid well above the objective. If the wind and tide are on the same beam, leeway must also be allowed for the course which is set an even greater amount above the objective. If wind and tide are on opposite beams, a nearly straight course can be laid, as the drift and leeway tend to blank each other out. Drift is usually somewhat greater than leeway. If the wind is astern, drift only must be allowed for.

In sailing *into* a foul tide the practice of lee-bowing will make for a faster passage. Set the course so as to take the tide on the lee bow, start the sheets slightly, and the tide will constantly be advancing the boat to windward—the desired direction. A straight course can be made to the objective. Oftentimes, remembering that drift is generally more than leeway over a given distance, it will be necessary to set the course to *leeward* of the objective.

When sailing in a tideway with a centerboard boat, only enough board is exposed to prevent leeway. More will merely increase the wetted surface or skin friction and make the boat harder to push against water already affecting the boat adversely.

It is a fallacy to assume that the direction of the tide reverses itself when flooding and ebbing. This is not so. Knowledge of local conditions is required to intelligently predict the tides. Lacking this, the publications entitled *Tide Tables* and *Current Tables* should be consulted.

The tide runs strongest in the middle of areas of water; weakest alongshore. In estuaries and sounds, the tide will sometimes flow one way in mid-channel, and the opposite way at the edges. Back eddies occur around points and headlands and underwater obstructions which the sailor can use in making progress against the tide. It flows much stronger in deep channels than over shallows. (*See* Chapter XI, paragraphs 1122 to 1127.)

When obliged to sail against a strong tide and light wind, put over to the lee shore, close under, and beat against it. Sail over shallow areas in preference to deep ones. If ground is still lost, there is no recourse but to anchor the boat.

Docking and Mooring a Sailboat

237. When a sailboat is in irons she will not sail. In making a landing or in picking up a mooring, the object is to sail the boat exactly to the spot and then sail no more. This is done by sailing the boat to a position where it is estimated that her own momentum will carry her forward, putting her in irons, and steering her to the desired dock, mooring, or small boat.

It can be successfully done only after the sailor has become thoroughly familiar with his boat; has learned her habits and her approximate distance of "shooting" under various wind velocities.

Whenever possible, and it usually is, the objective should be approached from leeward. Thus, if the boat is sailing toward a mooring

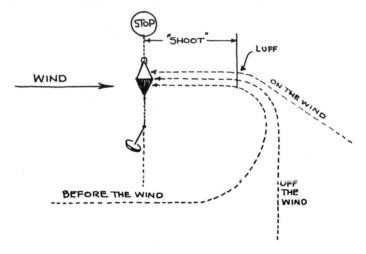

Figure 237A. Approaching a Mooring Under Sail

from windward, the course is held until it is *past* the mooring and well to one side of it. The boat is then put off the wind, swung quickly on the wind, and when it is at a point well to leeward of the mooring it is sharply put in irons (luffed), and the headway is depended upon to carry it to the mooring and to reach it without appreciable headway, leeway, or sternway. The jib is immediately lowered and the mainsheet let run. The boat will lie quietly, like a weather vane, and not sail thereafter. (Figure 237A.)

Casting off from a mooring and picking a mooring up are shown, step by step, in Figures 237B and 237C.

238. When a sailboat is anchored, the anchor is hove up short, then the sail set. As she is put on the wind, the cable is smartly handed in and the anchor lifted as the boat sails over it. If the anchor needs to be broken out, sail hard against it on one tack, drift to leeward, then

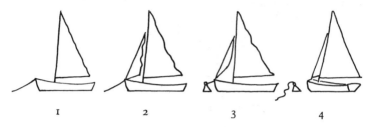

Figure 237B. Steps in Getting Away from a Mooring

1. Raise mainsail and ready all gear, lower centerboard, set backstays for desired tack. Bend jib but do not raise. Do not belay mainsheet; let run.
2. Raise jib. Do not belay jib sheet. Draw boat to mooring or prepare to cast off mooring warp.
3. Hold jib aweather on tack desired to sail on. As head pays off, cast off mooring.
4. Sheet in main; sheet in jib. Trim both.

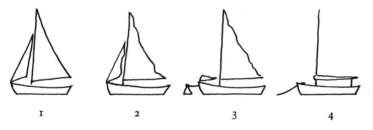

Figure 237C. Steps in Picking up a Mooring

1. Sail at mooring from leeward.
2. Luff and shoot into the eye of the wind, at mooring.
3. Let all sheets run. Pick up mooring and drop jib or vice versa.
4. Drift back on mooring warp, douse main and snug down.

get off on the other tack. The second jerk should break out the anchor. An anchor will break out easier with a short cable than with a long one.

239. When a sailboat wants to anchor, she is handled exactly as in picking up a mooring. As soon as she has stopped sailing and commenced making sternway, the anchor is put over and the cable payed out slowly as the leeward drift takes it. Leave the mainsail up until the cable is taut; it will set the anchor better than the drift of the uncanvased boat alone.

If it is required to set an anchor especially deep or well, drop it over the stern, sail it in hard; then, as the boat rounds to, lead it forward.

← ABOUT 6 FEET MORE THAN
BOAT AND WARP →

Figure 237D. Long Painter for the Boat Left at the Mooring
to Give Room for Maneuvering

240. In making a dock, it is approached from leeward whenever possible. (Figure 240.)

Immediately the dock is made let all sheets run, get a line from the bow to the dock, raise the centerboard, and lower the jib. She will lie there quietly.

In the event that too much way is on as the dock is approached, fenders should be kept handy. A boat hook can be used as a fender or to grab the dock in case the "shoot" has been too short.

In holding off with a boat hook, hold it on the side of the body, like a long-handled shovel—not with the inboard end pointing at your midriff. In holding off a boat with the feet, sit on the deck, bracing against the mast or a trunk, and fend with both feet.

Windward approaches to a dock are dangerous and should be attempted only if absolutely necessary. It requires the nicest timing and expert seamanship and helmsmanship. (Figure 240.)

In approaching a dock, the tide and current must often be reckoned with. Be certain that their effects upon the boat are completely forecast and, if favorable, fully used to help in the maneuver of docking. Both tide and wind can be of much use in getting a boat properly headed for leaving a dock. Stern lines from the boat to a turn around a dock bollard and thence back to the boat are very useful. One end of the line is cast off on deck and later hauled aboard.

In getting away from the windward side of a dock, sea room is gained by having someone ashore shove the boat to windward, using

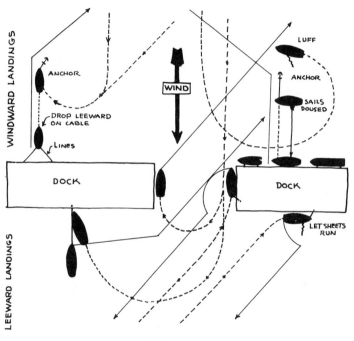

Figure 240

Dotted line—docking
Solid line—leaving the dock and returning to the original direction

the main boom. As soon as it is clear, sheet the sail home and get on the wind.

In getting away from the leeward side of a dock the boat can be backed out in the following ways:

1. By "fanning the jib." Hold the jib out. The wind will drive the

boat backwards and will drive the stern in the opposite direction. As this occurs, swing the jib to the other side. The course will be a series of "sashays" astern and can be kept up indefinitely, provided the stern is not permitted to swing too much.

2. By sailing the boat backwards. Jib and mainsail are trimmed absolutely flat amidships and the centerboard is raised entirely. The tiller is held (or lashed, if single-handed) about two inches to port or starboard. The boat is shoved off from the dock directly and exactly to leeward, and it will continue to so sail backwards until the helm is put over and the sheets started. It is important that trim be maintained during the maneuver, especially in the small boat.

Rules of the Road for Sailboats

241. (1) When two boats under sail are approaching one another so as to involve risk of collision, one of them shall keep out of the way of the other as follows:

(*a*) A boat which is running free shall keep out of the way of a boat which is close-hauled.

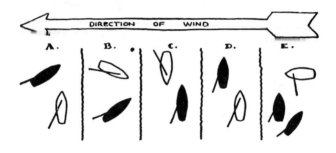

Figure 241. Article 17 of the Pilot Rules Illustrated. In Each Situation the White Boat Keeps Clear

(*b*) A boat which is close-hauled on the port tack shall keep out of the way of a boat which is close-hauled on the starboard tack.

(*c*) When both are running free, with the wind on different sides, the boat which has the wind on the port side shall keep out of the way of the other.

(*d*) When both are running free, with the wind on the same side, the boat which is to windward shall keep out of the way of the boat which is to leeward.

(*e*) A boat which has the wind aft shall keep out of the way of other boats.

(2) When a boat under power or oars and a boat under sail are proceeding in such directions as to involve risk of collision, the boat under power or oars shall keep out of the way of the boat under sail.

(3) Where, by any of these rules, one of the two boats is to keep out of the way, the other shall keep her course and speed.

(4) Every boat which is directed by these rules to keep out of the way of another boat shall, if the circumstances of the case permit, avoid passing ahead of the other.

(5) Every boat, whether under power, oars, or sail, when over-taking any other shall keep out of the way of the overtaken boat.

242. There are special rules for sailboats while racing, and each boat that is racing is obliged to observe them. Boats that are not racing are not bound by the rules (which are purely private), but as a matter of courtesy keep well away from racing boats, and so do not create situations requiring the application of any rules of the road.

The following racing rules are general but may be greatly varied by the committees governing the various races and classes of boats.

(1) The standard sailing course shall be a triangular course of three two-mile legs (total, six miles). If conditions make a triangular course undesirable, the total length shall be about six miles.

(2) Time of finish is marked when the foremast of two-masted, or the mainmast of single-masted, vessels crosses the line. Similarly, on the start, the position of the mast in regard to the starting line is to be used in determining whether or not the boat crosses before the gun is fired.

(3) Right of way. When one boat is approaching another boat, so as to involve risk of fouling, one of them shall keep clear of the other as follows:

(*a*) A boat free shall keep clear of one close-hauled.

When both boats are close-hauled, or both free, or both have the wind aft, and have wind on the opposite sides, the boat with the wind on the port side shall keep clear.

(*b*) When both boats are free, or have the wind aft and have the wind on the same side, the boat to windward shall keep clear.

(*c*) A boat with the wind aft shall keep clear of a boat on any point of sailing.

(*d*) An overtaking boat shall, as long as an overlap exists, keep clear of the boat which is being overtaken.

(*e*) An overlap is established when an overtaking boat has no longer a free choice on which side she will pass, and continues to exist as long as the leeward boat, by luffing, or weather boat, by wearing away, is in danger of fouling.

(*f*) When of two boats one is obliged to keep clear, the other shall not so alter her course as to involve risk of fouling.

(*g*) A boat may luff as she pleases in order to prevent another from passing her to windward, provided she begins to luff before an overlap is established.

(*h*) A boat shall not bear away out of her course so as to hinder another boat from passing to leeward.

(*i*) A boat shall not become entitled to her rights on a new course until she has filled away.

(*j*) When two boats, both close-hauled on the same tack, are converging by reason of the leeward boat holding a better wind, and when neither can claim the rights of a boat being overtaken, then the boat to windward shall keep clear.

(*k*) If an overlap exists between two boats when both of them without tacking are about to pass a mark on a required side, then the outside boat must give the inside boat room to pass clear of the mark. A boat shall not, however, be justified in attempting to establish an overlap and thus force a passage between another boat and mark after the latter has altered her helm for the purpose of rounding.

(*l*) A mark is any vessel, boat, buoy, or other object to indicate the course.

(*m*) When a boat is approaching a shore, shoal, pier, rock, vessel, or other dangerous obstruction and cannot go clear by altering her course without fouling another boat, then this latter shall, on being hailed by the former, at once give room; and in case one boat is forced to tack or bear away in order to give room, the other shall also tack, or bear away, as the case may be, at as near the same time as possible without danger of fouling. But should such obstruction be a designated mark of the course, a boat forcing another to tack under the provisions of this section shall be disqualified.

(n) Carrying away mast or gear through defect in the rigging due to the fault or negligence of the boat's crew, even though a foul has been committed, will not be considered a disability within the meaning of this rule. Carrying away mast or gear, when not fouled, will never be considered a disability within the meaning of this rule.

(4) If, in consequence of any foul committed any time after the warning gun, the *boat* which has been *fouled* be *disabled,* she may demand the right to sail the race again before another race can be sailed, or the original prize or prizes awarded in that race. The word *disabled* shall be understood to mean damage which would, in the opinion of the judges, materially affect the result of the race.

(5) (*a*) No means of propulsion other than sails shall be employed either in stays or free route except as follows:

(*b*) A boat running aground, or fouling a buoy, not marking the course, pier, vessel (other than another boat entered in the same or another race), or other object, may use her anchors, warps, or boat hooks to get clear; or she may, when aground, float herself by pointing her oars, but they shall not be used in any other manner than by pointing, and then only to get afloat. In no case is she allowed to receive any assistance except from the crew of the vessel which she fouls. Any anchor, warp, boat hook, or oar so used must be taken on board again before continuing the race.

(*c*) A boat shall not warp, kedge, pole, or make fast to buoy, pier, vessel, or other object.

OTHER TYPES OF SAILBOATS

243. Closely related to the sloop are the other types of single-masted boats. Their handling is essentially the same as for the sloop, since all are fore-and-aft rigs.

The Catboat

244. The cat is a single-masted boat with but one large mainsail, the mast being set far forward and the sail being gaff-headed. Usually the mast, since it has no shrouds, is very heavy, the deck at the mast being too narrow to give adequate "spread," and a jackstay is some-

Figure 243. Marconi Rig
Peak or jib-headed mainsail

Gaff Rig
Gaff-headed mainsail

times provided. In cats having shrouds the stays lead to channels or horns which extend the width somewhat.

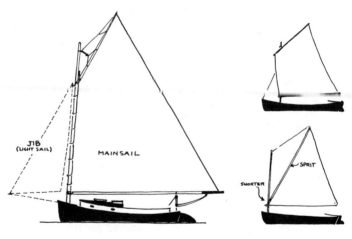

Figure 244. The Cat

Above—Standing Lug Rig
Below—Sprit Rig

While the rig is simple and easily handled by a small crew, the single sail is of tremendous proportions, and the long boom required is sometimes a danger when running in a beam sea or before the wind with a roll. The topping lift must be used more often than with the sloop or other types.

245. A cat sloop is a catboat which carries (as temporary or permanent fixtures) a bowsprit and a jib. Such headsails are properly in the light-air class, and most cats so equipped have a reefing bowsprit.

246. A cat yawl is a yawl minus the usual headsails but with the mast set forward as in a true cat.

247. A cat schooner is a schooner minus the usual headsails but with the mast set forward as in the true cat. (Examples are the Block Island boats and other obsolete types.)

All are bastard types, not generally seen now, but which were designed for some special use or condition in an era when a sailboat was a "beast of burden" and not a pleasure boat.

The Cutter

248. The cutter is essentially a sloop rig having her sails so arranged that many combinations of areas may be obtained. Originally the rig

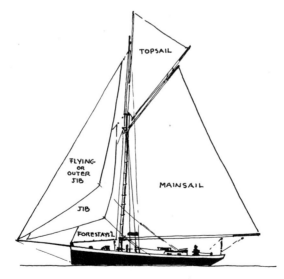

Figure 248A. Original Cutter Rig

carried a mainsail, two or three jibs, a topsail, and a square sail or course as well. It was a work-boat rig, much used by fishermen and pilots, and was pretty well able to meet any ordinary sea conditions, especially when fitted with a reefing bowsprit (as was usual in the past). (Figure 248A.)

A cutter with plain sail set carries a proportionately larger area than does a sloop with plain sail and is therefore faster than the sloop

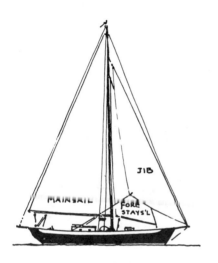

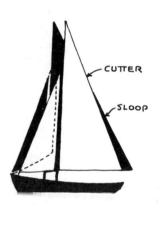

Figure 248B. A Modern Cutter Rig

Location of Rigs in Relation to Hull in the Sloop and Cutter

and will generally be slightly more weatherly. One advantage the rig has over the sloop is that under staysail it can be hove to better.

There is little difference between the modern cutter and the sloop. The cutter generally carries two or more headsails in the working rig and her mast is farther aft than that of a sloop. This location is about two-fifths of the waterline length aft. Her mast usually rakes aft more than a sloop's. (Figure 248B.)

Mainsail, staysail, and jib are the working sails; jib topsail and topsail the light airs. Under heavy weather conditions she may reduce sail handily to reefed main and full jib or staysail, or reefed main and reefed staysail, or reefed staysail alone.

The type presents no new problems in handling save in the trimming of the headsails. The jib is not self-trimming and must be sheeted after each new board. The staysail is set at a greater angle to the wind than the mainsail, and the jib at a greater angle than the staysail.

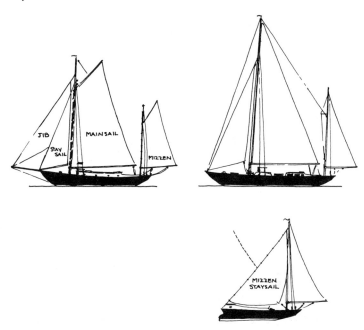

Figure 249A. The Yawl Rig

The Yawl and Ketch

249. The yawl and ketch (and schooner) make use of the divided rig which has the advantage of spreading a large area of canvas, and yet no one sail is too big to handle comfortably. Briefly, that is the why and wherefore of all divided rigs in small craft. Some divided rigs have the additional advantage of quick adjustment of sail area to replace reefing. The yawl in particular lends itself well to sailing under shortened canvas either under the mainsail alone or the jib and jigger (mizzen). (Figures 249A & 249B.)

All divided rigs on small boats have the disadvantage of requiring

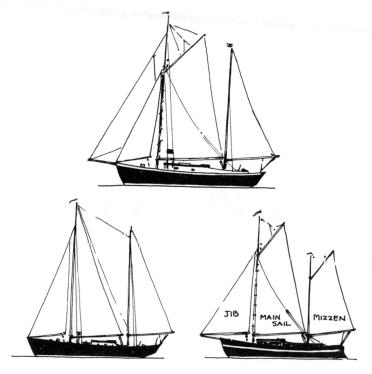

Figure 249B. The Ketch Rig

considerably more sparring, staying, and rigging than single-masted rigs. While they can carry more canvas than the undivided rig and work under shortened sail for some time after the single sticker has to reef, much of the additional sail drive merely goes to overcome this additional top hamper.

The divided rig has some marked advantages at sea and for cruising purposes in that repairs can be made aloft, a matter impossible on tall single masts. It is a "snug" rig, and, because it is very easily handled, greatly increases the limits of the "one-man boat." A small crew can handle a larger yawl or ketch than they can a sloop. However, any sail rig is a compromise or a personal preference, and the owner has his own good reasons for selecting the rig he has.

The yawl or ketch is sailed exactly as all fore-and-afters; the rig involves no new principles.

The yawl is generally designed to balance under full mainsail or under jib and mizzen and, of course, will still balance under jib mizzen and reefed mainsail. Light airs include the spinnaker, the ballooner, the Genoa; sometimes a jib topsail and often a mizzen staysail, a sail mastheaded to the mizzen when before the wind or on a broad reach.

The ketch does not lend itself so well to sailing under shortened canvas, and generally balance must be maintained by reefing all sails in heavy weather. The rig is basically a schooner rig and so handled. It carries the same light-air sails as the yawl. In addition, a fisherman is sometimes spread, hanked to the stay between main and mizzen-masts, or set flying. Such a sail is very powerful and makes use of the large triangle remaining when a jib-headed mainsail is used instead of a gaff-headed one.

250. A ketch is distinguished from a yawl (and vice versa) in the following ways:

1. The mizzenmast of a yawl is aft of the rudderhead; the mizzen-mast of a ketch is forward of the rudderhead.

2. The mizzen sail of a yawl is one fourth the area of the mainsail; the mizzen sail of a ketch is about two thirds the area of the mainsail (sometimes called foresail).

251. Marconi or peak-headed rigs are more efficient in the yawl or ketch rig than gaff-headed rigs. This is due to the fact that there is a proportionately greater "much-drive" area (luff), and because there is no part of the sail which sags excessively to leeward as does the head of a gaff sail. This sagging can be overcome fairly well, however, by use of a vang on the mainsail gaff which is led to a block on the mizzen and then to a cleat on or near the deck.

The Schooner

252. The schooner rig, while not having originated in America as it is so often stated, reached its highest development here and remains a typically American rig. (Figure 252A.)

The combinations of schooner sails are almost without end. The rig is basically three sails: a headsail, foresail, and mainsail. It can be

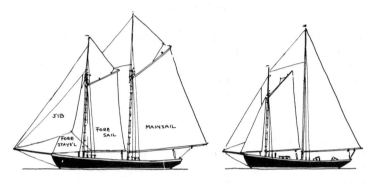

Figure 252A. Fisherman Schooner   Schooner Yacht

Figure 252B. Stays'l   Knockabout Schooner
Schooner

handled by a small crew, is fast and weatherly, and permits combinations of sail shortening and reefing to meet any sea conditions.

No new principles of sailing are involved in its handling. When running before the wind, the large mainsail is quite apt to blanket sail forward of it, and it is usual to set the main and foresail wing and wing and tack down wind. When on or off the wind, the foresail must be set at a greater angle to the wind than the mainsail. A loose-footed foresail or an overlapping foresail (boomless, of course) is a very effective and powerful schooner sail.

Under heavy weather conditions the schooner reduces to plain sail, then reefs, as required. She will lay to well under foresail or under

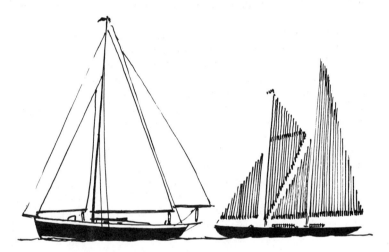

Figure 252C. Rig Oddments. *Left,* The Mizzen Staysail Yawl; *Right,* the "Wishbone" or Vamarie-Rig Schooner

reefed foresail alone; or under storm trysail; or quite often under bare poles, particularly if the mainmast is taller and more heavily rigged than the foremast. Light sails include fishermen, staysail, or balloon staysail hung between the masts. Spinnakers and light head-sails, while carried, are not as efficient as on other rigs because of the relatively short foremast.

A bald-headed schooner is one carrying gaff sails on both fore and mainmasts.

A knockabout schooner is one with the rig entirely inboard, i. e., no bowsprit. (Figure 252B.)

The staysail schooner is one on which the common foresail is absent, and in its place is a triangular sail hanked to a stay from the base of the foremast to the head of the mainmast. In the space above it, a huge staysail (or several smaller ones) is spread.

253. By far the greatest number of sailboats are engaged in the ancient sport of racing. Usually, fleets of one-design craft are organized, often sponsored by a yacht club, and strict rules are imposed and enforced so that the race, in fact, is between sailing brains and not sailing boats. This is as it should be, of course.

America has literally hundreds of racing classes, some numbering 4000 fleet units (the Snipe Class). More are added each year as new gimmicks and designs are developed. The trend at present is toward planing hulls—sailing craft which attain such high speeds that they rise, or plane, and skim not through but over the water. Some of the lasting contributions to sailing have come from the racing fleets and the sport is definitely the richer for their experiments and innovations.

254. Here is a rundown of the principal racing fleets of the United States. Since officers serve on a volunteer basis with few exceptions, the roster changes so rapidly that names and addresses cannot be included. To learn more about a fleet, write a builder or naval architect who advertises the fleet boat, or write the editor of any yachting periodical, who usually has these names up to date and on file.

CLASS	DESCRIPTION

Amphibi-con—26' x 8' Keel or CB sloop. 230 sq.ft. SA. Moderately large US fleet. To $7500. Strip planked hull.

Atlantic—30'-6" x 6'-6" Keel slope. 385 sq.ft. SA. About 120 in US fleet. To $3500. Planked wood or "glass."

Bull's Eye—15'-8½" x 5'-10" Keel sloop. 140 sq.ft. SA.

Cape Cod Mercury—15' x 5'-5" Keel or CB sloop. 119 sq.ft. SA. 16 US fleets. About $1250. Fiberglas.

El Toro International—7'-11" x 3'-10" CB cat. 36 sq.ft. SA. 1400 units, mostly West Coast. Plywood hull.

Finn Class—14'-9" x 5' CB cat. 114 sq.ft. SA. 110 units. $1735. Moulded plywood hulls.

Flying Dutchman—19'-10" x 5'-7" CB sloop. 176 sq.ft. SA. 458 boats in class. $995. Moulded plywood hulls.

Flying Scot—19′ x 6′-9″ CB sloop. 192 sq.ft. SA. 100 units in 12 fleets. $2200. Fiberglas, metal spars.

Hampton One Design—18′ x 5′-9″ CB sloop. 172 sq.ft. SA. 85 boats. About $1500. Wood hulls.

Highlander—20′ x 6′ CB sloop. 225 sq.ft. SA. 300 units in class. $2600. Moulded plywood hulls.

International—14′ x 5′-6″ or less to 4′-8″. CB sloop. 175 sq.ft. SA. About $1500. Wood.

International 110—13′-6″ x 5′-2″ CB sloop. 90 sq.ft. SA. 1800 boats in US. $1000 & up. Plywood hulls.

International 210—29′-6″ x 5′-10″ Keel sloop. 210 sq.ft. SA. 275 boats. About $3750. Plywood.

International Blue Jay—24′ x 4′-2″ Keel sloop. 155 sq.ft. SA. 2050 units in 32 fleets. $1595. Plywood hull.

International Dragon—29′-2½″ x 6′-5″ Keel sloop. 235 sq.ft. SA. 175 in US, 2000 in world fleets. $4-6500. Planked hulls only allowed.

International Flattie—18′ x 5′-3″ CB sloop. 157½ sq.ft. SA. About 950 units. Plywood or Fiberglas.

International L-16—26′ x 5′-9″ Keel sloop. 207 sq.ft. SA. 225 units. To $8000. Fiberglas. (Luders design)

Jet 14—14′ x 4′-8″ CB sloop. 113 sq.ft. SA. About 350 boats. To $2500. Moulded plywood or "glass."

Lightning—19′ x 6′-6¼″ CB sloop. 177 sq.ft. SA. 6200 active racers. $1950. Wood.

Moth—11′ x optional beam. CB sloop. 72 sq.ft. SA. 4000 units in world fleets. $750. Any material, no restrictions.

National One-Design—17′ x 5′-8″ CB sloop. 137½ sq.ft. SA. 760 boats. $1350 & up. Fiberglas over wood or plywood.

Penguin—11′-2″ x 4′-10″ CB cat. 72 sq.ft. SA. About 7000 units in world fleets. $650. Plywood or Fiberglas.

Raven—24′-3″ x 7′ CB sloop. 300 sq.ft. SA. About 320 boats. $3750 & up. Plywood or Fiberglas.

Rebel—16′ x 6′-6″ CB sloop. 166 sq.ft. SA. Fleet numbers 1200. $1400. Fiberglas.

Rhodes 18—18′ x 6′-3″ CB or keel sloop. 165 sq.ft. SA. 850 boats. About $2000. Wood or Fiberglas.

Rhodes Bantam—14′ x 5′-6¼″ CB dinghy. 120 sq.ft. SA. Fleet about 750. To $900. Wood, glass covered.

Sailfish—11′-7½″ x 2′-7½″ Daggerboard cat. 65 sq.ft. SA. About 13,000 sold. $375. Plywood.

Snipe—15′-6″ x 5′. CB sloop. 103 sq.ft. SA. 12,000 in world; 4000 in US. $1000. Plywood or plank.

Star—22'-8½" x 5'-8¼" Keel sloop. 281 sq.ft. SA. 4000 units in 86 fleets. $3750. Wood hulls.

Thistle—17' x 6' CB sloop. 175 sq.ft. SA. Fleet numbers 1230. $1750 & up. Moulded plywood.

Other smaller racing classes, organized for regional racing, are:

Acorn	Duet	Inland Scow	Pennant
Albacore	Falcon	Interclub	Pilot
Arrow	Farallon Clipper	Jollyboat	Renegade
Atalanta	Feather	Malibu Out-	Resolute
Barnegat Sneak-	Firefly	rigger	Sprite
box	Fish	Mass. "19"	Swallow
Bear	Folkboat	Maya	Town
Beetle Cat	Gannet	Melody	Treasure Island
Brutal Beast	Ghost	Naples Dink	Turnabout
Cadet	Golden Gate	Narrasketuck	Voyager
Chesapeake 20	HAJ (Hi's)	Nipper	Winabout
Cricket	Harpoon	Optimist Pram	Windmill
Cub	Hurricane	Osprey	Wood Pussy
Cutlass	Indian	Pelican	Y-Flyer
Delta			

GLOSSARY OF SAILBOAT TERMS

Aback—The position of the sails when the wind presses their surface toward the mast, tending to force the vessel astern.

Abaft—Toward the stern.

Abeam—On the side of the vessel, amidships, or at right angles.

Aboard—Within, on board the vessel.

About—To go on the opposite tack.

Abreast—Alongside of. Side by side.

Adrift—Broken from moorings or fasts.

Afloat—Resting on the surface of the water.

Aft—Near the stern.

Aground—Touching the bottom.

Ahead—In the direction of the vessel's bow. *Wind ahead* is from the direction toward which the vessel's head points.

Alee—When the helm is in the opposite direction from that in which the wind blows.

All Aback—When all the sails are aback.

All Hands—The entire crew.

All in the Wind—When all the sails are shaking.

Aloft—Above the deck.

Amidships—In the center of the vessel; either with reference to her length or to her breadth.

Apeak—When the vessel is hove taut so as to bring the vessel over her anchor.

Arm, Yardarm—The extremity of a yard.

Astern—In the direction of the stern. The opposite of ahead.

Athwart—Across.

Athwartships—Across the length of a vessel. The opposite to fore and aft.

Avast—To stop. "Avast heaving!"

Awning—A covering of canvas over a vessel's deck, or over a boat, to keep off sun and rain.

Back—To *back a sail* is to throw it aback. To *back and fill* is to alternately back and fill the sails.

Backstays—Rigging running from the masthead to the vessel's side, slanting a little aft.

Ballast—Heavy material, as iron, lead, or stone, placed in the bottom of the hold to keep a vessel steady.

Bar—Capstan bars are heavy pieces of wood by which the capstan is worked.

Bare Poles—The condition of a vessel when she has no sail set.

Bark, or Barque—A three-masted vessel having her fore and mainmasts rigged like a ship's, and her mizzenmast like the mainmast of a schooner, with a spanker and gaff topsail.

Battens—Put upon rigging to keep it from chafing. Battens are often used on yachts on the leech of a mainsail to make it set flat.

Beams—*On the weather* or *lee beam* is in a direction to windward or leeward, at right angles with the keel. *On beam ends*—The situation of a vessel when turned over so that her beams are inclined toward the vertical.

Bear—To *bear down upon a vessel* is to approach her from the windward.

Bearing—The direction of an object from the person looking.

Beating—Going toward the direction of the wind, by tacks.

Becalm—To intercept the wind. A vessel to windward is said to becalm another. So one sail becalms another to leeward of it.

Becket—A piece of rope placed so as to confine a spar or another rope. A handle made of rope, in the form of a half circle.

Belay—To make a rope fast; but not to hitch or tie it.

Belaying Pins—Movable pins placed in pinrails on which to belay running gear.

Bend—To make fast. *Bend a sail* is to put it on a yard, gaff, or boom. *Bend a cable*, make it fast to anchor. *Bend*, the knot with which one rope is made fast to another.

Bight—The double part of a rope.

Bilge—That part of a ship on which she would rest, besides the keel, if aground; also the part of the ship's interior over the bilge. *Bilgewater* is the drainage within the bilge; *bilged,* a ship resting on its bilges.

Bitts—Upright timbers running through the deck on which hawsers and other lines are secured.

Block—Land term is *pulley*. Round, boxlike, wooden or metal frame with a wheel within, through which ropes run.

Board—Course of a vessel on one tack. *Sternboard,* when a vessel is going astern. *By the board,* when a ship's masts fall over side.

Boat Hook—Staff with iron hook at one end, for holding small boats to wharves or ships' sides; also useful for picking up various floating objects.

Bobstays—Standing rigging running from bowsprit to cutwater or stem.

Bollard—Upright post, sometimes a cannon, half sunk in ground used for mooring lines. Sometimes called *dolphin* (Navy).

Boltrope—Outer edge of sail to which canvas proper is sewed.

Bonnet—Extra bit of canvas laced to foot of jib.

Booby Hatch—Small, raised hatchway.

Boom—Spar used to extend foot of a fore-and-aft sail.

Bow—Rounded part of a vessel forward.

Bowsprit—Heavy spar rigged from bow of vessel carrying the headsails.

Brace—Rope used to swing a yard about.

Brails—Ropes used to furl the spanker or spencer.

Breaker—Keg for drinking water used in small boats.

Breast Rope—Line passed around man who heaves the lead.

Brig—Square-rigged vessel with two masts.

Brigantine or *Hermaphrodite Brig* is square-rigged on foremast; fore-and-aft rigged on main; this is rarely seen.

Bring to—Throwing a vessel up into the wind.

Broach—To open a cask or box.

Broach to—To swing a vessel running before the wind broadside to wind or at right angles to course. A most dangerous thing if the sea be heavy.

Broadside—Side of a vessel.

Bull—A sailor's term for a small keg, holding a gallon or two.

Bull's-Eye—A small piece of stout wood with a hole in the center for a stay or rope to reeve through, without a sheave, and with a groove round it for the strap, which is usually of iron. Also a piece of thick glass inserted in the deck to let in light.

Bulwarks—Woodwork around a vessel above decks.

Bunting—Thin woolen stuff of which flags are made.

Buntlines—Ropes used for hauling up the body of a sail.

Bush—The centerpiece of a wooden sheave in a block.

Butt—The end of a plank where it unites with the end of another. *Scuttle butt,* a cask with a hole cut in its bilge and kept on deck to hold drinking water.

By the Head—When the head of a vessel is lower in the water than her stern. If her stern is lower, she is *by the stern.*

Cable—A large, strong rope, made fast to the anchor, by which the vessel is secured.

Canvas—Sailcloth; strength indicated by numbers o to 9. That numbered o is the heaviest. Also is used to mean sails ship may be carrying.

Cap—Heavy wooden block that forms connecting link of mast with one above it.

Capsize—Upset; overturn.

Careen—Heave a vessel on her side.

Carry Away—Break a spar or rope.

Carry On—To crack on all sail possible.

Cat's-paw—Light air.

Caulking Mat—Any canvas or other cloth on which a man takes a nap on deck.

Chains—Iron plates bolted to ships sides on which standing rigging is set up. *Rudder chains,* lead from rudder head to tiller ropes.

Channels—Broad planks bolted to outside of vessel to spread lower rigging.

Chockablock—When the lower block of a tackle is run close to the upper one, so that you can hoist no higher.

Clawing Off.—To work off close-hauled from lee shore.

Cleat—A piece of wood used to belay ropes.

Clew—The lower corner of square sails, and the after corner of fore-and-aft sails.

Clew Line—A rope that hauls up the clew of a square sail.

Close-Hauled—When a vessel is sailing as close to the wind as she will go.

Close-Reefed—When all the reefs are taken in.

Coamings—Raised work around the hatches, to prevent water from going into the hold.

Coat—Mast coat is a piece of canvas, tarred or painted, placed around a mast or bowsprit where it enters the deck, to keep out water.

Coil—To lay a rope up in a circle, with one turn or fake over another. A coil is a quantity of rope laid up in this manner.

Collar—An eye in the end or bight of a shroud or stay, to go over the masthead.

Companion—A wooden covering over the staircase to a cabin. Companionway, the staircase to the cabin. *Companion ladder,* leading from the poop to the main deck.

Conning, or *Cunning*—Directing the helmsman in steering a vessel.

Counter—That part of a vessel between the bottom of the stern and the wing transom and buttock.

Courses—Common term for the sails that hang from a ship's lower yards. The foresail is called the *forecourse* and the mainsail the *maincourse.*

Cranes—Heavy hoisting apparatus on ship's side to handle spars.

Cranky—Vessel that rolls a great deal and cannot carry much sail.

Cringle—Rope spliced into the boltrope of a sail to enclose iron ring or thimble.

Crossjack (pronounced crodgick)—Lower yard of a ship or its mizzenmast.

Crosstrees—Heavy bits of oak at mastheads to spread the rigging and sustain tops of lower masts.

Deadeyes—Bits of hardwood through which are rove lanyards to set up rigging.

Derrick—A single spar, supported by stays and guys, to which a purchase is attached; used to unload vessels, and for hoisting heavy objects.

Dogvane—A small vane, usually made of bunting, to show the direction of the wind.

Dolphin Striker—The martingale.

Douse—To lower suddenly.

Downhaul—A rope used to haul down jibs, staysails, and studding sails.

Drag—A sea anchor to keep the head of the vessel to the wind.

Draw—A sail *draws* when it is filled by the wind.

Drive—To scud before a gale, or to drift in a current.

Driver—A spanker.

Drop—The depth of a sail, from head to foot, amidships.

Duck—A kind of cloth, lighter than canvas, used for small sails.

Earing—A rope attached to the cringle, by which it is bent or reefed.

Even Keel—The position of a vessel when she is so trimmed that she rests evenly upon the water.

Eye—Shroud or stay where it goes over mast.

Eyebolt—Bar with circular hole at end projecting from ship's deck on side.

Eye Splice—Bit of rope spliced to form loop at end.

Eyes of Ships—Extreme forepart of bows.

Fag—Rope untwisted.

Fake—One of the layers of a coil of rope.

Fall—Ropes running through blocks by which a boat is hoisted.

Fast—Secured. *All fast, make fast* are common sea terms.

Fenders, Fender Spars—Rope rolls or wood hung from side of ship or boat to prevent chafing.

Fid—Wooden block at heel of mast holding it in place. Wooden marlinspike.

Fiferail—Rail around mast for belaying running rigging.

Flare—Temporary blaze made, usually by sailing vessels being overtaken, to indicate ship's position. Also used in small boats to attract attention.

Flat—A sheet is said to be hauled flat when it is hauled down close.

Flaw—A gust of wind.

Flowing Sheet—When a vessel has the wind free, and the sheets are eased off.

Flush—Level.

Fly—That part of a flag which extends from the union to the extreme end.

Foot—The lower end of a mast or sail.

Footrope—A rope upon which to stand when reefing or furling sail.

Fore—Used to distinguish the forward part of a vessel, or things forward of amidships; as, *foremast, forehatch*. The opposite to aft or after.

Fore and Aft—Lengthwise with the vessel. The opposite to athwartships.

Forecastle—That part of the upper deck forward of the foremast; or, forward of the afterpart of the forechannels. Also, the forward part of the vessel, under the deck, where the sailors live.

Forefoot—A piece of timber at the forward extremity of the keel, upon which the lower end of the stem rests.

Foremast—The forward mast of a vessel.

Forge—To forge ahead, to shoot ahead, as, in coming to anchor, or when going in stays.

Forward—In front of.

Foul—The opposite of clear.

Founder—When a vessel fills with water and sinks.

Free—Running before the wind. *Free of water,* clear of water.

Freeboard—Part of vessel out of water.

Freshen—When referring to ballast it means altering its position; when referring to a rope it means to ease it so it cannot chafe.

Full and By—Sailing order meaning to keep the sails full yet to steer a course as close to the wind as possible.

Furl—To roll a sail snugly on boom or yard.

Futtock Shrouds—Part of standing rigging leading from futtock plates on the top. The topmast rigging leads aloft from their upper ends.

Gadget—Any little handy contraption, such as a scraper, or special sailmaker's palm, etc.

Gaff—Spar to which head of fore-and-aft sail is bent.

Gaff Topsail—Light fore-and-aft sail rigged to gaff.

Gooseneck—An iron ring fitted to the end of a yard or boom.

Grating—Open latticework of wood. Used principally to cover hatches in good weather; also, to let in light and air.

Gripes—Bars of iron, with lanyards, rings, and clews, by which a boat is lashed to the ringbolt of the deck. Those for a quarter boat are made of long strips of canvas, going around her and set taut by a lanyard.

Grommet—A ring formed of rope, by laying around a single strand.

Gun-Tackle Purchase—A purchase made by two single blocks.

Gunwale—The upper rail of a boat or vessel.

Guy—A rope attached to anything to steady it, and bear it one way or another in hoisting.

Gybe—To change the position of the sails of a fore-and-aft vessel from one side to the other without going in stays.

Hail—To speak or call to another vessel or to men in a different part of the ship.

Halyards or Halliards—Ropes or tackle used for hoisting and lowering yards, gaffs, and sails.

Hand—*To hand a sail* is to furl it. *Bear-a-hand,* make haste; *lend-a-hand,* assist; *hand-over-hand,* hauling rapidly on a rope, by putting one hand before the other, alternately.

Handspike—A long wooden bar, used for heaving at the windlass.

Hatch, or Hatchway—An opening in the deck to afford a passage up and down. The coverings over these openings are called *hatches.*

Hatch Bar—An iron bar going across the hatches, to keep them down.

Haul—*Haul her wind,* when a vessel comes up close upon the wind.

Hawse Block—A block of wood fitted into a hawsehole when at sea.

Hawsehole—The hole in the bows through which the anchor cable runs.

Hawser—A large rope used for various purposes, as warping, for a spring, etc.

Head—Prow of a vessel. Also the upper end of a mast, called the *mast-head.*

Headsails—All sails that set forward of the foremast.

Heave in Stays—To go about, tacking.

Heave to—To put a vessel in the position of lying to.

Heel—The after part of the keel. The lower end of the mast or boom. Also, the lower end of the sternpost. *To heel* is to careen to one side.

Heeling—The square part of the lower end of a mast, through which the fid hole is made.

Helm—The machinery by which a vessel is steered, including the rudder, tiller, wheel, etc.

Helm Port—The hole in the counter through which the rudderhead passes.

Hog—A flat, rough broom, used for scrubbing the bottom of a vessel.

Holystone—A large stone, used for cleaning a ship's decks.

Home—The sheets of a sail are said to be *home* when the clews are hauled chock out to the sheave holes. An anchor *comes home* when it is loosened from the ground and hove in.

Horns—The jaws and booms and gaffs. Also, the ends of crosstrees.

Hounds—Projections at the masthead serving as shoulders for the trestle-trees to rest upon.

House—Lowering a mast and securing it to the spar below.

Irons—When a ship misses stays in tacking and hangs in the wind she is *in irons*.

Jacob's Ladder—Flexible ladder, made of rope with wooden rungs used far aloft. Smaller ones are used over ship's side for entering boats.

Jaws—Inner ends of gaffs and booms partly encircling the mast.

Jib—Chief headsail running on a stay to bowsprit. Flying jib and outer jib run on other stays.

Jib Boom—Boom rigged to bowsprit to which tack of jib is secured.

Jigger—Fourth mast in a square-rigged vessel; small tackle used for tautening sheets, halliards, etc.

Jury Mast—Temporary mast rigged to replace one lost.

Keel—Lowest and chief timber in a vessel, running its entire length.

Knightheads—Timbers next to the stem and running up to support the bowsprit.

Labor—A vessel is said to labor when she rolls or pitches heavily.

Lacing—Rope used to lash a sail to a spar, or a bonnet to a sail.

Landfall—Making land.

Lanyards—Ropes rove through deadeyes for setting up rigging. Also a rope made fast to anything to secure it.

Leading Wind—A fair wind. Applied to a wind abeam or quartering.

Lee—The side opposite to that from which the wind blows; if a vessel has the wind on her starboard, that will be the *weather* side, and the port will be the *lee* side. A *lee shore* is the shore upon which the wind is blowing. *Under the lee* of anything is when you have that between you and the wind.

Leeboard—A board fitted to the side of a flat-bottomed craft, to prevent its drifting to leeward.

Leech, or *Leach*—The border or edge of a sail, at the sides.

Leech Line—A rope used for hauling up the leech of a sail.

Leeward—The lee side. In a direction opposite to that from which the wind blows, which is called *windward*. The opposite of *lee* is *weather*, and of *leeward* is *windward*.

Leeway—What a vessel loses by drifting to leeward.

Lie to, or *Lay to*—To stop progress of a vessel at sea either by counter-bracing the yards or by reducing sail so that she will make little or no headway, but will merely come to and fall off by the counteraction of the sails and helm.

Life Lines—Ropes carried along yards, booms, etc., or at any part of the vessel to hold on by.

Lift—A rope or tackle, going from the yardarms to the masthead, to support and move the yard. Also a term applied to the sails when the wind strikes them on the leeches and raises them slightly.

List—Inclination of a vessel to one side; *heavy list to starboard* means much tilted over to the right.

Locker—Chest or box for stowing things. *Chain locker,* place for anchor chain; *bosun's locker,* storage place for small stuff used in ship's work.

Lubber's Hole—Opening in top through which green men climb; the smart sailorman goes up over futtock shrouds.

Luff—To bring the ship closer to the wind.

Luff Tackle—Purchase composed of a double and a single block.

Lugsail—Used in small boats; is bent to a yard or *lug* suspended from the mast.

Lurch—Sudden rolling of a vessel.

Main—Principal mast or sail.

Manropes—Safety lines used in going over the ship's side; also ropes between the gangway and the ship's rail proper.

Marlin—Fine two-stranded small stuff, usually tarred.

Marlinspike—Pointed instrument used in splicing rope.

Martingale—A short, perpendicular spar, under the bowsprit end, used for guying the headstays. Sometimes called a *dolphin striker.*

Mast—A spar set upright from the deck, to support rigging, yards, and sails.

Master—The commander of a vessel.

Mat—Made of strands of old rope, and used to prevent chafing.

Midships—The timbers at the broadest part of the vessel.

Misstay—To fail of going about from one tack to another.

Mizzenmast—The aftermost mast of a ship. The spanker is sometimes called the *mizzen.*

Monkey Block—A small single block strapped with a swivel.

Mouse—To put a turn of rope yarn or spun yarn around the end of a hook and its standing part when it is hooked to anything, so as to prevent it from slipping out.

Netting—Network of rope or small lines. Used for stowing away sails or hammocks.

Nip—A short turn in a rope.

Oakum—Stuff made by picking rope yarns to pieces. Used for caulking and other purposes.

Off and On—To stand on different tacks toward and from the land.

Offing—Distance from the shore.

Outhaul—A rope used for hauling out the clew of a sail.

Overhaul—Applied to rigging it means to examine and repair. Applied to rope it means to keep it clear from running through the blocks. To overhaul a ship is to catch up with or overtake it.

Painter—Rope at bows of a small boat to make her fast.

Part—To break. Also a section of rope when rove through a block, as the *standing part* and the *running part.*

Pay—To *pay off* is to let vessel go away from the wind. To *pay out* a line is to let it run. To *pay standing rigging* is to cover it with tar or pitch.

Peak—*Forepeak* is extreme forward part of the ship; *afterpeak,* extreme afterpart of ship; both below deck. *Peak of a sail* is the upper, outer edge.

Pennant, or *Pendant*—Narrow strip of bunting triangular in shape. Rope on which is hooked a purchase.

Pillow—Block supporting inboard end of bowsprit.

Pin—Center axis of a block. *Belaying pin,* iron or wooden bar used for making lines fast. Belaying pins are set in *pinrails.*

Pinrail—Oak ledges bolted inside the ship's rail to hold belaying pins.

Point—Reefpoints are small lines sewn in a sail with which to make it shorter or for shortening.

Poop—Raised deck at extreme end of vessel.

Port—Left side of vessel looking forward. A harbor. Also holes in vessel's side through which cargo is worked; *bunkerport,* holes leading to the coal bunkers.

Preventer—Additional stay or spar used to support one already in place.

Purchase—Extra power applied, usually by means of a block and tackle.

Quarter—Side of vessel toward the stern; opposite of bow.

Quarter-deck—That part of the deck aft of the mainmast.

Rack—To seize parallel ropes together, but not to "marry" them.

Rake—Angle at which masts or funnels are set.

Ratlines—Light lines running across the shrouds, thus forming a rope ladder.

Ready About—Order to stand by for tacking.

Reef—To shorten sail.

Reef Band—Extra width of canvas sewed in sail to support strain of *reef points.*

Reef Tackle—Small tackle used to stretch the leech of a reef tightly to yard or boom.

Reeve—To pass the end of a rope through a block.

Relieving Tackle—Extra tackles placed on rudderhead to take strain from rudder chains.

Rigging—The general term for all the ropes of a vessel. Also, the common term for the shrouds with their ratlines; as, the *main rigging, mizzen rigging,* etc.

Right—To right the helm, is to put it amidships.

Ring—The iron ring at the upper end of an anchor to which the cable is bent.

Ringbolt—An eyebolt with a ring through the eye.

Ringtail—A small sail, shaped like a jib, set abaft the spanker in light winds.

Roach—A curve in the foot of a square sail, by which the clews are brought below the middle of the foot. The roach of a fore-and-aft sail is in its forward leech.

Rope Yarn—A thread of hemp, or other stuff, of which a rope is made.

Round In—To haul in on a rope.

Round Up—To haul up on a tackle.

Roundings—A service of rope, hove around a spar or larger rope.

Rowlocks—The receptacles for the oars in rowing.

Royal—A light sail next above a topgallant sail.

Royal Yard—The yard from which the royal is set. The fourth from the deck.

Rudder—That by which a vessel or boat is steered, attached to the sternpost.

Run—The afterpart of a vessel's bottom, which rises and narrows in approaching the sternpost. *By the run,* to let go by the run is to let go altogether, instead of gradually.

Runner—A rope to increase the power of a tackle. It is rove through a single block, and a tackle is hooked to each end, or to one end, the other being fast. Also, a *cocoa mat.*

Running Rigging—The ropes that reeve through blocks and are pulled and hauled, such as braces, halyards, etc.; in contrast to the *standing rigging,* the ends of which are securely seized; such as stays, shrouds, etc.

Sag—To sag to leeward is to drift off bodily to leeward.

Sails—Are of two kinds: *square sails,* which hang from yards, their foot lying across the line of the keel, as the course, topsail, etc.; and *fore-and-aft sails,* which set upon gaffs, booms, etc., their foot running with the line of the keel.

Schooner—A vessel with two or more masts. A *fore-and-aft schooner* has only fore-and-aft sails. A *topsail schooner* carries a square-foot topsail, and frequently topgallant sail, and *royal schooners* are now built with two, three, four, and many with five masts.

Score—A groove in a block or deadeye.

Scud—To drive before a gale with no sail or only enough to steady the vessel. Also, low, thin clouds that fly swiftly before the wind.

Scuppers—Holes cut in the waterways for the water to run from the decks.

Scuttle—A hole cut in a vessel's deck, as a hatchway. Also, a hole cut in any part of a vessel. To *scuttle* is to cut or bore holes in a vessel to make her sink.

Scuttle Butt—Cask on deck containing drinking water.

Seize—To fasten ropes together by turns of small stuff, to secure hooks, etc.

Seizings—The fastenings of ropes that are seized together.

Sennit, or Sinnit—A braid, formed by plaiting rope yarns or spun yarns together.

Serve—To wind small stuff, or rope yarns, spun yarns, etc., around a rope to keep it from chafing. It is wound and hove around taut by a serving mallet.

Set—To *set up rigging* is to tighten it.

Shackles—Links in a chain cable fitted with a movable bolt so that the chain can be separated.

Shank—The main piece of an anchor; the stock is made fast at one end, and the arms at the other.

Sharp Up—Yards when braced as near fore and aft as possible.

Shears—Two or more spars, raised at angles or lashed together near their upper ends, used for lowering or hoisting heavy objects.

Sheave—Wheel within a block.

Sheepshank—Hitch used to shorten a rope without cutting it.

Sheer—Sometimes called *sheerstrake*. Top line of planking running fore and aft along a vessel's gunwale.

Sheet—Lines used to keep the lower parts of sails spread. In fore-and-afters, to hold booms from swinging too far.

Sheet Anchor—The ship's largest anchor; sometimes *best bower*.

Shell—Outside casing of a block.

Shore—Prop.

Shrouds—Standing rigging running from masthead to channel plates to support masts.

Sister Block—Block with two single sheaves, one above the other.

Slack—Anything loose. To *slack away* means to loosen gradually.

Slings—Rope support of a yard.

Sloop—Small vessel with one mast, carrying at least jib and mainsail.

Small Stuff—Spun yarn, marlin, and other light rope.

Snatch Block—Single block made so that the sheave can be opened and the bight of a rope led through.

Snub—To check a rope suddenly.

Spanker—Fore-and-aft sail on ship or bark farthest aft. Spanker booms, spanker brails, etc.

Spars—General term for masts, yards, gaffs, booms.

Spencer—Fore-and-aft sail on square-rigger, but not a headsail.

Spill—To shake wind out of sail by luffing.

Spindrift—Water swept from crests of waves. Flying clouds.

Spray—Water blown from waves.

Spring—To crack, as to "*spring*" a mast.

Sprit, and *Spritsail*—Sail used in small boats rigged on a sprit. Differs from *lug* and *lugsail* in that the sprit is stepped in a becket at foot of mast.

Spun Yarn—A rope formed by twisting together two or three rope yarns.

Square—Yards are *squared* when they are horizontal and at right angles with the keel. Squaring by the lifts makes them horizontal, and by the braces, makes them at right angles with the vessel's line. To *square a yard* means to bring it in square by the braces.

Square Sail—A temporary sail, set at the foremast of a schooner or the mainmast of a sloop when going before the wind.

Staff—A pole or mast used to hoist flags upon.

Stanchions—Upright posts of wood or iron placed so as to support the beams of a vessel. Also, upright pieces of timber placed along the sides of a vessel to support the bulwarks and rail. Also, any fixed, upright support.

Standing Rigging—That part of a vessel's rigging which is made fast to the sides.

Starboard—The right side of a vessel looking forward.

Stay—To tack a vessel, or to put her about, so that the wind, from being on one side, is brought upon the other, around the vessel's head. To *stay a mast* is to incline it forward or aft or to one side or the other, by the stays and backstays. A mast is said to be *stayed* too much forward or aft, or too much to port, etc.

Stays—Large ropes used to support masts, and leading from the head of one mast down to another, or to some part of the vessel. Those which lead forward are called *fore-and-aft stays,* and those which lead down to the vessel's sides *backstays. In stays,* or *hove in stays,* a vessel when she is *staying* or going from one tack to another.

Steady—To keep the helm as it is.

Stem—Extreme forward timber in a vessel.

Step—Block of wood at base of mast that holds its heel.

Stern—After end of vessel. (Never say rear, back, or behind.)

Sternboard—Motion of vessel backward. Also called *sternway.*

Sternpost—Aftermost timber in a vessel.

Stiff—Vessel able to carry plenty of sail safely. Opposite of cranky.

Strand—Part of a rope composed of smaller bits.

Strap—Rope or metal binding around a block.

Strip—Dismantle.

Surge—To *surge* a rope or cable is to slack it up suddenly where it renders around a pin, or around the windlass or capstan.

Sway—To hoist up.

Sweep—To drag the bottom. Also, large oars used in small vessels.

Swift—To bring two shrouds or stays close together by ropes.

Swifter—The forward shroud to a lower mast. Also, ropes used to confine the capstan bars to their places when shipped.

Swivel—A long link of iron, used in chain cables, made so as to turn upon an axis intended to keep the turns out of a chain.

Tack—To put a ship about, so that from having the wind on one side it is brought around on the other by way of her head. The opposite of wearing. A vessel is on the *starboard tack,* or has her *starboard tack* on board, when she has the wind on her starboard side. The rope or tackle by which the weather clew of a course is hauled forward and down. The *tack* of a fore-and-aft sail is the rope that keeps down the lower forward clew.

Tackle—A purchase; formed by a rope rove through one or more blocks.

Taffrail—The rail around a ship's stern.

Tail—A rope spliced into the end of a block and used for making it fast to rigging or spars is called a *tail block.* A ship is said to *tail up* or *down stream* when at anchor, according as her stern swings up or down with the tide; the opposite to *heading* one way or another.

Tail On—To take hold of a rope and pull.

Tail Tackle—A watch tackle.

Taut—Tight, snug.

Thimble—An iron ring, having its rim concave on the outside for a rope or strap to fit snugly.

Throat—The inner end of a gaff, where it widens and hollows in to fit the mast. Also, the hollow part of a knee. The *throat brails,* halyards, etc., are those that hoist or haul up the gaff or sail near the throat. Also, the angle where the arm of an anchor is joined to the shank.

Thrum—To stick short strands of yarn through a mat or canvas to make a rough surface.

Tier—The range of the fakes of a cable or hawser.

Tiller—A bar of wood or iron put into the head of the rudder, by which it is moved.

Timberheads—The ends of the timbers that come above the deck. Used for belaying hawsers and large ropes.

Toggle—A pin placed through the bight or eye of a rope, block strap, or bolt to keep it in its place, or to put the bight or eye of another rope upon, securing them together.

Top—A platform placed over the head of a lower mast, resting on the trestletrees, to spread the rigging and for the convenience of men aloft.

Topgallant Mast—The third mast above the deck.

Topgallant Sail—The third sail above the deck.

Topmast—The second mast above the deck. Next above the lower mast.

Topping Lift—A lift used for topping up the end of a boom.

Topsail—The second sail above the deck.

Traveler—Iron ring fitting to slide up and down rigging.

Triatic Stay—Heavy rope secured to heads of the fore-and-aft mainmasts.

Trice—To haul up by a rope.

Trim—The way a vessel floats. *Trimmed by the head* means with bows lower than they should be.

Truck—Uppermost end of the uppermost mast.

Trysail—Triangular fore-and-aft sail on a square-rigger; used in heavy weather.

Turn—*Half turn, round turn* applied to rope means *passing it about a pin. Turn in,* stop work or go to bed; *turn out,* get up or get on the job.

Unbend—To cast off, most frequently applied to sails.

Vane—Light bunting at masthead used as weather vane.

Vang—Rope leading from a gaff to ship's side to steady the gaff.

Veer—To pay out chain; also the wind *veers* when it changes against the compass (from westward to eastward); it *shifts* when it changes from eastward to westward.

Warp—To move a vessel from one place to another by means of a rope made fast to some fixed object, or to a kedge. A *warp* is a rope used for warping. If the warp is bent to a kedge which is let go, and the vessel is hove ahead by the capstan or windlass, it is called *kedging.*

Washboard—Light pieces of board placed above the gunwale of the boat.

Watch Tackle—A small luff purchase with a short fall, the double block having a tail to it, and the single one a hook. Used about deck.

Waterways—Long pieces of timber running fore and aft on both sides, connecting the deck with the vessel's side. The scuppers run through them.

Wear—To turn a vessel around so that from having the wind on one side, the wind will be on the other side, carrying her stern around by the wind. In *tacking* the same result is produced by carrying a vessel's head around by the wind.

Weather—In the direction from which the wind blows. A ship carries a *weather helm* when she tends to come up into the wind. A *weather ship* is one that works well to windward, making but little leeway.

Weather Roll—The roll which a ship makes to windward.

Whip—A purchase formed by a rope rove through a single block. To *whip* is to hoist by a whip. Also, to secure the end of a rope from fagging by seizing of twine.

Whisker Booms—The cross trees to a bowsprit.

Wing and Wing—The situation of a fore-and-aft vessel when she is going dead before the wind, with her foresail on one side and her mainsail on the other.

Work Up—To draw the yarns from old rigging and make them into spun yarn, foxes, sennit, etc. Also, a phrase for keeping a crew constantly at work upon needless matters, and in all weathers, and beyond their usual hours, for punishment.

Worm—To fill up between the lays of a rope with small stuff wound around spirally.

Yard—A long piece of timber, tapering slightly toward the ends, and hung by the center to a mast, to spread the square sails upon.

Yardarm—The extremities of a yard.

Yaw—The motion of a vessel when she goes off her course.

Yawl—A vessel with two masts, the small one aft.

⚓

CHAPTER III

HANDLING BOATS UNDER POWER

At Sea

301. The powerboat at sea, with plenty of space in which to navigate, constitutes no special problem in handling, save to steer and keep the course desired. A minimum of seamanship is required, and handling becomes simpler even than the handling of an automobile. This is because under ordinary conditions all the components of the problem remain relatively fixed (the surface of the sea, the power, the trim, for example) and are not constantly varying as when handling a boat under sail.

The navigator has but to know the peculiarities of his particular boat, her responsiveness to rudder and to power, and the boat may be handled in a carefree and effortless manner. In addition to the problems raised by navigation (which are thoroughly discussed in Chapter XI), only two situations might arise calling for special handling. One is the presence of traffic; the other, the coming of a storm.

Motorboat Rules of the Road

302. Inland and International Rules are similar in prescribing the conduct of each boat when meeting to prevent the possibility of collision. The five situations following cover all situations.

It should be noted that approximately the same standard rules of the road which apply to motor vehicles ashore apply to motorboats; that is, keep to the right; keep clear of the vessel approaching from the right; and indicate your intentions to the other boat involved. Note also that the law does not give either boat any "rights." It merely specifies which one is to "keep clear."

For full details of the law in every possible situation refer to the text of the law given in Chapter V.

Figure 302A. First Situation

Here the two colored lights visible to each will indicate their direct approach "head and head" toward each other. In this situation it is a standing rule that both shall direct their courses to starboard and pass on the port side of each other, each having previously given one blast of the whistle.

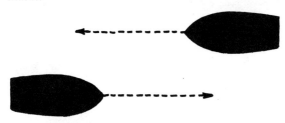

Figure 302B. Second Situation

In this situation the red light only will be visible to each, the screens preventing the green lights from being seen. Both vessels are evidently passing to port of each other, which is rulable in this situation, each pilot having previously signified his intention by one blast of the whistle.

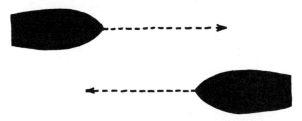

Figure 302C. Third Situation

In this situation the green light only will be visible to each, the screens preventing the red light from being seen. They are, therefore, passing to starboard of each other, which is rulable in this situation, each pilot having previously signified his intention by two blasts of the whistle.

Figure 302D. Fourth Situation

In this situation one steam vessel is overtaking another steam vessel from some point within the angle of two points abaft the beam of the overtaken steam vessel. The overtaking steam vessel may pass on the starboard or port side of the steam vessel ahead after the necessary signals for passing have been given with the assent of the overtaken steam vessel.

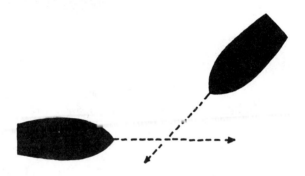

Figure 302E. Fifth Situation

In this situation two steam vessels are approaching each other at right angles or obliquely *in such manner as to involve risk of collision,* other than where one steam vessel is overtaking another. The steam vessel which has the other on her own *port* side shall hold course and speed, and the other shall keep clear by crossing astern of the steam vessel that is holding course and speed, or, if necessary to do so, shall slacken her speed, stop, or reverse.

General points of the law to remember are:
1. Motorboats are *always* to keep clear of boats under sail or oars.
2. A boat is under way when she is not moored or anchored, and is

to be treated as a vessel under way whether or not she is actually under power or moving.

3. An outboard motorboat is bound to observe the Rules of the Road exactly as a boat with permanent power.

4. Speed in rivers, narrow channels, along wharves, through canals, near fishing fleets or anchored boats, or *in any waters where her speed or wash* might cause damage or annoyance or danger is limited to not more than six miles an hour. There is no speed limit at sea.

Storm and Rough Water

303. Waves are of two forms; trochoidal and cycloidal. (Figure 303.) Trochoidal waves are the waves of deepwater, and, while they may be of tremendous dimensions, they are never dangerous until they begin to break at the crests. It takes a mighty storm to make them break, and the ordinary cruise will seldom find the motorboat so far offshore as not to have been able to run to shelter.

Cycloidal waves are the waves of shallow and confined waters. They are whipped up in shallow bodies (such as at inland lakes or in shallow coastal bays) by a comparatively moderate breeze and one which would have little effect upon deepwater waves. There is but a small span between crests, and consequently they "drop" from beneath a boat quickly and cause a short, jerky, and unpleasant motion, which makes steering difficult. They are dangerous to small open boats, and most uncomfortable to even the decked-in large boat, particularly when attacking on the beam. The cycloidal wave will

Trochoidal   Cycloidal

Figure 303. Wave Forms

break under wind velocities which would scarcely ruffle the trochoidal wave.

A sea may be composed of a combination of both types, as in shoal areas, or over a bar, or when a strong tidal current opposes the direction of the waves.

304. Some hints for handling the powerboat in seas follow:

Running Before a Sea

This is probably the most potentially dangerous of any position at sea. The boat is lifted by the stern, both steerageway and power are lost because the rudder and propeller are clear, or almost clear, of the water, and the boat goes into a wide and perhaps wild yaw. She may yaw to such an extent, as she is carried forward upon the breast of the wave, that she will broach to, or slither into the trough and

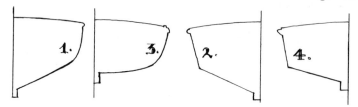

Figure 304. 1 and 2 Are Better Sea Boats than 3 and 4

broadside to the seas. In this position she is almost helpless for a period, and is liable to be boarded by the beam by the next sea, or rolled over.

Both yawing and broaching to can be avoided by a combination of careful, "compensating" steering and throttle control. At all costs the rudder must be used to keep the boat's stern to the seas. Abruptly checking speed will permit the sea to pass. Reduced speed is indicated always. Dragging a long hawser astern will help to slow the forward swing of the stern; or, in extreme cases, a hawser into which many figure-of-eight knots have been tied may be towed.

A combination of excessive speed imparted by the motor and the waves and a sharp lift of the stern may result in pitchpoling. The bow is completely submerged, and as it staggers the stern is lifted and the vessel turned over end for end. Heavy, 50-foot keelboats have been pitchpoled during violent storms. Open boats which are pitchpoled fill instantly. Careful helmsmanship, slow speed, and, if necessary, shifting of weights and ballast to the stern will reduce the likelihood of pitchpoling.

Running into a Sea

Running into a sea is wet and sloppy going, but is seldom dangerous if speed has been reduced to avoid strain on the boat, the engine, her gear, and her company. The speed must be regulated so that the bow lifts to the oncoming seas and is not driven into them. It helps, in unusually heavy or breaking head seas, to take them slightly on one bow. Some of the sea's energy will then be expended in a slight, rolling motion, and pitching will be lessened.

The great dangers in "slamming" into head seas are that (a) the hull will be strained to the point of springing a plank, or breaking some frames; (b) something might be torn adrift (ballast, engine, tanks, and particularly such fixtures on the ends) and will need to be tamed before pounding through the plank; and (c) the engine, or the gear, or the shaft may break down under the alternate heavy load of a submerged and then wildly racing wheel as the boat pitches.

Running in the Trough

If this becomes necessary, and the wind and seas attack on the beam, there is no course but to "take it" at reduced speed and with careful steering. The helmsman should be ready to meet the largest of the seas by quartering into it momentarily; that is, by receiving the force of the crest on the weather (windward) bow, then straightening to true course to take advantage of the calm which follows a particularly heavy sea.

If the seas are too heavy, a series of open legs must be made to the objective, first taking the seas on the weather bow and then steering the same distance on the opposite side of the true course and taking them on the weather quarter. It is often possible to set a course so that instead of running in the trough, a slightly windward course can be taken to a lee, and then the boat swung so that the lee-flattened seas will attack only the quarter.

The advantage and comfort of running under a lee shore, if a beam sea course lies ahead, should always be carefully considered. It is just as good (and far more comfortable and safe) to run to a lee, skirt it, and then run away from it at normal speed as it is to run in the trough half the distance at half the speed.

Heaving to

When headway becomes nil or the punishment too severe, there is nothing to do but heave the boat to (providing, of course, there is sufficient sea room). Small boats will not heave to without aid as steamers will, and a sea anchor, or drogue, becomes a necessity. Lacking a sea anchor, the motor may be hooked up just enough to give steerageway (but not headway), and the boat kept facing the seas at an angle on either bow. The use of oil will often help and is recommended. (*See* Chapter II for sea anchors and the use of oil.)

305. Cycloidal waves in a sea of generally trochoidal waves indicate a shallowing of the water under them, or the presence of an opposing or cross current of some strength, which, in effect, "shallows" the water, so far as wave making is concerned.

Run through such areas only if the cause is thoroughly understood and the bottom beneath known from experience, or from the chart. Cycloidal waves over coastal bars are common. Such breakers do not necessarily denote shallow or dangerous water, but it may be taken for granted that the smoothest of these areas are the deepest. In running into an area of breakers over a bar it behooves the helmsman to carefully study the wave groups and to count the light waves between the heavy ones. They will "make" in groups of at least three. The best time to cross the bar is directly after a large wave has passed and broken; then "gun" over in the relatively less violent other waves of the group.

Handling in Close Quarters

306. Considerably more knowledge and experience are required to maneuver a motorboat in congested waters or to dock or moor it than is required to handle it at sea. Here the action of the rudder and propeller, particularly in turning and backing, must be thoroughly understood. (Figure 306.)

The Rudder

307. A boat without rudder will (except as will be noted under *Propellers*) proceed in a straight line in still water and air because the water pressure is equal on both sides of the hull. In order to change the course, or to divert the boat from going in a straight line, the rudder is moved by means of a wheel or a tiller, either right or left, as desired. The effect is to throw the water pressures out of balance, and the boat will turn toward the side with the most pressure retarding it. (Figures 307A and 307B.)

What is actually happening is that water is "bunched" between the deadwood and the rudder and the *stern is being pushed away from a straight course*. As the stern swings, forcing the boat from a straight course, the bow moves slightly in the opposite direction, and, as the boat is still moving approximately along her original course but not now with her keel parallel to that course, an additional pressure comes into play against the bow, helping in the turning effect desired.

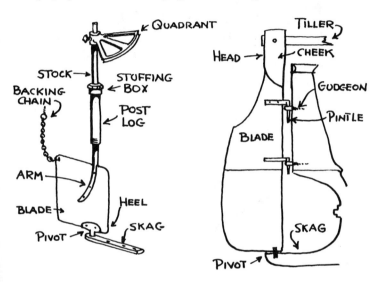

Metal balanced rudder with chain to stop blade 35° each side of amidships

Unbalanced wooden rudder

Figure 306

The bow never swings to as great a radius as the stern but both have a common center of arc, always forward of amidships, called the *pivoting point*. This is shown in Figure 307C. While the swing is shown as if the boat were stationary, swinging about the pivoting point, it must be remembered that the vessel is all the while moving along an arc of the turning radius.

Every boat has a different pivoting point, but it is *always forward of amidships*. Any turn made will therefore always move the stern a greater distance toward the outside of the turning circle than it will move the bow toward the inside of the turning circle. This is a cardinal rule to remember and must always be considered when maneuvering in limited spaces or in docking or getting away from a dock.

Figure 307A. The Propeller Stream Driving Ahead

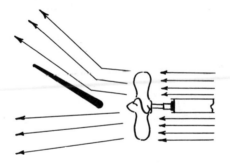

Figure 307B. The Propeller Stream Broken by the Rudder and Part of It Converted into "Side Motion"

308. The location of the pivoting is of minor importance. However, after handling a boat in various situations, the point is very soon "sensed," and thereafter any turn is visualized as revolving around this point, and the point itself following around the arc of the turn. Its exact location depends upon the design of the boat and the rudder. A boat with a deep forefoot will be slow on the bow swing, or a boat with little or no deadwood will be fast on the stern swing. It is a matter of side-resistance of the hull to the water. The shape and balance of the rudder will determine the "swing" of the boat as well. A boat that will "spin on a dime" is usually one with little deadwood or forefoot. Such a boat is hard to steer and needs constant watch, except at very high speeds, when other course-maintaining forces come into play.

A boat that turns slowly, "takes a long time to make up her mind," is usually one with a deep forefoot and a full deadwood. Such a boat is easy to steer and requires a minimum of wheel watch.

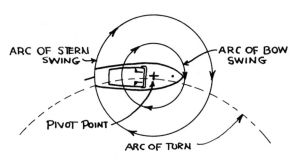

Figure 307C

Both types have their uses. Both types will require some special rudder handling when in wind.

309. A head wind will retard the progress of a boat but will not affect her course.

A wind on either bow will retard speed not only because of direct pressure but also because the helm must be carried to keep the boat headed on her true course; the boat will be slowed by the additional water pressure thus built up.

A wind on either beam will not directly retard speed, but the considerable amount of helm carried will.

Propellers

310. Practically all single-screw motorboats are equipped with a right-handed propeller. A right-handed propeller tends to throw the boat, with rudder amidships, slightly to the port, or left. This is due to the fact that upper and lower blades work in waters of different density, the lower blades exerting a thrust to port—which the upper blades cannot quite neutralize, even though turning in the same direction—and tending to throw the boat slightly to port, or left. If the propeller is left-handed, the effect will be just the opposite to the above.

The hand of a propeller is gauged by facing the propeller from aft, looking forward. A right-handed wheel, to move the boat forward, turns clockwise, or to the right at the top. A left-handed wheel is the reverse of the above.

In smooth water, therefore, the rudder will have to be moved slightly to compensate for this tendency to fall off. Sometimes this propeller force is enough to compensate for a beam wind without the aid of the helm.

Twin propellers balance each other (the screws turn in opposite directions, the tops turning outboard), and if revolutions are equal, the boat does not have this falling-off tendency. They may be used for steering, or manuevering, or turning without the helm; or to breast a wind or current by slightly increasing the speed of one.

Maneuvering

311. The most powerful steering effect is produced by the thrust of the propeller stream against the rudder. A quick "shot" of the engine against the rudder of a boat without headway will swing the boat without giving it substantial headway. This principle is used extensively in maneuvering in tight spaces. Full left or right rudder is required, and the *stern* will swing—not the bow. With a balanced or semibalanced rudder, which when hard over kills most of the propeller thrust except on itself, this maneuver becomes fairly simple.

Forward speeds constitute no problem in tight places. However, the seamanlike (but undramatic) manner of handling the boat is to send it ahead *slowly,* "ticking" the clutch or throttle rather than dashing forward and then snapping into high speed reverse. Such maneuvers are hard on the engine and are liable to stall it, with consequent disaster and damage to self and property.

Backing presents a peculiar situation for single-screw boats. Depending upon the propeller and design of the hull, a boat with a right-handed wheel will have a marked inclination to leave a straight backward course, even with the helm amidships and yaw off to the port. Sometimes no amount of opposite helm will straighten the boat out. She will always reverse with a swing to port (or to the right, if one is facing aft).

To back in a straight line, experimentation will produce a rudder position somewhere to port where rudder and propeller action become neutralized. The boat will always back, in turning, better to port than to starboard.

This principle, too, is used in maneuvering. A complete turn in confined areas is not attempted except clockwise, or from left to right,

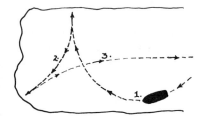 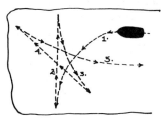

Figure 311. Complete Turn for Boats with Right-handed Wheels

Correct—clockwise   Incorrect—anticlockwise

1. Forward ⎤
2. Reverse ⎬ 3 moves
3. Forward ⎦

1. Forward ⎤
2. Reverse ⎮
3. Forward ⎬ 5 moves
4. Reverse ⎮
5. Forward ⎦

the easiest turning direction of the boat with a right-handed wheel. The extreme left-hand limit of the maneuver is approached first, the rudder put hard to starboard, stopped, and backed; then reversed, with the rudder hard to port. The inclination of the boat to back to port is here distinctly an advantage and will reduce the turning to one fifth of the moves necessary if it were made from right to left. (Figure 311.)

Twin-screw boats may be turned without *headway* or *sternway*, by going ahead on one wheel and reversing on the other. No helm is required.

Docking

312. Under ordinary conditions, docking is a simple enough matter if it is remembered always that the boat turns on a pivot; that sea room is required not only ahead or astern but on either side as well. Wind or tide or both are usually present, however, and must be taken into consideration. In the manuevers diagramed in the following figures it is assumed that the water and the air are still.

Both wind and tide can be *used* in docking maneuvers. The complete evolutions of the maneuver must be fully visualized, step by step, before attempting the first step. If the tide or wind will help or hinder any step, an estimate of that help or hindrance must be made and allowances made for it in the various steps.

Tide will move a boat over the bottom but will not alter its relative bearing to the compass points or the objective. Currents within the tide (or this moving body of water), such as around pierheads, will alter the relative bearing.

Wind will move a boat over the bottom *after* first swinging the boat broadside to the wind. The broadside angle will vary with the topside areas of the boat. Thus a raised-deck cruiser will move broadside but with the bow farther to leeward than the stern.

The judicious use of fenders is recommended for all docking maneuvers. Fenders are imperative when docking on the windward side of a dock. The use of the spring line and the proper mooring lines is shown in detail in Figure 1409A and 1409B, Chapter XIV.

It is always preferable to approach a dock or lie to it on the leeward side. Wind and tide shifts should be forecast and the berth chosen which will afford the best "lay" for the duration of the stay. If the boat must be shifted while at the dock, the diagrams following will give some helpful hints.

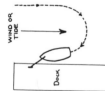

Figure 313

Approaching with the Wind. Turn to face the wind, get a bowline out first, let the stern drift alongside.

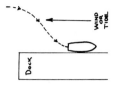

Figure 314

Approaching against the Wind. Maneuver alongside, get a bowline out first, let the stern drift alongside.

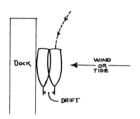

Figure 315

Approaching the Windward Side. Stop along side and parallel, drift into the dock. The bow will probably touch first.

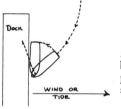

Figure 316

Approaching the Leeward Side. Touch with the bow, put a bow spring line out. Go forward under power with the rudder *away* from the dock to swing stern in.

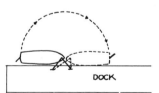

Figure 317

To Reverse the Heading While at a Dock. Put out double bowlines, swing rudder *toward* the dock, go forward under engine. When half way around, stop engine, reverse, then, as bow strains against the *opposite* bowline, proceed as before.

Figure 318

To Warp from a Pierhead to Alongside. Put out stern spring line, rudder toward dock and reverse on engine, *tending the bowline.* As the boat swings alongside, slack and tend spring line.

Figure 319

To Warp from Alongside to a Pierhead. Put out bow spring line. Go forward with rudder amidships, until pivoting point is beyond pierhead; then put rudder toward the dock and as the boat comes round put rudder away from the dock.

Figure 320

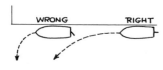

Right and Wrong Manner to Leave a Dock. Go forward with rudder amidships and, as speed is picked up, move it *slightly* away from dock, increasing the angle as the boat slowly bears away and clear. To set the rudder sharply and then go forward will swing the stern into the dock with considerable force, and be dangerous.

Figure 321

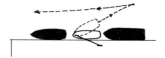

Clearing When Dockbound. Put out a bow spring line and with rudder toward the dock, go forward on engine. When clear, cast off and reverse; then go forward.

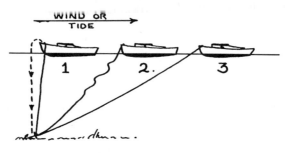

Figure 322. To Anchor

Run into the wind or tide until directly over the spot in which the anchor is to be set. Put over the anchor when *stopped*. Then sag back or move back under reversed engine, paying out the cable as needed (about five times the depth of the water); take a turn around the bitts or Samson post, and *set* the anchor under the momentum of reversed engine.

Figure 323. To Pick up a Mooring

Approach against the tide or wind, approaching the buoy or float without power (drifting) but with enough way on to steer. Do not sag back under power.

Figure 324. To Moor Between Two Stakes (or a stake and a dock)

Approach as in position number one. Put the rudder hard over and "kick" the stern over by a forward "shot" on the engine. Reverse (if necessary) and put a stern line on the stern stake that is at least as long as the distance between both stakes (position number two). Now run ahead, paying out the stern line to position number three. Put a bowline over the forward stake. Middle to position number four by hauling or power.

Fouling the Propeller

325. An ever-present danger when handling lines is that one will be sucked into the propeller. Whenever reversing or running ahead over a line, the line should be hauled taut and clear of the water. Dinghy painters must be watched very carefully when maneuvering, and good seamanship requires that the painter should be taken up short when planning to dock or moor. A series of net floats of wood or cork are often strung on the dinghy painter to keep it afloat. They should be spaced so that no bight may form between floats deep enough to reach the propeller.

A line which has become fouled in the wheel generally must be cut away. Reversing will sometimes help, but any power, forward or reverse, is liable to snub the line around the shaft or wheel blades, enough to throw them out of line, or spring them. A line is cut away best with a hacksaw, or a ragged knife blade.

If a lobster or net buoy is picked up, the mishap may be suspected of being more than merely a fouled propeller. Sometimes the wooden buoys jam between wheel and deadwood or hull, and cause split planks or other broken or strained underwater parts, and nearly always a bent propeller blade or blades.

Always be careful to pass to leeward, or around the "stern" of any pot buoy sighted. Watch also for a "trawl" of buoys or several buoys or warp floats secured together by underwater bridles, and do not pass between them.

Eelgrass and seaweed can generally be "reversed" off without damage. Specially designed antifouling wheels are required in weed or grass-infested waters.

Towing

SOME GENERAL NOTES ON TOWING

326. 1. A light dinghy will tow best on the forward breast of the second following wave.

2. A heavy tow, close up, should be towed with its center just slightly forward of the crest of one of the stern waves; never on the after breast of a wave.

3. In a broken or rolling sea a long towing hawser will provide the spring necessary between boats.

4. For maneuvering, always tow from the center line, rigging a bridle for the purpose if there is no center chock or bitts.

5. It is always better to tow a heavy boat from a point forward of the transom than from the transom, and thus permit the stern some side motion when steering.

6. In towing a boat from a position alongside, get to the leeward of her, and with the towing boat's rudder and propeller somewhat astern of the towed boat's stern.

7. Pushboats (as an outboard dinghy used for power of a sailboat in a calm) are rigged on either quarter, well fended off, with a bow spring line and a stern line, and headed slightly outboard of the course of the pushed boat. Stern pushboats are lashed bow to center line at

the transom, well fended, and lines are rigged from each quarter of the pushboat to the same quarter on the pushed boat.

Attraction (Suction)

327. Large vessels passing close aboard each other often experience a mutual attraction caused by the water's being "dragged" along with the boat's movement.

It is seldom dangerous when passing, as the situation changes too rapidly for either vessel to be swung enough to collide, though col-

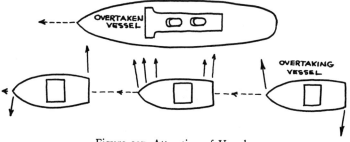

Figure 327. Attraction of Vessels

lision is possible, of course. However, when one vessel is overtaking another and the situation exists for several minutes, there is often a marked suction, described as follows: (Figure 327.)

As the overlap commences, the overhauling vessel may expect the bow to be slightly attracted toward the vessel overtaken. There will be a simultaneous repulsion of the stern. As the vessels haul abreast, the attraction forward increases, and repulsion astern changes gradually to attraction.

As the overtaking vessel hauls ahead, the bow attraction changes rapidly to repulsion, and the attraction of the stern becomes greater, diminishing only after a brief repulsion when entirely clear of the overtaken vessel.

The attraction of a large vessel for a small one may be so great as to cause the small one to yaw wildly and dangerously. The suction lessens in force at slow speeds and in deep water. Generally, there is little danger, at normal speeds, from small boats, except in very shallow water or in a narrow channel.

Running Coastal Inlets

328. The soundest seamanship plus local knowledge is required to run inlets in surf conditions. Inlet waves are as fast as 47 knots and as high as 52 feet! Figure 328A shows an average wave pattern in cross section. It may take other or reverse forms due to shoaling, channels and the state of the tide. The ideal manner in which to "ride in" is on the back of a wave. Avoid over-running by the use of the drogue and lagging by "gunning" the boat out of the reverse-current area under the following crests. (Figure 328B.)

Auxiliaries, in general, should avoid inlets in heavy weather. Twelve knots or better are required from a lively engine for safety. Do not attempt to tow small boats; collision will result. Under no circumstances attempt an inlet under sail alone. And do not hesitate to anchor or run off to await a favorable tide as the experienced surfmen do.

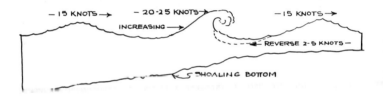

Figure 328A. Average Wave Section and Relative Wave Speeds over Bars and Shoaling Inlets. The reverse current is present in all troughs but strongest under crests.

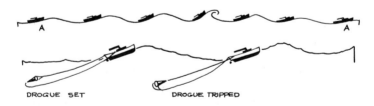

Figure 328B. *Top:* Select position on back of wave A as it forms well ahead of the breaker area and ride it beyond the breakers. *Bottom:* Use of the drogue to control speed and prevent "runs" when passing through breaker areas or inlets.

PART II
BOAT OPERATION

⚓

CHAPTER IV

GOVERNMENT REGULATIONS

401. For a number of years, government regulation of boating has been passing from Federal to state control. The transition, however, is not wholly complete; some ten states have so far not adopted a state boating law acceptable to the Federal authority. These states, if they contain Federal waters, remain under Federal law.

Those states having state boating laws are listed on page 178 - 185

In general, the Federal government, through the United States Coast Guard, has suggested to all states a minimum boating law, embracing such rules and regulations found in the past to have resulted in the greatest public benefit, and, further, has agreed that should a state enact such an approved state law, enforce it, and number boats, it will be exempt from Federal policing and enforcement. The base of the law which the Federal government approves as state law is the Motorboat Act of 1940 (Public Law 484, 76th Congress), familiar to yachtsmen and seamen for many years. However, an additional act, the so-called Bonner Act, or the Federal Boating Act of 1958, provides authority to correct and combat some of the problems raised by the current explosion in boating interest. These are in the area of legal responsibility for accidents, regulations calculated to reduce irresponsible and "hot-rod" boating and a better system of vessel numbering.

As stated above, not all states have as yet framed such a law, chiefly because there is not a convenient state agency to police and administer it, but it is predicted that all fifty states will have such laws within the next few years. Some states have passed the problem on to their Fish and Game Commissions, their Conservation Departments or to local sheriffs; others, more wisely, have created new Departments of Recreational Boating or similar authorities, by law responsible for and to the boatman. This, it would seem, is as it should be, for the new law provides, for the first time in history, a system of licensing fees, modest initially but undoubtedly due to slowly increase, which should have no destination but a fund for the benefit of the boatman who pays the tax. Too many states provide, as does the State of Arkansas, that the license receipts go "50% into the general County Fund and 50% to the State Game Protection Fund for administering and enforcing the act." Wiser states provide that the revenues go, as do those of Nebraska, into a "State Boating Fund for administering and enforcing the Act, and for the construction and maintenance of boating facilities, navigation aids and access to boating areas (launching ramps, for example), and such other uses as will *promote the safety and convenience of the boating public of Nebraska."*

While it is true that tax fees are presently very low and barely pay for enforcing the law, in time they will become a handsome source of revenue. Boatmen should now, through such associations as the Outboard Boating Club of America, the U. S. Power Squadron—and by writing to state congressmen—see that they are earmarked unmistakably for the use and benefit of the boating public.

As might be expected, those states with the oldest maritime tradition have resisted the change in boating laws, and the New England States at this writing are doing relatively little to co-operate with the Bonner Act. The Coast Guard is presently responsible for the numbering of boats and enforcing the law in Guam, U. S. Virgin Islands and Puerto Rico. It will probably remain so until these areas are declared nearer statehood.

At present the Federal government is disappointed in the application of the Bonner Act by many states, particularly in the matter of fairly uniform standards of legal equipment. However, it recognizes that change brings confusion and delay and has extended to April 1, 1963, the deadline for *all* vessels to be numbered in accordance with a Federal-approved state law. After that date the numbering of boats at least will have to conform to law or remain out of commission and action.

Under some recent codification of the Bonner Act, the Coast Guard has further explained some of its numbering rules as follows:

1. The hyphens or spaces required between the numerals and the prefix and suffix letters must be as wide as any letter except "I" or any number except "1."

2. The "forward half of the vessel" is defined as any part of the boat forward of a point halfway between its stem and stern.

3. On boats with a flaring bow, numbers must not be placed in a position where they will be hidden by the overhang of the bow. Numbers may be placed on the permanent superstructure of the vessel.

4. The "contrast" requirement means that numbers must be of a color different enough from their background so that they are "distinctly visible and legible." Pastel numbers, the Coast Guard notes, often do not provide sufficient contrast.

5. The background of the numbers includes the hull or superstructure to which they are applied, but does not include any border, trim, outlining, or shading. A backing plate is considered a suitable background.

Here, then is the Motorboat Act of 1940, the base of the law which applies to the boating public of some 39 states.

402. On April 25, 1940, the President of the United States approved Public Law No. 484, 76th Congress, which repealed the Motorboat Act of June 9, 1910, and provided for the better protection of life and property, increasing the standards for licensing of operators, fire and lifesaving equipment, ventilation, and other safety devices.

Public Law No. 484, 76th Congress, which might be properly termed the Motorboat Act of April 25, 1940, follows:

Be it enacted by the Senate and House of Representatives of the United States of America in Congress assembled, That the word "motorboat" where used in this Act shall include every vessel propelled by machinery and not more than sixty-five feet in length except tugboats and towboats propelled by steam. The length shall be measured from end to end over the deck, excluding sheer: Provided, That the engine, boiler, or other operating machinery shall be subject to inspection by the local inspectors of steam vessels, and to their approval of the design thereof, on all said motorboats, which are more than forty feet in length, and which are propelled by machinery driven by steam.

CLASSES

Sec. 2. Motorboats subject to the provisions of this Act shall be divided into four classes as follows:

Class A. Less than 16 feet in length.
Class 1. 16 feet or over and less than 26 feet in length.
Class 2. 26 feet or over and less than 40 feet in length.
Class 3. 40 feet or over and not more than 65 feet in length.

TABLE 401. SUMMARY OF EQUIPMENT REQUIRED BY REGULATIONS

U. S. Department of Commerce Bureau of Marine Inspection and Navigation

MOTORBOAT REGULATIONS (1940 LAW)

Requirements for Motorboats Not in Commercial Service

EQUIPMENT	Class A 0' to 16'	Class 1 16' to 26'	Class 2 26' to 40'	Class 3 40' to 65'
COMBINATION LIGHT	1—in forepart of boat showing red to port and green to starboard from right ahead to two points abaft the beam. Visible at least one mile.			
PORT SIDE LIGHT			1—on port side, properly screened to show red from right ahead to two points abaft the beam. Visible at least one mile.	
STARBOARD SIDE LIGHT			1—on starboard side, properly screened to show green from right ahead to two points abaft the beam. Visible at least one mile.	
STERN LIGHT	1—bright white light aft showing all around the horizon. Visible at least two miles.			
BOW LIGHT			1—bright white light in forepart of boat showing from right ahead to two points abaft the beam on both sides. Visible at least two miles.	
WHISTLE	none	1—hand-, mouth-, or power-operated. Audible one-half mile.	1—hand- or power-operated. Audible at least one mile.	1—power-operated. Audible at least one mile.
BELL	none	none	1—which produces, when struck, a clear bell-like tone of full round characteristics.	

EQUIPMENT	Class A 0' to 16'	Class 1 16' to 26'	Class 2 26' to 40'	Class 3 40' to 65'
LIFESAVING DEVICES	1—life preserver or ring buoy (20", 24" or 30") or buoyant cushion for each person on board.			1—life preserver or 20", 24" or 30" ring buoy for each person on board.
FLAME ARRESTERS	1—on each carburetor of all gasoline engines installed after April 25, 1940. (Note: Flame Arresters not required on outboard motors)			
VENTILATION	At least two ventilators with cowls or the equivalent capable of removing gases from the bilges in engine and fuel tank compartments of boats constructed or decked after April 25, 1940, using gasoline or other fuel of a flashpoint less than 110° Fahrenheit.			
FIRE EXTINGUISHERS (See Note)	1 B-I	1 B-I	2 B-I or 1 B-II	3 B-I or 1 B-II & 1 B-I

Note

Approved Fire Extinquishers

Class	Foam (Min. gallons)	Carbon Dioxide (Min. pounds)	Dry Chemical (Min. pounds)
B-I	1¼	4	2
B-II	2½	15	10

Carbon tetrachloride not approved. If machinery space has a fixed system, deduct one B-I extinguisher from above, except Classes A and 1.

LIGHTS

Sec. 3. Every motorboat in all weathers from sunset to sunrise shall carry and exhibit the following lights when under way, and during such time no other lights which may be mistaken for those prescribed shall be exhibited:

(*a*) Every motorboat of classes A and 1 shall carry the following lights:

First. A bright white light aft to show all around the horizon.

Second. A combined lantern in the fore part of the vessel and lower than the white light aft, showing green to starboard and red to port, so fixed as to throw the light from right ahead to two points abaft the beam on their respective sides.

(*b*) Every motorboat of classes 2 and 3 shall carry the following lights:

First. A bright white light in the fore part of the vessel as near the stem as practicable, so constructed as to show an unbroken light over an arc of the horizon of twenty points of the compass, so fixed as to throw the light ten points on each side of the vessel; namely, from right ahead to two points abaft the beam on either side.

Second. A bright white light aft to show all around the horizon and higher than the white light forward.

Third. On the starboard side a green light so constructed as to show an unbroken light over an arc of the horizon of ten points of the compass, so fixed as to throw the light from right ahead to two points abaft the beam on the starboard side. On the port side a red light so constructed as to show an unbroken light over an arc of the horizon of ten points of the compass, so fixed as to throw the light from right ahead to two points abaft the beam on the port side. The said side lights shall be fitted with inboard screens of sufficient height so set as to prevent these lights from being seen across the bow.

(*c*) Motorboats of classes 2 and 3, when propelled by sail and machinery, or by sail alone, shall carry the colored side lights, suitably screened, but not the white lights prescribed by this section: Provided however, That motorboats of all classes, when so propelled, shall carry, ready at hand, a lantern or flashlight showing a white light which shall be exhibited in sufficient time to avert collision: Provided further, That motorboats of classes A and 1, when so propelled, shall not be required to carry the combined lantern prescribed by subsection (*a*) of this section.

(*d*) Every white light prescribed by this section shall be of such character as to be visible at a distance of at least two miles. Every colored light prescribed by this section shall be of such character as to be visible at a distance of at least one mile. The word "visible" in this Act, when applied to lights, shall mean visible on a dark night with clear atmosphere.

WHISTLE, BELL AND LIFE PRESERVERS

Sec. 4. Every motorboat of class 1, 2, or 3, shall be provided with an efficient whistle or other sound-producing mechanical appliance.

Sec. 5. Every motorboat of class 2 or 3 shall be provided with an efficient bell.

Sec. 6. Every motorboat subject to any of the provisions of this Act and also all vessels propelled by machinery other than by steam more than sixty-five feet in length shall carry at least one life preserver, or life belt, or ring buoy, or other device of the sort prescribed by the regulations of the board of supervising inspectors with the approval of the Secretary of Commerce, for each person on board, so placed as to be readily accessible: Provided, That every such motorboat and every such vessel propelled by machinery other than by steam more than sixty-five feet in length carrying passengers for hire shall carry so placed as to be readily accessible at least one life preserver of the sort prescribed by the regulations of the board of supervising inspectors with the approval of the Secretary of Commerce, for each person on board.

LICENSED OPERATOR

Sec. 7. No such motorboat, while carrying passengers for hire, shall be operated or navigated except in charge of a person duly licensed for such service by a local board of inspectors. Whenever any person applies to be licensed as operator of any motorboat carrying passengers for hire, the inspectors shall make diligent inquiry as to his character, and shall carefully examine the applicant orally as well as the proofs which he presents in support of his claim, and if they are satisfied that his capacity, experience, habits of life, and character are such as to warrant the belief that he can safely be entrusted with the duties and responsibilities of the station for which he makes application, they shall grant him a license authorizing him to discharge such duties on any such motorboat carrying passengers for hire for the term of five years. Such license shall be subject to suspension or revocation on the same grounds and in the same manner and with like procedure as is provided in the case of suspension or revocation of licenses of officers under the provisions of section 4450 of the Revised Statutes, as amended (U.S.C., 1934 edition, Supp. III, title 46, sec. 239): Provided, That motorboats shall not be required to carry licensed officers except as required in this Act: And provided further, That licenses herein prescribed shall not be required of motorboats engaged in fishing contests previously arranged and announced.

FIRE EXTINGUISHERS

Sec. 8. Every motorboat and also every vessel propelled by machinery other than by steam more than sixty-five feet in length shall be provided with such number, size, and type of fire extinguishers, capable of promptly and effectually extinguishing burning gasoline, as may be prescribed by the regulations of the board of supervising inspectors, with the approval of the Secretary of Commerce, which fire extinguishers shall be at all times kept in condition for immediate and effective use and shall be so placed as to be readily accessible.

RACING OUTBOARDS EXEMPT

Sec. 9. The provisions of sections 4, 5, and 8 of this Act shall not apply to motorboats propelled by outboard motors while competing in any race previously arranged and announced or, if such boats be designed and intended solely for racing, while engaged in such navigation as is incidental to the tuning up of the boats and engines for the race.

FLAME ARRESTERS AND VENTILATION

Sec. 10. Every motorboat and also every vessel propelled by machinery other than by steam more than sixty-five feet in length shall have the carburetor or carburetors of every engine therein (except outboard motors) using gasoline as fuel, equipped with such efficient flame arrester, backfire trap, or other similar device as may be prescribed by the regulations of the board of supervising inspectors with the approval of the Secretary of Commerce: Provided, That this section shall apply only to such motorboats or vessels, the construction of which or the replacement of the engine or engines of which is commenced subsequent to the passage of this Act.

Sec. 11. Every such motorboat and every such vessel, except open boats, using as fuel any liquid of a volatile nature, shall be provided with such means as may be prescribed by regulations of the board of supervising inspectors with the approval of the Secretary of Commerce for properly and efficiently ventilating the bilges of the engine and fuel tank compartments so as to remove any explosive or inflammable gases: Provided, That this section shall apply only to such motorboats or vessels, the construction or decking over of which is commenced subsequent to the passage of this Act.

PILOT RULES

Sec. 12. Motorboats shall not be required to carry on board copies of the pilot rules.

RECKLESS OPERATION

Sec. 13. No person shall operate any motorboat or any vessel in a reckless or negligent manner so as to endanger the life, limb, or property of any person.

Sec. 14. Any person who shall operate any motorboat or any vessel in a reckless or negligent manner so as to endanger the life, limb, or property of any person shall be deemed guilty of a misdemeanor and on conviction thereof by any court of competent jurisdiction shall be punished by a fine not exceeding $2,000, or by imprisonment for a term of not exceeding one year, or by both such fine and imprisonment, at the discretion of the court.

Sec. 15. Any officer of the United States authorized to enforce the navigation laws of the United States, shall have power and authority to swear out process and to arrest and take into custody, with or without process, any person who may commit any act or offense prohibited by section 13, or who may violate any provision of said section: Provided, That no person shall be arrested without process for any offense not committed in the presence of some one of the aforesaid officials: Provided further, That whenever an arrest is made under the provisions of this Act, the person so arrested shall be brought forthwith before a commissioner, judge, or court of the United States for examination of the offense alleged against him, and such commissioner, judge, or court shall proceed in respect thereto as authorized by law in cases of crimes against the United States.

PENALTIES

Sec. 16. If any motorboat or vessel subject to any of the provisions of this Act is operated or navigated in violation of this Act or any regulation issued thereunder, the owner or operator, either one or both of them, shall, in addition to any other penalty prescribed by law than that contained in section 14 of this Act, be liable to a penalty of $100: Provided, That in the case of motorboats or vessels subject to the provisions of this Act carrying passengers for hire, a penalty of $200 shall be imposed on the owner or operator, either one or both of them, thereof for any violation of section 6, 7, or 8 of this Act or of any regulations pertaining thereto. For any penalty incurred under this section the motorboat or vessel shall be held liable and may be proceeded against by way of libel in the district court of any district in which said motorboat or vessel may be found.

REGULATIONS

Sec. 17. The board of supervising inspectors with the approval of the Secretary of Commerce shall establish all necessary regulations required to carry out in the most effective manner all of the provisions of this Act, and such regulations when approved by the Secretary of Commerce shall have the force of law. The Secretary of Commerce or any officer of the Department of Commerce authorized by the Secretary of Commerce may, upon application therefor, remit or mitigate any fine, penalty, or forfeiture incurred under this Act or any regulation thereunder relating to motorboats or vessels, except the penalties provided for in section 14 hereunder. The Secretary of Commerce shall establish such regulations as may be necessary to secure the enforcement of the provisions of this Act by any officer of the United States authorized to enforce the navigation laws of the United States.

Sec. 18. The proviso contained in the last paragraph of section 2 of the Act of May 11, 1918 (40 Stat. 549), shall apply also with like force and effect to motorboats as defined in this Act.

Motorboats as defined in this Act are hereby exempted from the provisions of Revised Statutes 4399, as amended (48 Stat. 125).

WHEN ACT TAKES EFFECT

Sec. 19. This Act shall take effect upon its approval as to all of the sections hereof except sections 6, 7, and 8, which sections shall take effect one year from the date of said approval, and for a period of one year from the date of approval of this Act sections 5, 6, and 7 of the Motorboat Act of June 9, 1910 (Public, Numbered 201, Sixty-first Congress; 36 Stat. 462), shall continue in full force and effect, except that from and after the date of the approval of this Act the Secretary of Commerce shall have authority to remit or mitigate all fines or penalties heretofore or hereafter incurred or imposed under sections 5 and 6 of the Motorboat Act of June 9, 1910. Except as hereinabove expressly provided, the Motorboat Act of June 9, 1910, above referred to, is repealed upon the approval of this Act and as to sections 5, 6, and 7 of said Act hereinabove continued the said sections are hereby repealed effective one year from the date of approval of this Act. Nothing in this Act shall be deemed to alter or amend section 4417a of the Revised Statutes (U.S.C., 1934 edition, Supp. IV, title 46, sec. 391a), the Act of August 26, 1935 (U.S.C., 1934 edition, Supp. IV, ch. 7A, secs. 178 and 179), the Act of June 20, 1936 (U.S.C., 1934 edition, Supp. IV, title 46, sec. 367), or repeal Acts of Congress or treaties embodying or revising international rules for preventing collisions at sea.

Sec. 20. There are hereby authorized to be appropriated such sums as may be necessary to carry out the provisions of this Act.

NUMBER CERTIFICATE TO BE KEPT ABOARD

Sec. 21. The provisions of section 210 of title II of the Anti-Smuggling Act, approved August 5, 1935 (49 Stat. 526; U.S.C., 1934 edition, Supp. IV, title 46, sec. 288), requiring a certificate of award of a number to be kept at all times on board of the vessel to which the number has been awarded shall not apply to any vessel not exceeding seventeen feet in length measured from end to end over the deck, excluding sheer, or to any vessel whose design of fittings are such that the carrying of the certificate of award of the number on such vessel would render such certificate imperfect, illegible, or would otherwise tend to destroy its usefulness as a means of ready identification.

APPENDIX AND EXPLANATORY NOTES TO TEXT OF GOVERNMENT REGULATIONS

Lights

403. All lights in use at present must conform to the Motorboat Act of 1940. Lights need be carried only at night and under way. No penalty is incurred for failure to have lights on board during daylight hours. They may be oil or electric but must fulfill the visibility requirements of the law.

Whistle

404. The foghorn (not required) is not a substitute for a whistle. Whatever the type the whistle must be capable of producing a prolonged blast, within the meaning of the law—or for at least two seconds.

Bell

405. A bell to come within the regulation requirements of "an efficient bell" should be at least eight inches in diameter at the bell.

Fire Extinguishers

406. Generally considered, the law provides that a fixed extinguishing system be provided for engine spaces, supplemented by a specified number of portable or hand extinguishers. Open outboards, if not carrying passengers for hire, need not carry an extinguisher. However, if the boat is outboard-powered and has an enclosed space, such as forward deck, a motor well or hood, or is a cabin cruiser or "hardtop," it must carry an extinguisher as if it were in Class 1.

Approved fire extinquishing materials in portable forms are as follows: (Note that carbon tetrachloride, formerly approved, is now forbidden.)

Class	Foam (Min. gallons)	Carbon Dioxide (Min. pounds)	Dry Chemical (Min. pounds)
B-I	1¼	4	2
B-II	2½	15	10

They are required as follows:

Class	Without fixed system in machinery space	With fixed system in machinery space
A	1 B-I	None
1	1 B-I	None
2	2 B-I or 1 B-II	1 B-I
3	3 B-I or 1 B-I and 1 B-II	2 B-I or 1 B-II

Ventilators and Flame Arresters

407. All engines installed in a permanent manner must be fitted with an approved flame arrester. Engine manufacturers equip their machines with such approved equipment. Outboard motors are excepted.

Any engine or fuel tankage enclosed (as under a bridge deck, cockpit floor, or boxed in) must be provided with means of ventilation. Ventilators need not be of common or standard types (such as cowl or clamshell types) but the provision made should be equal. The minimum required is for a pair of ventilators (two singles); and to be efficient these must be so fitted in relation to each other and the subject space as to "efficiently remove explosive gases."

Life Preservers

408. In general, the Coast Guard, authorized by the Motorboat Act of 1940, has codified the law and over the years established some tried and sound practices, one of them being the principle of "Coast Guard Approved Equipment." Thus the law, as applied, refrains from naming brands or manufacturers but, rather, defines standards to be met for approval. In the category of "Lifesaving Devices" the life preserver has come in for some special attention and at present the following forms are approved.

Buoyant Cushions, probably the commonest form of lifesaving device on pleasure craft, may have as floatation material fibrous glass, kapok, or plastic foam contained in cushion-shaped pads of various fabric or plastic materials and fitted with straps. Color may vary. It must be marked, by a sewn-in tab, as follows:

Buoyant Cushion

Size ....

Contains .... ozs. (kapok or fibrous glass) or ...... cubic inches of foam

Approved for use on motorboats of class A, 1 or 2 not carrying passengers
for hire

U. S. Coast Guard approval number ....

Lot number ....

Instructions for care of cushion ....

Name and address of manufacturer ....

Jacket Life Preservers are of jacket design, constructed with pads
of kapok, fibrous glass, cork or balsa wood, in a cloth covering fitted
with the necessary straps and ties. Sizes are for adults and children
and must be so marked. All must be orange in color. Each must bear
two markings, the manufacturers stamp indicating the approval
number and the inspector's stamp indicating the preserver has been
inspected and passed, as follows:

Life Preserver Jacket

Adult (or Child)

Model number ....

Manufacturer's name and address ....,,,

U. S. Coast Guard approval number ....

Inspected and passed   Date ....

        Place ....

        USCG inspector's initials ....

Ring Buoys may be of cork or balsa wood covered with canvas or
of foam with a special cover or surface. They may be white or orange
but must be fitted with grab lines and must be more than 20″ outside
diameter.

Cork and balsa wood rings must bear two tags, giving the same
information as for jacket life preservers (above). Plastic foam ring
buoys must bear a single metal plate attached to the buoy on which
appears the following:

Name and address of the manufacturer ....
Size of buoy (outside diameter) ....
U. S. Coast Guard approval number ....
Date ....
USCG inspector's initials ....

Buoyant Vests of approved design are vests (similar to a sleeveless, open front sweater) into which has been sewn pads of fibrous glass or kapok and having straps and ties. They may be any color. They are supplied in two child sizes and one adult size. Each bears a tab with the following information:

Buoyant Vest

Model ....
Adult (or Child) ....
Approved for use on motorboats of class A, 1 and 2 not carrying passengers
    for hire
U. S. Coast Guard approval number ....
Lot number ....
Instructions for care of vest ....
Name and address of manufacturer ....
Weight ranges for child sizes ....

Be it noted that *only* the above described devices are legal and approved. Bags of cork, pneumatic cushions, inner or other tubes, rubber buoyant toys, rafts, pine boards or cushions which are not boxed are illegal. On *all* boats carrying passengers for hire and on commercial vessels of 15 tons or over, the *only* type approved is the life preserver jacket.

Approved lifesaving devices, as well as other Coast Guard approved equipment is listed in the yearly publication, CG Booklet-190. It may be obtained free from any district Coast Guard office or any Officer in Charge, Marine Inspection. The booklet names brands and manufacturers, notes model numbers and gives much safety information.

The Federal Boating Act of 1958

409. This act, passed by Congress after considerable exploration into the boating explosion and its multiplying problems, is primarily an attempt to encourage individual states to administer and police the minimum law as embodied in the Motorboat Act of 1940, the soundest set of laws for the regulation of pleasure craft so far enacted. Such states as agree by enacting state laws approved by the provisions of the Federal Boating Act of 1958 may thereafter themselves administer the law of their own state, without interference from Federal authorities, and may, as well, collect and retain any licenses or taxes involved. Here are the highlights of the law:

This new law makes no change in the requirements respecting lifesaving equipment, fire extinguishers, lights, or other equipment, nor does it extend the water areas over which the Coast Guard has jurisdiction.

Numbers and certificates of number issued under this Act are for vessel identification only and do not authorize engaging in trade.

NUMBERING

On 1 April 1960, the Coast Guard commenced assigning new identification numbers to all undocumented vessels operating on the navigable waters of the United States which, regardless of length, are propelled in whole or in part by machinery of more than 10 horsepower (in the aggregate) unless the state in which the vessel is principally used has assumed numbering. The state may assume this function at any time by the enactment of a suitable law and the approval of its numbering system by the Secretary of the Treasury.

All numbering shall conform to an overall numbering system. In this new uniform system the first part of each number shall be an abbreviation of the state of principal use as indicated in the application. If principally used on the high seas, the vessel will be numbered according to the state in which it is usually docked, moored, housed, or garaged.

An undocumented vessel principally used in a state which has assumed numbering will not be numbered by the Coast Guard.

Unpowered vessels and those of 10 horsepower or less will be numbered upon request.

Vessels of more than 10 horsepower which have not previously been numbered will, pending receipt of a permanent certificate, be furnished a temporary certificate which must be carried on board whenever the vessel is in use.

Documentary proof of title and ownership is not required by the Coast Guard with application for number.

A numbering fee may be charged by the state. Estimated Coast Guard fees are: original numbering—$5; renewal of number—$3; reissue of lost or destroyed certificate of number—$1.

A number issued by a state may be valid for not more than 3 years. years from the date of the owner's birthday next occurring after the certificate is issued. Each renewal will be for 3 years.

A number issued by a State may be valid for not more than 3 years.

Certificates shall be pocket size, of water-resistant material, and must be on board whenever the vessel is in use.

A change of address must be reported within 15 days.

When a vessel is lost, destroyed, abandoned, or transferred to another person, the certificate must be surrendered within 15 days. If the certificate has been destroyed, notice to that effect must be given to the numbering authority.

A change of motor is not required to be reported.

If the state of principal use is changed, the owner must make application for a number for the new state and surrender the old certificate within 90 days.

A certificate may be canceled and the number voided prior to expiration for a false or fraudulent certification in the application.

Application for renewal of a Coast Guard issued number may be made within 90 days before expiration. If not renewed, a number is automatically invalid on the expiration date shown on the certificate. Applications for renewal received after expiration will be treated as original and involve the higher fee. The same number may be reissued if the renewal application is filed within 1 year after expiration.

Upon sale or transfer, where the vessel continues in use in the same state, the old number will be issued to the new owner.

The number awarded (and no other) shall be painted on, or attached to, each side of the bow (i.e. each side of the forward half of the vessel). They must be so positioned as to be clearly legible. The numbers shall be in block characters, at least 3 inches high, of a color which will contrast with the background, and so maintained as to be clearly visible and legible.

Numbers awarded to boat manufacturers or boat dealers may be printed upon or attached to a removable sign temporarily but firmly mounted upon the boat being demonstrated or tested.

Each state shall, for a period of at least 90 days, recognize the validity of a number awarded to a vessel by another state or by the Coast Guard.

Nothing in this law interferes with, abrogates or limits the jurisdiction of any state. Any state system will be approved which is compatible with the Federal numbering system.

BOATING ACCIDENTS

The operator of any boat involved in an accident must stop, render assistance, and offer identification. A written report must be filed within 48 hours if the accident caused death; if it injured any person so as to incapacitate for more than 72 hours or the accident resulted in physical damage to property in excess of $100, the report must be submitted in 5 days.

Boating accident report forms (CG—3865) are obtainable at any Coast Guard office or unit. They must be submitted by the operator to the nearest Coast Guard Officer in Charge, Marine Inspection, unless the operator is required to file an accident report with a state having an approved numbering system. Accident reports furnish information for use in accident prevention. Information from individual reports will not be publicly disclosed.

The Coast Guard will compile and publish statistics on vessels numbered and on boating accidents.

LAW ENFORCEMENT

Coast Guard boarding vessels will be identified by the Coast Guard ensign, and personnel will be in uniform. A vessel underway, upon being hailed by a Coast Guard vessel or patrolboat, is required to stop immediately and lay to, or maneuver in such a way as to permit the boarding officer to come aboard. Failure to stop to permit boarding may subject the operator or owner to a penalty of $100.

A civil penalty may be imposed by the Coast Guard for reckless or negligent operation, for failure to obey the rules of the road, failure to comply with the regulations, etc.

There is no change in the law which provides for a fine of up to $2,000 and imprisonment of not more than 1 year for the criminal offense of reckless or negligent operation of a vessel which endangers the life, limb, or property of any person.

NUMBERING AND RECORDING OF UNDOCUMENTED VESSELS

Item	*Old law*	*New law*
Undocumented vessels which are required to be numbered when upon the waters of the United States, except public vessels, ship's lifeboats, and motorboats designed solely for racing	All over 16 feet in length, propelled in whole or in part by machinery, and all having permanently attached motors regardless of length	All motorboats, irrespective of length, propelled in whole or in part by machinery *of over 10 horsepower* regardless of whether the motor is temporarily or permanently attached
By whom numbered	U.S. Coast Guard only	By the U. S. Coast Guard unless the state of principal use has assumed the numbering functions
Numbering pattern	Numbered according to Customs District in which the owner resides. The district number shown in the forepart of the number	Numbered according to the state in which the boat is principally used, regardless of where the owner resides
Period for which number is valid	Unlimited	Maximum of 3 years
Fee	None	Fixed by state or U. S. Coast Guard whichever does numbering
Certificate of number	Approximately 5 by 8 inches. Required on board vessels over 17-foot length except those of such open construction as would cause certificate to be destroyed	Of "pocket size" and required to be available for inspection at all times when vessel is in use

Text of the Federal Boating Act of 1958

410.

(*Public Law 85-911 85th Congress, H. R. 11078,*
September 2, 1958)

An act to promote boating safety on the navigable waters of the United States, its Territories, and the District of Columbia; to provide co-ordination and cooperation with the States in the interest of uniformity of boating laws; and for other purposes.

Be it enacted by the Senate and House of Representatives of the United States of America in Congress assembled, That this Act may be cited as the "Federal Boating Act of 1958."

DEFINITIONS

Sec. 2. As used in sections 3 to 5, inclusive, and sections 7 to 13, inclusive, of this Act—

(1) The term "undocumented vessel" means any vessel which is not required to have, and does not have, a valid marine document issued by the Bureau of Customs.

(2) The word "vessel" includes every description of watercraft, other than a seaplane on the water, used or capable of being used as a means of transportation on water.

(3) The word "Secretary" means the Secretary of the Department in which the Coast Guard is operating.

(4) The word "owner" means the person who claims lawful pos-session of a vessel by virtue of legal title or equitable interest therein which entitles him to such possession.

(5) The term "State" means a State of the United States, a Terri-tory of the United States, and the District of Columbia.

NUMBERING OF VESSELS

Sec. 3.(a) Every undocumented vessel propelled by machinery of more than 10 horsepower, whether or not such machinery is the prin-cipal source of propulsion, using the navigable water of the United States, its Territories and the District of Columbia, and every such vessel owned in a State and using the high seas, shall be numbered in accordance with this Act, except—

(1) foreign vessels temporarily using the navigable waters of the United States, its Territories and the District of Columbia;

(2) public vessels of the United States;

(3) State and municipal vessels;

(4) ships' lifeboats; and

(5) vessels designated by the Secretary under section 7 (*b*) of this Act.

(*b*) The owner of an undocumented vessel required to be numbered under subsection (*a*) of this section shall secure a number for such vessel in the State in which it is principally used, in accordance with the State numbering system approved by the Secretary in accordance with subsection (*c*) of this section, or if no such numbering system has been approved by the Secretary for the State where such vessel is principally used, shall secure a number for such vessel in accordance with subsection (*d*) of this section.

(*c*) The Secretary shall establish an overall numbering system for the numbering of vessels required to be numbered under subsection (*a*) of this section. He shall approve any State system for numbering vessels which is submitted to him which meets the standards set forth below:

(1) The system of numbering shall be in accordance with the overall system of numbering established by the Secretary.

(2) The certificate of number and the number awarded shall be valid for a period not exceeding three years, unless canceled or surrendered, and may be renewed for additional periods.

(3) The number awarded shall be required to be painted on, or attached to, each side of the bow of the vessel for which it was issued, and shall be of such size, color, and type, as may be prescribed by the Secretary. No other number shall be permitted to be carried on the bow of such vessel.

(4) The certificate of number shall be pocket size and shall be required to be at all times available for inspection on the vessel for which issued, whenever such vessel is in use.

(5) The owner shall be required to furnish to a designated State official, notice of the transfer of all or any part of his interest in any numbered vessel, and of the destruction or abandonment of

such vessel, within a reasonable time thereof. The owner shall be required to notify a designated State official of any change in his address within a reasonable time of such change.

(6) The State shall require that reports be made to it of accidents involving vessels numbered by it under its numbering system, and shall compile and transmit to the Secretary such statistics on such accidents.

(7) The State shall recognize the validity of a number awarded to any vessel by another State under a numbering system approved by the Secretary under this Act, or awarded a number by the Secretary, for a period of at least ninety days.

(8) In the case of a State having its numbering system approved after April 1, 1960, such State shall accept and recognize any valid certificate of number awarded under subsection (*d*) of this section for so long as such certificate would otherwise be valid under such subsection (*d*), except that where such a certificate would remain valid for more than one year after the date when such State's numbering system was approved, the State may accept and recognize the validity of such certificate for a lesser period, but such period shall not end sooner than one year from the date of approval of such system.

(9) The State may exempt any vessel or class of vessels from the numbering provisions of its system if such vessel or class of vessels has been made exempt from the numbering provisions of section 3 (*d*) by the Secretary under section 7 (*b*) of this Act.

(10) The States may charge fees in connection with the award of certificates of number and renewals thereof.

(11) The States may require that the operator of a vessel required to be numbered hereunder shall hold a valid safety certificate to be issued under such terms and conditions as may be provided by State law.

(*d*) The owner of an undocumented vessel required to be numbered under subsection (*a*) of this section who uses his vessel principally in a State which does not have a numbering system approved by the Secretary under subsection (*c*) of this section, shall make application to the Secretary, and upon payment of the fee established under section 5, such owner shall be granted a certificate of number containing the number awarded such vessel by the Secretary.

CERTIFICATE VALID THREE YEARS

(*e*) The certificate of number initially awarded to an owner under subsection (*d*) of this section shall be valid for three years from the date of the owner's birthday next occurring after the date the certificate of number is issued, unless surrendered or canceled pursuant to regulations of the Secretary. If at the end of such period such ownership has remained unchanged, such owner shall, upon application and payment of the fee established under section 5 of this Act, be granted a renewal of such certificate of number for an additional three-year period.

(*f*) The number awarded under subsection (*c*) or (*d*) of this section shall be painted on, or attached to, each side of the bow of the vessel for which it was issued, and shall be of such size, color, and type as may be prescribed by the Secretary. No other number shall be carried on the bow of such vessel.

(*g*) The certificate of number granted under subsection (*c*) or (*d*) of this section shall be pocket size and shall be required to be at all times available for inspection on the vessel for which issued whenever such vessel is in use, and shall constitute a document in lieu of a marine document that sets forth an official number issued by the Bureau of Customs.

(*h*) Whenever the Secretary determines that a State is not administering its approved system for numbering vessels in accordance with the standards set forth under subsection (*c*) of this section, he may withdraw such approval. The Secretary shall not withdraw his approval of a State system of numbering until he has given notice in writing to the State setting forth specifically wherein the State has failed to maintain such standards.

Sec. 4. The owner of any vessel numbered under section 3 (*d*) of this Act shall furnish to the Secretary notice of the transfer of all or any part of his interest in any numbered vessel, and of the destruction, or abandonment of such vessel, within a reasonable time thereof. The owner shall notify the Secretary of any change in his address within a reasonable time of such change.

Sec. 5. The Secretary may prescribe reasonable fees or charges for the numbering of a vessel, or renewal thereof, under subsections (*d*) and (*e*) of section 3 of this Act.

MOTORBOAT ACT AMENDED

Sec. 6.(a) Section *13* of the Act entitled "An Act to amend laws for preventing collisions of vessels, to regulate equipment of certain motorboats on the navigable waters of the United States, and for other purposes," approved April 25, 1940 (46 U. S. C. 526t), is amended to read as follows:

"*Sec. 13.(a)* No person shall operate any motorboat or any vessel in a reckless or negligent manner so as to endanger the life, limb, or property of any person. To 'operate' means to navigate or otherwise use a motorboat or a vessel.

"(*b*) In the case of collision, accident, or other casualty involving a motorboat or other vessel subject to this Act, it shall be the duty of the operator, if and so far as he can do so without serious danger to his own vessel, or persons aboard, to render such assistance as may be practicable and necessary to other persons affected by the collision, accident, or casualty in order to save them from danger caused by the collision, accident, or casualty. He shall also give his name, address, and identification of his vessel to any person injured and to the owner of any property damaged. The duties imposed by this subsection shall be in addition to any duties otherwise provided by law.

"(*c*) In the case of collision, accident, or other casualty involving a motorboat or other vessel subject to this Act, the operator thereof, if the collision, accident, or other casualty results in death or injury to any person, or damage to property in excess of $100, shall file with the Secretary of the Department within which the Coast Guard is operating, unless such operator is required to file an accident report with the State under section *3* (*c*) (*6*) of the Federal Boating Act of 1958, a full description of the collision, accident, or other casualty, including such information as the Secretary may by regulation require."

(*b*) Section *16* of such Act of April 25, 1940 (46 U. S. C. 526o), is amended by striking out "than that contained in section 14 of this Act."

(*c*) Such act of April 25, 1940 (46 U. S. C. 526–526t), is further amended by adding at the end thereof the following new section:

"*Sec. 22.(a)* This Act shall apply to every motorboat or vessel on the navigable waters of the United States, its Territories and the

District of Columbia, and every motorboat or vessel owned in a State and using the high seas.

"(*b*) As used in this Act—

"The term 'State' means a State of the United States, a Territory of the United States, and the District of Columbia."

Sec. 7.(*a*) The Secretary shall make such rules and regulations as may be necessary to carry out the provisions of this Act: *Provided,* That such rules and regulations shall be submitted to the Speaker of the House and the President of the Senate when Congress is in session, and shall not become effective until sixty days thereafter.

(*b*) The Secretary may, from time to time, and for such periods as he may prescribe, exempt any vessel or class of vessels from the numbering provisions of subsection (*d*) of section *3* of this Act.

VIOLATIONS AND PENALTIES

Sec. 8.(*a*) Whoever being the owner of a vessel required to be numbered under this Act, violates section *3* or *4* of this Act, or regulations established by the Secretary under section 7 of this Act, shall be liable to a penalty of $50 for each violation. Whoever operates a vessel in violation of section *3* of this Act, or regulations established by the Secretary under section 7 of this Act, shall be liable to a penalty of $50 for each violation.

(*b*) The Secretary may assess and collect any penalty incurred under this Act or any regulations prescribed pursuant to section 7 of this Act. The Secretary may, in his discretion, remit or mitigate any penalty imposed under this section, or discontinue prosecution therefor on such terms as he may deem proper.

(*c*) Commissioned, warrant, and petty officers of the Coast Guard may board any vessel required to be numbered under this Act at any time such vessel is found upon the navigable waters of the United States, its Territories and the District of Columbia, or on the high seas, address inquiries to those on board, require appropriate proof of identification therefrom, examine the certificate of number issued under this Act, or in the absence of such certificate require appropriate proof of identification of the owner of the vessel, and, in addition, examine such vessel for compliance with this Act, the Act of April 25, 1940, as amended, and the applicable rules of the road.

Sec. 9. It is hereby declared to be the policy of Congress to encourage uniformity of boating laws, rules, and regulations as among the several States and the Federal Government to the fullest extent practicable, subject to reasonable exceptions arising out of local conditions. In the interest of fostering the development, use, and enjoyment of all the waters of the United States it is further declared to be the policy of the Congress hereby to encourage the highest degree of reciprocity and comity among the several jurisdictions. The Secretary, acting under the authority of section 141 of title 14 of the United States Code, shall to the greatest possible extent enter into agreements and other arrangements with the States to insure that there shall be the fullest possible cooperation in the enforcement of both State and Federal statutes, rules, and regulations relating to recreational boating.

PUBLICATION OF ACCIDENT REPORTS

Sec. 10. The Secretary is authorized and directed to compile, analyze, and publish, either in summary or detailed form, the information obtained by him from the accident reports transmitted to him under section *3* (*c*) (6) of this Act, and under section *13* (*c*) of the Act entitled "An Act to amend laws for preventing collisions of vessels, to regulate equipment of certain motorboats on the navigable waters of the United States, and for other purposes," approved April 25, 1940 (46 U. S. C. 5261), together with such findings concerning the causes of such accidents and such recommendations for their prevention as he may deem necessary. Such information shall be made available for public inspection in such manner as the Secretary may deem practicable.

Sec. 11.(*a*) Except section *3* (*d*), this Act shall take effect on the date of its enactment.

(*b*) Section *3* (*d*) of this Act shall take effect April 1, 1960.

Sec. 12. The Act entitled "An Act to require numbering and recording of undocumented vessels," approved June 7, 1918, as amended (46 U. S. C. 288), and section 21 of the Act entitled "An Act to amend laws for preventing collisions of vessels, to regulate equipment of certain motorboats on the navigable waters of the United States, and for other purposes," approved April 25, 1940, as amended (46 U. S. C. 526t), shall not be applicable in any State having a numbering system approved by the Secretary under section *3 (c)* of this Act. Such Act of June 7, 1918, and such section 21 of the Act of April 25, 1940, are repealed effective April 1, 1960.

LAW ENFORCEMENT

Sec. 13. The applicability and the jurisdiction for enforcement, upon the navigable waters of the United States, its Territories and the District of Columbia, of the laws of the United States and of any State which require the numbering and otherwise regulate the use of undocumented vessels, shall be as follows:

(1) Such laws of the United States shall be applicable and enforced on such waters by law enforcement officers of the United States.

(2) Such laws of any State in a State having a numbering system approved by the Secretary under section *3 (c)* of this Act shall be applicable and enforced on such waters by law enforcement officers of the State or by law enforcement officers of the appropriate subdivisions of the State.

(3) Nothing herein shall preclude enforcement of State or Federal laws pursuant to agreements or other arrangements entered into between the Secretary and any State within the contemplation of section 9 of this Act.

(4) Nothing herein shall interfere with, abrogate or limit the jurisdiction of any State: *Provided, however,* That the Secretary shall not approve any State system for numbering which does not fully comply with the standards set forth in section *3 (c)*.

411. Excerpts from the Regulations drafted by the United States Coast Guard to implement the Federal Boating Act of 1958.

PART 171—STANDARDS FOR NUMBERING

GENERAL

§ 171.01–1 *Vessels to be numbered.* (a) Certain undocumented vessels are required to be numbered by subsection 3 (a) of the Federal Boating Act of 1958. (*see* paragraph 410.)

(b) Nothing in this section shall prohibit the numbering of any undocumented vessel, which may be propelled by machinery, upon request of the owner.

§ 171.01–5 *Exemptions.* Pursuant to subsections 3 (a) (5) and 7 (b) of the Federal Boating Act of 1958, the following are exempt from the requirement to be numbered:

(a) Undocumented vessels used exclusively for racing.

(b) Undocumented vessels operating under valid temporary certificates of number.

§ 171.01–10 *Determining horsepower of machinery.* (a) In general, for existing and new equipment, the manufacturer's rated horsepower at a stated maximum operating RPM as set forth on the nameplate attached to the engine, or as stamped on the engine, or as described in a "book of instructions" or other literature issued for such engine will be accepted as prima facie evidence of the horsepower of the machinery in question. In event the machinery does not have marked thereon or accompanying it any literature or tag setting forth the manufacturer's rated horsepower, or should the Coast Guard dispute the manufacturer's rated horsepower, then the Coast Guard's listing of horsepower will be accepted as prima facie evidence of the horsepower.

(b) In the event the owner or operator of a power propelled vessel disagrees with the findings of the Coast Guard as to horsepower, it shall be the responsibility of such owner or operator to prove to the satisfaction of the Coast Guard what is the actual horsepower of the propelling machinery.

VESSEL IDENTIFICATION

§ 171.05–1 *Numbering pattern to be used.* (a) The numbers issued pursuant to the Federal Boating Act of 1958 shall be in accordance with the pattern described in this section.

(b) The number shall be divided into parts. The first part shall consist of the symbols identifying the State of principal use, followed by a combination of numerals and letters which furnish individual vessel identification. The group of digits appearing between letters shall be separated from those letters by hyphens or equivalent spaces. As examples: AL–001–AA, or AK 99 AZ.

(c) The first part of the number shall be an abbreviation in capital letters of the State. The abbreviations of the States are as follows:

Alabama—AL
Alaska—AK
Arizona—AZ
Arkansas—AR
California—CF
Colorado—CL
Connecticut—CT
Delaware—DL
Florida—FL
Georgia—GA
Hawaii—HA
Idaho—ID
Illinois—IL
Indiana—IN
Iowa—IA
Kansas—KA
Kentucky—KY
Louisiana—LA
Maine—ME
Massachusetts—MS
Maryland—MD
Michigan—MC
Minnesota—MN
Mississippi—MI
Missouri—MO
Montana—MT

North Carolina—NC
North Dakota—ND
Nebraska—NB
Nevada—NV
New Hampshire—NH
New Jersey—NJ
New Mexico—NM
New York—NY
Ohio—OH
Oklahoma—OK
Oregon—OR
Pennsylvania—PA
Rhode Island—RI
South Carolina—SC
South Dakota—SD
Tennessee—TN
Texas—TX
Utah—UT
Virginia—VA
Vermont—VT
Washington—WN
West Virginia—WV
Wyoming—WY
Wisconsin—WS
District of Columbia—DC

(d) The remainder of the boat number shall consist of not more than four arabic numerals and two capital letters or not more than three arabic numerals and three capital letters, in sequence, separated by a hyphen or equivalent space, in accordance with the serials, numerically and alphabetically.

(1) As examples of the first alternative:

State designator	Maximum of 4 digits; numerical group	Maximum of 2 letters; alphabetical group
NY	1	A
NY	83	A B
NY	345	T R
NY	9999	Z Z

(2) As example of the second alternative:

State designator	Maximum of 3 digits; numerical group	Maximum of 3 letters; alphabetical group
NC	1	A
NC	83	A B
NC	345	P F
NC	999	Z Z Z

(e) Since the letters "I," "O" and "Q" may be mistaken for arabic numerals, all letter sequences using "I," "O" and "Q" shall be omitted. Objectionable words formed by the use of two or three letters will not be used.

(Sec. 3 (c), 72 Stat. 1754)

§ 171.05–5 *Display of number on vessel.* (a) Subsection 3 (f) of the Federal Boating Act of 1958 requires in part that "the number awarded * * * shall be painted on, or attached to, each side of the bow of the vessel for which it was issued * * * ."

(b) The numbers shall be placed on each side of the forward half of the vessel in such position as to provide clear legibility for identification. The numbers shall read from left to right and shall be in block characters of good proportion not less than 3 inches in height. The numbers shall be of a color which will contrast with the color of the background and so maintained as to be clearly visible and legible; i.e., dark numbers on a light background, or light numbers on a dark background.

(Sec. 3 (c) (3), (f), 72 Stat. 1754, 1755)

(c) Subsection 3 (f) of the Federal Boating Act of 1958 also provides "no other number shall be carried on the bow of such vessel."

§ 171.05–10 *Numbering livery boats.* (a) The numbering requirement of this part shall apply to livery boats.

(b) The certificate of number of a livery boat shall be plainly marked, "livery boat."

(c) The description of the motor and type of fuel will be omitted from the certificate of number in any case where the motor is not rented with the boat.

§ 171.05–15 *Numbering of manufacturers' and dealers' boats.* (a)

Numbering requirements of this part shall apply to boats operated by manufacturers and dealers.

(b) The description of the boat will be omitted from the certificate of number since the numbers and the certificates of number awarded may be transferred from one boat to another. In lieu of the description, the word "manufacturer" or "dealer," as appropriate, will be plainly marked on each certificate.

(c) The manufacturer or dealer may have the number awarded printed upon or attached to a removable sign of signs to be temporarily but firmly mounted upon or attached to the boat being demonstrated or tested so long as the display meets the requirements in § 171.05–5.

APPLICATION FOR NUMBER

§ 171.10–1 *To whom made.* (a) On and after April 1, 1960, the owner of any vessel required to be numbered and principally used in a State which has not assumed the functions of numbering under the Federal Boating Act of 1958 shall prior to its use apply to the U. S. Coast Guard for a number for such vessel.

(b) An undocumented vessel principally used in a State which has assumed the functions of numbering under the Federal Boating Act of 1958 will not be numbered by the Coast Guard.

§ 171.10–5 *Application requirements.* The application for a number shall include the following:

(a) Name and address of owner.

(b) Date of birth of owner.

(c) Present citizenship of owner.

(d) State in which the vessel is principally used.

(e) Present number (if any).

(f) Hull material (wood, steel, aluminum, plastic, other).

(g) Type of propulsion (outboard, inboard, other).

(h) Type of fuel (gas, diesel, other).

(i) Length of vessel.

(j) Make and year built (if known).

(k) Statement as to use (pleasure, livery, dealer, manufacturer, commercial-passenger, commercial-fishing, commercial-other).

(l) A certification of ownership by the applicant.

(m) Signature of owner.

§ 171.10–15 *State in which vessel is principally used.* (a) For the purposes of numbering, the statement of the owner with respect to the State in which the vessel is to be principally used, as set forth in the application for number, will be accepted, prima facie, as true.

(b) If the vessel is to be principally used on the high seas, then it shall be assigned a number for the State in which the vessel is usually docked, moored, housed, or garaged.

§ 171.10–20 *Application for renewal of number.* An application for renewal of a certificate of number shall be made by the owner on an application therefor which must be received by the Coast Guard within a period consisting of the last 90 days before the expiration date on the certificate of number and the same number will be issued upon renewal. Any application not so received shall be treated in the same manner as an original application except that the same number may be reissued if the application is received within one year from date of expiration.

§ 171.10–25 *Replacement of lost or destroyed certificate of number.* If a certificate of number is lost or destroyed, the owner shall, within 15 days, notify the Coast Guard office which issued the number. The notification shall be in writing, shall describe the circumstances of the loss or destruction and shall be accompanied by the fee prescribed in §171.17–1 (a) (3). The certificate of number issued as a result of such report will replace the certificate so lost or destroyed.

OWNERSHIP

§ 171.13–1 *Claim of ownership.* (a) The certified statement of ownership on the application for number shall be the minimum requirement for proof of ownership acceptable to the Coast Guard.

§ 171.13–5 *Liens.* Liens of all kinds, including reservations or transfers of title to secure debts or claims, will be disregarded in determining ownership under this subpart. A lienholder who acquires possession and title by virtue of default in the terms of the lien instrument, or any other person who acquires ownership through any such action of a lienholder, may apply for a number and shall attach to such application a signed statement explaining the fact in detail.

CERTIFICATE OF NUMBER

§ 171.15–1 *Information required on certificate.* The certificate of number shall include the following:

(a) Name and address of owner.

(b) Date of birth of owner.

(c) Present citizenship of owner.

(d) State in which the vessel is principally used.

(e) Present number (if any).

(f) Hull material (wood, steel aluminum, plastic, other).

(g) Type of propulsion (outboard, inboard, other).

(h) Type of fuel (gas, diesel, other).

(i) Length of vessel.

(j) Make and year built (if known).

(k) Statement as to use (pleasure, livery, dealer, manufacturer, commercial-passenger, commercial-fishing, commercial-other).

(l) A certification of ownership by the applicant.

(m) Signature of owner.

(n) Number awarded to vessel.

(o) Expiration date of certificate.

(p) Notice to the owner that he shall report within 15 days changes of ownership or address, and destruction or abandonment of vessel.

(q) Notice to the owner that the operator shall:

(1) Always carry this certificate on vessel when in use.

(2) Report every accident involving injury or death to persons, or property damage over $100.

(3) Stop and render aid or assistance if involved in boating accident.

§ 171.15–5 *Size and characteristics of certificate.* The certificate of number shall be pocket size (approximately $2\frac{1}{2}''$ x $3\frac{1}{2}''$) and water resistant.

§ 171.15–10 *Temporary certificate.* Pending the issuance of the original certificate of number, the owner of the vessel will be furnished a temporary certificate of number valid for 60 days from date of issue. This temporary certificate shall be carried on board when the vessel is being operated.

§ 171.15–15 *Period of validity of certificate.* The original certificate of number initially awarded by the Coast Guard shall be valid for a period ending 3 years from the anniversary of the date of birth of the applicant next succeeding the issuance of the certificate. Each renewal shall be valid for a period ending 3 years from the date of expiration of the certificate so renewed. A certificate issued to other than an individual shall expire 3 years from date of issuance.

§ 171.15–20 *Notification of changes required.* (a) When the owner of a Coast Guard numbered vessel changes the State in which the vessel is principally used, he shall within 90 days surrender the certificate of numbers to the Coast Guard. The owner shall also apply for another original number to the office issuing numbers for that State.

(b) When the owner of a Coast Guard numbered vessel changes his address from that shown on his certificate, but does not change the State in which the vessel is principally used, he shall notify the Coast Guard of his new address within a period not to exceed 15 days from such change.

(c) When a Coast Guard numbered vessel is lost, destroyed, abandoned, or transferred to another person, the certificate of number issued for the vessel shall be surrendered to the Coast Guard within a period not to exceed 15 days after such event. When the vessel is lost, destroyed, or abandoned and the certificate of number has been destroyed, the owner shall within 15 days notify the Coast Guard by letter or postal card of the change in the status of the vessel.

(d) The application for number by a new owner of a vessel shall, for purposes of fee, be regarded as an original application for number, but where the vessel will continue in use in the same State of principal use, the new number shall be identical with the previous one, except where a lienholder acquires title and lawful possession by virtue of his lien, in which case a new number shall be issued.

(e) A change of motor is not required to be reported to the Coast Guard.

§ 171.15–25 *One certificate for each vessel.* The intent of this subpart is that the owner of an undocumented vessel shall not have more than one valid number or valid certificate of number for any one vessel at any time. Therefore, the owner will violate the regulations if he retains more than one valid certificate of number for any one vessel.

§ 171.15–30 *Cancellation of certificate and voiding of number.* (a) Subsection 3 (e) of the Federal Boating Act of 1958 authorizes the cancellation of certificates of number, thereby voiding the numbers issued. This means that a certificate may be canceled and number voided by proper authority even though such action occurs before the expiration date on the certificate and such certificate is not surrendered to the issuing office.

(b) Certain causes for cancellation of certificates and voiding of numbers are:

(1) Surrender of certificate for cancellation.

(2) Issuance of a new number for the same vessel.

(3) Issuance of a marine document by the Bureau of Customs for the same vessel.

(4) False or fraudulent certification in an application for number.

(c) In the absence of an application for renewal as provided in § 171.10–20 a number is automatically void on the date of expiration as shown on the certificate of number.

FEES AND CHARGES

§ 171.17–1 *Fees and method of payment.* (a) The fees charged by the U. S. Coast Guard, based upon the estimated cost of the administration of the numbering system, are:

(1) Original numbering—$5.00.

(2) Renewal of number—$3.00.

(3) Reissue of lost or destroyed certificate of number—$1.00.

(b) All fees for numbering and renewal of numbers are payable to the U. S. Coast Guard and shall accompany the application.

AVAILABILITY OF RECORDS

§ 171.20–1 *Enforcement or assistance programs.* Upon request, information on ownership and identity of Coast Guard numbered vessels shall be available to Federal, State, and local officials, as needed in any enforcement or assistance programs.

§ 171.20–5. *Disclosure of information.* (a) The records pertaining to the numbering of undocumented vessels pursuant to this part are considered to be public records.

(b) Information based on such Coast Guard records may be released upon oral or written inquiry, subject only to reasonable restrictions necessary to carry on the business of the office. The Coast Guard may permit excerpts to be made or the copying or reproduction thereof by a private individual or concern authorized by the Coast Guard. The fees and charges for copying, certifying, or searching of records for information shall be assessed in accordance with 33 CFR 1.25.

PART 173—BOATING ACCIDENTS, REPORTS, AND STATISTICAL INFORMATION

BOATING ACCIDENTS

§ 173.01-1 *General.* (a) The provisions of this subpart shall apply (1) to all uninspected motorboats and (2) to all other uninspected vessels used for pleasure or recreational purposes. Uninspected vessels, other than motorboats, used for commercial purposes are not included.

(b) The provisions in this subpart are applicable in the United States, its Territories, and the District of Columbia, as well as to every such vessel which is owned in a State, Territory, or the District of Columbia and using the high seas.

§ 173.01-5 *Reportable boating accidents.* (a) Subsection 13 (c) of the Act of April 25, 1940, as amended (46 U. S. C. 526*l*), reads as follows:

In the case of collision, accident, or other casualty involving a motorboat or other vessel subject to this Act, the operator thereof, if the collision, accident, or other casualty results in death or injury to any person, or damage to property in excess of $100, shall file with the Secretary of the Department within which the Coast Guard is operating, unless such operator is required to file an accident report with the State under section 3 (c) (6) of the Federal Boating Act of 1958, a full description of the collision, accident, or other casualty, including such information as the Secretary may by regulation require.

(b) For the purpose of this subpart a "boating accident" means a collision, accident or other casualty involving (1) an uninspected motorboat or (2) any other uninspected vessel used for pleasure or recreational purposes.

(c) A vessel subject to this subpart is considered to be involved in a "boating accident" whenever the occurrence results in damage by or to the vessel or its equipment; in injury or loss of life to any person, or in the disappearance of any person from on board under circumstances which indicate the possibility of death or injury. A "boating accident" includes, but is not limited to, capsizing, collision, foundering, flooding, fire, explosion and the disappearance of a vessel other than by theft.

(d) A report is required whenever a vessel subject to this subpart is involved in a "boating accident" which results in any one or more of the following:

(1) Loss of life.

(2) Injury causing any person to remain incapacitated for a period in excess of 72 hours.

(3) Actual physical damage to property (including vessels) in excess of $100.

§ 173.01–10 *Written report required.* (a) Whenever death results from a boating accident, a written report shall be submitted within 48 hours. For every other reportable boating accident a written report shall be submitted within five (5) days after such accident.

(b) The operator(s) of the boat(s) shall prepare and submit the written report(s) to the Coast Guard Officer in Charge, Marine Inspection, nearest to the place where such accident occurred or nearest to the port of first arrival after such accident, unless such operator is required to file an accident report with a State under subsection 3 (c) (6) of the Federal Boating Act of 1958.

(c) Every written report shall contain the following information:

(1) The numbers and/or names of vessels involved.

(2) The locality where the accident occurred.

(3) The time and date when the accident occurred.

(4) Weather and sea conditions at time of accident.

(5) The name, address, age, and boat operating experience of the operator of the reporting vessel.

(6) The names and addresses of operators of other vessels involved.

(7) The names and addresses of the owners of vessels or property involved.

(8) The names and addresses of any person or persons injured or killed.

(9) The nature and extent of injury to any person or persons.

(10) A description of damage to property (including vessels) and estimated cost of repairs.

(11) A description of the accident (including opinions as to the causes).

(12) The length, propulsion, horsepower, fuel and construction of the reporting vessel.

(13) Names and addresses of known witnesses.

(d) The Coast Guard Form CG-3865 (Boating Accident Report) may be used for the written report required by this section.

The State Boating Laws Simplified

412. There exists such a vast variation in required equipment and operating laws, most still in formative stages, that no reliable table can possibly be compiled. When picking up your state number award, a digest of state laws is usually furnished. If in doubt, follow the Motorboat Act of 1940 (*see* paragraph 402.) and The Federal Boating Act of 1958. (*see* paragraph 410.)

STATE	WHERE TO APPLY FOR CERTIFICATE OF NUMBER	SPECIAL EXEMPTIONS	SPECIAL NUMBERS FOR BOAT MFRS. & DEALERS	ADMINISTERING AGENCY	DISPOSITION OF FEES
Arizona	Mot. Veh. Div., Dept. of Highways	—		Mot. Veh. Div., Dept. of Highways	—
Arkansas	Office of County Clerk	Boats with 10 hp. or less.	YES. Available only to licensed manufacturers and dealers.	Game & Fish Comm.	50% to counties' general funds, and 50% to State Game Protection Fund for use by G & F C in administration and enforcement of Act.
California	Dept. of Mot. Veh.	Undocumented vessels propelled solely by oars, paddles or electric motors of 10 hp. or less, and undocumented vessels 8 ft. or less propelled solely by sail.		Small Craft Harbors Comm., Dept. of Natural Resources	General Fund of State
Colorado	Director, State Parks & Recreation	Boats with 10 hp. or less.		State Park & Recreation Board	—
Delaware	Mot. Veh. Dept.	—	Dealers and livery owners shall have at their disposal blocks of numbers, and shall pay the	Comm. of Shell Fisheries, thru appointed Boat Safety Director	—

178

State		Exemptions	Registration	Enforcement	Fund disposition
Florida	Office of County Tax Collector, for pleasure boats; Game & Fresh-Water Fish Comm., or State Board of Conservation, for commercial boats	Boats with 10 hp. or less, motorboats used exclusively on private lakes, for racing, or for sightseeing.	YES	State Board of Conservation	Motorboating Revolving Fund—to cover administrative costs of Act. Further use to be determined by next legislature.
Idaho	Dept. of law enforcement	Boats with 10 hp. or less.	YES ($3.00)	State law enforcement department	50% general county funds, 50% state motor vehicle fund.
Illinois	Dept. of Conservation	—	YES	Dept. of Conservation	State Boating Act Fund—appropriations authorized only to Dept. of Conservation to cover costs of administering and enforcing this Act, building pleasure craft facilities, and promoting boating safety and boating safety education.
Indiana	Conservation Dept.	—	YES	Conservation Dept.	50% of all fees shall be earmarked for exclusive use of Conservation Dept. in the acquisition, establishment, operation and maintenance of public hunting and fishing sites.
Kansas	Forestry, Fish & Game Comm.	Boats with 10 hp. or less.	YES ($3 for each registration).	Forestry, Fish & Game Comm.	—

STATE	WHERE TO APPLY FOR CERTIFICATE OF NUMBER	SPECIAL EXEMPTIONS	SPECIAL NUMBERS FOR BOAT MFRS. & DEALERS	ADMINISTERING AGENCY	DISPOSITION OF FEES
Maine	Commissioner of Inland Fisheries & Game	Boats with 10 hp. or less; motorboats used exclusively on tidal waters; motorboats already under jurisdiction of Public Utilities Comm.; motorboats kept for use by any children's camp licensed by Dept. of Health and Welfare, provided not offered for hire to general public. Also, a motorboat owned by a non-resident may be operated for not more than 3 days in any calendar year without being numbered.	YES ($2 for each registration). Applicant must maintain permanent place of business in state, and is entitled to 4 sets of identification plates at $2 per set.	Commissioner of Inland Fisheries & Game	Funds of Dept. of Inland Fisheries & Game
Michigan	Sec. of State, or sheriff's dept. of each county.	———	YES ($5 for each registration).	Enforcement by sheriff's dept. of each county.	General Fund of State—appropriations authorized for water safety educational programs and for administration and enforcement of Act, including grants to counties.

State	Registration Agency	Exemptions	Registration Required	Administering Agency	Fund / Use
Minnesota	Commissioner of Conservation, or a county auditor or his agent	Duck boats during duck hunting season, sailboats, canoes, rice boats during harvest season, seaplanes.	YES	Commissioner of Conservation	For administration and enforcement of this Act, inspection of watercraft, and acquisition and development of sites for public access.
Missouri	Dept. of Revenue	Boats with 10 hp. or less, motorboats used exclusively on farm ponds not commercially operated for boating purposes.	YES ($10 for each registration).	Missouri Boat Comm.	Motorboat Fund—appropriations authorized for purposes of construction and maintenance of boating facilities, education and instruction in boating safety enforcement of Act, and reimbursement to counties for expenses incurred in enforcing Act—upon recommendation of the Boat Comm.
Montana	Fish & Game Comm.	Boats with 10 hp. or less.	YES	Fish & Game Comm.	—
Nebraska	Game, Forestation & Parks Comm.	—	YES ($3 for each registration).	Game, Forestation & Parks Comm.	State Boating Fund—appropriations authorized for administration and enforcement of Act, construction of maintenance of boating facilities, navigation aids and access to boating areas, and such other uses as will promote safety and convenience of boating public in Neb.

STATE	WHERE TO APPLY FOR CERTIFICATE OF NUMBER	SPECIAL EXEMPTIONS	SPECIAL NUMBERS FOR BOAT MFRS. & DEALERS	ADMINISTERING AGENCY	DISPOSITION OF FEES
New Mexico	State Park Comm.	Boats under 10 hp.	—	State Park Comm.	General Fund of State
New York	Conservation Commissioner	—	YES	Conservation Commissioner	State Boating Fund
North Carolina	Wildlife Resources Comm., or any N.C. certified hunting and fishing license agent	Boats with 10 hp. or less.	YES ($15 for initial certificate of number, and $6 for each additional certificate).	Wildlife Resources Comm.	Wildlife Resources Fund —appropriations authorized for administration and enforcement of Act, and for educational activities relating to boating safety and for no other purpose.
North Dakota	Game & Fish Dept.	Boats under 10 hp.	—	Game & Fish Dept.	State Game & Fish Fund —to pay for the costs of administering Act.
Ohio	Administrator, Div. of Watercraft, Dept. of Natural Resources. (In addition, person using outboard motor on a bailed or rented boat, must secure detachable outboard motor license)	—	YES ($20 annually for a dealer license and certificate of number).	Administrator, Div. of Watercraft, Dept. of Natural Resources	See Below

90% allocated to state departments, conservancy districts and political subdivisions having impounded waters upon which boating is permitted and authorized. It reimburses them for relinquishing to state collection of fees which they heretofore made under separate licensing systems. All applicants for certificate of number required to declare where they intend to principally use their watercraft as well as their principal place of mooring, and Administrator distributes license fees to political subdivisions in proportion to number of watercraft designating waters of a particular division as their principal place of use. Fees from watercraft owners designating Lake Erie as their principal place of use go to Waterways Safety Fund for purposes of acquiring, constructing and maintaining refuge and light-draft vessel harbor projects, channels, and facilities for vessels in navigable waters of state, and of operating and maintaining public boating facilities. 90% of total revenue from sale of outboard motor licenses allocated to state departments, conservancy districts and political subdivisions having impounded bodies of water upon which use of outboard motors is permitted, according to same percentage ratio employed for making reimbursements from sale of certificates of number.

Oklahoma	Planning & Resources Board (In addition, owner of any outboard motor of more than 10 hp. to be used on vessel required to be numbered in Okla., shall secure license and certificate of title for motor.)	A watercraft or motorboat used exclusively for racing; boat used solely on private lake or on any lake of 100 acres or less.	Annual dealer's license, $10.	Planning & Resources Board	Waterways Fund—to pay costs of administering and enforcing this Act.
Oregon	State Marine Board	Boats under 10 hp.	YES ($20 for first number applied for, and $5 for each additional number applied for in any application).	State Marine Director appointed by State Marine Board	State Marine Board Account in the General Fund—appropriations authorized for paying expenses of administering and enforcing Act, and for state aid to counties proportionate to number of certificates of number issued to residents of each county as compared to total number issued for entire state.

STATE	WHERE TO APPLY FOR CERTIFICATE OF NUMBER	SPECIAL EXEMPTIONS	SPECIAL NUMBERS FOR BOAT MFRS. & DEALERS	ADMINISTERING AGENCY	DISPOSITION OF FEES
Rhode Island	Div. of Harbors & Rivers, Dept. of Public Works	Motorboats used exclusively for racing.	—	Div. of Harbors & Rivers, Dept. of Public Works	For costs of administering Act, and for use of developing public boating facilities.
South Carolina	Div. of Boating, Wildlife Resources Dept.	Boats under 10 hp.	—	Div. of Boating, Wildlife Resources Dept.	For costs of administering and enforcing this Act.
South Dakota	Dept. of Game, Fish & Parks.	Boats with 6 hp. or less.	YES ($5 for each registration).	Dept. of Game, Fish & Parks	—
Texas	Mot. Veh. Div., Highway Dept.	Boats with 10 hp. or less, racing boats, provided they are operated only in a regulated and supervised race or exhibition.	YES ($25 for each registration).	Mot. Veh. Div., Highway Dept.	Special Boat Fund—to pay costs of administering this Act. Any funds remaining after administrative costs have been paid are to be used for purchasing public access sites and building and maintaining boat ramps.
Utah	Parks & Recreation Comm.	Racing boats during the three twenty-four (24) hour periods prior to, during and following any race authorized by the Comm.	YES	Parks & Recreation Comm.	Special Boating Fund—to pay costs of administration of this Act. Any funds in excess of amount necessary for administration of this Act may also be used for development and operation of boating and sanitation facilities. Any surplus reverts to General Fund.

State					General Fund of State
Vermont	Public Safety Dept.	Any Class A motorboat (less than 16 ft. in length) owned by a resident of a state which has no federally approved numbered system, provided it is operated in Vt. for not more than 7 consecutive days.	YES ($5 for a set of five certificates).	Commissioner of Public Safety	
West Virginia	Director of Conservation, Conservation Comm.	Boats with 5 hp. or less, racing boats while preparing for and participating in authorized races.	YES ($5 for each registration).	Director of Conservation, Conservation Comm.	Conservation Fund
Wisconsin	Conservation Comm.	—	YES	Conservation Comm.	Revolving appropriation for administration and enforcement of Act, Payment of state aids, and boating safety education program.

The following states are in the process of establishing state numbering systems and are presently exempt from federal numbering.

Georgia   Massachusetts
Kentucky   Mississippi
Louisiana   Nevada
Maryland   Virginia

The enactment of appropriate state law will follow and the boatman living in these states is advised to obtain copies of his state law when enacted.

In the few remaining states in which the Coast Guard still numbers boats, the procedure is to apply at the local post office for a boat numbering application. A Federal boating stamp is attached and the stub is post-marked, this being legal proof to an inspecting officer that the boat in question is legally registered. Evidence of ownership is required as well as receipt for payment of any local or sales tax involved. The above is a temporary measure only and may be abandoned at any time. Such numbers are presently issued in the states of Alabama, Alaska, Connecticut, District of Columbia, Hawaii, Iowa, New Hampshire, New Jersey, Pennsylvania, Tennessee, Washington and Wyoming.

The current status of this very pliable situation will be reported by the Coast Guard, by the states concerned and by the various yachting journals and the boatman is advised to obtain the latest data from local sources.

Exceptions to the Law

413. Boats operated solely on inland lakes or rivers, not on Federal waterways nor on a boundary between states or countries, are not required to observe the Federal law. They are required, however, to observe the state law, if there is one relating to motorboats or navigation.

Inspection

414. Inspection of motorboats to check required equipment and its condition is the duty of the Officer in Charge, Marine Inspection, United States Coast Guard. Voluntary inspection may be applied for from the nearest United States Coast Guard Auxiliary.

Under the Federal Boating Act of 1958, those states which have approved numbering systems also acquire the right to inspect boats. Such inspections will be made to discover if the vessel is observing *state* law, which may or may not be different from Federal law insofar as required equipment is concerned. Heave to when so ordered by an official patrol boat or officer of your state. It is a general rule that such patrol vessels shall be clearly identifiable by name or signal and its officers appear in regulation uniform. Acquaint yourself with the particular branch of your state government which is charged with administering your state boating law. The Coast

Guard also has the right to heave you to for inspection on Federal waters, whether or not your state has an approved boating act.

As a general rule, a boat may be inspected only when under way. *It may differ in your state.* Usually, government equipment need not be carried at moorings, nor at a wharf, nor while the boat is hauled. However, if a boat has been seen or reported under way and inspection is made immediately upon anchoring or tying up, the inspection officials are within their rights.

Inspectors' boats will fly the flag of the service to which the inspecting officer on board belongs.

Licensed Operators and Crew on Yachts

415. No motorboat under 300 tons, documented as a yacht and not carrying passengers or freight for hire, is required to carry any licensed officers or personnel.

416. Motorboats of 15 tons or more, which carry passengers or freight for hire, or yachts of 300 tons and over (seagoing), must carry the licensed personnel required by the certificate of inspection. Fishing vessels are exempt from this requirement.

417. Motorboats of 15 tons or over but less than 65 feet in length which carry passengers or freight for hire may be operated by personnel licensed under the Motorboat Law. On boats of such dimensions engaged in trade (commercial vessels, such as tugs, cargo carriers, etc.), as well as on vessels of 300 tons or over, and which are subject to hull and machinery inspection, a licensed pilot, or engineer, or other officers may be required, and will be so noted on the certificate of inspection by the local Officer in Charge, Marine Inspection, United States Coast Guard. (Thus, a steam-propelled boat of 40 feet, though documented as a yacht, is subject to inspection and might possibly require licensed operators, depending upon its use.)

License to Operate Motorboats Carrying Passengers for Hire

418. In general, a motorboat is carrying passengers for hire when, by *prearrangement,* some form of payment is made for the voyage or for use of the vessel. Payment may be in cash, gifts, services, or some other form.

419. Following are some opinions on typical situations:

These passengers are NOT being carried for hire.

1. Business associates, invited by the owner.

2. Passengers who take the owner ashore for entertainment, or food, or lodging, or who bring, as gifts, food, boat's gear, books, etc.

3. Passengers who have chartered the boat before it has been placed in commission and without crew, and who intend to use the vessel for pleasure, with or without a crew.

These passengers ARE being carried for hire.

1. Passengers who, in accepting an invitation to cruise or voyage, agree *in advance* to pay all or a proportionate share of the running

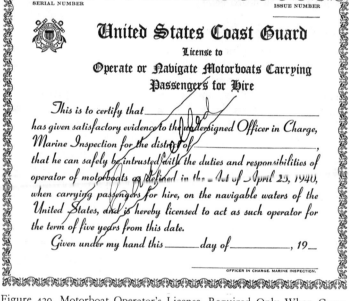

SERIAL NUMBER   ISSUE NUMBER

United States Coast Guard
License to
Operate or Navigate Motorboats Carrying Passengers for Hire

This is to certify that _____ has given satisfactory evidence to the undersigned Officer in Charge, Marine Inspection for the district of _____, that he can safely be intrusted with the duties and responsibilities of operator of motorboats as defined in the Act of April 25, 1940, when carrying passengers for hire, on the navigable waters of the United States, and is hereby licensed to act as such operator for the term of five years from this date.

Given under my hand this _____ *day of* _____, 19 __

OFFICER IN CHARGE, MARINE INSPECTION.

Figure 420. Motorboat Operator's License. Required Only When Carrying Passengers for Hire

expenses or other expenses (such as gasoline, canal tolls, stores, etc.).

2. Passengers who have chartered a boat for their exclusive use, the charter having included a crew.

420. For a license to carry passengers for hire, application is made to the Officer in Charge, Marine Inspection, United States Coast Guard. See next page for list of local depots.

The applicant (male or female) must be 18 years of age, must stand a physical examination by the United States Department of Health or a reputable private physician, and must pass an oral examination on boat handling and operating.

Physical examination consists of tests for color perception, blindness, impaired hearing, insanity, and certain diseases likely to affect the senses in the future.

Oral examination consists of questions relating to navigation laws, rules of the road, signals, elementary seamanship, safety on shipboard and at sea; and questions based on elementary first-aid knowledge. The examination is not difficult for the applicant familiar with boats and does not require a knowledge of extensive navigation, engineering, or maritime law.

Letters of character and ability are required.

Application is made on Form 866A. A license is issued, at no cost to the applicant, and is good for five years. It may be renewed during the 59th month, or within one year after expiration, upon showing proof of no major change in physical condition.

The license may be revoked upon the holder's being found guilty of endangering life, willfully violating laws or safety provisions, incompetency, unskillfulness, misbehavior, or negligence. When revoked, the license automatically expires.

Application offices of the United States Coast Guard are located as listed below:

District No.	Name	Depots or Offices at
1	Boston	Boston; Portland, Me.; and Providence, R.I.
2	St. Louis	St. Louis, Cairo, Dubuque, Cincinnati, Louisville, Memphis, Nashville, Pittsburgh, and Huntington, W. Va.
3	New York	New York, Albany, Philadelphia, and New London, Conn.
5	Norfolk	Norfolk, Baltimore, and Wilmington, N.C.
7	Miami	Miami, Charleston, Savannah, Tampa, Jacksonville, and San Juan, P.R.
8	New Orleans	New Orleans, Mobile, Port Arthur, Galveston, Corpus Christi, and Houston.

District No.	Name	Depots or Offices at
9	Cleveland	Cleveland, Buffalo, Oswego, Detroit, Duluth, Toledo, St. Ignace, Chicago, Milwaukee, and Ludington.
11	Long Beach	Long Beach, Calif.
12	San Francisco	San Francisco, Calif.
13	Seattle	Seattle, Ketchikan and Portland, Ore.
14	Hawaii	Honolulu.
17	Alaska	Juneau

There are no districts 4, 6, 10, 15 or 16 at present. However, the Coast Guard's latest charges, Guam, Virgin Islands, and Puerto Rico, may be assigned one or more of the above unused numbers, or possibly a number higher than 17.

Numbering

421. Numbers assigned by a state comply with a Federally approved numbering system. This includes a minimum letter size of 3″, of a color distinguishable against its background and a prefix denoting the state of issue. (Examples: ME for Maine, FL for Florida, etc.). These should be attached or painted forward of amidships and *on each side of the vessel.* Usually plastic or metal letters are used and often these are tacked to a panel which may be readily removed when topside painting is needed. The certificate of award, indicating the assignment of a particular number to a particular boat, must be kept on board at all times.

There is no law which provides that a pleasure craft must have a name and/or port of hail. If your boat has no name, note on the application "No name" or "Nameless." You may add a name and port of hail later and need not change the registration form. A documented vessel *must* have a name and a port of hail and *both* must be painted, or affixed if plastic or metal numbers, in letters at least 4 inches high *directly on the transom.* They may be on the bows as well, or on a wheel house panel, but *must* appear on the transom. The use of name boards or detachable panels on the transom is illegal for a documented vessel, although they will pass in any *other* location.

If, in those states not yet under state boating laws, the Coast Guard awards numbers, such numbers will start with a key number denoting the Coast Guard district from which the number has been issued, as follows:

Key Numbers	District Number	District Office at
1, 2, 4, 5	1	Boston, Mass.
2, 6, 10, 11	3	New York, N.Y.
7, 8, 9, 36, 37, 38, 39, 41	9	Cleveland, Ohio
12, 34, 35, 40, 42, 43, 44, 45, 46	2	St. Louis, Mo.
13, 14, 15	5	Norfolk, Va.
16, 17, 18, 49, 51	7	Miami, Fla.
18, 19, 20, 21, 22, 23, 24, 43	8	New Orleans, La.
25, 26, 27	11	Long Beach, Calif.
28, 47	12	San Francisco, Calif.
29, 30, 31, 33, 46	13	Seattle, Wash.
32	14	Honolulu, Ha.
(not determined)	17	Juneau, Alaska

Documenting

422. The provisions of the Numbering Act were framed primarily for and relate to boats used for pleasure. Boats so used (yachts) may not be documented unless they are 16 gross tons or over.

Documenting is indicated when:

1. A vessel of five gross tons or over is NOT used exclusively for pleasure.

2. A vessel under sixteen gross tons sails to a foreign port.

423. Documenting is in one of five forms, applicable to the following vessels and conditions:

1. A vessel in foreign trade, coastwise trade, or engaged in whaling should REGISTER.

2. A vessel of 20 gross tons or over, pursuing the business stated on her license or in the coasting trade, or mackerel fishery or cod fishery, or coastal trade and mackerel fishery should ENROLL AND LICENSE.

3. A vessel engaged as above but of less than 20 gross tons should LICENSE.

4. A vessel of over 20 gross tons, used exclusively for pleasure, and

desirous of proceeding from port to port in the United States, or to a foreign country, without reporting at the Customhouse should EN-ROLL AND YACHT REGISTER.

5. A vessel of between 16 and 20 gross tons, used exclusively for pleasure, desirous of proceeding as above should YACHT LICENSE.

It is to be noted that a yacht between 5 and 16 gross tons is NOT REQUIRED to register when sailing foreign. If she does, she becomes subject to all fees required of registered vessels.

Documented boats are not required to be numbered but must, if carrying passengers for hire, be operated by a licensed operator.

Document licenses are procured from the Bureau of Customs in the district in which the yacht is then lying.

Public vessels are vessels such as ferries, or liners, or accommodation boats, and must be documented.

Sailing Foreign (in Yachts)

424. Regulations for a pleasure yacht sailing foreign have been made relatively simple and consist merely of entering and clearing.

Permissions for entering and clearing are obtained from local customs officials. To clear the ship's registry papers or documentation must be exhibited. Upon entering the master or owner must report to the customs officials, meanwhile holding passengers and crew on board until the boat has been inspected. *All* boats must report to the immigration officials upon return to a United States port and no person landed until permission has been granted. If a paid crew is carried they must be reported on a Crew Manifest Form.

Note that:

A documented yacht need not clear an American port.

All yachts over 16 gross tons must enter when returning to an American port.

All yachts under 16 gross tons need enter only when they carry dutiable merchandise.

All yachts must clear an American port if there is dutiable merchandise aboard.

Any vessel of 5 gross tons or over not used for pleasure (i.e., not a yacht) must both enter and clear, whether documented or not.

A Bill of Health is not required when clearing an American port. However, to comply with vague and changing regulations of foreign ports, especially those of the West Indies, it is wisest to request a Bill of Health. It is furnished free by the Department of Health.

When a yacht of 16 gross tons or more enters she is required to file a manifest at the customhouse and pay a fee of $1.50. Yachts over 100 tons must pay $2.50. Additional charges are made if entry is on a holiday or if between the hours of 5 P. M. and 8 A. M. The matter must be taken care of within 48 hours of arrival.

Yachts clearing for Canada must secure a cruising permit which provides free entry and clearing from May 1 to October 1. The permit is obtained free at the first Canadian port entered and must be surrendered upon clearing for home. A similar exchange arrangement prevails for Canadian yachts entering the United States. No entry fees are assessed unless the yacht enters by sea. Thus the Great Lake ports of both Canada and the United States are "free ports" for pleasure vessels.

Upon request the Secretary of Commerce will issue a sea letter to a yacht engaged in ocean racing or a special single voyage. Such a letter is good only for the voyage specified and must be surrendered upon entering.

Customs regulations for lesser foreign countries (such as those of the Caribbean, Central America, etc.) change from time to time and seem to be interpreted more or less by individual port authorities and it is therefore wise to make a careful check. If there seem to be no regulations at a foreign port, assume that there are and take every document possible with you. Talk with yachtsmen, fishermen or shipping people at the last U.S. port; they have the "latest." Always carry in the flag locker the national ensign of the countries to be visited. Not only is this a courtesy—in some lands it is punishable by fine and imprisonment to fail to fly the flag of that nation!

Regulation of Motorboats During Wartime

425. Under war conditions, a captain of the port may prescribe and enforce any special regulations as well as general wartime regulations of pleasure and other small boats.

In general, such regulations consist of registering the boat and every member of the crew with the port authorities and, under certain conditions, every passenger as well. Proof of citizenship must be shown, address, age, occupation, and purpose of being on the sea. Photographs and fingerprints are required.

Such regulations apply to any person or any boat on the water, including rowboats, sailboats, and motorboats.

Coastal waters are under the jurisdiction of the United States Coast Guard, and application for permits, etc., is made to that service.

Certain sea areas, rivers or waters adjacent to maritime bases, factories, or wharves may be restricted or closed to boats. It may be required to report to guard vessels before entering or leaving areas, or in passing through mine nets, booms, or mined areas, or between and past forts, etc.

Boats may be restricted to use during daylight hours, or to certain days or weeks or seasons.

⚓

CHAPTER V

LIGHTS, WHISTLE SIGNALS, RULES OF THE ROAD AND NAVIGATION LAWS

(NOTE: *Simplified tables of whistle and fog signals for handy reference will be found in Chapter VIII*)

501. The light requirements for vessels under 65 feet in length have been changed recently and the old bugaboo of identifying a sailing vessel has been partially obviated. Lenses are no longer specified by lens area but, rather, by visibility.

32 Pts. White Vis. 2 mi.	20 Pts. White Vis. 2 mi.	12 Pts. White Vis. 2 mi.	20 Pts. R&G Vis. 1 mi. (Combination)	10 Pts. R&G Vis. 1 mi. (Separate)

0′–26′ LOA   **26′–65′ LOA**

Power

195

Sail and Power

Sail Alone

Figure 501A. Inland Rules (above)

These lights are legal only on inland waters, the Great Lakes and West-ern rivers. They must be shown by inboards, outboards, auxiliaries and straight sailboats.

Applies to power vessels under 40 gross tons and sail vessels under 20 gross tons. (An aux-iliary is legally a power boat.)

Figure 501B. International Rules (facing page)

These lights are required in international waters and the high seas and are legal, as well, on the Great Lakes, inland waters and Western rivers. Power boats over 40 gross tons *must* take the second option and the 20-point stern light must be visible for 5 miles. On the Great Lakes under sail alone, a stern light is not required. They must be shown by inboards, outboards, auxiliaries and straight sailboats.

20 Pts White
Vis. 3 mi.

12 Pts. White
Vis. 2 mi.

20 Pts. R&G
Vis. 1 mi.
(Combination)

10 Pts. R&G
Vis. 1 mi.
(Separate)

Option #1   **OR**   **Option #2**

Power

Sail and Power

Under sail alone there is no
option of side-lights. They
must be separated.

Sail Alone

Lights are required, lighted and visible as specified, between sunrise and sunset when *underway*. Stopped vessels or vessels at anchor (if not fishing) must display anchor lights except those under 65 feet in length and anchored or moored in a "special anchor area." Such areas are indicated on local charts and, in general, whether or not marked, are areas in which other and numerous vessels are anchored and, especially, moored. Such areas are likely to be off yacht clubs and marinas, near canal or waterway entrances and in "inner" local natural harbors normally associated with small craft.

Outboard powered craft are required to conform with these laws.

A manually propelled craft, such as a canoe, rowboat or a small sailing craft under oars in a calm, must have a white light ready to show an approaching boat in time to prevent collision. This light need be of no specified visibility and can be a lantern, flashlight or, in emergency, a white flare. Such a light need be displayed only "temporarily;" i.e., in time to avoid collision.

While it is unusual for an inspecting officer to actually test for himself the actual visibility of a light, this may be required in special cases. However, if your lights have a lens, either a Fresnel type (originally developed for oil flames) or a modern "wing tip" single or bull's-eye-type lens and an electric lamp of not less than 15 candle power behind it, the light will "pass" as legal. Anchor lights, from a practical viewpoint, need not meet the visibility requirements unless in an area not exempt from display of an anchor light. Usually, cruising men show, in an anchoring area, a lantern hung from a forestay, an electric portable device designed for anchor light service or the range light only of standard navigation lights.

A handy reference for quickly identifying the lights of a vessel at night at sea is found in the following light-identification tables.

Count the number of lights sighted and deduct one if both colored running lights are seen. Then refer to the table showing all the possible vessels and conditions under which that number of lights might be seen. If but one colored running light is seen, count the actual number of lights, and (making no deductions) refer to the correct table. (Example: Sighted two white range lights and port running light = three lights. The possibilities will be found in the table entitled *Three Lights*.)

As nearly as possible, the lights have been shown in their proper relation to each other as height above deck and each other. The arrow indicates the bow (or direction headed). It must be remembered that either a red or green running light may be seen, in which case the heading will be reversed. Lights of vessels being overtaken have not been shown, as few such combinations can be identified until 10- and 20-point lights are sighted from a position abeam.

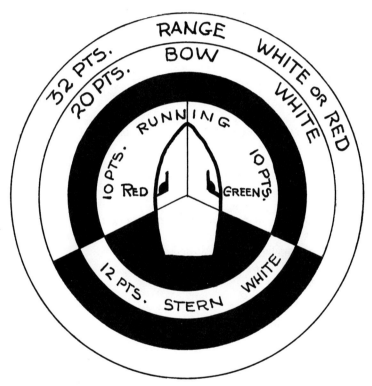

Figure 501C. Characteristics, Color, and Range of Navigation Lights. (Except Steam Trawlers which Carry Combination Masthead Lights, Red 8 Pts. on Port, White 4 Pts. Ahead and Green 8 Pts. on Starboard.)

Figure 501D. Key to Light Combinations

Color indicated by letter within light (R, red; G, green; W, white)

32 point range light

20 point bow light

12 point stern light

10 point red or green running light (this is not a combination light but signifies that either color may be seen)

10 point red (port) running light

10 point green (starboard) running light

heading of vessel when observed

NOTE: *A sailboat, under power alone, or under power and sail, displays the lights of a power boat.*

Figure 501E. One Light

Boat under 150 feet at anchor

Row or paddle boat (lantern or flash light)

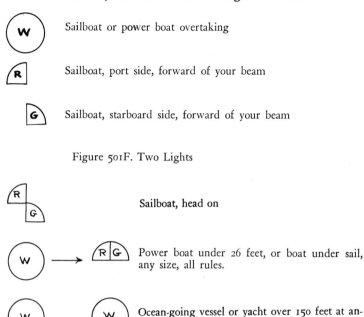

Sailboat or power boat overtaking

Sailboat, port side, forward of your beam

Sailboat, starboard side, forward of your beam

Figure 501F. Two Lights

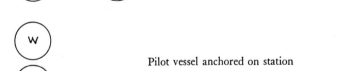

Sailboat, head on

Power boat under 26 feet, or boat under sail, any size, all rules.

Ocean-going vessel or yacht over 150 feet at anchor

Pilot vessel anchored on station

Vessel not under control

Figure 501G. Three Lights

Powerboat, under 26 feet, head on

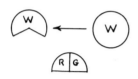

Powerboat, over 26 feet

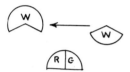

Steam vessel, under 40 tons

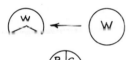

Sound or river steamer under Inland Rules

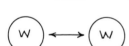

Ferry boat (may have line identification light amidships)

Fishing vessel underway and engaged in fishing

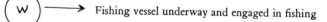

Figure 501G. Three Lights (*Continued*)

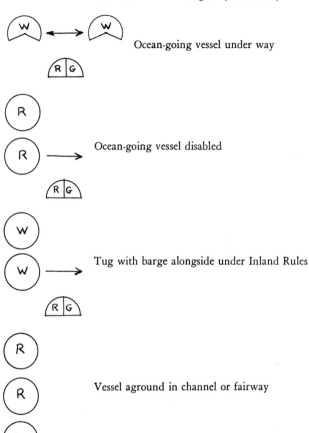

Ocean-going vessel under way

Ocean-going vessel disabled

Tug with barge alongside under Inland Rules

Vessel aground in channel or fairway

The Boatman's Manual

Figure 501H. Four Lights

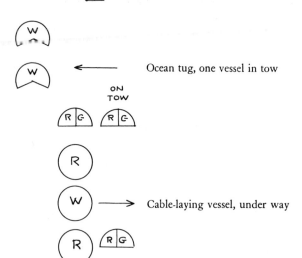

Powerboat, over 26 feet, head on

Fishing vessel, under way and engaged in fishing, head on

Ocean tug, one vessel in tow

ON
TOW

Cable-laying vessel, under way

Figure 501H. Four Lights (*Continued*)

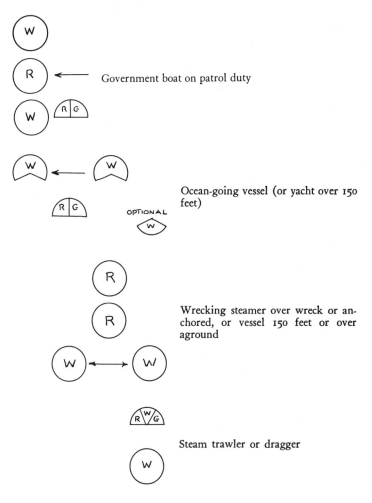

Government boat on patrol duty

Ocean-going vessel (or yacht over 150 feet)

OPTIONAL

Wrecking steamer over wreck or anchored, or vessel 150 feet or over aground

Steam trawler or dragger

Figure 501I. Five Lights

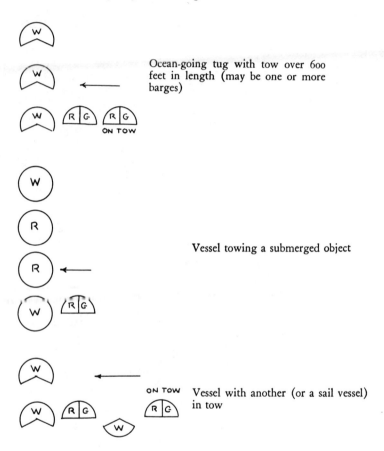

Ocean-going tug with tow over 600 feet in length (may be one or more barges)

Vessel towing a submerged object

Vessel with another (or a sail vessel) in tow

Figure 501J. Six Lights

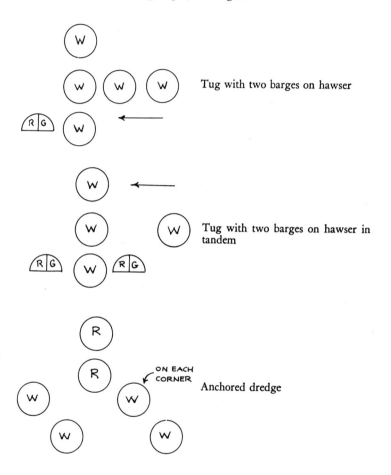

Tug with two barges on hawser

Tug with two barges on hawser in tandem

Anchored dredge

Figure 501K. Seven Lights

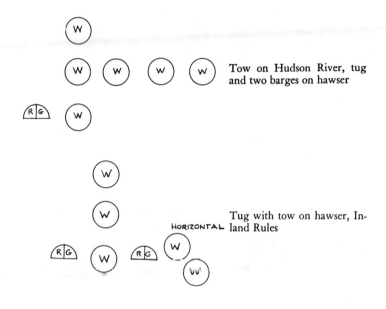

Tow on Hudson River, tug
and two barges on hawser

Tug with tow on hawser, Inland Rules

Figure 501L. More Than Seven Lights

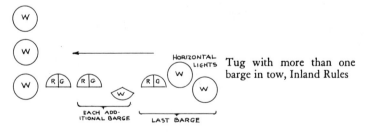

Tug with more than one
barge in tow, Inland Rules

NAVIGATION LAWS

Laws Relating to the Navigation of Vessels on All Harbors, Rivers, and Inland Waters of the United States, Except the Great Lakes and Their Connecting and Tributary Waters as Far East as Montreal and the Red River of the North and Rivers Emptying into the Gulf of Mexico and Their Tributaries [1]

AN ACT to adopt regulations for preventing collisions upon certain harbors, rivers, and inland waters of the United States

502. Whereas the provisions of chapter eight hundred and two of the laws of eighteen hundred and ninety, and the amendments thereto, adopting regulations for preventing collisions at sea, apply to all waters of the United States connected with the high seas navigable by sea-going vessels, except so far as the navigation of any harbor, river, or inland waters is regulated by special rules duly made by local authority; and

Whereas it is desirable that the regulations relating to the navigation of all harbors, rivers, and inland waters of the United States, except the Great Lakes and their connecting and tributary waters as far east as Montreal and the Red River of the North and rivers emptying into the Gulf of Mexico and their tributaries, shall be stated in one Act: Therefore,

Be it enacted by the Senate and the House of Representatives of the United States of America in Congress assembled, That the following regulations for preventing collision shall be followed by all vessels navigating all harbors, rivers, and inland waters of the United States, except the Great Lakes and their connecting and tributary waters as far east as Montreal and the Red River of the North and rivers emptying into the Gulf of Mexico and their tributaries, and are hereby declared special rules duly made by local authority:

PRELIMINARY

In the following rules every steam-vessel which is under sail and

[1] The Motorboat Act of 1940 supersedes Pilot Rules wherever they conflict in cases involving motorboats.

not under steam is to be considered a sailing-vessel, and every vessel under steam, whether under sail or not, is to be considered a steam vessel.

The word "steam-vessel" shall include any vessel propelled by machinery.

A vessel is "under way," within the meaning of these rules, when she is not at anchor, or made fast to the shore, or aground.

RULES CONCERNING LIGHTS, AND SO FORTH

The word "visible" in these rules, when applied to lights, shall mean visible on a dark night with a clear atmosphere.

Article 1. The rules concerning lights shall be complied with in all weathers from sunset to sunrise, and during such time no other lights which may be mistaken for the prescribed lights shall be exhibited.

Art. 2.[2] A steam-vessel when under way shall carry—(a) On or in front of the foremast, or, if a vessel without a foremast, then in the fore part of the vessel, a bright white light so constructed as to show an unbroken light over an arc of the horizon of twenty points of the compass, so fixed as to throw the light ten points on each side of the vessel, namely, from right ahead to two points abaft the beam on either side, and of such a character as to be visible at a distance of at least five miles.

(b) On the starboard side a green light so constructed as to show an unbroken light over an arc of the horizon of ten points of the compass, so fixed as to throw the light from right ahead to two points abaft the beam on the starboard side, and of such a character as to be visible at a distance of at least two miles.

(c) On the port side a red light so constructed as to show an unbroken light over an arc of the horizon of ten points of the compass, so fixed as to throw the light from right ahead to two points abaft the beam on the port side, and of such a character as to be visible at a distance of at least two miles.

(d) The said green and red side-lights shall be fitted with inboard

[2] Article 2 is amended by act of Congress approved June 9, 1910, effective on and after July 9, 1910, in rules for lights required to be carried by every vessel propelled by machinery and not more than 65 feet in length, except tugboats and towboats propelled by steam.

screens projecting at least three feet forward from the light, so as to prevent these lights from being seen across the bow.

(e) A sea-going steam-vessel when under way may carry an additional white light similar in construction to the light mentioned in subdivision (a). These two lights shall be so placed in line with the keel that one shall be at least fifteen feet higher than the other, and in such a position with reference to each other that the lower light shall be forward of the upper one. The vertical distance between these lights shall be less than the horizontal distance.

(f) All steam-vessels (except sea-going vessels and ferry-boats), shall carry in addition to green and red lights required by article two (b), (c), and screens as required by article two (d), a central range of two white lights; the after-light being carried at an elevation at least fifteen feet above the light at the head of the vessel. The head-light shall be so constructed as to show an unbroken light through twenty points of the compass, namely, from right ahead to two points abaft the beam on either side of the vessel, and the after-light so as to show all around the horizon.

Art. 3. A steam-vessel when towing another vessel or vessels alongside shall, in addition to her side-lights, carry two bright white lights in a vertical line, one over the other, not less than three feet apart, and when towing one or more vessels astern, regardless of the length of the tow, shall carry an additional bright white light three feet above or below such lights: *Provided,* That on the Red River of the North and the rivers emptying into the Gulf of Mexico and their tributaries, this article shall not affect the signal lights used on towing vessels which propel the tow by pushing at the rear of the tow. Each of these lights shall be of the same construction and character, and shall be carried in the same position as the white light mentioned in article two (a) or the after range light mentioned in article two (f).

Such steam-vessel may carry a small white light abaft the funnel or aftermast for the vessel towed to steer by, but such light shall not be visible forward of the beam.

Art. 5.[3] A sailing vessel under way and any vessel being towed, except barges, canal boats, scows, and other vessels of nondescript type, when in tow of steam vessels, shall carry the same lights as are

[3] Amended by act of Congress approved March 1, 1933.

prescribed by article 2 for a steam vessel under way, with the exception of the white lights mentioned therein, which they shall never carry.

Art. 6. Whenever, as in the case of vessels of less than ten gross tons under way during bad weather, the green and red side-lights can not be fixed, these lights shall be kept at hand, lighted and ready for use; and shall, on the approach of or to other vessels, be exhibited on their respective sides in sufficient time to prevent collision, in such manner as to make them most visible, and so that the green light shall not be seen on the port side nor the red light on the starboard side, nor, if practicable, more than two points abaft the beam on their respective sides. To make the use of these portable lights more certain and easy the lanterns containing them shall each be painted outside with the color of the light they respectively contain, and shall be provided with proper screens.

Art. 7. Rowing boats, whether under oars or sail, shall have ready at hand a lantern showing a white light which shall be temporarily exhibited in sufficient time to prevent collision.

Art. 8.[4] Pilot-vessels when engaged on their station on pilotage

[4] AN ACT relating to lights on steam pilot vessels.

Be it enacted by the Senate and House of Representatives of the United States of America in Congress assembled, That a steam pilot vessel when engaged on her station on pilotage duty and in waters of the United States, and not at anchor, shall, in addition to the lights required for all pilot boats, carry at a distance of eight feet below her white masthead light a red light, visible all around the horizon and of such a character as to be visible on a dark night with a clear atmosphere at a distance of at least two miles, and also the colored side lights required to be carried by vessels when under way.

When engaged on her station on pilotage duty and in waters of the United States, and at anchor, she shall carry in addition to the lights required for all pilot boats the red light above mentioned, but not the colored side lights.

When not engaged on her station on pilotage duty, she shall carry the same lights as other steam vessels.

SEC. 2. That this act shall be construed as supplementary to article eight of the act approved June seventh, eighteen hundred and ninety-seven, entitled "An act to adopt regulations for preventing collisions upon certain harbors, rivers, and inland waters of the United States," and to article eight of an act approved August nineteenth, eighteen hundred and ninety, entitled "An act to adopt regulations for preventing collisions at sea."

SEC. 3. That this act shall take effect on June thirtieth, nineteen hundred.

Approved, February 19, 1900.

duty shall not show the light required for other vessels, but shall carry a white light at the masthead, visible all around the horizon, and shall also exhibit a flare-up light or flare-up lights at short intervals, which shall never exceed fifteen minutes.

On the near approach of or to other vessels they shall have their side-lights lighted, ready for use, and shall flash or show them at short intervals, to indicate the direction in which they are heading, but the green light shall not be shown on the port side nor the red light on the starboard side.

A pilot-vessel of such a class as to be obliged to go alongside of a vessel to put a pilot on board may show the white light instead of carrying it at the masthead, and may, instead of the colored lights above mentioned, have at hand, ready for use, a lantern with a green glass on the one side and a red glass on the other, to be used as pre-scribed above.

Pilot-vessels, when not engaged on their station on pilotage duty, shall carry lights similar to those of other vessels of their tonnage.

Art. 9. (a) Fishing-vessels of less than ten gross tons, when under way and when not having their nets, trawls, dredges, or lines in the water, shall not be obliged to carry the colored side-lights; but every such vessel shall, in lieu thereof, have ready at hand a lantern with a green glass on one side and a red glass on the other side, and on ap-proaching to or being approached by another vessel such lantern shall be exhibited in sufficient time to prevent collision, so that the green light shall not be seen on the port side nor the red light on the star-board side.

(b) All fishing-vessels and fishing-boats of ten gross tons or up-ward, when under way and when not having their nets, trawls, dredges, or lines in the water, shall carry and show the same lights as other vessels under way.

(c) All vessels, when trawling, dredging, or fishing with any kind of drag-nets or lines, shall exhibit, from some part of the vessel where they can be best seen, two lights. One of these lights shall be red and the other shall be white. The red light shall be above the white light, and shall be at a vertical distance from it of not less than six feet and not more than twelve feet; and the horizontal distance between them, if any, shall not be more than ten feet. These two lights shall be of such a character and contained in lanterns of such construction as to be visible all round the horizon, the white light a distance of not less than three miles and the red light of not less than two miles.

(d) Rafts, or other water craft not herein provided for, navigating by hand power, horse power, or by the current of the river, shall carry one or more good white lights, which shall be placed in such manner as shall be prescribed by the Board of Supervising Inspectors of Steam Vessels.

Art. 10. A vessel which is being overtaken by another, except a steam-vessel with an after range-light showing all around the horizon, shall show from her stern to such last-mentioned vessel a white light or a flare-up light.

Art. 11. A vessel under one hundred and fifty feet in length when at anchor shall carry forward, where it can best be seen, but at a height not exceeding twenty feet above the hull, a white light, in a lantern so constructed as to show a clear, uniform, and unbroken light visible all around the horizon at a distance of at least one mile.

A vessel of one hundred and fifty feet or upwards in length when at anchor shall carry in the forward part of the vessel, at a height of not less than twenty and not exceeding forty feet above the hull, one such light, and at or near the stern of the vessel, and at such a height that it shall be not less than fifteen feet lower than the forward light, another such light.

The length of a vessel shall be deemed to be the length appearing in her certificate of registry.

Art. 12. Every vessel may, if necessary, in order to attract attention, in addition to the lights which she is by these rules required to carry, show a flare-up light or use any detonating signal that can not be mistaken for a distress signal.

Art. 13. Nothing in these rules shall interfere with the operation of any special rules made by the Government of any nation with respect to additional station and signal lights for two or more ships of war or for vessels sailing under convoy, or with the exhibition of recognition signals adopted by shipowners, which have been authorized by their respective Governments, and duly registered and published.

Art. 14. A steam-vessel proceeding under sail only, but having her funnel up, may carry in daytime, forward, where it can best be seen, one black ball or shape two feet in diameter.

SOUND SIGNALS FOR FOG, AND SO FORTH

Art. 15. All signals prescribed by this article for vessels under way shall be given:

1. By "steam-vessels" on the whistle or siren.

2. By "sailing-vessels" and "vessels towed" on the fog horn.

The words "prolonged blast" used in this article shall mean a blast of from four to six seconds duration.

A steam-vessel shall be provided with an efficient whistle or siren, sounded by steam or by some substitute for steam, so placed that the sound may not be intercepted by any obstruction, and with an efficient fog horn; also with an efficient bell. A sailing-vessel of twenty tons gross tonnage or upward shall be provided with a similar fog horn and bell.

In fog, mist, falling snow, or heavy rainstorms, whether by day or night, the signals described in this article shall be used as follows, namely:

(a) A steam-vessel under way shall sound, at intervals of not more than one minute, a prolonged blast.

(c) A sailing-vessel under way shall sound, at intervals of not more than one minute, when on the starboard tack, one blast; when on the port tack, two blasts in succession, and when with the wind abaft the beam, three blasts in succession.

(d) A vessel when at anchor shall, at intervals of not more than one minute, ring the bell rapidly for about five seconds.

(e) A steam-vessel when towing, shall, instead of the signals prescribed in subdivision (a) of this article, at intervals of not more than one minute, sound three blasts in succession, namely, one prolonged blast followed by two short blasts. A vessel towed may give this signal and she shall not give any other.

(f) All rafts or other water craft, not herein provided for, navigating by hand power, horse power, or by the current of the river, shall sound a blast of the fog-horn, or equivalent signal, at intervals of not more than one minute.

Art. 16. Every vessel shall, in a fog, mist, falling snow, or heavy rainstorms, go at a moderate speed, having careful regard to the existing circumstances and conditions.

A steam-vessel hearing, apparently forward of her beam, the fog-signal of a vessel the position of which is not ascertained shall, so far as the circumstances of the case admit, stop her engines, and then navigate with caution until danger of collision is over.

STEERING AND SAILING RULES [5]

Preliminary—Risk of Collision

Risk of collision can, when circumstances permit, be ascertained by carefully watching the compass bearing of an approaching vessel. If the bearing does not appreciably change, such risk should be deemed to exist.

Art. 17. When two sailing-vessels are approaching one another, so as to involve risk of collision, one of them shall keep out of the way of the other as follows, namely:

(a) A vessel which is running free shall keep out of the way of a vessel which is close-hauled.

(b) A vessel which is close-hauled on the port tack shall keep out of the way of a vessel which is close-hauled on the starboard tack.

(c) When both are running free, with the wind on different sides, the vessel which has the wind on the port side shall keep out of the way of the other.

(d) When both are running free, with the wind on the same side, the vessel which is to the windward shall keep out of the way of the vessel which is to the leeward.

(e) A vessel which has the wind aft shall keep out of the way of the other vessel.

Art. 18. Rule I. When steam-vessels are approaching each other head and head, that is, end on, or nearly so, it shall be the duty of each to pass on the port side of the other; and either vessel shall give, as a signal of her intention, one short and distinct blast of her whistle, which the other vessel shall answer promptly by a similar blast of her whistle, and thereupon such vessels shall pass on the port side of each other. But if the courses of such vessels are so far on the starboard of each other as not to be considered as meeting head and head, either vessel shall immediately give two short and distinct blasts of her whistle, which the other vessel shall answer promptly by two similar blasts of her whistle, and they shall pass on the starboard side of each other.

[5] *See also* Figure 241, Chapter II.

The foregoing only applies to cases where vessels are meeting end on or nearly end on, in such a manner as to involve risk of collision; in other words, to cases in which, by day, each vessel sees the masts of the other in a line, or nearly in a line, with her own, and by night to cases in which each vessel is in such a position as to see both the side-lights of the other.

It does not apply by day to cases in which a vessel sees another ahead crossing her own course, or by night to cases where the red light of one vessel is opposed to the red light of the other, or where the green light of one vessel is opposed to the green light of the other, or where a red light without a green light or a green light without a red light, is seen ahead, or where both green and red lights are seen any where but ahead.

Rule III. If, when steam-vessels are approaching each other, either vessel fails to understand the course or intention of the other, from any cause, the vessel so in doubt shall immediately signify the same by giving several short and rapid blasts, not less than four, of the steam-whistle.

Rule V. Whenever a steam-vessel is nearing a short bend or curve in the channel, where, from the height of the banks or other cause, a steam-vessel approaching from the opposite direction can not be seen for a distance of half a mile, such steam-vessel, when she shall have arrived within half a mile of such curve or bend, shall give a signal by one long blast of the steam whistle, which signal shall be answered by a similar blast, given by any approaching steam-vessel that may be within hearing. Should such signal be so answered by a steam-vessel upon the farther side of such bend, then the usual signals for meeting and passing shall immediately be given and answered; but, if the first alarm signal of such vessel be not answered, she is to consider the channel clear and govern herself accordingly.

When steam-vessels are moved from their docks or berths, and other boats are liable to pass from any direction toward them, they shall give the same signal as in the case of vessels meeting at a bend, but immediately after clearing the berths so as to be fully in sight they shall be governed by the steering and sailing rules.

Rule VIII. When steam-vessels are running in the same direction, and the vessel which is astern shall desire to pass on the right or starboard hand of the vessel ahead, she shall give one short blast of the steam-whistle, as a signal of such desire, and if the vessel ahead answers with one blast, she shall direct her course to starboard; or if she shall desire to pass on the left or port side of the vessel ahead, she shall give two short blasts of the steam-whistle as a signal of such desire, and if the vessel ahead answers with two blasts, shall direct her course to port; or if the vessel ahead does not think it safe for the vessel astern to attempt to pass at that point, she shall immediately signify the same by giving several short and rapid blasts of the steam-whistle, not less than four, and under no circumstances shall the vessel astern attempt to pass the vessel ahead until such time as they have reached a point where it can be safely done, when said vessel ahead shall signify her willingness by blowing the proper signals. The vessel ahead shall in no case attempt to cross the bow or crowd upon the course of the passing vessel.

Rule IX. The whistle signals provided in the rules under this article, for steam-vessels meeting, passing, or overtaking, are never to be used except when steamers are in sight of each other, and the course and position of each can be determined in the daytime by a sight of the vessel itself, or by night by seeing its signal lights. In fog, mist, falling snow or heavy rainstorms, when vessels can not see each other, fog-signals only must be given.

Art. 19. When two steam-vessels are crossing, so as to involve risk of collision, the vessel which has the other on her own starboard side shall keep out of the way of the other.

Art. 20. When a steam-vessel and a sailing-vessel are proceeding in such directions as to involve risk of collision, the steam-vessel shall keep out of the way of the sailing-vessel.

Art. 21. Where, by any of these rules, one of the two vessels is to keep out of the way, the other shall keep her course and speed.

Art. 22. Every vessel which is directed by these rules to keep out of the way of another vessel shall, if the circumstances of the case admit, avoid crossing ahead of the other.

Art. 23. Every steam-vessel which is directed by these rules to keep out of the way of another vessel shall, on approaching her, if necessary, slacken her speed or stop or reverse.

Art. 24. Notwithstanding anything contained in these rules every vessel, overtaking any other, shall keep out of the way of the overtaken vessel.

Every vessel coming up with another vessel from any direction more than two points abaft her beam, that is, in such a position, with reference to the vessel which she is overtaking that at night she would be unable to see either of that vessel's side-lights, shall be deemed to be an overtaking vessel; and no subsequent alteration of the bearing between the two vessels shall make the overtaking vessel a crossing vessel within the meaning of these rules, or relieve her of the duty of keeping clear of the overtaken vessel until she is finally past and clear.

As by day the overtaking vessel can not always know with certainty whether she is forward of or abaft this direction from the other vessel she should, if in doubt, assume that she is an overtaking vessel and keep out of the way.

Art. 25. In narrow channels every steam-vessel shall, when it is safe and practicable, keep to that side of the fair-way or mid-channel which lies on the starboard side of such vessel.

Art. 26. Sailing-vessels under way shall keep out of the way of sailing-vessels or boats fishing with nets, or lines, or trawls. This rule shall not give to any vessel or boat engaged in fishing the right of obstructing a fair-way used by vessels other than fishing-vessels or boats.

Art. 27. In obeying and construing these rules due regard shall be had to all dangers of navigation and collision, and to any special circumstances which may render a departure from the above rules necessary in order to avoid immediate danger.

SOUND SIGNALS FOR VESSELS IN SIGHT OF ONE ANOTHER

Art. 28. When vessels are in sight of one another a steam-vessel under way whose engines are going at full speed astern shall indicate that fact by three short blasts on the whistle.

NO VESSEL UNDER ANY CIRCUMSTANCES TO NEGLECT PROPER PRECAUTIONS

Art. 29. Nothing in these rules shall exonerate any vessel, or the owner or master or crew thereof, from the consequences of any neglect to carry lights or signals, or of any neglect to keep a proper lookout, or of the neglect of any precaution which may be required by the ordinary practice of seamen, or by the special circumstances of the case.

Art. 30. The exhibition of any light on board of a vessel of war of the United States or a revenue cutter may be suspended whenever, in the opinion of the Secretary of the Navy, the commander in chief of a squadron, or the commander of a vessel acting singly, the special character of the service may require it.

DISTRESS SIGNALS

Art. 31. When a vessel is in distress and requires assistance from other vessels or from the shore the following shall be the signals to be used or displayed by her, either together or separately, namely:

In the Daytime

A continuous sounding with any fog-signal apparatus, or firing a gun.

At Night

First. Flames on the vessel as from a burning tar barrel, oil barrel, and so forth.

Second. A continuous sounding with any fog-signal apparatus, or firing a gun.

Art. 32. All orders to helmsmen shall be given as follows:

"Right Rudder" to mean "Direct the vessel's head to starboard."

"Left Rudder" to mean "Direct the vessel's head to port."

Sec. 2. That the supervising inspectors of steam vessels and the Director of the Bureau of Marine Inspection and Navigation shall establish such rules to be observed by steam vessels in passing each other and as to the lights to be carried by ferryboats and by barges and canal boats when in tow of steam vessels, and as to the lights and day signals to be carried by vessels, dredges of all types, and vessels working on wrecks by [or] other obstruction to navigation or moored for submarine operations, or made fast to a sunken object which may drift with the tide or be towed, not inconsistent with the provisions of this Act, as they from time to time may deem necessary for safety, which rules when approved by the Secretary of Commerce are hereby declared special rules duly made by local authority, as provided for in article thirty of chapter eight hundred and two of the laws of eighteen hundred and ninety. Two printed copies of such rules shall be furnished to such ferryboats, barges, dredges, canal boats, vessels working on wrecks, and steam vessels, which rules shall be kept posted up in conspicuous places in such vessels, barges, dredges, and boats.

Sec. 3. That every pilot, engineer, mate, or master of any steam-vessel, and every master or mate of any barge or canal boat, who neglects or refuses to observe the provisions of this Act, or the regulations established in pursuance of the preceding section, shall be liable to a penalty of fifty dollars, and for all damages sustained by any passenger in his person or baggage by such neglect or refusal: *Provided,* That nothing herein shall relieve any vessel, owner, or corporation from any liability incurred by reason of such neglect or refusal.

Sec. 4. That every vessel that shall be navigated without complying with the provisions of this Act shall be liable to a penalty of two hundred dollars, one-half to go to the informer, for which sum the vessel so navigated shall be liable and may be seized and proceeded against by action in any district court of the United States having jurisdiction of the offense.

Sec. 5. That sections forty-two hundred and thirty-three and forty-four hundred and twelve (with the regulations made in pursuance thereof, except the rules and regulations for the government of pilots of steamers navigating the Red River of the North and rivers emptying into the Gulf of Mexico and their tributaries, and except the rules for the Great Lakes and their connecting and tributary waters as far east as Montreal), and forty-four hundred and thirteen of the Revised Statutes of the United States, and chapter two hundred and two of the laws of eighteen hundred and ninety-three, and sections one and three of chapter one hundred and two of the laws of eighteen hundred and ninety-five, and sections five, twelve, and thirteen of the Act approved March third, eighteen hundred and ninety-seven, entitled "An Act to amend the laws relating to navigation," and all amendments thereto, are hereby repealed so far as the harbors, rivers, and inland waters aforesaid (except the Great Lakes and their connecting and tributary waters as far east as Montreal and the Red River of the North and rivers emptying into the Gulf of Mexico, and their tributaries) are concerned.

Sec. 6. That this Act shall take effect four months from the date of its approval.

Approved, June 7, 1897.

PILOT RULES

Pilot Rules for All Harbors, Rivers, and Inland Waters of the United States, except the Great Lakes and Their Connecting and Tributary Waters As Far East As Montreal and the Red River of the North and Rivers Emptying into the Gulf of Mexico and Their Tributaries

---

Rules and regulations for the government of pilots of vessels propelled by steam, gas, fluid, naphtha, or electric motors, and of other vessels propelled by machinery, navigating the harbors, rivers, and inland waters of the United States, except the Great Lakes and their connecting and tributary waters as far east as Montreal, the Red River of the North, and rivers emptying into the Gulf of Mexico and their tributaries, as amended by the Board of United States Supervising Inspectors, Steamboat-Inspection Service, on February 27, 1912, and approved by the Secretary of Commerce, under the authority of an act of Congress approved June 7, 1897, and the acts of Congress approved February 14, 1903, and March 4, 1913, establishing the Department of Commerce.

THESE RULES SHALL BE EFFECTIVE ON AND AFTER MAY 1, 1912

PRELIMINARY

503. In the following rules the words *steam vessel* shall include any vessel propelled by machinery.

A vessel is *under way*, within the meaning of these rules, when she is not at anchor, or made fast to the shore, or aground.

Risk of collision can, when circumstances permit, be ascertained by carefully watching the compass bearing of an approaching vessel. If the bearing does not appreciably change, such risk should be deemed to exist.

SIGNALS

The whistle *signals* provided in these rules shall be sounded on an efficient whistle or siren sounded by steam or by some substitute for steam.

A *short blast* of the whistle shall mean a blast of about one second's duration.

A *prolonged blast* of the whistle shall mean a blast of from four to six seconds' duration.[6]

One short blast of the whistle signifies intention to direct course to own starboard, except when two steam vessels are approaching each other at right angles or obliquely, when it signifies intention of steam vessel which is to starboard of the other to hold course and speed.

Two short blasts of the whistle signify intention to direct course to own port.

Three short blasts of the whistle shall mean, "My engines are going at full speed astern."

When vessels are in sight of one another a steam vessel under way whose engines are going at full speed astern shall indicate that fact by three short blasts on the whistle.

Rule I. If, when steam vessels are approaching each other, either vessel fails to understand the course or intention of the other, from any cause, the vessel so in doubt shall immediately signify the same by giving several short and rapid blasts, not less than four, of the steam whistle, the DANGER SIGNAL.

Rule II. Steam vessels are forbidden to use what has become technically known among pilots as "CROSS SIGNALS," that is, answering one whistle with two, and answering two whistles with one.

Rule III. The SIGNALS FOR PASSING, by the blowing of the whistle, shall be given and answered by pilots, in compliance with these rules, not only when meeting "head and head," or nearly so, but at all times when the steam vessels are in sight of each other, when passing or meeting at a distance within half a mile of each other, and whether passing to the starboard or port.

The whistle signals provided in the rules for steam vessels meeting, passing, or overtaking are never to be used except when steam vessels are in sight of each other, and the course and position of each can be determined in the daytime by a sight of the vessel itself, or by night by seeing its signal lights. In fog, mist, falling snow, or heavy rainstorms, when vessels can not so see each other, fog signals only must be given.

SITUATIONS

Rule IV. When steam vessels are APPROACHING EACH OTHER HEAD

[6] Under the provisions of par. (a), sec. 4, of act of Congress approved June 9, 1910, "a blast of at least two seconds shall be deemed a prolonged blast within the meaning of the law," when given by vessels propelled by machinery and not more than 65 feet in length, except tugboats and towboats propelled by steam.

AND HEAD, THAT IS, END ON, OR NEARLY SO, it shall be the duty of each
to pass on the port side of the other, and either vessel shall give, as
a signal of her intention one short and distinct blast of her whistle,
which the other vessel shall answer promptly by a similar blast of her
whistle, and thereupon such vessels shall pass on the port side of each
other. But if the courses of such vessels are so far on the starboard
of each other as not to be considered as meeting head and head, either
vessel shall immediately give two short and distinct blasts of her
whistle, which the other vessel shall answer promptly by two similar
blasts of her whistle, and they shall pass on the starboard side of each
other.

The foregoing only applies to cases where vessels are meeting end
on or nearly end on, in such a manner as to involve risk of collision;
in other words, to cases in which, by day, each vessel sees the masts of
the other in a line, or nearly in a line, with her own, and by night to
cases in which each vessel is in such a position as to see both the side
lights of the other.

It does not apply by day to cases in which a vessel sees another
ahead crossing her own course, or by night to cases where the red
light of one vessel is opposed to the red light of the other, or where
the green light of one vessel is opposed to the green light of the other,
or where a red light without a green light or a green light without a
red light is seen ahead, or where both green and red lights are seen
anywhere but ahead.

Rule V. Whenever a steam vessel is NEARING A SHORT BEND OR CURVE
IN THE CHANNEL, where, from the height of the banks or other cause,
a steam vessel approaching from the opposite direction can not be
seen for a distance of half a mile, such steam vessel, when she shall
have arrived within half a mile of such curve or bend, shall give a
signal by one long blast of the steam whistle, which signal shall be
answered by a similar blast, given by any approaching steam vessel
that may be within hearing. Should such signal be so answered by a
steam vessel upon the farther side of such bend, then the usual signals
for meeting and passing shall immediately be given and answered;
but, if the first alarm signal of such vessel be not answered, she is to
consider the channel clear and govern herself accordingly.

WHEN STEAM VESSELS ARE MOVED FROM THEIR DOCKS OR BERTHS, and
other boats are liable to pass from any direction toward them, they
shall give the same signal as in the case of vessels meeting at a bend,

but immediately after clearing the berths so as to be fully in sight they shall be governed by the steering and sailing rules.

Rule VI. WHEN STEAM VESSELS ARE RUNNING IN THE SAME DIRECTION, and the vessel which is astern shall desire to pass on the right or starboard hand of the vessel ahead, she shall give one short blast of the steam whistle, as a signal of such desire, and if the vessel ahead answers with one blast, she shall direct her course to starboard; or if she shall desire to pass on the left or port side of the vessel ahead, she shall give two short blasts of the steam whistle as a signal of such desire, and if the vessel ahead answers with two blasts, shall direct her course to port; or if the vessel ahead does not think it safe for the vessel astern to attempt to pass at that point, she shall immediately signify the same by giving several short and rapid blasts of the steam whistle, not less than four, and under no circumstances shall the vessel astern attempt to pass the vessel ahead until such time as they have reached a point where it can be safely done, when said vessel ahead shall signify her willingness by blowing the proper signals. The vessel ahead shall in no case attempt to cross the bow or crowd upon the course of the passing vessel.

Every vessel coming up with another vessel from any direction more than two point abaft her beam, that is, in such a position with reference to the vessel which she is overtaking that at night she would be unable to see either of that vessel's side lights, shall be deemed to be *an overtaking vessel;* and no subsequent alteration of the bearing between the two vessels shall make the overtaking vessel a crossing vessel within the meaning of these rules, or relieve her of the duty of keeping clear of the overtaken vessel until she is finally past and clear.

As by day the overtaking vessel can not always know with certainty whether she is forward of or abaft this direction from the other vessel she should, if in doubt, assume that she is an overtaking vessel and keep out of the way.

Rule VII. When two steam vessels are APPROACHING EACH OTHER AT RIGHT ANGLES OR OBLIQUELY SO AS TO INVOLVE RISK OF COLLISION, other than when one steam vessel is overtaking another, the steam vessel which has the other on her own port side shall hold her course and speed; and the steam vessel which has the other on her own starboard side shall keep out of the way of the other by directing her course to starboard so as to cross the stern of the other steam vessel, or, if necessary to do so, slacken her speed or stop or reverse.

If from any cause the conditions covered by this situation are such as to prevent immediate compliance with each other's signals, the misunderstanding or objection shall be at once made apparent by blowing the danger signal, and both steam vessels shall be stopped and backed if necessary, until signals for passing with safety are made and understood.

Rule VIII. When a STEAM VESSEL AND A SAILING VESSEL are proceeding in such directions as to involve risk of collision, the steam vessel shall keep out of the way of the sailing vessel.

Rule IX. Every steam vessel which is directed by these rules to KEEP OUT OF THE WAY of another vessel shall, if the circumstances of the case admit, avoid crossing ahead of the other.

Rule X. In NARROW CHANNELS every steam vessel shall, when it is safe and practicable, keep to that side of the fairway or mid-channel which lies on the starboard side of such vessel.

Rule XI. In obeying and construing these rules due regard shall be had to all DANGERS OF NAVIGATION AND COLLISION, and to any SPECIAL CIRCUMSTANCES which may render a departure from the above rules necessary in order to avoid immediate danger.

SOUND SIGNALS FOR FOG, AND SO FORTH

Rule XII. In fog, mist, falling snow, or heavy rainstorms, whether by day or night, signals shall be given as follows:

A steam vessel under way, except when towing other vessels or being towed, shall sound, at intervals of not more than one minute, on the whistle or siren, a prolonged blast.

A steam vessel when towing other vessels shall sound, at intervals of not more than one minute, on the whistle or siren, three blasts in succession, namely, one prolonged blast followed by two short blasts.

A vessel towed may give, at intervals of not more than one minute, on the fog horn, a signal of three blasts in succession, namely, one prolonged blast followed by two short blasts, and she shall not give any other.

A vessel when at anchor shall, at intervals of not more than one minute, ring the bell rapidly for about five seconds.

SPEED TO BE MODERATE IN FOG, AND SO FORTH

Rule XIII. Every steam vessel shall, in a fog, mist, falling snow, or heavy rainstorms, go at a *moderate speed,* having careful regard to the existing circumstances and conditions.

A steam vessel hearing, apparently forward of her beam, the fog signal of a vessel the position of which is not ascertained shall, so far as the circumstances of the case admit, stop her engines and then navigate with caution until danger of collision is over.

POSTING OF PILOT RULES

On steam and other motor vessels of over 100 gross tons, two copies of the placard form of these rules (Form 803) shall be kept posted up in conspicuous places in the vessel, one copy of which shall be kept posted up in the pilot house. On steam and other motor vessels of over 25 gross tons and not over 100 gross tons, two copies of the placard form of the pilot rules shall be kept on board, one copy of which shall be kept posted up in the pilot house. On steam and other motor vessels of 25 gross tons and under, and of more than 10 gross tons, two copies of the placard form of the pilot rules shall be kept on board, and, where practicable, one copy thereof shall be kept conspicuously posted up in the vessel. On steam and other motor vessels of not more than 10 gross tons, two copies of the pamphlet form of the pilot rules shall be kept on board, and, where practicable, one copy thereof shall be kept conspicuously posted up in the vessel. (Authority: Sec. 2, act of Congress approved June 7, 1897.)

RULES FOR LIGHTS

Rules for Lights for Certain Classes of Vessels Navigating the Harbors, Rivers, and Inland Waters of the United States, except the Great Lakes and Their Connecting and Tributary Waters As Far East As Montreal and the Red River of the North and Rivers Emptying into the Gulf of Mexico and Their Tributaries

----

504. The following rules for lights to be carried by ferryboats, rules for lights for barges and canal boats in tow of steam vessels, rules for lights for rafts and other water craft navigating by hand power, horsepower, or by the current of the river, rule relating to use of search-lights, rule prohibiting unnecessary sounding of the steam whistle, rule prohibiting the carrying of unauthorized lights on steam vessels, and rule relating to drawbridges over navigable waters of the United States were adopted by the Board of Supervising Inspectors, Steam-boat-Inspection Service, and approved by the Secretary of Commerce.

These rules concerning lights shall be complied with in all weathers from sunset to sunrise.

RULES FOR LIGHTS TO BE CARRIED BY FERRY-BOATS NAVIGATING THE HARBORS, RIVERS, AND INLAND WATERS OF THE UNITED STATES, EXCEPT THE GREAT LAKES AND THEIR CON-NECTING AND TRIBUTARY WATERS AS FAR EAST AS MONTREAL AND THE RED RIVER OF THE NORTH AND RIVERS EMPTYING INTO THE GULF OF MEXICO AND THEIR TRIBUTARIES [7]

[Authority: Section 2, act of Congress approved June 7, 1897]

Ferryboats propelled by machinery and navigating the harbors, rivers, and other inland waters of the United States, except the Great Lakes and their connecting and tributary waters as far east as Montreal and the Red River of the North and rivers emptying into the Gulf of Mexico and their tributaries, shall carry the range lights and the colored side lights required by law to be carried on steam vessels navigating those waters, except that *double-end ferryboats* shall carry a central range of clear, bright, white lights, showing all around the horizon, placed at equal altitudes forward and aft, also on the starboard side a green light, and on the port side a red light, of such a character as to be visible on a dark night with a clear atmosphere at a distance of at least 2 miles, and so constructed as to show a uniform and unbroken light over an arc of the horizon of 10 points of the compass, and so fixed as to throw the light from right ahead to 2 points abaft the beam on their respective sides.

[7] See act of Congress approved June 9, 1910, effective on and after July 9, 1910, prescribing lights that shall be carried by certain classes of vessels of not more than 65 feet in length.

The green and red lights shall be fitted with inboard screens projecting at least 3 feet forward from the lights, so as to prevent them from being seen across the bow.

Local inspectors in districts having ferryboats shall, whenever the safety of navigation may require, designate for each line of such boats a certain light, white or colored, which will show all around the horizon, to designate and distinguish such lines from each other, which light shall be carried on a flagstaff amidships, 15 feet above the white range lights.

RULES FOR LIGHTS FOR BARGES AND CANAL BOATS IN TOW OF STEAM VESSELS AND FOR LIGHTS AND DAY SIGNALS FOR DREDGES, VESSELS WORKING ON WRECKS, ETC., NAVIGATING THE HARBORS, RIVERS, AND OTHER INLAND WATERS OF THE UNITED STATES, EXCEPT THE GREAT LAKES AND THEIR CONNECTING AND TRIBUTARY WATERS AS FAR EAST AS MONTREAL AND THE RED RIVER OF THE NORTH AND RIVERS EMPTYING INTO THE GULF OF MEXICO AND THEIR TRIBUTARIES

[Authority: Section 2, act of Congress approved June 7, 1897]

These rules concerning lights shall be complied with in all weathers from sunset to sunrise and shall be effective on and after September 1, 1914.

LIGHTS FOR BARGES AND CANAL BOATS IN TOW OF STEAM VESSELS ON CERTAIN INLAND WATERS ON THE SEABOARD, EXCEPT THE HUDSON RIVER AND ADJACENT WATERS AND LAKE CHAMPLAIN

On the harbors, rivers, and other inland waters of the United States, except the Great Lakes and their connecting and tributary waters as far east as Montreal and the Red River of the North and rivers emptying into the Gulf of Mexico and their tributaries, and except on the waters of the Hudson River and its tributaries from Troy to the boundary lines of New York Harbor off Sandy Hook as defined pursuant to section 2 of the act of Congress of February 19, 1895, the East River, and Long Island Sound (and the waters entering thereon, and to the Atlantic Ocean), to and including Narragansett Bay, R. I., and tributaries, and Lake Champlain, barges (except scows) and canal boats in tow of steam vessels shall carry lights as follows:

Barges and canal boats towing astern of steam vessels, when towing singly, or what is known as tandem towing, shall each carry a green light on the starboard side and a red light on the port side, and a white light on the stern, except that the last vessel of such tow shall carry two lights on her stern, athwartship, horizontal to each other, not less than 5 feet apart, and not less than 4 feet above the deck house, and so placed as to show all around the horizon.

When two or more boats are abreast, the colored lights shall be carried at the outer sides of the bows of the outside boats. Each of the outside boats in last tier of a hawser tow shall carry a white light on her stern.

The white light required to be carried on stern of a barge or canal boat carrying red and green side lights shall be carried in a lantern so constructed that it shall show an unbroken light over an arc of the horizon of 12 points of the compass, namely, for 6 points from right aft on each side of the vessel, and shall be of such a character as to be visible on a dark night with a clear atmosphere at a distance of at least 2 miles.

Barges or canal boats towing alongside a steam vessel shall, if the deck, deck houses, or cargo of the barge or canal boat be so high above water as to obscure the side lights of the towing steamer when being towed on the starboard side of the steamer, carry a green light upon the starboard side; and when towed on the port side of the steamer, a red light on the port side of the barge or canal boat; and if there is more than one barge or canal boat abreast, the colored lights shall be displayed from the outer side of the outside barges or canal boats.

The colored side lights referred to in these rules for barges and canal boats in tow shall be fitted with inboard screens, so as to prevent them from being seen across the bow, and of such a character as to be visible on a dark night, with a clear atmosphere, at a distance of at least 2 miles, and so constructed as to show a uniform and unbroken light over an arc of the horizon of 10 points of the compass, and so fixed as to throw the light from right ahead to 2 points abaft the beam on either side. The minimum size of glass globes shall not be less than 6 inches in diameter and 5 inches high in the clear.

Scows when being towed by steam vessels on the waters covered by the first paragraph of these rules shall carry a white light at each end of each scow, except that when such scows are massed in tiers, two or more abreast, each of the outside scows shall carry a white light on its outer bow, and the outside scows in the last tier shall each carry, in addition, a white light on the outer part of the stern. The white light shall be carried not less than 8 feet above the surface of the water, and shall be so placed as to show an unbroken light all around the horizon, and shall be of such a character as to be visible on a dark night with a clear atmosphere at a distance of at least 5 miles.

LIGHTS FOR BARGES AND CANAL BOATS IN TOW OF STEAM VESSELS ON THE HUDSON RIVER AND ADJACENT WATERS AND LAKE CHAMPLAIN [8]

All nondescript vessels known as scows, car floats, lighters, and vessels of similar type, navigating the waters referred to in the following rules, shall carry the lights required to be carried by barges and canal boats in tow of steam vessels, as prescribed in such rules.

Barges and canal boats, when being towed by steam vessels on the waters of the Hudson River and its tributaries from Troy to the boundary lines of New York Harbor off Sandy Hook, as defined pursuant to section 2 of the act of Congress of February 19, 1895, the East River and Long Island Sound (and the waters entering thereon, and to the Atlantic Ocean), to and including Narragansett Bay, R. I., and tributaries, and Lake Champlain, shall carry lights as follows:

Barges and canal boats being towed astern of steam vessels when towing singly shall carry a white light on the bow and a white light on the stern.

When towing in tandem, "close up," each boat shall carry a white light on its stern and the first or hawser boat shall, in addition, carry a white light on its bow.

[8] Adopted by the Board of Supervising Inspectors on January 27, 1933, and approved by the Secretary of Commerce on February 6, 1933.

When towing in tandem with intermediate hawser between the various boats in the tow, each boat shall carry a white light on the bow and a white light on the stern, except that the last vessel in the tow shall carry two white lights on her stern, athwartship, horizontal to each other, not less than 5 feet apart and not less than 4 feet above the deck house, and so placed as to show all around the horizon: *Provided,* That seagoing barges shall not be required to make any change in their seagoing lights (red and green) on waters coming within the scope of these rules, except that the last vessel of the tow shall carry two white lights on her stern, athwartship, horizontal to each other, not less than 5 feet apart, and not less than 4 feet above the deck house, and so placed as to show all around the horizon.

Barges and canal boats when towed at a hawser, two or more abreast, when in one tier, shall each carry a white light on the stern and a white light on the bow of each of the outside boats.

When in more than one tier, each boat shall carry a white light on its stern and the outside boats in the hawser or head tier shall each carry, in addition, a white light on the bow.

The white bow lights for barges and canal boats referred to in the preceding rules shall be carried at least 10 feet and not more than 30 feet abaft the stem or extreme forward end of the vessel On barges and canal boats required to carry a white bow light, the white light on bow and the white light on stern shall each be so placed above the hull or deck house as to show an unbroken light all around the horizon, and of such a character as to be visible on a dark night with a clear atmosphere at a distance of at least 2 miles.

When nondescript vessels known as scows, car floats, lighters, barges or canal boats, and vessels of similar type, are towed alongside a steam vessel, there shall be displayed a white light at the outboard corners of the tow.

PROPULSION OF BARGE OR BARGES BY PUSHING [9]

When under way between the hours of sunset and sunrise there shall be displayed a red light on the port bow and a green light on

[9] Adopted by the Board of Supervising Inspectors on January 25, 1935, and approved by the Secretary of Commerce on June 18, 1935.

the starboard bow of the head barge or barges, properly screened and so arranged that they may be visible through an arc of the horizon of 10 points of the compass; that is, from right ahead to 2 points abaft the beam on either side and visible on a dark night with a clear atmosphere at a distance of at least 2 miles, and be carried at a height sufficiently above the superstructure of the barge or barges pushed ahead as to permit said side lights to be visible.

Dump scows [10] utilized for the transportation and disposal of garbage, street sweepings, ashes, excavated material, dredgings, etc., when navigating on the Hudson River or East River or the waters tributary thereto between loading points on these waters and the dumping grounds established by competent authority outside the line dividing the high seas from the inland waters of New York Harbor, shall, when towing in tandem, carry, instead of the white lights previously required, red and green side lights on the respective and appropriate sides of the scow in addition to the white light required to be shown by an overtaken vessel.

The red and green lights herein prescribed shall be carried at an elevation of not less than 8 feet above the highest deck house, upon substantial uprights, the lights properly screened and so arranged as to show through an arc of the horizon of 10 points of the compass, that is, from right ahead to 2 points abaft the beam on either side and visible on a dark night with a clear atmosphere a distance of at least 2 miles.

Provided, That nothing in these rules shall be construed as compelling barges or canal boats in tow of steam vessels, passing through any waters coming within the scope of these rules where lights for barges or canal boats are different from those of the waters whereon such vessels are usually employed, to change their lights from those required on the waters from which their trip begins or terminates; but should such vessels engage in local employment on waters requiring different lights from those where they are customarily employed, they shall comply with the local rules where employed.

---

[10] Rule relating to dump scows adopted by the executive committee of the Board of Supervising Inspectors on November 18, 1924, and approved by the Secretary of Commerce on November 19, 1924. Later ratified by the Board of Supervising Inspectors and approved by the Secretary of Commerce.

Rules for Lights and Day Signals to be Carried by Vessels, Dredges
of All Types, and Vessels Working on Wrecks or other Obstructions
to Navigation, or Moored for Submarine Operations or Made Fast
to a Sunken Object Which May Drift with the Tide or be Towed [11]

[Authority: Section 2, act of Congress approved June 7, 1897, as amended by
act of Congress approved May 25, 1914]

RULE I. RULE FOR SIGNALS TO BE DISPLAYED
BY A TOWING VESSEL WHEN TOWING A
SUBMERGED OR PARTLY SUBMERGED OBJECT
UPON A HAWSER WHEN NO SIGNALS ARE DIS-
PLAYED UPON THE OBJECT WHICH IS TOWED

505. The vessel having the submerged object in tow shall display by
day, where they can best be seen, two shapes, one above the other, not
less than 6 feet apart, the lower shape to be carried not less than 10 feet
above the deck houses. The shapes shall be in the form of a double
frustrum of a cone, base to base, not less than 2 feet in diameter at the
center nor less than 8 inches at the ends of the cones, and to be not
less than 4 feet lengthwise from end to end, the upper shape to be
painted in alternate horizontal stripes of black and white, 8 inches in
width, and the lower shape to be painted a solid bright red.

By night the towing vessel shall display the regular side lights, but
in lieu of the regular white towing lights shall display four lights in
a vertical position not less than 3 feet nor more than 6 feet apart, the
upper and lower of such lights to be white, and the two middle lights
to be red, all of such lights to be of the same character as is now prescribed for the regular towing lights.

RULE 2. RULE FOR STEAMERS, DERRICK BOATS,
LIGHTERS, OR OTHER TYPES OF VESSELS
MADE FAST ALONGSIDE A WRECK, OR MOORED

[11] Adopted by executive committee of Board of Supervising Inspectors on July
22, 1914, and approved by the Secretary of Commerce on July 28, 1914. Adopted
by Board of Supervising Inspectors on January 20, 1915, and approved by the Secretary of Commerce on April 12, 1915.

OVER A WRECK WHICH IS ON THE BOTTOM OR PARTLY SUBMERGED, OR WHICH MAY BE DRIFTING

Steamers, derrick boats, lighters, or other types of vessels made fast alongside a wreck, or moored over a wreck which is on the bottom or partly submerged, or which may be drifting, shall display by day two shapes of the same character and dimensions and displayed in the same manner as required by the foregoing rule, except that both the shapes shall be painted a solid bright red, but where more than one vessel is working under the above conditions, the shapes need be displayed only from one vessel on each side of the wreck from which it can best be seen from all directions.

By night this situation shall be indicated by the display of a white light from the bow and stern of each outside vessel or lighter not less than 6 feet above the deck, and in addition thereto there shall be displayed in a position where they may best be seen from all directions two red lights carried in a vertical line not less than 3 feet nor more than 6 feet apart, and not less than 15 feet above the deck.

RULE 3. RULE FOR DREDGES WHICH ARE HELD IN STATIONARY POSITION BY MOORINGS OR SPUDS

Dredges which are held in stationary position by moorings or spuds shall display by day two red balls not less than 2 feet in diameter and carried in a vertical line not less than 3 feet nor more than 6 feet apart, and at least 15 feet above the deck house and in such a position where they can best be seen from all directions. By night they shall display a white light at each corner, not less than 6 feet above the deck, and in addition thereto there shall be displayed in a position where they may best be seen from all directions two red lights carried in a vertical line not less than 3 feet nor more than 6 feet apart, and not less than 15 feet above the deck. When scows are moored alongside a dredge in the foregoing situation they shall display a white light on each outboard corner, not less than 6 feet above the deck.

RULE 4. RULE FOR SELF-PROPELLING SUCTION DREDGES UNDER WAY WITH THEIR SUCTION ON THE BOTTOM

Self-propelling suction dredges under way with their suction on the bottom shall display by day the same signals as are used to designate any steamer not under control; that is to say, two black balls not less than 2 feet in diameter and carried not less than 15 feet above the deck house, and where they may best be seen from all directions.

By night they shall carry, in addition to the regular running lights, two red lights of the same character as the masthead light, in the same vertical plane and underneath the masthead light, the red lights to be not less than 3 feet nor more than 6 feet apart and the upper red light to be not less than 4 feet and not more than 6 feet below the white masthead light, and on or near the stern two red lights in the same vertical plane not less than 4 feet nor more than 6 feet apart, to show through 4 points of the compass; that is, from right astern to 2 points on each quarter.

RULE 5. RULE FOR VESSELS WHICH ARE MOORED OR ANCHORED AND ENGAGED IN LAYING PIPE OR OPERATING ON SUBMARINE CONSTRUCTION OR EXCAVATION

Vessels which are moored or anchored, and engaged in laying pipe or operating on submarine construction or excavation shall display by day, not less than 15 feet above the deck, where they can best be seen from all directions, two balls not less than 2 feet in diameter, in a vertical line not less than 3 feet and not more than 6 feet apart, the upper ball to be painted in alternate black and white vertical stripes 6 inches wide, and the lower ball to be painted a solid bright red. By night they shall display three red lights, carried in a vertical line not less than 3 feet nor more than 6 feet apart and not less than 15 feet above the deck, and in such position as may best be seen from all directions.

All the lights required by these special rules for dredges, wrecking boats, lighters, etc., shall be of such size and character as to be visible on a dark night with a clear atmosphere for a distance of at least 2 miles.

RULE 6. RULE FOR VESSELS WHICH ARE MOORED OR AT ANCHOR [12]

Vessels of more than 300 gross tons propelled by machinery when moored or anchored in a fairway or channel where traffic is liable to congestion or confusion shall display between sunrise and sunset on the forward part of the vessel where it can best be observed from other vessels one black ball or shape not less than 2 feet in diameter.

RULE 7. RULE FOR LIGHTS TO BE DISPLAYED ON PIPE LINES

Pipe lines attached to dredges, and either floating or supported on trestles, shall display by night one row of white lights not less than 8 feet nor more than 12 feet above the water, about equally spaced and in such number as to mark distinctly the entire length and course of the line, the intervals between lights where the line crosses navigable channels to be not more than 30 feet. There shall also be displayed on the shore or discharge end of the line two red lights, 3 feet apart, in a vertical line with the lower light at least 8 feet above the water, and if the line is to be opened at night for the passage of vessels, a similar arrangement of lights shall be displayed on each side of the opening. The lights shall be of the same size and character as specified in rule 5 above.

RULE 8. RULE FOR PASSING SIGNALS

Vessels intending to pass dredges or other types of floating plant working in navigable channels, when within a reasonable distance therefrom and not in any case over a mile, shall indicate such intention by blowing the passing signal prescribed in the local pilot rules for vessels under way, which shall be answered in the usual manner

[12] Rule 6 was adopted by the executive committee of the Board of Supervising Inspectors on May 19, 1923, and approved by the Secretary of Commerce on May 31, 1923. Adopted by the Board of Supervising Inspectors on January 16, 1924, and approved by the Secretary of Commerce on March 17, 1924.

from said plant if the channel is clear and the approaching vessel may pass on the course indicated; otherwise the floating plant shall sound the alarm or danger signal and the approaching vessel shall slow down or stop and await further signal from the plant.

When the pipe line from a dredge crosses the channel in such a way that an approaching vessel, owing to excessive draft or for other reasons, can not pass around the pipe line or dredge, a signal shall be given from the vessel by sounding 4 blasts of the whistle, which shall be answered by a like signal from the dredge. The pipe line shall then be opened for the passage of the vessel as soon as practicable; when the line is open ready for passage, the dredge shall so indicate by sounding the usual passing signal, and the approaching vessel shall promptly pass the dredge.

RULE 9. RULE FOR SPEED OF VESSELS PASSING FLOATING PLANT WORKING IN CHANNELS

Steamers, with or without tows, passing floating plant working in channels, shall reduce their speed sufficiently to insure the safety of both the said plant and themselves, and when passing within 200 feet of the said plant their speed shall not exceed 5 miles per hour. While passing over lines of the said plant, propelling machinery shall be stopped.

RULE 10. RULE FOR LIGHT-DRAFT VESSELS PASSING FLOATING PLANT

Vessels whose draft permits shall keep outside of the buoys marking the ends of mooring lines of floating plant working in channels.

RULE 11. RULE FOR AIDS TO NAVIGATION MARKING FLOATING-PLANT MOORINGS

Breast, stern, and bow anchors of floating plant working in navigable channels shall be marked by barrel or other suitable buoys. By night approaching vessels shall be shown the location of adjacent buoys by throwing a suitable beam of light from said plant on the buoys until the approaching vessel has passed, or the buoys may be lighted by red lights, visible in all directions, of the same size and character as specified in rule 5 above: *Provided,* That the foregoing provisions of this paragraph shall not apply to floating plant working in the following waters of New York Harbor and adjacent waters; namely, the East River, the North River (Battery to Spuyten Duyvil), the Harlem River, and the New York and New Jersey Channels (from the Upper Bay through the Kill Van Kull, Newark Bay, Arthur Kill, and Raritan Bay to the Lower Bay).

RULE 12. RULE FOR OBSTRUCTION OF CHANNEL BY FLOATING PLANT

Channels shall not be unnecessarily obstructed by any dredge or other floating plant. While vessels are passing such plant, all lines running therefrom across the channel on the passing side, which may interfere with or obstruct navigation, shall be slacked to the bottom of the channel.

RULE 13. RULE FOR PROTECTION OF MARKS PLACED FOR THE GUIDANCE OF FLOATING PLANT

Vessels shall not run over anchor buoys, or buoys, stakes, or other marks placed for the guidance of floating plant working in channels; and shall not anchor on the ranges of buoys, stakes, or other marks placed for the guidance of such plant.

NOTE—If it is necessary to prohibit or limit the anchorage or movement of vessels within certain areas in order to facilitate the work of improvement, application should be made through official channels for establishment by the Secretary of War of special or temporary regulations for this purpose.

RULE 14. RULE FOR CLEARING OF CHANNELS

When special or temporary regulations have not been prescribed and action under these rules and regulations will not afford clear passage, floating plant in narrow channels shall, upon notice, move out of the way of vessels a sufficient distance to allow them a clear passage.

Vessels desiring passage shall, however, give the master of the floating plant ample notice in advance of the time they expect to pass.

RULE 15. RULE FOR REVOCATION OF CONFLICTING REGULATIONS

All regulations or parts of regulations in conflict with these regulations are hereby revoked.

These rules shall be in full force and effect on and after May 19, 1928.

Special Rules & Regulations

RULES FOR LIGHTS FOR RAFTS AND OTHER WATER CRAFT NAVIGATING BY HAND POWER, HORSEPOWER, OR BY THE CURRENT OF THE RIVER, ON THE HARBORS, RIVERS, AND OTHER INLAND WATERS OF THE UNITED STATES, EXCEPT THE GREAT LAKES AND THEIR CONNECTING AND TRIBUTARY WATERS AS FAR EAST AS MONTREAL AND THE RED RIVER OF THE NORTH AND RIVERS EMPTYING INTO THE GULF OF MEXICO AND THEIR TRIBUTARIES

[Authority: Art. 9 (*d*), act of Congress approved June 7, 1897]

Any vessel, except rafts and rowing boats under oars, navigating by *hand power, horsepower, or by the current of the river,* shall carry one white light forward, not less than 8 feet above the surface of the water.

Rafts propelled by hand power or by the current of the river, or which shall be anchored or moored in or near a channel or fairway, shall carry white lights, as follows:

Rafts of one crib and not more than two in length shall carry one white light. Rafts of three or more cribs in length and one crib in width shall carry one white light at each end of the raft. Rafts of more than one crib abreast shall carry one white light on each outside corner of the raft, making four lights in all.

The *white light* required by these rules for rafts and other water craft shall be carried, from sunset to sunrise, in a lantern so fixed and constructed as to show a clear, uniform, and unbroken light, visible all around the horizon, and of such intensity as to be visible on a dark night with a clear atmosphere at a distance of at least 1 mile. The lights for rafts shall be suspended from poles of such height that the lights shall not be less than 8 feet above the surface of the water.

RULE RELATING TO THE USE OF SEARCHLIGHTS

The Board of Supervising Inspectors, at their annual meeting of January 1915, adopted the following rule relating to the use of searchlights:

Any master or pilot of any steam vessel who shall flash or cause to be flashed the rays of the searchlight into the pilot house of a passing vessel shall be deemed guilty of misconduct and shall be liable to have his license suspended or revoked.

RULE PROHIBITING UNNECESSARY SOUNDING OF THE STEAM WHISTLE

[Authority: Act of Congress approved February 8, 1907]

The Board of Supervising Inspectors, at their annual meeting of January 1907, adopted the following rule:

Unnecessary sounding of the steam whistle is prohibited within any harbor limits of the United States. Whenever any licensed officer in charge of any steamer authorizes or permits such unnecessary whistling, upon conviction thereof before any board of inspectors having jurisdiction, such officer shall be suspended from acting under his license as the inspectors trying the case may deem proper.

RULE PROHIBITING THE CARRYING OF UN-AUTHORIZED LIGHTS ON STEAM VESSELS

[Adopted by the Board of Supervising Inspectors on February 16, 1910, and approved by the Secretary of Commerce on March 9, 1910. Authority: Section 4450, Revised Statutes]

Any master or pilot of any steam vessel who shall authorize or permit the carrying of any light, electric or otherwise, not required by law, on the outside structure of the cabin or hull of the vessel that in any way will interfere with distinguishing the signal lights shall, upon conviction thereof before any board of inspectors having jurisdiction, be deemed guilty of misconduct and shall be liable to have his license suspended or revoked.

RULES GOVERNING THE OPERATION OF DRAW BRIDGES OVER NAVIGABLE WATERS OF THE UNITED STATES

It is suggested that pilots of all steamers navigating waters which are spanned by drawbridges under the jurisdiction of the War Department should provide themselves with the War Department rules governing the operation of these drawbridges, and observe the rules.

Act of September 4, 1890, in Regard to Collision at Sea, That Went into Effect December 15, 1890.

BY THE PRESIDENT OF THE UNITED STATES OF AMERICA

A Proclamation

506. Whereas an act of Congress in regard to collisions at sea was approved September 4, 1890, the said act being in the following words:

"Be it enacted by the Senate and House of Representatives of the United States of America in Congress assembled, That in every case of collision between two vessels it shall be the duty of the master or person in charge of each vessel, if and so far as he can do so without serious danger to his own vessel, crew, and passengers (if any), to stay by the other vessel until he has ascertained that she has no need of further assistance, and to render to the other vessel, her master, crew, and passengers (if any) such assistance as may be practicable and as may be necessary in order to save them from any danger caused by the collision, and also to give to the master or person in charge of the other vessel the name of his own vessel and her port of registry, or the port or place to which she belongs, and also the name

of the ports and places from which and to which she is bound. If he fails so to do, and no reasonable cause for such failure is shown, the collision shall, in the absence of proof to the contrary, be deemed to have been caused by his wrongful act, neglect, or default.

"*Sec. 2.* That every master or person in charge of a United States vessel who fails, without reasonable cause, to render such assistance or give such information as aforesaid shall be deemed guilty of a misdemeanor, and shall be liable to a penalty of one thousand dollars, or imprisonment for a term not exceeding two years; and for the above sum the vessel shall be liable and may be seized and proceeded against by process in any district court of the United States by any person; one-half such sum to be payable to the informer and the other half to the United States.

"*Sec. 3.* That this act shall take effect at a time to be fixed by the President by Proclamation issued for that purpose."

And whereas it is provided by section 3 of the said act that it shall take effect at a time to be fixed by the President by proclamation issued for that purpose:

Now, therefore, I, Benjamin Harrison, President of the United States of America, do hereby, in virtue of the authority vested in me by section 3 of the said act, proclaim the fifteenth day of December, 1890, as the day on which the said act shall take effect.

In testimony whereof I have hereunto set my hand and caused the seal of the United States of America to be affixed.

Done at the city of Washington this eighteenth day of November, in the year of our Lord one thousand eight hundred and ninety and of the Independence of the United States the one hundred and fifteenth.

[SEAL]   BENJ. HARRISON.

By the President:

JAMES G. BLAINE, *Secretary of State*.

Regulations for Tows of Seagoing Barges within Inland Waters

507. The following regulations limit the length of hawsers between towing vessels and seagoing barges in tow and the length of such tows within inland waters of the United States, designated and defined from time to time pursuant to section 2 of the act approved February 19, 1895. These regulations have been prepared and are approved by the Secretary of Commerce pursuant to section 14 of the act approved May 28, 1908, entitled "An Act to amend the laws relating to navigation, and for other purposes."

The suspension of these regulations on June 4, 1917, "for the duration of the war or until further notice," has expired by limitation, and said regulations are in full force and effect on and after December 21, 1923.

REGULATIONS

1.[13] Tows of seagoing barges navigating the inland waters of the United States are limited in length to five vessels, including the towing vessel or vessels.

2.[14] With the exceptions noted below, hawsers are limited in length to 75 fathoms, measured from the stern of one vessel to the bow of the following vessel; and should in all cases be as much shorter as the weather or sea will permit.

3.[15] In all cases where, in the opinion of the master of the towing vessel, it is dangerous or inadvisable, whether on account of the state of the weather, or sea, or otherwise, to shorten hawsers, hawsers need not be shortened to the prescribed length, except that hawsers must in any event be shortened to the prescribed length upon reaching the applicable locality named below:

(*a*) Tows from sea or Chesapeake Bay bound for Hampton Roads or beyond, before passing Thimble Light.

(*b*) Tows bound up the Chesapeake, to the northward of Baltimore Light.

(*c*) Tows bound up into New York from sea, at West Bank.

(*d*) Tows bound up the Delaware, between Fourteen Foot Bank and Cross Ledge Lighthouses.

(*e*) Tows from sea to Narragansett Bay, before reaching Rose Island.

[13] Section 1 and the first sentence of subdivision (*a*) of section 5 were amended pursuant to section 14 of the act approved May 28, 1908, and are effective on and after August 1, 1924.

[14] Amendments to sections 2 and 3 were adopted on February 16, 1938, and approved by the Secretary of Commerce on February 28, 1938.

[15] Sections 3 and 4 adopted February 25, 1936, and approved by Secretary of Commerce on April 6, 1936, under authority of section 14 of the act of Congress approved May 28, 1908.

(*f*) Hawsers may also be lengthened in the same places, under the same circumstances, when tows are bound out.

4. In all cases where tows can be bunched, it should be done.

(*a*) Tows navigating in the North and East Rivers of New York must be bunched above a line drawn between Robbins Reef Lighthouse and Owls Head, Brooklyn, but the quarantine anchorage and the north entrance to Ambrose Channel shall be avoided in the process of bunching tows. In the discretion of the master of the towing vessel, when tows are entering Long Island Sound from the westward, hawsers may be lengthened out after passing Fort Schuyler, and when entering Long Island Sound from the eastward, hawsers need not be shortened to the prescribed length until reaching Fort Schuyler.

(b) Tows must be bunched above the mouth of the Schuylkill River, Pa.

5. Section 15 of the act approved May 28, 1908, provides:

That the master of the towing vessel shall be liable to the suspension or revocation of his license for any willful violation of regulations issued pursuant to section 14 in the manner now prescribed for incompetency, misconduct, or unskillfulness.

6. Any violation of these regulations shall be reported in writing as soon as practicable to the board of local inspectors of steam vessels most convenient to the officer or other person who may witness the violation.

CHAPTER VI

GROUND TACKLE

The sailor throughout the ages has ever considered the anchor his stanch shipmate, ready to lower away and protect him when ill luck has driven his ship into a position of danger. In the symbolism of many races the anchor has appeared as the emblem of hope. No matter how bad conditions may appear, if the anchor can be firmly

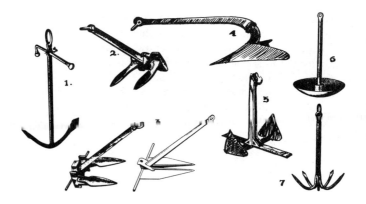

Modern Anchors

1. Yachtsman's Anchor.   2. Navy Type.   3. Two Improved Navy-Type Anchors.   4. CQR Plow Anchor.   5. Light Folding Anchor.
6. Mushroom Anchor (for Mooring).   7. Grapnel.

imbedded in something that will prevent matters from getting worse, there always is hope, and all is not lost.

Anchors were known to all maritime nations even in ancient times, and many of them were exactly like present-day anchors in principle. Seemingly, the old-fashioned anchor is the ultimate in a mechanism used to attach a ship to the ground beneath her.

601. The old-fashioned anchor is today the best and most efficient boat anchor. Others stow more easily, or are lighter, or cheaper, but none can equal this type as a general service anchor. On a boat having but one anchor, that anchor should be an old-fashioned one; on a boat having more than one anchor, the old-fashioned anchor should be one of them. (Figure 601B.)

It has two great faults, neither of which is of sufficient importance to abandon the type. (1) It is subject to fouling, that is, picking up

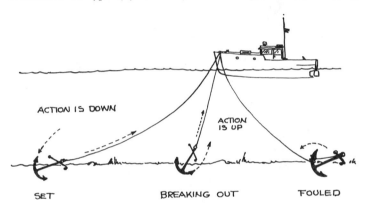

Figure 601A. The Action of an Old-fashioned Anchor Under Various Conditions

the anchor cable as the boat "walks" during anchored periods. There is no prevention for this, save to heave the cable up short after every 180° shift in the boat's heading, and, being sure the cable leads directly to the ring (or shackle, or jew's-harp), to pay the cable out as the boat sags against it; (2) it does not lend itself readily to stowing.

602. Modern design has removed the big objection of a fixed stock. The stock is now of metal, and by removing a metal key it can be folded parallel to the shank. It is stowed on deck on three chocks or pads of wood or metal, folded, and lashed down. It is sometimes carried slung from the bowsprit, hanging from the roller chock by the cable and being secured to the bobstay by a lashing. It would never be carried so at sea. (Figure 602.)

On large boats, the anchor is handled by an anchor davit, with a tackle leading to a balancing band. When fully hoisted, it is swung to the deck chocks or placed on the billboard and lashed. Very heavy anchors are first catted, then fished, then stowed. (Figure 602.)

603. The anchor is always washed free of mud before decking and the cable cast off if its immediate use is not planned. It must be lashed

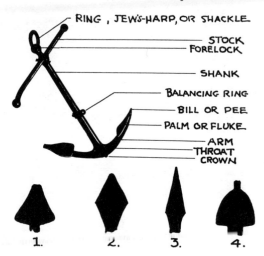

Figure 601B. Parts of the Old-fashioned Anchor

1. Spade palm—good general holding type except in rock
2. Herreshoff palm—good general holding
3. Sand palm—for sand and some types of weed (usually a light anchor)
4. Ship palm—general holding including rock (note the prominent bill)

down securely, otherwise pitching will surely send it adrift. An anchor adrift can do untold damage forward.

604. The stockless anchors (or patent anchors). This type of anchor has no stock and is therefore free of the danger of fouling the cable. Its action, however, is quite different from the old-fashioned anchor, and it has but 60 per cent of the holding power. Insurance requirements demand that stockless anchors be one fourth heavier than old-fashioned anchors for the same ship.

Both flukes are buried when properly set. To keep them so, a longer cable (more scope) is required than for anchors of the old-fashioned type. A dragging stockless anchor will capsize if one fluke hits a stone or boulder in the mud. If it is on too short a cable, and a sea is running, it will step itself out as the yawing ship brings stress on first one fluke and then the other.

The stockless anchor becomes efficient in very large sizes, such as those used on merchant or naval ships, and is further justified because

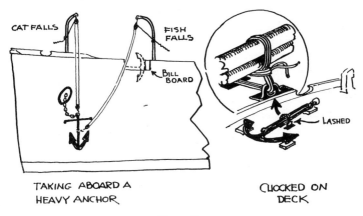

CAT FALLS

FISH FALLS

BILL BOARD

LASHED

TAKING ABOARD A
HEAVY ANCHOR

CHOCKED ON
DECK

Figure 602

it can be quite easily taken on board by bringing the shank right into the hawsepipe. It has no practical use on the small boat, and is in no way a general service anchor. It is useless in gravel, rock, or weed, and will hold fairly well only in soft mud.

605. The grapnel. This type of anchor makes an excellent rock anchor, its only recommendation as a service anchor. A trip (Figure 608) is usually required to free it.

The grapnel makes a good dinghy or tender anchor and will hold reasonably well in weed, sand, and gravel. Its chief use however, is as a retrieving hook. Dragged on a short warp it can be used to pick up lost cables or to trip a fouled or bound anchor.

Never leave a grapnel unattended. There is no type which fouls its cable more—or worse.

606. Other types. The demands of aviation have brought forth several types of lightweight anchors which have found their way to use on small boats. In general, these make use of the principle of the old-fashioned anchor in that they all have stocks in one form or another. (*See* illustration.) Improved flukes give extra "bite" and digging-in powers, and weight can therefore be sacrificed.

In the best of these types, the makers claim holding power at the rate of 30 to 1 over other types.

Most of these types have the advantage of very light weight (a 12-pound anchor is claimed to do the work of a 100-pound common anchor), and they fold down for easy stowing. It is this light weight which appears to be a great disadvantage, for these "hooks" rather readily slide over oyster banks, hardpan, or shallow silt on clay. In kelp or heavy weed bottoms they sometimes fail to reach the bottom. However, once bedded they have adequate fluke area to hold well. Efficiency is much increased by bending a fathom or two of chain between anchor and rope warp but light weight advantages are lost.

607. Anchors should be of malleable iron and hot dipped galvanized. The key should be secured to the shank or ring by a chain, with a small snap hook or bolt and nut to keep it set. Lifting bands, necessary for anchors of 50 pounds and upward, must be purchased separately.

608. Anchor trips are needed whenever the presence of rock is suspected. These are of two forms: (Figure 608.)

1. The cable is made fast at the crown, led along the shank, and secured to the ring by a few turns of light line. The cable should not lead through the ring. In the event that the anchor becomes wedged between rocks or in wreckage, an extra tug will break the ring lashing, and the lead will then be from the crown, and the anchor will break out easily.

2. A rope about half the diameter of the cable is bent to the anchor crown and led to the surface, where it is secured to a buoy. A fouled anchor can thus be freed by getting over it with a small boat or by picking up the tripping line from the bows with a boat hook. This method is to be recommended over number 1.

609. To determine the anchor's holding power required for various types of craft, the following formula is used:

For sailing cruisers—8% of the gross weight
For power cruisers—7%   "
For launches, light cruisers—6%   "
For centerboard sailers—5%   "

(Thus, a cruiser displacing [weighing] 8,000 pounds requires an anchor with a holding power of 560 pounds. The weight of the anchor will depend upon its style, and the makers usually have a table of holding powers for reference on various models of anchors.)

610. Bower anchors are those carried in the bow and are used for general anchoring purposes.

Stern anchors are carried in the stern for any purpose.

Sheet anchors are spare anchors of half the weight of the bowers.

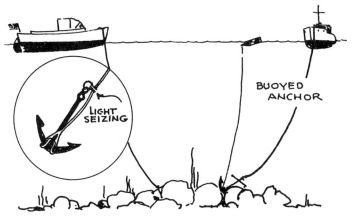

Figure 608. Anchor Trips

Stream anchors are medium-weight anchors, carried in the stern, and used to keep the boat from swinging by the stern (as in a stream).

Kedges are small old-fashioned anchors used for kedging or warping. (Kedging is the operation of moving a boat ahead a little at a time by carrying the anchor ahead in a small boat, letting go and then hauling up close to it. The same operation used to swing a boat by the stern is called warping.)

611. There is no exact way to calculate the proper weight of anchors for any given boat. The recommended anchors, indicated by the table in paragraph 609, while of sufficient size would be too large for easy and ordinary handling, i. e., while cruising or fishing. Small boats can be guided somewhat by the following rules:

1. Regular (light) anchor—one pound per foot of over-all length.

2. Kedge anchor—three-quarters of a pound per foot of over-all length.

3. Heavy anchor—two pounds per foot of over-all length. This rule applies to old-fashioned anchors only. Stockless anchors should be from 25 to 40% heavier. Fisherman or dory anchors should be 15% heavier.

Anchor Cables and Hawsers

612. Anchor cables are of chain (sometimes called chain cables or ship's cables).

Anchor hawsers are of manila rope (sometimes the outboard end will have a few fathoms of chain cable shackled to it to prevent undue

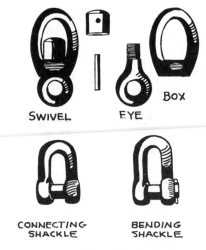

Figure 613A

chafing on the bottom). Hawsers are locally known also by the names of warps or anchor fasts.

Wire cable is sometimes used for anchor hawsers. It must be handled by a drum winch, not by hand, and is seldom seen on small boats.

613. Boat cables are generally of BBB chain, galvanized, and composed of but two to four shots. A shot is one of the lengths of chain making up the cable, and in the merchant service is 15 fathoms long.

Connections between shots are made by special links which permit the chain passing over the wildcat of the winch or windlass.

The outboard end is shackled to the anchor ring with the bow or rounded end of the shackle, called the bending shackle, facing the anchor. A stud link follows, then a swivel, then another stud link, then a shackle connecting to the first shot. Other combinations may be used,

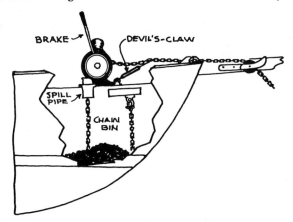

Figure 613B. Chain Cable—Handling and Stowing Gear

of course, providing the swivel is present. An old length of manila woven through the links of the first half fathom will do much to reduce wear of the chain here. (Figure 613A.)

The inboard end, called the bitter end, after dropping through the spillpipe to the chain locker is securely shackled to an eye or ring let into part of the boat's framing. Sometimes a pelican hook or release hook is placed between shackle and chain so that the cable may be slipped quickly should the need arise. (Figure 613B.)

614. Anchor windlasses are not usually found on small boats. However, when the anchor to be handled weighs 75 pounds or over, a windlass is necessary. Combination windlasses which handle chain cable or rope, or combination capstans having a chain wildcat can be purchased to operate by hand or by electricity. (Figure 614.)

Riding chocks are rarely found on small boats. These are steel chocks which guide the chain into the hawsepipe, and they have a locking device which is clamped to secure the chain and to take the strain from the windlass, leaving it free to be used for other purposes. A devil's-claw does the same thing. Sometimes the riding chocks are

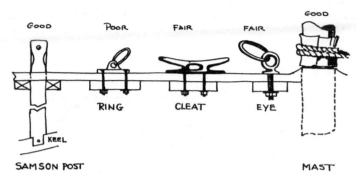

Figure 614. Small Boat Mooring "Bitts"

equipped with coil springs or rubber cushions, which take the shock of sudden jerks on the chain.

615. Chain is marked as follows, to permit the exact scope to be known as cable is payed out. Paint is used for the markings·

20 fathoms	shackle	painted	red
35	"	"	"	white
50	"	"	"	blue
65	"	"	"	red
80	"	"	"	white
95	"	"	"	blue
110	"	"	"	red
125	"	"	"	white

For the small boat, which seldom requires great scope, some other system of marking is more practical. While many privately developed systems are in use, the following is one often found:

1 fathom	1 red band (painted on a link)	5 fathoms	2 white bands
		6 "	3 "
2 fathoms	2 red bands	7 "	1 blue band
3 "	3 "	8 "	2 blue bands
4 "	1 white band	9 "	3 "

10 fathoms	1 red link		35 fathoms	3 white links
15 "	2 red links		40 "	1 blue link
20 "	3 "		45 "	2 blue links
25 "	1 white link		50 "	3 "
30 "	2 white links			

(Approximately three fathoms from the bitter end, about a half fathom of chain is painted yellow, indicating approach of the bitter end.)

616.

TABLE OF CHAIN SIZES FOR MEDIUM-HEAVY BOATS

WATERLINE LENGTH	DIAMETER OF CHAIN IN INCHES
For Motorboats	
25′	$\frac{3}{8}''$
35′	$\frac{7}{16}''$
45′	$\frac{1}{2}''$
55′	$\frac{9}{16}''$
For Sailboats (*Racing Type*)	
25′	$\frac{5}{16}''$
35′	$\frac{3}{8}''$
45′	$\frac{7}{16}''$
55′	$\frac{9}{16}''$
For Sailboats (*Cruising Type*)	
25′	$\frac{5}{16}''$
35′	$\frac{3}{8}''$
45′	$\frac{7}{16}''$
55′	$\frac{9}{16}''$

617. Chain cable is not subject to the rapid deterioration of rope. Its catenary curve (the curve of the chain between chocks and anchor) is greater than that of rope, and the chain, being of considerable weight, tends to act as a spring, and cushions the surge of the boat against the anchor. Even violent plunging of the boat against sufficient chain scope will not lift the chain very much from the bottom, thus keeping the strain in the position in which the anchor's holding power is best, i. e., pulling horizontally.

A chain anchor cable should be used on any boat large enough to carry the chain and its handling gear. A boat which regularly must anchor in rocky ground or in coral must always use chain cable or at least a chain cable pennant between anchor and warp.

Figure 617. Close Link   Stud Link

Rope Cable

618. Rope cable may be of manila or Nylon in accordance with the following table of recommended sizes:

WATERLINE LENGTH OF BOAT	DIAMETER OF MANILA	DIAMETER OF NYLON
25	$5/8$	$1/2$
30	$3/4$	$9/16$
35–40	1	$3/4$
45–50	$1\frac{1}{8}$	$7/8$
55–60	$1\frac{1}{4}$	$7/8$
65–70	$1\frac{1}{2}$	1

Manila will deteriorate much more rapidly than Nylon and is seldom good for more than two seasons in tidal waters.

SHACKLE, EYE OVER THIMBLE.   CHAFING GEAR   EYE SPLICE

ANCHOR BEND   TO JOIN CABLE USE SQUARE KNOT CARRICK BEND REEVING LINE BEND ALL WITH FALLS SEIZED TO THE STANDING PART   ANCHOR BOWLINE.

Figure 618

619. A knot in the rope weakens it about 25%. An eye splice in the rope does not weaken it at all. Chafing gear must be provided wherever the cable rests against any fixed object. Chafing can weaken a rope by 50% in a few minutes; it can part a rope in an hour.

620. Rope is subject to marine borers but may be somewhat protected from attack by painting it with a poisonous paint (such as copper paint). A rope cable will weaken first at the ends, between wind and water (between chocks and the water), and near the anchor, where it chafes the bottom at the anchor ring. Weakening action here is much speeded by the presence of particles of sand and grit in the lay.

Polluted water containing acid (especially uric acid) will attack rope, as will oil or gasoline scum. One of its greatest enemies is dampness. A rope cable should never be stowed below until thoroughly dry—*and then it should be kept dry.*

Anchoring

621. The anchor is let over crown first (not thrown) and held in an upright position until the boat begins sagging to leeward. Cable is payed out when it is apparent that the anchor will fall toward the boat, and is thereafter payed out only as needed, until the fully desired scope has been laid; then it is snubbed and the boat permitted to fully sag against the cable. (*Caution:* Never throw the anchor and follow it by a coil of rope. Fouling is certain to result.)

The stock will prevent the anchor from rolling and will assure the crown's being presented to the bottom in such a manner that the flukes can dig in and hold.

A bearing is taken on a fixed object ashore and noted. Frequent checking immediately after anchoring will indicate whether the boat is holding or not. If not, more scope, or better holding ground, or a heavier anchor is required.

If two anchors are required, the second one is set somewhat to port or starboard of the first and the same distance to leeward of it. It is set by carrying it out in a small boat, or, if possible, by hauling ahead on the cable of the first with the rudder hard over (or a small headsail set), and planting it from deck.

622. The general rule for scope (chain or rope) is: Anchor cable scope at least five times the depth of the water anchored in.

623. Anchoring with chain cable requires the same basic rules as the handling of anchor and cable. However, the chain is controlled by the winch brake instead of by hand, the pawl of the wildcat being off and the chain free to pass outboard. When sufficient scope has been veered out, a stopper is clapped on the cable, either by rigging the devil's-claw (a simple turnbuckle) or by tripping the pawl of the riding chock and then slacking off slightly on the windlass. The spillpipe is plugged, a conical stuffed canvas plug usually being used. (Figure 613.)

624. In congested anchorages, the practice of mooring will provide holding scope and yet keep the boat confined to a relatively small area of swing.

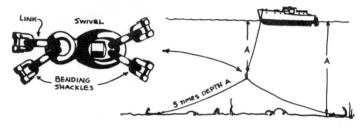

Figure 624. Mooring

Two anchors are used. The first is let go and its cable veered as the boat proceeds to the point where the second anchor is to be set, which point is distant from the first anchor by *twice* the scope of cable to be used on each anchor. The second anchor is let go; then the cable of the first is heaved in and the cable of the second veered out until the boat has the same amount of cable to each anchor (called *middling the cable*). Both cables are now shackled (or made fast) to a swivel piece, and a short cable is led from the swivel piece to the usual anchor bitts.

The anchors are layed out in line with the tide or with the heaviest winds to be expected. The scope from the swivel piece to each anchor is five times the depth of the water; the lead from the swivel piece to the boat is the depth of the water. A boat moored will swing to but one fifth of the scope of an anchored boat and still have the same security.

Kedging

625. To kedge an anchor means to carry it out by small boat some distance from the boat, where it can be used to help pull off a grounded boat, or to heave a boat down to lessen draught (as required when grounded), or for any number of purposes.

In the anchor weights liable to be found on boats, the elaborate methods of kedging a ship's anchor need not be explained. Figure 625 shows several methods of kedging anchors up to 300 pounds.

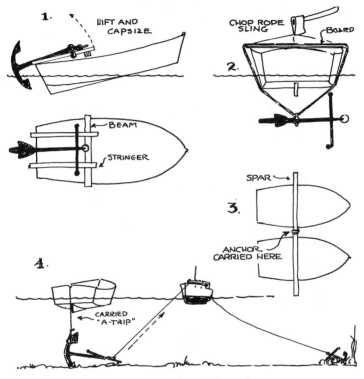

Figure 625. Kedging Light Anchors

The anchor should be set in such a place or in such depths as to be taken aboard directly to the mother ship. If this cannot be done, a tackle, which can be handled by man power, should be rigged to it and buoyed. A tripping line can be rigged. The anchor is tripped and held in a tripped position by making the tripping line fast to a small boat and heaving in on the anchor cable from the boat, an anchor first having been set off the stern.

Permanent Moorings

626. When a boat lies largely at a home port, it is usual to set a permanent mooring which is more secure than an anchor. The requisites of a permanent mooring are:

1. That it is of sufficient weight to hold in any likely blow or current.

2. That it is positively antifouling.

3. That it can be left set, without need of servicing or inspection for at least one season afloat.

4. That its warp (or bitter end) can be picked up under any conditions, night or day, with ease.

627. The commonest permanent mooring anchor is the mushroom anchor. (Figure 627.) It holds well in *all* types of bottoms, particularly

Figure 627.
Mushroom
Mooring
Anchor

mud or sand. The action is exactly the same as a fluked anchor; the pull must be horizontal so that the edge of the mushroom (or disk) bites into the bottom and buries itself. Some mushroom anchors are made with a bulb on the shank to assure the anchor's remaining capsized and not sitting upright.

628.

TABLE OF MUSHROOM ANCHOR WEIGHTS

WATERLINE LENGTH OF BOAT	LIGHT BOAT	CRUISING BOAT
25	50	100
30	75	125
35	100	150
40	125	175–200
50	200	300
60	250	4–450

629. The mooring cable, because it cannot be taken up often, is always of chain and generally ends in a short rope warp.

Its parts consist of a shackle between mooring anchor ring, then a swivel, then one-third the total length of the chain cable of heavy chain, then a swivel, then lighter chain, then a long link, then a bending shackle to the rope warp. The rope warp is of sufficient length to keep the boat clear of the mooring buoy, if one is used, or of sufficient length to reach bottom plus 25% of the depth if a float buoy (carried on deck) is used.

The scope of mooring cables is seven times the depth of the water; it is more under exposed-anchorage conditions or in swift tideways.

In crowded anchorages, such as most yacht anchorages are, there is seldom room to moor to the recommended scopes. Under such conditions the weight of the mooring must be increased as the scope is decreased. A ship mooring (Figure 624) is sometimes practical. If a lay can be found which permits mooring bow and stern to the prevailing winds or tides, the problem is easily solved. In such a case the stern mooring should be 10% or more heavier than the bow mooring. The bow should face the storm quarter. The boat should be middled between the buoys so as not to override either.

630. Various types of mooring buoys are shown in Figure 630.

If a rope pennant is used, it should be served for several feet fore and aft of the regularly used chock, remembering that rope changes its length as it becomes wet and dry.

If the mooring buoy can be taken on deck and lashed, it makes a more satisfactory rig and prevents paint-chafing and scarring as buoy

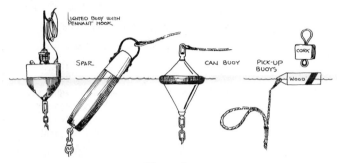

Figure 630

and boat collide between tides, or during calms, or when tides and winds come from opposite directions.

631. A very satisfactory permanent mooring, one that is particularly well suited to rocky anchorages, is a mooring anchor. This is simply an old-fashioned anchor, somewhat heavier in the shank and crown but having but one arm. It cannot foul the cable, and readily finds

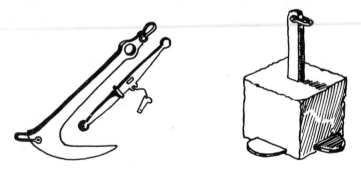

Figure 631. Mooring Anchor   The Cement Block Mooring Improved

holding crevices in rocky bottoms. Cutting off the arm of an anchor with a hacksaw makes an entirely satisfactory mooring anchor, provided it is about twice as heavy as the ordinary heavy service anchor.

632. Many other types of moorings, ranging from old auto engines, furnace castings, and cast cement, are in use. These types depend entirely upon dead weight for their holding power, and should be used only for anchoring in places known to be free of tides or heavy seas. Possibly lakes, some rivers, and same salt ponds might fall into this class. Few salt-water anchorages could be considered safe if lying to one of this type of mooring.

Any one of this type of mooring will be greatly improved in effectiveness if provided with some sort of a lever from which the cable lead

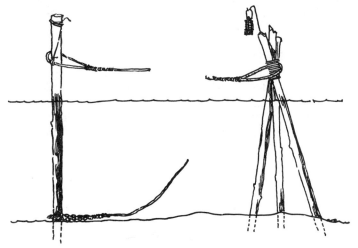

Figure 633. Mooring Stakes

can be taken. Anything which will tend to capsize the mooring object and make it difficult to drag through or over the bottom will help. An arrangement designed to dig in, as a fluke does, will also help greatly.

633. In deep mud bottoms, it is possible to drive a stake or stakes and lie to it with security and with a very short scope. The bottom must permit the stake to be driven in at least the depth of the water. One heavy stake will hold a small boat. Large boats require a "bundle," three or more stakes driven in somewhat like the frame of a wigwam and bound together at the common point of contact by several turns of rigging wire, well cleated. (Figure 633.)

The mooring cable is secured to the stakes by a large eye splice passed over them and well served. A hold-up line is attached to prevent the eye from dropping to the base of the stake. Fishermen in Peconic Bay, Long Island, use a similar arrangement but pass a chain loop over the stake and attach the mooring cable to this, thus putting the strain on the stake at about the bottom. The chain can be lifted at any time for inspection or renewal.

The scope of a cable when moored to a stake should be about three times the depth of the water. The cable should be twice the size ordinarily used, as it comes in for hard use as it dips between wind and water; and the strain, as the boat surges, is severe.

Red cedar makes the longest-lived stakes, with black birch and yellow pine following.

634. Moorings are generally moved by a scow equipped with a windlass, its tackle working through a large well amidships, over which is a sheer legs.

Lacking such a scow a mooring can be moved by lashing a spar or beam across two small boats. The rig is placed over the mooring at

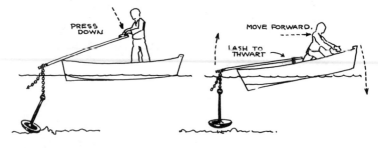

Figure 634. Breaking Out and Raising Small Moorings

low tide, the cable snubbed short and seized to the spar and let wait until high tide. Large moorings, even when deeply imbedded in the bottom, can thus be broken out and moved. To take such a mooring ashore, several tides are needed.

A boat lever can also be used. This rig is shown in Figure 634. A long boat of small beam is best. When securing or casting off the lever, beware of its swing and do not stand anywhere in its arc. When dropping a mooring from a boat lever, the lever will be shot a long distance astern. Be sure the water is clear of boats.

Moorings can also be raised by swamping a boat over them and rigging a bridle (*see* Figure 625) to the snubbed cable. As the boat is pumped free of water it will break out and raise the mooring.

Mooring and Anchoring Regulations

635. While at anchor, boats of all classes must show a white light visible all around the horizon. If under 150 feet in length the light must be not more than 20 feet above the water.

Exceptions are made in certain "anchorage areas" designated by the Secretary of War.

636. Vessels over 150 feet in length must show two white lights, one forward and one aft.

637. Vessels 65 feet in length or over must show anchor lights (or an anchor light) in any anchorage, including those designated as anchorage areas.

638. A boat lying to a permanent mooring is considered as being anchored.

639. No boat may lie at anchor in such a way as to obstruct the channel or close any area beyond to the free passage of other boats. Most areas bordering on Federal waters are under the direction of a Port Master, appointed by the government, who will assign permanent mooring locations upon application. He also hears complaints about offenders, may open or close an anchorage or mooring area, and investigate the types of moorings used, and forbid or permit their use.

In many local cruising harbors moorings are maintained for the free use of visitors by civic organizations, Chambers of Commerce and yacht clubs. These are generally white and marked "Guest." Always check to see what the mooring will hold. Leave it as found—including the warp sometimes attached.

⚓

CHAPTER VII

BRIDGE AND QUARTER-DECK

Since the days of the British sailing navy, the quarter-deck has been the traditional sanctuary of the "brains" of the ship. That these brains might function unhampered and uninterrupted, custom has decreed that no footstep, save in the rounds of duty, shall tread upon the quarter-deck to distract the master or his officers from their duty and their jobs. On modern vessels the bridge has the same sanctity.

Here, on bridge and quarter-deck, goes on the "extra" thought and planning so necessary to the success of any cruise, long or short. Those who do the brainwork of a cruise must know (and do know), first of all, the practical side of seamanship—every knot, and splice, and trick of sail handling; even the lowly swabbing of the deck. Every duty from that of the apprentice to the able-bodied seaman is thoroughly understood. In addition, such leaders must have a vast store of knowledge, much of it but distantly related to the sea. It is this knowledge, plus the ability to use it and to lead others, which constitutes the difference between officer and crew.

Roughly, this knowledge is divided into two major parts: one part, the knowledge required to solve the problems of the vessel while under way; the other, the knowledge required to meet the problems of a vessel while idle, or in port. And both parts overlap, of course.

Part one includes navigation (which is the subject of the three following chapters), weather lore, tide and currents, and many related subjects. Part two includes a knowledge of maritime law, insurance and insurance terms, stowage, port and clearance procedure, customs and immigration regulations, and like administrative matters.

Even the small-boat operator needs to know *some* of these things, and what follow, unrelated as they may appear, are the fundamentals of subjects which every merchant-marine officer knows intimately.

Weather Lore (Meteorology)

701. Meteorology and weather forecasting are today almost exact sciences. They have nothing whatsoever to do with the position of heavenly bodies, or the "color of Mars," or the behavior of sea birds, and like superstitions of not so long ago.

Unfortunately, weather data of a scientific nature is not available to the small-boat man at sea (save by radio), and, as weather is spot news, the highs and lows of pressure areas, wind directions, temperatures, etc., of thousands of square miles must be accurately known and the weather laws well understood in order to predict or forecast weather. However, while it is an interesting study, meteorology need not be studied or understood in order to safely plan a cruise, for the United States Government has made weather predictions available to anybody who is interested. Daily predictions and forecasting for weekly periods are made by experts and the information broadcast, by radio, to mariners, flyers, farmers, and others dependent upon the weather for their plans.

This information is available from the following sources:

1. By telephone from any Weather Bureau or Coast Guard station or base (at no charge).

2. From the daily press.

3. From flag signals from Coast Guard stations, in the form of storm warnings (*see* paragraph 811, Chapter VIII).

4. By radiotelephone in the form of a Marine Information Broadcast by the Coast Guard in co-operation with the United States Weather Bureau, the Hydrographic Office, the Navy and the U. S. C. G. Lighthouse Service.

Such Marine Information Broadcasts originate from official weather sources and are distributed by local broadcast stations. They are quite "official" and not to be confused with local forecasts which, at times, tend to favor the advertiser who wants a sunny weekend to move his vacation merchandise. The stations carrying these broadcasts are many and practically any small craft is within range of one or more at all times, except if far out at sea. Local newspapers carry the schedules, or you may phone any broadcasting station for its schedule or any Coast Guard station or depot.

Information is broadcast at stated times during the day, at regular entertainment frequencies, usually as part of a newscast. It is much appreciated by the hard-worked Coast Guard if yachtsmen listen to these broadcasts rather than call in at odd times and in odd circumstances. The ship-to-shore telephone earns its ugly reputation as a mere "yak-yak" instrument when it is used this way, as well as when it is used by bored yachtsmen or fishermen as much as the more obvious constant senseless chatter for "social" calls.

702. Marine Information Broadcasts include weather information and also other information of interest to the mariner (such as changes in navigational aids, obstructions to navigation, target practice near military bases, etc.). The broadcasts are first made at "copying rate," or 30 words per minute; then they are repeated at a normal speech speed, the entire broadcast taking about five minutes.

703. Local "signs" may be used to give a clue to the weather coming, but it should be remembered that (a) such signs are not always reliable, and, (b) such signs seldom will indicate the weather for more than the immediately succeeding 12 hours or less. Local signs may include the appearance of the sky, the clouds, direction and velocity of the wind, and barometric pressure.

704. The barometer is a reliable and trustworthy instrument which indicates the changes in atmospheric pressure as they occur. Changes in weather or future weather are always accompanied by (or because of) changes in barometric pressure. Note that in the following table, readings are "at sea level." While most small boats will make readings at approximately sea level, barometers above or below sea level should be read with the following correction:

For every 10 feet above or below sea level, add (or subtract) .01 inch.

Adjustment can be made on the barometer itself so that the pointer reading is correct at all times. Correct readings at the time of setting may be obtained by calling the Coast Guard or the Weather Bureau, or from the Broadcast of Marine Information.

Corrections for the Great Lakes follow:

Lake Superior .... ADD		0.64
Lakes Michigan & Huron .... "		0.62
Lake Erie .... "		0.61
Lake Ontario .... "		0.26

WEATHER SIGNS

Clouds

705. 1. Light, scud clouds alone indicate wind.

2. Light, scud clouds driving low under heavier cloud masses above indicate wind and rain.

3. Black, small clouds indicate rain.

4. Light, delicate clouds in soft fluffy masses foretell fine weather.

5. Hard clouds, sharply outlined and of bright hues promise rain and probably wind as well.

6. Misty, "wet" clouds forming about heights which remain or descend foretell wind and rain; if they disperse, improved weather may be expected.

7. High clouds which move against the direction of the lower clouds indicate the true future wind direction.

In general, the softer the cloud form, the less wind; the harder, more tufted, and sharper outlined, the more wind. The higher and more distant the clouds appear, the more gradual the weather change will come. Periods of bad weather are foretold by the breaking up into wisps, curls and patches of distant clouds; the breaking up gradually increasing and finally settling down over the sky as a murk, growing steadily in density.

Figures 705A and 705B show cross sections of cold and warm front approaches. The appearance and sequence of the several types and locations of clouds may, for the prudent mariner, foretell future weather. The practice of noting in the log the cloud disposition at the time of entry can lead to fairly accurate forecasting and serve as an alert in times of foul weather.

The local thunderstorm is really local, though many areas may experience "local" storms, locally born, at approximately the same time. Usually such a storm gives an advance "feel," confirmed by tumbling high, white cumulous clouds some hours before striking. When a thunderstorm is predicted, the problems of the sailor become many. He must, at the predicted time of striking, be off a windward shore, either anchored or snugged down to ride out the savage gusts usual to thunderstorms. He must also be in a position to reach port rapidly after the storm—for there will be little or no wind until the

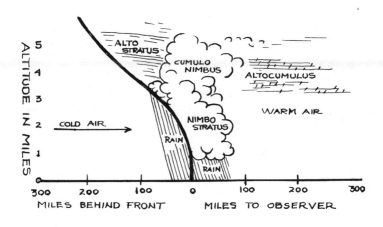

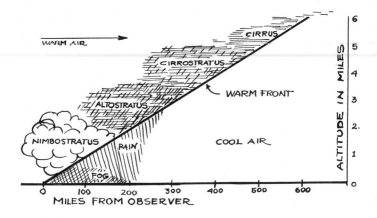

following day. Seas will not mount to dangerous heights because of the short duration of the storm, but winds may well be of almost hurricane intensity.

Figure 705C shows the general winds within a storm area as it moves along at average wind speed, usually toward the coast or a large body of water. The wind comes first; then the rain, knocking down the seas, then a cold or chilly front with diminishing wind and rain and finally an uneasy calm. Such a storm often awaits the arrival of high tide before descending. Sometimes it splits, sparing a small local area; sometimes it "hits" twice. If first observed inland at or over the head of two or more bays or rivers, it will often divide and your best position is to leeward and between the mouths of these rivers or sounds. Mountains will often channel storms within storms through ravines or gaps, and these may hit the adjacent waters with wild fury. Stay *behind* high land if possible, not *between* high land.

A sure sign of the approach of a local thunderstorm is the presence of "static" on the ship's radio. This will commence quite early in the morning, be definitely noticeable by noon and stop comfortable reception several hours before the storm strikes. After the storm the static will become weak or distant or cease, but if it does not, suspect a return engagement, possibly at night or at the next turn of the tide.

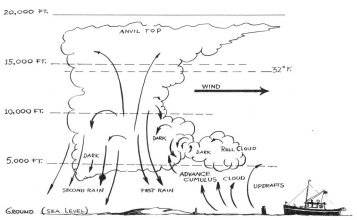

Figure 705C. A "Cross Section" of a Typical Summer Thunderstorm. It usually makes up in the west and the advancing anvil top and roll clouds are in evidence many hours before the storm strikes. The advance lower clouds "kill" the wind then reverse it. Violent cyclonic winds (really powerful updrafts) may be expected before the blackest clouds of all are overhead and release the rain in two distinct falls. This diagram shows what to expect from a storm and in what order as well as assisting in forecasting it. Obviously, sailing craft should prepare for the dangerous onslaught of the low cumulus clouds and the updrafts, which at sea level become heavy varying winds and threaten knockdowns and jibes.

Weather Predicting by the Barometer

706.

Wind direction	Barometer reduced to sea level	Character of weather indicated
SW to NW	30.10 to 30.20 and steady	Fair, with slight temperature changes, for one to two days.
SW to NW	30.10 to 30.20 and rising rapidly	Fair, followed within two days by rain.
SW to NW	30.20 and above and stationary	Continued fair, with no decided temperature change.
SW to NW	30.20 and above and falling slowly	Slowly rising temperature and fair for two days.
S to SE	30.10 to 30.20 and falling slowly	Rain within 24 hours.
S to SE	30.10 to 30.20 and falling rapidly	Wind increasing in force, with rain within 12 to 24 hours.
SE to NE	30.10 to 30.20 and falling slowly	Rain in 12 to 18 hours.
SE to NE	30.10 to 30.20 and falling rapidly	Increasing wind, and rain within 12 hours.
E to NE	30.10 and above and falling slowly	In summer, with light winds, rain may not fall for several days. In winter, rain within 24 hours.
E to NE	30.10 and above and falling rapidly	In summer, rain probable within 12 to 24 hours. In winter, rain or snow, with increasing winds, will often set in when the barometer begins to fall and the wind sets in from the NE.
SE to NE	30.00 or below and falling slowly	Rain will continue one to two days.
SE to NE	30.00 or below and falling rapidly	Rain, with high wind, followed, within 36 hours, by clearing, and in winter by colder.
S to SW	30.00 or below and rising slowly	Clearing within a few hours, and fair for several days.
S to E	29.80 or below and falling rapidly	Severe storm imminent, followed, within 24 hours, by clearing, and in winter by colder.
E to N	29.80 or below and falling rapidly	Severe northeast gale and heavy precipitation; in winter, heavy snow, followed by a cold wave.
Going to W	29.80 or below and rising rapidly	Clearing and colder.

Figure 707. Cloud Forms

1. Cirrus (Ci) Feather;
2. Cirrocumulus (Cc) Mackerel;
3. Cirrostratus (Cs) Web;
4. Altocumulus (Ac) Sheep;
5. Altostratus (As) Curtain;
6. Stratocumulus (Sc) Twist;
7. Stratus (St) Sheet;
8. Nimbostratus (Ns) Umbrella;
9. Cumulus (Cu) Wool Pack;
10. Cumulonimbus (Cn) Thunder.

273

Cloud definitions follow. (Figure 707.) The symbol in brackets is used in recording the cloud state when making out the ship's log, or reporting.

Cloud Definitions

707. 1. *Cirrus* (Ci)—Detached clouds of delicate and fibrous appearance; silky, white, without shading.

2. *Cirrocumulus* (Cc)—In layers and patches, white, flaky or small globular shapes, usually without shadows. In groups, lines, or ripples.

3. *Cirrostratus* (Cs)—Thin, whitish veil; sometimes quite diffuse, giving sky a milky look. Sun or moon shows through; halo often formed.

4. *Altocumulus* (Ac)—In layers or patches arranged in groups, lines or waves, following one or two directions with edges sometimes joining. *Altocumulus Castellatus* (Acc)—Same, vertical developments from common horizontal base.

5. *Altostratus* (As)—Fibrous veil, gray or bluish in color, similar to a thick cirrostratus but without halo phenomena. Sun or moon seen only vaguely. Sometimes very thick and dark with light patches. Surface never shows real relief and fibrous structure is always seen in the body of the cloud.

6. *Stratocumulus* (Sc)—In layers or patches, in masses and rolls which seem to twist; soft and gray, with darker shading. In groups, lines and waves in one or two directions. Often closely formed, edges joined, giving entire sky a wavy appearance.

7. *Stratus* (St)—Low uniform layers of clouds resembling fog but not resting on ground. When the lowest layer is broken into shreds and wisps it is called *Fractostratus* (Fs).

8. *Nimbostratus* (Ns)—Low, dark gray, uniform colored, rainy, feebly illuminated. Precipitation comes in the form of rain or snow, though precipitation may not reach the earth. If this is so, the cloud base appears diffuse and "wet."

9. *Cumulus* (Cu)—Dense clouds with vertical development; upper surface dome-shaped, with rounded edges, base nearly horizontal. With the sun against them they appear bright and fleecy in centers; with sun on side, strong light and shade is seen; with sun behind, the edges become luminous. If the formation is not hard and well defined, but ragged and changing, it is called *Fractocumulus* (Fc).

10. *Cumulonimbus* (Cn)—Heavy masses of clouds, with great vertical towering development; upper parts often fibrous and spreading out in the shape of an anvil. The base often has a layer of ragged low clouds below it. The thunder cloud.

Sky

708. A red sunset sky foretells tomorrow's fair weather. When, after a fine-weather day, the sun sets behind cloud banks, rain may be expected within 12 hours; if the barometer is dropping at the same time, rain is certain. After sunset, if the western sky is whitish and yellow far up, rain may be expected on the day following. If the western sky blends from a horizon of purple or lavender into a blue high up, expect fair weather tomorrow.

A yellow sunset means wind is coming; a faint yellow or reddish hue indicates that rain is coming. Greenish tints foretell both rain and wind. If the sun itself sets pale and white, bad weather is in the offing.

A "high dawn," or the sunrise's first light seen above a cloud bank, means wind is coming. A scorching morning sun, breaking from behind clouds, foretells thundershowers in the P. M. A morning gray sky means good weather. A morning red sky brings wind and rain. Bright, clear blues in the sky indicate fair weather.

Sun and Moon

709. A sun halo heralds bad weather. A moon halo indicates changing weather, usually bad before becoming good. A clear moon, seen in the daytime, means fair and cooler weather following shortly.

Fog and Dew

710. Fog and dew both foretell that fine weather is coming. Heavy dew in hot weather promises a continuation of fair weather. Absence of dew after a hot day means rain soon.

Sound and Sight

711. Rain is foretold when distant objects stand "above the horizon" and are unusually clear. This phenomenon is sometimes called (erroneously) a "water mirage."

An unusual brightness and twinkling of the stars means wind. Lunar rainbows, or winddogs, or fragmentary rainbows signify increasing wind and possibly rain as well.

A "good hearing day," especially unusually good hearing from the wet quarter, means that rain will follow. A "poor hearing day" indicates a low humidity or moisture content of the air, and consequently fair weather may be expected.

Some Sailor's Saws to Remember

712.

> When sound travels far and wide,
> A stormy day will like betide.

> The farther the sight
> The nearer the rain.

> Evening red and morning gray,
> Are certain signs of a fine day.

> A red sky in the morning
> Is the sailor's warning.
> A red sky at night,
> Is the sailor's delight.

Barometer

> First rise after low,
> Indicates a stronger blow.

> Long foretold, long last;
> Short warning, soon past.

> When the glass falls low,
> Prepare for a blow;
> When it rises high,
> Let all your kites fly.

> When the rain's before the wind,
> Halyards, sheets and braces mind
> When the wind's before the rain,
> Soon you may make sail again.

Scales of Wind Force, Visibility, State of Weather and Sea, and Symbols for Recording in Log

713.

THE BEAUFORT SCALE

Beaufort No.	Seaman's description of wind	Specifications for use on land	Miles per hour (statute)	Equivalent in knots	Terms used in U.S. Weather Bureau Forecasts
0	Calm	Calm; smoke rises vertically.	Less than 1	Less than 1	Light.
1	Light air	Direction of wind shown by smoke drift, but not by wind vanes.	1– 3	1– 3	
2	Light breeze .. (slight breeze)	Wind felt on face; leaves rustle; ordinary vane moved by wind.	4– 7	4– 6	
3	Gentle breeze .	Leaves and small twigs in constant motion; wind extends light flag.	8–12	7–10	Gentle.
4	Moderate breeze	Raises dust and loose paper; small branches are moved.	13–18	11–16	Moderate.
5	Fresh breeze ..	Small trees in leaf begin to sway; crested wavelets form on inland waters.	19–24	17–21	Fresh.
6	Strong breeze .	Large branches in motion; whistling heard in telegraph wires; umbrellas used with difficulty.	25–31	22–27	Strong.
7	Moderate gale . (high wind)	Whole trees in motion; inconvenience felt in walking against wind.	32–38	28–33	
8	Fresh gale	Breaks twigs off trees; generally impedes progress.	39–46	34–40	Gale.
9	Strong gale ...	Slight structural damage occurs (chimney pots and slate removed).	47–54	41–47	

10	Whole gale ... (heavy gale)	Seldom experienced inland; trees uprooted; considerable structural damage occurs.	55–63	48–55	Whole gale.
11	Storm	Very rarely experienced; accompanied by widespread damage.	64–75	56–65	
12	Hurricane		Above 75	Above 65	Hurricane.

Judging wind velocity on the water can only be roughly estimated, exact classification of the force depending upon whether it is open water, high seas, sheltered lake, river, etc. Here are some general rules:

	Force
Calm. Water surface smooth and glassy	0
Parts of water surface wind ruffled, with smooth patches interspersed	1
All surfaces ruffled	2
Small waves with occasional white caps	3
About half the wavetops breaking	4
Entire surface broken into whitecaps	4 plus
Tops of waves blowing off; spume	5-6
High waves, breaking on crests	7-9

(Revised Beaufort Scale adopted January 1, 1940, by the United States Government Service Departments.)

Visibility

714.

0.—Prominent objects not visible at 50 yards.

1.—Prominent objects not visible at 200 yards.

2.—Prominent objects not visible at 500 yards.

3.—Prominent objects not visible at ½ mile.

4.—Prominent objects not visible at 1 mile.

5.—Prominent objects not visible at 2 miles.

6.—Prominent objects not visible at 4 miles.

7.—Pron.inent objects not visible at 7 miles.

8.—Prominent objects not visible at 20 miles.

9.—Prominent objects visible above 20 miles.

State of Weather

715.

b.—Blue sky, cloudless.

bc.—Blue sky with detached clouds.

c.—Sky mainly cloudy.

d.—Drizzling, or light rain.

e.—Wet air, without rain.

f.—Fog, or foggy weather.

g.—Gloomy, or dark, stormy-looking.

h.—Hail.

l.—Lightning.

m.—Misty weather.

o.—Overcast.

p.—Passing showers of rain.

q.—Squally weather.

r.—Rainy weather, or continuous rain.

s.—Snow, snowy weather, or snow falling.

t.—Thunder.

u.—Ugly appearance, or threatening weather.

v.—Variable weather.

w.—Wet, or heavy dew.

z.—Hazy weather.

To indicate great intensity of any feature, its symbol may be underlined; thus: $\underline{r}.$, heavy rain.

State of the Sea

716.

B.—Broken or irregular sea.

C.—Chopping, short, or cross sea.

G.—Ground swell.

H.—Heavy sea.

L.—Long rolling sea.

M.—Moderate sea or swell.

R.—Rough sea.

S.—Smooth sea.

T.—Tide rips.

Storms

717. Wind is caused by the movement of air as it "spills" from an area of high pressure into an area of low pressure. If this difference in pressure is great, the wind moves with speed and violence and the result is a storm. The small boat, in storm periods, is endangered not only by the high wind, but by the sea which such winds make up. Storms are not to be confused with the normal sea and land breezes, caused by the air flowing upward from the heated earth during the daytime and permitting the cooler sea air to move inward toward the land and the reversal of this process during the night when the earth is cool.

Storms make the advance according to well-known laws and follow well-known paths. Any small boat contemplating an ocean voyage of any extent, particularly if in waters below 30° North, should carefully prepare against storm danger, and the navigator should thoroughly understand the laws of the storms he is likely to encounter.

Detailed information may be had from any of the following publications of the United States Department of Agriculture, Washington, D. C. They are sent upon payment with the order (money orders

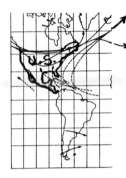

Figure 717. Principal Storm Tracks of the Western Hemisphere

———— Extratropical
- - - - - - Tropical (hurricanes)

or checks) and are sent post free to any address within the United States or any of its possessions.

The Hurricane—United States Department of Agriculture, Weather Bureau. Illustrated. 14 pages. 5 cents.

A paper dealing solely with the hurricane.

Florida Hurricanes—United States Department of Agriculture, Weather Bureau. Illustrated. 3 pages. 5 cents.

Discusses frequency, time, and starting point of Florida hurricanes. The great hurricanes that reached the Florida coast in the last 50 years are described.

The Daily Weather Map—with Explanation—United States Department of Agriculture, Weather Bureau. Illustrated. 8 pages. 5 cents.

Weather Forecasting—United States Department of Agriculture, Weather Bureau. Illustrated. 28 pages. 5 cents.

718. If caught at sea and a storm is brewing, the mariner has but to locate the storm center and make all possible speed away from it, and thus avoid its full intensity. Familiarity with the law of storms and with the habits of hurricanes and cyclonic storms enables this to be done.

The storm center may be roughly estimated, after its approach has been indicated by a rapidly falling barometer, by cirrus clouds radiating from a point of great cloud density. A long swell is apt to come from the direction of the storm. Another method is to face directly into the wind. The center will be approximately (in the Northern Hemisphere only) ten points to the observer's right. A ship heading

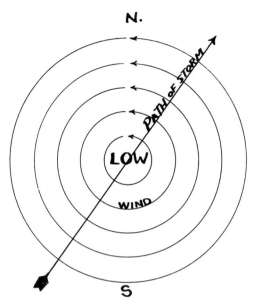

Figure 718

The cyclone (hurricane) in the Northern Hemisphere. It follows one of the storm tracks shown in Figure 717, rising from the south and generally dispersing at sea after recurving to the northeastward. Barometric pressures at the center range from 29.00 to 29.40 and at the outside edge 29.80 to 30.00. In low latitudes its diameter will be about 300 miles. After recurving and at about latitude 40 North it may be 1,000 miles in diameter. The center or "eye" is 10 to 15 miles in diameter, and the very "dead center" is always calm.

Such a storm moves along its track about 12 miles an hour at commencement, slows up around latitude 30 North and then, as it sweeps northward and eastward, increases to speeds as high as 35 miles an hour. The storm is most intense just before recurving.

The right half of the storm is known as the dangerous semicircle, and greater wind velocities prevail here than in the opposite half. Mariners always run for the left-hand semicircle when near the center if possible. Such a storm may find a pressure pocket inland or to the westward and northward and leave its usual course as did the great hurricanes of 1815 and 1938.

directly into the wind will therefore find the storm center two points abaft the starboard beam.

If such an observation is taken every hour or so, the course of the storm may be plotted and the speed at which the center is moving estimated. If the storm is definitely cyclonic (such as the West Indian hurricane), the following maneuvers will take the ship away from the danger of the storm center. This, as will be noted, takes advantage of the fact that such storms *always* (in the Northern Hemisphere) revolve around the center anticlockwise, or from right to left. The sailing directions will see the ship heading away from the center and to higher barometric readings.

Right or Dangerous Semicircle.—Steamers: Bring the wind on the starboard bow, make as much way as possible, and if obliged to heave to, do so head to sea. Sailing vessels: Keep close-hauled on the starboard tack, make as much way as possible, and if obliged to heave to, do so on the starboard tack.

Left or Navigable Semicircle.—Steam and sailing vessels: Bring the wind on the starboard quarter, note the course and hold it. If obliged to heave to, steamers may do so stern to sea; sailing vessels on the port tack.

On the Storm Track in Front of Center.—Steam and sailing vessels: Bring the wind two points on the starboard quarter, note the course and hold it, and run for the left semicircle, and when in that semicircle maneuver as above.

On the Storm Track in Rear of Center.—Avoid the center by the best practicable route, having due regard to the tendency of cyclones to recurve to the northward and eastward.

Tides

719. The tide is the diurnal, or twice daily, vertical rising and falling of the sea. It is caused by the attraction of the moon and sometimes by the sun and moon in combination.

While the moon affects tide the most, the sun has some influence, which is felt most when the attraction of sun and moon is combined. This occurs when both bodies are in the same or opposite quarters of the heavens, or at times of new and full moon, and result in the highest and lowest tides, called *spring tides*. At the first and third quarters of the moon the position of the sun and moon are such that high water of one body coincides with low water of the other. The result is that the tides then have the least range (or difference in level between high and low tide), and they are called *neap tides*.

Horizontal movements of the tide are called *tidal currents*. They flow inward to high-water levels (called the *flood tide*) and outward to low-water levels (called *ebb tides*). When vertical movement has ceased the tide is said to be at the *stand*. When horizontal movement has ceased (usually at or before the stand) the tide is said to be at the *slack*.

The rise of the tide is the amount in feet and inches that the tide rises above a normal point, or datum plane of mean low water. This datum plane is used in marking the depths on charts, and all soundings are given to it, or average (mean) low water.

The range of the tide is the extreme difference between high and low water (i. e., highest high water and lowest low water) expressed in feet and inches. This varies from zero (at the equator) to 40 or more feet (Bay of Fundy).

The set of a tidal current is the direction in which it flows.

The drift of the tidal current is the speed in which it sets, generally expressed in knots.

Tidal currents must be reckoned with when plotting courses for navigation and both set and drift considered. Tidal information and tables of datum are published by the United States Department of Commerce for every part of the United States coast line and must be referred to when plotting courses. (*See* Chapter XI.)

Units of Measure at Sea

720. *Yard*—3 feet. Distance off is expressed in yards (or cable lengths).

Fathom—6 feet. Depth is expressed in fathoms.

Cable length—1,200 feet. Distance from or to near-by objects, the shore, etc., is expressed by cable lengths (or yards).

Sea mile—6,080 feet. The distance between any two minutes of latitude, or between two minutes of longitude at the equator. Distance made good, lost, or away from, or toward is expressed in sea miles.

Note: The knot is not a unit of measurement but of speed and is equal to a speed of one nautical mile per hour.

The Ship's Log

721. A log is a continuous, minute-by-minute record of the progress and life aboard the boat and upon the sea about her. In it is noted *anything* of interest to the boat, though nothing trivial or in the nature of a diary entry.

A harbor log will merely record the goings and comings of the crew and officers, stores and fuel taken aboard or used, visitors and officials on board, inspections made and the findings of such inspections, orders received, accidents or *unusual* happenings, the depth of water in the well (leak rate), and general weather recording.

A sea or cruise log records, in addition to the items listed above, course, speed, engine revolutions, change of course and speed, ships sighted, etc.

The following items are essential to its keeping and usefulness:

Name of vessel, port of hail, where bound, date.
In command; names of crew and/or guests.
Amount of fuel in tanks, start and finish. Fuel consumed.
Amount of water in tanks, start and finish.
Running lights. Time of lighting and extinguishing.
State of weather.
State of sea.
Wind force and direction.   Recorded at fixed intervals, or at the
Visibility.   change of course, or change of watch.
Temperature.
Barometric pressure.
Where and when anchored (or moored).
Orders to the watch.
Orders for the morning.
Supplies or stores needed.

The actual recording of courses and distances run becomes valuable by comparing it with other similar runs and, of course, are absolutely necessary for running in fog or thick weather or away from the visible aids to navigation. Stock printed log forms for this purpose are many and may be procured from marine chandlers in bound blank form. One of the most useful and complete has the following headings (running horizontally across the top of the page):

Actual Time Abeam
Place Abeam
Distance Off
Log Reading
Course to Next ⎰ True Course
   Objective ⎱ Magnetic Course
           Compass Course
Current, Set, and Drift

Engine Speed (in r.p.m.)
Speed, Actual
Predicted Time to Be Abeam Next
  Objective
Elapsed Time on Course
Distance by Log (Log Reading)
Depths

On the left-hand edge of the page, vertically, and in the boxes provided, the navigator fills in the time; and opposite, under the proper heading, he makes the entry of the above items.

Thus a complete record of progress can be kept and used for comparison or for establishing position by dead reckoning if thick weather or night sets in.

A ship's log is legal and admissible evidence in any court of law and, when signed by the master at the time of its making, needs but certification as to its genuineness to help the court in rendering decisions upon legal action resultant from collision, property damage, etc.

Ship's Bells and Watches

722. Time is denoted on shipboard by striking the ship's bell as follows, each dot representing one stroke of the clapper. Time is taken from the flagship or senior officer present:

A. M.		P. M.	
12:30—1 bell	.	12:30—1 bell	.
1:00—2 bells	..	1:00—2 bells	..
1:30—3 bells	. . .	1:30—3 bells	. . .
2:00—4 bells	. . ..	2:00—4 bells	. . ..
2:30—5 bells	.. . . .	2:30—5 bells	.. . . .
3:00—6 bells	. . . ..	3:00—6 bells	. . . ..
3:30—7 bells	. . . . . .	3:30—7 bells	. . . . . .
4:00—8 bells	. . . .	4:00—8 bells	. . . .
4:30—1 bell	.	4:30—1 bell	.
5:00—2 bells	..	5:00—2 bells	..
5:30—3 bells	. . .	5:30—3 bells	. . .
6:00—4 bells	. . ..	6:00—4 bells	. . ..
6:30—5 bells	.. . . .	6:30—5 bells	.. . . .
7:00—6 bells	. . . ..	7:00—6 bells	. . . ..
7:30—7 bells	. . . . . .	7:30—7 bells	. . . . . .
8:00—8 bells	. . . .	8:00—8 bells	. . . .
8:30—1 bell	.	8:30—1 bell	.

9:00—2 bells ..	9:00—2 bells ..
9:30—3 bells . . .	9:30—3 bells . . .
10:00—4 bells	10:00—4 bells . . ..
10:30—5 bells	10:30—5 bells . . . . .
11:00—6 bells	11:00—6 bells . . . ..
11:30—7 bells	11:30—7 bells . . . .
12 Noon—8 bells	12 Mid. N.—8 bells . . . .

723. At sea, the day is divided into watches of four hours each, the period representing the time that various members of the crew are on duty. The crew usually is divided into two watches, the starboard

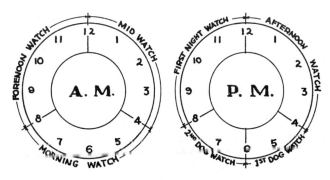

Figure 723. Order of Watches

or captain's watch (stood by the second mate) and the port or mate's watch, stood by the first mate. (Figure 723.)

In order to rotate the watches from day to day, the dogwatches of two hours each were instituted and are called first and second dogwatch (or dodge).

Billet System and Station Bills

724. Some manner of organization is required on every boat engaged in extended cruising. Division of duties and responsibilities is absolutely necessary to achieve the purposes of the cruise, which for the small-boat man, are fun, and pleasure, and relaxation.

By agreement in advance, each member of the ship's company should be made "head" of one of the boat's departments and take over the duties of that department (such as engine department, deck, bridge, or galley). If at sea, watches are stood in regular rotation, the agreement should indicate the relieving member and the time he is to relieve. Once a routine has been established, it should proceed without undue interruption of the ship's operation and without more than "bohunk" aid from other departments. The great advantage of such a system, even with a small crew of three or five men, is not that one man has to *do* everything in his department but that he is charged with *thinking and planning* for his department.

A routine cannot be laid down arbitrarily; it varies with ship, and crew, and cruising waters. In general it will be along the lines of the routine of a paid hand (*see* paragraph 1440, Chapter XIV), and the ordinary procedure of the navigator, engineer, and cook.

Men detailed to such positions should be selected with extreme care. Not only should they thoroughly understand the details of their department but must, if they are to work congenially with other crew members, be leaders, and cheerful, fair-minded companions. It is usual to have a round-table bull session before an important race or cruise and to thoroughly "hash over" all problems and duties, and thus eliminate the "kicks" from both sides at the beginning. Of all department heads, the navigator's is perhaps the most important to the ship, but by all the experiences of habitual cruisers, the cook's department is the most important to the ship's company, and the appointment of a cook and the fixing of his allowances for "grub," mealtimes, and rules should be with the consent of the entire party.

725. The small boat seldom needs an elaborate station-bill system. However, some organization is needed, and quickly, to meet common emergencies, and station bills, carefully planned, before such emergencies will avoid the confusion of orders and purposes which too often attend marine disasters or mishaps.

Crew members are each given a post and a duty for the several emergencies liable to occur on any boat and instructions that, when the alarm is given, it is their duty to proceed to the assigned station at once and there to do their assigned job or stand by for orders. The spirit of the station bill is simply that the various types of apparatus are manned and ready for use at the word of the leader. The leader has every right to consider the men under him as *part of the equipment* manned, and to expect them at their posts, ready to perform and carry out orders without question, and without other, or different, or "better" ideas. A poorly co-ordinated plan is far better than no plan, or a plan ruined because one man is not to be relied upon.

Some simple station bills are suggested below:

Fire

726. Upon the alarm:

1. Man fire extinguishers
2. Head boat so that fire is to leeward
3. Stand by signaling apparatus
4. Break out and rig emergency tiller
5. Launch and prepare small boat; distribute life preservers
6. Stand by engineer for instructions to shut fuel lines or plug fuel vents
7. Secure and be responsible for ship's papers, valuables, etc.

Collision

727. Upon alarm:

1. Stand by (and be prepared to man) all pumps
2. Stand by for inspection and repair duty
3. Stand by signaling apparatus
4. Put out all fires
5. Launch and prepare small boat; distribute life preservers
6. Stand by to assist other boat involved

Abandon Ship

728. Upon orders:

1. Launch and prepare small boat; distribute life preservers
2. Secure ship's papers, valuables, pets, etc.
3. Launch marker buoy for future locating of the wreck
4. Stand by distress signals

Man Overboard

729. Upon cry or alarm:

1. Launch life rings (with water lights, night or day)
2. Locate man overboard and keep pointing directly at him and in sight of the navigator
3. Prepare to launch small boat or raft

4. At night, man the searchlight
5. In daylight, send a man aloft to keep the man overboard in sight
6. Take 'bout-ship stations (on a sailing vessel)

"Jackass" Navigation

730. This inelegant name applies to the art of taking a boat from here to there without the use of formal navigation as such. It is akin to the term "flying by the seat of your pants." All small craft, operating inshore or in confined waters, use jackass navigation in some degree, quite often in combination with standard compass, log and lead practice. It refers to making good courses with the aid of local signs and knowledge, echo navigation and just plain sea sense. It is not offered as a substitute for scientific navigation but as a complement to it. After all many inshore courses are so short or varying that running a compass course and applying usual dead reckoning would result in error. Visible and audible "fixes" along such a course would be of great safety value to the skipper understanding "signs."

Off the Connecticut shore, for example, the local lobstermen make some astoundingly accurate runs in thick fog. Few of them ship compasses. Yet their secret is simple once understood. They run inshore, the general direction of which is indicated by tide or wind or both, stop their engines and listen. Always in this busy area, laced by highways, bridges, railroads and industry, they obtain not only audible lines of position but actual identification of the locale as well. The hoot of a train at a certain crossing, or bridge, the bleat of a factory whistle, the roar of traffic on a hill or its honking at a blind intersection, the rumble of a long freight over a trestle—all these sounds become lines of position to the alert skipper and give him a fix as accurate as one obtained from standard aids to navigation such as lighthouses, buoys and range marks.

To be sure, it requires an observant nature; the type which, in fair weather lays away many minute details, often quite unrelated, against a period of foul weather or stormy night. It is not impossible for the small craft skipper to have such intimate knowledge on tap for many miles about his home port and usual cruising grounds. Notes on charts are not uncommon; notes such as "You can see street light, corner Oak and Main, from here" or "Train blows three longs for Mystic Bridge."

In Maine local navigation is much dependent upon lobster buoys. These string along deep ledges, often quite close to shore and indicate a depth of water which at least a lobster boat can safely negotiate, usually about 15 feet at the ebb stage. Large buoys or buoys with stick handles indicate deep waters such as found a half mile or more off-shore. Warps with toggles (bottles, wooden floats or glass balls in nets) indicate swift currents, possibly identifying an entering gut or river. Buoys in a circle define a ledge; stay outside the circle for deep water. If you know the colors of the buoys used by various local lobster-men, or their license number which is burned into the buoy, you can, if you know the fishing grounds of these men, obtain a remarkably accurate fix.

Oyster stakes in other areas, notably the Chesapeake and eastern Long Island sound, indicate depths of about three fathoms and clear sand bottom. Fish weirs also indicate a two-fathom depth and sufficient water for the net boats and carriers to operate in.

The color of the sea is also a clue to water depth and location. Sand shows up in a lighter sea color. Mud and clay give a dark caste to the waters. Ledge and rocky bottom is revealed almost always by streamers of kelp and ribbon weed floating a fathom or more *above* the sunken danger. Study the bottom from aloft. In the West Indies it is rela-tively simple to con a ship through vicious coral heads from the cross-trees because of the clarity of the water.

In waters in which you catch flounders, you have a mud and probably level bottom. Mackerel sport in deep waters as a rule. Crabs come from deep but rocky bottoms. Cormorants (sometimes called "nigger-geese" or "shag") fish in about two fathoms. When you see one pop to the surface near by, you are in deep water. Porpoises play in mackerel waters—deep and moving—and this might indicate a main channel. Eel grass indicates shallowing waters; kelp deeper waters.

Tide rips, races or small wavelets imposed upon the general wave pattern might mean shallowing waters, bars or submerged ledge. Do not confuse these with wind galls which move over the surface.

The local wind and tide patterns also give broad fixes. In fog the wind almost always comes from the easterly quarter. Along the coast, the morning wind usually comes from the land, changes to southwest along the Atlantic and southeast along the Pacific coast during a normal day and backs off the land again in the evening. If the breeze smells of spruce woods or coke smoke or fish plant or hay, you have a pretty good idea of direction if you know the local terrain and com-munity. Inshore winds are apt to be "wet"; offshore dry.

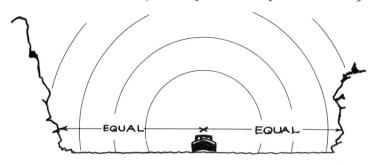

Figure 730A. A Mid-Channel Echo

The presence of garbage or wreckage floating in the tide may give a clue as to whereabouts. Brown waters, in Maine, identify one of the larger rivers which supports logging or textile mills. Spruce logs four feet long indicate a pulp mill; random trunks or slab edges indicate a lumber mill near by. If you know where these mills are you know that you are not far off. Oily waters, unfortunately, usually indicate a large city or town.

The use of echoes in close inshore navigation is well understood in some areas, notably the northwestern rivers and sounds. It is based on the speed of sound waves and measures, in time, the period required for a sound to be projected and bounce back to the point of origin; then convert the time into distance by the formula:

$$\frac{.18}{2} \times \text{time} = \text{distance off in miles}$$

Sound travels at the approximate rate of 1,100 feet per second or .18 miles per second. Since the echo must be bounced by a solid object, the distance off must be the distance from that object to the receiving point or one-half of the total distance travelled by the sound wave. For quick calculation merely multiply the total time in seconds between sending and receiving the signal by .09. A rough estimate may be made by counting ten seconds one mile.

In general a sharp, high-pitched signal works best. Use the electric horn, especially if it may be swiveled to direct the sound abeam. Foghorns and deep tones are not always reliable. A mouth whistle is

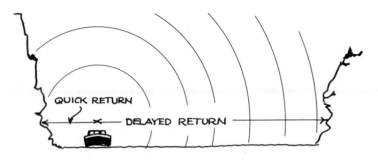

Figure 730B. A Side-Channel Echo

quite satisfactory, especially if blown through a speaking megaphone. A megaphone to the ear also assists in picking up the echo when the engines are running. Be careful to keep flat areas (such as sails, deck houses, etc.) in back of you as you signal. A gun shot returns a clear and distinct echo. However, unless blanks are shot this is a dangerous practice. *In extremis* beat a pail or dish pan lustily.

The type of echo will be a clue as to the type of reflector returning it. A long, muttering echo indicates low shore, trees, marsh or flats. Clear-cut echoes indicate cliffs, high ledges, steep shores or buildings. A weak echo, seemingly returned from a particular spot, may indicate another ship or an isolated object like a small islet, anchored craft or bridge footing. Test such an echo carefully and get a bearing on the object; it may be a vessel underway and in danger of collision from or with you. Sails return such an echo. When near by, cans and nuns return a soft whispering echo.

Dense fog dampens the echo and often distorts it. Wind, especially wind on the beam of the echo course, may whisk away all sound. By and large, echo navigation is a check, not a complete system of navigating unless you have extensive local experience under all weather conditions. It provides only *approximate* fixes. For accuracy combine echo navigation with sounding, compass courses and other conventional methods. (*See* Chapters IX, X and XI.)

Its most common use is for remaining in the middle channel of a river or sound. In Figure 730A a boat is shown in fog in mid-channel. A signal given on either side should result in the same distance off, sig-

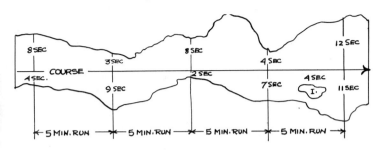

Figure 730C. Plotting an Echo Course with Distance Laid Off in Time

nifying that the boat is in the center of the river. Figure 730B shows the boat off its course. It will hear a quick echo on one side and a slow echo on the other. To be sure, it may be desirable to follow a veering channel by using this very method. If so, lay out, on the chart, at regular time intervals, the time count you expect to receive at these points; in this case converting distance to time. (*See* Figure 730C.)

It is possible to make a change in course by keeping an echo abeam during the turn. Plot the limit of the turn and convert it to compass a course. When the boat steadies on the corrected course, the echo should be directly abeam, thereafter fall to the quarter, and eventually be left astern.

Know the shoreline and coast contours. There is always danger that the echo signal may pass over a low beach or marsh and be returned by some higher elevation far inland. You may readily obtain a fix in this manner, of course, provided you *know the coast*. (Figure 730D.)

Here on the coast of Maine we have what is probably the strangest echo known. Coming in from Pemequid toward Friendship in a thick o' fog, we run out our time to Cranberry Island and to confirm the dead-reckoned fix, a man goes forward and howls like a dog. Almost immediately a dog howls or barks back. We're on course—for no matter when you howl at Mord Libby's dog on Cranberry Island he howls right back.

Boundary Lines of the High Seas

731. The boundary lines between the High Seas and Inland Waters were defined by Congress in 1895. They are presently being revised and

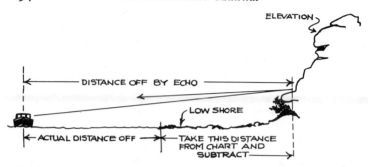

Figure 730D. Why It Is Important to Identify the Shore Returning the Echo

copies will be available from the Superintendent of Documents, Washington, D.C. The subject interests the yachtsman only from the viewpoint of the coastal sailor who from time to time passes over the boundary line and is therefore under changing Rules of the Road.

The Congress defined the boundaries by exact lines, running between known places on the standard chart (such as buoys, islands, headlands, lighthouses, etc.).

INLAND WATERS ON THE ATLANTIC, GULF, AND PACIFIC COASTS OF THE UNITED STATES

General rule.—At all buoyed entrances from seaward to bays, sounds, rivers, or other estuaries for which specific lines are not prescribed, Inland Rules of the Road shall apply inshore of a line approximately parallel with the general trend of the shore, drawn through the outermost buoy or other aid to navigation of any system of aids.

Pilot Rules for Western Rivers apply in rivers flowing into the Gulf of Mexico (with some exceptions).

Reporting Marine Accidents and Casualties

732. Motorboats of not over 15 gross tons or over 65 feet in length and carrying neither passengers nor freight for hire must report casualties of a "serious" nature. This would include loss of vessel, serious injury to anyone on board or death on board. Minor accidents such as collisions, fouls, stranding or fire, causing no serious personal injuries or material loss beyond such as would be normally adjusted between the boats involved need not be reported.

Report is made to the District Commander of the nearest Coast Guard District office or the service's Washington, D.C., office. The notice may be in the form of a brief message by phone, telegram, radio or First Class mail. In addition the owner or master shall promptly complete and file Coast Guard form N.C.G. 2692 if the accident involved a death. If not, form N.C.G. 924 must be filed. Both are filed at the Coast Guard headquarters of the district in which the accident occurred or in that to which the vessel proceeded after the accident. Forms may be obtained from the Officer in Charge, Marine Inspection, of any Coast Guard district.

The regulation further provides that any witness of a marine accident shall bring his information, if material, to the attention of the U.S. Coast Guard.

It is required that the vessels involved in a marine accident preserve logs, copies of radiograms, records of radiotelephone calls, navigator's work books or marked charts, crew and passenger lists and compass deviation cards. These may be demanded by Coast Guard examiners who investigate the occurrence.

Caution is given that nobody is interested in minor mishaps of the week-end variety between yachts. However if an accident involves a death, injury causing hospitalization, abandonment of the vessel, a foreign, commercial or war vessel, full report should be made as a matter of protection to self as well as to comply with maritime law.

Salvage

733.

"The right of salvage depends on no contract. A salvor who rescues valuable ships or cargoes from the grasp of wind and wave, the embrace of rocky ledges or the devouring flame, need prove no bargain with its owner as the basis of recovering a reward.

"He is paid by the courts from motives of public policy—paid not merely for the value of his time and labor in the special case, but a bounty in addition, so that he may be encouraged to do the like again."

(From *Hughes on Admiralty*.)

In any case, the matter of determining salvage fees, rights, and other questions is for the court to decide. The spirit of the law is that all parties involved were functioning during an emergency and unable because of the urgency of the situation to mutually agree on terms. Salvage questions seldom crop up in the small-boat fleet.

However, it is wise never to request a tow or ask for aid when disabled without being certain that a salvage situation is not being created. If wrecked and in dire danger, a salvage or potential salvage situation exists the moment that, without agreement, witnessed or in writing, the wrecked mariner accepts a line from the rescuing boat. Yachts performing such aid seldom consider it a salvaging job but commercial vessels or towboats might.

In any event, should the rescuer claim salvage, the courts will decide the amount of the award. This award is arrived at by a careful consideration of the actual danger that the wrecked vessel was in, the likelihood of her getting off without aid, etc. No salvage award is ever made for saving life, or for removing passengers or crew from a wrecked ship.

A towboat, or other boat which has been called to the scene by telephone or signal, is substantially "under a contract" even though the amount of payment for the service has not been specified, and her charges must be made accordingly and not as a salvage fee. Salvage generally can be claimed only when the wrecked ship has been "given up," or obviously should be given up, or if by not salvaging, she would shortly become a total loss.

Tows accepted from the Coast Guard or other government craft never constitute a salvage situation. Police or state boats may charge for services but not on a salvage basis. Under no interpretation of the law can it be called salvage when: (1) A sailboat is becalmed and in no danger and requests a tow; (2) a powerboat, suffering an engine breakdown and in no danger, requests a tow; (3) any boat, without crew or passengers on board, becomes "adrift" and is towed to another mooring, or her own anchors let go, or her engine started or sail raised and she is taken to a place of security.

Draft and Plimsoll

734. Draft numerals appear on the stem or sternpost or both of some vessels (mostly commercial freighters) and indicate the draft of the vessel for loading and trimming purposes. The draft is read to the *top* of the numeral. Large vessels have the numerals exactly six inches high, and the bottom of the numeral therefore becomes the half-foot (or six-inch) mark.

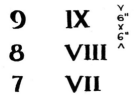

Figure 734. Draft Numbers

735. The Plimsoll mark is a safe-load mark required on merchant vessels. It assures the vessel's not being loaded beyond her safe point of buoyancy. If loading for a voyage on the North Atlantic in winter, she is loaded to the mark WNA, giving her more stability than her normal mark (in the circle). If she is loading in fresh water, she may load deeper, as, upon entering salt water which is more buoyant than fresh

Figure 735. Plimsoll Mark

water, she will rise to her normal mark. (Figure 735.) Other marks concern loading in the Indian Sea, etc.

· The mark is painted about amidships, on each side. The horizontal line must be parallel to the waterline, and the lines on either side must be the same distance in or above the water to assume fore-and-aft and athwartships trim.

Tonnage

736. Gross tonnage is the internal capacity of the vessel expressed in units of 100 cubic feet. Moorsom's system of ship measurement arbitrarily establishes this space as being required to accommodate one ton of average general merchandise. It is strictly a measure of volume, not weight, and includes all spaces below the main deck, and all permanently enclosed spaces above the main deck.

737. Net tonnage is the measurement of the volume, not weight, of the useful cargo-carrying spaces left after deducting from the gross tonnage all the spaces required for machinery, crew accommodation, galley, etc. It is, in other words, the capacity of the spaces on board which have earning power.

738. Gross tonnage is used as a basis of classifying vessels. Net tonnage is used as a basis of charging vessel tolls (such as harbor dues, canal tolls, cargo insurance, etc.). Pilotage is charged by the foot of draft, not tonnage.

Displacement and Deadweight Tonnage

739. Displacement, or displacement tonnage, is the actual weight in long tons (2,240 pounds) of the vessel and all that is in her. It varies with the draft. It is figured by calculating the volume of the vessel under water in cubic feet and dividing by 35 for fresh water and 36 for salt water. The answer will be in tons.

740. Deadweight tonnage is the carrying capacity of the vessel in long tons. It is the difference between the vessel light and with stores and fuel aboard, and the vessel loaded to her marks.

Thames Measurement

741. Small boats are arbitrarily measured for tonnage by applying the Thames Tonnage Rule:

$$\text{T.M. (in tons)} = \frac{\text{Length} - \text{beam} \times \text{beam} \times \frac{1}{2}\,\text{beam}}{94}$$

Example: A vessel 30 feet overall with a beam of 9 feet.

$$\text{tonnage} = \frac{30 - 9 \ (\text{or } 21) \times 9 \times 4\frac{1}{2}}{94} = 9 + \text{tons}$$

Ship Measurement

742. *Length overall* is the extreme length measured from the foremost part to the aftermost part of the hull.

Length between perpendiculars is the length measured between the forward part of the stem and the after part of the rudder post. In the case of a raked stern or rudder post the measurement is taken from the intersection through the upper deck.

Length registered is the length measured between the foreward part of the stem and the after part of the sternpost.

Breadth moulded is the breadth of the hull at the widest part, measured between the outer surfaces of the frames.

Breadth registered or extreme breadth is the breadth of the hull at the widest part measured between the outer surfaces of the shell plating.

Depth moulded is the depth measured between the top of the keel, or lower surface of the frame at the center line, and top of the upper deck beam at the gunwale.

Depth registered is the depth measured amidships between the top of the floors, and the top of the upper deck beams.

List of Ship's Papers

743. *The Register.* Ship's evidence of nationality. Gives hailing port, name of the master, description of the vessel as to type, size, etc., and the owners.

The Articles of Agreement. The agreement between the ship, represented by the master, and the mariners, and other persons shipped on board for the voyage, or for a certain period of time. It recounts the limits of the voyage, the names and ratings of the crew, their compensation, and the time of the commencement of their service.

The Crew Manifest. A separate paper, simply giving the names and ratings of the crew for purposes of health and Customhouse examination.

Clearance Papers. The official permission to sail from her port of departure. Shows that all port dues and charges have been paid. Gives ports of destination.

Bill of Health. Shows condition of the health of the country and part from whence the vessel sails.

Charter Party. The contract between owner of the vessel and charterer, or shipper. Carried when a vessel is under charter.

Cargo Manifest. This is a detailed list of the cargo on board, names of the consignees, consignors, ports of lading, ports of discharging, marks, numbers, etc.

Bills of Lading. These are receipts signed by the master, owner, or agent, certifying to the lading of the goods on board ship.

Passenger List. If a passenger vessel this list must contain the names and destination of all passengers. It is really a part of the manifest.

Stores List. Contains list of the ship's stores. Must be complete when entering port, showing all unbroken and broken stores. Such stores not subject to duty.

Invoice. This document must contain a detailed account of the cargo, stating the number of packages, value, charges, freight, insurance, marks, numbers. Also the name of the vessel, her master, port of destination, and name of consignee.

The following certificates are also commonly carried: Certificate of Classification, issued by a classification society, such as Lloyd's Register, showing that the vessel is approved as to construction, etc. Certificate of Freeboard, shows the assigned position of the load-line disc (Plimsoll Mark). Certificate of Inspection, issued by the United States Steamboat Inspection Service. States that the inspectors approve the vessel and her equipment. It must be framed and placed in a conspicuous place. Tonnage Certificate is a document of measurement, used in the Panama and Suez Canals, for the purpose of establishing the toll rate. A Seaworthy Certificate may be issued by a surveyor of a classification society, on the request of the master. It attests the good and seaworthy condition of the vessel.

Sea Letter. A document issued to unregistered vessels owned by citizens of the United States. It is issued by the Customs Authorities. It certifies to the nationality and ownership of the vessel.

Commercial Ship's Business

744. *Charter Party.* A form of contract, or lease. It is a specified contract by which the owners of the vessel let the entire vessel to another person, to be used by him for transportation on his own account, either under their charge or his. When the vessel remains in charge of the owners it constitutes a Contract of Affreightment.

The Charter Party takes various forms.

Time Charter. The owner hires his ship out for a definite time and usually supplies crew, fuel, and stores.

Voyage Charter. The owner hires the vessel out for a definite haul, as, for example, a run between two ports, or a round voyage between two ports, with intermediate stops in both or one direction. Owner furnishes crew, coal, and stores.

Tonnage Charter. Charterer pays a certain rate per registered ton, or per ton, deadweight capacity.

Bare Boat, or Bare-Pole Charter. Charterer furnishes crew, coal, and stores. Partial bare-boat charter sometimes occurs wherein the charterer agrees to the owner's furnishing the crew, in which case he is also responsible for their welfare.

Lump-Sum Charter. The charterer pays a lump sum or fixed price for the ship.

Lay Days. The days allowed by the charter party for loading or unloading a vessel. The vessel being detained beyond the lay days, the charterer becomes liable for demurrage.

Demurrage. The compensation to be paid for the detention of a ship beyond the lay days allowed in the Charter Party. It must be claimed daily, as due.

Protest, or "Writ of Protest." The declaration made by the master of a vessel before a notary, or consul, if in a foreign port, within twenty-four hours after the arrival of the vessel in port, after a period of heavy weather, or a disaster, stating that he anticipates that the ship or cargo, or both, are damaged, and that the same was not due to any fault of the vessel, her officers, or crew, but to the perils of the sea, and protesting against them. It must be signed by the master and some member of the crew.

Extension of Protest. A protest may be extended to show particulars of storms, etc., that caused the damage. The logbook should support the statements made in the Protest and Extension of Protest.

Survey. After noting a protest, a survey of the ship and cargo must be made before breaking bulk and to begin by opening hatches.

Hatch Survey. To prevent any claim on the ship for damage by water, the surveyors must certify that the hatches were properly secured, the cargo properly dunnaged, and to make a claim on the underwriters, or enable the consignor to make such a claim, the surveyors must certify that the cargo was damaged by sea water.

A copy of the protest must be promptly sent to the owners of the vessel.

General Average. This is the principle of law which requires that parties interested in a marine venture shall contribute to make up the loss of the sufferer when there is a voluntary sacrifice of part of the venture, made by the master or representative of all concerned, for the benefit of all.

For instance, to safeguard the ship, a certain amount of cargo may have to be thrown overboard, or jettisoned. Evidence must be produced that the sacrifice was necessary, that it was not due to the goods jettisoned. The entries in the logbook must show the facts.

Particular Average. Signifies the damage or partial loss happening to the ship, or cargo, in consequence of some fortuitous or unavoidable accident, and it is borne by the individual owners of the articles damaged, or by their insurers.

Mortgage. A transaction whereby the ship is given as security for money advanced to the owner. He may use this money in any manner he sees fit.

Bottomry Bond. A contract in the nature of a mortgage, by which the owner of the ship, or the master, or his agent, hypothecates (to pledge without delivery of title, or possession) and binds the ship and sometimes the freight, as security for the repayment of money advanced, or lent, for the use of the ship, if she terminates her voyage successfully.

If the ship is lost by the perils of the sea, the lender loses the money. If the ship arrives safely he is to receive the money lent, with the interest and premium stipulated, although it may be, and usually is, in excess of the legal rate of interest.

Respondentia Bond. When sufficient money cannot be borrowed on the ship and freight (freight money) the cargo itself may be given as security. This is given under a respondentia bond. It should never be resorted to if it is at all possible to avoid it. The contract is of the same nature as bottomry, but has priority to such claims.

Freight. This word is sometimes wrongfully used as a term meaning cargo. It is the amount agreed upon in payment for the transportation of cargo and should never be used in any other sense. The freight may be demanded before the cargo is delivered to the consignee. It is generally paid when the cargo is on board, at the port of departure.

Dead Freight. When a charterer agrees to give a ship a full cargo and for any reason does not do so, he must also pay the freight on the quantity that would have been required to finish the loading. This is known as dead freight. After this payment, which must be collected at the port of loading, the ship must not take on board any more cargo, and must proceed to her port of destination without unnecessary delay.

Pratique. A certificate given after compliance with the quarantine regulations permitting a newly arrived ship to land her passengers and crew.

Port Charges. Pilotage, port, harbor, and hospital dues. Based on tonnage, and in the case of pilotage, on draft.

CHAPTER VIII

SIGNALS AND SIGNALING

Whistle Signals

801. Whistle signals are given on the steam whistle, air whistle, or the electric whistle, which is required by law as part of the equipment of every motorboat.

A short blast is defined as being of one second's duration.

A prolonged blast is defined as being from four to six seconds' duration, but under no circumstances less than two seconds' duration.

INTERNATIONAL RULES

One short blast—I am directing my course to starboard.
Two short blasts—I am directing my course to port.
Three short blasts—My engines are going full astern.

(NOTE: These are the only whistle signals permitted under International Rules.)

PILOT OR INLAND RULES

One short blast:

1. When changing course to starboard.
2. When maintaining a course to starboard of a passing vessel.
3. When on a crossing course, privileged vessel so signifies she will hold her course and speed.
4. When on a crossing course, burdened vessel so signifies she will give way to the privileged vessel.
5. When overtaking vessel desires to pass another on the overtaken vessel's starboard side.
6. When overtaken vessel grants request (5).

Two short blasts:

1. When changing course to port.
2. When maintaining course to port of a passing vessel.

3. When overtaking vessel desires to pass another on the overtaken vessel's port side.

4. When overtaken vessel grants request (3).

Three short blasts:

My engines are going full astern.

Danger signal (four or more short blasts):

1. When the course or intention of another vessel is not understood.

2. When answering the request of an overtaking vessel to pass in the negative. (As soon as the situation preventing passing has cleared, the usual overtaking signals are made, one or two short blasts, depending upon the passing side of the original request.)

3. When immediate compliance with a whistle-signal request is impossible for any reason.

Warning signal (one long blast):

1. When leaving a dock or berth.

2. When visibility, because of bends, high banks, or other obstructions, has been reduced to one-half mile or less. (The signal must be answered before passing signals are exchanged.)

GREAT LAKES RULES

Rules for the Great Lakes are exactly the same as Inland Rules. Unofficially, three short blasts, by usage, is recognized as a request for a passing vessel to slow down; also to indicate sternway. The danger signal is sometimes used to indicate that the course which another vessel has signified is not considered safe.

Fog Signals

802. Fog signals are given in day or night in thick weather of any kind (snow, heavy mist, fog, or heavy rain or smoke). Signals are made on the steam whistle, siren, foghorn, or bell as provided in the various regulations following.

INTERNATIONAL RULES

Equipment—Steam vessels are required to have a steam whistle (operated by steam or air) or a siren, mechanical foghorn and bell.

Sailing vessels must have a foghorn and bell. Boats under 20 tons require only equipment to make an efficient sound signal.

Signals under Way:

Steam vessels—One prolonged blast at intervals of not more than two minutes. (If under way but stopped—two prolonged blasts at intervals of not more than two minutes.)

Sailing vessels—Starboard tack—one blast. Port tack—two blasts. Wind abaft the beam—three blasts. Intervals in each case not more than one minute.

Signals at Anchor:

All vessels—Bell rung rapidly for five seconds at intervals of not more than one minute.

Signals for Towed or Towing Vessels:

One prolonged blast followed by two short blasts at intervals of not more than two minutes.

Boats under 20 Tons:

Exempt from above rules but must make an efficient sound signal at intervals of not more than one minute.

PILOT OR INLAND RULES

Equipment—Steam vessels must have a steam whistle (operated by steam or air) or siren, mechanical foghorn and bell. Sailing vessels of 20 tons or over must have a bell and foghorn. Rafts, current boats, etc., must have a foghorn or the equivalent.

Signals under Way:

Steam vessels—One prolonged blast at intervals of not more than one minute (on whistle or siren).

Sailing vessels—Starboard tack—one blast. Port tack—two blasts. Wind abaft the beam—three blasts. Intervals in each case of not more than one minute (on foghorn).

Signals at Anchor (or Not under Way):

All vessels—Bell rung rapidly for five seconds at intervals of not more than one minute.

Signals for Towed or Towing Vessels:

One prolonged whistle blast followed by two short blasts at intervals of not more than one minute. (Towed vessels make the same signal but on a foghorn.)

Rafts, Current Boats, Rowboats, etc.:

One blast of the foghorn, or equivalent, at intervals of not more than one minute.

GREAT LAKES RULES

Equipment—Steam vessels must have a steam or air whistle, audible two miles, and a bell. Sailing vessels must have a foghorn and bell. Boats under 10 tons may have a foghorn or the equivalent. Steamers towing rafts must have a screeching or Modoc whistle.

Signals under Way:

Steam vessels—Three blasts at intervals of not more than one minute (except when towing raft).

Sailing vessels—Starboard tack—one blast. Port tack—two blasts. Wind abaft the beam—three blasts. Interval in each case of not more than one minute.

Signals at Anchor:

All vessels—Bell rung rapidly for from three to five seconds at intervals of not more than two minutes. Grounded or stranded vessels near a channel or fairway make the same signal.

Signals for Towed or Towing Vessels:

A vessel towed makes four bells on the fog bell (thus: .. ..), at intervals of one minute.

A steamer towing a raft must sound the screeching or Modoc whistle for from three to five seconds at intervals of not more than one minute.

Boats under 10 Tons—fishing boats, current, and rowboats, etc.:

One signal at intervals of not more than one minute on the foghorn or other sound apparatus.

WESTERN RIVER RULES

Equipment—Steam vessels must have a steam whistle; sailing vessels must have a foghorn; both have fog bells.

Signals under Way:

Steam vessel—One blast at intervals of not more than one minute.
Sailing vessel—One blast at intervals of not more than one minute.

Signals at Anchor:

All vessels—Bell rung at intervals of not more than two minutes.

Signals for Towing Vessel:

Towing steamer sounds three blasts at intervals of not more than one minute.

Fishing Boats, Barges, Current, and Rowboats, etc.:

When anchored or under way (but not anchored in port) they must sound the foghorn or equivalent (equal to steam whistle), at intervals of not more than two minutes.

Distress Signals

803

INTERNATIONAL RULES

By Day:

1. A gun or other explosive signal fired at intervals of about a minute.
2. The International Code signal of distress indicated by NC.
3. The distance signal, consisting of a square flag, having either above it or below it a ball or anything resembling a ball.
4. Continuous sounding with any fog-signal apparatus.
5. The signal SOS made by radiotelegraphy, or by any other distress-signaling method.

By Night:

1. A gun or other explosive signal, fired at intervals of about a minute (for vessels only).

2. Flames on the vessel, as from a burning tar barrel, oil barrel, etc. (for vessels only).

3. Rockets or shells throwing stars of any color or description, fired one at a time, at short intervals (for vessels only).

4. A continuous sounding with any fog-signal apparatus; in the case of aircraft, sound apparatus.

5. The signal SOS made by radiotelegraphy, or by any other distance-signaling method.

INLAND RULES

By Day:

1. A continuous sounding with any fog-signal apparatus, or firing a gun.

By Night:

1. Flames on the vessel, as from a burning tar or oil barrel, etc.

2. Continuous sounding with any fog-signal apparatus, or firing a gun.

For Aircraft Only:

1. The signal consisting of a succession of white lights projected into the sky at short intervals.

2. The international distress call "MAYDAY" by means of radiotelephony.

International Lifesaving Signals

804. 1. Upon discovery of a wreck by night, the lifesaving force will burn a red pyrotechnic light or a red rocket to signify "You are seen; assistance will be given as soon as possible."

2. A red flag waved on the shore by day, or a red light, red rocket, or red Roman candle displayed by night, will signify "Haul away."

3. A white flag waved on shore by day, or a white light slowly swung back and forth, or a white rocket or white Roman candle fired by night, will signify "Slack away."

4. Two flags, a white and a red, waved at the same time on shore by day, or two lights, a white and a red, slowly swung at the same time, or a blue pyrotechnic light burned by night, will signify "Do not attempt to land in your own boats; it is impossible."

5. A man on shore beckoning by day, or two torches burning near together by night, will signify "This is the best place to land."

Submarine Distress Signals

805. A submarine of the United States Navy which may be in need of assistance releases a red smoke bomb.

A submarine which may be compelled to surface in the vicinity of surface craft releases a yellow smoke bomb. Surface vessels should keep clear of the yellow smoke bombs.

Any person sighting a red smoke bomb rising from the surface of the water should report the time and location immediately to the nearest naval authority or Coast Guard unit.

Signals for a Pilot

806. A pilot may be obtained by displaying any of the following:

By Day:

1. The International Code Signal G, meaning "I require a pilot."
2. The International Code Signal P. T., meaning "I require a pilot."
3. The Pilot Jack hoisted at the fore.

By Night:

1. The pyrotechnic light (blue light) every 15 minutes.
2. A bright white light, flashed or shown at short or frequent intervals just above the bulwarks for about a minute at a time.
3. The International Code Signal P. T. by flashing light.

Engine Room, Telegraph or Bellpull Signals

807.
Engine stopped—one bell for ahead slow.
Engine running slow—jingle for full speed ahead.
Engine running full speed ahead—one bell to slow down.
Engine running ahead slow—one bell to stop.
Engine stopped—two bells for astern.
Engine running astern—jingle for full speed astern.
Engine running astern—one bell to stop.
Engine running full speed ahead—four bells for full speed astern.
Engine running ahead slow—three bells for full speed astern.

Distance Signals

808. Whenever two vessels desiring to communicate with each other are separated by distances too great to be bridged by ordinary signaling methods but are still in sight of each other, the "distance signals" shown in Figure 808 can be used.

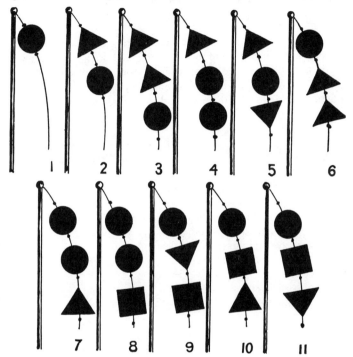

Figure 808. International System of Distance Signals (by Combining Balls, Cones, and Drums, or by Square Flags, Balls, Pennants, and Wefts) Used When the "Code" Cannot Be Read

1. "Preparative," "Answering," *or* "Stop" *after each complete signal.* 2. "Aground, want immediate assistance." 3. "I am on fire." 4. "Yes," *or Affirmative.* 5. "No," *or Negative.* 6. "Assistance is coming." 7. "Want a pilot." 8. *Asks the name of ship* (*or signal station*) *in sight or,* "Show your distinguishing signal." 9. "Repeat signal, or hoist it in a more conspicuous position." 10. "Cannot distinguish your flags, come nearer, or make distance signals." 11. *Cyclone, Hurricane, or Typhoon expected.*

Such signals are made from the highest practical point, preferably not to the masthead, as the mast, crow's-nest, etc., sometimes tend to distort the shapes. A usual place to make such signals is from a stay between the foremast and stack, the signals halyards being led to the bridge wing. Care should be exercised so that the signals are not raised into the smoke or outpouring heat of the funnels.

Day Marks

809. Day marks are shown by boats operating under special conditions, such as towing or being towed, fishing and dredging. The signal is made by a ball or cone shape. (Figure 809.) Small boats are not required by law to show day marks, but every operator should understand and be able to read them when displayed on other vessels.

Radio Time Signals

810. Radio time signals are sent daily from several United States naval radio stations. In the event of failure or error of the signal, it will be repeated one hour later.

The time signal consists of the transmission of dots (.) and the omission of the dots (o) for various seconds preceding the hour signal. The hour signal is the beginning of the transmission of a dash (–) which is much longer than the others (i. e., 1.5 seconds).

In all cases the beginnings of the dots and the dash indicate the beginning of the seconds, and the ends of the dots and the dash are without significance.

The number of dots sounded in the group at the end of any minute indicates the number of minutes of the signal yet to be sent.

TABLE OF NAVAL RADIO TIME SIGNALS

Minute interval during preceding hour	Seconds of Minute Intervals												
	1 to 28	29	30 to 50	51	52	53	54	55	56	57	58	59	60
Min.													
55 to 56	Dot (.)	o	Dot (.)	o	.	.	.	.	o	o	o	o	.
56 to 57	every	o	every	.	o	.	.	.	o	o	o	o	.
57 to 58	second 1	o	second	.	.	o	.	.	o	o	o	o	.
58 to 59	to 28	o	30 to	.	.	.	o	.	o	o	o	o	.
59 to hour	incl.	o	50 incl.	o	o	o	o	o	o	o	o	o	—

A vessel not under control shows a day mark consisting of two black balls vertically arranged placed in a position where they can be best seen. The same day signal shall be displayed by self-propelled suction dredges underway with their suctions on bottom.

 Vessels which are moored or anchored and engaged in laying pipe or operating on submarine construction display in daytime two balls in a vertical line, the upper ball being painted with alternate black and white vertical stripes and the lower ball in bright red.

 A steam vessel under sail alone shows a day mark consisting of one black ball.
This same signal is used on vessels of over 300 gross tons when anchored.

 A cable vessel in the daytime shows a day mark consisting of three shapes, the upper and lower of which are red balls and the center shape is in the form of a double cone base to base, painted bright white.

 Dredges held in a stationary position show two balls in the daytime, vertically arranged and placed in a position where they can best be seen.

 A vessel towing a submerged boat in daytime shows two shapes, one above the other, in the form of two double cones base to base, the upper cone being painted with alternate horizontal stripes of black and white and the lower shape being painted bright red.

 Steamers, lighters, and other vessels made fast alongside a wreck or moored over a wreck display two double cones base to base, both of which are painted bright red.

 A fishing vessel in the daytime may display a basket in the rigging.

Figure 809. Day Marks

Storm and Weather Signals

811. The storm flags are a red pennant or a red square with a black center flown in various combinations. These are shown, together with their meanings, in Figure 811. At night certain lantern combinations, hoisted vertically, give the same information and this also is shown in Figure 811.

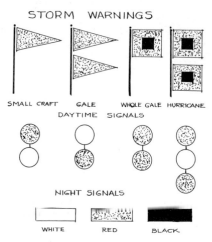

Figure 811. Storm-warning Signals

EXPLANATION OF SMALL CRAFT, STORM, AND HURRICANE WARNINGS

Small craft warning: One red pennant displayed by day and a red light above a white light at night to indicate winds up to 38 mph (33 knots) and/or sea conditions dangerous to small craft operations are forecast for the area.

Gale warning: Two red pennants displayed by day and a white light above a red light at night to indicate winds ranging from 39 to 54 mph (34 to 48 knots) are forecast for the area.

Whole gale warnings: A single square red flag with a black center displayed during daytime and two red lights at night to indicate winds ranging from 55 to 73 mph (48 to 63 knots) are forecast for the area.

Hurricane warning: Two square red flags with black centers displayed by day and a white light between two red lights at night to indicate that winds 74 mph (64 knots) and above are forecast for the area.

Both night and day storm signals are displayed at all Coast Guard stations, from the larger of the Coast Guard vessels (such as tugs, buoy tenders, cutters, etc.), from lightships on station, but *day signals only,* and from many private shore points. It is common for a yacht club, marina, shipyard or other boating facility to keep in touch with the local Coast Guard unit and, as a local service, display storm warnings. For full lists of display points as well as weather broadcasts, see "Storm-Warning Facilities Charts." These are in the form of eleven charts (soon to be 12) covering coastal waters and the Great Lakes and cost five cents each. Source is the Superintendent of Documents, Washington 25, D.C.

812. Storm-warning signals are displayed by the Weather Bureau in maritime communities and ports, and by the United States Coast Guard on some of their vessels, and by Coast Guard shore or surf stations. The various Coast Pilots contain local lists of points at which signals are displayed.

In some localities weather signals are displayed. Their meanings follow:

SQUARE FLAG	MEANING
All white	Clear and fair
All blue	Rain or snow
Upper half white, lower half blue	Local rain, snow or showers
White, square black center	Cold wave

A black pennant shown with the weather flag indicates temperature change. If above the weather signal, the temperature will rise; if below, it will fall.

Canada has a somewhat different storm warning code, based on the positions of certain forms of cones and cylinders by day and colored lights by night, as follows:

Moderate gale, commencing in the east
    By day: a cone, apex down
    By night: a single red light
A gale, commencing in the west
    By day: a cone, apex up
    By night: a red light over a white light
A heavy gale, commencing in the east
    By day: a cylinder over a cone, apex down

By night: a single red light
A heavy gale, commencing in the west
    By day: a cone, apex up, over a cylinder
    By night: a red light over a white light

International Code Signaling

813. Flag signaling is the oldest of the existing methods of visual signaling between vessels or between vessels and shore. The code used is international and standard in all civilized maritime nations.

The International Code consists of 26 letter flags, 10 numeral pennants, 3 repeater flags, and a code or answering pennant. The message, called a *hoist,* is read from top to bottom, and is sent aloft, if possible, in one string using a tack line (a length of halyard about one fathom long) to separate words, numbers, or meanings.

Messages often require more than one hoist. They are read in the following order:

First	Masthead
Second	Triatic stay
Third	Starboard yardarm
Fourth	Port yardarm

If all hoists are flown from the yardarm, the outboard hoist is the first read. If all hoists are flown from the triatic stay, the forward one is read first.

Signals remain flying until answered.

A signal is said to be *superior* to another if hoisted before the latter; it is *inferior* if hoisted after. It is also superior if hoisted in a preferred position (such as at the masthead), and inferior if hoisted in a secondary position (such as at the port yardarm).

How to Call

814. Unless the signal letters of a particular vessel are hoisted superior to the message, the message is understood to be addressed to all vessels. In the event that it is impossible to determine the signal letters of the ship desired to be addressed, the group VH is displayed superior. (Meaning: Hoist your signal letters.) At the same time the signal letters of the inquiring ship are displayed.

If this fails the group NMJ is displayed. (Meaning: I wish to signal to vessel—or vessels—on bearing blank from me.)

How to Answer Signals

815. The ship (or ships) addressed hoists the answering pennant *at the dip* (halfway up the halyard) as soon as it has seen each hoist made; and *close up* (fully hoist the answering pennant) as soon as read and understood. As soon as the hoist is hauled down on the transmitting ship, the answering pennant is lowered to *at the dip* on the receiving ship. Each hoist is so acknowledged until the message is completed.

Inasmuch as it is often difficult to distinguish between *at the dip* and *close up,* the answering pennant is not hoisted on the triatic stay signal halyards but rather to the masthead or a yardarm.

How to Complete a Signal

816. The transmitting ship hoists the answering pennant alone after the last message hoisted to indicate that the message has been completed. The receiving ship answers this in a similar manner to answering all other hoists; then makes the reply.

If the Signal Is Not Understood

817. If the receiving ship cannot distinguish or understand the signal made, the answering pennant is kept at the dip and an appropriate signal made, informing the transmitting ship of the reason.

If the hoist can be distinguished but not understood the pennant is kept at the dip and the signal VB made. (Meaning: Signal is not understood though flags are distinguished.)

818. Signaling, signaling practices, and code letters are given in full detail in the publication H.O. No. 87, entitled *International Code of Signals, Volume I, Visual and Sound,* which may be obtained from the Hydrographic Office, Washington, D.C., or its agencies in principal cities.

All the codes are given. In general they are divided as follows:

One-letter codes	Urgent or common use
Two-letter codes	Distress and maneuvering signals
Three-letter codes	Common words, phrases, and sentences
Four-letter codes	Those commencing with letter A are geographical locations; the remaining ones the signal letters of ships, shore stations, etc.

U.S. Ensign

Yacht Ensign

Jack

Club Burgee

Owner
Absent
Flag

Private Signal

Guest
Flag

Owner's
Meal
Flag

Officers' Flag

Crew Meal
Pennant

Yacht Flags

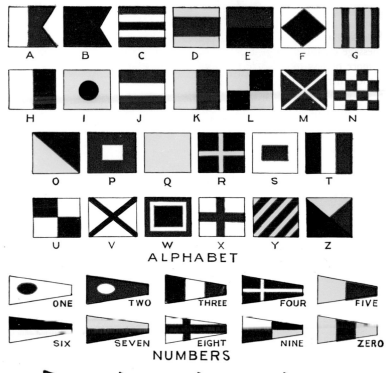

ALPHABET

NUMBERS

INTERNATIONAL CODE FLAGS AND PENNANTS

NAMES OF INTERNATIONAL ALPHABET FLAGS

A	ALFA	J	JULIET	R	ROMEO
B	BRAVO	K	KILO	S	SIERRA
C	CHARLIE	L	LIMA	T	TANGO
D	DELTA	M	MIKE	U	UNIFORM
E	ECHO	N	NOVEMBER	V	VICTOR
F	FOXTROT	O	OSCAR	W	WHISKEY
G	GOLF	P	PAPA	X	X RAY
H	HOTEL	Q	QUEBEC	Y	YANKEE
I	INDIA			Z	ZULU

819. In order to avoid confusion as the signalman calls off the letters of a flag hoist to the yeoman (or the person taking down the message on the message blank), the United States Navy has evolved a more or less foolproof system. Each letter is given a word sound rather than a letter sound, so that B, for example, cannot be confused with E, C, D or T. Its word sound is *Bravo,* a word unlike any other word in the code. These letter names are tabulated under the illustration on the preceding page.

The Semaphore Code of Flag Signaling

820. Semaphore or hand-flag signaling may be used for short distances for intership or ship-shore communication. It is very much faster than signaling by International Code hoists, and only one signalman is required at each end. Eight to ten words per minute is considered average sending speed. (Figure 820B.)

The flags may be of any color or combination of colors, and are usually selected to stand out from the background against which they will be seen.

All letters are made with the flags fixed, not fluttering. The cornet or attention sign alone is given by waving the flags. It is acknowledged by the letter C (answering sign) and the message given at once.

821. The letters of the semaphore code have additional meanings as follows:

Letters A to J	Numerals 1 to 10
A	Error
C	Answering sign
I	Execute
K	Negative

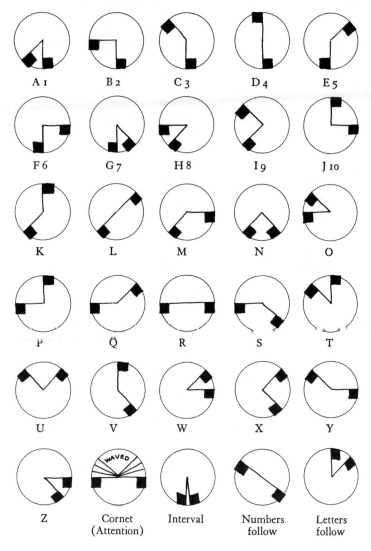

Figure 820A. The Hand Semaphore Code

L	Preparatory
N	Annulling
O	Interrogatory
P	Affirmative
R	Acknowledge

Figure 820B. Hand Semaphore

822. Large vessels and permanent short-signal stations are some-times equipped with a mechanical semaphore-sending device. This is

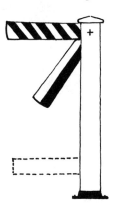

Figure 822A. The Semaphore Machine

usually located near the bridge and may be revolved to face the receiving ship. (Figure 822A.)

The code is exactly the same as for hand signaling. It has the advantage of fixed arms (or flags) and may be easily read even if to windward

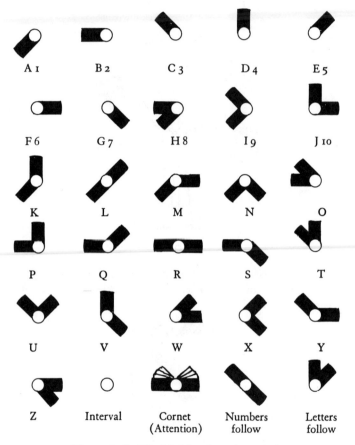

Figure 822B. The Machine Semaphore Code

or leeward, positions in which the hand flags are sometimes blown in such a manner as not to be easily read.

The International Morse Code (Dot and Dash Signals)

823. The international Morse code is truly international, and may be used to communicate with a ship or the shore in any civilized land

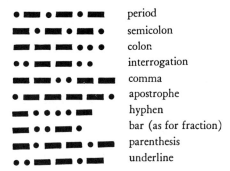

A • ━	M ━ ━	Y ━ • ━ ━
B ━ • • •	N ━ •	Z ━ ━ • •
C ━ • ━ •	O ━ ━ ━	1 • ━ ━ ━ ━
D ━ • •	P • ━ ━ •	2 • • ━ ━ ━
E •	Q ━ ━ • ━	3 • • • ━ ━
F • • ━ •	R • ━ •	4 • • • • ━
G ━ ━ •	S • • •	5 • • • • •
H • • • •	T ━	6 ━ • • • •
I • •	U • • ━	7 ━ ━ • • •
J • ━ ━ ━	V • • • ━	8 ━ ━ ━ • •
K ━ • ━	W • ━ ━	9 ━ ━ ━ ━ •
L • ━ • •	X ━ • • ━	0 ━ ━ ━ ━ ━

Figure 823A. The International Morse Code

with a reasonable chance of the message's being understood and answered. It is used in radio, blinker light, sound, and visual signaling.

The code is shown in Figure 823A above.

• ━ • ━ • ━	period
━ • ━ • ━ •	semicolon
━ ━ ━ • • •	colon
• • ━ ━ • •	interrogation
━ ━ • • ━ ━	comma
• ━ ━ ━ ━ •	apostrophe
━ • • • • ━	hyphen
━ • • ━ •	bar (as for fraction)
━ • ━ ━ • ━	parenthesis
• • ━ ━ • ━	underline

Figure 823B. International Morse Code Punctuation

German-Spanish

■■ ■■ ■■ ■■ CH

Spanish

■■ ■■ ● ■■ ■■ Ñ

Spanish-Scandinavian

● ■■ ■■ ● ■■ Á or Å

French

● ● ■■ ● ● É

German

● ■■ ● ■■ Ä

■■ ■■ ■■ ● Ö

● ● ■■ ■■ Ü

Figure 823C. International Morse Code Language Letters

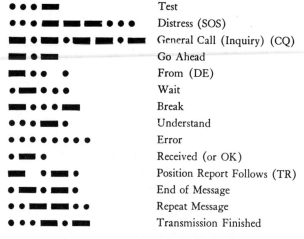

● ● ● ■■	Test
● ● ● ■■ ■■ ■■ ● ● ●	Distress (SOS)
■■ ● ■■ ● ■■ ■■ ● ■■	General Call (Inquiry) (CQ)
■■ ● ■■	Go Ahead
■■ ● ● ●	From (DE)
● ■■ ● ● ●	Wait
■■ ● ● ● ■■	Break
● ● ● ■■ ●	Understand
● ● ● ● ● ● ● ●	Error
● ■■ ●	Received (or OK)
■■ ● ■■ ●	Position Report Follows (TR)
● ■■ ● ■■ ●	End of Message
● ● ■■ ■■ ● ●	Repeat Message
● ● ● ■■ ● ■■	Transmission Finished

Figure 823D. International Morse Code Calls

824. Blinker code is sent, using the Morse code, by various types of lights. Emergency blinker messages may be sent with a flashlight, a lantern and screen, or by using the main or navigating light switches as keys.

Messages are divided into five component parts as follows:

Component	Transmitting Vessel Makes	Receiving Vessel Makes
1. Call	AA AA AA (general call)	TT TT TT (answer)
2. Identity	DE—signal letters or name	Repeats
3. Break sign	BT (text follows)	BT
4. Text	Message	Acknowledges each group of words or codes by TT TT
5. Ending	AR (message finished)	R (message received)

After a vessel has established her identity (if requested) future messages are carried on by the parts 1, 3, 4, and 5 only.

H.O. 87 should be referred to for complete details of blinker signaling, especially if communication with naval vessels or bases is contemplated.

825. Sound signals by Morse code may be made on the whistle, foghorn, or other sounding device. It is to be considered purely as an emergency form of signaling, as such signals would create confusion in fog or in waters having heavy traffic.

The signals are made as follows:

Component	Transmitting Vessel Makes	Receiving Vessel Makes
1. Call	AA AA AA	TT TT TT
2. Break sign	BT	(No acknowledgment)
3. Text	Message	"
4. Ending	AR	R

NOTE: If the message is not understood by the receiving ship she makes UD (repeat); otherwise the message is considered as having been understood and so acknowledged by making R.

Wigwag Morse Code Signaling

826. The Morse code may be used in a system of flag manipulations which are basically very simple. The flag may be of any color easily seen against the background and should be bent to a staff about five feet long. (Figure 826.)

Attention is called by waving, and is answered by TT TT.

The start is made by holding the staff vertical, flag up. Dots are made by dipping the flag to the right (of the signalman making the message), and dashes are made by dipping the flag to the left. The interval (flag down) is made between words or sentences.

AR signifies message completed and R message received.

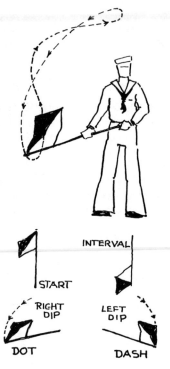

Figure 826. Wigwag Signaling, Using International Morse Code

Private Signal Codes

827. Private codes are used by some nautical organizations, particularly yacht clubs when racing or moving in squadron formation. A private signal-code book must be used, and a signal made from it is preceded by the international code hoist NMM, indicating that the message is not to be interpreted from the International Code book.

In general, signals in the club code consist of:

Special, racing, and emergency signals (one of two flags, from A to Z, and A to AZ).
General signals (two flags, BA to GZ).
Designation (two flags, HA to HZ).
Days of the week (two flags, IQ to IZ).
Hours of the day (two flags, JA to KY).
Names of places (two flags, NA to WZ).
Compass signals (three flags, AQD to AST).

Radiotelephone

828. Radiotelephone equipment and service are now available for even the smallest boats. Six, 12, 32, and 110 volt circuits are standard. Some equipment includes radio direction-finding apparatus as well as short wave and standard broadcast bands.

The smaller sets operate on from two to ten frequencies, four being considered the least required for practical communication purposes.

The frequencies are shown in the tables on the following pages.

On small sets switching is not automatic, and the antenna must be manually switched from sending to receiving by a phone-piece button, or by operation of the main switch. The call is received on small sets by means of a loud speaker, the set being tuned to the shore station by the receiver; or by calling the shore station at regular periods and picking up waiting calls. Large sets have usual telephone bell-ringing systems, and the station can be called at any time.

Through shore stations, connection may be made with any land telephone in the world, or with another or a chain of shore stations, thus making transmitting possible over distances far greater than the range of the set by land or radio hookup with more powerful sets. Rates are approximately the same as for general telephone calls for equal zone distances plus a marine call charge. Calls on the ship-to-ship frequency are made without charge if they have not gone through a shore station.

Shore Stations

829. The daylight range of a 50-watt transmitter is about 300 miles; of a 15-watt set about 175 miles. Range increases at night. Range may increase or decrease very much with change in atmospheric conditions.

FREQUENCIES USED FOR THE MARINE RADIO TELEPHONE SERVICE

SERVICE	SHIP TRANSMITTER	SHIP RECEIVER	RECEIVER CRYSTAL FREQUENCY
Ship to Ship	2738	2738	2283
Ship to Ship	2638	2638	2183
Coast Guard	2670	2670	2215
Harbor Stations:			
Boston	2110	2506	2051
New York	2198	2590	2135
New York	2126	2522	2067
Wilmington	2166	2558	2103
Norfolk	2142	2538	2083
Miami	2118	2514	2059
Tampa	2158	2550	2095
New Orleans	2206	2598	2143
Charleston	2174	2566	2111
Galveston	2134	2530	2075
San Pedro	2174	2566	2111
San Francisco	2110	2506	2051
Astoria	2206	2598	2143
Portland	2206	2598	2143
Seattle	2126	2522	2067
San Juan, P.R.	2134	2530	2075
Kahuku, T.H.	2134	2530	2075

GREAT LAKES

SERVICE	SHIP TRANSMITTER	SHIP RECEIVER	RECEIVER CRYSTAL FREQUENCY
Ship to Ship			
Channel #40	2738	2738	2283
General Calling, Safety			
Channel #51	2182	2182	1727
Ship to Shore, Vessels under 1,000 tons			
Channel #39	2118	2514	2059
Ship to Shore, Vessels over 1,000 tons			
Channel #30	2158	2550	2105
Ship to Shore, Canadian Vessels			
Channel #38	2206	2582	2127

SERVICE	SHIP TRANSMITTER	SHIP RECEIVER	RECEIVER CRYSTAL FREQUENCY
Ship to Shore Channel #60	4422.5	4282.5	3827.5
Ship to Shore Channel #20	6660	6470	6015
Ship to Shore Channel #10	8820	8585	8130

MISSISSIPPI VALLEY

SERVICE	SHIP TRANSMITTER	SHIP RECEIVER	RECEIVER CRYSTAL FREQUENCY
Ship to Ship Channel #4	2738	2738	2283
Ship to Shore Channel #5	2782	2782	2327
Ship to Shore Channel #1	4162.5	4162.5	3707.5
Ship to Shore Channel #2	6455	6455	6000
Ship to Shore Channel #6	8840	8840	8385
Ship to Shore Channel #7	11090	11090	10635

The following frequencies are used for communication with the stations indicated:

COASTAL STATION FREQUENCY	SHIP FREQUENCY	USE
2182 kc.	2182 kc.	For calling, answering, and safety purposes.
2514 kc.	2118 kc.	Primarily for communication with U.S. and Canadian ships of 1,000 gross tons and less.
2550 kc.	2158 kc.	Primarily for communication with U.S. ships of over 1,000 gross tons.
2582 kc.	2206 kc.	For communication with Canadian ships only.

The following frequency is used for communication with the stations indicated:

2738 kc.	2738 kc.	Primarily for communications relating to safety of navigation to ship's business.

The following frequencies may be used for communication with U.S. Coast Guard stations:

COASTAL STATION FREQUENCY	SHIP FREQUENCY	USE
2182 kc.	2182 kc.	Great Lakes only.
2670 kc.	2670 kc.	Elsewhere (emergency only).

Note: The air is becoming crowded and frequent changes are ordered in operating ranges. The tables appearing here are subject to change and the ship's radio desk should be furnished with the latest frequency assignments.

Making a Call

830. The owner will first have duly registered with the telephone company, given the boat's call signal, set up an account, and requested the type of service desired (for yachts and noncommercial boats this is the General Service).

831. A call *from* the boat is made by merely listening to hear if the channel is clear and if so, giving the answering operator the name of the boat calling and the number desired. If a ship is being called, give its call letters and probable location. Upon completion of the call the operator is given the calling boat's letters and the information that it is signing off.

832. A call from land *to* a boat is made by requesting Long Distance and then the Marine Operator. Give the called boat's name (or call letters and name), its probable location; then follow the operator's instructions.

833. A call to the *Coast Guard* is made only in emergencies or for information which the Coast Guard usually gives. Request for weather information would hardly be fair (considering that it is sent out at frequent intervals anyway). Requests for medical advice, assistance, conditions over bars or in storm areas, or reporting vessels in distress are all legitimate reasons for using the Coast Guard frequency.

Any shore station will relay a call to the Coast Guard free of charge.

Telegrams may be sent via radiotelephone.

Licenses Required

834. 1. A license to operate a ship's radio station, and a request for assignment of call letters. Good for one year and renewable upon application.

2. A Restricted Radiotelephone Operator's Permit. Good for three years and renewable upon application. Examination is extremely simple and requires no technical knowledge or knowledge of code. It does require a familiarity with regulations affecting radio traffic and elementary radio law.

Both licenses are free and are obtainable from the Federal Communications Commission (F.C.C.) at Washington, D.C., or its local office.

835. Any person, licensed or not, may freely use the radiotelephone. The law requires only that someone on board must be licensed (master, owner, etc.).

836. The operator's permit referred to does not give authority for the holder to make any frequency or other changes to the set. The experimenter or radio "ham" requires a second- or first-class license, obtainable only after technical examination. Any adjustments to the set must be made by or in the presence of a holder of a more advanced license. The restricted license is a license to *use* the radiotelephone only.

Installation

837. In addition to an antenna (usually a single wire) a copper ground plate of about ten square feet in area is necessary on the wooden-hulled boat. The shrouds of sailing vessels may be used as antennas if insulated from the hull.

The installation must be made by a licensed radio worker, and frequencies tested for compliance with all regulations.

The ordinary battery system will seldom stand the heavy drain of even a low-powered transmitting set, and booster batteries or a separate battery and generator plant are required.

In General

838. If you have a *legitimate* priority call, you may use the following to clear the channels and get attention.

Distress: Mayday, Mayday, Mayday (repeat until air is clear).
Urgent and concerning safety of vessel or crew: Pan, Pan, Pan.

Weather information (needed promptly) or safety (i.e., condition of the sea over a bar, or at an inlet): Security, Security.

You are required by the Federal Communications Commission to keep a log of every call in or out. (Rule 8.368)

You are also required to maintain a radio watch on 2182 kc. (Rule 8.223). This is hardly practical on small craft because there simply aren't the power reserves. In a crowded yachting area, you probably can assume that *somebody* is monitoring the air at any given moment. However, at sea or in lonely areas, it becomes a duty to listen. If the battery won't stand a constant drain, click in every five minutes. Reception does not consume much power and somebody may be in trouble—and so may you someday.

Inspecting officers may request to examine the radio log and to see your license. Keep these handy.

Do not break in on conversations. When you get the air, be brief and concise, identify yourself by call number and/or yacht name each time you speak. If possible, sometime in the message work in your approximate position. (*See* sample radio conversation following.) This may help if you strike trouble or break down, for the Coast Guard is listening and picks just this kind of information out of the babble that pervades the radio air. Watch your language. No one will blame you for getting mad at the inane conversations that fill the small-craft channels, but don't—repeat DON'T—damn them. It is a criminal offense to use profanity or obscene language on the air.

If you carry, even temporarily, passengers for hire and they number more than six, your vessel *must* be equipped with a radiophone. You will need at least a Third Class license and a set which puts out not less than 25 watts. Vessel operator's licenses are also required as indicated in Chapter IV. If your boat is chartered, it is not carrying passengers for hire if you go with the boat as a *guest* of the charterer. The charterer may use your radiophone under your license, but you are responsible for him and what he does or says.

Example of Form for a Ship-to-ship Conversation

839. Remember—wait for a break; then be brief.

CALLING VESSEL

VESSEL CALLED

Calling W 2 877. This is CD 335, the yacht *Dog Star*. Come in please. (Repeat 3 times and end with "Over.")

CD 335, the yacht *Dog Star*. This is W 2 877, the ketch *Windigo*. I read you loud and clear. Over.

This is CD 335. Good morning, W 2 877. I have a message for you. (Repeat message twice; then add "Over" and listen.)

This is W 2 877. I have your message and thank you. There is no reply at present but I will call you at 2300 if agreeable. Over:

This is CD 335. Yes—I will listen for you on this channel at 2300. This is CD 335, the yacht *Dog Star,* heading 145 true from Cape Porpoise Sea Buoy. Signing off. Over and out.

This is W 2 877, the ketch *Windigo*. To CD 335. Acknowledge. This is W 2 877, off Thatcher's, 3 miles, heading for Rockport. Over and out.

PART III
PILOTING AND NAVIGATION

⚓

CHAPTER IX

THE INSTRUMENTS OF
PILOTING

In broaching the subject of navigation, let it be understood that the approach in this *Manual* is entirely from the viewpoint of the small-boat man. His navigating is done almost entirely by visible aids to navigation or by soundings (called piloting); when overtaken by thick weather or when making the occasional hundred-mile leg offshore he relies upon his compass, and log, and lead—and perhaps more than any of these, upon his lookout. And this is as it should be.

To introduce into this *Manual* a complete treatise on navigation (the average technical volume dealing with the subject reaches a thousand pages of this size) would be but to obfuscate the simple elements of the subject which are all that the small-boat man needs to get from "here to there" in safety. Gyrocompasses and pitometer logs and fathometers are interesting and necessary to the deepwater navigator, but in no way concern the 'long-shore navigator; nor is his vessel likely to be equipped with such apparatus. Celestial navigation, too, while interesting to the student and necessary to the yachtsman who regularly makes long ocean passages, is of no use to the coastwise navigator. In extremis, celestial navigation for the small-boat man is what Alfred Loomis so soundly defined it: the ability to distinguish sunrise from sunset, then to steer toward the sunset until a large continent looms in sight! It may be pointed out that on the Pacific Coast it would be best to steer toward the sunrise. In either case, the navigator will come upon some aid to navigation, or a familiar coast line, and it behooves him then to thoroughly understand piloting.

901. The following instruments are required for piloting.

Compass	Magnetic, at least 4″ card.
Lead and line	5 to 14 pounds and line marked to about 20 fathoms.
Log	Patent or taffrail (or chip).
Course protractor	Single arm.

Dividers	About 5″ legs.
Binoculars	7 x 35 (or 50), prismatic best.
Time piece	Accurate watch or chronometer.
Deviation card	For the compass and boat used.
Charts	Local.
Publications	Light List, Tide Tables, Current Tables, Coast Pilot for the locale.
Logbook	Or paper or notebook for calculations and record.

Other tools desirable but not absolutely necessary are: parallel rulers, drawing compass, straight edge, Notices to Mariners, pelorus (preferably to fit on standard compass), thermometer, stop watch, etc. Radio navigation requires a direction finder and a radio-beacon chart, and a standard broadcast receiver is helpful at times.

The Magnetic Compass

902. The magnetic compass is a mechanical contrivance making use of the electrical attraction of the magnetic poles. Basically it is a freely suspended magnet which tends always to point toward the magnetic North Pole. To this magnet is attached a circular card, graduated, and which is read at the lubber's line, which is simply the vessel's heading marked conveniently near the card on the inside of the bowl. Thus a fixed pointer (the only such pointer on a vessel) is obtained. *It is always fixed and the boat always moves around it.* It is of the utmost importance that the novice firmly fix this truth in his mind—in relation to the earth *the compass card never moves;* the boat *moves around it to the extent shown by the lubber's line.*

Various methods of suspending this magnet are in use; liquids are introduced to slow or steady the pointer and the entire device suspended in gimbals, permitting it to remain level and accurate regardless of angle of heel or pitch. It is often enclosed in a binnacle for protection and fitted with various hoods, magnifiers, and lighting devices for easy reading and for night use.

The compass is always installed, with the lubber's line and the center of the pivot on which the magnet and its attached card rotates, on the fore-and-aft line of the boat. This line may be any distance from the center fore-and-aft line but must be parallel to it. It must never be assumed that a thwartships bulkhead is at perfect right angles to the center line and that the compass, affixed to such a bulkhead, will be accurate. A line must be stretched from the exact center of the stem to the exact center of the transom, and the lubber's line and the center of the pivot be equidistant from such a line.

If the compass is thus placed accurately, a reading at the lubber's line will be the compass course of the boat.

903. The compass card is marked in several ways, two of which are in common use. Figure 903 shows these. The inner card is that of the age of sailing and was accurate enough for the wandering courses of sailing vessels. The outer card, marked in degrees, is most commonly used today.

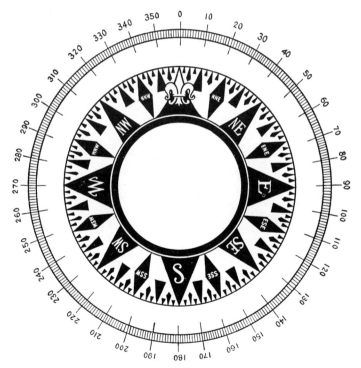

Figure 903. The Mariner's Compass

Inner—the quarter-point card
Outer—the 360° (or Navy) card

The circumference of the card is divided into 32 points of $11\frac{1}{4}$ degrees each. North, south, east, and west are the cardinal points, and midway between each cardinal point is an intercardinal point, northeast, southeast, southwest, and northwest. Between each cardinal and intercardinal point is an intermediate point. There are 16 intermediate points always recognized by the sign "x" or "by." An easy way to remember the intermediate points is to regard the "x" as saying "but." Thus NW x W is northwest (the intercardinal or cardinal point first) *but* west of it. S x W is S *but* west of it. The distance in the direction indicated from the cardinal or intercardinal point by the second component of the intermediate point is always one point, or $\frac{1}{32}$ of the circle.

The quarter points are the four divisions of each point, named as in the following table:

1ST QUADRANT	2ND QUADRANT	3RD QUADRANT	4TH QUADRANT
North	*East*	*South*	*West*
N ¼ E	E ¼ S	S ¼ W	W ¼ N
N ½ E	E ½ S	S ½ W	W ½ N
N ¾ E	E ¾ S	S ¾ W	W ¾ N
NxE	ExS	SxW	WxN
NxE ¼ E	ESE ¾ E	SxW ¼ W	WNW ¾ W
NxE ½ E	ESE ½ E	SxW ½ W	WNW ½ W
NxE ¾ E	ESE ¼ E	SxW ¾ W	WNW ¼ W
NNE	ESE	SSW	WNW
NNE ¼ E	SExE ¾ E	SSW ¼ W	NWxW ¾ W
NNE ½ E	SExE ½ E	SSW ½ W	NWxW ½ W
NNE ¾ E	SExE ¼ E	SSW ¾ W	NWxW ¼ W
NExN	SExE	SWxS	NWxW
NE ¾ N	SE ¾ E	SW ¾ S	NW ¾ W
NE ½ N	SE ½ E	SW ½ S	NW ½ W
NE ¼ N	SE ¼ E	SW ¼ S	NW ¼ W
NE	SE	SW	NW
NE ¼ E	SE ¼ S	SW ¼ W	NW ¼ N
NE ½ E	SE ½ S	SW ½ W	NW ½ N
NE ¾ E	SE ¾ S	SW ¾ W	NW ¾ N
NExE	SExS	SWxW	NWxN
NExE ¼ E	SSE ¾ E	SWxW ¼ W	NNW ¾ W
NExE ½ E	SSE ½ E	SWxW ½ W	NNW ½ W

NExE ¾ E	SSE ¼ E	SWxW ¾ W	NNW ¼ W
ENE	SSE	WSW	NNW
ENE ¼ E	SxE ¾ E	WSW ¼ W	NxW ¾ W
ENE ½ E	SxE ½ E	WSW ½ W	NxW ½ W
ENE ¾ E	SxE ¼ E	WSW ¾ W	NxW ¼ W
ExN	SxE	WxS	NxW
E ¾ N	S ¾ E	W ¾ S	N ¾ W
E ½ N	S ½ E	W ½ S	N ½ W
E ¼ N	S ¼ E	W ¼ S	N ¼ W
East	*South*	*West*	*North*

Boxing the compass includes the ability to name the opposite (across the card) point from any other point. First the cardinal and inter-cardinal points are thoroughly memorized, then the intermediate points, then the quarter points. The navigator should know how to box the compass, always visualizing the card as fixed and the lubber's line revolving about it.

The 360° or Navy card is divided into 360 degrees starting with zero (north) and proceeding clockwise. It is the most accurate of all the cards and makes fine steering possible, and is considered the correct card for modern times. (Figure 903.)

Commercial vessels and the United States Navy all use the degree card for steering. However, wind and weather occurrences are referred to in relation to the compass points. The double card having both degree and compass points is in common use, and is perhaps the most widely used whether steering by degrees or points. It would seem that the navigator, who has probably worked the navigational problems in points, would do best, when acting as helmsman, to steer by points. However, when giving the course to another there will be less con-fusion (especially to the nonsailor) and more accuracy by steering a degree course.

904. Degree and Compass-Point Table

Compass Points	Degrees	Points	Compass Points	Degrees	Points
North	0° 00′ 00″	0	NxE	11° 15′ 00″	1
N¼E	2° 48′ 45″	¼	NxE¼E	14 03 45	1¼
N½E	5 37 30	½	NxE½E	16 52 30	1½
N¾E	8 26 15	¾	NxE¾E	19 41 15	1¾

Compass Points	Degrees	Points	Compass Points	Degrees	Points
NNE	22° 30′ 00″	2	SE	135° 00′ 00″	4
NNE¼E	25 18 45	2¼	SE¼S	137 48 45	3¾
NNE½E	28 07 30	2½	SE½S	140 37 30	3½
NNE¾E	30 56 15	2¾	SE¾S	143 26 15	3¼
NExN	33 45 00	3	SExS	146 15 00	3
NE¾N	36 33 45	3¼	SSE¾E	149 03 45	2¾
NE½N	39 22 30	3½	SSE½E	151 52 30	2½
NE¼N	42 11 15	3¾	SSE¼E	154 41 15	2¼
NE	45 00 00	4	SSE	157 30 00	2
NE¼E	47 48 45	4¼	SxE¾E	160 18 45	1¾
NE½E	50 37 30	4½	SxE½E	163 07 30	1½
NE¾E	53 26 15	4¾	SxE¼E	165 56 15	1¼
NExE	56 15 00	5	SxE	168 45 00	1
NExE¼E	59 03 45	5¼	S¾E	171 33 45	¾
NExE½E	61 52 30	5½	S½E	174 22 30	½
NExE¾E	64 41 15	5¾	S¼E	177 11 15	¼
ENE	67 30 00	6	South	180 00 00	0
ENE¼E	70 18 45	6¼	S¼W	182 48 45	¼
ENE½E	73 07 30	6½	S½W	185 37 30	½
ENE¾E	75 56 15	6¾	S¾W	188 26 15	¾
ExN	78 45 00	7	SxW	191 15 00	1
E¾N	81 33 45	7¼	SxW¼W	194 03 45	1¼
E½N	84 22 30	7½	SxW½W	196 52 30	1½
E¼N	87 11 15	7¾	SxW¾W	199 41 15	1¾
East	90 00 00	8	SSW	202 30 00	2
E¼S	92 48 45	7¾	SSW¼W	205 18 45	2¼
E½S	95 37 30	7½	SSW½W	208 07 30	2½
E¾S	98 26 15	7¼	SSW¾W	210 56 15	2¾
ExS	101 15 00	7	SWxS	213 45 00	3
ESE¾E	104 03 45	6¾	SW¾S	216 33 45	3¼
ESE½E	106 52 30	6½	SW½S	219 22 30	3½
ESE¼E	109 41 15	6¼	SW¼S	222 11 15	3¾
ESE	112 30 00	6	SW	225 00 00	4
SExE¾E	115 18 45	5¾	SW¼W	227 48 45	4¼
SExE½E	118 07 30	5½	SW½W	230 37 30	4½
SExE¼E	120 56 15	5¼	SW¾W	233 26 15	4¾
SExE	123 45 00	5	SWxW	236 15 00	5
SE¾E	126 33 45	4¾	SWxW¼W	239 03 45	5¼
SE½E	129 22 30	4½	SWxW½W	241 52 30	5½
SE¼E	132 11 15	4¼	SWxW¾W	244 41 15	5¾

Compass Points	Degrees	Points	Compass Points	Degrees	Points
WSW	247° 30′ 00″	6	NWxW	303° 45′ 00″	5
WSW¼W	250 18 45	6¼	NW¾W	306 33 45	4¾
WSW½W	253 07 30	6½	NW½W	309 22 30	4½
WSW¾W	255 56 15	6¾	NW¼W	312 11 15	4¼
WxS	258 45 00	7	NW	315 00 00	4
W¾S	261 33 45	7¼	NW¼N	317 48 45	3¾
W½S	264 22 30	7½	NW½N	320 37 30	3½
W¼S	267 11 15	7¾	NW¾N	323 26 15	3¼
West	270 00 00	8	NWxN	326 15 00	3
W¼N	272 48 45	7¾	NNW¾W	329 03 45	2¾
W½N	275 37 30	7½	NNW½W	331 52 30	2½
W¾N	278 26 15	7¼	NNW¼W	334 41 15	2¼
WxN	281 15 00	7	NNW	337 30 00	2
WNW¾W	284 03 45	6¾	NxW¾W	340 18 45	1¾
WNW½W	286 52 30	6½	NxW½W	343 07 30	1½
WNW¼W	289 41 15	6¼	NxW¼W	345 56 15	1¼
WNW	292 30 00	6	NxW	348 45 00	1
NWxW¾W	295 18 45	5¾	N¾W	351 33 45	¾
NWxW½W	298 07 30	5½	N½W	354 22 30	½
NWxW¼W	300 56 15	5¼	N¼W	357 11 15	¼

905. It will be noted that the system of relative bearings also makes use of 32-point division of the imaginary circle around the vessel. They are definitely related to the compass bearings.

Thus a vessel heading north, having a stern wind, would refer to the wind as a 180° or a south wind. If the vessel were heading west with a stern wind, the wind would be a 90° or an east wind. If heading west with the wind broad on the port quarter, the wind would be a 135°, or southeast wind.

Example of relative bearings compared to compass bearings of a vessel headed north (north to south, or starboard side).

RELATIVE BEARINGS

Wind

N ....Ahead.
NxE ....One point on starboard bow.
NNE ....Two points on starboard bow.
NExN ....Three points on starboard bow.
NE ....Broad on starboard bow.

NExE ....Three points forward on starboard beam.
ENE ....Two points forward on starboard beam.
ExN ....One point forward on starboard beam.
E ....Abeam, or, broad on starboard beam.
ExS ....One point abaft starboard beam.
ESE ....Two points abaft starboard beam.
SExE ....Three points abaft starboard beam.
SE ....Broad on starboard quarter.
SExS ....Three points on starboard quarter.
SSE ....Two points on starboard quarter.
SxE ....One point on starboard quarter.
S ....Astern.

It is necessary to know the boxing of the compass to convert such bearings. For example, the boat is heading NNE: What is the compass bearing of a wind three points on the port bow?

Emergency Direction Finding

906. If the compass fails or becomes lost or broken, the navigator has two simple methods to give him general direction.

By Day. North by Watch.

With a watch or clock known to be reasonably accurate, hold it level and in such a position that the hour hand points to the sun. Exactly halfway between the hour hand and twelve o'clock will be

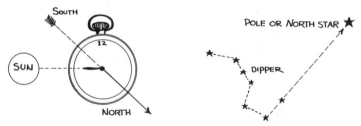

Figure 906. Emergency Direction Finder

south, and directly opposite, of course, north. (South of the equator, the halfway mark will be north.)

By Night. North by the Pole Star.

The Dipper (7 stars in the shape of a common water dipper and which are always visible in clear weather from most of the northern hemisphere) is found in the constellation of the Bear. A line drawn through the two front stars of the dipper's bowl will lead to a conspicuously bright star, which is Polaris, the North Star. (Figure 906.)

COMPASS ERROR

Variation

907. Magnetic north and geographic or true north (to which all navigational charts are oriented) do not coincide. True north and south (the poles) are used as the chart poles because both are fixed and unvarying. Magnetic north is some 400 miles south of geographic north and is constantly, though predictably, changing its exact location.

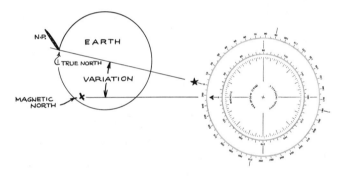

Figure 907. Variation

Therefore, when the compass needle points north it is not pointing to the north of the chart but to a different (magnetic) north. The amount of separation between these two points is called variation, and is expressed in degrees.

The amount of this variation varies with the locality, as it follows certain magnetic channels between the poles; it may vary east or west of the true meridian, or there may be no variation at all.

On coastwise charts the amount of variation in the locality shown on that chart is shown by a combination compass rose. This is a triple graduated circle (*see* Figure 907), the two outer roses marked in degrees and the inner marked in compass points. The outer circle is oriented to true or geographical north; its zero degrees is *true north*. The inner circle is oriented to magnetic north of the year noted in the center; its "north point" is *magnetic north*. The difference between the two points is the variation in the year noted in the center of the rose, top half.

The variation in the year *read* is obtained by multiplying the annual increase or decrease noted in the lower half of the center by the number of years elapsed between printing and reading. Thus, on the chart rose shown in Figure 907 the variation in 1948 was 12° west (note information in left-hand circle) and the variation increases 4′ each year (note information in the right-hand circle). The variation in 1951, therefore, equals 3 x 4′ or 12′ (years elapsed x annual increase), and the total variation in 1951 is 12° 12′ west. Had the annual variation been decreased the amount would be subtracted.

When a magnetic course is changed to true course *east* variation is always *added* and *west* variation is always *subtracted*. East variation is always shown to the right of the true north, and west variation to the left.

Unless the chart used is very old and the total annual increase or decrease amounts to a substantial part of a degree, the coastwise cruiser may safely disregard annual changes in variation on short courses. In practice, normal errors in steering and in estimating drift and windage will greatly outweigh the annual error in variation. Long sea courses should, however, take the annual variation into consideration.

Deviation

908. Deviation is another form of compass error. It is caused by magnetism within the vessel which affects the accuracy of the compass and must be corrected by placing compensating magnets about the compass—which nullify its effects—or by calculating a table showing the deviation error on various headings (as the magnetism moves about the fixed compass needle). It is usual to eliminate as much of the deviation as possible by placing surrounding magnets; then calculate a deviation chart for the remaining error. This error is applied to the correct course and results in the compass course, which is the course steered, and is neither a magnetic nor a true course.

All boats have varying magnetic characteristics peculiar to themselves and caused by a combination of factors, such as induced magnetism in iron ballast, in the iron masses of the machinery, in electrical apparatus, and in the hull, even though itself of wood.

Strong magnetic influences sometimes affect the compass sufficiently to make it worthless, but most of these can be eliminated by the careful location of the compass itself. It should be as far away as possible from the engine, and, especially, from such influences as the coil, generator, or other apparatus having a magnetic field. No part of the compass or binnacle should be electrically grounded. Wires passing near by should be twisted around themselves to neutralize their fields, and iron or steel objects (such as knives, marlinspikes, etc.) should be kept away from the vicinity of the compass and out of the pockets of the helmsman. Magnetic energy will pass through anything and therefore shielding is of no avail.

Commercial vessels and some yachts engage a professional compass adjuster (cost $50 or thereabouts) who places the compensating magnets about the compass where needed and who furnishes the ship with a card showing residual compass errors. These must be taken into consideration when laying out courses in the manner to be later detailed.

While there are several methods of compensating compasses the simplest for the small-boat man is the following ("Hoke" method).

909. Provide the boat with two bar compensating magnets (permanently magnetized small bars, usually enclosed in a copper sheath pierced for nailing). With the compass in its usual position and free of magnetic influences (including the two bars) take the boat out to a buoy (during slack water and preferably on a still day) about which there is a mile or more of sea room. Prepare, meantime, several large wads of balled newsprint, or a child's balloon weighted with about six to eight ounces on a three-foot line.

From the buoy, put the boat on a due north compass course and run, without change, for about 600 yards (zero course). Toss the balloon into the wake, make a quick complete turn, run over the balloon, and head directly back to the buoy. (Figure 909A.)

The compass should read 180°, or south. If it does not (and it probably will not) it will require compensating.

This is done at once by placing one of the bar magnets ahead or astern of the compass with its long axis on an exact thwartship line and with its center exactly on the fore-and-aft (or lubber) line of the compass. It is turned end for end until the error is decreased; then moved toward or away from the compass until the compass course reads exactly halfway between south and the reading without the bar, and here lightly secured by tacks. The boat, meantime, must have been on a course exactly on the buoy. (Figure 909B.)

Repeat the entire maneuver again. The compass course of zero, reversed, should be the compass course 180°. If it is not, repeat again eliminating the last remaining error by careful and minute adjust-

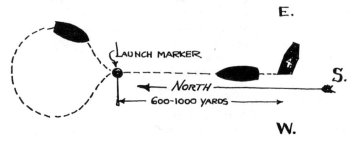

Figure 909A. "Hoke" Method of Compensating the Compass

ment of the bar magnet, permanently fastening the bar only after perfection.

A similar procedure is followed for an east-west or west-east course (whichever is most convenient), but the compensating magnet is placed with its long axis on a fore-and-aft line, on either side of the compass, but with its center on a thwartship line passing through the center of the compass.

Many modern compasses have built-in compensating magnets easily adjusted with a screwdriver or thumb turn. They are recommended.

910. Heeling error is the compass error caused by the change of the relative position of large ballast castings. It is compensated for by placing a magnet *under* the compass, locating it with the north (red) end up in the Northern Hemisphere.

As the greatest heeling error is found on north and south courses the ship is so headed, and the compensating magnet moved toward or away from the compass until the compass does not deviate as the boat heels. Heeling error adjustment should be made before other adjustments. The heeling magnet has no effect on the compass when the boat is on level keel.

911. Compensating the compass does not cure all the problems of deviation; it merely reduces them to an irreducible minimum. As the amount and direction of deviation vary with every course or bearing, a further correction is required to arrive at accurate true courses.

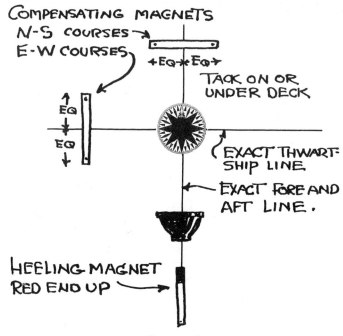

Figure 909B.

Finding the deviation on various headings requires the comparing of compass bearings with magnetic bearings as the ship is headed on various courses. This is done by taking magnetic bearings on the sun, or by running over known ranges, maintained for the purpose by the government, or by running between any objects, such as buoys which have a known magnetic bearing, or by swinging ship and noting the bearings of some fixed object.

In any case, the difference between the magnetic bearing and the observed compass bearing on that heading is the deviation on that heading. The deviation is noted for each heading on some convenient form. Deviation is east if the magnetic bearing is greater than the compass bearing. Deviation is west if the magnetic bearing is less than the compass bearing.

Swinging ship is the simplest for the small-boat man. (Figure 911.) The boat is anchored, bow and stern, off some prominent object

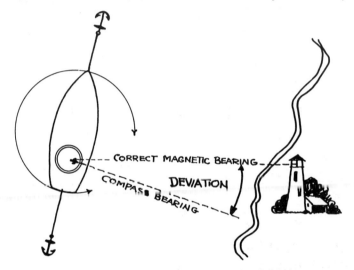

Figure 911. Swinging Ship to Determine Deviation

(such as lighthouse, steeple, etc.) about five miles off. By cross bearings, or soundings, or other methods, the exact location of the boat is established, and the magnetic bearing of the shore object to the boat noted. The difference between this magnetic bearing and the compass bearing as the ship is headed and steadied at various positions over the same spot will show the deviation on the respective heading.

The ship may be swung using a near-by object as well. In this case the boat's compass is taken ashore and the bearing noted from object to boat. This bearing is then reversed, the compass taken back on board and the ship swung as described. A chart is not required, as the compass ashore has indicated the correct magnetic bearing in reverse (it being free of the causes of the deviation on board).

While a complex pelorus form is used by professionals for taking bearings of distant objects, the average small-boat man will be well served by a simple azimuth attachment on the steering compass. It is

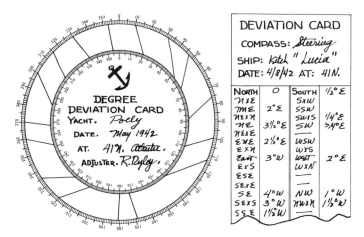

DEGREE
DEVIATION CARD
YACHT. *Poely*
DATE. *May 1942*
AT. *41N. Atantic.*
ADJUSTER. *R. Ryley.*

DEVIATION CARD
COMPASS: *Steering*
SHIP: *Ketch "Lucia"*
DATE: *4/8/42* AT: *41N.*

North	0	South	½° E
N x E		S x W	
NNE	2° E	SSW	
NE x N		SW x S	¼° E
NE	3½° E	SW	¾° E
NE x E		—	
ENE	2½° E	WSW	
E x N		W x S	
East	3° W	West	2° E
E x S		W x N	
ESE		—	
SE x E		—	
SE	4° W	NW	1° W
SE x S	3° W	NW x N	1½° W
SSE	1½ W	—	

Figure 912. Deviation Cards

merely a device for naming a bearing by reference to the compass. (*See* Figure 919.)

912. A deviation card or table is made for handy reference so that the navigator can quickly apply deviation error for any course. For the coastwise sailor a card in one of the forms shown in Figure 912 will suffice.

The card type is the one provided by professional compass adjusters.

The double rose type is used generally by yachtsmen. Note that the outer rose shows the magnetic course from the chart and that the inner shows the course to steer. Thus any course taken from the chart as the correct one, is correct only if not connected to the inner one by a line. If such a line is present (and it is likely to be on all save the cardinal points), steer the course indicated on the inner rose to which it points.

When swinging ship as described, the powerboat should have its motor in operation (but not in gear, of course). Every iron or steel object belonging to the boat should be in its normal position exactly as it would be at sea.

The auxiliary vessel will often require two deviation cards, one made from errors noted with the engine in operation and one made without the engine.

As the ship is swung, near-by lights, searchlight, binnacle light, and the radio should be snapped on to be certain that their electrical fields do not disturb the compass. Low-tension disturbances (lights, horns, etc.) can be neutralized by twisting the feed wires or running them parallel to each other. High-tension coils, magnetos, etc., might seriously offend. Separation from the compass is the only cure; if this is impossible a deviation card will be necessary.

Any shift of iron ballast, re-engining, rewiring, installation of an iron mass, such as a stove, relocation of the battery system, etc., should make the navigator view the deviation card with suspicion and cause him to check its accuracy on several headings.

Total Error

913. By combining the errors of variation and deviation the navigator obtains the total compass error which must be applied to correct a compass course or bearing to true.

The rules for combining are:

When the names are alike, *add* and give the total error the same name. (Example: Dev. W 10° and Var. W 5° = Error W 15°.)

When the names are unlike *subtract* the lesser from the greater and give the total error the name of the greater. (Example: Dev. W 10° and Var. E 5° = Error W 5°.)

Error east is marked + (plus).

Error west is marked – (minus).

Examples:

RULE: When correcting *add* east, subtract west.
When uncorrecting *subtract* east, add west.

Correcting: Compass to True

Compass Course		135°	Compass Course		212°
Dev. W	− 8		Dev. E	+ 4	
Var. E	+17		Var. E	+11	
Error		+ 9°	Error	+	15°
True		144°	True		227°

Uncorrecting: True to Compass

True		144°	True		227°
Dev. W	+ 8		Dev. E	− 4	
Var. E	−17		Var. E	−11	
		− 9°			−15°
Compass		135°	Compass		212°

(*Note all signs reversed*)

Course Conversion Examples

True	142°	Magnetic	277°
Variation	13° E	Deviation	3° E
Magnetic	129°	Compass	274°
Compass	88°	Magnetic	199°
Deviation	9° W	Variation	12° E
Magnetic	79°	True	211°

The Sounding Lead

914. The hand lead is the most convenient device for obtaining soundings for the small boat. It is essentially a weight of lead which carries a marked line to the bottom, and which, in a tallow-filled pocket, picks up a sample of the bottom. Both the depth markings and the bottom sample help the navigator to fix position or estimate progress by referring to the chart.

The hand lead, its markings and handling, is throughly described in paragraph 1427, Chapter XIV.

Weights of five to seven pounds are adequate for soundings up to 40 feet. The standard 14-pound coasting lead is ample for ordinary coastal uses.

The leadsman will report the actual depth from the bottom to the surface of the water. The navigator must make his own calculations to correlate the readings with the chart depths, which are for mean low water. The stage of the tide at the moment of sounding must be subtracted (or occasionally added) from the reported depth to coincide with the chart depths.

While sounding, speed should be somewhat reduced, depending upon the depth of the water, to, usually, around five miles an hour.

Log

915. To navigate accurately, the mariner requires some means of knowing his speed over the bottom. The most practical devices for small boats all indicate speed through the water, and therefore allow-

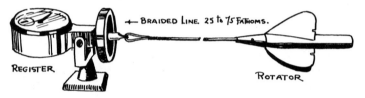

Figure 915. Patent or Taffrail Log

ances must be made for tide, current, and leeway (which will be detailed later).

The patent or taffrail log is the most practical. It is a device consisting of a propeller-shaped rotator towed at the end of a long line attached to a mechanism which, by means of a pointer, indicates on a dial the distance sailed. (Figure 915.)

The common type is calibrated for nautical miles of 6,080 feet each. The large dial shows the miles run and the small dial the tenths of miles. The distance run is the difference between readings, of course.

The patent log is seldom completely accurate, and its error should be ascertained and recorded upon various runs in still water. It will underread in drifting calms and is quite likely to be very far "off" in heavy weather. Any erratic reading should make the navigator suspicious of a fouled rotator (seaweed, rubbish, or an attack by a fish), or of bent rotator blades, or of mechanical failure of the recorder. Any inclination for the rotator to skip along the surface can be cured by either introducing a balanced tubular sinker some feet ahead of it or by giving the towing line more scope. The line should always be long enough to drop the rotator entirely clear of the wake and its eddies (about 100 feet at 10 knots), and at sea it can well be twice that length.

The log is streamed by paying the rotator quickly over the stern; not by casting it as a sounding lead.

When the log is taken in, the line is unhooked from the wheel and, as the rotator is handed *in* the line is let to pay *out;* the line will thus untwist and may be properly coiled down as it is hauled aboard. The recorder requires oiling frequently, and, if salt-water soaked, it should be plunged into fresh hot water, then dried and oiled, before stowing.

916. Various other types of speed- and distance-measuring devices are in use, some applicable to the small boat. One is a delicate sub-surface pressure device, indicating speed. It is manufactured for sail-boats 0 to 7 mph and for powerboats up to 40 mph. Other devices are geared to the engine shaft and are calibrated to convert revolutions per minute to miles per hour on a dial similar to the speedometer of an automobile.

Any powerboat equipped with a revolution counter may have its speed accurately charted on a conversion card. The calibration is made at various engine speeds over a measured course, or between buoys, etc., of known distances apart. Such measurements are preferably made in still water. However, if a current is suspected, the course may be run; then reversed, and the mean taken as the still-water time and distance.

CONVERSION CARD

Motor Vessel Viking

R.P.M.	M.P.H.
600	5.25
650	6.50
700	8.10
750	9.25
800	9.87
(etc.)	

917. A log entirely suited for small-boat use, especially at speeds for two to five miles an hour, is the chip log. (Figure 917.)

It consists of a quadrantal segment of wood weighted on the arced side to hold it just awash when afloat. A bridle leads from this to the log line, the upper part being the bridle proper and the lower parts being pendants, leading to a pine plug which fits snugly into a wooden socket seized to the log line. With the three parts rigged, the chip, when launched, will assume a vertical position and rest there approximately stationary. Upon hauling in, the log line is jerked sharply,

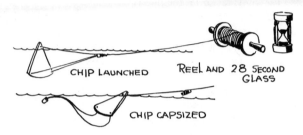

Figure 917. Chip Log

disengaging the plug and capsizing the chip so that it may be easily hauled aboard.

The log line is loosely laid, untarred hemp, similar to a lead line, and is marked (after being wetted and put on a stretch) as follows:

15 fathoms from the chip (marking the end of the "stray line")	One piece red bunting.
At every 47 feet 3 inches thereafter	Fish line seized to the log line.

Each piece of fish line is knotted; one knot for the first piece, two knots for the second piece, three knots for the third piece, etc. The log line is stored on a free-running spool with a handled axel and permitted to run freely out over the stern. Time is taken (or the sand glass capsized) when the red bunting leaves the reel. The line is checked when 28 seconds have elapsed (or the glass run out). The number of knots which have unreeled during the 28-second period is the *speed* of the boat in knots.

(It is almost impossible to purchase a chip log today. However, it is easily made by the boatman. The chip is of varnished three-eighths-inch soft wood, about six to eight inches in radius, and a quarter circle in area. The lead weight is usually a strip, sewn in leather, weighing about two ounces.)

918. A speed formula for emergency use is as follows (the Dutchman's Log):

Between known distances abreast the length of the boat, take the amount of time it takes for a chip, paper, or other floating object to reach from the bow mark to the stern mark; then calculate—

Distance in feet is to feet per hour as the time in seconds is to the hour in seconds (3,600 seconds).

Example: Distance between marks 30 feet

Time between marks 4 seconds

30 : ? :: 4 : 3,600 = 27,000 feet per hour

To convert to nautical miles per hour divide by 6,080 (answer: 4.4 knots.)

To convert to statute miles per hour divide by 5,280 (answer: 5$\frac{1}{7}$ statute miles per hour).

Accessories

919. The transparent course protractor has largely replaced the clumsy parallel rules today. To use, set the grommet over the point of departure, being sure that the rose is oriented to chart north, swing the

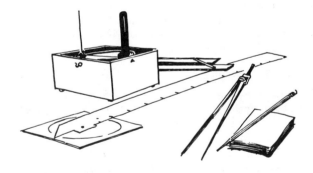

Figure 919. Arm Course Protractor or Parallel Rules, Dividers, Azimuth Circle or Sighting Vane (Vane Shown), Pencil and Scratch Pad

arm on the course line desired and read the course from the rose. Distance scale for No. 1200 coast series charts is marked on the arm. A large chart table is unnecessary.

Any accurate timepiece is suitable for coastwise work. A chronometer is unnecessary and, unless carefully rated, is probably not as accurate on a small boat as a good wrist watch. Such a wrist watch should have a sweep secondhand, and might be luminous and waterproof for sea use. A stop watch is very useful, especially for racing navigators and for timing light flashes.

Dividers should be of adequate span and of brass; not steel.

Binoculars are of two types: Galilean field and prismatic. Both are used extensively for navigating. Coastwise work requires a better binocular than offshore work.

Galilean field glasses of the better grade will magnify about five times, but they have small fields and uneven illumination. A field of 200 at 1,000 yards, bright in the center and ragged at the edges, is the best to be hoped for. They do not serve well as night glasses.

Prismatic glasses with the same magnification power as a Galilean glass will provide a much larger field, and a field of approximately the same relative brightness. Powers of 7×35 or 7×50 are perfect for marine use and make excellent night glasses.

All binoculars require extreme care in handling. They should be cleaned regularly, kept out of the direct sun and wet, and in general handled as a precision instrument.

The telescope or "spy glass" has fallen into disfavor in modern times. However, while it is a clumsy instrument to use, there is no reason why a good one should not be used if desired.

Charts and Chart Reading

920. A chart is a detailed picture or representation on durable paper of the navigable waters of the world. All charts are projections, so projected to overcome the curvature of the earth's surface and show it on a plane medium. Three methods are used: the Mercator, the Polyconic, and the Gnomonic.

The Mercator is generally used, and it is *always* used for coastwise charts. For the navigator, because its parallels of latitude and meridians of longitude are square to each other (which in reality they are not), the chart is simplicity itself, and as a projection, offers no problems. (Figure 920A.)

The chart is always oriented to true or geographic north. Coastwise charts, however, are oriented to magnetic north as well and the year of the orientation noted on the chart rose, upper half. Measurements of distances are taken, with the dividers, from the scale of miles (nautical) and yards printed on all coastwise and harbor charts. It may also be taken from the latitude scale of minutes on the east and west perimeters of the chart. On Mercator charts of large areas, the minutes of latitude will be unequal, and there will be no scale on the

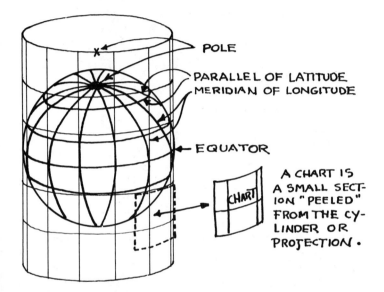

POLE

PARALLEL OF LATITUDE
MERIDIAN OF LONGITUDE

EQUATOR

A CHART IS
A SMALL SECT-
ION "PEELED"
FROM THE CY-
LINDER OR
PROJECTION.

CHART

Figure 920A. A Mercator Projection

The Mercator projection (to which all large-scale and coastal charts are made) simply expands the spherical surface of the earth into a cylinder. The chart is a detailed representation of the expansion, made from the *cylinder.*

The advantage to the navigator is that the meridians of longitude are parallel to each other and at right angles to the parallels of latitude, thus permitting the course or track of a ship to be represented by a straight line. North is anywhere along the perimeter of the cylinder.

chart. Distance is then measured from the latitude scale at a point opposite the area being worked. (Figure 920B.)

The chart shows in detail *everything* of possible interest and aid to the mariner, including the depth and character of the bottom over

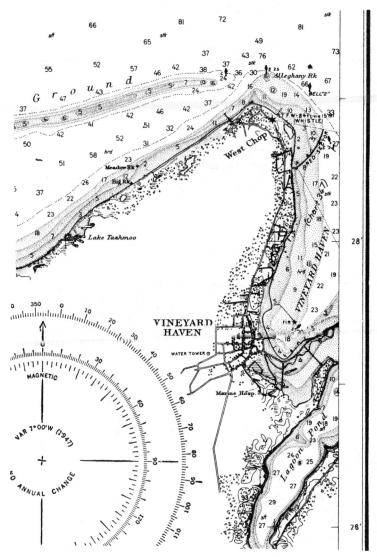

Figure 920B. Section of a Coast Chart

which he sails, the near-by shore line, land contours, and objects to be used for bearings; aids and dangers to navigation, tidal and other currents, anchorages, radio stations, towns, Coast Guard stations, tidal interval and height, and many other things.

A careful study of the standard chart symbols and abbreviations will reveal the extent of the information to be gleaned from a chart.

Standard Symbols Used on Charts

921.

AIDS TO NAVIGATION

Life saving station .... ✦L.S.S.
Life saving station (Coast Guard) .... ✦ *C.G.165*
Lighthouse .... ✹
Lighthouse on small-scale chart .... •
  (light sectors shown by dotted lines)
Light vessels showing number of mast lights .... ⚓ ⚓
Radio station .... R.S.⊙
Radio compass station .... R.C.⊙
Radio tower .... R.T.⊙
Radio beacon .... R.Bn.⊙
Water gage .... ⚓

Beacons (sectors shown by dotted lines) { Lighted .... ★
                                          Not lighted ..... ▲ ⚐ ⚑ ⚐ ⚑ ⚑
                                          (sample of distinctive top marks) }

Buoys {
Buoy of any kind (or red buoy) .... ◊

Black .... ●

Striped horizontally (in general) .... ◓

Striped horizontally (red and black) .... ◒

Striped vertically .... ◐

Checkered .... ◕

Perch and square .... ◻

Perch and ball .... ◯

Whistling (or use first six symbols with word "whistling"). ..... ◊
}

921.   AIDS TO NAVIGATION (*Continued*)

Buoys { Bell (or use first six symbols with word "bell") .... $\overset{\dot{\phi}}{}$

Buoys { Lighted .... $\overset{Q}{*}$

Anchorage { Of any kind (or for large vessel) .... $\updownarrow$

Anchorage { For small vessels .... t

Mooring .... ⚓

Range or bearing line .... - - - - - - -

Track line .... ──────

Dry dock .... ⊃──<

Floating dry dock .... ⊂──⊃

Cable area (in red) .... - - - - - - -

HYDROGRAPHY, DANGERS, OBSTRUCTIONS

In general ....|.......................................

Rocky ledges ....

Coral reefs ....

Gravel and rocks ....

Mud ....

921.

HYDROGRAPHY, DANGERS, OBSTRUCTIONS (*Continued*)

Tidal flats ....

Salt marsh ....

Bluffs and contour lines ....

Shore lines { Surveyed ....
{ Unsurveyed ....

Kelp or eelgrass ....

Ice limits (ice packs or barriers) ....
Rock under water .... +
Rock awash (at any stage of the tide) .... *

Breakers along shore ....
Fishing stakes ....

Fish weir ....

Overfalls and tide rips ....

Limiting danger line ....

Whirlpools and eddies ....

Wreck (any portion of the hull above low water) ....
Sunken wreck ....
Sunken wreck (not dangerous to surface navigation) .... +++
Submarine cable ....
Current, not tidal, velocity 2 knots ....

921.

HYDROGRAPHY, DANGERS, OBSTRUCTIONS (*Continued*)

Tidal currents {
Flood, 1½ knots .... *1½ kn* →
Ebb, 1 knot .... *1 kn* →
Flood, second hour .... ●→→
Ebb, third hour .... ●●→
}

No bottom at 50 fathoms 50

Depth curves:

1-fathom or 6-foot line ....
2-fathom or 12-foot line ....
3-fathom or 18-foot line ....
4-fathom line ....
5-fathom line ....
6-fathom line ....
10-fathom line ....
20-fathom line ....
30-fathom line ....
40-fathom line ....
50-fathom line ....
100-fathom line ....

Abbreviations Used with Hydrographic Symbols

922.

F. fixed	**(U)** unwatched	**R.Bn.** radio beacon
Fl. flashing	**ev.** every	**F.H** foghorn
Occ. occulting	**m.** miles	**F.S** fog siren
Alt. alternating	**min.** minute	**F.T** fog trumpet
Gp. group	**sec.** seconds	**R.C** radio direction
R. red	**vis.** visibility	finder
W. white	**F.B** fog bell	**F.W** fog whistle
G. green	**F.D** fog diaphone	**S.B** submarine bell
sec. sector	**F.G** fog gun	

Special Notes on Chart Reading

923. 1. Elevations given on land are from mean high water.

2. Depths given on water are to mean low water (feet or fathoms). Sailing and general charts give fathoms; coastal and harbor charts give feet. If combinations are used, the depths given in feet will be confined to a shaded inshore area.

3. The center of the base line of any symbol presenting a horizontal line is the exact location (such as a light vessel, etc.).

4. The dot under the buoy symbol shows the exact location.

5. The bearings of ranges are given as true, in degrees, from north.

6. Bluffs are shown by a hatched band, the width denoting the height of the bluff, not the plan view. Thus a high bluff would be indicated by a wide band, a low bluff by a line or narrow band.

7. Any feature which is above high water at all times (such as a rock or reef) is named with VERTICAL lettering.

8. Any feature which is definitely part of the hydrography (such as character of the bottom, aids to navigation, etc.) is named with *leaning* lettering.

924. Coast charts are on the scale of 1:80,000. Harbor charts are still larger to show all necessary information as sailing waters become restricted and therefore more dangerous.

925. Charts bear three dates, in the following locations:

Center, below border—shows the exact date of the edition.

Lower left, below border—shows date of the latest correction to the chart plate.

Right of subtitle, below border—shows the exact date of issue.

Charts show all necessary corrections as to lights, beacons, buoys, and dangers which have been received to the date of issue, being hand corrected since the latest date printed in the lower left-hand corner. All small but important corrections occurring subsequent to the date of issue of the chart are published in *Notice to Mariners* and should be applied by hand to the chart immediately after the receipt of the notices. The date of the edition of the chart remains unchanged until an extensive correction is made on the plate from which the chart is printed. The date is then changed and the issue is known as a new edition. When a correction, not of sufficient importance to require a new edition, is made to a chart plate, the year, month, and day are noted in the lower left-hand corner. All the notes on a chart should be read carefully, as in some cases they relate to the aids to navigation or to dangers that cannot be clearly charted.

926. Charts are issued by the following departments of the government:

1. The Coast and Geodetic Survey, Department of Commerce—coastal and other navigation charts.

2. Hydrographic Office (H.O.) United States Navy—foreign charts.

3. The War Department, Engineer Corps—Great Lakes and certain inland waters.

A free catalog (*Catalog of the United States Coast and Geodetic Survey*) is available to mariners from the Department of Commerce. In addition to listing all the charts published, and their prices, charts are thoroughly discussed, and the dealers who retail them listed.

Inland waters charts are listed in free catalogs as follows: Great Lakes, Lake Champlain, New York Canals; U.S. Engineer Office, 930 Ellicott Sq. Bldg., Buffalo 3, N.Y. The Mississippi and Tributaries (only from) Mississippi River Commission, Box 665, Vicksburg, Miss. *See also* Par. 934.

Charts cost from 50–75 cents and are the only accurate representation of the coast available to the navigator. No trust should be placed in charts which are presented free to the public on a "road-map" basis, nor do the publishers expect that such charts will serve the navigator in lieu of government-published and corrected charts.

Most large cities have an official chart sales outlet. Ship chandleries, marine supply depots, and book stores, lacking the official sales list, could be expected to supply charts. The local Customhouse will supply the names of near-by dealers to anyone on request.

Publications

927. The navigator will find the following publications supplementing information given on the chart.

United States Coast Pilot *Tide Tables* *Current Tables*	*United States Coast and Geodetic Survey*
Notice to Mariners *Light Lists*	*United States Coast Guard*

928. *Notice to Mariners* is sent free, weekly, to any applicant if application is made to the nearest Coast Guard District Commandant. It is a bulletin, noting both permanent and temporary changes to all charts issued. Permanent changes (such as relocating of buoys, or a collapse of dredged channel walls, etc.) should be marked on the chart at once in India ink. Temporary changes (such as the placing of temporary buoys, notice of a dredge working, etc.) should be merely noted in the proper location on the chart in pencil and the notation erased upon the situation's again becoming normal.

Copies are on file at all Customhouses, chart agencies, consulates, Coast Guard district offices, etc., and may be examined by navigators without cost.

929. *Tide Tables* are published annually in advance, in two volumes, covering the Atlantic, Pacific, and Indian Oceans.

They contain tables showing the times of high and low water at scores of reference stations, and tables showing the differences and

NEW YORK (The Battery), N. Y., 1942

	JANUARY					FEBRUARY					MARCH			
	HIGH		LOW			HIGH		LOW			HIGH		LOW	
DAY	Time	Ht.	Time	Ht.	DAY	Time	Ht.	Time	Ht.	DAY	Time	Ht.	Time	Ht.
	h. m.	*ft.*	*h. m.*	*ft.*		*h. m.*	*ft.*	*h. m.*	*ft.*		*h. m.*	*ft.*	*h. m.*	*ft.*
1 Th	7 28	4.5	1 17	−0.2	1 Su	8 14	4.5	2 16	−0.3	1 Su	7 14	4.5	1 09	−0.2
	7 55	3.6	2 00	−0.4		8 43	3.8	2 53	−0.6		7 39	4.1	1 42	−0.5
2 F	8 03	4.5	1 57	−0.2	2 M	8 45	4.5	2 55	−0.4	2 M	7 49	4.6	1 52	−0.4
	8 31	3.6	2 40	−0.5		9 17	3.9	3 30	−0.7		8 16	4.3	2 22	−0.6
3 Sa	8 33	4.5	2 37	−0.2	3 Tu	9 20	4.5	3 33	−0.5	3 Tu	8 25	4.7	2 34	−0.6
	9 06	3.6	3 18	−0.5		9 56	4.0	4 05	−0.7		8 51	4.5	3 00	−0.7
4 Su	9 04	4.4	3 14	−0.2	4 W	10 00	4.4	4 09	−0.4	4 W	9 01	4.7	3 14	−0.7
	9 42	3.6	3 54	−0.5		10 40	4.1	4 38	−0.6		9 29	4.6	3 37	−0.8
5	9 36	4.3	3 48	−0.1	5	10 43	4.2	4 45	−0.3	5	9 45	4.6	3 54	−0.7

Figure 929A. Example of Table from *Tide Tables, Atlantic Coast*

constants at several thousand subordinate stations. It is thus possible to predict the exact time of high water and low water, and the stage of each on any given date in any waters of navigational importance.

In reading the table of reference stations, the bold-faced type always denotes P.M. time; the light-faced type A.M. time; and all time is standard time. The heights (marked Ht.) indicate the difference in height of that tide from the depths given on the chart. Unless preceded by the sign − (minus) the height is always *added*.

In reading the table of subordinate stations (Table 2) the reference is to the reference station shown at the head of the table. The difference in time and height is shown, which is to be added or subtracted from the same tide at the reference point to obtain the time and height of the tide at the subordinate point.

The publication fully explains the workings of the tables.

While the tide information is accurate for all practical purposes the navigator should realize that the weather (which is not predictable) may greatly affect the tides. Offshore winds may very materially lower the high-water stage; inshore winds may raise the stage. Such con-

TABLE 2.—TIDAL DIFFERENCES AND CONSTANTS

New York and New Jersey	Lati-tude	Longi-tude	Tidal difference		Ratio of ranges	High water inter-val	Mean range of tide	Spring range of tide
			Time of tide	Height of high water				
NEW YORK AND NEW JERSEY								
New York Harbor								
Coney Island	40 34	73 59	−0 10	+0.1	1.0	7 35	4.7	5.7
Norton Point, Gravesend Bay	40 35	74 00	0 00	+0.1	1.0	7 35	4.7	5.7
	Reference station, **New York**							
Fort Wadsworth, The Narrows	40 36	74 03	−0 35	+0.2	1.0	7 40	4.6	5.6
Fort Hamilton, The Narrows	40 37	74 02	−0 35	+0.3	1.1	7 40	4.7	5.6
Bay Ridge	40 38	74 02	−0 25	+0.1	1.0	7 49	4.5	5.4
St. George	40 39	74 04	−0 20	+0.1	1.0	7 53	4.5	5.4
Bayonne	40 41	74 06	−0 15	+0.1	1.0	7 55	4.5	5.4
Gowanus Bay	40 40	74 01	−0 20	0.0	1.0	7 56	4.4	5.3
Governors Island	40 42	74 01	−0 10	0.0	1.0	8 04	4.4	5.3
New York, The Battery	40 42	74 01	0 00	0.0	1.0	8 15	4.4	5.3
Hudson River ‡								
New York, The Battery	40 42	74 01	0 00	0.0	1.0	8 15	4.4	5.3
Jersey City, Penn. R. R. Ferry, N. J.	40 43	74 02	+0 05	0.0	1.0	8 22	4.4	5.3
New York, Desbrosses Street	40 43	74 01	+0 10	0.0	1.0	8 25	4.4	5.3
New York, Chelsea Docks	40 45	74 01	+0 15	−0.1	1.0	8 32	4.3	5.2
Hoboken, Castle Point, N. J.	40 45	74 01	+0 15	−0.1	1.0	8 32	4.3	5.2

‡Values for the Hudson River above George Washington Bridge are based upon averages for the six months, May to October, when the fresh-water discharge is a minimum.

Figure 929B.

siderations become important when crossing a bar, or navigating shallow water.

Coastal charts give limited tidal information in a legend, usually appearing in a lower corner.

Example: Chart # 215, Connecticut River

Tide (referred to mean low water)

	Saybrook Light	*Essex*	*Deep River*
Mean high water	3.6 ft.	2.7 ft.	2.5 ft.
Mean sea level	1.8 ft.	1.4 ft.	1.2 ft.
Lowest tide to be expected	−2.5 ft.	−2.5 ft.	−2.5 ft.

This gives the information that, at Essex, the high-water depths will probably be 3.6 feet above those shown on the chart, that the average level will be 1.8 feet above those shown on the chart, and that lowest depths to be expected may reach 2.5 feet below those shown on the chart.

TABLE FOR FINDING HEIGHT OF TIDE ABOVE LOW WATER AT ANY HOUR OF THE EBB OR FLOOD

1. Find rise of tide for given day in *Tide Tables* (difference between heights of nearest high and low tides)
2. Enter column 1 or 3 on line corresponding to time for which height of tide is to be calculated
3. In column 2 find constant given for that time
4. Multiply constant obtained in (2) by total rise of tide

1 RISING TIDE Hours after low water	2 CONSTANT Ebb or Flood	3 FALLING TIDE Hours after high water
6	1.0	0
5½	0.98	½
5	0.92	1
4½	0.84	1½
4	0.75	2
3½	0.63	2½
3	0.50	3
2½	0.38	3½
2	0.26	4
1½	0.16	4½
1	0.08	5
½	0.025	5½

930. *Current Tables* are also published annually in advance for both the Atlantic and Pacific Oceans. They are similar to the *Tide Tables* in that two tables (reference and subordinate) are used. The time of maximum flood and maximum ebb, and slack ebb and flood ebb are given, as well as the velocity and direction of the current.

It should be remembered that the direction of a current is that toward which the current moves, or sets. Most coastwise currents are caused by the rise and fall of the tides, rather than meteorological phenomena, and therefore flood directions are toward the land, and contributaries and ebb directions away. Offshore, tidal currents are unconfined by channels and never reach a slack, flowing in any and all directions, and are known as rotary currents.

Tidal current charts are available for active boating areas (New York, Long Island Sound, San Francisco, etc.) which, together with

THE NARROWS, NEW YORK HARBOR, N. Y., 1942

	JANUARY							FEBRUARY					
Day	Slack; Flood Begins Time	Maximum Flood Time	Ve-locity	Slack; Ebb Begins Time	Maximum Ebb Time	Ve-locity	Day	Slack; Flood Begins Time	Maximum Flood Time	Ve-locity	Slack; Ebb Begins Time	Maximum Ebb Time	Ve-locity
	h. m.	h. m.	knots	h. m.	h. m.	knots		h. m.	h. m.	knots	h. m.	h. m.	knots
1	3 10	5 53	2.0	8 56	. . .	. . .	1	4 08	6 40	2.1	9 54	0 42	2.0
Th	3 59	6 18	1.5	9 04	12 15	2.1	Su	4 51	7 06	1.7	10 06	1 14	2.2
2	3 51	6 26	2.0	9 38	0 23	1.9	2	4 48	7 22	2.1	10 36	1 26	2.1
F	4 41	6 51	1.5	9 47	1 00	2.1	M	5 30	7 48	1.7	10 52	1 56	2.3
3	4 30	7 04	2.0	10 21	1 07	1.9	3	5 30	8 04	2.0	11 19	2 08	2.1
Sa	5 22	7 29	1.5	10 32	1 42	2.2	Tu	6 08	8 33	1.7	11 39	2 35	2.3
4	5 09	7 44	2.0	11 02	1 50	1.9	4	6 14	8 52	1.9	. . .	2 50	2.1
Su	6 02	8 12	1.5	11 16	2 22	2.2	W	6 49	9 21	1.8	12 01	3 14	2.2
5	5 50	8 29	1.9	11 45	2 31	1.9	5	7 03	9 41	1.8	0 27	3 33	2.1

Figure 930A. Example of Table from *Current Tables, Atlantic Coast*

the *Current Tables,* give direction and velocity of the current for any year and for various stages of ebb and flood.

Eldridge's *Tide and Pilot Book* also gives information relative to the general subject and contains tide tables.

931. *United States Coast Pilot* is a publication, in series, giving extremely minute and detailed information of value and use to the navigator. It is published about every five years, but corrected between publications by free supplements and by notes contained in the weekly *Notice to Mariners.* It is necessary to any navigator sailing outside of local waters, and provides exactly the type of information which enables the navigator to sail safely in his *own* local waters.

Example of information given for a harbor:

Stonington Harbor is well sheltered by the breakwaters, and is available for vessels of about 11 ft. (3.4 m) or less draft at low water. Anchorage can be selected between the West Breakwater and *Penguin Shoal,* where the depths are 15 to 18 feet (4.6 to 5.5 m), taking care to keep the south end of Wamphassuck Point bearing northward of 270°

true (WNW ⅞ W mag.). Vessels of about 10 feet (3 m) or less draft can anchor in the inner harbor from Penguin Shoal and Inner Breakwater to the steamboat wharf, taking care to give the western shore a berth of 250 yards. Small vessels of less than 8 feet (2.4 m) draft can anchor in the eastern half of the harbor, above the steamboat wharf, taking care to avoid a rock which bares at low water, about 50 yards to the southward of the railroad wharf. There is an old dolphin, in ruins, with a red barrel atop, near the rock.

West Breakwater extends 2,000 feet in a southeasterly direction from off *Wamphassuck Point,* and is marked at its eastern end by a flashing green light.

Inner Breakwater is about 400 yards northward of Stonington Point, on the east side of the entrance. It extends westward about 250 yards, and is marked at its western end by a flashing red light.

Stonington is a town with railroad communication, and there is bus service to Westerly and New London. A motorship runs to Block Island

TABLE 2.—CURRENT DIFFERENCES AND CONSTANTS

Station or locality	Latitude	Longitude	Time difference	Velocity ratio	At strength of current			
					Flood interval	Flood direction (true)	Average velocity	Spring velocity
	° ′ North	° ′ West	h. m.		h. m.	Deg.	Knots	Knots
Outer coast			Time meridian, **The Narrows,** New York Harbor, p. 52					
			Reference station, **The Narrows,** New York Harbor, p. 52					
Fire Island Lightship*	40 29	72 11						
Fire Island Inlet, 22 miles south of ¹	40 16	73 16						
Moriches Inlet	40 46	72 44	−0 20	0.7	6 40	345	1.3	1.6
Shinnecock Canal, railroad bridge	40 53	72 30	²−0 40	²0.8		²180	²1.5	
Ponquogue bridge, Shinnecock Bay	40 51	72 30	+0 40	0.4	7 40	250	0.7	0.8
Shinnecock Inlet	40 51	72 29	−0 20	1.3	6 30	350	2.4	2.9
Fire Island Inlet, inside, near Democrat Pt.	40 38	73 17	−0 20	1.3	6 35	115	2.3	2.8
Fire Island Inlet, near Oak Beach	40 38	73 18	+0 45	1.3	7 45	35	2.3	2.8
Jones Inlet	40 35	73 34	−1 00	1.6	5 55	35	2.9	3.5
Long Beach, inside, between bridges	40 36	73 40	0 00	0.3	6 55	75	0.6	0.7
East Rockaway Inlet	40 35	73 45	−1 30	1.3	5 25	40	2.3	2.8
Ambrose Channel Lightship*	40 27	73 49						
Scotland Lightship*	40 27	73 55						

Figure 930B.

the year round. Coal, water, and boat supplies can be obtained at the wharves, where the depths are 7 to 12 feet (2.1 to 3.7 m). There is one marine railway about 110 feet long and one smaller one, and there are facilities for repairing small craft. Larger vessels go to Noank. A towboat may be ordered by telephone from Westerly.

Directions, Stonington Harbor.—The harbor is approached from southeastward and westward. Vessels with local knowledge sometimes cross Noyes Shoal and approach from the southwestward. The southeastern approach is the best, having fewer dangers, and the lights serve as guides to avoid them. In the daytime, with clear weather, no difficulty should be experienced in entering by any of the approaches.

From southeastward.—Pass 100 yards southward of Napatree Point Ledge lighted bell buoy and steer 298° true (NW ⅜ W mag.) for about one mile until about 250 yards west of the red buoy at the southwest end of the Middle Ground. Then steer a 354° true (N ⅝ E mag.) course for the lighthouse on the east end of West Breakwater, which leads about midway between Middle Ground buoy No. 6 and the bell buoy marking the east end of Noyes Shoal. Pass over 250 yards westward of the light on the west end of East Breakwater, 100 yards or more eastward of the lighthouse on the east end of West Breakwater, and enter the harbor between Inner Breakwater and the black buoy marking the eastern end of Penguin Shoal.

From westward.—From Ram Island Reef lighted bell buoy steer 51° true (NE by E ¾ E mag.) for White Rock, passing about midway between Ellis Reef south buoy No. 1 and the red buoy at the northwest end of Eel Grass Ground. Pass 200 yards southward and about ¼ mile eastward of White Rock, and bring the rock in range with the stone building with red roofs on Baker Island astern, course 88° true (E by S mag.), which leads 200 yards northward of Noyes Rock, marked at its north and south ends by horizontally striped buoys. Pass southward of the fish weirs which extend 100 yards or more southward from West Breakwater, pass 100 yards or more eastward of the lighthouse on its east end, and enter Stonington Harbor between Inner Breakwater and the black buoy marking the eastern end of Penguin Shoal.

932. Inland waterways for the Atlantic Coast are fully covered in the following publications:

Inside Route Pilot (including charts).

Atlantic Intracoastal Waterway (United States Engineer's Office).
Gulf Intracoastal Waterway. (United States Engineer's Office).

933. *Light Lists* for all navigable waters of the United States published and issued by the United States Coast Guard may be obtained from the Superintendent of Documents, Washington, D. C.

All lighthouses, lightships, buoys, radio beacons, etc., maintained are listed and their characteristics, official names, signaling devices, appearance, position, and dimensions fully described. They are arranged in geographical order, as the mariner comes upon them in regular order, lighted aids forming one list and unlighted aids another.

While the *Light Lists* are not absolutely necessary to the navigator it is extremely convenient, and will save much searching of the chart, and eliminate the possibility of overlooking a light or buoy when making a coastwise run.

Government Publications of Use to the Mariner

934.

CATALOGS

Circular No. 3.—Hydrographic Office, Navy Department, Washington, D.C. Describes latest publications of the H.O., foreign charts, pilots and light lists. Free.

Catalog of U.S. Coast and Geodetic Survey Nautical and Aeronautical Charts, Coast Pilots, Tide Tables, Current Tables, Tidal Current Charts—U.S. Department of Commerce, Coast and Geodetic Survey. Illustrated. 48 pages. Free. Obtained from U.S. Coast and Geodetic Survey and Authorized Sales Agencies.

General Catalog of Mariners and Aviators Charts and Books—Hydrographic Office, Navy Department. $1.20.

Catalog of Charts of the Great Lakes, Lake Champlain, New York Canals, Lake of the Woods—Obtained from War Department, United States Engineer Office, 930 Ellicott Sq. Bldg., Buffalo, N.Y., or War Department, U.S. Lake Survey Office, 630 Federal Building, Detroit, Michigan. Free.

Map and Navigation Data, Mississippi and Tributaries—Obtained only from Mississippi River Commission, P.O. Box 665, Vicksburg, Mississippi. Free.

Descriptive Price-list of Maps Published by the Mississippi River Commission—Obtained only from Mississippi River Commission, P.O. Box 665, Vicksburg, Mississippi. Free.

NAVIGATION LAWS

Navigation Laws of the United States (Latest Edition)—U.S. Coast Guard, Washington, D.C. 491 pages. $1.25.

Pilot Rules—U.S. Coast Guard, District Coast Guard Offices. 60 pages. Illustrated. Free.

Nautical Rules of the Road—U.S. Coast Guard, Washington, D.C. 136 pages. Illustrated. Free. Discusses differences in the four "Rules" applying in U.S. waters in text and drawings.

MOTORBOAT LAW

Motorboat Regulation—U.S. Coast Guard. 77 pages. Free. Copies may be obtained from local Coast Guard District Offices or U.S. Coast Guard, Washington, D.C.

AIDS TO NAVIGATION

Buoys in Waters of the United States—U.S. Coast Guard. Illustrated. 10 pages. Free. Obtainable from the U.S. Coast Guard, Washington, D.C.

Significance of Aids to Marine Navigation—U.S. Coast Guard. Illustrated. 33 pages. Free. Obtainable from the U.S. Coast Guard, Washington, D.C.

Reprint of Hydrographic Information No. 10 (Revised). The Use and Interpretation of Charts and Sailing Directions—Hydrographic Office, Navy Department. Free.

Light Lists—U.S. Coast Guard. Five light lists are published annually by the Coast Guard. They are:

Atlantic and Gulf coasts of United States. $1.75.

Intracoastal Waterway—Inside waters from Hampton Roads, Virginia, to the Rio Grande. $.75.

Pacific Coast—United States, Canada, and Hawaiian (Midway, Guam) and Samoan Islands (Tutuila and Aunuu). $1.25.

Great Lakes—United States and Canada. $1.00.

Mississippi and Ohio rivers and tributaries. $1.00.

TIDE AND CURRENT TABLES

Tide Tables and Current Tables—U.S. Department of Commerce, Coast and Geodetic Survey.

Tide Tables, Atlantic Ocean. 50 cents.

Tide Tables, Pacific Ocean and Indian Ocean. 50 cents.

Tide Tables, East Coast, N. & S. America.

Tide Tables, West Coast, N. & S. America.

Current Tables, Atlantic Coast, North America. 25 cents.

Current Tables, Pacific Coast, North American and Philippine Islands. 25 cents.

Tidal Current Charts—U.S. Department of Commerce, Coast and Geodetic
Survey.

Boston Harbor (1938). 25 cents.

New York Harbor (1946). 25 cents.

San Francisco Bay (1943). 25 cents.

Long Island Sound and Block Island Sound (1943). 25 cents.

Narragansett Bay to Nantucket Sound (1945). 25 cents.

Puget Sound, two parts. Ea. 25 cents.

Delaware Bay and River. 25 cents.

UNITED STATES COAST PILOTS

United States Coast Pilots and Intracoastal Waterways Pilots—U.S. Department of Commerce, Coast and Geodetic Survey.

Notice to Mariners for the Atlantic, Gulf and Pacific coasts, and

Local Notice to Mariners are published by the U.S. Coast Guard in various
Coast Guard Districts on the Atlantic and Pacific Coasts, the Gulf of
Mexico and the Great Lakes. Copies are free to those actually requiring
them for use. Requests to be placed on the mailing list should be addressed to the nearest Coast Guard District Commander.

NAVIGATION

H.O. No. 9 American Practical Navigator—(Bowditch) Hydrographic Office, Navy Department, Washington, D.C. $3.75.

The American Nautical Almanac (Latest Edition)—United States Naval
Observatory. 304 pages. Copies purchased from the Superintendent of
Documents. $.75.

RADIO

H.O. 205—Radio Navigational Aids—U.S. Navy Department, Hydrographic
Office, Washington, D.C. $2.00.

Marine Radiobeacons—U.S. Coast Guard, Washington, D.C. Illustrated.
16 pages. Free.

H.O. 88—International Code of Signals. Vol. II (Radio)—Hydrographic
Office, Navy Department. 418 pages. $1.80.

H.O. 206—Radio Weather Aids to Navigation—U.S. Navy Department,
Hydrographic Office, Washington, D.C. $2.00.

Radio Direction Finder

935. The radio direction finder (Figure 935) for the small boat is a self-contained device which utilizes the directional characteristics of the loop antenna. A movable loop is manipulated by hand so that it rests at a null or silent point on the beam of a known radio wave. Its shaft is connected to a pointer from which a bearing may be taken

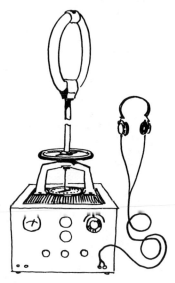

Figure 935. Radio Direction Finder

from a dumb compass card, so mounted that readings can be taken from the ship's head in degrees or compass points. By applying the compass course, either a magnetic or true bearing of the radio beacon may be figured.

Direction finders are supplied by several different manufacturers, and come with operating instructions relating to the particular type and model. The instrument is subject to error caused by deviation and must be calibrated upon installation and a deviation card calculated. This is usually done by observing radio bearings of a visible beacon and making the proper corrections on various headings on a direction-finder deviation card or circle.

It is affected by high land and by night reception. If over 100 miles from the beacon, corrections must be made to convert the great circle bearings to Mercator bearings. Any other radio antenna must be open while radio bearings are being taken.

The radio direction finder serves to give the navigator bearings and cross bearings from invisible marks, and thus to obtain a "fix." In some cases the beam may be followed for a distance by log, or by time, until usual methods of obtaining a "fix" are available (soundings, fog signals, lights, etc.). This is called *homing*. The danger, of course, is of over-running and crashing on the shore or the radio-beacon ship.

Loran (Long Range Navigation) is a public service system which projects micro-waves over large sea areas from two or more stations keyed to each other. Equipment (rather expensive and heavy for small craft) measures the time difference and converts it into distance; roughly, obtaining a fix from electronic lines of position. In England Decca and Console systems serve similarly and require their own type receivers.

Radar is an electronic navigational aid which, from a masthead revolving grid, projects a radio beam to slightly beyond the horizon. Upon reaching a solid object such as a reef, ship, shore (and sometimes a whale!), the signal "bounces" back and is recorded on a scope on the sending vessel. The shape of the object is shown and recognized by experienced operators as well as its distance off and compass bearing, the center of the scope being the position of the vessel. Frequent bearings give fixes and indicate the position of the object, its direction, speed, etc. Radar "lighthouses" impose an identifying signal on the scope thus giving their bearing from the vessel.

The so-called Fathometer electronically measures and records the depth of water in which the vessel is floating on a "one shot" dial or on a printed recording tape. Small wheelhouse models for yachts are available and are of considerable service to fishermen in finding certain bottoms.

While electronic aids to navigation may be desirable in some cases their cost, weight and power drain are prohibitive for most small yachts. If only one is carried the RDF (direction finder) is the most useful.

CHAPTER X

AIDS TO NAVIGATION

The Buoyage System

1001. All Federal waters of the United States of importance to navigation are marked as to dangers, obstructions, best channels, etc., by an intricate buoyage system. The system is maintained by the United States Coast Guard (since 1940). All buoys of a permanent nature are shown on local charts and in the *Light Lists*. However, buoys tell their own story by shape, color, and number, and so, in a sense, chart the waters within sight of the navigator.

The system calls for the coloring, numbering, and shaping of the various buoys in reference to the channels which they define when such channels are *entered from seaward* and followed to the head of navigation. Thus, the right-hand side of a channel is marked by buoys which are colored red, and with conical (or nun) shapes, and with even numbers; the left-hand side is indicated by buoys which are colored black, and with flat (or can) shapes, and with odd numbers—and this is true when entering from seaward. When leaving, proceeding to seaward, *exactly the reverse is true*.

Buoys having vertical black and white stripes are mid-channel buoys, and indicate that the channel is directly beneath. They are to be passed close aboard. Buoys having horizontal black and red stripes indicate junctions, or middle grounds, or obstructions beneath, and are to be passed on either side with a *wide berth*.

Figure 1001 gives the full meanings of all types of buoys when coming from seaward.

Special Notes on Daytime Aids and Buoys

1002. Can and nun buoys are divided into three types—tall, regular, and special; and each type is divided into three classes—first, second, and third, the first class being the largest of the type. This division is merely to standardize buoys for all possible uses and locations (such as

Buoy	Chart Symbol	Description and Meaning

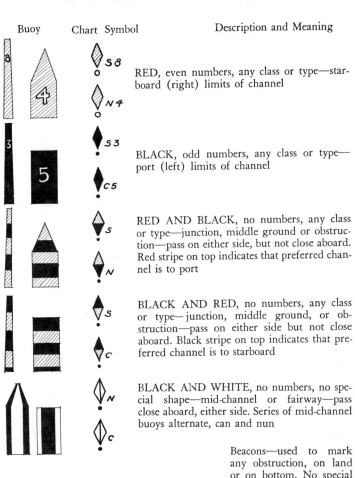

RED, even numbers, any class or type—starboard (right) limits of channel

BLACK, odd numbers, any class or type—port (left) limits of channel

RED AND BLACK, no numbers, any class or type—junction, middle ground or obstruction—pass on either side, but not close aboard. Red stripe on top indicates that preferred channel is to port

BLACK AND RED, no numbers, any class or type— junction, middle ground, or obstruction—pass on either side but not close aboard. Black stripe on top indicates that preferred channel is to starboard

BLACK AND WHITE, no numbers, no special shape—mid-channel or fairway—pass close aboard, either side. Series of mid-channel buoys alternate, can and nun

Beacons—used to mark any obstruction, on land or on bottom. No special shape, though color indicates passing side if possible. Bush marks are usually locally set, and generally indicate the starboard limits of the channel. Dolphins, sometimes with pointers, also local marks, colored as government buoys; if not colored leave to starboard

Figure 1001. The Buoyage System

at sea, or in shallow waters, etc.), and neither type nor class changes the meaning in any way.

Spar buoys are divided into four classes, class one being the largest. The size in no way changes the meaning of the buoy.

A yellow buoy of any type indicates quarantine areas.

A white buoy of any type indicates limits of anchorage grounds, or may be an experimental buoy, or may mark out a torpedo range off a naval base.

A white buoy with a green-banded top indicates dredging areas.

1003. Buoys are numbered, starting from *seaward,* in sequence. Sometimes, a buoy will carry a letter, such as 16 A, indicating that buoys have been added to the series, and the series are not renumbered. Isolated sea buoys are sometimes given a number and letter, such as I CS, the letter indicating its station name (Cerebus Shoal).

Sometimes only letters are given to fairway or obstruction buoys.

1004. Warning is here made that the chart symbol for a buoy of *any shape* is a diamond, over a dot (indicating the anchor ring or exact location). The symbol shows only the color, the legend near by indicates the type and number. (C = can, N = nun, S = spar.)

1005. Black and white horizontally striped spars mark the limits of legal areas for the setting of fish nets or weirs. Such marks are numerous in the Chesapeake.

Bush stakes, with white or colored bunting flags, indicate private oyster beds and are purely private marks. They are numerous in such oyster areas as Gardiners Bay, Long Island. They are generally in water of at least 16 feet deep and on bottoms of sandy character and uniform depths. At night, they constitute a real hazard to propellers and sails with sheets started.

1006. Unlighted buoys are frequently fitted with reflectors, which are very useful in picking up a buoy at night with a searchlight. The reflector color is always white, red, or green, and has the same meaning as lights of these colors.

1007. In Maine waters, the black buoys are passed to starboard when entering a "thoroughfare" from the eastward. When proceeding south along the Atlantic Coast, red offshore buoys are passed on the right; on the Pacific Coast, on the left; the reverse when proceeding north on either coast.

1008. Beacons are placed on shore or on sunken or awash obstructions where a floating buoy cannot be stationed. They may be of any shape, and are often cairns, wooden shapes, baskets, kegs, dolphins, or standing parts, on which are perched a cage, fish trap, flag, etc. If possible, the color will indicate the passing side.

1009. Local marks (which are supposedly erected with the approval and under the direction of the harbor master) are often placed by fishermen and others using obscure local channels, creeks, and salt coves. They may be dolphins, bush stakes, anchored oil tins, or kegs, or merely wooden floats. If colored at all, they will be colored as the government buoys are. If not, they are generally (*not always*) to be

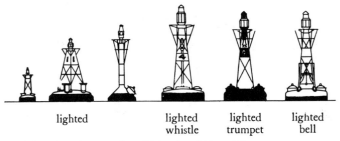

| lighted | | lighted whistle | lighted trumpet | lighted bell |

Figure 1011A. Lighted and Sound Buoys

left to starboard on coming from seaward. Lanterns, or pointers, or both, sometimes indicate turning points and the direction of the turn.

Mistrust local marks until they have been clearly explained by some local boatman, or until a boat of equal draft has entered or cleared within sight of you.

1010. At nighttime or in thick weather, when color is indistinguishable, proceed by shape, and (if a searchlight is available) by shape and number. If uncertain of the color or number (as between a channel can buoy and an obstruction or fairway buoy) pass it to starboard on entering for safety. Obstruction buoys are sometimes given a white-painted top. This is merely to facilitate picking it up by searchlight and in no way changes its meaning. Warning is given that gull guano often discolors a black buoy enough to be confusing at night. Running strange buoys at night always calls for slow speed and dependence upon log, lead, and lookout.

Buoys are liable to shift, to capsize from ice or collision, or to sink,

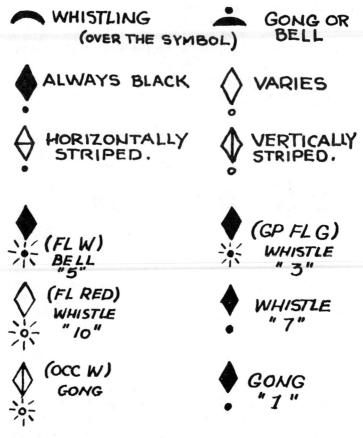

or to have been shifted from the chart location because of shoaling or channel changes, and the navigator should proceed with caution

Figure 1011B. Chart Symbols for Various Combinations of Sound-Light Buoys

Note that the rays at the anchor ring denote that the buoy is lighted and the light color and characteristics are described in brackets near by. Type of sound apparatus, if any, is given, as well as the number of the buoy.

and the help of the *Notice to Mariners* whenever buoyage conditions vary from the chart.

Light and Sound Buoys

1011. The more important of the buoys are lighted, or are provided with a sound-making device, or both. (Figure 1011A.)

The painted color of all buoys is according to the standard buoyage system, whether lighted or unlighted. The addition of light or sound merely increases their usefulness in thick weather or at night, and in

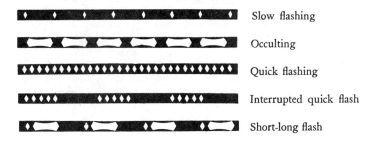

Slow flashing

Occulting

Quick flashing

Interrupted quick flash

Short-long flash

Figure 1011C. Characteristics of Buoy Lights

no way changes the meaning of the buoy considered from the usual angle of color and numbering. The shape alone will vary and will mean nothing.

The light, however, will definitely give the buoy a characteristic as indicated in the following table:

Red or black buoys: When marking the sides of channels—slow-flashing or occulting lights, at regular intervals. When marking turns, or dangerous spots—quick-flashing lights.

Horizontally banded red and black buoys: When marking junctions, obstructions, or middle grounds which may be passed on either side—interrupted, quick-flashing lights.

Vertically striped black and white buoys: When marking fairway or mid-channel—short-long flashing light. (Fixed lights on buoys are not the rule but may be occasionally found particularly on red or black buoys.)

Red buoys show white or red flashes.

Black buoys show white or green flashes.

Obstruction buoys show green or white if the preferred channel is to starboard, and red or white if the preferred channel is to port.

Fairway buoys show white only.

(Note Figure 1011C for light characteristics.)

1012. The following table presents the meaning of various light patterns. Note that buoys never flash two colors, as that is a characteristic reserved for lighthouses.

Characteristic of Flashing	*Purpose Indicated*
1. Flashing: Less than 30 light periods per minute.	Channel sides and coasts.
2. Quick flashing: Not less than 60 flashes per minute.	Sudden constriction or sharp turns in channel. A distinctly cautionary significance is indicated.
3. Interrupted quick flashing (group): Quick flashing as above but interrupted by eclipse periods of four seconds at regular intervals about eight times per minute.	Obstructions, middle grounds, junctions, or wrecks. A distinctly cautionary significance is indicated.
4. Short-long flashes: Groups of a short and a long flash. Groups are repeated about eight times per minute.	Mid-channels and fairways.

1013. Any lighted or unlighted buoy may be equipped with a sound-producing device. This serves as further identification, and is especially useful in fog, or in the case of the unlighted buoy.

Figure 1013. Sound Buoys

Devices include the trumpet or "groaner," the bell, gong, and whistle. Most of them are operated by the motion of the sea, although mechanical clappers are being introduced which operate by compressed air or electricity. Bells are usually located in harbors or tidal currents where a slight sea motion will actuate them. Gong buoys consist of

STARBOARD HAND BUOYS. RED, NUN

DENOTES STAR-
BOARD SIDE OF
OBSTRUCTION

PORT HAND BUOYS - BLACK OR CHECKERED, CAN

DENOTES PORT
SIDE OF
OBSTRUCTION

MIDDLE GROUND BUOYS - BLACK & WHITE, SPHERICAL

← INNER LIMIT OF SHOAL
OUTER " " " →

BELL AND LIGHT BUOYS

STARBOARD HAND · RED

PORT HAND · BLACK

CHECKERED
OR
STRIPED

MIDDLE GROUND
BEACON · BLACK
AND WHITE

WRECK

GREEN WRECK
FLAGS

4 FLAGS · PASS EITHER
SIDE
3 FLAGS · PASS TO PORT
2 FLAGS · PASS TO
STARBOARD

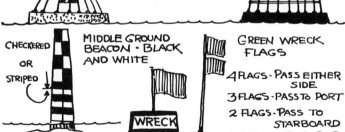

Figure 1015. British Buoyage System

four gongs of different tone and are used to avoid confusion in an area where there are several bell buoys. The whistle types are generally placed offshore where the normal seas provide sufficient motion to operate the self-contained air-compressing device.

No sound has special significance. It merely serves to locate and identify the buoy.

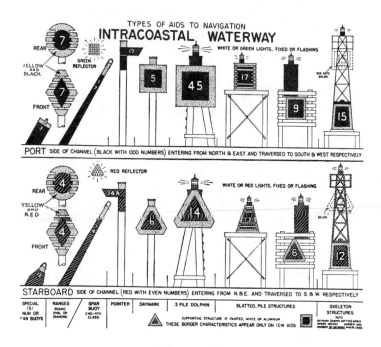

Figure 1016A

Foreign Buoyage Systems

1014. The Canadian buoyage system is basically the same as that of the United States.

1015. The British buoyage system varies slightly from that of the United States, especially in the matter of the markings of the buoy. It is shown in its essential details in Figure 1015. Buoys are read from seaward as in the American system, with black buoys to be passed to port and red buoys to starboard when entering.

Intracoastal Waterway Buoyage System

1016. Intracoastal waterway buoys, while having the color appropriate to the location, have a distinguishing yellow band or, in the case of day-marks, have a yellow border. (Figure 1016A.)

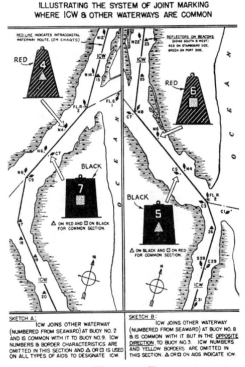

ILLUSTRATING THE SYSTEM OF JOINT MARKING
WHERE ICW & OTHER WATERWAYS ARE COMMON

SKETCH A:
ICW JOINS OTHER WATERWAY (NUMBERED FROM SEAWARD) AT BUOY NO. 2 AND IS COMMON WITH IT TO BUOY NO.9. ICW NUMBERS & BORDER CHARACTERISTICS ARE OMITTED IN THIS SECTION AND △ OR ▣ IS USED ON ALL TYPES OF AIDS TO DESIGNATE ICW.

SKETCH B:
ICW JOINS OTHER WATERWAY (NUMBERED FROM SEAWARD) AT BUOY NO. 8 & IS COMMON WITH IT BUT IN THE OPPOSITE DIRECTION TO BUOY NO.3. ICW NUMBERS AND YELLOW BORDERS ARE OMITTED IN THIS SECTION. △ OR ▣ ON AIDS INDICATE ICW.

Figure 1016B

They are numbered from north to south along the Atlantic, and from east to west along the coast of the Gulf of Mexico.

When the intracoastal and regular coastal waters join or overlap, special markings are used as follows:

On black can buoys—a yellow-painted triangle to indicate that the buoy is to be regarded as a red nun buoy.

On red nun buoys—a yellow-painted square to indicate that the buoy is to be regarded as a black can buoy.

Thus, vessels sailing the intracoastal waterways use the conversion markings above when navigating in an overlap, while vessels sailing regular harbor or river routes use the buoys in their original meanings. (Figure 1016B.)

Lighthouses

1017. Lighthouses, unlike buoys, are in definitely fixed and known locations on land, and they become therefore the mariner's prime nighttime aid in determining his position.

The chart gives all essential information about the particular light, its light characteristics, visibility, height above high water, and sound-signal character. The *Light List* gives further information, including the phase characteristic.

CHESAPEAKE BAY

No.	Name Character and period of light	Location Latitude, N. Longitude, W.	Light above [illegible]	Miles seen
		° ′ ° ′	*Feet*	
1574	*Little Creek Harbor Approach Lighted Bell Buoy 1.* Fl. W., 5 sec.	In 19 feet, off entrance to Little Creek Harbor.	10	-----
1575	LITTLE CREEK HARBOR JETTY 1. U. Fl. W., 5 sec.	On outer end of east jetty--- 36 56.0 76 10.6	70	-----

VIRGINIA AND NORTH CAROLINA NORFOLK DIST.

No.	Candlepower Apparatus	Light characteristic	Structure, vessel or buoy [illegible]	Rebuilt
			Feet	*Year*
1574	70 200 mm a	Flash 0.5 sec. BELL, on buoy.	Black.	
1575	2, 100 500 mm a	Flash 1 sec. WHISTLE; air blast 2 sec., silent 16 sec. Bell, 1 stroke every 15 sec., if whistle is disabled. Maintained by Pennsylvania Railroad Co.	Skeleton tower.	1929

Figure 1017. Examples from the *Light List*

Day identification of a lighthouse is made by the painted color (always one or a combination which stands out from the background seen from sea), the type of structure, and location, such as on land, bluff, shoal, sandspit, etc. The lantern itself is on the exact geographic spot stated in the *Light List,* and the height stated is from high water to the center of the lantern.

Night identification is made by the phase, period, and color of the light.

1018. The period of a light (flashing or occulting, not fixed) is the time required for it to proceed through a full set of changes.

The phase of a light is the exact duration of the interval of light and darkness (or eclipse) which makes up the period.

The color of the light is the color, or colors, actually observed. Red, green, and white, or red or green in combination with white, are used, never green and red.

1019. Abbreviations, meanings, and phases used on charts and *Light Lists* for the description of lights are:

LIGHTS WHICH DO NOT CHANGE COLOR	CHARACTERISTIC PHASES	LIGHTS WHICH DO CHANGE COLOR
F.—Fixed.	A continuous steady light.	Alt.—Alternating.
Fl.—Flashing.	(a) Showing a single flash at regular intervals, the duration of light being always less than that of darkness. (b) A steady light with, at regular intervals, a total eclipse; the duration of light being always less than that of darkness.	Alt. Fl.—Alternating flashing.
Gp. Fl.—Group flashing.	Showing at regular intervals, a group of two or more flashes.	Alt. Gp. Fl.—Alternating group flashing.
Occ.—Occulting.	A steady light with, at regular intervals, a sudden and total eclipse; the duration of light being always greater than, or equal to, that of darkness.	Alt. Occ.—Alternating occulting.
Gp. Occ.—Group occulting.	A steady light with, at regular intervals, a group of two or more sudden eclipses.	Alt. Gp. Occ.—Alternating group occulting.
F. Fl.—Fixed and flashing.	A fixed light varied, at regular intervals, by a single flash of relatively greater brilliancy. The	Alt. F. Fl.—Alternating fixed and flashing.

F. Gp. Fl.—Fixed and group flashing.	flash may, or may not, be preceded and followed by an eclipse. A fixed light varied, at regular intervals, by a group of two or more flashes of relatively greater brilliancy. The group may, or may not, be preceded and followed by an eclipse.	Alt. F. Gp. Fl.—Alternating fixed and group flashing.

1020. Upon first sighting a navigation light, extreme caution should be used in making identification. The visibility given on the chart and *Light List* is figured in miles from an observer's eye *15 feet above high water*. The vessel must be definitely known to be within the area of visibility of the light when its direct rays are seen; if definitely outside such an area, the light is to be but *tentatively* identified.

Correction for eye height above water is made with the aid of the Table of Distances of Visibility found in the *Light List*. The formula for obtaining distance of visibility follows:

$$\sqrt[2]{\text{height of light (ft.)}} \times 1.15 + \sqrt[2]{\text{height of observer's eye (ft.)}} \times 1.15$$
$$= \text{distance of visibility in miles}$$

Or:

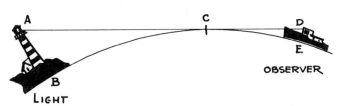

Figure 1020

$\tfrac{8}{7}\ \sqrt[2]{AB}$ in feet = AC in miles.

$\tfrac{8}{7}\ \sqrt[2]{DE}$ in feet = CD in miles. Therefore: AC + CD = visibility (in nautical miles).

Table of Visibility at Sea

1021.

Height	Visibility		Height	Visibility		Height	Visibility	
Feet	Stat. Miles	Naut. Miles	Feet	Stat. Miles	Naut. Miles	Feet	Stat. Miles	Naut. Miles
5	2.96	2.55	60	10.25	8.85	130	15.08	13.03
10	4.18	3.61	65	10.67	9.21	140	15.65	13.52
15	5.12	4.43	70	11.07	9.56	150	16.20	14.00
20	5.92	5.11	75	11.46	9.90	200	18.71	16.16
25	6.61	5.71	80	11.83	10.22	250	20.92	18.07
30	7.25	6.26	85	12.20	10.54	300	22.91	19.80
35	7.83	6.76	90	12.55	10.84	350	24.75	21.38
40	8.37	7.23	95	12.89	11.14	400	26.46	22.86
45	8.87	7.67	100	13.23	11.43	450	28.06	24.24
50	9.35	8.08	110	13.87	11.99	500	29.58	25.56
55	9.81	8.48	120	14.49	12.52			

1022. The glare of the light will usually be seen before the light itself, being reflected downward by the atmosphere, and it may take on an orange or reddish color.

Fixed lights, when first observed in a seaway, may appear to be flashing, or the phase or period of a flashing light made irregular or destroyed. An observation from a more lofty point will usually bring a new light into clearer focus at once.

Two colored lights (as red and white flashing) are often obscured by atmospheric conditions, causing but one color to be seen at first. Fixed *and* flashing lights usually show the flash alone when it is first picked up, the lower-powered fixed light only appearing later.

When in doubt whether the light first sighted is a lighthouse or a vessel, observe it from a point below that from which it was first observed. The lighthouse light will disappear, or become erratic, or off-color. The vessel's light will remain as before.

It should always be remembered that the weather and atmospheric conditions at a distant lighthouse might be quite different from those prevailing at the point of observation and due allowance made.

1023. Lights may have a light sector of color different from the light itself. This sector is usually red and covers an area of danger (Figure 1023). Such sectors are shown on the chart by dotted lines and a legend, and their bearings read from the chart rose. When passing into the sector, note that the color will not change at once but be gradual. Example: From white to red, the white will pass through stages of pink, orange, red orange, etc.

When such a light having a sector is located on an island or a headland, it may be first seen from such an angle that its sector alone is seen and is to be identified by the sector rather than its major characteristics. An example is North Dumpling light in Fisher's Island Sound. When approaching from the east, this light, which is fixed

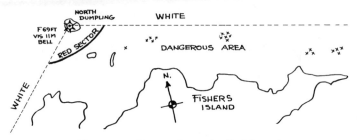

Figure 1023. Danger Sector (or Red Sector)

white, is first observed as red because of the red sector which covers Fisher's Island and its dangerous clumps and hummocks to northward. (*See* Figure 1023.)

Lightships

1024. Lightships serve the same purpose as lighthouses and are different only in that they are floating lights. They are fully described in the *Light List;* also on the chart.

			SEACOAST						VIRGINIA		NORFOLK DIST.
No.	Name Character and period of light		Location Latitude, N. Longitude, W.	Light above water	Miles seen	No.	Candlepower Apparatus Illuminant	Light characteristic Fog signal		Structure, vessel or buoy Top of lantern Established above ground Rebuilt	
				Feet						Feet Year	
1380	CAPE CHARLES............ Gp. Fl. W., 60 sec. Flashes "4-5."		On Smith Island, north side of entrance to Chesapeake Bay. 37 07.4 75 54.4	180	20	1380	740,000 1 e	Flashes "4-5" every 60 sec.; 4 flashes 0.3 sec. each, eclipse 6.8 sec., 5 flashes 0.3 sec. each, eclipse 32.3 sec.		Octagonal, pyramidal, skeleton structure. Upper part black, lower part white. 191 1827 1895	
										Coast Guard station near.	
1381	Cape Charles Lighted Whistle Buoy 7½. Fl. W., 5 sec.		In 40 feet, south of Smith Island Shoal. 37 04.7 75 44.2	10	9	1381	390 375 mm a	WHISTLE, on buoy.		Red.	
1382	CHESAPEAKE LIGHTSHIP. Occ. W., 4 sec. Radiobeacon. Distance-Finding Station. (Chesapeake Bay, see No. 1449.)		In 63 feet, 15 miles 78° from Cape Henry Lighthouse. Off entrance to Chesapeake Bay. 36 58.7 75 42.2	66	14	1382	16,000 500 mm e	Light 2 sec., eclipse 2 sec. Light shown from mainmast if foremast light is inoperative. Riding light, F. W. 40 cp., on forestay. DIAPHONE, two-tone, air; blast 3 sec., silent 27 sec. Bell, hand, if diaphone is disabled. RADIOBEACON: Transmits on 312 kc., groups of dot, 2 dashes, dot (• ▬ ▬ •). Antenna lead-in at center of ship.		Red hull, "CHESAPEAKE" on sides; two tubular masts with lantern and gallery at each masthead. (See p. 7.) Station buoy 600 yards north of lightship. 1928 Code flag signal and radio call NNBF. DISTANCE-FINDING STATION. For method of operation, see p. 10. Radio messages of importance in the maintenance of aids to navigation or on other urgent matters will be received during the first 15 minutes of each hour from 0800 to 2015, standard time.	

Figure 1024A

As the lightship swings to an anchor, the light is not fixed but is some feet off the station shown on the chart, usually about seven times the depth of the water shown at the chart location or the *Light List* and in the direction of the tide, or wind, or both at the time of observing. In addition to the navigation light, the lightship carries a riding light forward (characteristics described in the *Light List*), and from this may be ascertained the heading and the approximate distance off station.

A lightship is identified at daytime by a huge white-lettered station name on each topside, as well as its description as to shape, superstructure, color, number of masts, etc.

Regular station ships, red hull, white station name, port and starboard, white superstructure, stacks, spars, etc., buff

Relief ships red with "relief" lettered port and starboard

Figure 1024B. Light Ships

Some lightships are equipped with a submarine bell which strikes a distinctive signal. (Example: Ambrose Channel lightship strikes groups of two and two strokes every 12 seconds.) Special sound-detecting apparatus is required, although it is said that such signals may be heard over short distances by placing the ear or a stethoscope on the inside of the boat's planking, well under water and with the engine stopped. Finding the bearing by such means would be extremely inaccurate, and would place the vessel merely in the proximity of the submarine bell, and would locate the bell as off either port or starboard beam.

Range Lights and Marks

1025. Channels are sometimes shown by two marks, often lighted at night, placed some distance apart as on shore, or on shore and a breakwater, or headland, etc. They are so placed that the mariner has but to keep the two marks in line to remain in the channel.

Both day and night identification is learned from the chart and *Light Lists*. Lights may be fixed or flashing and be colored. Their lenses usually direct the most brilliant rays along the correct course, and, therefore, when running a range, a dimming of the light may be taken to mean that the boat is not on the range. Ranges marking straight channels are not difficult to follow. However, if the channel is sweeping, or dog-legged, extreme care should be excercised and the chart thoroughly studied before attempting the channel.

Lighted Beacons

1026. Beacons on land or over shoals are often lighted, and are classified somewhere between lighthouses and lighted buoys. In so far as possible, their painted coloring and light characteristics indicate their position in relation to the channel.

Characteristics are noted on the chart and in the *Light Lists*.

If reflectors are placed on them, the letters REF appear adjacent to the symbol. If lighted, the symbol is a five-pointed open-center star (distinguished from a lighthouse, which has a six-pointed star as a symbol).

Aviation Lights

1027. Aviation lights likely to be within range of water-borne traffic are listed in the *Light List* and shown on charts. They may be used exactly as lighthouses are, and, because of their great power and height, are often seen before navigational lights are raised. Listed characteristics and color identify them, and they are extremely useful in getting a fix far offshore.

Fog Signals

1028. Practically all lighthouses and lightships have fog-sounding equipment, the type being noted on the chart. Devices used include:

The bell—On inshore stations and for short warning distances.

The gong—In areas in which there are other and many near-by sound signals in operation as a distinguishing signal. Four tones are sounded.

1029.   CANDLE POWER OF BRIGHTEST UNITED STATES LIGHTHOUSES

Station	C.P.	Station	C.P.	Station	C.P.
Navesink, N.J.	9,000,000	Cape Charles, Va.	740,000	North Point, Wis.	300,000
Hillsboro Inlet, Fla.	5,500,000	Sankaty Head, Mass.	720,000	Stratford Pt., Conn.	290,000
Liston Range, Del.	5,000,000	Whitefish P't, Mich.	670,000	Fire Island, N.Y.	280,000
Cape Cod, Mass.	4,000,000	Marcus Hook, Del.	640,000	Pensacola, Fla.	280,000
White Shoal, Mich.	3,000,000	30-Mile Point, N.Y.	620,000	Cape Arago, Ore.	270,000
Molokai, T.H.	2,500,000	Anacapa Isl., Calif.	600,000	Braighill Ch'n'l, Md.	260,000
Farallon, Calif.	2,200,000	Kauhola, Hawaii	566,000	Cape May, N.J.	250,000
Cubit's Gap, La.	2,000,000	Cape Elizabeth, Me.	500,000	Mifflin Bar, N.J.	240,000
Pully Point, Wash.	2,000,000	Point Tuna, P.R.	490,000	Horseshoe Range, Pa.	240,000
Santa Barbara, Calif.	1,200,000	Deepwater Pt., N.J.	450,000	Chester Range, Pa.	240,000
Cape Kumukahi, T.H.	1,700,000	Cherry Is., Del. Riv.	450,000	No. Manitou Sh'l, Mich.	240,000
Hog Island, Va.	1,500,000	New Castle Range, Del.	450,000	Tinicum Island, N.J.	240,000
Dry Tortugas, Fla.	1,500,000	Cape Canaveral, Fla.	430,000	Bellevue Range, Del.	240,000
Point Arguello, Calif.	1,200,000	Marquette, Mich.	400,000	Beavertail, Rhode Isl.	240,000
Nawiliwili, Hawaii	1,200,000	Rock of Ages, Mich.	400,000	Twin River Pt., Wis.	240,000
Reedy Island, Del.	1,200,000	Cape Romain, S.C.	390,000	Sturgeon Bay Can., Wis.	240,000
Kilauea, T.H.	1,100,000	Pt. Arena, Calif.	390,000	Ponce de Leon Inlet, Fla.	220,000
Hereford Inlet, N.J.	1,100,000	The Graves, Mass.	380,000	Montauk Point, N.Y.	220,000
Point Cabrillo, Calif.	1,000,000	Sabine Pass, La.	380,000	Two Harbors, Minn.	220,000
Jupiter Inlet, Fla.	1,000,000	Del. Breakwater	370,000	Umpqua River, Oreg.	210,000
Chapel Hill, N.J.	1,000,000	Split Rock, Minn.	370,000	E. River Range, N.Y.	200,000
Point Sur, Calif.	1,000,000	Harrison Crib, Ill.	360,000	Cape Spencer, Alaska	200,000
Cape St. Elias, Alaska	1,000,000	Staten Island, N.Y.	350,000	C'p. Hinchinbrook, Ala.	200,000
Buffalo, N.Y.	1,000,000	Marblehead, Ohio	330,000	St. Clair Hts., Mich.	200,000
Hecata Head, Calif.	950,000	4-Mile Crib, Ill.	320,000	Manhattan Range, I.	200,000
Piglon Point, Calif.	900,000	Cape Blanco, Oregon	320,000	Point Loma, Calif.	200,000
Point Vicente, Calif.	900,000	Cape Flattery, Wash.	300,000	Mt. Desert Rock, Me.	200,000
Barbers P't, Hawaii	750,000	Devils Island, Wis.	300,000	Fort Gratiot, Mich.	200,000

The whistle—On lightships. Steady note, possibly chimed.

The horn—On any lighthouse or ship. May be of reed or diaphragm type but always a steady tone. (Also listed as oscillator, tyfon, reed horn, and nautaphone.) Generally marked HORN on charts.

The diaphone—On any lightship or lighthouse. Two-toned note, ending on the lowest pitch.

The siren—On any lighthouse or lightship. Typical siren sound but pitch rises and falls very quickly; not prolonged like a fire siren.

| Name | Light characteristic | Structure, vessel or buoy | |
Character and period of light	Fog signal	Top of lantern above ground	Established Rebuilt
AMBROSE CHANNEL LIGHTSHIP. Gp. Fl. W., 8 sec. 3 flashes. Radiobeacon. Distance Finding Station.	3 flashes 1 sec. each, 2 eclipses 1 sec. each, 1 eclipse 3 sec., shown from foremast head. Fixed white light of 520 cp. shown if flashing light inoperative. Riding light, bow, F. W., 250 cp., 21 feet high. HORN, diaphragm, air; blast 3 sec., silent 12 sec. RADIOBEACON: Transmits on 286 kc, dots (• etc.). SUBMARINE BELL: groups of 9 and 2 strokes "22" every 12 sec.	Black hull, "AMBROSE" in white, on sides, two white masts, black circular grating at each masthead. 1908 Code flag signal and radio call, WRG. DISTANCE FINDING STATION. For method of operation see p. 7. Radio messages of importance in the maintenance of aids to navigation or on other urgent matters will be received during the first 15 minutes of each hour from 0800 to 2015, standard time.	

Figure 1030A. Radio Navigational Aids on a Typical Lightship

While the chart denotes the type of sound, the period and phase of the sound, which is timed, is listed in the *Light List* only. The station may, of course, be identified by the sound characteristics.

Fog signals are put into operation when visibility reaches about six miles. The vagaries of sound in fog are unpredictable, and the mariner should not place too much reliance on sound signals for determining direction. The signal may skip large areas quite close to the source, or may be misdirected and deflected upwards or sidewards. Half of

a two-toned signal may be lost, or distorted. Direction may be reversed; or the signal may be justifiably estimated close aboard when
it is quite distant, or quite distant when it is close aboard. The true
signal and direction is best heard from the highest point aboard, away
from superstructure, as on a mast.

Lead, log, and lookout are by all means more important than fog
signals to the navigator. Fog signals are intended as *warnings* only;
not directional aids.

Radio Aids to Navigation

1030. On most lightships and lighthouses (and occasionally other
coastal points) the United States Coast Guard maintains radio beacons.

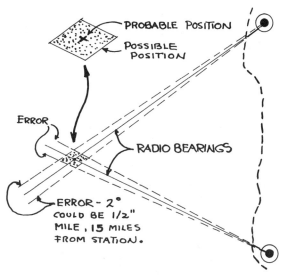

Figure 1030B. Probable and Possible Position from Two
Radio Bearings

These are simply radio transmitting sets which project an identifying
signal by which the navigator whose boat is equipped with a radio
direction finder (*See* Figure 935) may orient himself. Signals are sent
on the 285–315 kc. band during thick weather and during one or two

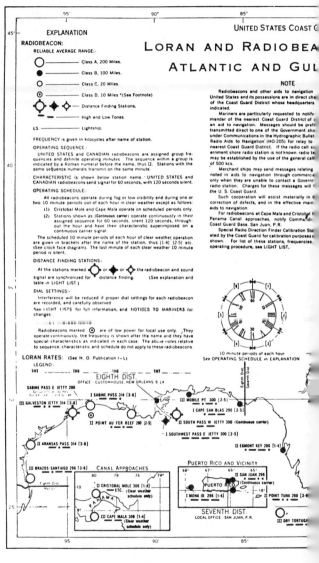

Figure 1030C

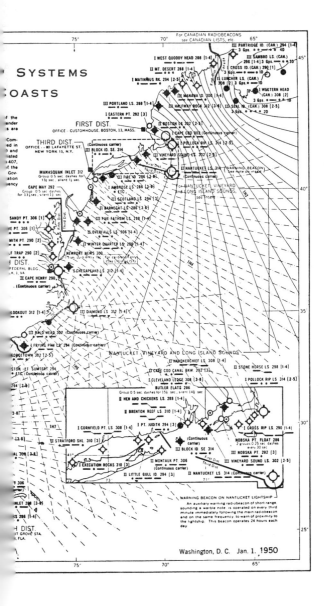

ten-minute periods each hour of clear weather. Each such station has an identifying signal. (Example: Cape Cod sends — — . —).

Full information is contained in the *Light List* and on the radio-beacon charts (*See* Figure 1024A), with changes posted in the *Notice to Mariners*.

To take a bearing, the navigator merely tunes the direction finder to the listed frequency of the station desired, adjusts the pointer until the faintest (or no) signal is heard, and reads the bearing. Depending upon the type of instrument, this bearing may be a degree bearing from the ship's head or a true bearing on the station. A simple procedure indicates which of the two possible bearings (180° separated) is the correct one.

As the bearing or bearings so ascertained are in no way different from visual bearings, methods of working a fix or line of position are exactly the same. What applies to working visual bearings in the following chapter, applies also to radio-beacon bearings; the methods are interchangeable. It should be noted, however, that radio bearings are assumed to have a plus or minus error of about two degrees, and that a fix is liable to a small error. This is shown, for illustrative purposes, in Figure 1030B.

This is true only when the fix has been obtained by all radio bearings (as in fog). By crossing a radio bearing or bearings with a visual bearing or bearings, an *approximately* exact position may be determined.

1031. Radio bearings may be taken on standard broadcasting stations of known location, or on any of the directional air-navigation radio beacons, as well as on marine radio-beacon stations. The air-navigation beams operate continuously 24 hours a day and have an identifying signal superimposed upon the constant beam—letters A and N. However, warning is given that such beams are extremely wide and therefore subject to great errors in exact position fixing, and are to be regarded as auxiliary to the regular marine radio beacons. They are useful, generally, only if *happened* upon and serve to check, or roughly estimate, position.

1032. Radio-compass stations are simply direction finders on shore. The ship communicates with one, requests bearings, and, after several shore stations have taken a bearing on the *ship,* the position is transmitted to it. Small boats do not use the radio-compass stations, and they are not to be confused with radio beacons.

1033. Distance-finding stations are radio-beacon stations equipped to transmit a *sound* signal simultaneously with the radio signal. The interval between the reception of the radio signal and the sound signal (read by a stop watch) is converted into distance. The radio and the sound signal are identical, the sound signal being made by the station's foghorn, or siren, or whistle.

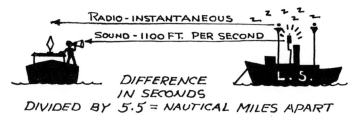

Figure 1033

Another system makes use of the submarine bell of a lightship and her radio beacon, the submarine bell being heard through an electrical receiving apparatus composed of port and starboard underwater microphones.

For the small boat the following table shows the distance from the sending station. Direction is taken (one bearing only required) in the usual way.

Interval between radio and sound signal, in seconds	Distance away in nautical miles
1	0.2
2	0.4
3	0.5
4	0.7
5	0.9
6	1.1
7	1.3
8	1.4

9	1.6
10	1.8
20	3.6
30	5.4
40	7.2
50	9.0
60	10.8

1034. To approximate the distance, divide the time between signals in seconds by 5.5 for nautical miles, or 5 for statute miles.

1035.

Sound travels as per the following table:

at 40 degrees F.	1,100 ft. per sec.	or 1 mile in	4.8 sec.
50 "	1,110 "	"	4.78 sec.
60 "	1,120 "	"	4.73 sec.
70 "	1,130 "	"	4.68 sec.
80 "	1,140 "	"	4.63 sec.
90 "	1,150 "	"	4.59 sec.

CHAPTER XI

COASTAL AND INLAND NAVIGATION

1101. Navigation is the art of conducting a vessel from "here" to "there" at any place on the earth's ocean surfaces, and of determining the vessel's position at any time.

Navigation is subdivided into:

Celo—(or celestial) navigation—which is the art of navigating solely with the aid of celestial bodies.

Geonavigation—which is the art of navigating with the aid of visible or audible objects.

Geonavigation is called *piloting,* and is the branch with which small-boat men and coastwise sailors are concerned. Piloting is divided (as is celonavigation) into two branches, observation and dead reckoning.

Both branches solve the problems of navigation, that is, the problems of position, direction, and distance.

1102. Observation makes use of observed objects and their bearings from which one or more *lines of position* are plotted, and from which is obtained a *fix,* or the exact location of the vessel at the time of the observation. A line of position is a line, straight or circular, somewhere along which the vessel must be. A second line of position which crosses the first is obviously, therefore, the exact spot along the first line at which the vessel is, and is called a *fix.*

A line of position may be established from seen or heard objects, radio beacons, foghorns (with caution), buoys, lighthouses, headlands, prominent objects, etc., of known location (determined, of course, from the chart). A line of position established by visible objects may be crossed with a line of position established by audible objects, a radio bearing with a sighted bearing, a sighted bearing with a sound bearing, a sound bearing with a depth reading, etc., ad infinitum.

Visible bearings are the most reliable and the most desirable, and are the commonest in use for ordinary piloting. Radio bearings are equally reliable, and the *only* reliable bearings in thick weather.

The method of determining the fix is a matter for the navigator alone to decide. The important thing to remember is that it must be as exact as is humanly possible.

1103. When lines of position are unobtainable (as at night, or in thick weather, or offshore), the fix is determined by dead reckoning. Dead reckoning is the navigator's best guess, made in the light of the course, speed, sea condition, current, wind, etc., as to the vessel's exact position. It is not correct—but it is as correct as it can be until a fix by observation can be obtained. The vessel's position between observations at any time or under any conditions of visibility is a dead-reckoning position; each fix by observation is corrected dead reckoning. Piloting is therefore a healthy combination, dictated by circumstances, of observation and dead reckoning.

1104. Any voyage starts from a fix, proceeds along the desired direction, at the desired speed, for the desired distance. En route, as the course is changed, as land is dropped or sighted, new fixes are required, either to check or locate the vessel's exact position.

The actual plotting of the course of the vessel is called the *track* and is done, graphically, on the appropriate chart of the waters sailed in. Fixes are noted at the intersection of two or more lines of position by a prick of the dividers, or a penciled dot or cross, and is labeled and the time noted. Courses are straight lines drawn from a fix to a future desired or estimated fix, and are drawn in pencil, aided by the parallel rule, and are labeled *above the line* as to direction (in degrees or points) and *below the line* as to speed and distance. Lines of position (which form the fix at their intersections) are labeled *above the line* as to bearing and *below the line* as to the time of the observation.

A bearing is always expressed as from the ship; not from the object observed. (Exception: Bearings given by a radio-compass station to a ship.) A magnetic bearing is expressed in points; a true bearing is expressed in degrees, unless otherwise noted. ($285°$ is considered a true bearing. $285°$ M would be a magnetic bearing. SE × E is considered a magnetic bearing. SE × E true would be a true bearing.)

The Course Line

1105. The course line is drawn from a fix to some distant point to which it is desired to proceed, the direction being determined by the topography, the water depths, intervening dangers, currents, leeway allowances, etc. It is a graphic straight line from a known "here" to a known "there" and represents an *intended* course.

The direction of the course is obtained as follows:

With the parallel rulers, transfer the course line to the nearest chart rose, so that one edge touches the exact center of the rose (marked +). Where this same edge touches the perimeter of the rose will be found the direction of the course.

If the course is read from the inner rose it will be a magnetic course and will need to be corrected only for deviation error.

If the course is read from the outer rose it will be a true course and must be corrected for both deviation and variation error.

Either may be used. Magnetic is generally used for coastwise work and short distances. In either case the resultant course will be the steering course.

It will be seen that a sailing vessel may or may not be able to lay a course and make it good. If not (as when close-hauled), she must establish herself on the best course possible toward the objective and then lay down the course line. The course is taken from the compass, corrected to magnetic or true, and then, with the course protractor, the course line is drawn on the chart.

Abbreviations Used in Coastal Chart Work

A—ante meridiem, before noon	M—miles
C—course	P—post meridiem, afternoon
Corr—corrected	R—running (as R fix)
DR—dead reckoning, or dead-reckoning position	S—speed
	Var—variation
Dev—deviation	Yd—yards

1106. Distance or run is worked on a coastwise chart by the dividers, stepping off the scaled units of distance on the course line, between fixes. The scale is obtained from the scale of nautical miles printed on every coastwise chart. While distance may be obtained from the border (which is marked off in degrees and parts of degrees of latitude and longitude), there is no practical advantage in this on a large scale chart.

Distance is shown on the chart in nautical miles (6,080 feet per mile). Distance is measured on the course line in nautical miles and tenths of nautical miles (not fractions). A scale of yards is also shown as a convenience, as the *Coast Pilot* often gives distances in yards.

1107.

CONVERTING NAUTICAL MILES TO STATUTE MILES

The following shows the difference between the nautical mile, 6,080 feet, and the land or statute mile, 5,280 feet:—

Nautical Miles.	Statute Miles.	Nautical Miles.	Statute Miles.
1	1.151	22	25.333
2	2.303	23	26.484
3	3.454	24	27.636
4	4.606	25	28.787
5	5.757	26	29.938
6	6.909	27	31.090
7	8.060	28	32.242
8	9.212	29	33.392
10	11.515	30	34.544
11	12.666	35	40.302
12	13.818	40	46.060
14	16.121	45	51.818
15	17.272	50	57.574
16	18.424	60	69.088
17	19.575	70	80.604
18	20.727	80	92.120
19	21.878	90	103.636
20	23.030	100	115.148
21	24.181		

1108. Dead reckoning commences immediately upon leaving a fix. Careful record is kept of speed, log readings (distance), course, and changes of these, and the record converted into graphic plottings along the course line. In a sense the course line is a line of position, but it is a very uncertain one. In thick weather it is of some comfort, but of very little practical use. This is because the errors of steering and the effects of current and leeway have made it anything but a straight course. Any course must be corrected for current and leeway if subject to their effects. Methods are given later in order not to interrupt the development of the subject here.

Lines of Position

1109. The simplest line of position is that taken from a range. Two objects of known location are "lined up," a pencil line extended seaward from them on the chart, and the ship will be somewhere along that line. No compass bearings are required, and there can therefore be no compass errors.

To obtain an exact fix, one or more lines must be crossed with the first. It would be unusual (and highly unlikely) to obtain two ranges for a fix. However, a single bearing and a range are usually possible.

This is obtained by sighting across the compass (aided by a pelorus, though not necessary) to any prominent charted object and noting its compass bearing. If a degree bearing, it must be uncorrected for variation and deviation, if a magnetic bearing, it must be uncorrected for deviation only. With the parallel rulers, step off the corrected direction from the chart rose to the object sighted; then extend the line seaward. The ship will be somewhere along that line.

The exact point of intersection of two lines of position will be the fix. The center of the triangle formed by the intersection of three lines of position will be the fix.

A circular line of position is obtained by determining the distance off from any object. The ship will be somewhere on a circle of which the object is the center. A fix on this circle can be obtained by another line of position crossing it, including a line of position to the object itself.

Fix by Bearings

1110. Left, right, and *A* are true ranges. *B* is not a range but a bearing. The compass bearing from boat to buoy must read exactly the

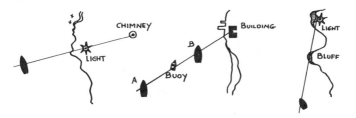

Figure 1110. Line of Position from Ranges

opposite of the bearing from boat to building. Sight alone cannot take such a bearing with accuracy. The right-hand situation is the familiar *open-up* range, expressed as *open up the light on the bluff* (or over the bluff, etc.).

1111. A line of position from a single bearing. Another crossing bearing is needed for an exact fix. The course is often used as a line of position, but, because of the vagaries of a steered course, is inexact and might result in a fix at any one of many points.

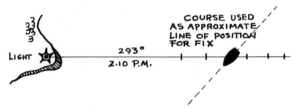

Figure 1111. Single Bearing

1112. A circular line of position is established by calculating the distance off. A bearing on the object sighted and used as the center of such a circle will give a fix on the circle. The right-hand situation shows how a bearing taken to an object outside the circle might result

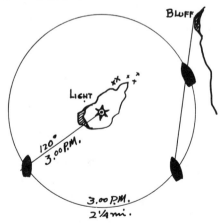

Figure 1112. Circular Line of Position

in two possible fixes. Bearings must be taken on another object, or the center object, to determine in which of the two possible positions the vessel may be.

Distance off is determined by a sextant and certain Bowditch tables, or by bow and beam bearings (Figure 1118–9), or by a running fix (Figure 1116), or by a distance-off calculator, which is a simple graphed card from which the fix may be calculated on the one-bearing principle. The card is obtainable from marine supply houses under various names at very slight cost.

1113. Two cross bearings provide a reasonably accurate fix. It is to be noted that the less the degree of intersection, the greater the likelihood of error.

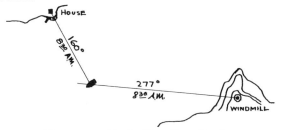

Figure 1113. Fix by Two Cross Bearings

1114. A fix by three bearings is desirable whenever possible, as the error is averaged by locating the fix in the center of the triangle resulting

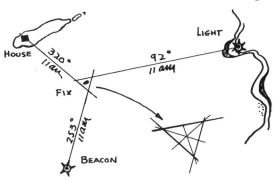

Figure 1114. Fix by Three Bearings

because of error. The smaller the triangle, the more accurate the fix. If the triangle is large, its center may be found by the same methods by which triangular sail centers are found.

1115. Advancing a bearing line to get a running fix is a method of obtaining a fix from two objects observed at different times. A single bearing is taken and the position ticked off on this line of position. The distance off must be a dead-reckoning position, of course (A). Course and distance are dead reckoned when the ship finds herself able to take another bearing, the position ticked off, and through this point a line parallel to the original line of position is drawn. The running fix is then made exactly as any two-bearing fix (B).

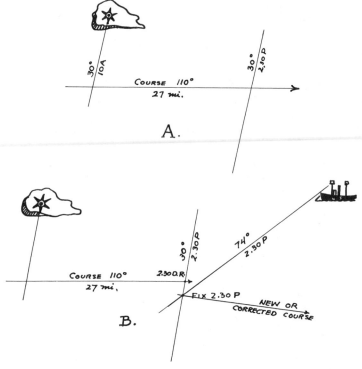

Figure 1115. Running Fix

It is a thoroughly accurate and reliable method, provided that the course and distance are carefully dead reckoned and are the ship's exact progress and direction *over the bottom*.

1116. Two bearings on one object to get a running fix and distance off are diagramed. By noting the log reading between two bearings on a straight course and advancing the original bearing by that course

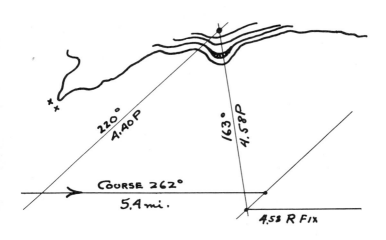

Figure 1116. Two Bearings on Same Object

and distance, a cross of this line with the second line of position will provide running fix.

1117. Course and two bearings are plotted on the chart. With the dividers scaled to the distance run between the bearings, adjust the two legs each on a line of position, both being equidistant along a right angle from the course line. The ship's position will be indicated on the second line of position.

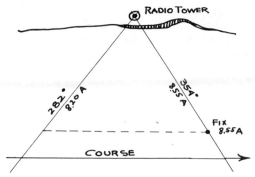

Figure 1117. Two Bearings and a Run Between

1118. Bow and beam bearings may be taken from the compass, considering it merely as a protractor, or by relative bearings. When the object bears 45° (or four points), read the log. When the object bears 90° (or eight points) read the log.

The distance off on the line of position A-B is equal to the distance run between B-C.

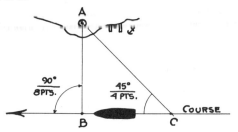

Figure 1118. Bow and Beam Bearings

1119. Another method of finding distance off is called *doubling the angle on the bow*. Bearings are taken as above. The log is read when the object bears 22½° (two points). It is read again when the angle has doubled, or at 45° (four points). The distance run between C-D equals C-A or the distance off.

Distance off A-B will equal $\frac{7}{10}$ths of the distance run between C-D.

This method is valuable in that it *predicts* the distance off when abeam.

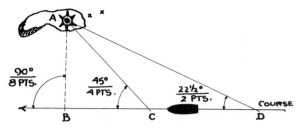

Figure 1119. Doubling the Angle on the Bow

The above problem is merely an example. Any angle observed from D to A may be doubled and logged to obtain C-A. (Example: If D is 30°, C would be 60°.) However, the $\frac{7}{10}$ths rule holds good only for the $22\frac{1}{2}$°–45° bearings.

Fix by Sounding

1120. A sounding can be used as one component of obtaining a fix, and is especially useful for finding distance off. A one-point bearing and a sounding at the same time as the observation provide a reliable fix. A fix on a circular line of position can often be obtained by a sounding.

A series of soundings (called a chain) is the most certain method of obtaining a thick-weather fix for the ship without radio direction-finding equipment. A chain of soundings is taken and applied as follows (Figure 1120):

Make and log a series of soundings along the ship's course, noting the time of each cast, depth of water, and distance between.

Example: Course NNE $\frac{1}{2}$ E 9.00 A 68 ft. 14.5 m.
9.10 71 14.9
9.30 64 16.2

Graph this on a small piece of tracing paper, marking the course line oriented to a meridian, or to north. Along the course line, mark the depths, space the log readings apart by the chart scale (done with the dividers, of course). Now lay the tracing paper on the chart, the course lines matching, and the first sounding over the dead-reckoning position at the time the sounding was made.

If the chart soundings agree with the graphed soundings, the ship

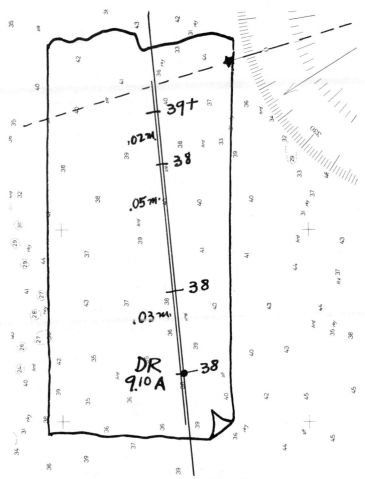

Figure 1120. Chain of Soundings

is on that course. If they do not agree, move the chain around, keeping it properly oriented until a place of agreement is found. As it is impossible to find two places on the chart where that exact chain of soundings on that course can be obtained, a little searching about the dead-reckoning position is bound to produce a fix.

If the estimated position is in an area of changing bottom, taking samples of the bottom will aid in proving the fix. Bottoms do not change in composition very rapidly in passing along a coast. They do change coming on to the coast, or when approaching a river mouth, sound, etc.

Danger Bearing

1121. A danger bearing is a convenient way in which to keep clear of hidden dangers (shoals, reefs, etc.) without frequent fixes or reliance on dead reckoning.

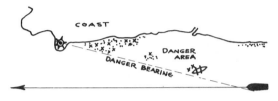

Figure 1121

Draw a line from some prominent landmark well ahead so as to clear all dangers (as the dotted line, Figure 1121) and note its direction by compass rose. Take frequent bearings on the object as the ship proceeds. As long as the bearings are to the right of the dotted line's bearings, the ship is to the left and safe side of the danger bearing.

Current and Leeway

1122. All courses, fixes, lines of position—in fact every feature of the chart—are shown in relation, or drawn in relation, to the bottom, a fixed, permanently oriented quantity. The water through which the boat moves (except in some inland lakes, etc.) is not fixed but moves *as a mass* in accord with tidal and current laws. The course, it might be said, is laid out on the *bottom,* not on the surface of the water. Yet the vessel attempts to sail that course through a moving element. Obviously, the course must be corrected by the amount of such movement and its direction.

Correcting for current in coastwise sailing is an extremely difficult procedure, involving a thorough knowledge of the tidal flow, its slacks, reverses, and directions. Tidal set and drift is fully tabled in the government publications previously listed and discussed. The information gleaned from them must be applied by the navigator to his particular problem.

It is by all means best done graphically, on the chart, and to the same scale as the chart. In practice it becomes quite foolish to plot courses corrected for current for any but long courses, or courses to be made good in thick weather. There are so many opportunities for getting fixes in coastwise sailing that it is far wiser to depend upon even a hasty fix than a course corrected for current on the average coastal run. River mouths, depths of water, submerged topography, backeddies around headlands, bays, and islands all contort the tidal currents into waters little short of whirlpools, varying by the minute and the yard in drift, set, and behavior, and by no means decently reversing themselves upon the change of the tide. Obviously, it would be impractical and well-nigh impossible to anticipate the effect of the current upon a course were its direction and velocity to change six times in an hour; yet there are many coastal locations where it does change this often, and more.

However, in a long run (as eastward or westward through Long Island Sound), it would be folly to disregard the current completely. It should be stated, however, that a 100% current-corrected course can be achieved only with the aid of local tidal knowledge, and that the average coastwise navigator has learned to select the *main* and *important* factors of the problems raised by current and to apply only these in correcting his course.

Tidal and current predictions in government or other publications are for normal weather. The amount by which the predictions will be affected by periods of wind, storm, rivers in flood, ice conditions, etc., can only be estimated. Such estimates are best made by persons having local knowledge: fishermen, boatmen, ferrymen, Coast Guard stations, etc.

Current Dead Ahead or Dead Astern

1123. The effect of currents parallel to the course is on speed over the bottom alone. It has no effect whatsoever on course, and in neither case does any course correction have to be made.

However, since speed is movement through the water at a stated rate per hour for that boat, and since the water itself is moving in relation to the bottom (over which speed or distance is measured for chart purposes), the velocity of the current will directly affect speed over the bottom.

A head current will reduce speed over the bottom by the speed of the current.

Examples:

Vessel, still-water speed	10 k.	4.5 k.
Head current, drift	−2 k.	−2.8 k.
Speed over bottom	8 k.	1.7 k.

A stern current will increase speed over the bottom by the speed of the current.

Vessel, still-water speed	9 k.	6.3 k.
Stern current	+2 k.	.9 k.
Speed over bottom	11 k.	7.2 k.

Current Broad on the Beam

1124. To graphically solve the problem of correcting the compass course between two points so as to allow for current and for steering a corrected course between the two points (Figure 1124A):

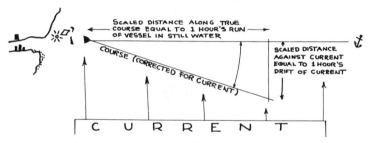

Figure 1124A. Correcting the Course for Current

Draw on the chart a straight line between the point of departure and the destination. Mark, to the chart scale, a distance along this line from the start equal to the distance the boat will cover in one hour (determined by the planned speed).

Draw from this point, parallel to the line of current but against the direction of its flow, a straight line. Mark, to the chart scale, a distance along this line from the intersection equal to the distance the current will flow in one hour.

By completing the triangle, the resultant hypotenuse enables the navigator to:

1. Find the corrected course by measuring the angle between the hypotenuse and the original course line and by transferring this angle to the compass rose to obtain the correct steering course in degrees or points.

2. Find the time to sail this course for the distance scaled on the original course by measuring and scaling the hypotenuse, then converting this distance into time by the usual methods.

Any proportional part of an hour's run scaled on the original course line may be used, providing the hour's drift of the current is scaled in proportion. It is thus possible to correct a very short course of less than an hour's run.

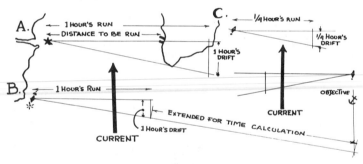

Figure 1124B

Examples of this and other methods are shown in Figure 1124B. All are based on the above, however, and are merely worked out in this manner because of chart limitations, convenience, or the navigator's preference.

1125. There is a minor and inconsequential error inherent in the formula which has no effect upon the accuracy of the result unless the speed of the current is 33% or more of the speed of the boat. The error is generally disregarded by coastwise navigators, and is in any case very slight. Even over a long course the error would not result in the vessel's being so far off course that expected visible aids to navigation, or means of getting a fix, would be denied the navigator.

The usual course corrections for deviation, variation, or both must be applied to the course corrected for current, of course.

It should be unnecessary to state that current drift and set (velocity and direction) are obtained from the *Current* and the *Tide Tables*. It is highly unlikely that a run will encounter a uniform drift and set for its entire distance. Judgment alone can estimate allowances to be made for such conditions. Current vagaries are mostly near shore, and it is therefore sound navigation to calculate correct courses to steer from between offshore marks, such as buoys, fixes, etc., between which the current will often be found more uniform than 'longshore.

Long courses may see the current lessen, increase, change direction, etc., and such changes must be considered in laying down the steering course. In some localities it is possible to take advantage of a rotary current, which is more or less constant in direction at least.

Current on the Bow

1126. Any current forward of the beam retards the progress over the bottom.

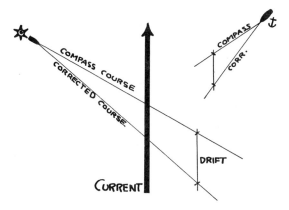

Figure 1126. Current on the Bow

To graphically solve the problem and lay a corrected course, the same basic principles apply as in calculating a beam current.

Figure 1126 shows the method. Note that its graphic solution varies only in laying down the current line. This *must* be parallel to the direction of the current, and, of course, against it.

Current on the Quarter

1127. Any current aft of the beam helps the progress over the bottom. The graphic solution is no different from the one above.

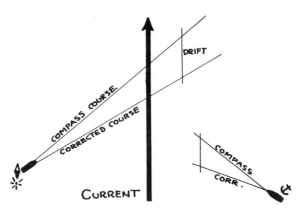

Figure 1107. Current on the Quarter

Leeway

1128. Leeway is the leeward drift of the vessel due to wind or the heave of the sea. The amount of leeway is measured by the angle between the course steered and the course made good. It varies with wind, state of the sea, and the vessel itself. It is a matter to be estimated by the navigator, based upon his experience and judgment.

If leeway can be estimated, it is applied exactly as current to correct the course. If it is disregarded, the error will appear when the next fix is made, and the course and distance then corrected.

Somewhat the same basic laws as the laws of current apply, but the amount must always remain an inexact quantity. A vessel with wind on the bow or aft makes no leeway. A beam wind causes maximum leeway. A wind on the quarter causes but slight leeway. Deep vessels make less leeway than shallow ones. Leeway in rough water, or when hove to, greatly exceeds leeway in calm water.

Navigators may be guided somewhat in estimating by observing the angle between the vessel's wake and a long line, or the log, towed astern. Such an observation is useless, of course, in broken seas or slow speeds.

A "ground log" is sometimes used to show approximate drift. This is simply a lead and line of some weight. The vessel is stopped, the lead dropped to bottom, and the rate of drift or leeway noted from a reading of the line. Thus, if a vessel drifts nine feet by line reading per minute, she will make 540 feet of leeway in an hour. This is applied to the course, especially a course of several hours' run, exactly as current corrections are.

As a conclusion to this section on coastal navigation, let the navigator and the mariner never forget a basic truth, unalterable by human emotion, weather conditions, or anything else, short of an explosion of the universe:

The Compass Never Lies.

Have a good compass, properly adjusted for deviation; take care of it; and from that moment on

Trust Your Compass Over All Else.

It is impossible, within the scope of this *Manual,* to discuss celonavigation, nor would it be of much use to the boatman, who is 99% of the time a coastwise or inland mariner.

It might be stated that a knowledge of the sailings (middle latitude, traverse, etc.) would be of considerable use to the offshore navigator. Additional instruments of navigation are required, including the sextant.

Navigational methods have advanced considerably in the last thirty years, and the modern navigator no longer requires an intricate knowledge of mathematics to solve the problems of celestial navigation. Perhaps the greatest advance has been made in the methods of working by the publication of certain tables necessary to the art. Of these, the latest is known as *H.O.* (Hydrographic Office) *214,* or

Tables of Computed Altitude and Azimuth, and it is quickly replacing the older types: *H.O. 208,* and *H.O. 211,* and others.

Its great advantage lies in the fact that only two tables need be referred to and that calculation consists of but simple and very brief arithmetic, thus almost eliminating the chance of error, as well as speeding up the entire working out of position. Yachtsmen who have used *H.O. 214* are enthusiastic, and report time savings of 50% or more over older methods, with error practically nil for anyone who can add and subtract.

In its latest form *H.O. 214* is known as *H.O. 218;* exactly as the original except that it is based on the Air Almanac rather than the Nautical Almanac and thereby still further streamlined.

However, all these "methods" are not short cuts, in the sense that observations and sights are no longer required. Basically, there has been no change in the science of nautical astronomy, and up to the point of referring to the tables, the navigator must today know everything he had to know thirty years ago, or a hundred years ago.

Navigating the Inland Waterways

1129. The small-boat owner with his home port located on or near the 34,000 miles of improved waterways and countless natural and man-made lakes that abound in the United States has some special problems; indeed handling a small boat in inland waters is as different from coastal navigation as night is from day. Most of our inland waterways have been improved to a six-foot draft and have commercial uses vital to the economy of the entire continent. Yet yachting is equally important and there is no one area in the United States with as many boat units as the Midwest. The St. Louis district of the Coast Guard has more yachts numbered than any other district in the nation. In this vast system are the Great Lakes, Lake Champlain and many lakes as yet unnamed but rapidly forming behind power dams. An increasingly popular long cruise is from an Ohio port, down the Mississippi, say in October when the current is quiet, through the inland waterways to Carrabelle; thence across the Gulf to Tarpon Springs, Florida, through the waterways or across Lake Okachobee to the east coast of Florida, north through the inland waterways to the Chesapeake, the Delaware, the Hudson, the Erie Canal, through the Great Lakes to Chicago, down the Illinois

River to Cairo on the Mississippi and back up the Ohio. This is some 7000 miles of cruising and less than 10% of it is in ocean waters! No ocean cruiser on a coasting cruise can equal this distance and remain in new and virgin waters.

Our inland waterways are all free and open to pleasure craft; there are no tolls, few permits necessary and the depth of your boat alone fixes your route. For the most part these inland routes, so-called, are on improved rivers or bays, are fresh water and demand some special considerations by the navigating department of the average cruiser.

Following are presentations of these problems and their solutions. However, just as the coastal cruiser should use as his "bible" both charts and the various *Coast Pilots,* so should the inland voyager use his special inland charts and the several helpful booklets distributed by the various government agencies concerned. Sources for inland navigation information are listed at the end of this chapter.

Local Lore and Knowledge

1130. Unlike the salt-water navigator for whom it has been possible to compile more or less standard aids and procedures, the inland navigator depends very much on local knowledge, i.e., that vast store of information never set down in print but existing only in the minds and experience of local boatmen, pilots, lock tenders, fishermen and the river engineers. Your job, in a new and strange area, even though it is apparently amply charted, is to—somehow—discover the essentials of this information.

For example, an aid to navigation, clearly defining a channel, can become utterly useless and false within six hours after a thunderstorm 100 miles upriver. Bars build and melt, chutes open and shut. Sawyers fetch up and lie in wait for you in swept channels and entire islands move, disappear or are formed between sun up and sun down.

It is therefore of paramount importance to ask questions before you attempt what seems a simple and safe passage. Study the charts. Read all you can. Draw on your own experience. And then ask questions. It is expected and you are respected for asking. Read Mark Twain's *Life on the Mississippi* if you would like to find out what a a working river pilot must know before he can appear in his own middle window and pass steering orders to his wheelman.

Inland waters are not subject to direct tidal effects. However, water levels may and do change, at times rather unpredictably, in areas near the confluence of tidal waters or other rivers. While the tidal range may not be great—only 18 inches at the mouth of the Mississippi for example—winds and other local conditions may build a high on a high so that the water level change is actually 36 inches. A sudden rain-swollen current may blank out an incoming tidal current, negate a low tide or create a high stage ten times that of a normal tide. Again, your best course is to ask questions of those who know the river.

Wind affects water stages. This is especially true on the shallower lakes where waves build into trochoidal forms, soon become large and powerful and result in far greater danger to a boat than the smooth cycloidal seas of the coast which may be five times higher.

Inland waters are navigated with constant reference to the "stage of the water" or, on rivers, to "the pool stage." This simply means how much plus or minus you have from the datum for that lake or pool. It is somewhat akin to allowing for the stage of the tide in coastal waters, except that the stage is not predictable by ordinary observation or by tables. On rivers, pool stages are often noted on bulletin boards located at dams or along the river banks. River charts indicate their location. Usually 9 feet is taken as normal pool depth and a pool noted as minus 0.5 would be 5 inches below normal or a pool depth of 8 feet, 7 inches.

Lake waters are subject to wind and also to barometric pressures, which sometimes cause a noticeable alteration in water level called a *seiche.* Many artificial lakes feed powerhouse dams and levels will become markedly lower in dry spells. Dams and locks will usually post the stage; a call to the engineers will give you the stage and, sometimes, any contemplated changes in the immediate future.

Inland rivers or improved rivers usually have a constant current downward, interrupted only by wind of backing-up tide. The current varies greatly, depends much upon upriver rain or drought conditions and, in places, may raise the river stage 50 feet in a few days. This occurs often during the spring snow runoff and sometimes results in devastating floods. This ever-present current, even when calm and confined, works constantly to change the river bottom and its course. When speeded up by melting snow or rain, river currents not only scour the bottom and move vast quantities of sand and mud in a few days, but also nibble into banks, create new river channels, widen rivers, and cast up sand or mud bars in former channels. When at last the current meets opposition in the form of tide or wind, it meekly slows down and drops its suspended silt and sand—and a new bar is formed!

The Western rivers carry downstream at a slow pace a great mass of mud and muck, not much compressed, called *flocculation,* which at times rolls surfaceward and appears to be a new or forming bar. Commercial vessels plough through it; most pleasure boats glide over it. It is unpleasant stuff indeed to draw into your engine jackets and pumps. A little like chilled consommé, it contains sand and grit which can ruin engines, strut bearings and propeller shafts in short order.

River Currents

1131. River currents have a pattern familiar to men who know the rivers, and many pilots use this pattern to their advantage. Here are the general rules:

1. Run downstream in mid-stream, following the deepest channels where the current is swiftest.

2. Run upstream as close as possible to the banks.

3. Running upstream, cut into coves and behind points where counter (upstream) currents lurk to help you.

4. Work river tides. In the Hudson River, for example, you can start at such time that you carry a favorable, helping tide the entire 153 miles to Troy. This is possible because as you ride north on a rising tide, it neutralizes the river current, and you do not at any time oppose either tidal or river current. The trick is to ride the crest of high tide as nearly as possible since it takes some hours to travel the length of the river, even as you do.

The meanderings of a river such as the Mississippi are punctuated by points and capes almost continuously. At these places, the current usually crosses to the *outside* of the curve and follows close to the bank opposite the cape or point. As it crosses it scours a deep channel and this is usually the recommended and/or marked channel. At times of higher stages, however, the current is driven toward the inside of the curve, but at a slower rate than in its deep, normal channel. Hence, it drops sand and mud and the *inside* of most of such curves should be assumed to be shallow or barred.

Remembering always that the current has probably swept out the natural and best deepwater channel, and that any improvements or dredging have probably been made to and in this natural channel, you should try to traverse these channels in a natural swing rather than in a straight course from buoy to buoy. Watch your wake and if it curls, seemingly "bucking" a counter or side current, you are probably off to one side of the channel, though not necessarily in shallow or dangerous waters. The natural channel will most likely be ideally balanced between *all* the factors which affect its course. You have many of these factors on your local chart—bluffs, heights of land, nature of the bottom, adjacent swamps or lowlands, entering or leaving estuaries or creeks and the contour of the bottom which is shown on some but not all inland charts. The stage of the river, the direction of the wind, your own draft, the velocity of the current; all these inform you of what is probably the natural—and therefore the best—channel.

River currents create islands and bars in mid-river, which are seen only at low-water stages. Currents will visibly flow over these, often with a distinct ripple or crest on the upriver edge, and such areas are likely to appear lighter than the deeper waters. Roots and bushes are sometimes grounded on them and serve as warnings.

When a river cuts behind a bank it forms a "towhead" and the upriver entrance is apt to be shoal or barred. When a river cuts across a cape or point, literally forming a new river, it is called a "chute." Chute water is apt to be foul with stumps and snags. Avoid both chutes and towheads as channels, however inviting. They should be used as overnight anchorages with caution.

Even in main channels you may encounter a snag, which is a water-logged stump, often of some hard wood such as gum or walnut. Avoid any current aberration as possibly caused by a snag, or by a sawyer, which is an entire tree caught on the bottom by the roots and lying in the current, literally sawing from side to side in a wide and destructive swath. Government sweepers work the Western rivers year 'round in an attempt to reduce snags and sawyers.

In general, a river should be navigated by pleasure craft only under the best conditions and it is no disgrace to lay over because of current conditions. Vessels which "bull" through find all manner of trouble at times—sand-ruined pumps and bearings, strandings and minor collisions, docks and landings under water, fuel pumps submerged and the riverbanks deserted. October is the best month on the Western rivers with channels cleared and current at low velocities. April and May are the hard months with high currents, much floating debris and flocculation sluicing downstream and jamming coves. Marine services are often suspended until later in the year when the river is safe.

Anchoring

1132. The easy way to anchor is, of course, in one of the many marinas on the Western and inland waterways. But to actually lie to a hook is sometimes a problem on inland waters.

The bottoms of most rivers are unstable and it is alway wise to seek out an anchorage free of current and wind, present or anticipated. It is usual to lie under banks, especially at bends where you can get out of the main channel. Beware of traffic. The big tows do not lay over at dark and, by means of radar and twin search-lights, churn on course in fog and on the darkest of nights.

Favorite river anchorages are: behind a towhead, especially one which has developed a bar on the upriver end and has become a quiet cove; a short way into a creek or tributary which does not have much current; in the "lesser channels" usually found behind river islands, these being on the side of the island opposite the main or marked channel; and behind a wooden or cement pile dike, constructed in the river by engineers to protect the banks. In times of flooding waters it may become necessary to anchor with a view toward avoiding debris; the dike and towhead are particularly good at such times.

If the stage is stable, river boats freely tie up to any shore, frequently to islands or sand bars. The deepest water is usually on the upriver side or edge. River boatmen run a line from the bow to a tree or buried anchor ashore, cut a 25-foot sapling and with it hold out the stern, and then run a preventer line from the stern to shore.

Anchorages on lakes are no problem. The charts will indicate coves, local fleets will be moored in some and entering creeks and rivers often have a deep spot immediately behind the bar usually found off the mouth. Select an anchorage away from traffic swells and from the sudden "northers" which spring up on most fresh water lakes in summertime. A tie-up to shore, or trees, or rock ledges, is common; indeed many lakes, such as Lake Champlain are so deep that an average cruiser would not carry sufficient cable to anchor in a safe manner in many of its rocky coves.

For river anchoring you will require a "hook" with broad flukes and of some weight. Very light patent anchors or wispy "dory" anchors are not sufficient. In most cases, it is necessary to penetrate considerable bottom muck or flocculation, and the rule that scope equals at least 5 times the depth becomes essential.

River bottoms, particularly in areas of slow or sluggish current, are apt to be foul and studded with water-logged stumpage and vegetation. It behooves the prudent skipper *always* to rig an anchor trip. Chapter VI on ground tackle discusses anchoring and anchor trips and buoys.

Modern light-weight anchors, while having sufficient fluke area to hold, frequently do not have the weight to penetrate to a holding bottom. The old dodge of rigging a fathom or two of chain immediately ahead of the anchor will usually solve the problem. But it raises the obvious question of why not stick to the old-fashioned heavy anchor in the first place.

Dragging and grounding is a real threat on Western rivers. The considerable wake of passing traffic gives the anchor an uneasy hold. The heave and surge impose heavy strains which can break out an anchor while you snooze. A sudden current—perhaps stemming from an up-country rain—can also break out an anchor. If you drag and ground there is usually no tide to assist in getting off. If, after power has failed to move you, the boat still remains grounded, you must wait for a friendly haul or a wake. As the first swells of a wake hit, gun the boat into deeper water. The *second* swell may be too late since it will tend to wash you further aground. Another trick is to create a wake by running around the grounded boat in circles with the dinghy and an outboard. Each time its small wake hits the grounded boat, gun her off and, little by little, you can gain deeper water.

The normal practices of carrying out a kedge anchor or towing off with the dink and outboard should also be tried. During all of this guard against sucking sand and silt into your engine cooling system.

Aids to Inland Navigation

1133. These differ greatly from coastal navigational aids and marks and from each other. All inland waters are adequately charted and these should be consulted for chart symbols. River charts are in the form of strip maps, sometimes bound in volumes. They indicate north but do not show a compass rose, for compass courses on most Western rivers are impractical. The Great Lakes are charted in the more familiar Coast and Geodetic Survey forms and a *Great Lakes Pilot,* sister to the *United States Coast Pilot,* gives all pertinent information. Many inland charts do not indicate water depths because of the great variance in pool and river stages. However, they do show in most cases the favored channel (often buoyed or on a range as well), and these are maintained at project depth or pool depth, plus or minus the water stage at the moment.

Aids to navigation are numbered from a common point and the number of the aid is the number of miles from this point. On the Illinois River, for example, Barry Island Light would be noted in this way:

Barry Island Light	255.1 miles from	On right bank
Fl.W. 2 sec.	Grafton	(descending)

It will also be noted that this mark is visible 360 degrees with a 3-degree directional beam oriented upstream.

On the lower Mississippi the reference point is A.H.P. which means "above head of passes." On the Ohio, mileage is reckoned from Pittsburgh. On the Champlain Canal, mileage is reckoned from Lock #1, which is the Federal Lock at Troy, N.Y., and must be traversed by all traffic whether bound in or out of the Erie or the Champlain canals.

It would be foolhardy to attempt to describe all the navigational aid systems used on the various inland waters. There are just too many of them, each either slightly or greatly varying from the universal buoyage systems of coastal and tidal waters. The Great Lakes, the Erie Canal, Lake Champlain and the Champlain Canal, the Ohio, the Mississippi, upper and lower, the Missouri, the Tennessee and its man-made lakes, Lake Mead, the Willamette—and lakes as yet unmade and unnamed—all have their peculiar systems of navigational aids.

There is no sounder advice than to obtain all the information and charts pertaining to the waters you plan to cruise well in advance of the cruise. (*See* the publications list following.) Study these and become familiar with the basics. There is good reason for the changes from standard or from Federal systems; usually it is because of the fluctuation of water levels and the relatively small and narrow waters involved. Most inland waters cannot be related to the heavens, to celestial navigation, to magnetic north and to predictable tidal ranges. They are therefore related to other fixed values such as mileage, visible marks (towns, bridges, dams etc.), to the character and topography of the surrounding observable country, and to the buoyage system found to be best and safest for that particular water.

In order to indicate the extent of the difference between these systems and the Federal system, some basic variations are shown in Figures 1133A to 1133D. *These are not complete.*

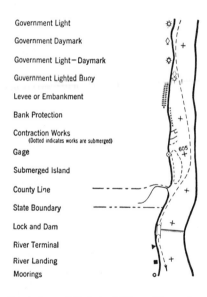

Government Light	
Government Daymark	
Government Light—Daymark	
Government Lighted Buoy	
Levee or Embankment	
Bank Protection	
Contraction Works	
(Dotted indicates works are submerged)	
Gage	
Submerged Island	
County Line	
State Boundary	
Lock and Dam	
River Terminal	
River Landing	
Moorings	

Figure 1133A. Symbols on Mississippi River Charts Between Cairo and Minneapolis, Printed in Black and White

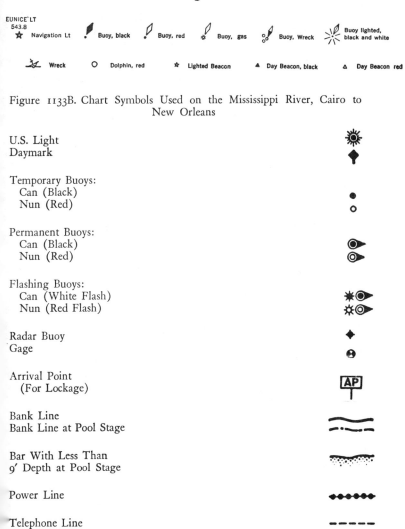

Figure 1133B. Chart Symbols Used on the Mississippi River, Cairo to New Orleans

U.S. Light	
Daymark	
Temporary Buoys:	
Can (Black)	
Nun (Red)	
Permanent Buoys:	
Can (Black)	
Nun (Red)	
Flashing Buoys:	
Can (White Flash)	
Nun (Red Flash)	
Radar Buoy	
Gage	
Arrival Point	
(For Lockage)	
Bank Line	
Bank Line at Pool Stage	
Bar With Less Than	
9′ Depth at Pool Stage	
Power Line	
Telephone Line	

Figure 1133C. Chart Symbols Used for the Ohio River

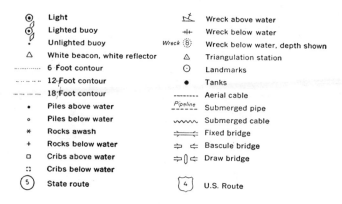

Figure 1133D. Symbols Used on Charts of the New York State Canal System. Ascending Leave White Buoys to Port, Red to Starboard

One basic and common characteristic of river aids is that most are not in the form of floating buoys but in driven piles; or they are distinctive marks on trees, bridge abutments or posts on the banks. Ranges, properly marked with targets, are quite common. At all times there are vessels at work on the river—dredging, clearing snags and sawyers, building up levees and revetments and servicing navigational aids—and their signals should be heeded if anchored in a fairway or working a main channel. The favored passing channel, if the vessel has made no signal, is the one toward deepest middle water.

The aids are lighted at night sufficiently to indicate the channel and course to *pilots of experience,* men who have run the river by daylight. No novice should attempt night navigation, for the tendency at night is to run from light to light in straight lines and, as previously noted, the channel is apt to follow a natural curve and be anything but a straight line except in dredged areas. It might be safe to navigate at night on a lake, or on deep water such as found in sections of the Tennessee system.

A fathometer is of considerable practical use in river navigation. So is a knowledge of echo navigation and, of course, that ancient and reliable standby, local knowledge. Larger craft employ radar with success and commercial traffic so equipped drives on through fog, mist and snow which should see small craft tied up. A direction finder is of use on the Great Lakes, but not on the rivers.

Throughout the literature of river pilotage the terms left and right bank are used. Aids are noted as being on the left or right bank. *In all cases,* the left bank is the bank to your left as you face or head *downstream.* Steaming upstream, you must make the conversions, and an aid noted as on the right bank will appear on your left side. Exceptions to this rule are found on the Champlain Canal, where the term "starboard" (right) is used and this means the right-hand or east side of the channel leaving the Federal lock at Troy. (Below Troy the coastal buoyage system prevails.) If bound into the Erie Canal the right-hand side becomes north. *Both hands are reversed when approaching the Troy lock.*

Regulations

1134. While Inland Rules prevail for the regulation of navigation and traffic on inland waters, there are the following exceptions to be remembered:

1. On the Mississippi River system, Inland Rules hold to the Huey Long Bridge, 16 miles north of New Orleans. From there to its source, and including its tributaries and also the Red River of the North, the regulations of the Pilot Rules for Western Rivers prevail.

2. On the Great Lakes and its tributaries, as far east as Montreal, the entire system is under the regulations of the Great Lakes Rules. No part of these lakes are under Inland Rules though some are under Canadian law, which differs little from United States regulations. Canadian navigational aids near U.S. waters are marked with the letter "C."

Many special or local rules have crept into use, some of them not codified into law. Here are some to remember:

1. General lock signals are one long and one short blast as the vessel approaches a lock of the Mississippi system. It will be answered by the lock tender but is not necessarily a signal to enter. Entrance may be controlled by lights, similar to traffic lights, or by hand or sound signals.

On the New York State Barge Canal system (Erie and Champlain canals), the signal is three "distinct" blasts and the entrance permission is a green signal light.

2. Special lock signals on the Ohio River:

    (*a*) Light signals mean:

        Flashing red .... Do not enter, stay clear
        Flashing amber .... Approach, slowly and under control
        Flashing green .... Enter and prepare to lock

    (*b*) Multiple locks (2 or more). Lockmaster makes sound signal on air or other horn:

        1 long .... Enter landward lock
        2 long .... Enter riverward lock
        1 short .... Leave landward lock
        2 short .... Leave riverward lock

3. The order of entering locks for locking through are as follows:

    First .... U. S. military or naval craft
    Second .... Vessels carrying U. S. mail
    Third .... Commercial passenger craft
    Fourth .... Commercial tows, full or empty
    Fifth .... Commercial fishermen
    Sixth .... Pleasure craft

The great number of pleasure craft using the locks has made it necessary to revise these rules at some locks, as those controlling pools near populous centers such as St. Louis or Cincinnati. Some have adopted a rule to lock through all accumulated and waiting pleasure craft once every hour. On the Ohio, every fourth locking through operation is for pleasure craft. Sometimes a single tow, 1200 or more feet in length, requires 5 or 6 lockings for all its barges, which must be broken and then reassembled below the lock—an operation consuming half a day!

4. Any craft but pleasure craft, when giving a sound or whistle signal, must at the same time flash an amber light synchronized with the sound signal.

5. Fog signals for power vessels on Western rivers:
    2 short and 1 long blast once every minute, on *whistle.*

6. Fog signals for sailing vessels on Western rivers:
    2 short and 1 long blast once every minute on *horn.*

7. Fog signals for tows on Western rivers (signal given by tow or push boat and, if push boat, by leading barge also):

3 blasts of equal length every minute

8. Power vessels at anchor or lying to, upon the approach of another vessel, in fog, give the following bell signals:

1 tap every minute if lying against the right bank.

2 taps every minute if lying against the left bank.

9. Meeting vessels, by law, assume the following rights and burdens:

Downstream-bound vessel has the right of way and is privileged.

Upstream-bound vessel is burdened and must sound the first passing signal.

However, cross signals here are not illegal and the vessels *pass on the side signalled by the privileged (downstream) vessel.*

10. Vessels bound upstream and approaching a narrow channel occupied by, or *about to be occupied by,* a vessel bound downstream must lay to and allow the descending vessel to pass through.

11. At the junction of two navigable waterways or channels, the vessel having the other to port must give the first signal.

12. A privileged vessel in any situation (as if bound downstream) is obliged to *hold its course* but may reduce or increase its speed. However, if risk of collision exists, *both or all* vessels involved must reduce speed or stop if necessary.

13. On Western rivers, the signal when approaching a bend, or other "blind" feature which reduces visibility ahead to less than 600 yards, is three "distinct" blasts. Any approaching vessel, whether or not seen, must reply by the same signal.

Only when the vessels sight each other do they exchange the usual passing signals in the usual manner.

On inland lakes, the same situation calls for one long blast on the whistle (as do *all* other pilot rules).

14. Commercial tows (sometimes composed of forty barges laced together and pushed by a modern triple-screw Diesel "towboat") are by courtesy given certain rights by pleasure craft in recognition of the difficulty of stopping, steering and controlling such a "vessel." It takes such a tow up to a mile to stop, even with engines rung down to full astern. Loss of way at critical points, such as in a narrow

channel or in a bend, can strand and even damage such a tow. They must be given—if only for the safety of the pleasure craft involved—the power of steering, which stems only from their engine power.

The pilots of these tows see you and want to know where you are. Don't "hide" under their barges, or pace them just ahead of the lead barge; don't cut circle around them. If you must pass, do so in a long straight stretch; in a bend you are likely to be pushed or washed into the bank because of the swing of such a vast tow. When two tows meet, each pilot has his problems; don't complicate them by demanding at this time the rights which by law may be yours. As someone once pointed out, the vast new inland cruising area came to us because commercial interests promoted and needed it, not because your Congressman or anybody else was much concerned about giving a few thousand yachts some new thrills.

Locks and Locking

1135. Until a few decades ago, our Western rivers were, by and large, unnavigable. Only special types of vessels, such as the old Mississippi River steamboat and the Missouri stern-wheeler could negotiate the natural Western rivers. To go where commercial vessels do now used to require a flat boat or a raft—or just reasonably high boots! By building a complex system of dams and by controlling the depths of connecting lakes and waterways at all times, we have created a continuous navigable pathway from the heartland of our country to the ports of the world. (Figure 1135A shows the TVA system.) And, right along with inland waterways, we have created an unlimited source of hydro-electric power.

The connecting link for the inland boatman is the lock, a simple device which, with a vessel afloat on its "locked-in" water, raises or lowers the water and the vessel to the level of a new body of water. The common lock form on our Western rivers is the gate lock, the operation of which is shown in Figure 1135B.

The small craft skipper has some problems—not great—in the art of "locking through."

Lock signals have been given in paragraph 1134. When waiting for clearance into the lock, keep the boat well under control. If a wait seems indicated, tie up at the lock wings; that's why they are there. Keep far away from the gate and allow space for the vessel locking

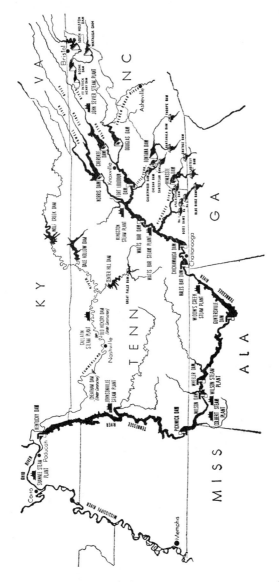

Figure 1135A. An example of the vast new waterways created in the Tennessee Valley (TVA) by a system of dams, impounded waters and connecting rivers. All are navigable to the furthermost dam and carry a minimum depth of 9 feet.

437

HOW A LOCK WORKS

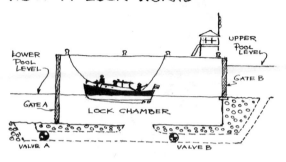

Figure 1135B. A Simplified Diagram of the Operation of a Canal Lock. Valves A and B are electrically controlled from the lockmaster's station. In this diagram the vessel entered the lock at upper pool level, with Gate B open and Gate A closed and chamber level the same as the upper pool. Gate B and Valve B were then closed and Valve A opened. The chamber water level was allowed to lower until it matched the water level of the lower pool. Valve A was then closed and Gate A opened and the vessel proceeded on her course.

against you, and probably causing the delay, to clear the lock wings, the dam boom and to enter the regular channel. On the Mississippi, there is a "dead line" clearly marked and noted beyond which no vessel is to proceed without the lockmaster's permission. On some locks, at this point, there is a whistle cord to alert the lock tender and for use by very small craft.

The down-current end of a lock is likely to have considerable current near the lock entrance and genuine turbulance when the lock is emptying and before the downstream gates open. Fenders, needed inside the lock, might be useful here as well.

Enter the lock slowly and watch for the lockmaster's signal as to your berth. Proceed there and stay there. In some locks lines are passed down to you; in others you receive a hauling line ending in a monkey fist to which you make your own lines fast. Send your lines aloft, with the hauling line secured to the eye of your line, and the lock attendant will pass the eye over one of the many bollards studding the lock wall. Use good line, with a large-sized eye splice rove in (say

18″ in diameter), and be *very* sure it is long enough. It must be as long, plus 50%, as the rise of the water in the lock. Obviously, this is important or you are going to loose control of the boat on a lock drop.

Locks are of concrete, usually rough, often dirty or oil-smeared and probably dripping wet. You will need fender protection. Fancy yacht fenders are not the thing unless you use them inside a fender board, and a fender board is not to be trusted unless tended at all times. They have a tendency to catch or trip on the rough lock wall. Tires, covered with canvas, are excellent fenders but are forbidden in some lock systems. On the New York State canals, it is common to take a gunny sack or two, pack it full of grass or hay and use these as disposable fenders.

LOCKING THROUGH SEQUENCE ★

A VESSEL ENTERS FROM POOL TO LOCK CHAMBER - BOTH AT 0 LEVEL

B WATER FROM LEVEL +15 IS VALVED INTO CHAMBER TO +15 LEVEL

C CHAMBER LEVEL IS NOW AT +15, GATE IS OPENED AND COURSE RESUMED.

Very few locks, even large and deep ones such as the one at Whitehall, N.Y., or the easterly lock on the Lake Okachobee waterway, throw up a disturbance great enough to endanger small craft. The lockmasters carefully control the inlet valves, and the stories sometimes batted around about maelstroms inside lock gates are fantasies. While there is a beam current tending to move the boat toward or away from the lock wall, it is at no time strong enough to take control of a yacht-sized vessel. (The writer and his wife, with *no* fenders of any kind, have many, many times locked through with no more than a line to a bollard and a boathook or a sneakered toe to hold her off the wall.)

Figure 1135D. How to Handle Locking Lines When Single-Handed

Ease yourself up by hand or boathook, have a fender ready if you are super-careful and stand by for orders from the lockmaster. Do *not* ease yourself up by boathook on the rungs of the iron ladders found in verticle channels; some lock keepers positively forbid it, others just think it's a nice way to break your arm and its your own business if you want to. Be prepared to give the attendant your boat name, port, registration number, last port and destination. All Western river and TVA locks are free. No permit is required to use them. New York State canals are also free but a permit is required. This may be obtained at no cost from the lock tender of the first lock you encounter.

Do not under any circumstances cleat your locking lines down to your deck. Boats have been damaged and capsized by this thoughtless practice. Tend your lines, bow and stern, every moment of the time in the lock. Some cruising men carry a double length locking line which the lock tender passes over the bollard. When ready to leave the lock, it is necessary only to haul in on the fall and you are free. This device is not practised by some cruising men because the line often brings down a bushel of grass clippings and a faceful of pebbles and dust. It becomes dirty and oily by contact with the lock wall and, finally, the er l may fall into the water and the rope must be dried before stowing—or, possibly, unwound from the propeller.

Guard gates may sometimes be found closed in a stretch of canal before a lock. These are lowered while lock gates are under repair and since repair schedules are known, such information is noted at locks and in appropriate nautical publications.

Watch, when canaling and locking, your overhead clearances. It is generous for yachts in all places but the Champlain Canal, $15\frac{1}{2}$ feet being the limiting height here. Sailing boats unstep spars and carry them on deck. Cruisers fold back small spars. It is a good precaution to measure your boat height above water and note it in the log. A gentleman we know on Lake Oneida can enter the lake only with full fuel and water tanks—but he knows it and is never in trouble.

On the Western rivers, it is often possible—indeed so ordered—to go over the dam rather than through the lock. At periods of extra high water, when both pools connected by a lock are at the same level, wickets, normally upright to protect vessels from going over the dam, are lowered and the navigating channel is then through the so-called "bear trap." The sill depth in the dam passage will be at least the depth of the controlling pool, and when the signals are up to use the bear trap, it applies to all traffic, including big tows and tugs. Knowing these craft can slide over the dam should ease the minds of the small craft skipper who can't get used to the idea of sailing over a dam.

On the Ohio, where many such dam wickets are found, lock information is posted on a conspicuous bulletin board well above the lock entrance. The board is scarlet, the lettering is white and the heading of the bulletin is always the word "PASS." At night distinguishing lights give the same information and the bulletin board is brightly spot-lighted.

Even if one lock has its wickets open, there is no assurance that others adjacent to it will also be open. Carefully study each lock as you approach and handle it as a separate and unrelated navigating problem.

In some locks you are requested not to smoke. In others you are required to shut down your engines while locking through. In no locks or lock approaches may you tie up for the night. Near some locks there are terminals for commercial use and, if not in use, there is no objection to lying there. Most canal towns have a town landing or stage and invite the passing yachtsman to leave a few dollars in their community. It is usually difficult to find anchorages near locks, or their canalized approaches, and therefore the day's run should be planned with overnight stops in mind. If you *must* lay over, pick a creek entry, or a bight well away from the wash of passing tows, which operate around the clock. Beware also of proximity to railroad tracks or major truck arteries; there is not much sleep in such places.

Locks become dangerous for small craft when ice begins forming or drifts downstream. In many areas locks are closed to vessels under certain tonnages for periods of up to 10 weeks. High water loaded with debris may also close a lock to small craft. If closed, the information will be noted in appropriate bulletins to mariners.

1136. The following publications are of particular interest and use to river and inland pilots:

For sources of charts and river information, write Mississippi River Commission, Corps of Engineers, U. S. Army, P.O. Box 80, Vicksburg, Miss. Its list covers all Western rivers and the Great Lakes. A list of charts and river bulletins pertaining only to the Ohio River is published, free, by the Division Engineer, Ohio River Division, P.O. Box 1159, Cincinnati, Ohio.

River Charts as well as *Navigation Bulletins* and *Notices to Navigation Interests* are distributed by the various offices of the Corps of Engineers, U. S. Army, in the areas over which they have jurisdiction. They are located at:

Memphis District—P.O. Box 97, Memphis 1, Tenn.

Vicksburg District—P.O. Box 60, Vicksburg, Miss.

New Orleans District—Foot of Prytania Street, New Orleans, La.

St. Louis District—420 Locust St., St. Louis 2, Mo.

Rock Island District—Clock Tower Building, Rock Island, Ill.

St. Paul District—U. S. Post Office & Customhouse, 180 E. Kellogg Blvd., St. Paul 1, Minn.

Missouri River Division—Farm Credit Bldg., 206 So. 19th St., Omaha 1, Neb.

Chicago District—475 Merchandise Mart, Merchandise Mart Plaza, Chicago 54, Ill.

North Central Division—536 So. Clark St., Chicago 5, Ill.

Ohio River Division—P.O. Box 1159, Cincinnati 1, Ohio.

Pittsburgh District—925 New Federal Bldg., Pittsburgh, Pa.

Huntington District—237 Fourth Ave., P.O. Box 2127, Huntington 18, W. Va.

Louisville District—830 West Broadway, P.O. Box 59, Louisville 1, Ky.

Nashville District—306 Federal Office Bldg., P.O. Box 1070, Nashville 1, Tenn.

Southwestern Division—1114 Commerce St., Dallas 2, Texas.

Galveston District—606 Santa Fe Bldg., Galveston, Texas.

Mobile District—2301 Grant St., Mobile 7, Ala.

Charts—Tennessee River—Available from the Tennessee Valley Authority, Maps and Engineering Records Section, 102A Union Building, Knoxville, Tennessee. Bound sets available from District Engineers at Cincinnati, Nashville and Louisville.

Charts—Great Lakes and connecting rivers, Lake Champlain, New York Canals and Minnesota-Ontario Border Lakes (including some Canadian waters)—U. S. Lake Survey, Corps of Engineers, U. S. Army, 630 Federal Building, Detroit 26, Mich.

Charts—Canadian Waters—Chart Distribution Office, Canadian Hydrographic Service, Department of Mines and Technical Surveys, Bolo Drome Building, 249 Queen St., Ottawa, Canada.

Notice to Mariners—Data for up-to-date corrections to coastal charts, Coast Pilots, etc. U. S. Hydrographic Office, Navy Department,

Washington, D.C. (Local daily notices available from Commanders of the various Coast Guard Districts. For the Mississippi, from St. Louis and New Orleans offices.)

Light Lists—Separate volumes for Mississippi River System, Great Lakes, and coastal waters. Superintendent of Documents, Government Printing Office, Washington 25, D.C., and local Coast Guard offices at St. Louis and New Orleans.

Great Lakes Pilot—U. S. Lake Survey, Corps of Engineers, U. S. /Army, 630 Federal Building, Detroit 26, Mich.

Your Key to the Lock—U. S. Army Engineer District, Corps of Engineers, Room 322, Federal Building, P.O. Box 991, Albany 1, N.Y. Pamphlet prepared for the guidance of yachtsmen passing through the Federal Lock at Troy, N.Y.

Rules of the Road—Separate volumes for Inland Waters of Atlantic and Pacific Coasts and Gulf of Mexico; Great Lakes; and Western Rivers. U. S. Coast Guard Headquarters, Washington 25, D.C. For Western Rivers available also from local Coast Guard offices at St. Louis and New Orleans.

Regulations to Govern the Use, Administration and Navigation of the Ohio River, Mississippi River above Cairo, Ill. and Their Tributaries—District Engineer, St. Louis, Mo. (Also available at any lock.)

Rules and Regulations to Govern the Operation of Drawbridges Crossing the Mississippi River and All Its Tributaries and Outlets —District Engineer, Chicago, Ill.

Rules and Regulations Governing Navigation and Use of the New York State Canal System—Superintendent of Operation and Maintenance, State Department of Public Works, Albany, N.Y.

New York State Canals and Waterways—Official map, with condensed information on canal system, navigational aids, pleasure boat regulations, data on locks, etc. Superintendent of Operation and Maintenance, State Department of Public Works, Albany, N.Y.

Mississippi River Navigation—Division Engineer, Lower Mississippi Valley Division, Corps of Engineers, U. S. Army, P.O. Box 80, Vicksburg, Miss.

Locking Through—Things you should know if you use navigation locks, District Engineer, St. Louis, Mo.

Ohio River Handbook—Piloting information pertaining to the Ohio and its tributaries. Young & Klein, Inc., 1351 Spring Lawn Ave., Cincinnati 23, Ohio.

Your Ohio—Pamphlet of general interest. Corps of Engineers, Ohio Division.

Radio Aids to Navigation, Great Lakes—U. S. Coast Guard, 9th District, Main Post Office Building, Cleveland 13, Ohio.

Inland Waterway Guide. Great Lakes Edition—Inland Waterway Guide, Inc., 25 West Broward Blvd., Fort Lauderdale, Fla.

Recreation in TVA Lakes—Tabulates boat docks and related services, with map. Information Office, Tennessee Valley Authority, Knoxville, Tenn.

Boating and fishing guide to the Great Lakes of the South—The Nashville Tennessean, Nashville, Tenn.

Map, Principal Waterways of the United States—Chief of Engineers, Department of the Army, Operations Division, Civil Works, Washington 25, D.C.

Charting the Great Lakes—The story of the United States Lake Survey, United States Lake Survey, 630 Federal Bldg., Detroit 26, Mich.

Navigation Locks and Dams, Mississippi River—District Engineer, St. Louis, Mo.

Tips on River Safety—District Engineer, St. Louis, Mo.

Mississippi River, Chain of Rocks Canal and Locks—District Engineer, St. Louis, Mo.

PART IV
BOAT MAINTENANCE

⚓

⚓

CHAPTER XII

MARLINSPIKE SEAMANSHIP

The care, handling, knotting, splicing, and use of rope, both fiber and wire, is called *marlinspike seamanship*. The small-boat man will require some knowledge of marlinspike seamanship, especially the sailboat man. There are some 1,500 knots, hitches, and splices. About a dozen of them will serve the small-boat man all his days afloat and in any situation. All the others are either trick or fancy knots or special-purpose knots, left over from square-rigger days when there was possibly more need for a knowledge of marlinspike seamanship than there is today.

It is far better to understand rope and its care, and to thoroughly understand a *few* useful knots (in darkness, ice, or snow!) than it is to know several hundred knots only slightly. Old shellbacks, sitting in the lee of the dory shop love to while away time by recalling or inventing knots, but in their days aloft they found fifteen sufficient to sail the ship and keep them in jobs.

Fiber Rope

1201. The chief fiber ropes are made of manila, hemp, cotton, and flax. Manila, or abaca, comes from a plant resembling the banana tree and is grown chiefly in the Philippines. It is peculiarly suited to resist the action of salt water, and its long fibers do not fatigue as quickly as other types of rope. Hemp, or sisal, comes from the sisal plant of North America and Russia. In the days of rope standing rigging, it was tarred and so used, but it is almost useless when required to pass over sheaves, or be hitched and bent. It is used today as an inferior grade of rope, and is sometimes mixed with manila.

Sisal lacks gloss and is stiff and harsh. The fibers are short, only two to four feet, and have a greenish tinge; manila is glossy, has a brilliant sheen, a smooth, pliable, round fiber from six to twenty feet long. The difference in strength is so great that manila should always be inspected for sisal fillers before full manila strains are placed on a line.

Coir rope is made from a coconut fiber. It is coarse and red and floats and is therefore sometimes used as a hawser. Its strength and life cannot be compared with manila rope.

Cotton and flax ropes are used for small lines, such as signal halyards, log line, lead line, etc.

Nylon rope is used extensively today and is a highly satisfactory, though initially expensive form of cordage. It has the great advantage of not only enormous strength but it is impervious to wet or dry rot and if necessary can be stored wet. As a mooring line it does not rot between wind and water (where the rope dips and alternates between wet and dry). Nylon will stretch, as much as one third, and is therefore a good anchor or dock line since it will take sudden surges or snaps. For the same reason it does not make an ideal halyard or backstay; these lines need to be fairly stable once cleated down.

Nylon's enemy, like manila, is wear and chafing, and it should be protected by serving at points of wear (chocks, etc.). When unreeling, handle it like wire rope and do not take the end from the center of the coil as you would manila or coil rope. Special techniques, discussed later, are required to splice Nylon.

Its strength in relation to manila is approximately as follows:

$\frac{3}{8}''$ dia. Nylon equals $\frac{1}{2}''$ dia. manila
$\frac{5}{8}''$ dia. Nylon equals $\frac{7}{8}''$ dia. manila
$\frac{3}{4}''$ dia. Nylon equals $1\frac{1}{8}''$ dia. manila
$1''$　dia. Nylon equals $1\frac{1}{2}''$ dia. manila

1202. Rope is made by machinery by twisting the fibers into yarns or threads, then twisting the threads into strands, and finally the strands into finished rope. As the rope is built each successive part is twisted on an opposite direction. Right-handed yarns make left-handed strands and right-handed rope, called *plain-laid rope*. Rope twisted to form another rope will be left-handed, called *cable-laid rope*. Four-stranded rope, for ease in passing over sheaves and for longer life, is right-handed, and has a small strand or heart laid in the center as a core. (Figure 1202.)

Right-handed rope, held vertical, runs　////////
Left-handed rope, held vertical, runs　\\\\\\\\

Plain-laid right-hand rope	Cable-laid left-hand rope	Four-strand right-hand rope

Figure 1202

1203. A coil is a standard method of coiling a rope for shipment from the ropewalk and is 200 fathoms or 1,200 feet in length no matter what the size. If a vegetable rope, not Nylon, it must be uncoiled in the following manner in order to avoid kinks: Loosen the burlap cover and lay the coil, flat down, with the inside end nearest the deck. Reach down through the center and draw this end up and out. Coil down in lengths required in a clockwise direction, i.e., from left to right. Any other method will put additional turns in the rope, in which case it will have to be thoroughfooted.

1204. To thoroughfoot a rope, it is coiled down *against* the lay (a right-handed rope is coiled from right to left). Then reach down into the center (exactly as in uncoiling properly), draw the end up and out, and coil down *with* the lay. If one end is belayed, coil opposite the lay from the belaying point, dip the end down through the coil, capsize the coil, and coil with the lay.

1205. Once out of the coil, rope is coiled except when in use.

Straight coil: Lay a circular bight on the deck, following it with additional bights to the bitter end. Pass kinks and turns aft, coiling with the lay. Capsize the coil and it will be clear for running.

Flemish down: Make a small tight circle of the free end and continue to lay down circles outside each other. The coil will be flat and will resemble a wound clock spring.

Fake down: Lay the free end out in a straight line (as along the waterways), then turn back a loop to form a close flat coil. Continue to lay flat coils with the ends on top of the preceding coil.

1206.

MANILA ROPE TABLE

SIZE, WEIGHT AND STRENGTH OF MANILA ROPE

Circumference Inches	Diameter (Nominal) Inches	Length of Coil (Approx.) Feet	Gross Wgt. of Coil (Approx.) Pounds	Length per Pound (Min.) Feet	Breaking Strength (Min.) Pounds
⅝	3/16 (6 thd.)	2,650	35	76.0	450
¾	¼ (6 thd.)	1,920	35	55.0	600
1	5/16 (9 thd.)	1,935	55	35.0	1,000
1⅛	⅜ (12 thd.)	1,690	65	26.0	1,350
1¼	7/16 (15 thd.)	1,200	63	19.0	1,750
1⅜	15/32 (18 thd.)	1,200	75	16.0	2,250
1½	½ (21 thd.)	1,200	90	13.3	2,650
1¾	9/16	1,200	125	9.61	3,450
2	⅝	1,200	160	7.52	4,400
2¼	¾	1,200	200	6.00	5,400
2½	13/16	1,200	234	5.13	6,500
2¾	⅞	1,200	270	4.45	7,700
3	1	1,200	324	3.71	9,000
3¼	1 1/16	1,200	375	3.20	10,500
3½	1⅛	1,200	432	2.78	12,000

Cir-cum-ference Inches	Diameter (Nominal) Inches	Length of Coil (Approx.) Feet	Gross Wgt. of Coil (Approx.) Pounds	Length per Pound (Min.) Feet	Breaking Strength (Min.) Pounds
3¾	1¼	1,200	502	2.40	13,500
4	1⁵⁄₁₆	1,200	576	2.09	15,000
4½	1½	1,200	720	1.67	18,500
5	1⅝	1,200	893	1.34	22,500
5½	1¾	1,200	1,073	1.12	26,500
6	2	1,200	1,290	0.927	31,000

To determine the thread of a rope: Number of yarns per strand × number of strands = thread.

Strength. Manila rope strength may be roughly figured by squaring the circumference and multiplying by 150 lbs. For instance, a three-inch rope—3 × 3 = 9, 9 × 150 = 1,350 lbs. as safe working load.

For Nylon rope use the same formula but multiply by 250 instead of 150.

1207. A hawser is any rope more than five inches in circumference.

1208. Rope sizes are correctly given or called by their *circumference* in inches. (Thus a three-inch rope is one inch in diameter.)

1209. Rope will last a long time if properly cared for. Such care includes:

1. Keep dry—and never stow away unless dry.

2. Use chafing gear where it passes any fixed object. Worm, parcel, and serve large ropes and hawsers.

3. Keep rope away from oil, gasoline, acids, and sand and grit. Always wash out an anchor cable by swishing or hosing.

4. Avoid knots, especially tight ones. A knot reduces the strength of rope about 25%.

These remarks apply also to Nylon rope even though this material will take much more punishment than vegetable ropes.

1210. A worn or weak rope will look bleached and possibly hairy. The true condition may be seen by driving a marlinspike into a strand

and opening it up. If it is powdery, the fibers broken or easily broken, or the strands pulled greatly out of a round shape, the rope may be considered weak and not to be trusted. Look for first wear *inside the rope,* especially in the way of blocks and lizzards.

A worn or weak spot in a Nylon line will have visible broken strands, usually pin sharp and readily discovered by feeling the area. Look for wear at points of flex, such as at a block or lizzard. Suspect any Nylon that has been exposed to acid, its worst enemy. In unclean harbor waters, near large cities and industrial areas, acid may well be present and dangerous to Nylon line.

Small Stuff

1211. Small stuff (or cordage) are lines of $1\frac{3}{4}$ inches in circumference or less, and are usually designated by "threads," 24 thread or $1\frac{3}{4}$-inch rope being the largest. Halyards, sheets, and other running rigging lines are not considered small stuff, but lines.

Small stuff includes the following cordage:

Marlin: For seizings and general service. It is two-stranded and laid left-handed. Untarred, it is used for sennit. Tarred, it is used in rigging.

Spun yarn: Loosely laid, multistranded, tarred, spun yarn is used for seizings and general service of a temporary or emergency nature.

Seizing stuff: Heavy seizing line. A finished rope, usually right-handed and three-stranded. It is tarred.

Ratline stuff: As above but in sizes 6–24 thread.

Houseline: Three-stranded, left-handed for general uses.

Roundline: Three-stranded, right-handed for general uses.

Hambroline: Two-stranded, right-handed, of fine-quality yarns.

Whiteline or codline: Small stuff, untarred.

Sail twine: Small, light-cotton stuff, for sewing canvas.

Parts of a Rope

1212. Any rope, when being knotted, or bent, or hitched, divides itself into three parts. It is customary to refer to these parts when giving instructions in knot tying. They are:

The standing part: The long unused or belayed end.

The bight: The loop, or half loop, formed by turning the rope back on itself.

The end: The remaining short end. (If passing through a block it is called the *fall*.)

Knots, Hitches, and Bends

1213. The knots, hitches, and bends following are all that the average boatman will require. They should be thoroughly and well understood; then used in the right place. At least the bowline, reef knot, half

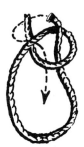  

Figure 1213. How to Tie the Bowline

hitch, and clove hitch should be used and the user able to tie these in the dark, under water, behind the back, or with one hand and the teeth. A "good" knot is not always the one which serves the situation best, but the one which can be securely tied under the circumstances, which will not jam if it becomes wet or frozen, and which will not chafe the line unduly.

Overhand Knot
Stopper knot to keep the end of a rope from fraying or running through a block.

Reef or Square Knot
Strong, will not slip, is easily tied and easily cast off, even when wet or frozen, by pushing the standing parts and ends against each other. Not recommended except for tying ropes of the same circumference.

ˡ Sheet or Becket Bend
Used for securing a small rope to the bight of a larger rope. May be double for extra holding power.

Double Carrick Bend

Used for joining large ropes, such as hawsers. As there are no sharp bends, it does not cripple the rope fibers. It passes through chocks and hawseholes easily. The ends must be seized to standing parts for security.

Bowline

Called the king of knots. It will not slip. A double turn is taken around rings, etc., to prevent chafing.

Bowline on a Bight

A strong secure loop which can be made in a rope, both ends of which are to be belayed.

Cat's-Paw

A good "hook" hitch for a rope which has no ends. Make two bights, one in each hand, twist on themselves, and slip over the hook. It is secure, and will not slip with strain on either fall.

Blackwall Hitch

A "hook" hitch for a single-part rope. Double it for extra security.

Two Half Hitches

A temporary fastening to a spar or Samson post. For extra security, or on a line not under constant strain, seize down the end.

Clove Hitch

A secure fastening which can be made over a post or yardarm even with the ends belayed. It will not slip either way. Recommended only for a line on which there is a constant strain.

Fishermen's Bend

Used for making fast to a spar or ring. It is popular, with ends seized to standing part, as an anchor knot.

Timber Hitch

Good fastening and will hold when hauled at acute angles to a spar, or when hauling a spar, or sending aloft.

Rolling Hitch

A hitch that can be moved along the spar by slacking off, then putting strain on again. Also used to make fast to the standing part of another rope.

Belaying to a Cleat

Make the turn around the cleat first; then form a bight in the fall, turn half over, and slip over the cleat ear.

Mousing

A seizing to prevent a hitch or sling from accidentally jumping off the hook.

Whipping and End Knots

1214. All rope ends require either whipping or back splicing or one of the crown knots to prevent the rope from unlaying. Whipping is used if the rope is to be passed through a block. A knot is used to prevent the rope from passing through a block by accident (such as the end of a sheet or halyard) as well as to keep the lay intact.

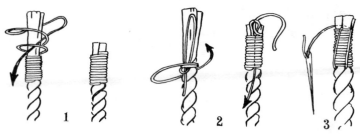

Figure 1214. Whipping

Whipping is done by one of the methods shown in Figure 1214. The whipping is small stuff; for most small boats codline or sail twine will be suitable. A dab of paint or varnish will prevent the whipping from wearing or slipping off.

Nylon line may be handled quite differently—by flame. A match or soldering iron or hot knife, touched to the strands of a line or the yarns of a strand, will effectively fuse the end together. This is *always* done when splicing Nylon. Because Nylon has such a large stretch factor, the ends, after tucking the splice, are left quite long. Later, after the splice has seated itself and worn in, the ends are trimmed and sealed by flame. It is usual, however, to whip even Nylon line after sealing with flame. Such whips must be especially tightly drawn up as Nylon is slippery. The sewn whip shown in Figure 1214 is best for Nylon.

The Backsplice
The crown is made as shown, hauled taut, and the ends tucked over and under the strands of the standing part. It will not pass through a block.

The Wall Knot
Make the crown, haul taut, relay the strands, and whip the end. A wall and crown knot is made by laying a backsplice crown over the wall crown and cutting off the ends.

Splices

1215. Splicing is the art of joining any two parts of a rope together permanently. Splicing introduces all the strands involved to each other in such a manner that a continuation of this introduction will result in relaying the rope with equal tension on all the strands.

The most important step in splicing is the start. Introduce (or marry) the strands correctly and the remaining steps follow almost automatically.

To prepare the rope for splicing, unlay the end for several feet, whip each end, if the rope is over 21 thread, with a temporary whipping or seizing of small stuff. If the rope is four-stranded, the heart is cut off short where the unlaying commences.

A tapered tool of wood or steel (called a fid or marlinspike) is used to aid in opening the lay of the rope at the point where a strand is to be introduced. On small rope mere twisting of the rope *against* the lay will open it sufficiently for hand tucking.

Four tucks will hold any splice providing they are full strands, i. e.,

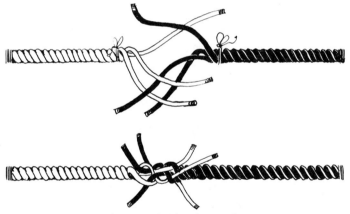

Figure 1216. The Short Splice

not tapered off. Tapering off is made after the fourth tuck, and is done by reducing all strands by one third, tucking, reducing by another one third, and finally tucking and trimming off close. For neatness, or to prevent chafing (as in the eye splice of a mooring line), the splice may be served with small stuff. Serving is started at the "thin" side of the splice and proceeds outward, served against the lay, and ended as in a whipping. A serving board is used for ropes of large circumference; and worming or parceling or both may be done under the serving.

Three splices are sufficient to meet any needs on the small boat.

The Short Splice

1216. For joining two ropes which do not have to pass through a block, or small chocks, or spill pipe, etc. (Figure 1216.)

"Marry" the ropes first (with a seizing around the standing part if there is an inclination to unlay), then seize down one set of strands and proceed with tucking in the other set, over and under for four tucks. Cast off the strand seizing and tuck the first set, over and under. Do not trim too short if untapered. Shape the splice by rolling underfoot. Very large ropes may require pounding with a wooden mallet as the tucks are made to preserve shape.

The Long Splice

1217. For joining two ropes together without enlarging the diameter (as for a rope which is to pass through a block):

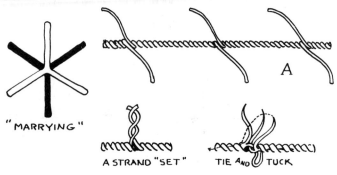

Figure 1217. The Long Splice

Unlay six to eight times the circumference of each rope and "marry" exactly as for the short splice. Now, unlay one strand carefully and lay in the matching strand from the opposite side. Repeat now with *two strands* but in the opposite direction. Two strands will remain in the center and the splice appear as in A, Figure 1217.

Each set of strands is now cut short, divided and an overhand knot tied with them. Each end is then tucked once *with the lay,* reduced again, tucked and trimmed. The splice must be rolled or pounded into shape and size. Well made, it should appear as a continuous length of rope.

The Eye Splice

1218. The eye splice is used to form a permanent loop in rope, the end being spliced into the standing part. "Marrying"is the important

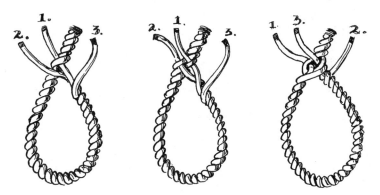

Figure 1218. The Eye Splice

step and is shown in Figure 1218. The first two tucks are shown left and middle; the right-hand cut shows the splice turned over, strand three tucked and the strands all hove taut.

Proceed now over and under, as in short splicing, in rotation. May be tapered and served.

Four-Stranded Rope

1219. The short splice is made exactly as for the three-stranded rope. Marry, hitch over and under.

Granny

Carrick Bend

Fisherman's Knot

Figure of Eight

Reef Point or Slippery Reef

Rope Yarn
or Marlin
Knot

Heaving
Line Bend

Reeving
Line Bend

Figure 1220A

The long splice is made exactly as for the three-stranded rope save that about 30% more end is unlayed as there will be four tucks instead of three.

The eye splice is made by dividing the strands, two on each side of the standing part. Tuck the two top strands into the top lay of the standing part, turn over and tuck the two remaining strands in the remaining lay. Continue, over and under, as in the usual eye splice.

Additional Knots, Hitches, and Bends

1220. Granny (or lubber's) knot. A misformed reef knot and dangerous because it slips.

Single carrick bend, for joining large ropes and hawsers. The absence of sharp bights makes it easy on the rope.

Reef point (or slippery reed or draw knot). For tying in reefs in sails. May be quickly cast off by jerking the fall.

Fisherman's knot. For securing leaders or trolling lines together.

Figure of eight. A stopper knot.

Rope-Yarn knot (or marlin knot). Small and tight knot for tying small stuff together.

Heaving-line bend. To tie a small rope to a large one, and for making fast the heaving line to a hawser.

Reeving-line bend. For connecting two hawsers or cables. The ends must be seized securely.

Running bowline. Slip noose.

French bowline. Useful for sending men aloft or over the side. The man sits on one loop, passing the other under the armpits and leaving both hands free.

Spanish bowline. Two loops, neither of which will slip.

Openhand knot. A quickly formed loop, but dangerous as it will jam.

Fisherman's eye. Another loop form.

Midshipman's hitch. A useful knot. It will not "set up" until hauled taut over an object within the loop; thereafter hold.

Crabber's eye. A no-slip noose.

Tomfool knot. Two loops both of which can be drawn taut and held.

Jury masthead knot. Placed over the masthead, each loop may be used to secure stays or halyards to. Sometimes used on sheer legs.

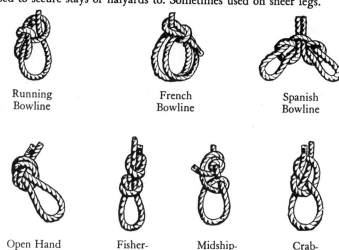

Running
Bowline

French
Bowline

Spanish
Bowline

Open Hand
Knot

Fisher-
man's
Eye

Midship-
man
Hitch

Crab-
ber's
Eye

Sheepshank

Toggled Sheepshank

Tomfool
Knot

Jury Masthead
Knot

Marlinspike
Hitch

Figure 1220B

Marlinspike hitch. A turn in which to insert a marlinspike or other object, and so to get a good grip on the line for hauling.

Sheepshank. Used for shortening rope. Will hold as long as there is strain on the rope.

Toggled sheepshank. Same as sheepshank but will hold even if rope is slacked away. Can be bent in when both ends are fast.

Slippery clove. A clove hitch that can be quickly released.

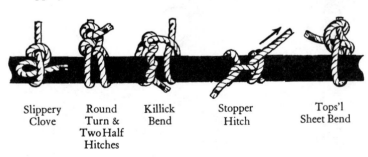

Slippery
Clove

Round
Turn &
Two Half
Hitches

Killick
Bend

Stopper
Hitch

Tops'l
Sheet Bend

| Tops'l
Halyard
Bend | Stuns'l
Tack
Bend | Stuns'l
Halyard
Bend | Lifting Hitch |

Figure 1220C

Round turn and two half hitches. The double turn relieves the strain on the hitches.

Killick bend. For extra security. The left-hand part of the bend is the timber hitch.

Stopper hitch. Used to fasten a rope to a spar or the standing part of another rope. Can be slid, then hauled taut.

Tops'l sheet bend. For bending a sheet to the clew of a sail.

Tops'l halyard bend. To make a rope fast to anything.

Stuns'l tack bend (buntline hitch). Strong, providing there is constant strain on it.

Stuns'l halyard bend. A simpler and quicker form of the tops'l halyard bend.

Lifting hitch. For lifting, or when the strain is to be exerted parallel to the spar.

Seizings

1221. Seizings are lashings of small stuff of a more or less permanent character, such as the seizing used for rattling down shrouds. Any small stuff is suitable and should be tarred if it is expected to remain exposed for any length of time, or if it is part of the standing rigging.

Clinch (or throat seizing). Use a bight on the standing part of a rope to take another rope, or a block or a tackle.

Round seizing. Used to hold two or more ropes together or in a bight. Ten to twelve round turns are layed around the parts and

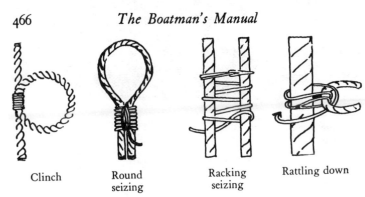

Clinch   Round seizing   Racking seizing   Rattling down

Figure 1221

these secured by two or three frapping turns taken around the round turns.

Racking seizing. Another method of securing several lines together. It is very strong and nonslip. Note the eye at the start.

Rattling down. Used for rattling down shrouds. On steel shrouds, a few frapping turns are taken around the seizing for extra power.

End Knots

1222. Double wall knot (*See* page 396.) Made exactly as the wall knot, but each strand is followed around again until the end comes out on top.

Diamond knot. Made exactly as the wall knot, but each strand is brought up through the bight of the second strand.

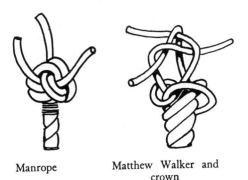

Manrope   Matthew Walker and crown

Figure 1222A

Manrope knot (Double Wall and Crown). Make a single crown, then *underneath* it make a single crown around the standing part.

Matthew Walker knot. Start as a single wall knot but each strand is taken under the two other strands and brought up alongside their own parts. *Keep the twist in the strands.* (Figure 1222A.)

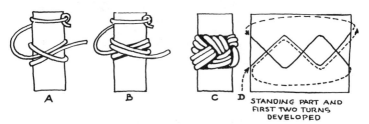

A   B   C   D STANDING PART AND
FIRST TWO TURNS
DEVELOPED

Figure 1222B. Three-strand Turk's-head

The three-strand Turk's-head. A separate knot, not made with the

rope's own strands. Used for rope's ends, tiller handles, stanchions, and for other ornamental uses. (Figure 1222B.)

Tie short end out of the way as in A and make the end into a clove hitch. Follow the clove hitch around, making a two plait; then follow again, making a three plait. This is the principle of making the knot. To make the overlays or convolutions of the knot, several hitches of

Start   Completed
Sailmaker's Splice

Flemish
Eye Splice

Cut Splice　　　　　　　　　　　　　　　Chain Splice

Figure 1223

the bight, over and under are taken as in D and the lay of it followed for three or four strands round. The ends are tucked under and cut off.

Additional Splices

1223. Sailmaker's splice. Make the first tuck in the same manner as the ordinary eye splice. Follow with the other strands, then, but *around* the strands of the standing part and *with the lay* (not over and under). Two full tucks, then taper for four tucks, makes a long neat splice and takes leather serving well.

Flemish eye splice. Unlay all strands for about a foot; then unlay one strand further for the full length of the bight to be made. Form the eye by looping the two (paired) strands around to the point where

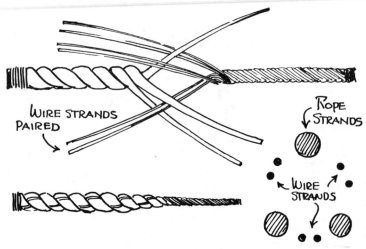

WIRE STRANDS PAIRED

ROPE STRANDS

WIRE STRANDS

Figure 1224. Rope to Wire Splice

the single strand has been unlaid. Lay up the single strand in its own groove but in the opposite direction. Finish by tucking the three strands as in the common eye splice. It gives additional strength and a short splice, as two tucks are sufficient to hold it.

Cut splice. Each end is made as in the common eye splice, the standing part of one end splicing into the standing part of the other. Both sides of the eye should be the same length.

Chain splice. Unlay the end and reeve two of the strands through the chain link or shackle. Unlay the third strand back still farther, following it and filling its groove by one of the first two (rove) strands as in the long splice. Tie overhand knot and tuck, exactly as in long splice. The remaining end is tucked and tapered where it is.

Rope to Wire Splice

1224. This is a handy but very difficult splice, and most professional riggers have a self-developed method for making it. The rope part is unlaid and the strands tapered *at once*. Then the wire part is unlaid *in pairs* and the two parts married as for the short splice. Proceed, over and under, with the wire part only for *several feet,* halving the wire pair to one at the finish. The splice must be very tightly served for its entire length. Professionals sometimes (as with 6×19 wire) end the splice by sewing in the wire strands individually, using a sail needle.

Protecting Rope from Wear

1225. Rope requires protection from wear (as hawsers) when subject to handling on deck, on docks, or where it passes over fixed objects, such as bollards or chocks. Serving usually offers ample protection and has the advantage of not stiffening the rope as complete protection does.

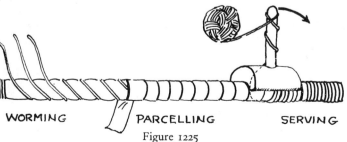

WORMING   PARCELLING   SERVING

Figure 1225

For rope standing rigging and to keep moisture, dampness, and frost out of the rope, it is wormed, parceled, *and* served. This makes a very stiff rope, hardly flexible enough for rope which must run.

Worming is done with small stuff which fills the lay evenly and presents a fairly uniform surface for the *parceling,* which is done with strips of canvas. Sometimes, as in the case of standing rigging, the parceling may be wrapped so as to shed water, like shingling, the lap being down. Parceling is sometimes painted with red or white lead, or hot tar, and immediately *served*. This is small stuff, often tarred, wound tightly over the parceling with the aid of a serving mallet.

The turns proceed as in the following jingle:

> Worm and parcel with the lay,
> Turn and serve the other way.

Wire Rope

1226. Standard wire rope consists of a center around which is laid six strands. Strands consist of 7, 12, 19, 24, or 37 wires each (Figure 1226). Wires are made of galvanized iron, cast steel, plow steel, and sometimes copper, bronze, or Phosphor bronze. The coppers are generally much less strong than iron wire of the same diameter. For fine

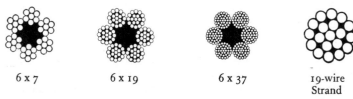

6 x 7   6 x 19   6 x 37   19-wire
                                              Strand

Figure 1226. Common Wire-rope Forms

yacht work enduring wire is made of stainless steel and other alloys, usually nonrusting and very much stronger than ordinary steel wire.

Wire rope is always designated by the *diameter* of the rope, not the circumference as in fiber rope. It is put out in reels or coils. Reels should be placed on a spindle and the wire used directly from it. Coils should first be rolled (like a hoop) and the wire taken from it in this way, not as from fiber rope coils.

If wires and strands are laid in the same direction, it is called *lang-lay* wire rope; if in opposite directions, it is called *regular-lay* wire rope. Most small-yacht rigging rope is regular lay.

1227. To form it into terminals or to join it together, three methods are in use; splicing, wire-rope sockets, or wire-rope clamps. The use of clamps is for a temporary joining or eying only and it is considered lubberly to set up any of the standing rigging so.

Wire Splicing

1228. Wire in sizes up to about ½″ may be spliced with the aid of the following tools:

1. One large steel marlinspike.
2. Two small steel splicing pins (small marlinspikes).
3. Knife for cutting out the core.
4. Wire cutters for nipping off the strands.
5. A wooden mallet for beating the splice into shape.

Larger wires, which are stiffer, require the following tools in addition:

1. Wooden block (or another mallet) for shaping.
2. Hemp-rope grommet and wooden twisting bar (to seize onto the standing part of the wire rope for a twist against the lay to open the strands).
3. A rigger's screw or a rigger's vice. (Figure 1228.)

Seizing wire will be required in the following sizes:

Diameter of Rope	Size of Serving Wire
⅛″—³⁄₁₆″	.040
¼″—⅜″	¹⁄₁₆″
½″—⅝″	³⁄₃₂″
¾″—1″	⅛″

A seizing is correctly made as shown in Figure 1228. From one to four seizings may be needed. Strands are seized with small stuff or sail twine to prevent them from springing apart.

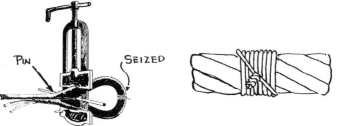

Rigger's screw   Figure 1228   Correct wire seizing

TABLE OF BREAKING STRENGTHS—WIRE ROPE

6 x 7 CONSTRUCTION

Diameter, Inches	1/16	3/32	1/8	5/32	3/16	7/32	1/4	9/32	5/16	3/8	7/16	1/2	9/16	5/8	3/4
Bronze	77	172	306	478	688	940	1,225	....	....	....	....	....	....	....	....
Galv. Iron	236	459	711	980	1,220	1,580	1,980	2,400	2,720	3,900	5,280	6,860	8,640	10,600	14,200
Galv. Cast Steel	....	....	....	....	....	....	3,500	4,300	5,600	7,800	10,600	13,600	17,000	20,800	29,600
Galv. Plow Steel	....	....	....	....	....	....	4,200	5,300	6,570	9,270	12,400	16,200	20,300	24,800	35,600
Galv. Imp. Plow St.	355	780	1,150	2,000	2,750	4,000	4,800	6,100	7,500	10,600	14,200	18,500	23,400	28,800	36,900

6 x 19 CONSTRUCTION

Diameter, Inches	1/8	5/32	3/16	7/32	1/4	9/32	5/16	3/8	7/16	1/2	9/16	5/8	3/4
Phosphor Bronze	....	....	....	....	2,400	....	3,310	4,720	6,370	8,300	10,400	12,700	18,000
Galv. Cast Steel	....	....	....	....	3,200	4,300	5,600	7,800	10,600	13,600	17,000	20,800	29,600
Galv. Plow Steel	....	....	....	....	4,290	5,400	6,840	9,650	12,800	16,500	20,500	25,400	36,100
Galv. Imp. Plow Steel	1,280	2,000	2,900	3,950	5,890	6,700	7,900	11,100	14,700	19,000	23,800	29,100	41,500

6 x 37 CONSTRUCTION

Diameter, Inches	1/4	5/16	3/8	7/16	1/2	9/16	5/8	3/4	7/8	1
Galv. Cast Steel	3,600	5,600	8,000	10,800	13,600	17,000	20,800	29,400	39,600	51,400
Galv. Plow Steel	4,080	6,400	9,000	12,200	15,600	19,500	23,800	33,600	45,200	58,600
Galv. Imp. Plow Steel	4,800	7,400	10,400	14,300	18,000	22,400	27,400	38,800	54,000	67,200

19-WIRE STRAND

Diameter, Inches	1/16	3/32	1/8	5/32	3/16	7/32	1/4	9/32	5/16	3/8	7/16	1/2
Galv. Imp. Plow Aircraft Strand	500	1,100	2,100	3,200	4,600	6,100	8,000	10,000	12,500	17,500	23,500	28,500

6×12 RUNNING ROPES   6 STRANDS OF 12 WIRES EACH—7 HEMP CENTERS

Diameter, Inches	1/4	5/16	3/8	7/16	1/2	9/16	5/8	3/4	13/16	7/8	1
Phosphor Bronze	1,330	2,050	3,040	4,120	5,330	6,700	8,210	11,500	12,900	14,900	. . . . .
Galv. Cast Steel	2,000	3,520	4,940	6,580	8,460	10,520	12,920	18,520	21,600	25,000	32,600
Galv. Plow Steel	3,000	4,260	6,020	8,020	10,200	12,860	15,800	22,600	26,600	30,800	40,000

TILLER ROPES 6×6×7   6 STRANDS—42 WIRES EACH—7 HEMP CENTERS

Diameter, Inches	3/16	1/4	5/16	3/8	7/16	1/2
Bronze	. . . .	1,285	1,875	2,900	3,900	5,700
Phosphor Bronze	. . . .	1,500	2,400	3,500	4,500	6,000
Galv. Iron	. . . .	1,125	1,759	2,520	3,438	4,300
Galv. Cast	. . . .	2,050	3,180	4,570	6,190	8,020
Galv. Plow	1,700	2,440	3,830	5,490	7,430	9,590

WEIGHT AND COMPARISON OF MANILA WITH WIRE ROPE

| GALVANIZED IRON RIGGING AND GUY ROPE | | | | | GALVANIZED STEEL MOORING LINES AND HAWSERS | | | | |
| Composed of 6 Strands and a Hemp Center, 7 Wires to the Strand | | | | | Composed of 6 Strands and a Hemp Center, each Strand composed of 24 Wires and a Hemp Core | | | | |
Diameter in inches	Approx. circum. in inches	Approx. weight per foot	Breaking strength in tons of 2,000 lbs.	Circum. of manila rope of nearest strength	Diameter in inches	Approx. circum. in inches	Approx. weight per foot	Breaking strength in tons of 2,000 lbs. Plow steel	Breaking strength in tons of 2,000 lbs. Cast steel
1¾	5½	4.60	37.00	10	2 1/16	6½	5.87	118.00	98.00
1⅝	5⅛	3.96	32.40	9	2	6¼	5.52	112.00	92.00
1½	4¾	3.38	27.70	8½	1 13/16	5¾	4.53	92.30	76.20
1⅜	4⅜	2.84	23.70	7½	1¾	5½	4.23	86.20	71.20
1¼	3⅞	2.34	19.90	7	1⅝	5⅛	3.64	74.50	61.60
1⅛	3½	1.90	16.50	6	1½	4¾	3.11	63.60	52.60
1 1/16	3⅜	1.70	14.80	5½	1⅜	4⅜	2.61	53.60	44.40
1	3⅛	1.50	13.20	5¼	1¼	3⅞	2.16	44.40	36.70
⅞	2¾	1.15	10.20	4¾	1⅛	3½	1.75	36.00	29.90
¾	2⅜	.84	7.10	3¾	1	3⅛	1.38	28.50	23.70
⅝	2	.59	5.30	3¼	⅞	2¾	1.06	22.00	18.30
9/16	1¾	.48	4.32	3	¾	2⅜	.78	16.40	13.60
½	1⅝	.38	3.43	2½	⅝	2	.54	11.60	9.59
7/16	1⅜	.29	2.64	2¼	½	1⅝	.35	7.63	6.37
⅜	1⅛	.21	1.95	2	⅜	1⅛	.194	4.40	3.67
5/16	1	.15	1.36	1½					
9/32	⅞	.125	1.20	1⅜					
¼	¾	.090	.99	1¼					
7/32	11/16	.063	.79	1⅛					
3/16	⅝	.040	.61	1					

1230. To open wire. Clap a clove hitch over the wire rope or make strap and several round turns with the rope grommet, insert the twisting bar and pull against the lay and lash the bar so. (As to a floor staple if the splicing is to be done with a bench vice.)

Further opening is done with the splicing pins (or marlinspike when handling very small rope) and the strand inserted in the opening ahead of the pin. The strand thus introduced is hauled taut and laid neatly before the pin is withdrawn.

1231. To shape a splice. After the full tucks have been completed, beat into shape with a wooden mallet (never a hammer), turning the splice as it is done. The splice should be approximately cylindrical. Then middle the strands, tuck one half the middling, beat, and nip off the unused middling, again beating the ends into the lay. Middle again and repeat. The splice is then served with annealed serving wire (*see* table, paragraph 1228) ending at the crotch. The entire splice may be well painted or varnished and then served with small stuff or a sewn rawhide serving.

Short Splice in 6 x 7 Wire

1232. Place temporary seizings at the point where the strands are to be unlaid on each rope. Unlay each strand, opening them to appear like an umbrella blown inside out. Cut off the hemp heart very close. Marry the strands, exactly as in fiber-rope short splice. Cast off one seizing. Starting with any strand of one side (the other side being held in a bench vice or lashed to a spar or some fixed object), tuck over *one* and under *two* against the lay. Continue with the five remaining strands; then put in the second row of tucks.

Now place the tucked side in the vice, cast off the remaining seizing, and splice the remaining side. Continue each side until four full tucks have been done, each over one and under two.

Shape as directed in paragraph 1231.

Eye Splice in 6 x 7 Wire

1233. The commonest eye splice is the Liverpool splice, easily made and as strong as any.

The standing parts are placed in the vice, the end unlayed and seized, and the two parts lightly seized together. The end is then divided into two bundles of three strands each and the heart cut away. The inside

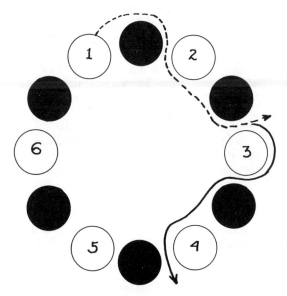

Figure 1232. The Short Splice in Wire Diagramed

Black strands are those of the standing part; white, those of the part being tucked. They are shown as a cross section of the married position. Strands 1 to 6 each tucked (over one and under two) as shown at strand No. 1. The dotted line shows the first, third, and fifth tucks, and the solid line the second, fourth, and sixth tucks.

"bundle" is tucked first, in the order shown in the diagram. Note that all the strands *enter* between the same strands of the standing part. The remaining bundle is then tucked in the order shown.

After the first tuck, there should be a strand emerging from between each of the lays of the standing part. Following tucks are made by passing each strand *around and under* the strand of the standing part, following the lay. Three tucks are sufficient; middle and shape as for other splices.

This splice can be made over a thimble or as an open eye.

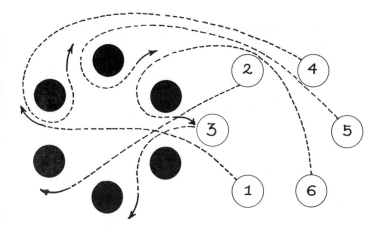

Figure 1233. The Eye Splice in Wire Diagramed

Black strands are those of the standing part; white, those of the end being tucked. They are shown as a cross section of the two parts of the wire rope laid together, ready for tucking, with the bight toward the observer. Tucking is done in the order shown. Succeeding tucks are made around and under the strands of the standing parts, following the lay.

The Grommet Splice

1234. This is a very simple form of wire splice, related to the Flemish splice, and can be done only with preformed wire (common yacht-rigging wire). Great care must be used in the serving, using only annealed serving wire of the correct size (*see* table, paragraph 1228) layed on with a wire serving tool. If made over a thimble, the ends should be tucked once, then served.

Wire-Rope Sockets

1235. Wire-rope sockets to take the place of eye splices are of two general types:

1. A hollow basket fitting, having an eye for a shackle, into which the frayed strands of the wire are inserted, spread, and then filled with

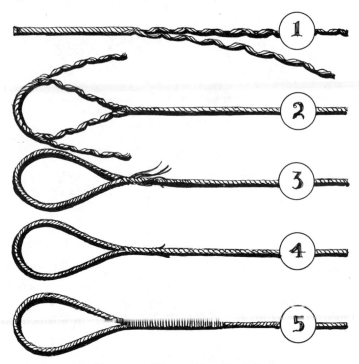

Figure 1234. How to Grommet Splice

1. Cut wire rope off clean. There is no need to whip the ends as pre-formed rope will not spring apart. Unlay, three strands on either side, carefully retaining natural curves, a length just twice the circumference of the eye to be formed. 2. Draw the two groups toward each other without unnatural bending and tie a simple overhand knot. The knot will form a small-sized section of complete rope at the top of the bight. 3. Now lay each strand into the loop, letting the strands fall in their grooves. The fiber heart should be worked in carefully as the laying up proceeds. Bring the ends snug to the crotch and cut the individual strands off at varying short lengths from 1″ to 2″. 4. Work these ends into the lay of the standing part by tapping with a wooden mallet. 5. Serve the ends down tightly with stainless steel annealed serving wire, drawing it taut with a wire serving tool. Properly done this splice is just as strong as a tucked splice and can be finished in one quarter of the time.

molten zinc. In making such a terminal it is essential that the wires be absolutely clean and oil-free and spread so that the zinc flows down and around each individual wire of the strand. Caution is made not to use babbitt or other antifriction metal. Lead is too soft. The molten zinc should not be over 825° F., so that the fine wires are not melted.

2. A basket fitting into which the frayed wire ends are placed, and which has a screw with a cone-shaped tip screwed against the wire rope. The strand wires are evenly spread and gripped between the cone of the screw and a beveled shoulder, thus clamping it firmly and with uniform tension.

Both types are for sale at marine chandleries, and either makes a neat yacht finish without loss of wire strength. Streamlined basket fittings may be obtained for racing yachts. These are generally attached by the wire-rope manufacturer by special patented methods, and it is necessary to give accurate lengths for all parts of the rigging wire.

Wire-Rope Clamps (Clips)

1236. These are U-shaped units, used to make temporary splices or eyes, with or without a thimble. The correct-sized clip must be ordered for both the size and type of wire.

They are correctly applied only when the U (or staple) grips the end and the shoulder grips the standing part. Any other manner of applying will crush the standing part and weaken the entire line. All clips are put on the same way, not staggered. Three clips are sufficient for any splice so made.

Another form of wire-rope clamp is made (especially for tiller cables), both parts of which are scored and which exert equal pressure on both parts of the wire. They have the advantage of not crushing the wire at any point. One is sufficient for tiller cables. In general, they have not the strength of a U-clip because the setup is by slotted screw and not by hex-nut and bolt.

Glossary of Rope Terms

1237.

Becket.—A rope eye for the hook of a block. A rope grommet used as a rowlock; any small rope or strap serving as a handle.

Belay.—To make fast to a cleat or belaying pin.

Bend.—The twisting or turning of a rope so as to fasten it to some object, as a spar or ring.

Bight.—Formed by bringing the end of a rope around, near to, or across its own part.

Bitter end.—The last part of a rope; the last link of an anchor chain.

Chafe.—To wear the surface of a rope by rubbing against a solid object.

Coil.—To lay down rope in circular turns.

Cord.—A small rope made by twisting several strands together.

Cordage.—Ropes or cords; anything made of ropes or cords; used collectively as in speaking of that part of the rigging of a ship composed of ropes, etc.

End seizing.—A round seizing at the end of a rope.

Fid.—A tapered wooden pin used to separate the strands when splicing heavy rope.

Frapping turns.—Cross turns; turns taken around and perpendicular to the turns of a lashing or seizing.

Hawser-laid.—Left-handed rope of nine strands, in the form of three three-stranded, right-handed ropes.

Heart.—The inside center strand of a rope.

Heave.—To haul or pull on a line; to throw a heaving line.

Heave taut.—To haul in a line until it has a strain upon it.

Irish pennant.—The frayed loose end of a line.

Jam.—To wedge tight.

Kink.—A twist in a rope.

Knot.—A twisting, turning, tying, knitting, or entangling of ropes or parts of a rope so as to join two ropes together or make a finished end on a rope, for a certain purpose.

Lanyard.—A line attached to an article to make it fast, as a knife lanyard.

Lashing.—A passing and repassing of a rope so as to confine or fasten together two or more objects; usually in the form of a bunch.

Line.—A general term for light rope.

Loop.—Same as *Bight.*

Marlinspike.—An iron or steel pin that tapers to a sharp point, used to splice wire rope.

Marry.—Temporarily holding two lines together side by side or end to end.

Nip.—To pinch or close in upon.

Part.—To break.

Pay out.—To slack off on a line, to allow it to run out.

Pointing.—Any of numerous ways of working the end of a rope into a stiff cone-shaped point.

Rack.—To seize two ropes together with crossed turns of spun yarn.

Rigging.—A term applied to ship's ropes generally.

Round seizing.—To seize two ropes together.

Secure.—To make fast.

Seize.—To bind two ropes together.

Sennit.—Braided spun or rope yarns commonly named according to their shape or design.

Slack.—The part of a rope hanging loose; the opposite of taut.

Splice.—The joining of two ends of a rope or ropes by intertwining the strands so as to increase the diameter of the rope as little as possible.

Standing part.—That part of a line which is secured.

Stopper.—A short line, one end of which is secured to a fixed object and used to check or stop a running line, as a boat fall stopper.

Strap.—A rope ring or sling, made by splicing the two ends of a short piece of rope. Used to handle heavy objects. Small straps used to attach a handy-billy to the hauling part of a line.

Take a turn.—To pass a line around a cleat or belaying pin to hold on.

Taut.—Tight; snug; tightly drawn; opposite of slack.

Thimble.—An iron ring with a groove on the outside for a rope grommet or splice.

Toggle.—A small piece of wood or bar of iron inserted in a knot to render it more secure, or to make it more readily unfastened or slipped.

Trice.—To haul up and secure.

Unbend.—To untie or cast adrift.

Veer.—To allow rope or chain to run out; to slack off.

⚓

CHAPTER XIII

BLOCKS AND TACKLES

1301. A block is a mechanical device to change the direction of the pull of a rope, wire, or fiber. It may be desired to change the direction of pull to "give a better lead" (make it more convenient) or to multiply the power of the pull.

When blocks and rope are combined to multiply power it is called a *tackle*. The following terms are used in connection with a tackle:

Falls.—That part of the tackle made of rope.
Standing part.—That part of the falls made fast to one of the blocks.
Hauling part.—The end of the falls to which the power is applied.
Round in.—To bring the two blocks together.
Overhaul.—To separate the two blocks.
Reeve.—To pass the rope through the block, over the sheave.
Two-block.—To bring the two blocks together (or choc-a-block).

Blocks

1302.

TABLE OF BLOCK SIZES

Length Shell Inches	Size Sheave Inches	For Dia. Rope Inches
3	1¾ x ½ x ⅜	⅜
4	2¼ x ⅝ x ⅜	½
5	3 x ¾ x ⅜	⅝
6	3½ x 1 x ½	⅝–¾
7	4¼ x 1 x ½	⅞
8	4¾ x 1⅛ x ⅝	1
9	5½ x 1⅛ x ⅝	1

1303. Wire rope should pass over sheaves of very much larger diameter than fiber rope to reduce fatiguing. Special wire-rope blocks are manufactured, usually with iron or steel shells and sometimes with specially designed sheave grooves, to accommodate the various lays of wire rope. A wire rope ending in a manila-rope pennant should pass over a sheave grooved for the manila rope and having a wire-rope groove scored into it.

All types of blocks can be had with ball bearing or other types of frictionless bearings. They are desirable for any block handling fiber rope over two inches and wire rope over one-quarter inch.

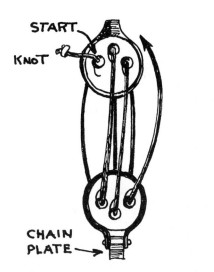
Reeving deadeye lanyards

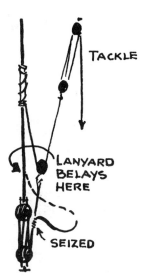
Setting up rigging

Figure 1303

Cheek blocks are made to be permanently fastened, sheave against the flat of the object fastened to, and are usually lead blocks (such as those at the foot of a mast used to lead halyards aft). They are generally of all-metal construction.

Deadeyes are a type of sheaveless block, used to set up standing rigging. A tackle is first clapped on the two ends to be set up, then a lanyard rove between the upper and lower deadeyes more or less permanently; it, too, having been set up with the aid of a tackle.

1304. Blocks are generally iron strapped, though occasionally rope-strapped blocks are still seen, especially aloft. Yacht blocks are often of bronze and all metal. They are called by the number of their sheaves (single, double, triple, fourfold, etc.), or, when part of the rigging of a

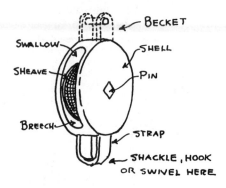

Figure 1304A. The Parts of a Block

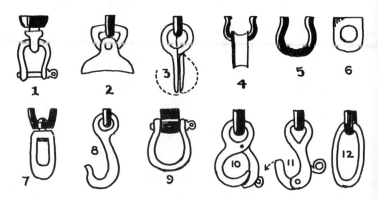

Figure 1304B. Block Fittings

1. Swivel with upset front shackle
2. Flat sheet bridle
3. Front sister hooks
4. Eye and thimble
5. Lashing eye
6. Solid eye
7. Swivel eye
8. Front backstay hook
9. Front shackle
10. Front Coleman hook
11. Anchor trip hook
12. Front ring (or link)

vessel, by their purpose (sheet block, tops'l halyard block, jib halyard lead block, etc.).

If the block has a latching device, permitting the rope to be rove without passing it through the swallow, it is called a *snatch block*. These are often used for lead blocks, as when changing direction of the pull between a capstan and a tackle. Single iron bound blocks are called *gin blocks*. A *secret block* is one having a casing entirely around it, the parts of the falls emerging from two holes in the casing. *Cargo blocks* are of steel, the shell being diamond-shaped.

1305. A general formula for selecting the correct block size follows:

Length of block—three times the circumference of the rope.

Sheave diameter—twice the circumference of the rope.

Tackles (Pronounced Tayckles)

1306. Tackles are used to multiply power. Such multiplication can go on almost indefinitely, or until friction becomes so great that there remains no further advantage in multiplying the power. Power is gained at the expense of time; a tackle which increases power by four, for example, must be hauled four times as far (requiring four times as much time) but requires but one fourth the power, friction not considered.

1307. Fixed blocks do not increase power; they merely change the lead. The movable blocks alone provide gain in power.

1308. The block having the greatest number of parts should be placed at the weight to be moved. The number of rope parts leading from the movable block indicates the number of times the power has been theoretically increased.

1309. To determine the power required to raise a given weight with a tackle, divide the weight to be raised by the number of rope parts at the movable block (or blocks). The quotient will be the power required to produce a balance, friction not considered.

Example:	Weight to be moved	1,200 pounds
	Tackle parts	4
	Power required for balance	300 pounds (pull)
	Estimated loss by friction	20%
	Pull required for balance (300 plus friction)	360 pounds

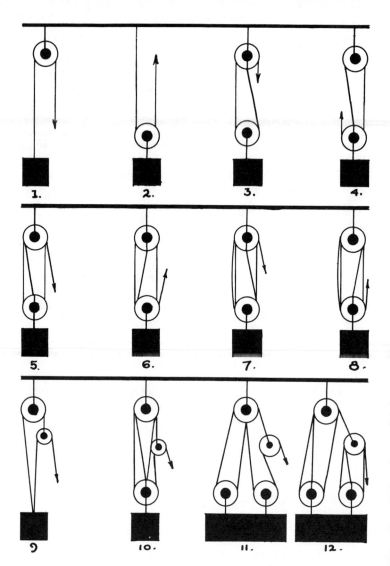

Figure 1306A

Table of Purchases

	Friction Not Considered	Friction Considered	Power Required
No. 1, Single whip	$P = W$	$\dfrac{P}{W} = \dfrac{11}{10}$	1 W
No. 2, Single whip, inverted	$\dfrac{P}{W} = \dfrac{10}{20}$	$\dfrac{P}{W} = \dfrac{12}{20}$	½ W
No. 3, Gun tackle	$\dfrac{P}{W} = \dfrac{10}{20}$	$\dfrac{P}{W} = \dfrac{12}{20}$	½ W
No. 4, Gun tackle, inverted	$\dfrac{P}{W} = \dfrac{10}{30}$	$\dfrac{P}{W} = \dfrac{13}{30}$	⅓ W
No. 5, Luff tackle	$\dfrac{P}{W} = \dfrac{10}{30}$	$\dfrac{P}{W} = \dfrac{13}{30}$	⅓ W
No. 6, Luff tackle, inverted	$\dfrac{P}{W} = \dfrac{10}{40}$	$\dfrac{P}{W} = \dfrac{14}{40}$	¼ W
No. 7, Double purchase	$\dfrac{P}{W} = \dfrac{10}{40}$	$\dfrac{P}{W} = \dfrac{14}{40}$	¼ W
No. 8, Double purchase, inverted	$\dfrac{P}{W} = \dfrac{10}{50}$	$\dfrac{P}{W} = \dfrac{15}{50}$	⅕ W
No. 9, Spanish Burton	$\dfrac{P}{W} = \dfrac{10}{30}$	$\dfrac{P}{W} = \dfrac{13}{30}$	⅓ W
No. 10, Double Spanish Burton	$\dfrac{P}{W} = \dfrac{10}{50}$	$\dfrac{P}{W} = \dfrac{15}{50}$	⅕ W
No. 11, Bell purchase	$\dfrac{P}{W} = \dfrac{10}{70}$	$\dfrac{P}{W} = \dfrac{17}{70}$	⅐ W
No. 12, Luff on Luff	$\dfrac{P}{W} = \dfrac{10}{160}$	$\dfrac{P}{W} = \dfrac{26}{160}$	1/16 W

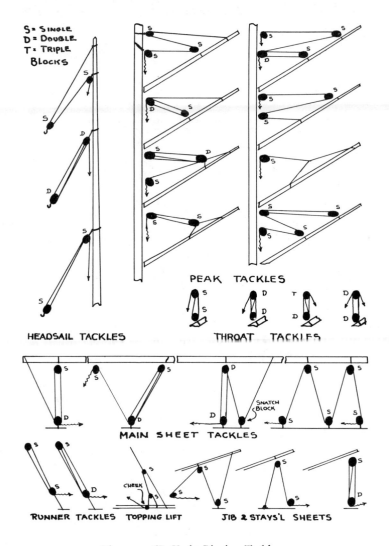

S = SINGLE
D = DOUBLE
T = TRIPLE
BLOCKS

HEADSAIL TACKLES

PEAK TACKLES

THROAT TACKLES

MAIN SHEET TACKLES

SNATCH BLOCK

RUNNER TACKLES   TOPPING LIFT   JIB & STAYS'L SHEETS

CHEEK

Figure 1306B. Yacht Rigging Tackles

488

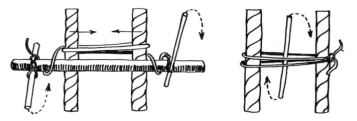

Figure 1314. Two Forms of the Spanish Windlass

1310. To determine the amount of purchase (power of tackle) required to raise a given weight with a given power, divide the weight by the power. The quotient will be the number of rope parts required at the movable block.

Example:	Weight to be moved	1,200 pounds
	Power available	400 pounds (pull)
	Rope parts needed, therefore	3
	For friction	1
	Total rope parts	4

1311. A man can pull about 150 pounds maximum, providing he has a firm foothold and is in such a position as to exert his fullest power. This may be down, up, or sideways, and is made up of deadweight pull and muscular pull, the back muscles being the most powerful.

1312. To determine the weight a given tackle will raise, the weight that a single rope will bear should be multiplied by the number of parts at the moving block.

Example:	Single rope will bear	400 pounds
	Tackle parts	3
	Weight the tackle will move	1,200

1313. When one tackle is clapped upon another, multiply the two powers together to obtain the total amount of purchase gained.

Example:	Tackle #1	3 powers
	Tackle #2	2 powers
	Total power	6

1314. The Spanish windlass is a blockless tackle, oftentimes handy. (Figure 1314.) It is used mainly for rigging jobs.

1315. The Parbuckle (Figure 1315) is a blockless tackle for taking spars or casks up the side or up an incline (as the gangplank).

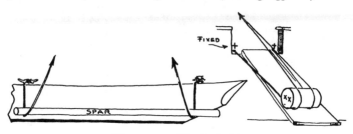

Figure 1315. The Parbuckle

To Make Up a Tackle

1316. Place the blocks about three feet apart, hooks pointing up, and coil down *with the sun,* coiling around the blocks. With the end of the fall, clove hitch the tackle about midway between the blocks. Store only if thoroughly dry.

To Fleet a Tackle

1317. Place on deck exactly in the position as when made up. Cast off the hitch, lift the coil clear, and capsize. Separate the two blocks.

CHAPTER XIV

DECK SEAMANSHIP

Deck seamanship is that branch of seamanship embracing the practical side, from the simplest rudiments of marlinspike seamanship up to navigation. It does not include engineering knowledge. The good deck seaman understands and can expertly practice his part of the following maneuvers and operations covered in other chapters of this *Manual*.

Small-Boat Handling	Chapters I, II, III
Handling Ground Tackle	Chapter VI
Marlinspike Seamanship	Chapter XII
Rigging	Chapter XIII
Maintenance and Repairs	Chapter XV
Safety at Sea	Chapter XVI
Custom and Etiquette	Chapter XVIII

In addition, some elemental knowledge of other departments will help to round out the subject. These include, for example, taking soundings by the lead, reading the log, signaling, rules of the road, and quartermaster duties (steering and steering orders).

The subject of deck seamanship is not completely covered in this chapter. What is presented is merely in addition to the deck seamanship presented in the above-listed chapters.

Handling Cargo and Stores

1401. Loading the small boat is generally not a job calling for complicated cargo-handling gear. What cannot be carried can be handled easily by a jury boom rigged to the masts, or use of the existing spars fitted with special tackles.

In rigging such jury booms it is essential that the boom-hoisting tackle be secured to the boom at approximately the same point at which the cargo tackle or sling is attached. It would not do, for example, to attach a load to the middle of the main boom and hoist it with the topping lift.

Whips may be rigged (Figure 1401) and are very convenient for taking on a deck load.

1402. For vessels without spars, some form of the sheer legs make handy derricks. (Figure 1402.) In guying such hoisting rigs, the sheer legs must rest on a chafing pad of wood or folded canvas to protect the deck, and the fitting to which every guy is fastened must be carefully examined for strength. Many deck fittings, such as ring bolts and cleats, will stand a tremendous side strain but very little direct pull against the fastenings. Do not trust a fitting fastened with a "dry

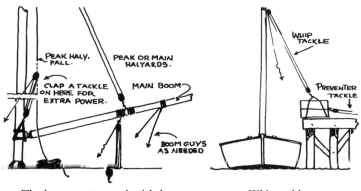

The boom used as a derrick boom   Whip tackle

Figure 1401

bolt," that is, one not fitted with a washer and nut or headed over a washer. Ring bolts, which are often placed on a deck as a convenient place to hook a block to change the direction of a *horizontal* lead, should not be used, as they are very often dry-bolted (especially in fishing and commercial type vessels).

Guys, well padded, secured to a fixed part of the vessel (as a mast, bitts, Samson post) or to a round turn around the vessel's counter itself, are the most secure.

1403. By remembering always that the vessel is a movable object or platform, many handling problems become simple. To shift a deck load while moored to a dock, for example, it is simple to hoist the load by means of a derrick *from the dock* and move the boat under it.

In unloading (as barreled fish) it is simplest to drop the barrels under the arc of the boom on the dock; then shift the boat astern and make available another cleared space.

This principle is used in removing heavy engines forward from under a bridge deck, up and then aft, through the hatch, and onto the deck or dock, and saves rigging skids and horizontal purchases.

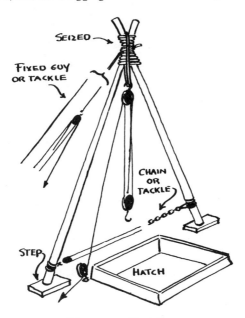

Figure 1402. Sheer Legs

1404. Slings are usually endless ropes, spliced together for providing a bight for the lifting block hook. The object moved must be raised with a pinch bar to adjust the sling and set down on a block or roller, the sling thrown off and then set fully down. (Figure 1404.) Engines and machinery should be handled with chain slings or spark-plug hole balancing eyes, screwed into the head of the engine. Many engines are manufactured with lifting rings. The purchase must be made fast above the shaft line in order not to capsize the machine.

In making a rope sling the turns should be taken out of the line

before splicing. This is done by coiling the line down *against* the lay
and bringing the bottom end up through the coil and short-splicing
the ends. A chain sling should have a ring or long link on one end
and a hook on the other. A swivel between load and movable block
will permit better handling and placing of the load.

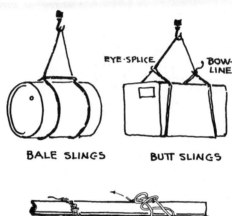

BALE SLINGS   BUTT SLINGS

NON-SLIP SPAR HITCH

Figure 1404

1405. Dunnage is loose wood and wooden blocks laid under and
between items of cargo and other items or structural parts of the boat
(as mast heels, bulkheads, etc.).

It serves the further purpose of raising the cargo above any bilge
water and affords ventilation between items. Dunnage is absolutely
necessary for the laden vessel putting to sea. It should serve to prevent
the cargo from moving in any *direction*. Wedges are used in addition
to hand-placed dunnage on steel-hulled ships only. The first layer of
dunnage is always placed thwartships to permit the free passage of
water as the ship rolls.

1406. Cargo is stowed with liquid always below the dry cargo;
barrel bungs *up;* all case markings *up.* Carboys of acid or barrels of
fuel are stored on deck, ready to be jettisoned in case of fire or other
emergency. The small boat (such as a cruiser storing up for a long

ocean passage) should have the heaviest cargo on the bottom, concentrated amidships and near the center line.

In stowing stores to be used during the voyage, great care must be used to make the stores available as might be needed. Careful marking of cases, concentration of like items together (foods grouped, spare parts grouped, tools grouped, etc.), and a full and detailed cargo list

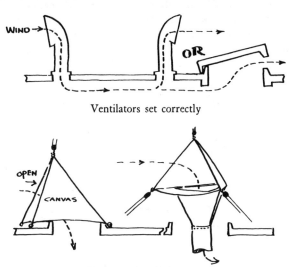

Ventilators set correctly

Figure 1406. Wind scoops

and cargo plan are required. Ventilation is of the utmost importance, and a good day at sea should see hatches opened and a wind scoop rigged. The principle of ventilation is to create a draught. A ventilator merely turned to catch the breeze will not ventilate unless there is an outlet.

Deck Cargoes and Stowage

1407. The disposal of cargo on deck is always secondary to the safe operation of the boat. No cargo should ever make useless the lifeboats, main bilge pump, winches, etc.; or close up hatches or companionways. In general, and especially if the cargo is heavy, it is best stored amidships, and adequately protected by tarpaulins in such a manner (by lashing) as to positively not shift as the boat rolls and pitches, or as attacked by boarding seas.

Dunnage should be placed under it always. Wooden barrel heads should be wet down each day to keep them swelled. Cases should be permanently marked with paint, not gummed labels. No baled or inflammable cargo should be placed in the lee of galley stacks or exhaust stacks. Casks and barrels should be stowed forward of cased items to form a protection from spray.

1408. If cargo must be jettisoned (as under storm conditions) heave it to windward and from a point as far aft as possible. Heave floating cargo into the top of a sea, not the trough, or it might "come back." It is dangerous to lighten liquid loads by broaching the casks (except water casks). If it must be done to save time, close all hatches and openings to below decks to prevent fumes, possibly explosive, from collecting in the hull.

Mooring to a Dock

1409. When a boat is moored alongside a dock in a more or less permanent manner, mooring lines are put out as follows:

Bowlines. Lines run from the inshore bow to the dock bollard (or cleat or pile head) at an angle of about 30° to the keel.

Stern lines. The same, except that a stern line may lead from an offshore chock.

Breast lines. Lines which lead from the bow and stern chocks, or chocks of their own, at right angles to the keel.

Spring lines. Run from chocks at the bow or stern to the dock at an angle to pull opposite to the bow or stern lines.

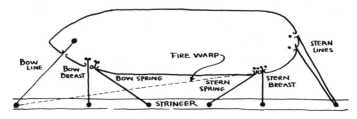

Figure 1409A. Mooring a Vessel

The line between chock and dock bollard is called the *drift*. After a ship is moored, the drift should be of equal tension on all lines so that the strain is equally divided. If the tide or wind is liable to set the vessel against the dock, lines must be run to another dock of the slip, or to mooring piles, or stream anchors.

Under such circumstances a boat may be breasted off by suspending short spars between dock and hull. Fenders may also be used, rigged as shown in Figure 1409B, but it must be certain that there is no pos-

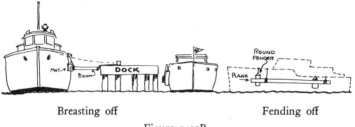

Breasting off   Fending off

Figure 1409B

sibility of their "hanging up" on the piles, where there is a rise and fall of tide.

1410. Mooring a ship is not merely a matter of tying it up. The lines serve at first in conjunction with the rudder and screw to warp the vessel sideways into her berth, and the order of passing lines will come from the navigator (or bridge).

A boat approaching a dock bow first will first need the bowline passed, then the bow spring. As her stern swings abreast, the stern line will be required, then the stern spring, and, lastly, the breast lines.

If she is approaching as above with a strong tide or wind setting her against the dock, other maneuvers may be called for, possibly fenders and breast lines first.

1411. A mooring line is passed as follows: Prepare the heaving line by coiling about one third of the knotted end loosely in the right (or heaving) hand, with the knot (usually a weighted knot or "monkey fist") hanging at the outside turn of the coil and below the same level. Coil the remaining line loosely over the palm of the free hand, arranged so that the outside turns will run out smoothly and without fouling. The heave is made with a sweeping side motion, full arm extended, and using the body to add to the swing.

The heaving line is attached to the hawser with a heaving line bend and hauled across to the dock. If the hawser is too heavy to be handled by the heaving line, a messenger is first bent on of about three-inch line, hauled across, and the hawser bent to it.

1412. If it is necessary to slack off a hawser from the bitts (as when leading it to a winch) a stopper is clapped on to take the strain while the change over is being made. Such a stopper is shown in Figure 1412. The fall must be held onto or belayed.

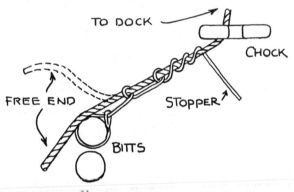

Figure 1412. Clapping a Stopper on a Mooring Hawser

1413. Fire warps are sometimes rigged for emergencies. This is a long lead from the stream end of a dock aft to the stern chocks and thence along deck to the winch or coiled handy. In case of a dock fire, the fire warp can be hauled from the *deck* by the stand-by crew and, as the regular mooring lines are let go, the boat hauled ahead and into the stream where she can be anchored, or signal for a tow.

1414. For bending two eyeless hawsers, use a double-sheet bend; or a double-carrick bend, ends stopped down. If the hawser must pass through solid chocks, use a reeving-line bend. Replace a parted eye quickly by a bowline.

Dinghy Booms

1415. Only large boats are equipped with boat booms, yet the dinghy on a stern painter constitutes a problem as wind and tide swing it against the boat. (Figure 1415.)

While it can often be kept clear by setting a light anchor or some drag off the dinghy's stern, or hanging a bucket with the bottom punctured from the transom, thus discouraging its "nursing the ship," one of the booming methods in Figure 1415 is more satisfactory.

Cut A shows the spinnaker or other light spar lashed to the main boom and the dinghy sent to its outboard end on an endless line.

Figure 1415. Jury Boat Booms

Cut B shows the spinnaker pole guyed as a regular boat boom. The dinghy painter may be rove to an endless line or merely made fast while the boom is alongside, it being controlled by the forward guy.

In a swift tideway, a sea painter may be led over the dinghy's inboard bow and it will ride away from the ship. However, when there is tide enough to accomplish this, the boat will stay astern. It is a useful wrinkle in a crowded anchorage, or if a dinghy light cannot be set at night when the dinghy is moored astern.

To Rig a Bosun's Chair

1416. When work aloft or over the side is to be done, the worker may be hauled there in a bosun's chair. (Figure 1416.) The important part of the chair is the gantline and its belaying in a safe manner, or making yourself fast aloft.

This is done, once you have reached the point at which the work is to be done, by reaching up above the bend in the bridle eye and seizing both the hauling and standing parts of the gantline in the left hand, taking a good grip calculated to hold your weight. The tender on deck now slacks off the hauling part. Reach down and take a generous bight of the slack, pull it through the bridle, slip it over the head, down over the shoulders, and under the chair and the legs. Let the slack overhaul itself until the bight is brought tight and jammed inside the bridle.

To lower away, pay up the hauling part of the gantline and let yourself down gently.

If there is no gantline affording communication to the deck (as on

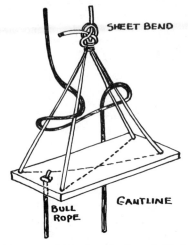

Figure 1416. Rigging of a Bosun's Chair

a spar), take a bull rope aloft, fastened to a leg of the bridle. Paint, tools, etc., can then be hauled aloft as needed.

To Rig a Scaffold

1417. Scaffolds, or hanging stages, are rigged as shown in Figure 1417. Plank should be at least two inches by twelve inches and not more than ten feet between bridles nor extending more than two feet beyond bridles. Yellow pine or spruce, absolutely clear of knots, is suitable. Beware of fir, white pine, or soft woods. The bridle horns are of hardwood (oak or elm) and should extend about twelve inches on each side of the plank.

Rig the bridle into a bowline with the turns shown at the horns; then lead to the hooks, down, around the plank several turns and belay on the outboard horns. Pad the inside horn ends to protect the ship's side.

A scaffold can be breasted in (as under the counter) by heaving inboard with lines made fast to deck. Breasting into the side may be done with the help of a hook into a port light frame.

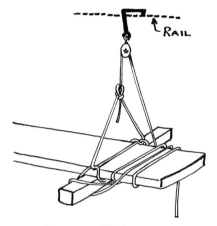

Figure 1417. Rigging a Stage

To Rig a Gangplank

1418. The small-boat gangplank need seldom be more than a two inch by twelve inch sound plank, rigged between the boat and the dock. If there is a rise and fall in tide, the boat end should be securely lashed permitting the dock end to move. A cleat nailed under the boat end will catch the rail or toe mould, preventing slipping outboard. Steep gangplanks should be covered with fiber matting or should have light battens nailed across as treads. If possible rig a manrope 'longside, as a handrail.

A loading plank must be extra heavy (or doubled planks) and have no cleats. If material is being taken aboard in hand wheelbarrows, nail two parallel cleats along the center of the plank as wheel tracks.

SPECIAL DUTIES OF DECK SEAMEN

Lookout

1419. Lookouts, wherever stationed, must be on the alert for, and immediately report, vessels, land, rocks, shoals, discolored water, buoys, beacons, lighthouses, floating objects, signals being made, or *anything else which might be of interest to the navigator.*

The lookout is to assume that the bridge has not seen the subject of his report until his report is acknowledged. The report should be made by word of mouth (or telephone) if possible. Reporting by bell, supplemented by a verbal report if requested, is made as follows:

One bell—Object seen on starboard side.

Two bells—Object seen on port side.

Three bells—Object seen dead ahead.

1420. Lookouts report anything so sighted in relation to the vessel; not the compass nor the wind. This system of reporting is called *relative bearings from the ship.* The outboard perimeter of the ship (the rail) is considered a circle divided into 32 sections or points; 16 from ahead to astern on each side.

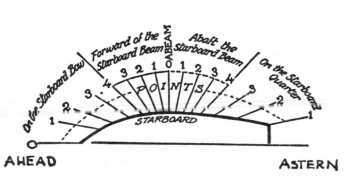

Figure 1420. Relative Bearings

The Bearings on the Port Side are Designated the Same Way

When reporting an object, it is reported as, for example, "Nun buoy two points on the port bow." Further description may at times be required as, "Floating object," "Object awash," "Moving object, possibly a whale," or, "On the horizon," or, "Close aboard."

General Instructions for Lookouts

1. Be alert and attentive.

2. Do not divide your attention.

3. Remain where posted until regularly relieved; then report to the bridge stating that you have been relieved.

4. Keep on your feet. Do not lounge.

5. Repeat a hail or a report until acknowledged by the bridge.

6. One lookout is detailed to strike the time on the ship's bells. Be thoroughly familiar with bell time.

7. Report to the bridge every 30 minutes, inspecting all running lights just before reporting. The correct report, if all lights are lit, is, "All the lights are burning bright."

1421. A dim light can be seen quicker at night by first looking at the sky *above* the horizon, then dropping the eyes *to* the horizon. Sweep the horizon, then the sky just above the horizon.

Stand in the dark and be careful that no light shines in the eyes. Lighting a match, or a flashlight, or tending a coal-stove fire all cause temporary blindness, lasting for several minutes.

"Lookout" with the ears as well as the eyes. In fog or thick weather, take a post away from engine and other noises and listen only. Report even the *suspicion* of a fog warning. Fog plays tricks with sound— it may not be heard again, it may be farther away or much nearer than it sounds, or in a different direction.

Quartermaster

1422. When acting as quartermaster (steersman) on a boat under sail, the steering instructions may be in one of the following forms:

1. Make the best course—Steer "by the luff" or the best course possible as to speed with due regard to tide, sea, etc. This order puts the quartermaster on his own and requires a knowledge of sailing as well as steering.

2. By the helm—Steer as ordered by the navigator, your concern being only the position of the helm. The helm, within the meaning of these orders, is the tiller, not the rudder.

Helm down—Push the tiller to leeward.

Helm up—Push the tiller to windward.

Ease the helm—Hold it more amidships.

Steady—Approval of the boat's course; continue to keep her sailing on it, using the helm without direction from the navigator.

3. By the compass—Keep the boat sailing on the course given. Remember that she will not necessarily stay there but must be averaged. If she swings slightly to port, an equal swing should be made to starboard, usually done by timing the first swing; only so can an offshore course be made good.

1423. When acting as quartermaster on a power vessel the steering instructions may be in one of the following forms:

1. Make the best course—A straight course is indicated to a range, or landmark, or visible aid to navigation.

2. By the rudder—Handling the rudder by means of the wheel (and possibly a rudder indicator, consisting of a pointer geared to the rudder mechanism which indicates, on a scale, the angle of the rudder in degrees) as directed.

The terms "port" and "starboard" are no longer used in steering orders. It is against the law to use them on merchant vessels. "Right" and "left rudder" are used exclusively.

Right rudder means that the wheel is to be turned to the right (with the clock) so that the rudder and the bow of the vessel go right.

Left rudder means that the wheel is to be turned to the left (against the clock) so that the rudder and the bow of the vessels go left.

UNITED STATES NAVY STEERING ORDERS

The first part of the command designates the direction of movement, i. e., *right* or *left*. This enables the man at the wheel to start putting on rudder before the second part of the command, stating the amount to be used, is given.

COMMANDS:

Right (left) full rudder.
Right (left) standard rudder.
Right (left) standard half rudder.

Full rudder commonly designates 30-degree rudder. When the rudder is thrown full or hard be careful not to jam it against the stops. Standard rudder and standard half rudder vary on different ships.

Right (left), 3, 5, 10, etc., degrees of rudder.—This indicates the angle in degrees which the rudder is to be offset.

Right (left), handsomely.—"Handsomely" is defined as "carefully." It is used in orders to the steersman when only a very slight change of course is desired.

Give her more rudder.—Increase the rudder angle already on. This order is sometimes given when it is desired to turn the ship more rapidly, in the direction she is already turning.

Ease the rudder.—Decrease the rudder angle which is on. This order may be given, *Ease to 15, 10, 5,* etc.

Rudder amidships.—Place the rudder on the center line.

Meet her.—Check, but do not stop, the swing. This is done by putting the rudder in the opposite direction. This order is usually used when it is desired to keep the ship from swinging past her new course.

Steady, Steady so, Steady as you go.—Steer the course you are on, if the ship is swinging, the course should be noted at the time the order is given and the ship steadied on that course.

Shift the rudder.—Change from right to left rudder. This order is usually given when a ship loses her headway and commences to gather sternboard, if it is desired to keep her turning in the same direction.

Mind your rudder.—Steer more carefully or stand by for an order to the wheel.

Mind your right (left) rudder.—Use more right (left) rudder from time to time. This order is used when the ship shows a marked tendency to get off her course more to one side than to the other.

Nothing to the right (left).—Do not steer anything to the right (left) of the ordered course. This is given when the course to be made good is a shade to one of that set.

Keep her so.—Steer the course which you have just reported; given, following a request for the course.

Very well.—The situation is understood; used in reply to a report made by the steersman.

As soon as the steering order is given, the quartermaster must repeat it exactly and then execute it. As soon as the boat is on the course ordered, the quartermaster so reports.

3. By compass—Such a course is given by compass degree point and the quartermaster himself expected to interpret the orders into wheel orders. Example: "Course 168." "Course 168, sir" (executes order). "Steady on course 168, sir."

Methods 2 and 3 are often combined, straight or leg courses being given by compass and turns or maneuvers by wheel orders. Method 3 is very simple and demands no further information to the quartermaster than the exact course (corrected by the navigator) and possibly the order (example), "Course 230, nothing right (or left)," indicating that no tolerance is allowed to the right (or left) of the course ordered.

1424. When being relieved, always give the relief the exact course and have him repeat it; then report to the navigator that you have been relieved. If any peculiarities of steering have developed, such as a tide or wind set, or a change of trim, the new quartermaster should be told about it.

Follow the orders of the captain under all conditions, even if they conflict with those of the pilot.

Engine speeds, towed vessels, keeping squadron position, and other problems related to steering are not problems of the quartermaster. If he is steering under orders, his duty is to steer only. If he is "in charge" of the boat and steering as well, he may (and on the small boat is quite likely to be expected to) take full command of the ship's movement along the course given.

To Heave a Life Ring

1425. The life ring is thrown overboard at the cry of "Man overboard," or before the cry, if the man is discovered. If a self-igniting water light is attached this is thrown with the ring, *night or day*. By day the thick smoke of such a light helps the swimmer find the buoy, and the boat, after doubling back, to find it as well. If the swimmer is still within range throw the ring *near* him, not *at* him. A heavy ring or its light can stun a man easily.

It is the duty of the man nearest the life ring (or rings) to get it overboard at once, without orders; then to raise the cry (if not already raised), and keep his eye on the man overboard and his arm pointed at the swimmer.

If not under way, a ring buoy with a line may be thrown. This is thrown exactly as a heaving line is thrown. If the line is fitted with a lemon, it is placed under the left instep. If with a loop, it is slipped over the left wrist. Be very sure that the line will reach the swimmer's position before throwing it. If the buoy fetches up on a short line it will be hurled *backwards,* away from the swimmer.

Use of Line-Throwing Gun

1426. Coastwise (commercial) vessels of between 150 and 300 tons must be equipped with a shoulder line-throwing gun, capable of "shooting" at least 400 feet of a three-eighths inch circumference laid-up flexible cotton or flax line. Part of the gear is an auxiliary one-inch line of manila, .45 or .50 caliber shells, projectiles, and cleaning tools. The gear must be kept in its case and accessible at all times.

In using the shoulder line-throwing-type gun, the following precautions should be observed:

(1) Care should be taken to prevent fouling of the line in rigging, ridge ropes, etc., which have a tendency to rise or jump up when the gun is fired.

(2) The projectile should be seated in the end of the cartridge case.

(3) If fired near the ship's side, the gun must be held firmly to prevent it from "jumping" overboard.

(4) The line should be wet thoroughly for two or three feet from the shank to prevent burning.

(5) The use of a "reduced-load" cartridge is recommended, containing 50 grains of powder instead of 70.

(6) After using, the line should be thoroughly dried before rewinding or faking.

(7) In using this equipment the instructions furnished by the manufacturer shall be followed.

Heaving the Lead

1427. When detailed to "take soundings" by the hand line the small lead or blue pidgeon (7–14 pounds) is used.

A position is taken slightly forward of amidships on the windward side. The line is held about six to ten feet from the lead at the toggle (not always provided) and swung fore and aft; then, when sufficient momentum has been achieved, swung twice around with the clock and released on the forward upswing. As the lead enters the sea ahead of the leadsman's position the slack is taken in until the leadsman "feels bottom" or the line is straight up and down; the depth quickly read and reported to the navigator and then the line taken in handsomely.

It must be handed in rapidly and kept clear of the wheel. As the water shallows, soundings are taken more frequently. If directed by the navigator (as in making a soundings track) it is done by time casts, and the time to sound will come from the bridge.

The depth is read from the marks (Figure 1427) *at the waterline*. If at night, the line markings are *felt* (or felt with the tongue) at the

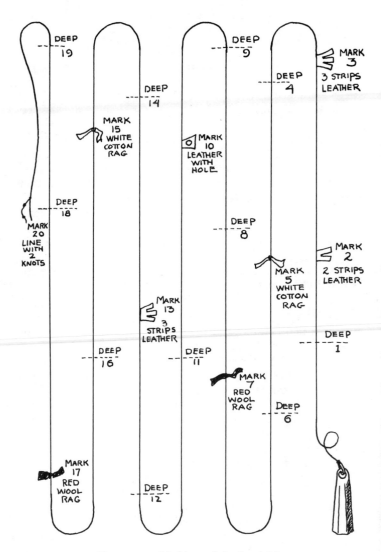

Figure 1427. Markings of the Lead Line

508

rail, the distance from rail to water deducted, and the true depth at the waterline reported.

The first two casts are not reported. These are the "soaking casts" and serve to shrink the line to its length when the markings were first attached (always attached to a wet line).

The following terminology is used in reporting soundings:

When the depth corresponds to any mark on the lead line it is reported as: "By the mark 7," "By the mark 10," etc.

When the depth corresponds to any fathom between the marks on the lead line it is reported as: "By the deep 6," "By the deep 8," etc.

When the depth is judged to be a fraction greater or less than that indicated by the marks it is reported as: "And a half 7," "And a quarter 5," "Half less 7," "Quarter less 10," etc.

Arming the Lead. This is done by filling the concavely grooved depression in the bottom of the hand lead with tallow, grease, or some similar substance. A sample of the bottom is thus brought up for examination and is reported, following the sounding report, to aid the navigator in determining his position by comparing the bottom reported with his chart. After reporting, the tallow is wiped clean or the lead rearmed if the tallow is below the surface of the depression.

Bottoms are reported, after examination of the sample as follows:

Clay	Shell	Mud (soft, red, black, etc.)
Coral	Stones	Rock (may be "felt" by
Gravel	Weed	bouncing the lead)
Sand (fine or coarse)	No sample	

Use of Oil for Modifying the Effect of Breaking Waves

1428. Many experiences of late years have shown that the utility of oil for this purpose is undoubted and the application simple. The following may serve for the guidance of seamen whose attention is called to the fact that a very small quantity of oil skillfully applied may prevent much damage, both to ships (especially of the smaller classes) and to the boats, by modifying the action of breaking seas. The principal facts as to the use of oil are as follows:

1. On free waves—that is, waves in deep water—the effect is greatest.

2. In a surf or waves breaking on a bar, where a mass of liquid is in actual motion in shallow water, the effect of the oil is uncertain,

as nothing can prevent the larger waves from breaking under such circumstances, but even here it is of some service.

3. The heaviest and thickest oils are most effectual. Refined kerosene is of little use; crude petroleum is serviceable when nothing else is obtainable; but all animal and vegetable oils, and generally waste oil from the engines, have great effect.

4. A small quantity of oil suffices, if applied in such a manner as to spread to windward.

5. It is useful in a ship or boat, either when running or lying to or in wearing.

6. No experiences are related of its use when hoisting a boat at sea or in a seaway, but it is highly probable that much time would be saved and injury to the boat avoided by its use on such occasions.

7. In cold water the oil, being thickened by the lower temperature and not being able to spread freely, will have its effect much reduced. This will vary with the description of oil used.

8. For a ship at sea the best method of application appears to be to hang over the side, in such a manner as to be in the water, small canvas bags capable of holding from one to two gallons of oil, the bags being pricked with a sail needle to facilitate leakage of the oil. The oil is also frequently distributed from canvas bags or oakum inserted in the closet bowls. The positions of these bags should vary with the circumstances. Running before the wind they should be hung on either bow—for example, from the cathead—and allowed to tow in the water. With the wind on the quarter the effect seems to be less than in any other position, as the oil goes astern while the waves come up on the quarter. Lying to, the weather bow, and another position farther aft seem the best places from which to hang the bags, using sufficient line to permit them to draw to windward while the ship drifts.

9. Crossing a bar with a flood tide, to pour oil overboard and allow it to float in ahead of the boat, which would follow with a bag towing astern, would appear to be the best plan. As before remarked, under these circumstances, the effect cannot be so much trusted. On a bar with the ebb tide running it would seem to be useless to try oil for the purpose of entering.

10. For boarding a wreck it is recommended to pour oil overboard to windward of her before going alongside. The effect in this must

greatly depend upon the set of the current and the circumstances of the depth of water.

11. For a boat riding in bad weather from a sea anchor it is recommended to fasten the bag to an endless line rove through a block on the sea anchor, by which means the oil can be diffused well ahead of the boat and the bag readily hauled on board for refilling if necessary.

Yachts find that oil may be effectively distributed to quiet seas by freeing it through water-closet or galley-sink discharges. If the toilet is used, the oil should be fed into the bowl in small quantities and pumped out by the hand pump. The pump will in all probability require overhauling after such use, as oil ruins the rubber gaskets and "joker" valve.

Perhaps a better method is to feed through the galley sink. Puncture an oil-filled can and wrap it in canvas or rags to prevent too rapid flow and place in the sink. When shorthanded this method has much to recommend it. If the oil breaks into patches or islands (caused by cold water) thin it with kerosene. In following seas the cockpit scuppers may be used.

1429. The proper use of various types of fire extinguishers likely to be found on small craft is as follows. (*See* Figure 1429.)

1. Soda-acid (Foam) type. This is for use in extinguishing wood, paper or fabric fires and its fumes are detrimental to fabrics and paint. The motion of the vessel tends to mix the chemicals within the extinguisher and it may be found to be "dead." This kind of fire can be better fought with the newer types of extinguisher—a CO_2-operated cartridge or a pressurized water unit. Water is very effective against alcohol fires.

The Foam type is also effective against oil or gasoline fires in *static pools*. It will not subdue flames from burning lacquer thinner or some solvents. (For this use the Dry Chemical type.)

Warning. The Foam type is dangerous to use on electrical fires or near electrical apparatus.

2. The Carbon-tetrachloride type. This is the familiar "Pyrene" type of hand-pumped or pressurized extinguisher heretofore found on most small craft. It is effective on electrical fires up to 5000 volts and on all other kinds of fire in *confined spaces*.

To operate, turn the handle and pump, directing the stream toward the flames or a heated surface above the flames. The liquid when vaporized by heat developes phosgene gas which smothers the fire if there is no draft or wind present.

Warning. This type developes a highly poisonous gas which can kill the operator. For this reason it, as well as the type using Chlorobromethane, has been outlawed by Coast Guard regulations and many state boating laws and it does not pass under any circumstances as an approved and legal fire suppressor. (The deadline to get them off pleasure craft was January 1, 1962.)

3. The Carbon-dioxide (CO_2) type. This type is effective on all kinds of fire, including electrical fires, if not too deep-seated. It is the extinguisher to use when fire is first discovered and it readily extinguishes liquid or gasoline fires. It is non-poisonous and will not injure fabrics, paint, clothing or food. Automatic or manually operated systems are available which flood the bilges, tank and engine spaces, and sometimes are piped over the entire ship. Installation of this type, if an approved make, will result in appreciable savings in insurance costs.

4. Dry Chemical type. This extinguisher discharges finely powdered bicarbonate of soda under high pressure and is an extremely efficient fire suppressor for all kinds of fires. It is far less costly than other

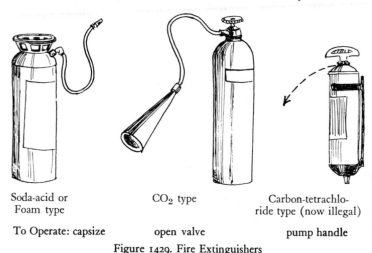

Soda-acid or Foam type	CO_2 type	Carbon-tetrachloride type (now illegal)
To Operate: capsize	open valve	pump handle

Figure 1429. Fire Extinguishers

types; or, at least, the refills are. An objection is that it leaves a residual dust which must be picked up by vacuum cleaner. This type is probably most commonly used on boats today.

Discharge all extinguishers (except number 2 above) into the base of the fire first; then work upward. Aim to take advantage of wind or draft. Do not let the fire get between you and your escape. If explosion seems imminent or certain, get off the ship, you can't save her anyway but you may save your life. Read the directions on your extinguishers and make certain that you and anyone likely to handle them understand how they work. Try a practice run—it doesn't cost much. And, after practice or fire, *refill the extinguisher*.

Alarm Signals

1430. Standard emergency alarm signals follow:

(1) *Fire-alarm signals.*—(*a*) The general-fire-alarm signal shall be a continuous rapid ringing of the ship's bell for a period not less than ten seconds supplemented by the continuous ringing of the general alarm bells for not less than ten seconds. (*b*) For dismissal from fire-alarm stations, the general-alarm bells shall be sounded three times, supplemented by three short blasts of the whistle.

(2) *Boat-station or boat-drill signals.*—(*a*) The signal for boat drill or boat stations shall be more than six short blasts and one long blast of the whistle, supplemented by the same signal on the general-alarm bells. (*b*) Where whistle signals are used for handling boats, they shall be as follows: To lower boats, one short blast of the whistle; to stop lowering the boats, two short blasts of the whistle; for dismissal from boat stations, three short blasts of the whistle.

(3) *Other emergency signals.*—(*a*) The master of any vessel may establish such other emergency signal, in addition to the above, as will provide that all the officers and all the crew and passengers of the vessel will have positive and certain notice of the existing emergency.

If a station bill has been posted or agreed upon, proceed to that alarm station and carry out the duties agreed upon. If no station bill exists, report to the person in command.

Do Nots for Deck Seamen

1431. Never smoke on deck while taking on fuel, or near open hatches.

Never go up or down ladders with both hands full.

Never work in the hot sun without protecting the head.

Never walk under a hoisting boom, or sheer legs.

Never walk on the weather side in a heavy sea.

Never walk on oily or slippery decks with rubber soles or heels.

Never wear sea boots on deck if it can be avoided.

Never stand in the bight of a line or cable.

Never work aloft or overside without a safety line.

Never trust a line or tackle until tested as safe and secure.

Never enter the bridge or the quarter-deck unless on duty or invited.

Never enter the engine room unless on duty or invited.

Never go on deck, knowing that you will get wet, without protection.

Never assume anything: investigate, inspect, and test.

HELPFUL HINTS FOR DECK SEAMEN

To Fold the Ensign

1432. Fold it lengthwise four folds (Figure 1432); then fold in triangular form toward the cannon. Three stars should show. The flag must never touch the deck and should be gathered in the arms as it falls. Stow it in the flag locker, not between staff and halyards.

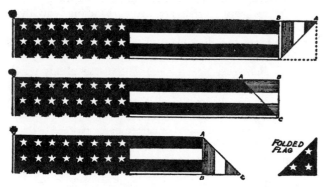

Figure 1432. How to Fold the Ensign

Stowing Other Flags and Pennants

1433. These are rolled around themselves or around the staff. If stowed in a flag locker, the canvas tabling strip is outside, the bottom of the flag toward the opening, and the name of the signal clearly inked on the tabling strip.

Order of Making and Dousing Colors

1434. The ensign is always raised before any other flags (such as club or private signals), and lowered after them. (*See* Chapter XVIII for correct flags to fly, and when.)

Folding Sails

1435. After thoroughly dry, sails may be folded as shown in Figure 1435 for rapid bending when again used. Note that two edges will show sail slides; the foot and the luff.

All battens must be removed first and puckering lines slackened. After folding, stow in the sail bag and keep dry.

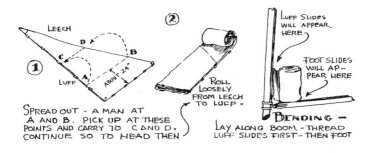

Figure 1435. How to Fold Sails

Covering Sails

1436. Small headsails or yawl mizzens should be taken in. It is simpler than covering them.

Sails to be covered should be carefully furled and stopped down, and not depend upon the cover to hold them secure.

Lay the cover (unroll it) along the boom; then fit and lace the throat, making all snug at the gooseneck, halyards outside the cover and the neck drawn tight to shed rain and dew. Then work aft, unrolling, drawing taut against the throat and tying down with slippery reef knot.

Folding Seamen's Uniforms

1437. To keep wool or work uniforms neat and pressed, and to appear with the correct collar and other creases, fold as in Figures 1437A and 1437B. Brush the uniform as it is smoothed and rolled.

Cleaning White Hats

1438. The Bob Evans type of canvas hat is best cleaned by a thorough soaking, then a scrubbing inside and out. It is then stretched over a sphere (globe, football, bottle, round fender), common table salt rubbed into it, then set in the sun for a quick dry.

TURN INSIDE OUT . PLACE ONE SLEEVE DIRECTLY OVER THE OTHER, FRONT OF JUMPER BEING ON INSIDE OF FOLD , COLLAR EXTENDING ABOVE NECK WITH TWO SIDE EDGES TOGETHER ON INSIDE OF COLLAR. FOLD COLLAR LENGTHWISE OF JUMPER — FOLD ARMS BACK OVER COLLAR TWICE AND ROLL BACK FROM NECK TOWARD LOWER EDGE OF JUMPER. ROLL JUMPER TIGHTLY, SMOOTHING WRINKLES & SECURE WITH COTTON STOPPERS .

Figure 1437A. Folding Uniform Jumper

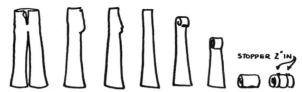

STOPPER 2˝ IN

BRUSH CLEAN . TURN INSIDE OUT . FOLD ONE LEG OVER THE OTHER SO THAT SEAM ON INSIDE OF LEGS COME TOGETHER . TURN WAIST BAND BACK TO THE MIDDLE OF THE LEG —— TUCK IN THE SEAT —— AND ROLL TOWARDS BOTTOM OF THE LEG AND SECURE .

Figure 1437B. Folding Uniform Trousers

Body and Soul Lashings

1439. Storm clothing is worn to keep dry, not warm. Warm woolen clothing, not too bulky, should be underneath and then every attempt made to keep it dry. Deck work under storm conditions will soon see the average suit of oilers "leaking" due to wind. Lashings may be placed as shown in Figure 1439 to make wind stops.

A small Turkish towel around the neck will help keep water from trickling down inside. "Fisherman" type waterproof canvas gloves are soft, flexible, and waterproof, but not too warm for summer wear. In winter, wear warm gloves under them.

The secret of keeping warm is keeping dry.

Figure 1439. Storm Clothing Lashing

Yacht Deck Routine of the Paid Hand

1440.

6.00 A. M.   Turn out. Douse all night lights.
Check anchor and cable.
Sound the well.
Post log (weather, wind, temperature, barometric pressure).
Adjust ventilators to wind. Ventilate engine room.

6.30 A. M.   Hose down with fresh water (if at dock).
Sponge down with fresh water if at moorings (using a

large chamois).

Wash all windows, port lights, windshields.

Tidy the bridge, chart table, deck.

Polish brass.

7.30 A. M. Swig up all halyards (if now dry); remove catharpins.

Bail and make ready the dinghy.

8.00 A. M. Make colors, taking time from flagship, senior officer, or yacht club. (*See* Chapter XVIII for correct colors.)

9.00 A. M. Regular chores which may include the following:

Pump ship.

Dry sails.

Fill lamps.

Charge batteries (if no engineer on board).

Watch for shore or other signals. Make owner signals.

Deck-gear maintenance and repair.

Maintain paint and varnish work.

Check anchor cable at swing of tide or wind.

Stand by (forward or forward below).

7.00 P. M. Break out night lights, ready to rig.

Tidy ship (coil down lines, stow dinghy gear, secure and cover sails).

Make small boats secure.

Slack off halyards and sheets; rig catharpins if required.

Put hoods on binnacle, wheel, etc. Cover what brass work possible.

Check anchor and cable; chafing gear.

8.00 P. M. Douse colors, taking time as in making colors.

Set night lights.

During the night check lights, cable, and barometer several times. Call owner (or an officer) if a storm brews or a sea makes. Get failing lights burning at once.

1441. In washing down bright work or paint, use fresh water only, no soap. If dried salt spray is present, wring the chamois in a second bucket of fresh water; then wet in clean fresh water. Decks should be swept or swept and swabbed first. Clean topsides at freeing ports or scuppers. Glass is cleaned best with a chamois, well wrung out and a spot of ammonia in the water.

Brass work should first be rid of dried salt spray, then polished with a good yacht brass polisher. Weathered brass or stubborn spots may be brightened by a touch of muriatic acid. Weatherproof waxes applied to the surface will provide a more durable polish.

Extensive paint cleaning is done with a commercial cleaner and plenty of water. High-gloss paint should not be cleaned with an abrasive powder; flat paint may be. Stains or waterline oil streaks may be softened with a paste made of soft water and Gold Dust or an equal amount of powdered soap.

Rubber matting may be cleaned by rubbing the spot with steel wool. Paint spots may be removed by applying a hot knife to the spot. Seagull guano should be removed immediately and the spot well washed with water. (It will "eat" into paint, varnish, or canvas in short time.) Rust spots through paint (nail sickness) can be cured only by digging out the putty or bung, painting the rusting fastening with thick red lead or white lead; then reputtying or rebunging and touching up the spot with surface paint. Gasoline will remove exhaust smudge on the transom. A fine wire brush will remove scum and growth along the waterline.

1442. Few small yachts ship "straight" deck seamen. The paid hand is expected to lend a helping hand in navigating, general ship maintenance, possibly act as engineer, or cook, or steward. Duties should be clearly understood at the time of taking the berth, and all details of the employment definitely settled. Owners are usually obligated to employ paid hands "all found" (providing meals on shipboard or on shore at the owner's expense), uniforms, and work topclothing, storm clothes, and laundry service. A predetermined number of hours per day or week belong to the ship while at moorings; all the time (within reason) while at sea.

Compensation and social-security insurance must be carried by the owner. He must observe wage-hour laws when requesting maintenance or fitting out work of the paid hand.

All licenses are at the employee's expense; as are dues for seamen's organizations and social security payments (taken at the source, by the employer, and placed to the employed person's account). The greatest source of complaint against the paid hand by the owner is liquor and women. No paid hand has the right to drink on his employer's time nor invite his friends on board without permission. The wise paid hand will practice sobriety while on duty and be careful not to overstep the social barriers (often very difficult to recognize within the confines of a small boat).

⚓

CHAPTER XV

BOAT AND ENGINE MAIN-
TENANCE AND REPAIR

General Repair and Maintenance Work

1501. Every boat, however small, should be equipped to make minor repairs at sea. Tools needed in addition to a full complement of engine tools and the usual splicing tools should include the following at least:

SMALL-BOAT TOOL KIT

Ax or hatchet
Hammer with 8″ handle (but full-weight head)
Hacksaw and frame, about 10 inches
Small combination wood saw
Several-sized screw drivers
Several-sized chisels
Several-sized files
Wrecking bar
Electrician's pliers
Snips
Hand awl with assortment of bitts
Small hand drill with assortment of drills
Caulking iron and wooden mallet

A small bench vice is always handy, as well as a square and ruler. Tools not regularly used should be oiled to prevent rust and kept in the dryest locker, above the waterline.

The paint locker should include several sealed jars of matching paint so that odd spots can be touched up during the season. White lead, putty, liquid marine glue, and turpentine come in handy. Several small sash brushes, a varnish brush, and an artist's or lettering brush will serve for touching up.

Nothing is useless at sea. A general but small "junk box" should be kept for all manner of small string, nails, wire, bolts, etc. As a foundation for such a store box there should be an assortment of nails, screws, nuts and bolts, leather and metal washers, spare wire, a "snake" for cleaning plugged lines and pipes, a length of rubber tubing for syphoning, a small funnel, spare bulbs and fuses, etc. A few lengths of board, a piece of plywood, piece of inner tube, cork, sail canvas, sheet lead, and strip brass may each have their uses in emergency repairing.

The type and combinations of repairs at sea are unpredictable—but "anything might happen." In the following pages some of the more common types of repair work and maintenance are explained.

How to Caulk

1502. (Figure 1502.) A shows a hollow seam which can never be made tight. B shows a seam that has been caulked too tightly and which will "throw" its putty. C shows a seam correctly caulked.

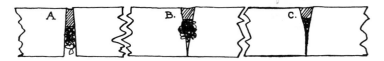

Figure 1502

Note that the cotton has been driven down securely but has not scarred the plank edges. After caulking, the cotton is payed with paint and when set, puttied over. For "hooking out" old caulking there is nothing better than a file tip, heated and bent into a sharp reverse hook.

To Keep Decks Tight

1503. (Figure 1503.) Souse down frequently with sea water. The deck depends upon the swollen condition of the planks for its tightness. Annoying small leaks can sometimes be stopped for a long period by injecting linseed oil into the seams (especially where putty is chipped out) with an ordinary squirt can.

To Re-cover a Canvas Deck

1504. (Figure 1504.) Start off with a smooth clean deck and tack the canvas along the center line or outboard coaming line so that the canvas is always stretched outward. Use copper tacks only. Make joints by a double overlap as shown. If laid in oil paint, immediately paint the canvas, thus bonding the canvas between two coats of paint

Figure 1503

which will dry together. If laid in a deck glue or mastic, do not paint until glue is thoroughly dry. Use a waterproof marine glue under all mouldings.

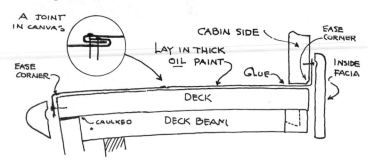

Figure 1504

Electrical Connections Through the Deck

1505. (Figure 1505.) One of the two methods of bringing a wire on deck (as to the running lights, horn, etc.) will provide a seatight connection. Keep the loop type in the lee of some fixed deck member, like a cabin trunk, or the shroud turnbuckles for protection, and make the loop high enough to get the deck mop under it.

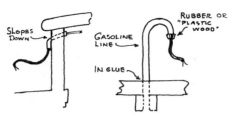

Figure 1505

Watertight Vent

1506. (Figure 1506.) A simple water-trap arrangement which will give ventilation without soaking the below-deck spaces. The drawing is self-explanatory.

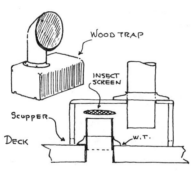

Figure 1506

To Set a Mast Coat

1507. (Figure 1507.) The proper manner of putting on a mast coat is shown. Make the lashing with several turns of strong tarred marling and set the bottom and the lead gasket in thick paint or marine glue.

To Make a Temporary Patch in Planking

1508. (Figure 1508.) Any heavy, firm bundle of rags or clothing or sails stuffed into a hole in the planking will very much reduce the

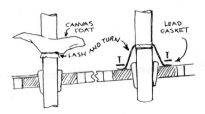

Figure 1507

rate of the leak. With it so under control, prepare a piece of odd wood (floor board, box side, etc.) to fit between the frames at the point of the leak. Using a woolen cloth, or anything convenient as a gasket between the temporary patching piece and the inside of the planking, fasten the patch by some means. It can often be braced to some adjacent part of the frame, or a batten and wedge can be rigged as shown in the cut. Such bracing should be nailed in place, for the hull of a

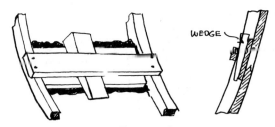

Figure 1508

boat "works" while under way. The patching piece could be screwed into the planking as well.

The leak will thus be reduced to a seepage which can only be further controlled by caulking (rope yarns, cotton line, fish line, unraveled woolen garments, etc.).

A split plank can usually be caulked temporarily from the inside. A sprung plank can sometimes be forced back in place by knocking off the butt block and strapping it in by a line passed completely around the boat and set up with a Spanish windlass.

One of the handiest materials to stop leaks or close up punctures is sheet lead. It can be peened into almost any crevice, and when laid over thick white lead or pitch and tacked around the edges will serve for small leaks.

To Make a Permanent Patch in Planking or Plywood

1509. (Figure 1509.) Set in a graving piece which is secured to a butt block behind the planking. Use screw fastenings from the inside

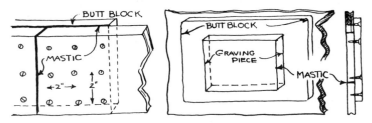

Figure 1509

for a puncture; on the outside for a butt joint (as when fitting in a length of new planking). If in plywood, make a wood-to-wood fit and set in marine glue. If in solid wood, make "caulking joints" (which fit wood to wood only on the inboard edges); then caulk, pay, and putty.

To Set a Boat Plug

1510. (Figure 1510.) Use soft, clear, white pine. Taper to fit the hole exactly when handtight. Drive in snugly from the *outside,* then saw off flush. Do not glue in if it is to be taken out again. If the hole

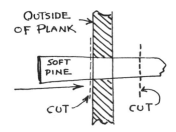

Figure 1510

is ragged, rebore it a larger size. Let the plug extend inside at least the thickness of the planking if possible.

Driving Fastenings

1511. (Figure 1511.) While few "dry" fastenings will have to be driven in ordinary or emergency repair work, the method is shown in case such a fastening might have to be substituted for a bolt or nut

Figure 1511

and bolt. Any metal rod can be so driven for a temporary fastening (as for fishing spars). It can be headed on both ends, making a secure fastening.

When coming across such fastenings in repair work, it is useless to attempt to remove them by pulling. In wet wood, or after having been set for a long time (especially in oak), they can sometimes be driven through with another and smaller rod after the head has been hacksawed off. Beware of such fastenings when making a saw cut in wood; they must be hacksawed through with a saw having greater set than the wood saw. Such fastenings, often unsuspected by the novice, are usually found in rudders, centerboards, centerboard cases, watertight bulkheads, deadwood, etc. Look for them in any wide surface. The heads are often covered with a wooden boat plug or putty. They can be located by a magnet or the compass, used to search out the wood.

To Keep Limbers Free

1512. (Figure 1512.) Plugged limbers in inaccessible places may be kept clear by rigging the simple gear shown, passing through *all* limbers. Use brass fittings only.

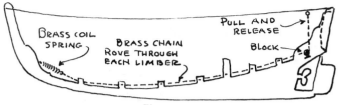

Figure 1512

Pipe Plugs

1513. (Figure 1513.) Any outboard pipe connection may let go because of corrosion or breaking at any time. If lead, it is simple to pinch it together and peen it closed with a hammer and block. If a rigid metal, a universal pipe plug of soft pine can be used. Several are carried, each having tapers from the largest to the smallest diameter outboard pipe on the boat.

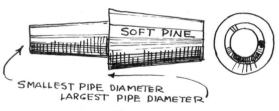

Figure 1513

Care of the W.C.

1514. Few of the shipboard mechanical parts "get out of order" as often as the hard-used water closet. The repair kit of every boat should have in it a complete replacement kit of gaskets, springs, and washers for the particular w.c. on board. Emergency repairs are impossible save with these patterned parts.

The w.c. is a sturdy affair but suffers so much because the lubber seldom understands its operation and consequently does considerable damage in his ignorance. The best assurance that it will continue to perform is to post operating rules near by. One of the best and least offensive, yet good-naturedly effective, is the Long Island Sound classic by Peterkin, which pertains to a common type.

DIRECTIONS FOR LANDLUBBERS

It seems this type of bathroom is restricted to a boat,
So follow these directions and don't let them get your goat.
You grasp the handle firmly and work it to and fro,
To make the water in the bowl all disappear below;
Next press the pedal gently, when the tide is almost out,
Pumping in the old Atlantic that the poets rave about.
Release the pedal when it's full, and pump with might and main,
Until you hear the last of it go gurgling down the drain.
A surge of satisfaction will now grace your beating heart,
As you find yourself the master of this oceangoing art.

To Make a Temporary Wooden Cleat

1515. (Figure 1515.) Emergency cleats may be easily made to replace one torn out by following the direction in the sketch. A hard wood will serve best. Through-bolt a cleat if at all possible.

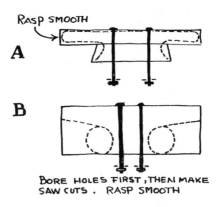

Figure 1515

To Secure Light Boards to Shrouds

1516. (Figure 1516.) Several methods are shown for securing these troublesome fixtures. Adjustable fastening methods are to be preferred, making leveling simple in the event shrouds must be adjusted.

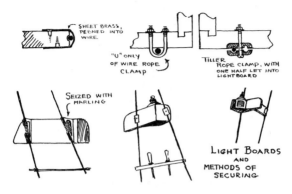

Figure 1516

Fishing Spars

1517. (Figure 1517.) If the broken spar can be shortened and still be of use, a good and permanent fish can be made, as shown in sketch A. A mast broken at or below the partners can be fished, as shown in sketch B.

The broken spar which cannot be shortened (as a main boom or gaff) must be put in "splints," as shown in sketch C. The splints may be of anything handy, such as floor boards, oars, other lighter spars, etc. The greatest strain on a boom or gaff is at the after end. If possible to do so, reverse the spar so that the fish comes as far forward as possible.

If the fish is made with a single-tapered spar, short cleats should be tacked to the broken spar and the sound spar lashed to it securely, taking a few turns around the seizing between the spars. If two tapered spars are used, lash them opposite each other (port and starboard, not top and bottom) and put the heel of one forward and the other aft. (Sketch D.)

It might be necessary to hold the fractured ends together, in which case a line or several lines are rigged, as shown. Use a stopper hitch or a killick hitch for fastening to the spar, and set the line up by twisting, and then lashing the twisting bar to the spar.

A fished spar is naturally very much weaker than a sound spar, and a great strain occurs at the point of fracture. If possible change the

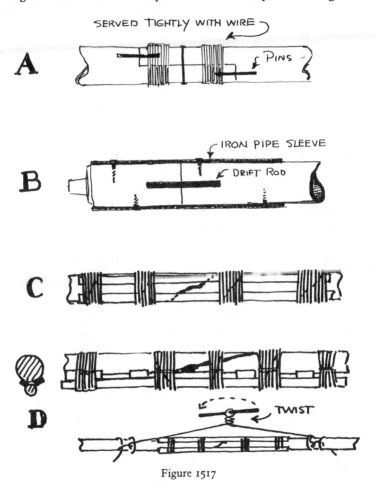

Figure 1517

leads (as of a main sheet or one of the gaff peak halyard leads) so as to bring its tension at or very near the fracture.

Jury Rudder

1518. (Figure 1518.) The loss of rudder is not an uncommon occurrence. The figure shows several methods of utilizing boat parts for a jury rudder.

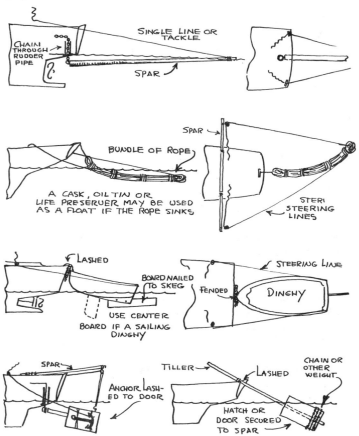

Figure 1518. Jury Rudders

Towing a sail astern, with line from outboard corners to the quarters, can be used as a rudder by hauling in on one corner, thus making a purse or pocket. Deck buckets with holes punched in the bottoms and towed from one of the quarters will steer a small boat. Small boats can also be steered by shifting ballast or live weight. A sail raised on a rudderless powerboat will act as a rudder within limits.

Correct Way to Pack a Stuffing Box

1519. (Figure 1519.) Cut the packing into complete circles, ends butted and staggered. Do not make the common mistake of "winding" it in. Put in enough rings to have three complete threads still

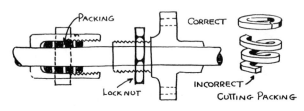

Figure 1519

exposed but not less than three rings of packing. No lubrication other than in the packing is needed.

Dinghy Fending Rail

1520. (Figure 1520.) Use old soft line of manila or new cotton line. Tack every second strand *inside* the rope with a pot nail, hauling the rope taut as the nailing proceeds. A tapered short splice at the bow and quarters will give additional protection. Such a rope may be covered with several thicknesses of canvas or old fire hose, in which case it is first tacked to the sheer strake, the bed moulding set over the tacks, the rope attached and the covering drawn tightly over the gunwale and fastened inside, as shown upper left.

"Splicing in" Buttons

1521. (Figure 1521.) New buttons are set in mattresses and cushions as shown in the figure. A composition button will outlast those covered with material or tin caps, and will not "rot" the surrounding material.

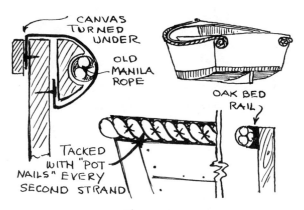

CANVAS TURNED UNDER

OLD MANILA ROPE

OAK BED RAIL

TACKED WITH "POT NAILS" EVERY SECOND STRAND

Figure 1520

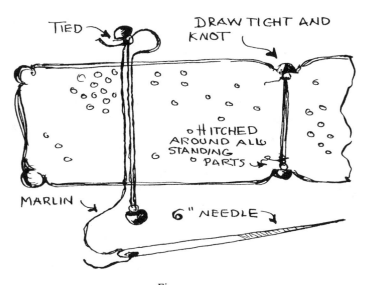

TIED

DRAW TIGHT AND KNOT

HITCHED AROUND ALL STANDING PARTS

MARLIN

6" NEEDLE

Figure 1521

CANVAS WORK AND SAIL REPAIR

Weights of Sail Canvas

1522. The weight of the canvas refers to the weight in ounces per linear yard.

Sail canvas is cut 22 inches wide. To find the weight per linear yard number 8 canvas is taken as a reference point. This weighs 11 ounces per yard (width divided by 2).

For each number above number 8 deduct 1 ounce.

TABLE OF SAIL-CANVAS WEIGHTS, 22 INCHES WIDE

00	20 oz.	5	14 oz.	10	9 oz
0	19	6	13	11	8
1	18	7	12	13	7
2	17	8	11	14	5
3	16	9	10	15	4
4	15				

Standard Canvas Numbers for Boats

1523.

Waterline length	Mainsails, fores'ls in schooners, mizzens in ketches	Heads'ls and yawl jiggers	Storms'ls
20 ft.	#15	#14	——
30	#11	#12	#8
35	# 9	#11	#7
40	# 9	#10	#5
45	# 8	# 9	#4
50	# 6	# 9	#3
60	# 4	# 7	#2

1524. Canvas-sewing equipment consists of the following essentials:

1. (*a*) *Sail needles.* Long spur needles, triangular in shape, rounded at the eye end for general sewing. Number 15, which is two and a half inches long is a favorite.

(*b*) *Roping needles.* Short spur needles, stockier than sail needles. Used for sewing to boltropes and other heavy work.

2. *Twine.* Cotton twine of four to eight ply for general canvas work, the heavier ply for heavier canvas. Comes in a ball of one half pound. Roping is done with nine- to twelve-ply twine.

3. *Palm.* A heavy leather half glove worn over the hand. The palm has a lead casting sewn in, which is used to push the needle through the canvas or rope.

4. *Pricker.* A long, sharp, steel-pointed tool, used to puncture a needle hole in several thicknesses of canvas.

5. *Creasing stick.* A tool having a slot at one end used to crease the seams preparatory to sewing; made of metal, bone, wood, or scrimshaw.

6. *Sail hook.* A large barbless hook on a length of line which is fastened to any handy object and hooked into the canvas to hold it in a convenient working position.

1525. Canvas is not generally cut but ripped. A sharp knife is used, the blade almost parallel to the canvas. A thread or two is picked up ahead of the knife and the knife followed closely as the thread is pulled away from the user.

Canvas Seams

1526. The flat seam (Figure 1526A) is the commonest seam used for joining two pieces of canvas together. Patches in sails are made with it as follows: Make the patch generously larger than the hole; then sew the patch to the hole edge and the patch edge to the sail, using flat stitches.

The round seam. Used for joining two edges together but leaves a ragged edge on one side. Excellent for sea bags, binnacle and wheel jackets but not often used for sail work.

The herringbone stitch. To sew a rip in canvas.

The baseball stitch. The same.

The shoemaker's stitch. Used for leather serving or for fastening oar leathers. Two needles are required, as shown. (Figure 1526B.)

The boltrope stitch. Used for sewing canvas to a boltrope. The stitch picks up each successive rope strand and its length is therefore governed by the strand twist. Doubled twine is often used for boltrope sewing.

FLAT STITCH

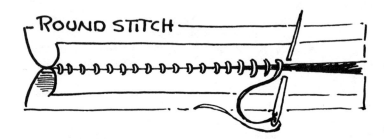

ROUND STITCH

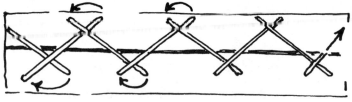

HERRINGBONE STITCH

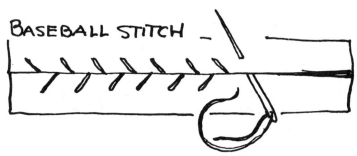

BASEBALL STITCH

Figure 1526A

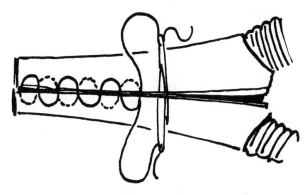

Figure 1526B

Sail Repair

1527. Cloth seams are sewn with flat stitches, the canvas being doubled under itself. Batten pockets and reef-point doubling are put in with herringbone stitches. The canvas is never sewn to the boltrope without folding under twice. Occasionally the selvage edge is sewn directly to the boltrope.

Reinforcing or doubling is called *tabling* and is used extensively at the head, tack and clew to take the extra strain at these parts. Grommets are generally shaped over a small brass ring but may be made without the ring by folding the canvas back several times and following around the edge with a round stitch. Middle stitching is a row of stitches between the seam stitches for extra strength.

Sailmaking

1528. Sails are not flat areas of canvas as they seem but have definite shape and draft depending upon their use. The novice should not attempt sailmaking without the aid of some technical advice beyond the scope of this *Manual*. Machine sewing will hasten the work much and make a more satisfactory job in general. A few general hints follow:

Arrange the cloths in main and foresails so that they parallel the boom or make about a 15° angle with the waterline. The cloths in headsails usually follow both the angle of the mainsail cloths and a

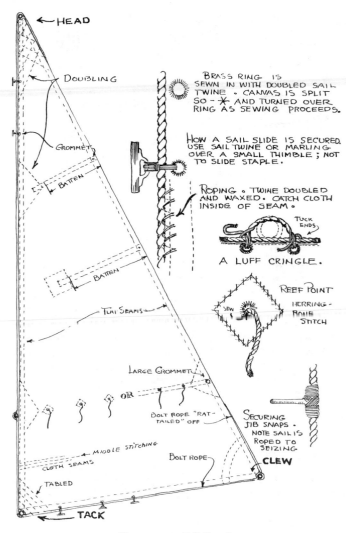

←HEAD

DOUBLING

BRASS RING IS
SEWN IN WITH DOUBLED SAIL
TWINE. CANVAS IS SPLIT
SO - ✕ AND TURNED OVER
RING AS SEWING PROCEEDS.

GROMMET

BATTEN

HOW A SAIL SLIDE IS SECURED.
USE SAIL TWINE OR MARLING
OVER A SMALL THIMBLE; NOT
TO SLIDE STAPLE.

ROPING. TWINE DOUBLED
AND WAXED. CATCH CLOTH
INSIDE OF SEAM.

TUCK
ENDS

BATTEN

A LUFF CRINGLE.

REEF POINT

HERRING-
BONE
STITCH

SEW

TWIN SEAMS

LARGE GROMMET

OR

BOLT ROPE "RAT-
TAILED" OFF

SECURING
JIB SNAPS.
NOTE SAIL IS
ROPED TO
SEIZING

MIDDLE STITCHING

CLOTH SEAMS

BOLT ROPE

CLEW

TABLED

←TACK

Figure 1527. Sail Repair

vertical line, meeting at the bisected angle of the clew. Use genuine "boltrope" for the boltrope, not common manila which stretches and shrinks too much for this use. Make batten pockets several inches

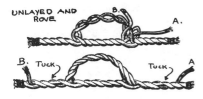

| Turning in a reef cringle over a round brass thimble | Turning in a head, tack, or clew cringle. Note that bolt-rope goes *outside* |

Figure 1528

longer than the batten. On racing sails the reef points are not rove until needed. Sails will stretch considerably and should be made about 8% less than spar limits.

Canvas Protection

1529. Mildewproofing canvas is simply waterproofing it to resist the moisture which encourages mildew.

UNITED STATES DEPARTMENT OF AGRICULTURE WATERPROOFING FORMULA

Petroleum asphalt	8½ pounds
Vaseline (amber)	1½ pounds
Dry-earth pigment (ochre or umber)	5 pounds
Gasoline	3 gallons
Kerosene	2 gallons

Melt the first two items slowly over a fire while stirring constantly. Remove far away from flame and pour into the mixed gasoline and kerosene. A small amount is withdrawn and made into a paste with the pigment. When smooth it may be further thinned and finally mixed with the main batch. If the waterproofing material settles to the bottom, the batch must be reheated by setting in a tub of hot water—*never over a flame.*

This quantity will be a khaki color and will cover about 450 square feet of canvas, one side. It may be sprayed or painted on and permitted to dry thoroughly. Folding and stowing away before completely dry may cause spontaneous combustion.

If a white treatment is desired use zinc oxide in place of the earth pigment.

Another waterproofing mixture is made as follows:

Boiled linseed oil	2 quarts
Bronzing powder	½ pound
Japan drier	¼ pint

Dissolve the powder first in a small quantity of oil; then add to the mix. No heating is necessary and it may be used at once. The quantity above will cover about 75 square feet, one side, in a light khaki color. It will make a much stiffer surface than the first formula and is best used on standing panels, dodger cloths, etc., rather than on sail covers, jackets, etc.

Another formula is merely a mixture of one gallon of turpentine to one half pound of refined beeswax. The canvas is soaked in it and dried thoroughly for a long period. The color will be quite yellow. This is the dressing used on most oilers and storm clothing with canvas unrubberized fabric. Old oilers may be restored by so treating.

PAINTING

There probably can be no more important thing said about small-boat painting than to caution the boatman to *use only marine paints*. Any other paint than one labeled a marine paint by a reliable manufacturer is utterly useless and lifeless on shipboard. House paints simply will not stand up on the sea, and to use them is to waste the time and effort put into the work, and, often enough, to definitely affect the appearance and value of the boat.

The next most important thing is that the undersurface be properly prepared before painting; that it is dry, oil-free, and firm, and that the paint is applied under fair-weather conditions.

Preparing the Surface

1530. Remove all scaled or powdery paint, using a paint or varnish remover or a blowtorch. If a paint remover has been used, wash down thoroughly with gasoline, turpentine, or a thinner. Then sand the surface thoroughly until smooth, even, and firm. Check back then for loose putty and reputty where necessary. If a new raw place is to be puttied, prime first with thin paint or shellac to stop the suction which would soon draw the oil from the putty and permit it to powder. Shellac over knot holes, give a final light sanding over, *dust well,* and then only apply the first paint.

Metal surfaces must be chipped, scraped, and wire-brushed free of scale or rust. Paint applied over rust will not stop the rust nor will the paint long remain bonded to the spot. Once clean, smooth, and dry, a first coat of red lead should be applied; then finish coats. Red lead alone will fully seal iron against the action of oxidization, or rust.

Galvanized surfaces by nature repel paint. A good prime coat, after a wash down with vinegar, is shellac. Ammonia washes are used before prime coats of paint. Old galvanized surfaces which have been exposed to the weather for a period of time will form a far better bonding surface than new galvanizing.

It is not usual to paint bronze or brass work. If it must be, however, all trace of the polishing agent must be removed before the paint will hold. Bronze surfaces can be roughened somewhat by painting with muriatic acid, permitting it to "eat" slightly; then wash off and paint.

Varnished surfaces should be prepared as for painting. A hand hook-type scraper will come in handy here and bite into ancient varnish that sandpaper won't touch. Sand well, then dust and touch up and even the color (if not natural) with an oil stain.

Canvas decks are treated as woodwork. If they are badly checked, they are hopeless and a recanvasing is indicated. To remove the paint by a paint remover from such a deck requires immense quantities of remover. Burning off will result in burned-through areas even when done by experts. Both methods will destroy the bond of the canvas to the deck beneath it.

When to Paint

1531. Paint and varnish only when:

1. The surface is absolutely dust-free.

2. Work above it has been completed.

3. The surface is thoroughly dry.

4. The weather is fair, with no prospect of change, and the temperature at least 50°.

5. The wind, or the possible future winds, will not bring dust, sand, or insects.

6. The coat beneath is thoroughly dry and set.

7. A painting, not a scrubbing, is indicated.

Painting Tools

1532.

CHECK LIST FOR FITTING OUT PAINTING

Brushes	Paint Cleaner
Sandpaper	Wiping Rags
Steel Wool	Mixing Buckets
Turpentine	Wire Brush
Reducing Oil	Scrapers
Paint & Varnish Remover	Putty Knives
Naphtha	Blowtorch

Clean paint and varnish brushes in turpentine; then wash with ordinary "brown soap" and dry thoroughly. Clean shellac brushes in alcohol. Never stand a brush on end. Suspend (in a can of clean turps if desired) in such a way that the bristles do not touch the bottom of the can. A hole bored through the handle as illustrated in Figure 1533 provides a handy way to suspend brushes in turpentine. If a brush has been softened by a commercial brush reconditioner, wash it *many* times before again using. A very slight trace of softener will destroy a paint job done with the brush later.

Tool Set

1533. Tool set for a 35-footer, painting crew of three men.

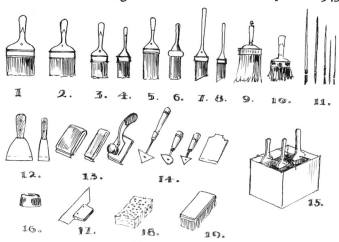

Figure 1533

1–4, flat brushes 2 to 4 inches. 5–6, long-bristled varnish brushes, oval or round. 7–8, bevel-point sash tools. 9, dusting brush. 10, old brush for paint and varnish removing. 11, assorted flat and round lettering and artists' brushes. 12, putty knives. 13, hook scrapers. 14, knife scrapers. 15, brush reservoir. 16, rubber antidrip caps for overhead painting. 17, sheet-metal guard for painting sash and corners and around fittings. 18, sponge rubber or cork sanding block. 19, wire scrub brush.

Applying Paint and Varnish—Hints

1534. 1. To mix prepared paint. Pour off most of the vehicle (liquid). Stir and paddle the pigment thoroughly, adding small quantities of the liquid from time to time, until all the liquid and pigment are combined. Then box the paint by pouring back and forth until smooth and without lumps.

2. Do not mix in driers (if to be used) until immediately before ready to paint.

3. Thin paint and varnish with turpentine; shellac, with alcohol.

4. Hard-pulling enamels spread easier if naphtha or high-octane gasoline is poured thinly over the surface of the can as used. It will aid in spreading the enamel but evaporate almost immediately. Watch the ventilation when so doing.

5. Paint should be brushed out thin, not flowed on, with the grain, and with brush strokes underneath, and with the "long" way of the surface or panel.

6. Varnish should be flowed on and not brushed out too thin.

7. Sand lightly between coats of both paint and varnish. Dust.

8. Keep paint well mixed during use. Do not mix varnish or enamel during use as it will form bubbles and "foam" at the brush stroke.

Putties and Cements

1535. Nail holes, seams, etc., are best puttied with white lead putty, not ordinary "sash" putty. A small quantity of litharge will cause putty to set quickly and dry very hard. Blemishes, scrapes, and other hull "nicks" are best patched with such a mixture.

Professionals handle the putty as shown in Figure 1535. The palm of the left hand is used as a magazine for a "sausage" of putty, and it

Figure 1535. Puttying

is fed between the thumb and the second joint of the forefinger and pressed firmly into the crack with the thumb; then cut off with a quick motion of the knife. A long seam is done in exactly the same way, from right to left, hitching the hand along and following with the putty knife.

Seams which are subject to "motion," like deck seams, should be puttied with a commercial elastic seam cement, applied exactly like white lead putty. Paying seams with pitch or hot marine glue requires special equipment and furnaces and is not for the novice to attempt. Liquid and plastic woods are not used in seams but are excellent for patching holes and scars. When dry either type can be sanded, sawn, and screws driven into it.

1536.

PAINT REQUIREMENTS FOR VARIOUS TYPES OF BOATS

	Din-ghies	Row-boats	Plain Launches	Run-abouts	Cruis-ers	Sail-boats	Auxil-iaries	Yachts
Average Length (feet) ...	10	15	25	25	30–32	20	35	60
Top-Side Paint ...	1 qt.	—	2 qts.	—	2 gals.	2 qts.	2 gals.	9 gals.
Varnish ...	2 qts.	—	—	1½ gal.	1 gal.	1 qt.	2 gals.	5 gals.
Deck Paint..	—	2 qts.	1 gal.	1 qt.	1 gal.	1 gal.	2 gals.	5 gals.
Interior Enamel ..	—	—	—	—	2 qts.	—	3 qts.	3 gals.
Bottom (Anti-fouling)..	—	1 qt.	2 qts.	1 gal.	1½ gal.	3 qts.	3 gals.	6 gals.
Boot-Topping	—	—	—	½ pt.	½ pt.	½ pt.	½ pt.	1 pt.

The above quantities are for one painting of two coats. Double the quantities required for painting and varnishing from the bare wood.

Bottom Paints

1537. Whenever a boat is used in waters which support marine growth or barnacles or teredo worms, a copper or "poisonous" paint is used on the hull below the waterline. There are many grades of such paint on the market. The cheapest, which is a brown color, is satisfactory for its prime purpose, discouraging growth and attack. The most expensive, some of which are guaranteed on a money-back basis to keep a hull clean for a normal season, are finely ground and compounded paints, and provide a racing surface as smooth as an enamel.

Each section of the country has its favorite color and brand. As the manner and intensity of growth and attack vary with the water and water temperatures, it is always wise to use the favorite in that section. Commercial boats and fishermen have usually discovered the best type and are using it.

Seasonal repainting of the bottom seldom requires that the old copper paint be removed. It is powdery and usually, when dry, flakes and falls away. However, the under surface should be prepared and made as smooth as any other painting surface, in order to reduce skin friction to a minimum. Wire brushing and sanding are generally required, and possibly reputtying of some of the seams and fastening holes. A white lead litharge putty may be used on the holes but a white lead putty is best for the seams. When cleaning off copper paint,

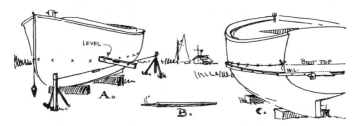

Figure 1537A. Marking Waterlines

the throat must be protected by a mask or by a wet cloth tied over the nose and mouth as the powder is highly poisonous, especially those paints having mercury in them.

Depending upon the protection necessary, every part of the underwater surface is copper painted, including rudder, propeller, and outside ballast castings. The only exception is the small zinc block sometimes let into the deadwood to discourage electrolysis and the copper plate of a radio ground.

The waterline may be "sprung" as shown in Figure 1537A. The boat must be plumb but need not be level. The line (sketch A) is level with the bow and stern painted waterlines, and a series of reference points, level with the line, marked off on the hull. A batten is now sprung through these points (sketch C) and the waterline permanently marked with a hook file (sketch B) or a backsaw. A curved waterline or boot-top is swung by letting a line "drape" naturally and marking its curve on the hull. The ends of such a curved waterline sweep upward from the level in about the same proportion as the sheer does, usually more at the bow than the stern. The boot-top on a flat transom stern is always level and never follows the deck crown.

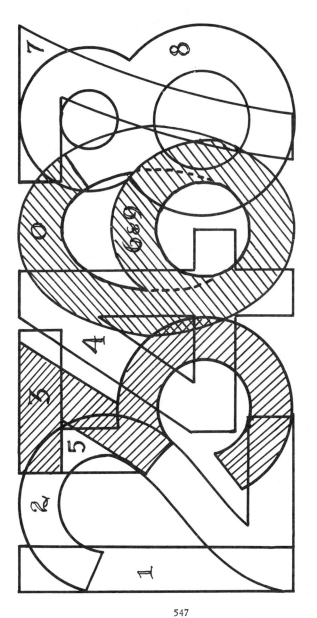

Figure 1537B

These numerals are exactly three inches high as required by the Motorboat Numbering Act. They may be transferred to the boat by tracing or cutting out and painted with a lettering or artist's brush

HANDY FORMULAS

Red Lead
   1538.

   To make one gallon
   Dry red lead   20 pounds
   Raw linseed oil   5 pints
   Turpentine   ½ pint
   Liquid driers   ½ "

Pure White Lead Paint
   1539.

   To make approximately six quarts
   White lead paste   25 pounds
   Raw linseed oil   6 pints
   Turpentine   1 pint
   Liquid driers   ¼ "

Marine Gloss White (Outside)
   1540.

   To make approximately one gallon
   White lead paste   5 pounds
   White zinc paste   9 "
   Raw linseed oil   3 pints
   Turpentine   3 gills
   Liquid driers   7 ounces

Hull Black
   1541.

   To make approximately one gallon
   Red lead paste   4¼ pounds
   Carbon black in oil   .33 gallons
   Prussian blue in oil   .08 "
   Raw linseed oil   .40 "
   Turpentine   .06 "
   Liquid driers   .06 "

Solvent Type Paint Remover
1542.

To make approximately one gallon
Benzol	2 quarts
Household paraffin (shave and dissolve into benzol)	1½ pounds
Denatured alcohol	1 quart
Acetone	1 "

Starch Type Paint Remover
1543.

Caustic soda (98%)	4 pounds
Bolted whiting	4 "
Cornstarch	2 quarts
Water	2 "

(Mix together and use as a thick paste. This mixture should not be used on oak as it will discolor the wood.)

Paint Cleaner

1544. Mix as above but add three to five times the quantity of water. Use on a scrub brush or a sponge rubber pad with a circular motion and wash off with clean salt or fresh water.

THE MARINE ENGINE

1545. Marine gasoline engines are either of the two-cycle or four-cycle type. The basic operating principles of each, regardless of make or model, are exactly the same. The variation in engine styles is chiefly a matter of the engine accessories, such as carburetors, starters, electrical equipment, etc. It is impossible to describe and list each of the hundreds of different accessories separately. However, the service pamphlets and booklets of instruction supplied with the engine contain the peculiar instructions, tables of clearances for valves, bearings, points, spark plugs, and lists of replacement parts. These references should be kept on board at all times.

The following information is applicable to all motors:

HOW THE ENGINE OPERATES

The Four-Cycle Motor

1546. In a four-cycle engine, four piston strokes are required to complete each power cycle. During the exhaust and intake strokes the piston functions as an air pump and this operation actually consumes

Figure 1546A. The Cycle of a 4-Cycle Engine

power. Each new air charge must be "stretched" into the cylinder. (Figure 1546A.)

NOTE: When the engine is operating at 2,500 rpm, the above cycle of operations is repeated 1,250 times per minute in each cylinder. The complete cycle of intake, compression, explosion and scavenging is therefore completed in 1/1,250 of a minute, or roughly 1/20 of a second. Any single stroke, involving only one-fourth of the cycle, thus requires only a small instant of time, about 1/80 of a second. From this, it will be clear why it is necessary to set valve tappet clearances accurate to measurements of a thousandth of an inch.

The Two-Cycle Motor

1547. In a two-cycle engine, a charge of fuel is burned every time the piston comes to top dead center, and consequently there is one power impulse per cylinder for each revolution of the crankshaft. In other words, a two-cycle engine with six cylinders has twice as many power impulses as a four-cycle engine with six cylinders operating at the same speed.

In a two-cycle engine, intake and exhaust take place simultaneously at the bottom of each stroke. The two-cycle engine, therefore, does not function as an air pump during any part of the cycle, so an external means of supplying air must be provided.

In the two-cycle gasoline motor, air and fuel are taken into the crankcase, through a check-valved breather, by the upstroke of the

AIR AND
FUEL
ADMITTED

INTAKE
VALVE
OPEN

Intake stroke: Intake valve starts to open just before top dead center, connecting this particular cylinder with intake manifold and carburetor. Piston, in descending, forms a vacuum which pulls fuel through the carburetor, and draws into the cylinder a charge of the air and gasoline from the intake manifold.

BOTH
VALVES
CLOSED

Compression stroke: On the upstroke of piston, following intake, both valves are closed and the explosive mixture of air and gasoline is compressed into a small space between the top of piston and the cylinder head.

BOTH
VALVES
CLOSED

Power stroke: At the instant the piston reaches its highest point of travel, and compression is greatest, a spark is timed by the distributor to occur across the points of the spark plug, igniting the mixture. The subsequent burning of the inflammable mixture, which is commonly called the "explosion" because it occurs within a very small fraction of a second, causes a very large increase in gas volume; and the resulting pressure on the top of the piston forces the piston downward, producing work. Through the connecting rod, this power is transmitted to the crankshaft.

EXHAUST
VALVE
OPEN

Exhaust stroke: Exhaust valve opens during the latter part of the power stroke, so that the pressure in the cylinder can equalize with atmospheric pressure, then the burned gases are pushed out through the exhaust valve and into the exhaust manifold by the rising piston. At the top of this stroke, the operating cycle is completed, and intake starts again.

Figure 1546B. Operation of a 4-Cycle Engine

piston; then driven, through a by-pass and air port, into the cylinder on the downstroke. In the two-cycle Diesel motor, mechanical means, such as blowers or air injectors, supply the air directly to the cylinder and at the proper time. The principle in both is the same, though Diesel engines make use of mechanical valves while the two-cycle

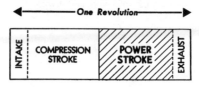

Figure 1547A. The Cycle of a 2-Cycle Engine

gasoline motor is valveless as a rule. Outboard motors and lighting-plant motors are generally of the two-cycle type and operate on the same principle. (Figure 1547B.)

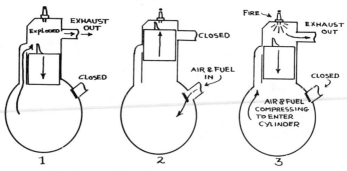

Figure 1547B. Operation of a 2-Cycle Gasoline Engine

The Operation of a Modern Diesel Engine

1548. The engine represented in Figure 1548 is the Gray Marine Diesel.

Maintenance Instructions for a Typical Four-Cycle Gasoline Engine

1549.

DAILY

Check lubricating oil level in crankcase, and when necessary refill to high-level mark on depth stick.

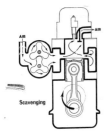

A series of ports cut into the circumference of the cylinder wall above the piston in its lowest position admit the precompressed air from the blower into the cylinder as soon as the top face of the piston uncovers these ports. The one-way flow of air toward the exhaust valves sweeps out the exhaust gases, leaving the cylinder full of clean air when piston covers the ports again.

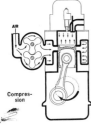

As the piston continues on the upward stroke, the exhaust valves close and the charge of fresh air is compressed to one-sixteenth of its initial volume. This happens on every upward stroke of the piston in a two-cycle engine.

Shortly before the piston reaches its highest position, the required amount of atomized fuel is sprayed into the combustion space by the unit fuel injector. The intense heat generated during the high compression of the air ignites the fine fuel spray immediately, and the combustion continues as long as fuel enters the cylinder. The resulting pressure forces the piston downward until the exhaust valves are opened again.

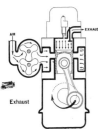

The burnt gases escape into the exhaust manifold and the cylinder volume is swept with clean scavenging air as the downward piston uncovers the inlet ports. This entire combustion is repeated in each cylinder for each revolution of the crankshaft. The quantity of fuel burned each cycle is controlled by the injector, and is varied by the operator or the governor.

Figure 1548. Operation of a Diesel Engine

Give grease cup on water pump one-half turn per day. Use waterproof grease. If running continuously this should be done every four hours.

Check overflow water every time the engine is started to make certain that pump is functioning.

EVERY 50 HOURS OF OPERATION

Remove oil from crankcase, using sump pump, and refill to high mark on oil-depth gauge.

Check water level in battery. Proper fluid gravity is 1.275.

Remove cap of oil cooler and clean out any accumulated dirt or debris.

Put three or four drops of engine oil (S.A.E. 30) in oiler on generator, and two drops in oiler on starting motor.

Put three to five drops of engine oil (S.A.E. 30) in the oiler on the outside of distributor body.

Check oil level in housing for driving gears on sea-water pump. Refill as necessary to level of inspection plug.

ONCE A MONTH

Inspect flame arrester to make sure the air passages are clean and free from oil or lint. If dirty, remove and wash in kerosene. Blow out with compressed air if available.

Check adjustment of clutch and reverse gear.

Clean sediment bowl on fuel pump.

EVERY 150 HOURS

Replace cartridge in lubricating-oil filter, regardless of apparent condition.

Apply one drop only (no more) of light engine oil (S.A.E. 10) to the breaker-arm hinge pin in distributor.

Remove the distributor rotor and apply three to five drops of light engine oil (S.A.E. 10) to the felt in the top of the breaker cam.

TWICE A SEASON "TUNE UP"

Clean and adjust breaker points on distributor. Points should contact evenly.

Remove the distributor head and smear a bit of vaseline or grease the size of a match head on the lobes of the breaker cam.

Check spark plugs and set gap, using feeler gauge. Clean fouled plugs and search for cause of fouling. Replace cracked or doubtful plugs.

Check distributor setting.

Check carburetor adjustment.

Inspect all wiring for loose connections or worn insulation. Clean battery terminals with soda solution and coat lightly with vaseline or grease.

Check engine coupling for misalignment. Tighten lag screws holding engine to bed.

Remove clean-out plate and look for signs of sludge in oil sump. Inspect oil pick-up screen. If you find sludge, the motor is running too cold, or there may be a leak in oil cooler.

Check valve-tappet adjustment.

Clean the engine thoroughly.

EVERY 1000 HOURS OR ONCE A SEASON

Give engine a thorough going over.

Grind and adjust valves.

Check valve stems for carbon.

Clean commutator on generator, using No. oo sandpaper.

If compression is weak, look for imperfectly seating valves or rings stuck in grooves on piston.

EVERY 2500 HOURS

Time for a major overhaul.

Install new piston rings. Check piston clearance.

Check bearings. When oil pressure drops below 20 pounds, this is an indication of worn bearings.

Maintenance Instructions for a Two-Cycle Engine

1550. The simplicity of the two-cycle gasoline engine makes maintenance a matter of external oiling and cleaning only. As there is no lubricating oil in the crankcase (it is mixed with the gasoline in the fuel tank in the proportions recommended by the manufacturer), maintenance may be reduced to the following daily operations:

Turn down all grease cups.

Refill drop oiler (if so equipped) every 50 hours of operation.

Drain carburetor bowl or strainer for water.

With sump pump, draw off raw gas and oil from crankcase.

Clean points of make-and-break mechanism, or, if equipped with high-tension system, proceed as for four-cycle engines.

Tighten all hold-down bolts.

Check shaft alignment.

Check carburetor adjustment.

Renew batteries (or recharge if storage type).

Remove carbon from cylinder by scraping.

The two-cycle engine will operate for years if properly maintained without the overhauls necessary to the four-cycle type. Once the correct carburetor and timing adjustments have been reached, the engine requires little more than daily oiling of external moving parts, such as pump plunger, timing mechanism, and thrust bearing.

Outboard motors are lubricated through the carburetor. Ignition parts may be inspected and cleaned by removing the flywheel or rope-starter plate and exposing the magneto and timer built into the flywheel, and serviced as for high-tension systems (*see* four-cycle motor instructions). External greasing is done by removing the screw caps and injecting the grease by means of the tube in which the grease is packaged. Waterproof grease must be used for underwater transmission parts.

The outboard motor which has become soaked or has been submerged should be serviced as described in paragraph 1554.

Diesel Engines

1551. Diesel engines vary greatly in operating principle, and no general remarks may be made which would serve as a complete guide of maintenance. The manufacturer's recommendations, as they apply to his motor, should be followed.

However, lubricating-oil levels in crankcase and transmission should be checked daily, and all grease cups turned down. Fresh-water cooling systems should be checked for content (if so equipped) and, if in winter, the freezing point checked. Every 24 hours of operation, the sediment and water should be drawn off from oil and fuel filters.

Every 50–75 hours of operation, the crankcase oil should be changed, all air screens cleaned. Transmission oil will last for 250–350 hours of operation. Elements in fuel and lubricating-oil filters should be replaced about every 500 hours. Intake ports in some types require cleaning about every 2,500 hours, and possibly new cylinder liners, or piston rings, or both.

Electrical starting and generating equipment on the Diesel is serviced exactly like similar equipment on gasoline engines.

Overhauling an Engine after Submersion in Salt Water

1552. It is important to understand that damage is done primarily by the action of air (oxygen) on the surfaces exposed to salt water. The damage can be minimized by leaving the engine submerged until you are ready to do the entire job. If the engine has been flooded only, not sunk, treat it as soon as possible with Tectyl (*see* instructions below), or if this chemical is not readily available, the best procedure is to leave the water in the engine, or to submerge the engine in fresh water at once, until ready to proceed with the overhauling.

Regardless of what precautions are taken or how long the engine has been under water, it is well to bear in mind that the sooner these precautions are taken after the engine is exposed to the air, the less likely it is that pitting and serious corrosion of the parts will have taken place.

EMERGENCY TREATMENT WITH TECTYL

Tectyl is the name of a new chemical which is of particular value in salvaging engines after exposure to salt water, having the property of displacing water from contact with metal, leaving a tenacious, moisture-resisting film. Tectyl is said to do two things: (1) it separates water from iron or steel, (2) it forms an oily protective coating on the metal. It is electromagnetically attracted to steel, and forms what are known as *polor films*. There are four grades forming thin, adherent films ranging from .0002 to .0008 of an inch in thickness.

Tectyl grade No. 511 is recommended for marine engines.

As soon as possible after the engine has been immersed or flooded it should be drained of oil and water and treated with Tectyl 511 as follows:

1. Fill the base of the engine with Tectyl 511 and circulate it through the engine's oil system by cranking the engine over, either with the starter or by hand. After the Tectyl is removed from base, the water will separate out from it, and the undiluted Tectyl can be saved and used again.

2. Remove the spark plugs and slush the cylinders with Tectyl 511, cranking the engine over by hand to aid in spreading the compound. CAUTION: Do not replace spark plugs during this operation, because the liquid above the pistons will be compressed and may break something.

3. Remove the cover to the valve chamber and slush the entire chamber thoroughly with Tectyl 511, using a brush or a spray gun.

4. Squirt some Tectyl 511 into the flame arrester on the carburetor.

5. Remove cover on reverse-gear housing, and flush clutch and reverse gear, also inside of housing, thoroughly with Tectyl 511.

6. Spray or paint all accessories and exterior surfaces with Tectyl 511. Wipe off at once from electrical parts, as it has a tendency to cause the insulation to swell.

7. Remove Tectyl from base of engine and refill to high-level mark on depth stick with regular lubricating oil of the correct grade, to which a pint of Tectyl 511 has been added. (Tectyl is soluble in oil or gasoline.)

8. As soon as possible, give the engine a complete dismantling and thorough cleaning.

OVERHAULING THE ENGINE AFTER SUBMERSION

Materials: Necessary wrenches, etc.; plenty of soft dry rags (do not use cotton waste); a gallon or so of light machine oil or Tectyl; a plentiful supply of fresh water, under pressure if possible.

Procedure: Remove engine complete; take off cylinder head, valve-cover plate, oil pan, clutch housing complete, flywheel cover if any. Also remove the carburetor, starter, generator, distributor, coil, spark plugs, and all other attached parts. Then turn a stream of fresh water on the engine and the removed parts, and do a thorough, quick job of rinsing and flooding all the salt water out of them. If water under pressure is not available, submerge the entire engine and all the parts in a tank of fresh water, and after an hour or so change the water, or keep a stream flowing through the tank. Thoroughly flush out the water jackets and piping.

If no tank large enough is available, rinse all small parts and accessories removed from engine in a large bucket or tub of fresh hot water, sousing them thoroughly. (CAUTION: Give starter and generator a quick dipping; do not leave them in hot water, as this may damage the insulation.) Use a brush or cloth to scrub the inside and outside of the cylinder block, until you are sure all salt has been dissolved and washed away.

After you are convinced that no more salt remains on any part of the engine or accessories, the job is reduced to a simple process of drying, covering the surfaces with a protective film of oil or Tectyl, and assembling.

All electrical parts should, if possible, be taken after the rinsing to a manufacturer's agent or reliable electrical-repair shop for expert treatment. They must in any case be disassembled, each part thoroughly rinsed, wiped dry and clean with all traces of sand, grit, etc., removed. Then they should be dried further by dry heat, not over 175° F., for several hours. Shellac all interior insulation in starter and generator; wipe all metal surfaces with thin oil or Tectyl. Refill oil cups, grease cups, etc.—carefully removing all old grease—then reassemble and test on a battery. Install new breaker points in distributor.

Storage Batteries will usually require replacing.

The engine proper, including clutch and reverse gear, should be thoroughly dried by wiping all surfaces, inside and out, with soft rags until they are perfectly clean and dry. As each part or section is cleaned, cover it with light machine oil or Tectyl to exclude air. Do a particularly good and careful job on valve mechanism, gears and timing chain if any, and recesses. Wash out the oil pan with kerosene. Disassemble carburetor and blow out the jets with compressed air. If possible, have manufacturer's agent or authorized service station clean and reassemble it. Pay special attention to this if carburetor body is die-cast aluminum, or zinc alloy:

Assembly: With every part of the motor thoroughly washed free of salt, dirt, etc., dried and covered with light oil, the assembly may be commenced. It always pays to use new gaskets if possible, particularly on cylinder head and oil pan. New wires should be used on both high-tension and low-tension circuits, unless they were practically new when the accident took place. Use new ignition coil. Install new packing or oil seals at rear end and on clutch cross shaft. If valves need grinding, now is the time to do it.

Storage: If engine is to be stored for some time or laid up for the season, plug all water outlets in cylinder block and head, and fill the water jackets with kerosene or fuel oil, through the water outlet tube. A quantity of No. 30 oil should be put into each cylinder through the spark-plug holes.

Warning: An engine that has not been properly gone over, after being submerged in salt water, will often run after even a sketchy and superficial cleanup. It will look OK on the outside. But do not let this deceive you, for some salt and moisture will remain in the pores of the metal. Slow rusting and pitting will continue until some part breaks suddenly or a rust flake plugs up an oil feed to a bearing. You will be wise if you take no chances.

"Laying-up" Suggestions for Winter Storage

1553. 1. First run the engine, under load with clutch engaged, until it is completely warmed up. (Hot oil is thinner and will drain better; also it has the accumulated impurities held in suspension.) Then shut it off and remove crankcase oil, using the sump pump. Reason for removing the old oil is that it may have an acid content, because most fuels have a trace of sulphur, and sulphur-dioxide gas (SO_2) which is a product of combustion, plus water (H_2O), plus heat, and forms sulphurous acid (H_2SO_3). Refill slightly over the "full" mark with fresh oil of the correct viscosity.

2. Then start up the engine again to distribute clean oil through the engine, and while it is running at good speed, choke it off by pouring a cupful of regular No. 30 engine oil into the air intake on the carburetor. This will have the effect of making the engine a trifle hard to start in the spring, but not if you clean the spark plugs, and it will coat the combustion chamber as well as the carburetor jets with a protective film of oil. Turn off ignition switch.

3. Drain all water jackets and piping, and don't forget the drain cock on the oil cooler, if your engine has one. Prodding the drain

cocks with a piece of wire after draining will make sure they are fully open and not clogged with sediment. Then close all drain cocks, and fill all the water passages with kerosene or fuel oil, through the water-outlet tube. This is particularly important if the boat has been operated in salt water, as this treatment will exclude oxygen and this retards rusting. After filling, open the lowest petcock and drain out about a quart; water, being heavier than oil, will be forced out at the bottom. Close petcock and refill.

4. Drain the fuel tank, gasoline lines, and carburetor dry. This will prevent "sweating" and consequent water in the gasoline next spring. Most yards require this as a precaution against fire. Remember also that gasoline will get "stale," losing its more volatile fractions by evaporation; also ethyl gasoline has a chemical property of depositing a rubberlike gum or jell which will foul up the fuel pump and carburetor. Clean the gas tank now: it will be easier than in the spring.

5. Protect cylinder walls by coating them with a thin film of lubricating oil S.A.E. No. 30. Simplest way to do this is to remove spark plugs and pour a half cupful of oil into each cylinder. Then crank the motor over a few times by hand, with the spark plugs out, to distribute this oil evenly over the cylinder walls. CAUTION: If you use the electric starter for cranking the motor at this time, the spark plugs *must be out,* otherwise the oil may be compressed enough to break the pistons.

6. Care of Electrical Equipment: Remove the coil, the high-tension wires, and the magneto (if any). These parts can best be kept clean and dry in some safe place at home. Starter and generator may also be removed, but if they are left on the motor they should be cleaned and wrapped with rags. Spark plugs should be replaced in the cylinder head and tightened down firmly. These protect the threads and seal out dirt. Do not use corks in spark-plug holes.

7. Care of Batteries: Replenish water to bring level $\frac{3}{8}''$ above the plates. Fully charge the battery to 1.275 gravity, then store in a clean dry place and keep charged. Battery should be inspected once a month during the winter: your marine dealer will take care of this for you at small cost. Clean the cable terminals by dipping

them in a solution of baking soda, then dry them and coat lightly with vaseline or thin grease. Badly corroded terminals should be replaced.

8. External Care of the Engine:

   A. Cover all surfaces having a tendency to rust by painting or spraying with oil. Use an oily rag, a paint brush or a spray gun, and pay particular attention to rusty spots. Remove the valve-cover plate, and paint or spray the valve springs, valve stems, and all exposed metal parts which are not painted. (A valve spring which is protected against rust will seldom, if ever, break.)

   B. Examine the paint on the outside of the engine, and repaint any damaged spots before rust appears.

   C. Always disconnect the propeller shaft from the engine at the coupling *before hauling boat from the water*. This is to prevent straining or bending the shaft. Now is a good time to check your propeller for bent blades.

   D. Put a tarpaulin or waterproof canvas cover loosely over the engine to protect it from water drips and snow. Be sure the covering is not too tight, because good ventilation is desirable; this discourages rust and condensation.

9. How about overhauling? If your engine has been in use for several years, its performance will be improved by a general overhaul. Winter is the time to do it. Don't wait until the spring rush season.

10. Order spare parts at this time through your dealer: you will get best service. Be sure to supply identification of model and serial number. These will be found on a brass plate, usually riveted to the cylinder block, manifold, or reverse-gear cover.

YOU'LL WANT TO THINK OF THESE THINGS IN THE SPRING

1. Fill the tanks with a good grade of clean gasoline, of the octane rating recommended for your engine.

2. Double check your gasoline line and fittings for leaks.

3. Check the lubricating oil, and make sure the crankcase is filled

to the high-level mark on depth stick, with any good nationally advertised oil of the correct viscosity, as recommended in the instruction book for your engine.

4. Put new grease in all grease cups, and a few drops of oil in the oil cups of generator and starter, also on all control joints. Remove all old grease carefully from grease cups before refilling.

5. Brighten up the terminal posts on the batteries, using steel wool, and attach cables. After tightening down the clamps, smear lightly with vaseline or grease to exclude acid and air. Do not put vaseline on the battery posts *before* attaching the cables, as vaseline is a nonconductor.

6. Clean all contacts inside the distributor with fine sandpaper (No. 00) or a small file. If the points are pitted, dress them down evenly on an oil stone, or better still replace them with a new set of points; these are inexpensive and easily installed. Wipe inside of distributor clean, and rub a very thin film of cup grease around the cam and the terminals inside the cap.

7. Inspect top of pistons by looking through the spark-plug holes, using a flashlight, and make sure there is no excess oil standing on top of the pistons. Inspect spark plugs and check to make certain they are set for the correct gap, as specified in instruction book. If they look doubtful, replace them with new plugs of the correct heat range, or have them sandblasted and tested. One faulty plug can cause you no end of trouble.

8. Now is a good time to check over your stock of spares. It is good policy to carry on board an extra condenser, distributor rotor, distributor cap, coil, set of distributor points, and set of spark plugs. These are inexpensive items, and having them may save you a day's cruising sometime. Some owners also carry a spare water pump and spare propeller.

9. Tighten down all bolts, nuts, screws, etc., paying particular attention to the cylinder head studs, the lag screws holding engine to the bed, and electrical connections.

10. Reconnect the coupling *after* the boat is put in the water, and check the alignment. Tighten up on stuffing boxes and water-pump packing glands.

11. CAUTION: Before starting the motor, open the hatches and let the boat "air out." If boat is equipped with an engine-room ventilating

fan, let the fan run long enough to insure a complete change of air. Make sure the bilge is dry. Be sure there is no possible cause of fire—rags, gas or oil leaks, open tins of kerosene or gasoline, etc.—anywhere around the boat.

12. Finally, with gas in the tank, oil in the base, propeller tight on the shaft, stuffing boxes tight, and the motor hitting on every cylinder, water coming freely through the overflow, oil gauge and ammeter readings OK, you will be ready for a trial run. It is very important to check your clutch and reverse gear carefully at this time to make sure they are properly adjusted. A loose clutch will wear prematurely.

Propeller Sizes

1554. Printing suggested propeller sizes in table form is an unusual procedure. However, the following tables have been prepared by the Gray Marine Motor Company, of Detroit, Michigan, after many years of experience in the marine motor field and in the light of many thousands of individual problems which this large manufacturer has solved for the boatowner. The Gray Marine Motor Company points out that to apply these charts intelligently is to remember that the sizes given are *average;* also that for the extreme economy and for special cases, larger sizes are often used to advantage. These suggested wheel sizes will not fit all boats, and it should be remembered that diameter and pitch have to be varied according to the characteristics of the hull. Propeller sizes given are for three-blade wheels. For auxiliary two-blade propellers, increase diameter. Wheel sizes given are mostly unsuited for towing service, which requires more diameter and less pitch. The general rule when slip is excessive is to increase diameter and decrease pitch. When highest economy is wanted, use more diameter or pitch. Twin-screw installations usually need a higher ratio of pitch to diameter, because one engine takes the load off the other.

Engine manufacturers generally maintain a service for their users which recommends proper propeller sizes. In requesting such information, provide the manufacturer with length, beam, and draft; type of boat and uses; speed desired and size of the present wheel (if any). A picture of the boat, out of water if possible, helps greatly, as well as any general information, such as thickness of deadwood, distance from it to wheel, and type of rudder. Naturally, the make, horsepower,

LARGE CENTER FIGURES REFER TO AVERAGE DIAMETER AND PITCH. THE LOWER FIGURES COVER SUGGESTED RANGES.

Horse-power	Med. & Hvy. Duty Eng.	Direct Drive	1.5:1 Ratio	2:1 Ratio	2.5:1 Ratio	3:1 Ratio	3.5:1 Ratio
16	69 cu. in.	12 x 8 / 14 x 8—10 x 10		16 x 12 / 18 x 10—15 x 13			
22	91 cu. in.	12 x 10 / 15 x 8—11 x 8		17 x 12 / 19 x 10—15 x 14			
27	112 cu. in.	13 x 10 / 15 x 9—12 x 11		18 x 12 / 20 x 12—15 x 15			
37	140 cu. in.	14 x 10 / 16 x 9—12 x 12	15 x 13 / 17 x 11—16 x 12	18 x 14 / 21 x 14—18 x 16	20 x 16 / 22 x 16—18 x 18	20 x 18 / 20 x 20—18 x 20	22 x 20 / 20 x 22—20 x 20
42	162 cu. in.	15 x 10 / 17 x 10—13 x 12	16 x 13 / 18 x 11—15 x 12	22 x 14 / 20 x 14—18 x 18	22 x 18 / 22 x 20—22 x 16	22 x 20 / 24 x 20—24 x 18	24 x 20 / 26 x 20—22 x 22
55	200 cu. in.	14 x 11 / 16 x 9—13 x 12	16 x 13 / 18 x 10—15 x 12	20 x 14 / 19 x 14—16 x 18	22 x 16 / 20 x 18—18 x 20	24 x 18 / 22 x 20—20 x 22	24 x 22 / 28 x 20—22 x 24
68	218 cu. in.	15 x 11 / 16 x 10—13 x 12	16 x 14 / 17 x 12—15 x 14	20 x 15 / 22 x 16—18 x 16	22 x 18 / 24 x 16—20 x 20	24 x 20 / 22 x 22—22 x 20	26 x 22 / 28 x 20—24 x 24
83	244 cu. in.	15 x 12 / 17 x 10—14 x 12	17 x 13 / 18 x 12—15 x 15	20 x 16 / 24 x 16—18 x 18	24 x 18 / 26 x 18—22 x 24	26 x 20 / 28 x 18—24 x 24	28 x 26 / 30 x 26—28 x 28
87	290 cu. in.	16 x 10 / 17 x 10—14 x 12	17 x 14 / 19 x 12—17 x 15	22 x 18 / 26 x 16—20 x 18	24 x 20 / 26 x 18—22 x 24	26 x 22 / 28 x 20—24 x 24	30 x 24 / 32 x 22—28 x 28
96	330 cu. in.	16 x 11 / 18 x 10—15 x 11	18 x 14 / 20 x 12—18 x 18	20 x 20 / 26 x 18—24 x 20	26 x 20 / 28 x 18—24 x 24	28 x 22 / 30 x 20—26 x 26	32 x 24 / 34 x 22—30 x 26
101	383 cu. in.	18 x 10 / 18 x 13—16 x 14	20 x 18 / 22 x 16—20 x 16	26 x 22 / 28 x 24—24 x 24	30 x 24 / 28 x 26—28 x 28	34 x 24 / 30 x 28—32 x 26	36 x 26 / 32 x 28—34 x 28
122	372 cu. in.	15 x 14 / 18 x 12—17 x 11	19 x 16 / 22 x 14—18 x 17	24 x 20 / 22 x 20—22 x 22	24 x 24 / 26 x 22—26 x 24	26 x 26 / 28 x 24—28 x 22	28 x 28 / 32 x 24—30 x 26

Figure 1554. Table of Propeller Sizes

drive, and all information about the motor including the rated r.p.m. and piston displacement is necessary as well.

WHEEL SIZES FOR HIGH-SPEED DIRECT-DRIVE ENGINES

Horse-Power	Wheel Size
45	10 X 10
	10 X 9
62	11 X 11
	11 X 12
75	11 X 12
	12 X 12
86	12 X 12
	11 X 12
90	12 X 12
	12 X 13
103	12 X 13
	12 X 12
125	13 X 14
	13 X 13
140–160	12 X 14
	13 X 14
	12½ X 16
	13 X 15
175	15 X 14
	15 X 15

PART V
SAFETY

⚓

CHAPTER XVI

SAFETY AT SEA

1601. Safety at sea is the twin art of *keeping out of trouble* and *getting out of trouble* if you get into it.

The more the boatman is prepared by experience and equipment and common sense to keep out of trouble, the less he will have to get out of trouble. Very few of the troubles that beset the ship at sea are to be dismissed by that all-inclusive phrase "dangers of the sea." A storm at sea is no particular hazard if the boat is seaworthy and the ship and crew prepared for the blow. Yet a mild gale at sea can be a disaster to the ship which ought never to venture from smooth water because of design or condition, and whose crew have not suspected the breeze until it descended upon the unprepared ship. A fire on shipboard is a disaster; yet most fires anywhere are preventable, not by the use of an extinguisher, but rather by proper design and insulation, and safe and sane equipment, thought of long before the extinguisher is needed.

Keeping out of trouble starts with an intelligent and unemotional survey of the boat in which every possible contingency is understood, and means taken to prevent that contingency. The means taken include the following:

1. Correction of the basic elements of a hazard or a danger.
   (Examples: Clear, unobstructed decks to make tripping and falling overboard impossible. Backfire traps on carburetors.)
2. Proper equipment at hand to fight or control a danger.
   (Examples: Life preservers, accessible and usable. Means of signaling. Fire extinguishers.)
3. Training and experience.
   (Examples: Thorough understanding of the Rules of the Road. Knowledge of the use of danger-fighting equipment. Common sense and sanity applied to weather, speed, organization, etc.)

The last mentioned is the most important. The boatman of experience and judgment seldom has to worry about getting out of trouble because he doesn't often get into it. He sails only when his boat is in top-notch condition, fully equipped; when the weather present and predicted is suitable and safe for *his* boat; when he is prepared to meet any possible danger—including the danger of boatmen not of his own experience and common sense.

On board will be the equipment peculiarly suited to his boat and his problems in meeting danger. The skeleton of such equipment will be the required items of equipment by the government. To them he will add whatever is still needed to make his vessel as safe as possible. Government equipment is required to prevent collision at night or in fog, to fight fire, to prevent gasoline fire and explosion, and to sustain persons afloat in the water. (Paragraph 402, Chapter IV.) Voluntarily, the boatman must provide his own means of anchoring, signaling, prevention of fire or explosion from other sources than the engine, laying to, calming waves, stopping leaks, and a great many other things. The amount, utility, and fitness of all this equipment, plus the amount of knowledge and experience in the crew, make a ship safe or not safe.

Two of every known safety device on board and a lubber at the wheel do not make a safe ship.

No safety devices on board and an experienced seaman and navigator at the wheel do not make a dangerous ship.

Getting out of trouble starts with a basic knowledge of seamanship and the ability to use, under emergency conditions, safety devices and maneuvers. It means preparation by drill and organization, and having ready and in usable condition the devices required to control or remedy the trouble.

When trouble comes at sea, it is usually complex; a combination of several troubles. There are few situations for which a specific can be prescribed. Only by understanding the nature of each trouble can the vessel again be put into a safe condition. Thus, a fire might disable the engine and burn away the steering control. Putting the fire out saved the ship for the moment but a jury sail and rudder are still needed, or signals must be made, the vessel anchored, a tow called, to save the life of the boat and its company.

FIRE

Keeping out of Trouble

1602. Government regulations for motorboats require a backfire trap on every marine engine except an outboard motor. These traps must be of approved make, and those sold with marine plants are of approved make. Lighting plants or gasoline-driven pumps must have the carburetors so fitted.

As an additional precaution, the safe installation will always see a drip pan placed under the carburetor. This is covered with a fine flame-arresting mesh and a sump pipe led to the intake manifold to draw off any raw gasoline which collects.

Government regulations also require that the motor which is boxed in (as under a bridge deck, cockpit floor, etc.) must be ventilated outboard. Cowl or equal-type ventilators are required, and are so arranged as to form a positive draught. General ventilation of the hull is desirable, not only to disperse dangerous gases but to prevent dry rot in the hull parts and to keep the boat "sweet."

1603. Both the backfire trap and ventilator regulation are aimed at preventing gasoline explosion.

Gasoline fumes may come from leaking or ruptured fuel lines or from improperly installed tanks.

Fuel lines should be strapped down with broad metal straps, screwed to woodwork (not nailed) at frequent enough intervals to prevent any movement of the line. A chafing pad should be inserted between strap and pipe. In the way of bulkheads or structural members, the pipe should pass through a hole several times its own diameter. Shut-off valves, manufactured for gasoline lines, should be at the tank outlets, fuel pump, or vacuum tank and carburetor.

Fuel tanks should be most securely chocked and strapped in place. The filler pipes should positively be outboard, so that spilled gasoline and gasoline fumes will pass overboard. Vent pipes for tanks should positively be outboard, so that fumes are drawn away from the boat. The same precautions are to be observed in the installation of other fuel tanks (cooking fuels, lighting-plant fuels, etc.). Diesel oil tanks are not excepted.

1604. Fire may start by an electric spark. Switches and fuses, if at all possible, should be kept out of the small engine compartment and at least three feet above the floor level. Power ventilators should be equipped with a motor shielded against sparking or, if not, located outside the exhaust duct. Inspection of the electrical system should frequently be made to locate the ruptured or weakened wire before it breaks and sparks and becomes a potential danger.

1605. Any minute spark may explode gaseous fumes if present in the boat. Such fumes are heavier than air and settle into the lowest and most difficult to ventilate parts of the boat; hence the required backfire traps and ventilation requirements.

Such fumes are generated chiefly while fueling. Unless the wind is blowing outboard from the filling pipe (not forward, aft, or inboard) all hatches and companions should be closed lest such fumes be whirled into the ship's below decks. Watch also boats which are fueling near by. Fumes may be undetected by ordinary methods yet be present in dangerous quantities or mixtures. It is safest to assume that they are present and to ventilate carefully before any fire is lighted or engine started. It should be needless to point out that, when fueling, all fires should be out, engine stopped, and smoking on board and near by strictly prohibited.

There are commercial devices for sale which detect the presence of dangerous gaseous fumes, including fumes from cooking gas, alcohol, turpentine, etc.

1606. Overheated engine parts may cause fire on shipboard. The exhaust line should be lagged with asbestos wherever not watercooled, especially the engine end of it. Sheet asbestos should line the engine compartment and underneath side of hatches, etc. Shaft bearings should be frequently lubricated. An overheated one can cause fire, especially if the inflammable parts surrounding it have been allowed to become oil-soaked.

1607. Heating and cooking stoves can cause fire. Pressure stoves using gasoline or alcohol for fuel must be most carefully handled at all times. Under no circumstances fill a near-by fuel tank while the stove is lighted. The stoves seldom fail if kept clean and in an unleaky condition. Stove fires are almost always the fault of a careless operator. Any wick or open-fount-type oil stove is dangerous on shipboard and should be replaced by a stove approved by the Underwriter's Laboratories.

Gas is one of the most dangerous fuels for shipboard use. Being heavier than air it is apt to settle deep in the bilges.

Coal, briquet, and wood-heating stoves should be of a "marine" variety and design. This will see adequate provision made for lashing and securing them and that all doors are equipped with a seagoing latch, not to be easily or accidentally opened by heeling or pitching.

All stoves should have pot rails to hold cooking pots securely. A spilled pot will cause the flame to jump and make possible the igniting of some near-by object. All sailing vessels should have pot rails and the stove hung in gimbals, preferably athwartships. If the stove is not equipped with gimbals, no cooking should be done at sea. If the stove is not equipped with gimbals or pot rails, no cooking should be done on board at all.

Woodwork adjacent to stove spaces should be protected from the danger of fire by asbestos covering, or metal stove shields, or a similar device. Stovepipes should pass through the deck in a water iron, *kept filled with water at all times,* to prevent scorching the deck and deck beams in their way. The head of the smoke pipe should be fitted with a Charlie Noble or a similar screened device to prevent sparks from flying.

1608. Spontaneous combustion has caused many shipboard fires. Any oil-soaked material may self-ignite under conditions of warmth and absence of ventilation. Suspect paint rags, storm clothing, wiping rags, oil mops, and waxing rags. Usually such fires smolder until given air by opening a locker or bin; then they burst into furious flame. Old oil skins are the gravest offenders. Discard them when the finish becomes tacky. Store new ones in ventilated lockers only and after thorough drying.

Getting Out of Trouble

1609. The types and quantity of required legal fire-fighting apparatus are listed for classes of boats in Chapter IV. These are *minimum* requirements and may be quite inadequate on all types of boats within the class. Every vessel's fire-fighting equipment should suit that particular vessel.

Any boat with enclosed engine spaces should be equipped with a permanently installed basic fire-suppression system of the carbon-dioxide type. These may be obtained to operate automatically or manually; the former affording protection 100% of the time, the latter only when an operator is on board.

Fire extinguishers and controls for manually operated CO_2 systems should be located "handy." "Handy" is not in such a position as to necessitate reaching *through* a fire area for them, or to have to open lockers, or to have to do more than *reach* from the position the operator is in when fire is most likely to occur. Thus, the galley extinguisher should be located between the stove and the exit, not beyond or above the stove, nor in a corner opposite to the exit. The main extinguishing system should be within reach of the helmsman on the average small boat.

Some thought of fighting fire should be exerted *before* an emergency. A fire-station bill can be very simply worked out for the organized cruise. Fire drill might be engaged in at the outset of a cruise. (A sample fire-station bill is given in paragraph 726, Chapter VII.)

While the actual methods of using the various types of fire extinguishers are given in detail in paragraph 1429, Chapter XIV, all are dependent upon a smothering action, and, upon the outbreak of a fire, it is good to close hatches, portholes, and ventilators in order to keep the fire-suppressing agent at the fire, not blown away.

If the fire breaks through to the deck, head the burning end of the boat to leeward, at slow speed if forward of the steersman. At all costs keep it from spreading toward the wheel or the life preservers or the lifeboat. A fire can be fought effectively from windward even after extinguishers have become useless (as they usually are in the open at sea) by water or soaked blankets or chopping away. A burning boat headed to windward will catch completely in a few seconds and drive the crew overboard without a chance of fighting or securing life preservers. If the air is calm, do not hesitate to reverse. Getting to shore is of secondary importance. Maneuvering to control the fire is first.

Auxiliary fire-fighting gear, even on the small boat, might well include a fire ax, several buckets of sand, water pails (to which a short filling line has been rove), and possibly a pump and hose. A simple system of Y-switches on the electric-bilge pump, or cooling water pump or hand pump can provide a small stream of water of sufficient strength to reach any part of a small boat.

MAN OVERBOARD

Keeping Out of Trouble

1610. In the ordinary operation of a boat, many situations develop which require taking the risk of falling overboard. There is little to be done about the matter save to remember the old adage of the square-riggers, "One hand for the ship and one for yourself."

Beyond that only a few precautions can be observed to lessen the possibility of such an accident.

Life lines should be rigged on any vessel, sail or power, which goes to sea in any place on deck which does not afford a foothold and a *handhold*. Life lines serve two purposes: one is to provide a handhold (as in going forward along the waterways); the other to serve as a net in the event that one is swept outboard by a boarding sea. The life line (or storm rails) should therefore be rigged to exceptionally strong stancheons, should be of wire rope, and should be spaced vertically no more than 12 inches apart. A height of 26 to 30 inches from the deck is sufficient. They should positively extend around the stern.

If permanently installed rails or life lines are absent, every man on deck during rough weather or at night should have an individual life line harnessed from himself to some firm part of the ship. It should be in the form of a broad leather or canvas belt around the middle, to which is attached a stout line of about two inches circumference, of sufficient length not to hinder normal movement about deck, and having the end terminate in a husky snap hook.

It should be a habit to snap the line to a ring, reaching to the deck from the companionway, before going on deck. A line fastened to the boat at both ends along the center line, or one along each waterway, should have been rigged before the weather made up. Individuals required to go forward on duty snap their life lines to this, changing them to shrouds or bowsprit rigging, etc., while working. Naturally, only men who can swim should be detailed to any duty where there is risk of falling overboard.

Untidy decks, or decks cluttered with cleats, halyard leads, uncoiled rope, or ship's gear, cause tripping and should certainly be redesigned with as few tripping hazards as possible.

Proper footgear must be carefully selected to wear only a nonslip type. Rubber boots are slippery and almost impossible to swim in as they fill and weight down the feet. Any boat liable to an "icing-up" should carry ice creepers for attaching over ordinary footgear. Rubber-soled sneakers, the common shipboard footgear of the pleasure boat, are dangerous when worn smooth. They should be kept in a roughened condition by cutting cross slices, or branding in a grid with hot wire or a soldering iron, or by painting with benzol in uneven patches (which will soften and dissolve the rubber).

It should be needless to state that life jackets should be worn by every man having deck duty during rough weather. The soft "racing jacket" is most comfortable and does not retard the movements.

1611. Life preservers are required equipment on motorboats. While the Motorboat Law does not specify life preservers for sailboats, under the regulations of the Coast Guard (which cover *all* vessels) they are legally required equipment.

1612. The jacket-type life preserver is required on all boats carrying passengers for hire. There must be child's-sized life preservers

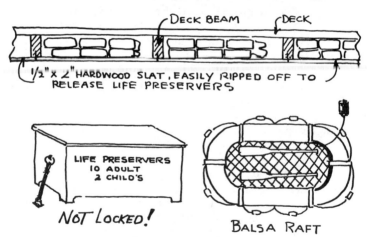

Figure 1612

available if children are in the passenger list. Life preservers should be kept instantly available, either in racks or in plainly marked boxes or lockers.

Pleasure boats are permitted to count a ring buoy as a life preserver, and below 41 feet may substitute box-type buoyant cushions for jacket-type preservers. However, the proper life preserver cannot be specified by over-all length or any such arbitrary standard. It must fit the worst emergency to which the particular boat might be subjected. Thus, a 20-footer which goes to sea, while permitted to consider a buoyant cushion an approved life preserver, should most certainly be equipped with the jacket type.

All life preservers must be approved by the proper inspecting agencies and so stamped. Inspection is made at the manufacturing source. The preserver is purchased with the approval marked or tagged to it, and inspectors boarding the boat will consider such markings as legal. It is illegal to remove the approval tag.

Supplementary (but not required) lifesaving equipment might include a balsa raft (easily stowed and easily launched and capable of supporting four to eight persons in the water) as well as at least one conveniently located ring buoy and attached water light. Pine planks are allowed as legal equipment only on commercial motor fishing-boats.

Getting Out of Trouble

1613. The life-preserver jacket is worn exactly as a vest with the lashing in *front*, the corks (if a solid-cork type) overlapped and securely and snugly tied to the body with square knots. It is of the utmost importance that the jacket fit tightly. Many persons have died with a broken neck from jumping into the sea with a loosely tied life preserver which had been driven upward sharply upon reaching the water.

1614. The ring buoy should be used as shown in Figure 1614. The shoulders may be let through a large ring buoy and the weight rests on the arms. Putting the head through the ring helps somewhat to break the seas and permits easier breathing. Avoid the fumes of the water light if possible.

1615. The first duty upon the call "Man Overboard" is to get a ring buoy or raft launched. Launch *near* not *at* the swimmer. The helmsman should stop the propeller at once and head sharply toward the side from which the person fell, thus swinging the propeller away from the man overboard. A member of the crew should point to the

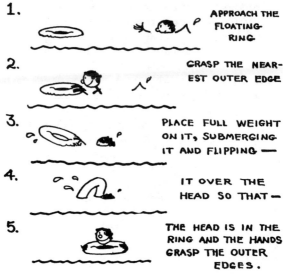

1. APPROACH THE FLOATING RING

2. GRASP THE NEAREST OUTER EDGE

3. PLACE FULL WEIGHT ON IT, SUBMERGING IT AND FLIPPING —

4. IT OVER THE HEAD SO THAT —

5. THE HEAD IS IN THE RING AND THE HANDS GRASP THE OUTER EDGES.

Figure 1614. How to Get into a Ring Buoy

man overboard and keep pointing for the benefit of the helmsman and, if it is launched, the life boat. The water light will cast a light by night and thick smoke by day. Man the searchlight at once if at night. (*See* Man Overboard station bill, paragraph 729, Chapter VII.)

It is generally quite useless to launch a small boat of the dinghy type at sea in a storm. Attempt the rescue from the large boat, taking the person aboard on the lee side. If a search must be made mark the course by any handy means, such as leaving a trail of oatmeal, an oil slick, or paper, or by taking shore ranges, so that the same water is not covered twice.

SHIPWRECK

Keeping Out of Trouble

1616. Shipwreck is usually caused by faulty navigation or poor seamanship or a combination of both. There is no positive way in which to keep out of such trouble except to know the boat, its habits and peculiarities and capabilities, and to have the knowledge, judgment, sense, and courage to operate it under safe and sane conditions of weather and sea, and in a safe and sane manner.

It is largely a matter of what has been done and planned long before the moment of danger; the preparation and skill of the skipper and the seaworthiness and condition of the vessel. To elaborate would be to run in circles. Suffice to mention that, in the final analysis, a vessel is no better or safer than the human beings who operate her. She will seldom meet with shipwreck, grounding, stranding, or dismasting unless she has been placed in such danger by ignorance, or stupidity, or carelessness, or drunkenness by the hand at her controls.

No boat need strand on a strange coast if the skipper is a navigator and seaman in fact, not theory.

No boat need suffer a "licking" at sea if the skipper is a seaman and sailor in fact, not theory.

No boat need suffer any form of shipwreck if her skipper has fitted her out and equipped her for the purposes of her use, wisely and generously.

Experience, knowledge, judgment, sense, and courage—and of these courage is probably the greatest. It takes courage to remain in port when the barometer predicts a storm beyond the pleasant sky. It takes courage to abandon a sail because of some minor failure of gear. It takes courage to refuse to make a night run because of lack of navigational skill. But boats skippered like that do not get into trouble very often.

Dismasting or Being Swept

1617. The great danger after such a disaster is that spars and loose gear will batter the boat. Cut everything away as soon as possible, saving what can be *safely* saved only. Get hatches on at once (tarpaulin, boards, overturned tables, mattresses) and pump the ship dry. The use of oil, laying to, jury rigs and rudders are discussed elsewhere in this *Manual*.

Stranding and Grounding

1618. Such accidents on a rising tide are seldom more than annoying providing the hull has not been punctured. If it has been, judgment must decide whether to abandon ship, or make temporary repairs, or remain on board until help comes.

On a falling tide, it may become far more serious than at the moment of striking. The boat can sometimes be placed in a better situation by jettisoning cargo or ballast, or shifting them for balance. Sound the water near by. A channel may be found ahead or astern and, with weights shifted, the boat might be pried or kedged off, or run out under her own power or sails.

Kedge anchors should be taken out in the proper direction and the warp led to a winch, the capstan or a block and tackle. A lead from an anchor to the masthead, or a parbuckle arrangement, will often heel a stranded boat to the point that she will float off a reef or shoal. Sometimes it is possible to swamp a small boat in such a manner that she will lift the stranded boat as it is pumped dry. Every such accident presents its own peculiar problem, and an effective solution depends upon the skipper's knowledge of seamanship and engineering, as well as his resourcefulness and ingenuity.

Upon stranding check the well at once. Put out all fires. Plug tank vents if the boat has heeled enough to cause spillage. Get a lifeboat or raft over and ready for use. Ventilate or jettison the batteries (salt water and batteries form chlorine gas in lethal quantities). Take means to prevent the wreck from settling into a still worse position.

Make distress signals. (Paragraph 803, Chapter VIII.)

Do not hesitate to ask and take the assistance of the Coast Guard. Such assistance is the primary function of that service and accepting its aid does not create a salvage situation. The Coast Guards are experts in the matter of shipwreck. They should be considered as "in charge" after their appearance; they well understand their duties— the first of which is to save life in danger, then to rescue property.

1619. If the use of a breeches buoy or life car is necessary the following instructions should be complied with:

A shot with a small line attached will be fired across your vessel. Get hold of the line as soon as possible and haul on board until you get a tail block with a whip or endless line rove through it. The tail block should be hauled on board as quickly as possible to prevent the whip drifting off with the set or fouling with wreckage, etc. Therefore, if you have been driven into the rigging, where but one or two men can work to advantage, cut the shot line, and run it through some available block, such as the throat or peak halyards block, or any block which will afford a clear lead, or even between the ratlines, so that as many as possible may assist in hauling.

Attached to the tail block will be a tally board with the following directions in English on one side and in French on the other:

"Make the tail of the block fast to the lower mast, well up. If the masts are gone, then to the best place you can find. Cast off shot line, see that the rope in the block runs free, and show signal to the shore."

The above instruction being complied with, the result will be shown in Figure 1619A, Detail A.

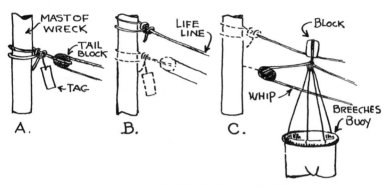

Figure 1619A. Wreck End of a Breeches Buoy

As soon as your signal is seen a three-inch hawser will be bent onto the whip and hauled off to your ship by the lifesaving crew.

If circumstances permit, you can assist the lifesaving crew by manning that part of the whip to which the hawser is bent and hauling with them.

When the end of the hawser is got on board, a tally board will be found attached, bearing the following directions in English on one side and in French on the other:

"Make this hawser fast about two feet above the tail block; see all clear and that the rope in the block runs free, and show signal to the shore."

These instructions being obeyed, the result will be shown in Figure 1619A, Detail B.

Take particular care that there are no turns of the whip line around the hawser. To prevent this, take the end of the hawser up between the parts of the whip before making it fast.

When the hawser is made fast, the whip cast off from the hawser, and your signal seen by the lifesaving crew, they will haul the hawser taut, and by means of the whip will haul off to your vessel a breeches

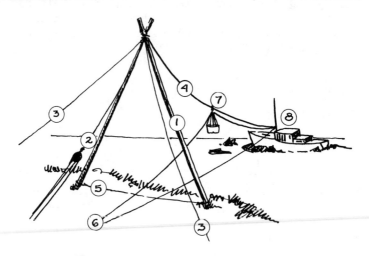

Figure 1619B. The Breeches Buoy (shore end)

1. Sheer legs	5. Foot rope
2. Tackle	6. Whip
3. Guys	7. Breeches buoy
4. Life line	8. Wreck

buoy suspended from a traveler block, or a life car, from rings running on the hawser.

Figure 1619A, Detail C, represents the apparatus rigged, with the breeches buoy hauled off to the ship.

If the breeches buoy be sent, let one man immediately get into it, thrusting his legs through the breeches. If the life car be sent, remove the hatch, place as many persons therein as it will hold (four to six) and secure the hatch on the outside by the hatch bar and hook; signal as before, and the buoy or car will be hauled ashore. This will be repeated until all are landed. On the last trip of the life car the hatch must be secured by the inside hatch bar.

In many instances two men can be landed in the breeches buoy at the same time by each putting a leg through a leg of the breeches and holding onto the lifts of the buoy.

Children when brought ashore by the buoy should be in the arms of older persons or securely lashed to the buoy. Women and children should be landed first.

In signaling as directed in the foregoing instructions, if in the daytime, let one man separate himself from the rest and swing his hat, a handkerchief, or his hand; if at night, the showing of a light and concealing it once or twice will be understood; and like signals will be made from the shore.

Circumstances may arise, owing to the strength of the current or set, or the danger of the wreck's breaking up immediately, when it would be impossible to send off the hawser. In such a case a breeches buoy or life car will be hauled off instead by the whip or sent off to you by the shot line, and you will be hauled ashore through the surf.

If your vessel is stranded during the night and discovered by the patrolman—which you will know by his burning a brilliant red light —keep a sharp lookout for signs of the arrival of the lifesaving crew abreast of your vessel.

Some time may intervene between the burning of the light and their arrival, as the patrolman may have to return to his station, perhaps three or four miles distant, and the lifesaving crew draw the apparatus or surfboat through the sand or over bad roads to where your vessel is stranded.

Lights on the beach will indicate their arrival, and the sound of cannon firing from the shore may be taken as evidence that a line has been fired across your vessel. Therefore, upon hearing the cannon, make strict search aloft, fore, and aft for the shot line, for it is almost certain to be there. Though the movement of the lifesaving crew may not be perceptible to you, owing to the darkness, your vessel will be a good mark for the men experienced in the use of the wreck gun, and the first shot seldom fails.

Important.—Remain by the wreck until assistance arrives from the shore, or as long as possible. If driven aloft, the inshore mast is the safest.

If not discovered immediately by the patrol, burn rockets, flare-ups, or other lights, or if the weather be foggy, fire guns or make other sound signals.

Make the shot line fast on deck or to the rigging to prevent its being washed into the sea and possibly fouling the gear.

Take particular care that there are no turns of the whip line around the hawser before making the hawser fast.

Send the women, children, helpless persons, and passengers ashore first.

Make yourself thoroughly familiar with these instructions, and remember that on your coolness and strict attention to them will greatly depend the chances of success in bringing you and your people safely to land.

Instructions to Aid in Rescue by Lifeboat or Surfboat

1620. The patrolman, after discovering your vessel ashore and burning a warning signal, hastens to his station or the telephone for assistance. If the use of a boat is practicable, either the large lifeboat is launched from its ways in the station and proceeds to the wreck by water, or the lighter surfboat is hauled overland to a point opposite the wreck and launched, as circumstances may require.

Upon the boat's reaching your vessel the directions and orders of the officer in charge (who always commands and steers the boat) should be implicitly obeyed. Any headlong rushing and crowding should be prevented, and the captain of the vessel should remain on board, to preserve order, until every other person has left.

Women, children, helpless persons, and passengers should be passed into the boat first.

Goods or baggage will positively not be taken into the boat until all are landed. If any person be passed in against the remonstrance of the officer in charge, he is fully authorized to throw the man overboard.

General Information from the United States Coast Pilot

1621. Coast Guard (lifesaving) stations and houses of refuge are located upon the Atlantic and Pacific seaboards of the United States, the Gulf of Mexico, and the Lake coasts.

The stations are manned throughout the year by crews of experienced surfmen.

All lifesaving stations are fully supplied with boats, wreck guns, beach apparatus, restoratives, and clothing provided by the Blue Anchor Society, Women's National Association for the shipwrecked requiring it, etc.

Houses of refuge are supplied with boats and restoratives, but not manned by full crews; an officer in charge, and at places, one or two additional men reside in each, who are required to make extended excursions along the coast after every storm, with a view of ascertaining if any shipwreck has occurred and finding and succoring any persons that may have been cast ashore.

Houses of refuge are located exclusively upon the east coast of Florida, where the requirements of relief are different from those of other portions of the seaboard.

The lifesaving stations are provided with the International Code of Signals, and other means of visual signaling, and vessels can, by opening communication, be reported; or obtain the latitude or longitude of the station, where determined; or information as to the weather probabilities in most cases; or, where facilities for the transmission of messages by telephone or telegraph are available, requests for a tug or Coast Guard cutter will be received and promptly forwarded.

All services are performed by the lifesaving crews without other compensation than their pay from the Government.

Destitute seafarers are provided with food and lodging at the nearest station by the Government as long as necessarily detained by the circumstances of shipwreck, and, if needed, with clothing provided by the Blue Anchor Society.

The station crews patrol the beach from two to four miles each side of their stations between sunset and sunrise, and if the weather is foggy the patrol is continued through the day. A continuous lookout is also maintained at every station night and day.

Each patrolman carries warning signals. Upon discovering a vessel standing into danger he ignites one of these, which emits a brilliant red flame of about two minutes' duration, to warn her off, or, should the vessel be ashore, to let her crew know that they are discovered and assistance is at hand.

If the vessel is not discovered by the patrol immediately after striking, rockets, flare-up lights, or other recognized signals of distress should be used. If the weather be foggy, some recognized sound signal should be made to attract attention, as the patrolman may be some distance away at the other end of his beat.

Masters are particularly cautioned, if they should be driven ashore anywhere in the neighborhood of the stations, to remain on board until assistance arrives, and under no circumstances should they attempt to land through the surf in their own boats until the last hope of assistance from the shore has vanished. Often when comparatively smooth at sea a dangerous surf is running which is not perceptible 400 yards off-shore, and the surf when viewed from a vessel never appears as dangerous as it is. Many lives have been lost unnecessarily by the crews of stranded vessels being thus deceived and attempting to land in the ship's boats.

The difficulties of rescue by operations from the shore are greatly increased in cases where the anchors are let go *after entering the breakers,* as is frequently done, and the chances of saving life correspondingly lessened.

Boarding a Wreck—Hints

1622. It is best in most cases to approach and board a vessel, whether stranded or afloat, from the lee side. The greatest danger lies in the sea's crashing the boat against the vessel or in being swamped as the sea breaks away from it. The sea is always more violent on the weather side of the vessel. A vessel stranded broadside to the sea presents such hazards as wreckage alongside, which may damage the boat, and the possibility of a falling mast, a stove in lifeboat, or other gear that may have become awash. The presence of these dangers may make it advisable to carry out rescue from bow or stern. To board a wreck that is stranded on a smooth beach it is well to anchor the lifeboat to windward and veer down with caution until close enough to reach the vessel with a heaving line.

To carry out rescue from a drifting wreck, come in from leeward keeping a sharp lookout for floating wreckage. In a strong wind lay off and heave a line aboard. Instruct a seaman aboard the wreck (if there be one) to secure the line to one person's body with a French bowline and have the person jump overboard. Haul him aboard and repeat the operation. Remember that there is great danger of swamping if you take your boat alongside a wreck that is rapidly drifting to leeward. If you must go alongside do so with bow or stern to sea ladder or gangway and hold your boat at right angles to the wreck. From this position it will be much safer when pulling away.

A wrecked craft with very low freeboard is best boarded from the weather quarter. This action cuts down the danger from her main booms, chains, etc.

Fog

1623. Fog has no terrors for the capable navigator. He knows exactly where he is at all times and proceeds in such a manner as to be in a position to avoid collision, indicating his position and course to other traffic.

Rules of the Road provide that speed in fog or thick weather should be reduced or maintained at "moderate," with due regard to circumstances and conditions. When any fog signal is heard forward of the beam, the law provides that the vessel hearing it must stop and then navigate with extreme caution until danger of collision is past.

Motorboats of Class I must be equipped (and use as a fog signal) a whistle capable of being heard one half mile. On Classes II and III, the whistle must be audible at least one mile, and a fog bell must be carried as well. No motorboat makes fog signals on a foghorn. Class A boats need not carry whistle or bell.

Sound Signals for Fog

1624.

MOTORBOATS (On Whistle)

1. Under way.—A prolonged blast at least once every minute.
2. Towing.—One prolonged blast and two short blasts, in succession, at least once every minute.
3. Towed.—Same (but no other signal).
4. At anchor.—A rapid ringing of the bell for at least five seconds at least once every minute.

SAILBOATS (On Foghorn)

1. Starboard tack.—One blast at least once every minute.
2. Port tack.—Two blasts at least once every minute.

3. Wind abaft the beam.—Three blasts at least once every minute.

4. At anchor.—Same as motorboat.

Fog distorts, blankets, and magnifies sound in unpredictable ways, and bearings taken from sound signals during thick weather are not to be relied upon. The cautious and experienced navigator relies upon the three L's of navigation in thick weather—log, lead, and lookout. Radio bearings, on the radio-equipped boat, are reliable during fog.

1625. Fog in itself is in no way dangerous. Fog combined with poor navigation or seamanship can be dangerous and may cause shipwreck or collision. Beyond that the worst that can happen is to become lost —and the only way to get out of such trouble is to anchor. Deepwater men of long experience do not fear fog. They navigate to the best of their ability—and the moment they become lost, they humbly and wisely anchor.

There is no alternative within the bounds of prudence or good seamanship.

Safety Equipment for Small Boats in Addition to Required Equipment

1626. Auxilary fire-suppression apparatus.

Life rafts, balsa rafts, lifeboats.

Water lights.

Shoulder gun (for throwing line).

Very pistol (for signaling and lighting dangerous waters at night).

Signaling gear (such as a gun, blinker, flares, etc.).

Sheet and storm anchors (and hawsers).

First-aid kits.

Auxiliary lights (may be oil, or spare standard lights).

⚓

CHAPTER XVII

FIRST AID AND SANITATION

FIRST AID

General Directions for Giving First Aid

1701. First aid is the immediate temporary treatment given in case of accident or sudden illness before the services of a physician can be secured. It is exactly what the name implies, but a good first-aider will know what *not* to do as well as what to do.

The prime purpose of first aid is to prevent further damage to the injured person, and only when this is accomplished can the first-aider be considered competent.

Never move the victim nor raise him to a sitting position until the extent of his injuries is known. Even then, do not move him unless he is liable to additional injury where he is. A measure of good judgment is required of all good first-aiders to know when it is necessary to chance additional injuries to the victim by moving him at all.

Treat for shock first. Keep the victim on his back, his head slightly lower than his feet. Keep him warm, using any means available. If he is conscious, administer hot liquid stimulants.

Cover the victim enough to keep him warm.

Remove clothing from about the wound. Cut the clothing; removal in the ordinary manner may add to the injury.

Look for bleeding and check it, using digital pressure or a compress; use a tourniquet only if absolutely necessary.

If breathing has stopped, apply artificial respiration immediately.

Do not move the victim until it is certain that no bones have been fractured. If there are fractures, splint first.

Apply sterile compresses to wounds and bandage them.

For serious burns, apply clean sheeting strips dipped into warm water and baking soda or Epsom salts; *nothing else.*

If vomiting is desired, give lukewarm salt water or mild soapsuds.

Wounds

1702. All wounds are in danger of infection.

Small wounds should be made to bleed by rubbing the skin gently toward the wound, encouraging the cleansing action of free bleeding. Then apply mild tincture of iodine *around and in* the wound. Permit the iodine to dry; then apply a sterile compress and bandage securely but not tightly. Freely bleeding wounds will not require iodine; nor will the iodine do any good.

Punctured wounds especially require free bleeding and iodine swabbed deep into them. Also, the advice of a physician should be sought immediately upon reaching shore for it is in this type of wound that tetanus is most likely to develop.

Profuse bleeding requires pressure at once to stop off the main flow of blood. This is done by digital pressure (Figure 1702) after it has been determined whether the bleeding is arterial or venous. Arterial bleeding alone is in spurts and is bright red. Venous bleeding alone is in a steady stream and somewhat darker. Capillary bleeding is in the form of an ooze and can usually be stopped by direct pressure on a sterile compress over the wound.

Arterial and venous bleeding often occur together, and pressure must be applied to both arteries and veins.

Pressure is *always* applied between the wound and the heart in arterial bleeding; where necessary in venous bleeding.

Raising the injured member to the heart level or above helps to control the blood flow.

The tourniquet is used only when digital pressure is not sufficient. It is dangerous to use in that circulation may be too long cut off and permanent damage result. It is applied only at two places: on the arm, about four inches below the shoulder; or on the thigh, about four inches below the groin point.

It is tied loosely (of a wide material, cravat, etc.), then tightened by the Spanish-windlass method (a stick is inserted in the loop and twisted). It is tightened only enough to stop the flow of blood, *never tighter,* and loosened every 15 minutes *even if the wound again bleeds.* The blood must not be cut off from the injured member for longer.

Large wounds of the abdomen or chest should be treated with a mild antiseptic, such as boric-acid solution, or peroxide, and a wet dressing containing the same solution placed to cover the entire area.

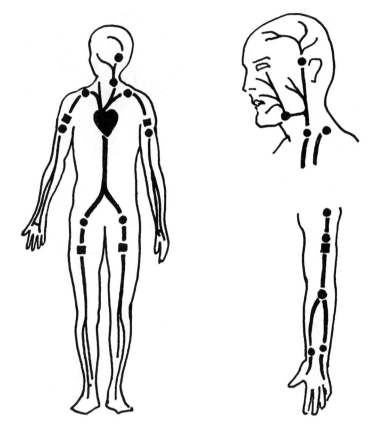

● Point for applying digital pressure

■ Point for applying tourniquet

Figure 1702

Under no circumstances should the first-aider attempt to push pro-truding organs back into the body. The physician only has the knowl-edge and experience to do this properly. Every severe wound needs a physician's attention.

Shock

1703. Shock of varying intensity follows all accidents and may be serious enough to cause death. If shock is not already present, the victim should be treated for prevention of shock by giving the same treatment as for shock. It may be assumed that it is present if the following symptoms appear or any combination of them:

Color: face gray; lips pale; nails blue.

Pulse fast and weak.

Cold sweat, especially on forehead and palms.

Exhaustion.

Violent shaking (chills).

Nausea or vomiting.

Treatment

Lay victim down; head low.

Apply heat (hot-water bottles, warm bricks or plates, wrap in blankets).

Stimulants: Aromatic spirits of ammonia, hot coffee or hot tea. Never force an unconscious person to drink. If he is unconscious, an ammonia ampule, or smelling salts, or aromatic spirits should be introduced under the nose.

Warning. Do not give a stimulant in the case of a severe head injury, or in cases of severe bleeding, until after bleeding has ceased.

Fainting

1704. The symptoms and treatment are similar to those for shock, except that they need not be so vigorous. Fainting can often be prevented by lowering the head (as below the knees while sitting down) and by forced coughing.

Bandages

1705. Bandages are of cloth or gauze of various shapes, used for any of the following purposes:

To hold dressings and compresses in place.

To hold splints in place.

To control bleeding by pressure.

To support, as a sling, a broken member.

The triangular bandage has many uses, open or folded as a cravat.

It is about 36 inches square, diagonally folded. It is never used directly on a wound under any circumstances.

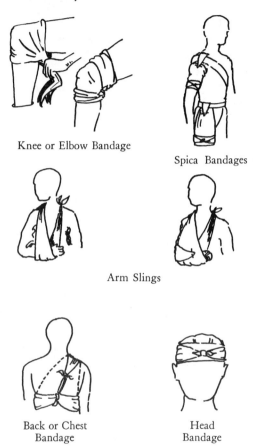

Knee or Elbow Bandage

Spica Bandages

Arm Slings

Back or Chest
Bandage

Head
Bandage

Figure 1705. Bandaging

The roller bandage is of various widths, and is used for the binding of injured toes and fingers.

Bandages of any kind are made tight enough to hold the dressing, but never tight enough to stop the circulation. They are never applied wet, nor applied and then wetted, as shrinking will occur which will stop circulation. After bandaging, frequent inspection is necessary to see that the wound has not swelled and so cause undue tightness.

Compresses and Dressings

1706. These are sterilized cloth swatches to be placed directly upon the wound after it has been made ready for dressing and bandaging. They are assumed to be sterile if the wrapping has not been broken, and if the first-aider has not fingered or dropped them before applying. Do not open until needed; then place upon the wound immediately.

Splints

1707. Splints are materials of wood, wire, paper, etc., used to prevent broken bones from moving at the point of fracture. They may be improvised from any rigid object or material (rolled magazines and newspapers, sail battens, floor board, oars, etc.).

Splints must be long enough to prevent movement of the joints above and below the fracture, and as wide as the thickness of the limb.

In applying, the splint should be padded, having first been measured on the sound limb (not the injured one). The most comfortable position for the victim will be the one in which you find him, and he should be splinted in exactly that position. Do not attempt to reduce the fracture—you may cause additional damage. If the limb is deformed put a pillow or a sweater under it so that it can be fastened above and below the joints on either side of the break. Use a roller bandage or a wide strip of cloth, not rope or small stuff, and immobilize the break by making the sound parts of the limb fast to the splint. Square knots are used, the knot being tied against the splint, not the limb. No binding is placed near the fracture as swelling will occur here very soon.

Fractures in which the bone protrudes are treated as wounds and are compound fractures. The first-aider should never attempt to set bones.

Fractures

1708. A fracture is a broken bone or bones.

A simple fracture is one in which the broken bone does not pierce the skin. There is no danger from infection.

A compound fracture is one in which the broken bone does pierce the skin. There is great danger of both bone and flesh infection.

The first-aider must use care that improper handling of the injured person does not make a compound fracture of a simple one.

SIMPLE FRACTURE

Symptoms

The victim may have heard or felt the bone snap.

Pain at the point of fracture.

Tenderness at the point of fracture.

The limb deformed.

Voluntary movement limited or completely lost.

Swelling.

Shock.

Treatment

Apply splints.

Move only as necessary.

Lay the patient down if possible.

Treat for shock.

Transport to doctor (splinted), or call doctor (before splinting).

NOTE: If in doubt, treat as for fracture.

COMPOUND FRACTURE

Symptoms

The same as for a simple fracture PLUS:

A wound from the break out.

Protruding bone.

Bleeding.

Severe shock.

Treatment

Treat as for a wound.

After bandaging, treat as for a simple fracture.

WARNING: Never apply water to a compound fracture.

1709. Fractured Ribs

Symptoms

Pain on breathing following injury.

Tenderness at point of fracture.

Treatment

Apply cravat bandages, hauled quite tightly, with the victim in full expiration.

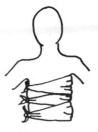

Figure 1709

1710. Fracture of the Upper Arm

Figure 1710

Use two padded splints. Place the arm in a narrow sling, and bind the arm to the body with a wide cravat bandage.

1711. Fracture of the Forearm and Wrist

Figure 1711

Use two padded splints, back and front. Place in a sling with the thumb up and the hand raised slightly above the elbow.

1712. Fracture of the Collarbone

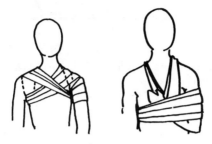

Figure 1712

Apply an arm sling, raised high. Bind the arm to the body.

1713. Fracture of the Elbow

Figure 1713

Splint the upper and lower arms; then place in a sling. But never force the elbow into a right-angle position if it does not do so easily.

1714. Fracture of the Leg

Figure 1714

Use two splints, well padded, top and bottom. Roll in a blanket or bed pad.

1715. Fracture of the Kneecap

Figure 1715

Use one splint on the back of the leg. Place **extra** padding under the knee and at the heel.

1716. Fracture of the Thigh

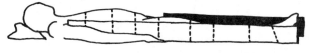

Figure 1716

Use two splints—one from the armpit to the heel on the outer side, and the other from the crotch to the heel. These should be heavy ($\frac{3}{4}'' \times 5''$) and well padded. In emergencies in which long splints are not to be found, use the short splint only and bind the injured leg to the sound one.

Fracture of the Skull

1717.

Symptoms

Bruise (likely).

Bleeding from the ears, nose, or eyes.

Depressed bone.

Dizziness.

Loss of consciousness.

Repeated vomiting.

Double vision (likely).

Treatment

Lay the victim down with the head elevated.

Treat for shock, but *do not give any stimulant.*

Do not attempt to stop the bleeding of the ears unless it is excessive. Check the bleeding of the bruise or wound, being careful not to place too much pressure on the compress, and thus on the brain. Cold cloths on the head will help.

There is always a question to the first-aider whether such an injury is a concussion or a fracture or both. Great care is required, and *immediate medical assistance and hospitalization*.

Dislocations

1718. A dislocation needs a physician's care at once. Cold may be applied to the joint. Do not attempt to reset the joint.

Sprains

1719. A sprain should be elevated. Cold should be applied; and after several hours hot water may be applied by soaking. Epsom salts in the water will aid. The joint should be kept at rest.

INJURIES DUE TO HEAT AND COLD

Burns

1720. Burns may be caused by dry heat and wet heat; when due to the latter, they are called scalds.

Burns are divided into three degrees, depending upon their severity.

Skin reddened	First degree
Skin blistered	Second degree
Deep burns, cooking, or charring	Third degree

Treatment of first-degree burns:

The skin is not broken, making strict antiseptic measures unnecessary. (However, many first-degree burns later become second-degree burns.)

A good burn ointment is indicated; then proper dressing. These include vaseline, vaseline mixed with baking soda into a paste, carbolated petrolatum, olive, castor, or lubricating oil, butter or frying fats.

Cold water will effectively relieve the pain.

Never use iodine on a burn.

Treatment of second- and third-degree burns:

Burns of these degrees should be treated as open wounds and only dressings known to be sterile used on them. Soak in tap water, luke warm, with 3 tablespoons of baking soda or Epsom salts. A 5% solution of tannic acid in water may be used to soak the burn if not in the area of the head or hands. Boric acid, once a popular treatment agent, is no longer considered effective. Very strong tea (which is about 5% tannic acid), if freshly made, is effective. Do not remove waxlike or metallic substances if within the burn. Do not break blisters. The first-aider's job, in a burn case, is to keep the burn moist and ready for medical treatment.

It is best to use one of the solutions if possible, as burn ointments sometimes prevent certain other treatments which the physician may consider necessary. Great care must be exercised in removing clothing in the region of a burn or scald. If it adheres to the skin, cut around it, and let the physician remove it from the burned areas. Do not use butter, lubricating oils or greases, or vaseline on a second-degree burn unless the solutions are unavailable.

Shock is usual in second- and third-degree burns, and the first-aider should treat for it whether it is present at the moment or not.

Sunburn

1721. Sunburn is treated as a first-degree burn, occasionally as a second-degree burn. Calomine lotion is soothing. If blistering develops, as in second-degree burns, treat as a wound, liable to infection. If fever occurs as a result of an extensive sunburn, medical aid is required.

Sunstroke and Heat Exhaustion

1722. These two conditions are often confused. The comparison below should be studied and treatment used only after a positive diagnosis has been made.

SUNSTROKE	HEAT EXHAUSTION
CAUSE	CAUSE
Exposure to heat—particularly sun's rays.	Exposure to heat—either sun's rays or indoor heat.

SYMPTOMS

SYMPTOMS

Headache.

Red face.

Skin hot and dry, no sweating.

Pulse strong and rapid.

Temperature, very high.

Unconscious, usually.

TREATMENT

Lying with head elevated.

Cool body with bath or cold applications.

No stimulants.

Pale face.

Skin moist and cool, sweating profuse.

Pulse weak.

Temperature, low.

Often faint, but seldom remain unconscious for more than a very few minutes.

TREATMENT

Lying with head level or low.

Often requires external heat.

Stimulants always indicated.

Frostbite

1723.

Symptoms

Considerable pain if the hands or feet are frosted; less or none if the ears or nose.

The frosted area becomes a grayish white, the tissues actually containing ice.

Treatment

Very gentle and slow thawing, in cool air or cold water or by applying heat under the armpit. Wrap the frosted member in blankets of *room temperature*. Avoid quick thawing at all costs; never thaw at a heating unit.

WARNING: After freezing, snow rubbed on the frozen part will not result in thawing.

Exposure to Cold

1724.

Symptoms

Numbness—movement difficult or impossible.

Drowsiness, failing eyesight.

Staggering.

Treatment

Place the victim in a *cool* room. Give artificial respiration if breathing has ceased. Rub the limbs briskly with cool cloths. Raise the room temperature as the victim commences to react; then give hot drinks and place in a warm bed.

COMMON EMERGENCIES

Foreign Bodies in the Eye

1725.

Treatment

Do not rub.

Close the eye. Grasp the lashes of the upper lid and pull out and down over the lower lid, causing tears, and the likelihood that the foreign body will be washed into the corner of the eye, from whence it can be easily removed. If seen, the object may be removed with the tip of a clean cloth or sterile bandage.

Failure to so locate it should indicate an inspection of the inside of the lids. The lower lid is retracted and examined, with the victim looking up; the upper lid is rolled back over a match or toothpick, with the victim looking down; the object is then removed as above.

Complete failure to remove the offending object should see the victim placed in the doctor's care immediately. Meanwhile, a cold wet compress will help, and the placing of a few drops of mineral, olive, or castor oil in the eye will ease the pain.

All chemicals reaching the eye should be washed out thoroughly with large quantities of water, using an eyecup if possible.

Foreign Bodies in the Throat

1726.

Treatment

Immediate removal of the foreign body.

Hanging victim by the feet or knees and sharply slapping him between the shoulders will often dislodge the object.

If breathing is severely labored or has ceased, give artificial respiration at once. When calling for help, report the nature of the complaint so that the physician can bring the proper instruments. Ordinarily these are not carried.

Do not probe with a finger unless the object can be seen and it is apparent that a *sure* hold may be taken on it.

Do not eat crackers or dry bread or drink water until there is a certainty that such measures will dislodge the object.

Hiccough

1727.

Treatment

Hold the breath for extended periods.

Drink water very slowly.

Pull the tongue out for 30 seconds as far as possible.

Breath in and out of an ordinary brown paper bag for four or five minutes.

These methods failing, vomiting may be encouraged by giving an emetic followed by soda in water, or milk of magnesia.

Severe or persistent hiccoughing requires medical care.

Food Poisoning (Ptomaine)

1728.

Symptoms

Discomfort in the upper abdomen.

Pain and cramps.

Nausea and vomiting; purging.

Prostration.

Treatment

Dilute by swallowing large quantities of water.

Induce vomiting. (An emetic plus tickling the back of the throat will cause immediate vomiting.)

Treat for shock.

Toothache

1729.

Search for cavities and clean out, using a toothpick and a bit of cotton.

Apply and pack in cotton soaked in oil of cloves.

If infection of the tooth is suspected, apply heat or cold, whichever relie/es pain best.

Cramps

1730. WARNING: Never treat for common cramps (diarrhea) until assured that the complaint is not appendicitis.

Appendicitis is to be suspected if the pain is general over all or most of the abdomen, attended by nausea and vomiting (possibly of only short duration), and accompanied by pain, tenderness, and rigidity in the lower right part of the abdomen, and slight rise in temperature.
Treatment

If Appendicitis Is Suspected

Put such persons to bed at once.

Get immediate medical aid. (*See* chapter on Signaling.)

Do not give a laxative.

Do not give food.

Do not apply heat to abdomen.

Operation at once is indicated, and the patient must be sent ashore in the *quickest possible manner*.

If Appendicitis Is Not Present

Do not attempt to stop diarrhea at once.

Give plenty of water.

Withhold food for 24 hours.

Treatment of the Ordinary Cold

1731. While not generally serious, the ordinary cold is common and will seldom send the boatman ashore for medical aid. Prompt measures will often break it up in its early stages.

Avoid unnecessary exposure.

Drink plenty of fluids.

Take bicarbonate of soda (baking soda). A full teaspoonful in a full glass of water every two hours for three or four doses.

Take any good laxative but not a violent one.

Take a hot bath and a hot drink; then turn in. Do not get chilled.

Gargle (if the throat is sore) with the hottest water possible to which has been added salt. Gargle often. Sea water which has been first boiled is satisfactory.

Rest is the best remedy known.

If the cold persists, or if a serious cough develops and the temperature remains above normal, seek medical aid. Any cold which seems to be traveling toward the chest or lungs and is *more than a head cold* should be regarded as serious.

A person having a cold should always sleep alone. He should guard against coughing or breathing heavily near other persons. Individual towels, utensils, and bedding should be provided, and these sterilized before being used by others. Frequent washing of the hands by the victim and his mates will prevent the spread of the cold.

1732. A severe cold, especially following exposure or injury, may develop into pneumonia.

Symptoms

Severe chill and rapidly rising temperature.

Head and body pains, particularly a stabbing pain in the chest.

Bloody or "rusty" sputum (sticky in nature).

Delirium.

Treatment (By a physician *immediately*)

Plenty of fresh air.

A fluid or semifluid diet.

Bowels must be kept open (by enemas, if necessary).

If the pulse is weak, give strong tea or coffee.

Under no circumstances attempt to nurse through a pneumonia case. Special drugs and care are needed.

Removing Fishhooks in the Flesh

1733. Paint the exposed part of the hook with iodine; push it entirely through the flesh; cut off the eye with a nippers and draw it free. If it is necessary to draw it out toward the eye, nip off the hook beyond the curved part, paint it with iodine and draw it out backwards.

Make the wound bleed and treat as an open wound.

Artificial Respiration

1734. Certain accidents, particularly drowning, cause the breathing to stop before the heart stops beating. Artificial respiration should follow immediately upon discovering that breathing has ceased after submersion, gas exposure (asphyxiation), or electric shock. Do not waste time trying to detect pulse or heartbeat. Apply artificial respiration at once (if possible sending someone for a doctor), and keep it up until the victim begins to breathe for himself, or until a physician pronounces him dead, or until he appears to be dead beyond any doubt.

THE MOUTH-TO-MOUTH METHOD

It is generally agreed that the mouth-to-mouth (or mouth-to-nose) technique is the most practical method of artificial respiration, particularly when the rescuer is alone.

1. If there is any foreign matter in the victim's mouth, wipe it out quickly with your fingers or a cloth wrapped around your fingers.

2. Lay the victim on his back. Tilt his head back so that his chin is pointing upward. Use your hands to push or pull his lower jaw forward so that it juts out. This procedure moves the base of the tongue away from the back of the throat and prevents obstruction of the air passage.

3. Place your mouth tightly over the victim's mouth. Pinch the victim's nostrils shut or close his nostrils with your cheek. Blow into the victim's mouth.

4. Remove your mouth, turn your head to the side and listen for the return rush of air that indicates an air exchange. If the exchange occurs, continue to blow into the victim's mouth. For an adult, blow vigorously at the rate of about 12 breaths per minute. For a child, use shallow breaths at the rate of about 20 per minute.

5. If an air exchange does not occur, recheck the position of the head and jaw, and repeat blowing efforts. If there is still an obstruction, turn the victim quickly on his side and administer several sharp slaps between his shoulder blades to dislodge foreign matter. Again remove foreign matter from his mouth with your fingers, readjust the head and jaw position and repeat blowing efforts. Continue as long as necessary, until the victim begins to breathe for himself.

THE BACK PRESSURE-ARM LIFT (HOLGER-NIELSON) METHOD

If the mouth-to-mouth method is not used, a manual method of artificial respiration must be applied. There are several manual methods, and the nature of the victim's injury often determines the method that is most effective. The Back Pressure-Arm Lift (Holger-Nielson) Method is generally recommended.

1. Wipe foreign matter out of the victim's mouth quickly with your fingers.

2. Put the victim on his stomach. Bend his elbows and place his hands one on top of the other. Turn his head to the side and place it on his hands. Extend his head as far as possible and make sure that his jaw juts out.

3. Kneel directly above the head of the victim. Put your hands on the flat of his back so that your open palms lie just below an imaginary line running between the victim's armpits.

4. Rock forward until your arms are almost vertical, allowing the weight of the upper part of your body to exert a steady, even, downward pressure on the victim's back.

5. Release the pressure and rock slowly backward, moving your hands to the victim's arms just above his elbows.

6. Leaning backward, lift the victim's arms upward and toward you until you feel resistance and tension in his shoulders. Then lower his arms to the ground. This completes the cycle. Immediately resume the back pressure position and repeat the cycle at the rate of about 12 times per minute. Check the head and jaw position frequently and watch for any obstructions. Continue the cycle until the victim begins to breathe for himself.

POINTS TO REMEMBER

1. Always check for tight clothing around the victim's neck, chest or waist and loosen immediately.

2. Do not move the victim any more than is absolutely necessary until he is breathing normally of his own volition. If he must be moved, because of extreme weather conditions, etc., artificial respiration should continue during the time he is being moved.

3. Always be alert to any obstruction that blocks the victim's breathing. This is particularly necessary when the victim has swallowed great quantities of water. If regurgitation occurs, immediately clear the mouth of any foreign matter and resume artificial respiration.

4. If a second rescuer is on the scene, he should continually check the victim's mouth for obstructions and see that his jaw is kept in the jutting-out position. He should also be prepared to take over the artificial respiration.

5. If it is necessary to change operators during the course of artificial respiration, it must be done without losing the rhythm of the

respiration.

6. When the victim first begins to breathe, time the rhythm of the artificial respiration to coincide.

7. As soon as the victim starts breathing of his own volition, stop artificial respiration. But if his recovery is only temporary and he stops breathing again, resume artificial respiration at once.

8. Recovery of the victim is normally rapid, except in certain cases such as electric shock, drug poisoning or carbon monoxide poisoning. The rescuer should be prepared, however, to continue artificial respiration as long as necessary—sometimes for many hours.

9. Keep the victim from being chilled at all times.

10. When the victim revives he should be kept quiet, warm and otherwise treated for shock until the doctor arrives.

11. A doctor's care is necessary during the recovery period to prevent respiratory or other disturbances that may develop. If a doctor is not on the scene, the victim should be taken to one when he has resumed normal breathing and can be moved safely.

Transportation of the Injured

1735. Unless it is absolutely necessary, it is wisest not to move the injured person. Provide comfort as best as possible (pillows, cover, heat, or shade), and wait for the physician.

If removal is essential, the victim, in every case of injury except to the arms or hands, should be transported in a lying position. Lacking a stretcher, the following improvised carrying devices may be used.

1. A blanket. Carried by four or six persons under the command of a leader, who directs the movements and synchronizes them.

2. Shirts, overcoats, or a mattress cover might be rove over two oars or short spars, thus making a "stretcher."

3. Use a pipe berth, a hatch cover, or a floor rack of a small boat.

In transporting an injured person from ship to ship in a rough sea, lash him to a firm rigid base (hatch cover, battened planks, etc.). He may be placed in a small light dinghy and the dinghy regarded as the stretcher. Coast Guard rescue planes and ships have special basket stretchers which will be brought to the ship by the boarding party.

First-Aid Kits

1736. A good first-aid kit contains such articles as the following:

1-inch compress on adhesive in individual packages.
* Sterile gauze squares—about 3″ × 3″—in individual packages.
* Assorted sterile bandage in individual packages.
* Triangular bandages.
  Sterile gauze in individual packages of about one square yard.
  Roll of ½-inch adhesive.
* Burn ointment.
  Inelastic tourniquet.
* Aromatic spirits of ammonia.
  Scissors.
  3-inch splinter forceps.
  1-inch and 2-inch roller bandages.
  Wire or thin board splints.
  Castor oil or mineral oil, for use in eyes. This should be sterile; may be obtained in small tubes.

The boat kit may well include the following items also:

Thermometer	Olive oil
Aspirin tablets	Tannic acid powder
Oil of cloves	Eyecup
Bicarbonate of soda	Boric acid
Epsom salts	

A first-aid kit is useless unless kept in order and stocked up. Ship inspection should include the checking of the kit and the immediate replacing of items used.

Medicine Chest

1737. Few small boats require a medicine chest. However, should one be required, the following representative list will suffice in addition to the first-aid kit for coastwise needs. The use of these drugs and medicines is not recommended except under unusual emergency circumstances, or as directed by radio or signaling by medical authorities.

* These items provide a simple first-aid kit for canoes and open boats.

CAUTION.—Preparations containing opium, such as paregoric, laudanum, camphor and opium pills, etc., should be given only when absolutely necessary as they are habit-forming.

Antiseptics and Disinfectants

Bichloride of mercury
  (7½-grain tablets and bulk)
Chloride of lime
Tincture of iodine
Solution of cresol (compound)
Formalin
Argyrol solution (20%)
Mercurochrome solution (1%)
Picric acid (½% solution)
Cocaine solution (1%)

Ointments

Vaseline
Mercury ointment (External use only)
Ichthyol ointment (20%)
Sulphur ointment
Glycerine base burn ointment

Liniments

Turpentine
Camphorated oil

Permanganate of potash
  (1-grain tablets or crystal form)
Soap liniment

Powders

Calomel (½ grain)
Boric acid
Bismuth subnitrate

Cathartics

Compound cathartic pills
Castor oil
Epsom salts

Internal Medicines

Aromatic spirits of ammonia
Bicarbonate of soda (baking soda)
Bromide of potash
Copaiba and Santal oil (5-grain tablets)
Sweet spirits of niter
Ipecac (alcresta) (5-grain tablets)
Aspirin (5-grain tablets)
Quinine sulphate (5-grain capsules)
Paregoric

Shipboard Sanitation

1738. Any boat, especially a cruising boat having living quarters in the usual cabin forecastle, etc., may become infested. The presence of any object carrying in, or on it, fleas, lice, bedbugs, etc., and rats and mice is a potential "infested object." It may harbor and spread dangerous diseases.

Most small boats have no serious pest problem. However, the boat which berths near large foreign vessels, or at waterside docks, shipyards, or bulkheads known to harbor rats may very easily become the home of one of these pests not uncommon in the large vessels of the merchant marine.

No government regulations for the control of small-boat sanitation exist, save when that boat has entered from a foreign port. Such a vessel must present a consular bill of health certifying the state of any quarantinable disease at the port of clearance. Quarantine may be required upon recommendation of the health officer making the inspection of the boat's crew.

1739. The disinfection of an infested boat can be accomplished by boiling or steaming (at 20 pounds pressure for 15 minutes) all objects, clothing, etc., from the boat or the part of the boat which is suspect. With cabins stripped bare, bulkheads, ceilings, decks, and all furniture are washed with a disinfectant. Bichloride of mercury (1:500) is recommended. Mix one part bichloride of mercury with 500 parts of sea water. A 5% carbolic-acid solution (50 parts of carbolic acid to 50 parts of alcohol, mixed and added to 900 parts of sea water) is also effective.

1740. Fumigation is not practical for the small boat. Fumigation is used for disinfestation, not disinfection. The average small boat can be freed of infestation by simpler methods.

1741. Rats and mice can be trapped on small boats with ordinary baited traps set in the galley or near food lockers. Flooding the boat by opening sea cocks, letting the water reach the level of the floor boards, will drive these pests into places where they can be caught. In laying to any dock or wharf infested by rodents, always put out booms and have rat guards on them and all hawsers; also draw in the gangplank whenever possible, especially at night.

1742. Fleas normally live on rats and mice as well as on the ship's pet. Animals which have died of the bubonic plague (Black Death) may be considered as having freed fleas whose bite may transmit the disease to man. Fleas can be gotten rid of by pouring boiling water in crevices and cracks in sleeping quarters. Kerosene so applied will also kill them. A very effective method is to place a small animal on board for several days (cat, dog, or monkey) and then fumigate the animal. The fleas will have taken the animal as host. Bedding should be boiled or steamed.

1743. Cockroaches carry disease. Commercial powders will rid the boat of them.

1744. Lice are found on human beings and may transmit disease from diseased to other persons. The person having head lice, body lice, or pubic lice (crabs) should be deloused, his clothing and bedding disinfested, and his surroundings disinfected.

1745. Bedbugs are gotten rid of as fleas by pouring boiling water or kerosene in cracks and disinfesting clothing and bedding.

1746. Flies and mosquitoes both carry disease. Sanitation and comfort are both achieved by complete screening of every opening in the boat. The unscreened boat may control these pests by liberal use of antifly sprays or an insect repellent placed at all openings.

Drinking Water

1747. Clean and sterile drinking water is absolutely necessary on shipboard, especially on long offshore cruises. The secret is clean tanks and clean piping, and a sterilizing agent in the water, no matter how pure when first tanked.

Tanks should be mechanically cleaned often (through the handholes) and then filled with a one-ounce solution of hypochlorate of lime to each 300 gallons of water. Pipes are filled as well. Let it stand for 24 hours; then discharge, flush, and fill with pure water.

1748. Drinking water should be treated in one of the following ways to assure disinfection and sterilization:

A. Add one-quarter teaspoonful of dry hypochlorate of lime (bleaching powder) to 50 gallons of water. It will not affect taste.

B. One tablespoonful of tincture of iodine to 50 gallons of water. Stir and do not use for 30 minutes thereafter.

Small boats which have tanks not readily cleaned should use tank water exclusively for cooking and washing and carry drinking water in glass containers, kept clean. Water should never be carried in copper tanks unless the tank has been tinned inside.

PART VI
CUSTOM AND ETIQUETTE

⚓

⚓

CHAPTER XVIII

NAUTICAL ETIQUETTE AND FLAGS

FLAG ETIQUETTE

The United States Ensign

1801. This (the regular United States flag) is properly flown by all except documented yachts, which fly the yacht ensign. It is properly flown only at anchor, and shown under way when passing or saluting other vessels, lighthouses, or signal stations, or upon entering a harbor, or fortification.

It is flown from a taffrail staff on all boats at anchor. A sailing vessel having a boom which interferes with such a staff carries the staff slightly to starboard of the boom. Under way, a powerboat may carry the ensign from a gaff of the aftermost mast. Under sail, the ensign is flown from the peak of the aftermost sail. Marconi-rigged boats carry the ensign about two thirds of the length of the leech from the clew, or about where the flag would be were the rig gaff headed.

It is always hoisted by halyards and is two-blocked. It may be dipped for saluting when required. If it is flown at half-mast (as on Memorial Day from 8 A.M. until noon), it is first hoisted fully aloft, then lowered to the half-mast position. The ensign is always broken out flying, never bundled into a ball, and broken from stops or halyard hitches arranged to release it after hoisting aloft.

The ensign is flown from 8 A.M. until sunset; never at night.

It is never used as a signal of any kind, save with one exception. It is universally recognized as a distress signal if flown from any part of a vessel upside down (canon to the bottom).

The ensign should be flown when entering a foreign port or foreign territorial waters, or when meeting any vessel on the high seas. Showing the ensign, however, does not exempt or protect any vessel from further revealing her identity. Before law, the papers and documents

615

alone reveal identity, and the flag in itself is not sufficient proof of nationality to any challenging vessel or station.

The Yacht Ensign

1802. This is the familiar ensign, exactly like the United States ensign, except that the canon contains a circle of 13 stars and a fouled anchor, in white against a blue field. It is authorized by law as a yacht signal for documented yachts of 16 tons or over, and indicates that such a yacht is exempt by law from certain port clearing and entering regulations.

However, its use has become general for all yachts, and custom has sanctioned it as an ensign replacing the United States ensign on vessels of the pleasure class. When used in place of the standard United States ensign it must be accorded the same respect and flown from the usual positions on shipboard.

Its use in territorial or inland waters is in no way frowned upon by law or by custom. However, any vessel sailing foreign, or sailing upon the high seas (*see* paragraph 731, Chapter VII, for boundaries) should meticulously observe the law, flying the United States ensign only and the yacht ensign, *in addition,* as a signal, if documented as a yacht.

The Jack

1803. This flag is similar to the canon and stars of the United States ensign and is, strictly speaking, a naval flag and not a yachting or small-boat flag. It is flown only from a jack staff—a staff on the cap of the bowsprit—never from the bow staff of any powerboat. It may be properly flown from the bow staff of a two-masted sailing vessel or auxiliary (which assumes the presence of a bowsprit), or from the jack staff of a clipper-bowed steam vessel.

It is hoisted only on festive occasions, or Sundays and holidays, and *never* under way; nor is it shown at any time unless the boat is ready for visitors and all deck and other work done, wash taken in, and owner and crew "off duty."

The jack has fallen into disuse among small-boat men.

The Private Signal or Owner's Flag

1804. This is generally a swallowtail upon which is worked certain devices and colors, in patterns selected by the owner, and which serves as an identification signal.

By mutual agreement, the signal is designed so as not to duplicate any other private signal, and, before adopting it, the design is submitted to the publishers of *Lloyd's Registry of American Yachts* who rule upon the appropriateness of the design. When accepted it may be registered with this publisher, who then publishes it, together with other American owner's flags. The publication is therefore the key for identifying owner's flags.

Owner's signals are located in *Lloyd's Register* by simply noting the color combinations of the observed signal. All color combinations are shown together (such as all the white and blue flags, or all the red and black flags). In the correct color-combination lists will be found the identifying designs, devices, or initials, and the name and other information concerning the owner of the signal.

It is flown from the points shown in the diagrams following.

The Burgee

1805. The burgee, or club flag, is generally a pennant upon which have been worked the colors and devices selected by yacht clubs (or other clubs having a yachting division) as their own identifying signal. Its design and selection and registry follow the *Lloyd's Register* procedure of the private signal, and club burgees are shown in that publication.

It is flown from the points shown in the diagrams following.

Officer's Flag

1806. This is a flag of varying design and color flown by a yacht club officer on his own boat. It is flown only upon a boat belonging to the same club as the officer flying it; never, for example, when on a cruise with another club. It flies night and day as long as the yacht is in commission, and is hoisted to the points diagramed hereinafter. Some clubs show this flag from the yardarm of the shore signal mast when the officer whose flag it is is on the grounds.

The officer's flag becomes his private signal and is flown as the private signal while the owner holds club office.

Owner Absent Flag

1807. A blue rectangular flag is shown from the starboard yardarm or spreader to indicate that the owner is not on board. It is never flown under way, whether the owner is on board or not. At night, the signal is made by a blue electric light or lantern, hung in the same place.

Guest Flag

1808. A blue rectangular flag, diagonally crossed by a white stripe, is used to show that the boat is being used by guests of the owner. It is flown from the starboard yardarm or spreader during their stay but is lowered at night, whether or not the guests are on board. It is flown *under way* and at anchor.

Owner's Meal Flag

1809. Flown from the starboard yardarm or spreader during daylight hours, this white rectangular flag indicates the fact that the owner is at table and not to be disturbed. Flown only when at anchor.

Crew's Meal Pennant

1810. A red pennant, flown from the foremost mast, at the port yardarm or spreader, indicating that the crew is at table and cannot, for the moment, be expected to render usual services. Flown only when at anchor and during daylight hours.

Other Flags

1811. A night or wind pennant is sometimes hoisted to the truck of the aftermost mast as a hawk. This pennant may also be used during daylight hours as a hawk, while under way.

A rectangular yellow flag is used as the quarantine flag.

A rectangular red flag is hoisted when fuel is being taken aboard as a warning. All near-by fires are put out and smoking on or in the vicinity of the boat that is fueling is prohibited.

Dressing ship is done with the International Code flags, bent alternatingly, a flag and a pennant, on national holidays and for special occasions, such as a regatta or a launching. (Figure 1813.) The ensign, the private signal, or the burgee are never part of such a hoist.

Ship is dressed while at anchor only; never while under way. It is highly improper to dress ship at any time with college banners, or any flags having letters or words, and especially advertising pennants such as those sometimes supplied with stock boats.

1812. The ensign may be half-masted on any day of national mourn-

COMMODORE   **VICE-COMMODORE**

WHITE ON   WHITE ON
BLUE   RED

REAR COMMODORE FLEET CAPTAIN
RED ON WHITE   BLUE ON WHITE

Figure 1811. Common Forms of Yacht Club Officers' Flags

ing and always on Memorial Day. The burgee may be half-masted upon the death of a club officer or member. The private signal may be half-masted upon the death of the owner or a member of his immediate family.

When half-masting any flag or signal, it is always first hoisted and then secured at half-mast. Upon lowering, it is first run up; then lowered and taken in.

1813. Flags are displayed from 8 A. M. until sunset. It is considered courteous to take the time of making and lowering from the yacht club in whose harbor the boat is lying or from the boat of the senior officer present. The usual signal is a gun.

Flags are raised in the following order; ensign, burgee, and private signal; and lowered in the reverse order. If sufficient hands are present, all flags should be handled simultaneously, immediately upon the signal. Upon lowering, the night pennant is sent up at once and anchor

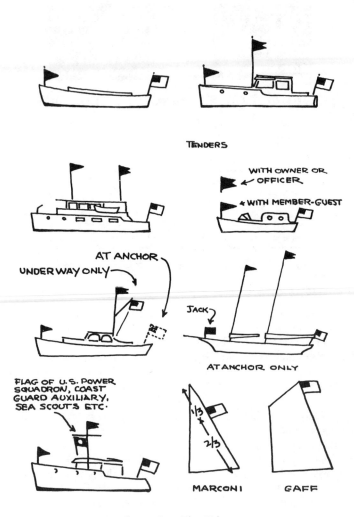

KEY · ◻ = ENSIGN ▶ = PRIVATE SIGNAL

TENDERS

WITH OWNER OR OFFICER
WITH MEMBER-GUEST

AT ANCHOR
UNDER WAY ONLY
JACK

AT ANCHOR ONLY

FLAG OF U.S. POWER SQUADRON, COAST GUARD AUXILIARY, SEA SCOUTS ETC.

1/3
2/3
MARCONI
GAFF

Figure 1813. Flag Etiquette

620

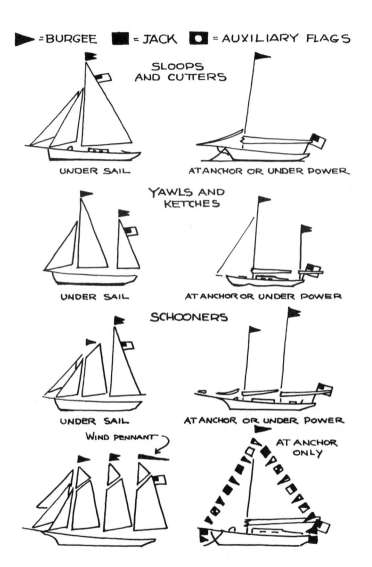

Figure 1813. Flag Etiquette (*continued*)

lights lighted and set. Power vessels generally show their range light as an anchor light. Sail vessels hang a lantern from the forestay.

If a passage is started before 8 A. M. or finished after sunset, it is proper to have flags set until coming to anchor, but under no circumstances are they to be flown during darkness (officer's flags and wind pennant excepted).

Salutes

1814. Formal salutes are made with a gun or the ensign. In any case the junior always salutes first and is answered promptly by the senior, and in the same manner in which it is made.

A gun salute is one gun.

A flag salute is one dip of the ensign.

It is usual to salute American and foreign naval vessels.

It is courtesy to salute senior officers upon meeting afloat or upon their arrival at an anchorage, and to salute upon arriving at the home anchorage of another yacht club.

Gun salutes are never made on Sunday.

No salute is ever made by whistle or foghorn.

The standard three blasts, calling a shore boat or club ferry, is not a salute and is permissible.

It is a nice courtesy to hand salute the quarter-deck upon boarding any boat.

Boat salutes are made to seniors by breaking the stroke for a moment and resting upon the oars, or by tossing the oars, or, in a sailboat, by letting the sheet fly for a moment. Boats (as power tenders) salute with the ensign. (NOTE: No rowingboat rowing less than four oars flies the ensign, and therefore salutes as provided above.)

Boat Hails

1815. Upon coming alongside a boat (as in a dinghy or tender) the hail is generally "Boat Ahoy!"

It is proper to reply as follows:

If a flag officer—"Fleet."

If an owner (or guest)—"Name of your boat."

Paid officers—"Aye, aye."

Crew member—"Hello."

If passing—"Passing."

Custom

1816. The owner and his guests (and his paid officers, if licensed) use the starboard gangway (or ladder or boat steps) upon boarding or leaving the boat.

The paid crew, shore, mail, ice and service boats use the port side.

Both the bridge and the quarter-deck are sacred to the owner (captain or master) and are not to be entered without invitation. The starboard side of the quarter-deck and the starboard bridge wing are reserved for the owner, and chairs or settees located there are not to be used except by invitation, or after asking permission.

Paid hands, when off duty, remain forward, or in the forepeak quarters below. The usual call is a stroke on the bell, or one short blast of the whistle. Engineers remain in the engine room or on the forecastle deck. Stewards remain within voice or buzzer call. Wash, sails, deck mops, etc., are dried forward. Crews swim from the forward deck and use the port side (when possible) for traversing the length of the boat.

Boat courtesies require that juniors board a small boat first and leave last. The boat owner is considered senior to all on board, of either sex or of any age, except in the event that a senior flag officer is on board, or a club member older than he.

Flag Etiquette on Shore

1817. The signal mast of a yacht club or other nautical shore station displays flags as follows:

	STAFF WITH YARD	STAFF WITH GAFF	STAFF WITH YARD AND GAFF
U.S. Ensign	Masthead	Gaff	Gaff
Burgee	Starboard yardarm	Masthead	Masthead
Jack	——	——	Port yardarm

The jack is flown only on Sundays and holidays. Flags are made at 8 A. M. and lowered (to a single gun) at sundown. The distinguishing colored light signals of the club are immediately raised after lowering the flags. The ensign is made first and lowered last. (*See* paragraph 1432, Chapter XIV, for folding the ensign.) Boat call or code signals are made to the port yardarm and lowered immediately upon being acknowledged by the boat called.

Racecourses

1818. While a boat racing has no legal rights over a boat not racing, it is courteous to not only give racing boats every right but to try to forecast the rights she may desire and *keep well out of her way.* Do not enter the limits, present or future, of any racecourse. Avoid any wave making or wash that might hinder the racing boats. Follow racing sailboats on the leeward side and well astern of the *last* boat. Keep turning points clear. Large vessels under sail should keep well clear of smaller racing sailboats, so as not to create eddies or disturb the free flow of the wind to the racing boat.

Yachting Uniform

1819. Service dress for formal or other appropriate wear is in general based on the rules relating to the subject of the New York Yacht Club.

The coat is a double-breasted navy-blue garment. The trousers are of the same material and without cuffs. For summer or tropical wear, an all-white suit may be worn, cut the same. Either the blue or white cap may be worn with the blue uniform, but the white uniform calls for only the white cap. Black shoes are worn with the blue uniform, and white shoes (not sneakers) worn with any uniform combination having white trousers. The blue-uniform jacket is often worn with white trousers.

The style of uniform, or "dress of the day," is indicated by the senior officer, and other offiers and members dress as he does. White and blue cap-tops are alternated upon orders from the senior officer, or by date, generally the white top indicated between May first and October first.

The formal yachting dress is worn at all regattas, when visiting a yacht club, and at all social occasions connected with cruising or yacht-club activities. Guests are received on board in the uniform as well as visiting officers of any yacht club. It is entirely appropriate when visiting customs or port officials on boat business.

A simple work uniform, usually of khaki, is prescribed by the code of many clubs for general service, especially for the owner-skipper, who may dispense with the formal dress except for the special social and other occasions noted above. The cap is worn with the work uniform, and footgear may be of the utility type.

Yacht Insignia for Cap and Uniform

1820. Members of yacht and similar nautical clubs (but not the United States Power Squadron or Sea Scouts) follow the general insignia rules given below.

Paid hands wear only the cap devices, in gold bullion, shown in Figure 1820. While these are actually officers' insignia, the paid hand on small boats, whose status is somewhere between crew and officer and who at times acts as each or both, is generally permitted by custom to wear them.

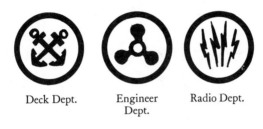

Deck Dept. Engineer Dept. Radio Dept.

Figure 1820. Paid Officers' Cap Insignia

Paid hands who serve as officers only (as on a large yacht) may wear the cap device shown in Figure 1820, also of gold bullion. Inside the wreath may be the owner's flag only, or the crossed owner's and club flag, both in enamel.

1821. The device of the club member but nonboatowner is the simplified insignia with the club disk, shown in Figure 1821, left. The right-hand device, same figure, is worn by the member who is a boatowner but not a club officer. Both are in gold bullion, with the club disk in enamel.

626 *The Boatman's Manual*

Cap insignia of
club member but
not boat owner

Cap insignia of club
member who is a
boat owner (not an
officer)

Figure 1821

1822. Club officers wear the same basic device, to which is added the gold-bullion devices showing rank, as in Figure 1822. The in-

★ ★ ★ Commodore
3 Stars

★ ★ Vice-Commodore
2 Stars

★ Rear Commodore
1 Star

Secretary
Maple Leaf

Treasurer
Acorn

OR M Measurer
Bar or "M"

Figure 1822. Cap Insignia worn in Addition to Crossed Anchors (Figure
1821) to Show Rank

Fleet Surgeon
Medical Cross

Race Committee
Vertical Anchor

Fleet Captain
Horizontal Anchor

Figure 1822. Cap Insignia worn in Addition to Crossed Anchors (Figure 1821) to Show Rank (*Continued*)

signia of rank is worn only during incumbency. Occasionally, local rules permit past flag officers to wear the insignia devices of rank, but in silver.

1823. Sleeve insignia (Figure 1823) is worn on the uniform jacket, both sleeves, as follows:

Figure 1823. Sleeve insignia of a Commodore

Commodore	four plain stripes, one stripe with trefoil, three stars
Vice-commodore	three " " " " " " two stars
Rear-commodore	two " " " " " " one star
All other flag officers	one " stripe " " " " no stars
Nonofficer member	" " " " " " " " "

(Past flag officers wear the stripes of their former office but not the stars.)

The Boatman's Manual

The sleeve braid is usually three eighths of an inch wide, and local regulations establish the distance between, the distance from the cuff and the size of the stars. Black stripes are worn on the blue-uniform jacket, and white stripes on the white-uniform jacket. The stars are gold in any case. Sleeve insignia are not worn on work-uniform jackets of any kind; nor on topcoats or storm clothing.

Military Insignia.

1824.

Boatmen often come in contact with Coast Guard or naval officers and their insignia of rank are therefore given in Figure 1824.

Warrant officers are addressed as chief or sir. Commissioned officers are addressed as sir until the rank of commander, after which they are addressed by rank (as Commander Jones, Admiral Smith, etc.).

Insignia of Navy and Coast Guard are alike.

Rank	Sleeve Insignia	Shoulder-Strap Insignia
Warrant Officer	¼ in. gold	On black background same width and type of stripes
Chief Warrant Officer	½ in. gold	Same as sleeve

(NOTE.—Warrant officer stripes are broken at 2 in. intervals by ½ in. dark-blue silk thread.)

Ensign	½ in. gold	Same as sleeve
Lieutenant (Junior Grade)	One ½ in. gold with one ¼ in. gold above	Same as sleeve
Lieutenant	Two ½ in. gold	Same as sleeve
Lieutenant Commander	Two ½ in. gold with one ¼ in. between	Same as sleeve
Commander	Three ½ in. gold	Same as sleeve
Captain	Four ½ in. gold	Same as sleeve
Rear Admiral	One 2 in. gold with one ½ in. gold above	Anchor with 2 stars on gold lace background
Vice-Admiral	One 2 in. gold with two ½ in. gold above	Anchor with 3 stars, etc.
Admiral	One 2 in. gold with three ½ in. gold above	Anchor with 4 stars, etc.

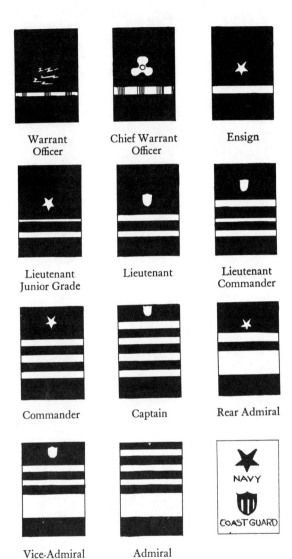

Warrant Officer

Chief Warrant Officer

Ensign

Lieutenant Junior Grade

Lieutenant

Lieutenant Commander

Commander

Captain

Rear Admiral

Vice-Admiral

Admiral

NAVY

COAST GUARD

Figure 1824. Navy and Coast Guard Sleeve Insignia

INDEX